TEARS *of* RANGI

TEARS *of* RANGI

EXPERIMENTS ACROSS WORLDS

ANNE SALMOND

AUCKLAND
UNIVERSITY
PRESS

Royalties from this work are donated to the Longbush Ecological Trust.

A note about textual conventions:
In this book, italics have been used when quoting longer Māori
texts, but not for proper and place names, individual words or short
Māori phrases now familiar in New Zealand English. Macrons for
Māori words have been used throughout (unless names – place,
personal, tribal). The Taura Whiri convention has been followed
with regards to the application of hyphens in Māori words.

First published 2017
Reprinted 2017, 2018
This paperback edition first published 2020

Auckland University Press
University of Auckland
Private Bag 92019
Auckland 1142
New Zealand
www.press.auckland.ac.nz

© Anne Salmond, 2017

ISBN 978 1 86940 929 6

Publication is assisted by creative nz
ARTS COUNCIL OF NEW ZEALAND TOI AOTEAROA

A catalogue record for this book is available from
the National Library of New Zealand

This book was printed on FSC® certified paper and other controlled material

Book design by Katrina Duncan
Cover design by Keely O'Shannessy

Cover images:
Top: The Whanganui River with a Māori canoe in the foreground, James D. Richardson.
Middle: Waitangi, Tamara Voninski / oculi.
Bottom: The Wounded Chief Honghi and His Family, Augustus Earle.

Printed by 1010 Printing Co. Ltd

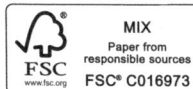

FSC
MIX
Paper from
responsible sources
www.fsc.org   FSC® C016973

CONTENTS

Whanganui woman demonstrating plaiting and weaving flax.

Whakarongo! Whakarongo! Whakarongo	Listen, Listen, Listen
ki te tangi a te manu e karanga nei	to the cry of the bird calling
Tui, tui, tuituia!	Bind, join, be one!
Tuia i runga, tuia i raro,	Bind above, bind below
Tuia i roto, tuia i waho,	Bind within, bind without
Tuia i te here tangata	Tie the knot of humankind
Ka rongo te pō, ka rongo te pō	The night hears, the night hears
Tuia i te kāwai tangata i heke mai	Bind the lines of people coming down
I Hawaiki nui, i Hawaiki roa,	From great Hawaiki, from long Hawaiki
I Hawaiki pāmamao	From Hawaiki far away
I hono ki te wairua, ki te whai ao	Bind to the spirit, to the day light
Ki te Ao Mārama!	To the World of Light!

— CHANT BY ERUERA STIRLING

E paru i te tinana, e mā i te wai,   If you're touched with mud,
                                         you can wash it off,
E paru i te aroha, ka mau tonu ē.   If you're touched with aroha,
                                         it lasts always.

— EREURA STIRLING

When I was sixteen, I met Peggy Kaua and Lady Lorna Ngata in Gisborne, my home town. They were leading experts in kapa haka (ancestral dance) and friends with my mother. I was about to head off for a year in the States as an American Field Service scholar, and they taught me some action songs. They were elegant and dignified, very kind and a little amused by my efforts. During that year in the States when I talked about my own country, I began to glimpse the depths of my ignorance about te ao Māori (the Māori world).

The following year at the University of Auckland, I began to learn Māori and joined Māori Club. I met Eruera and Amiria Stirling, leading elders in Auckland, at a party, and Amiria invited me to their house in Herne Bay. Eruera was an orator, trained in ancestral knowledge by the last tohunga (priestly expert) from the Kirieke whare wānanga (schools of learning) in the Eastern Bay of Plenty. For the next 20 years, Eruera and Amiria guided and taught me, not just about tikanga Māori (Māori ways of living) but about life in general. My debt to them is incalculable.

Later that year, I attended a tukutuku (woven wall-panel) school at Tikitiki on the East Coast, run by the master carver Pine Taiapa. A group from Ngati Whatua, tāngata whenua (people of the land) in Auckland, were learning to weave tukutuku panels for their chapel in Okahu Bay, the last remnant of their tribal estates in the heart of Auckland. This was the first time I had stayed on a marae, and during the tukutuku school I met Bill and Connie Davis, elders of Ngati Whatua. Afterwards I used to visit them in Kitemoana Street, or 'Boot Hill' as they called it, where Ngati Whatua had been sent (booted) after their village in Okahu Bay was taken by the government in 1951 and burned to the ground. During that same year, I met Merimeri Penfold, who was teaching te reo (Māori language) at the university. She was a brilliant teacher, poet and writer who became my close friend, advisor and confidant until her death in 2014.

These were life-changing meetings. I became captivated by the depths and intricacies of te ao Māori, and in awe of the mana (ancestral power) of its experts. I began to learn about the pain of the colonial experience for Māori, from those who were living through it, and about courage and resilience in the face of adversity. I came to see that in exploring Māori ways of being, understanding is elusive – always partial and never final. This has been (and still is) an amazing journey. This book is dedicated to those who have been teachers and friends, guides and guardians along the way, past and present, in gratitude for their generosity, patience and kindness:

Peggy Kaua	Linda and Graeme Smith
Lady Lorna and Sir Henry Ngata	Tracey McIntosh
George and Pare Marsden	Michael Walker
Darcy Ria	Lee Cooper
Hine and Paul Weka	Kori Netana
Eruera and Amiria Stirling	Hone Sadler
Merimeri Penfold	Ann Sullivan
Bill and Connie Davis	Margaret Mutu
Bruce and Joy Biggs	Rangimarie Rawiri
Sir Hirini and Lady June Mead	Mere Gillman
Sir Hugh and Lady Freda Kawharu	Manuka and Diane Henare
Patu Hohepa	Paul Tapsell
Ngapare Hopa	Merata Kawharu
Ranginui and Deidre Walker	Kingi Snelgar
Sir Tamati and Lady Tilly Reedy	Kiri Toki
Wharetoroa and Ngarungatapu (Bea) Kerr	Dan Hikuroa
Witi Ihimaera	Libby Hakaraia and Tainui Stephens
Maxine and Hone Ngata	Wayne Ngata
Roimata and Rauru Kirikiri	Hera Ngata-Gibson
Sir Pita Sharples	Che Wilson
Sir Robert Mahuta	Jim Schuster
Dame Mira Szazy	Amber Dunn
Taimihinga Potaka	Richard Brooking
Waerete Norman	Wirangi Pera
Selwyn Muru	Lisa Reihana
Ngawhira Fleet	Fiona Pardington

A heartfelt mihi, too, to my colleagues in the research project, Te Ao Tawhito: The Ancient Māori World, supported by the Marsden Fund from the Royal Society of New Zealand, which made this book possible. During the project, Hone Sadler, Jane McRae, Jeny Curnow, Robert Pouwhare and Joe Te Rito located and translated early Māori manuscripts, while Hazel Petrie and Christine Jackson scoured the archives for relevant materials from the early contact period in English and Māori. A catalogue of many of these sources by Hazel Petrie has been lodged in various research archives.

Te Ao Tawhito team members also produced their own works on the ancestral Māori 'world' – Hone Sadler's *Ko Tautoro: Te Pito o Tōku Ao. A Ngāpuhi Narrative* (2014); Hazel Petrie's *Outcasts of the Gods?: The Struggle Over Slavery in Māori New Zealand* (2015); Jeny Curnow's translations with Robert Pouwhare and Joe Te Rito of Te Rangikaheke manuscripts, lodged in the Auckland Public Library in 2012; and Jane McRae's *Māori Oral Tradition: He Kōrero nō te Ao Tawhito* (2017). Their remarkable inquiries have enriched my thinking about ancestral ways of being.

I am deeply indebted to friends and colleagues in Māori Studies, Ngā Pae o te Māramatanga Centre of Research Excellence and the Waitangi Tribunal for their inspiration and support; to Wayne Ngata, Raewyn Dalziel, Deidre Brown, Angela Middleton, Manuka Henare, Billie Lythberg, Ron Crosby and Sir Geoffrey Lloyd for their generosity in offering expert feedback on drafts of the manuscript; and to several anonymous readers for their wise advice.

In bringing the book to press, Christine Jackson researched the images, Mike Wagg did an astute, fastidious job of editing, Sarah Ell and Nicola Makiri van Aardt meticulously checked the text and Sam Elworthy showed great faith in the work and helped to shape it.

My thanks to two brilliant artists, Robert Sullivan for his permission to quote from his poem *Star Waka*, and Brett Graham for permission to reproduce his work *Nebula 11*, based on a sketch of a takarangi double spiral by Pei Te Hurinui Jones.

I also owe a great deal to my daughter Amiria Manutahi Salmond, whose work on the 'ontological turn' in anthropology helped to inspire this book. I've loved our debates and shared projects, and *Tears of Rangi* took shape around them.

As Ranginui Walker once said of scholarly work, it should be like a marae (ceremonial centre for kin groups), where 'people stand to be blown about by the wind and shone on by the sun'. In a series of keynote lectures, academic papers, newspaper articles, broadcasts and talks in New Zealand and Europe, different sections of this work have been drafted and tested. I am grateful to to those listeners and readers who engaged in debate and discussion with me, offering corrections and new insights.

Thank you, too, to those who shared their experience and wisdom in various real-life experiments 'across worlds' – the founding Board of the Museum of New Zealand Te Papa Tongarewa, the Board of the New Zealand Historic Places Trust, the Expert Advisory Panel for the World Heritage nomination of Taputapuatea Marae in Ra'iatea, the Longbush Ecological Trust and the Te Ha Trust in Gisborne, Te Awaroa: Voice of the River project, the Starpath Partnership for Excellence, the Air New Zealand Sustainability Panel and the Council of the Royal Society of New Zealand – *e hoa mā, tēnā koutou katoa!*

As always, my love to the family – Jeremy, our children and their families, and our large, irreplaceable whānau, the Thorpe and Salmond clans.

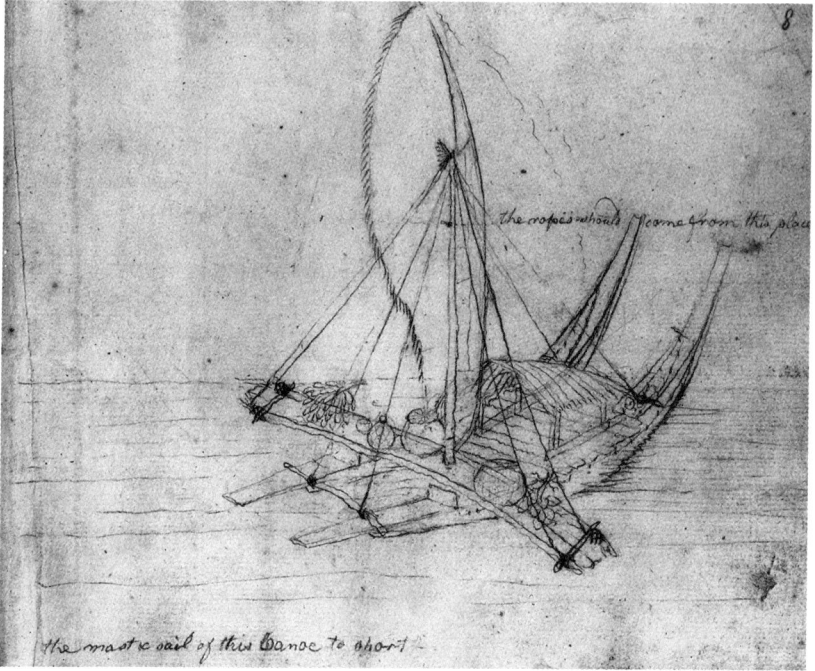

A tiipaerua (double canoe) sketched by Sydney Parkinson
during the Endeavour's *visit to Ra'iatea in 1769.*

Voyaging Worlds

I<small>N THE TWENTY-FIRST CENTURY PACIFIC, THE MOST ICONIC IMAGES</small> of the Earth are those taken from outer space. A blue globe hangs in a pool of darkness, spinning in the sun. When the Pacific Ocean comes into sight, its scatter of islands is barely visible. Edged by the continents of Asia, Australia and the Americas, the scale of this great ocean is impressive. Marbled by drifts of cloud, the Pacific covers almost a third of the earth's surface. In the far southern reaches, one can see the islands of New Zealand, the last significant land mass on Earth to be found and settled by people.

The ancestors of Māori invented blue-water sailing. As they sailed across the Pacific, stars, comets, clouds, the sun, the moon and birds appeared at different heights in the heavens. At night, successions of stars rose up in the sky, guiding them on their voyages. As winds blew and waves and swells slapped against the hulls of their canoes, it seemed that they stood still in the ocean while islands floated towards them.[1]

The Brazilian anthropologist Viveiros de Castro has argued for the 'ontological self-determination' of the world's peoples.[2] Here, he is not talking about 'world views' (as though despite our different visions, there is just one world after all), or even 'humanity' or 'the planet', but suggesting that different peoples may explore different realities, and have the right to do so. For the Polynesian voyagers, a layered, curved universe in which islands sailed across the sea and stars across the sky was not a myth, but based on experience. Their explosive migrations east to Easter Island and the west coast of South America, north to Hawai'i and south to New Zealand were made possible by a navigation system based on deep knowledge of the sea, winds and stars; fast, resilient canoes;[3] a portable suite of plants and animals; and kin-based forms of order that allowed them to transplant themselves in new and unfamiliar lands.

When the first star navigators arrived in New Zealand in about the early fourteenth century,[4] they had to rapidly adapt to plants and animals, land-scapes and climatic conditions very different from those in their tropical homelands. By the time the first Europeans came ashore perhaps four hun-dred years later, Māori had developed many new technologies, along with new dialects, art forms and philosophical ideas. Far from a static 'traditional' society, early Māori life was dynamic and rapidly changing.

In order to reach these remote islands, the first Western explorers, Abel Tasman in 1642 and Captain James Cook in 1769–70, faced similar challenges. They had to master the art of sailing for long periods across great distances, along with technologies (including projectile weapons) that allowed them to survive the challenges from island warriors.[5] At the time of the *Endeavour*'s arrival, life in Europe was also in a phase of explosive inno-vation. The settlers who arrived in the wake of the early European explorers brought with them new repertoires of plants and animals,[6] habits of mind and ways of living, casting up realities that, like those of their Polynesian precursors, made it possible for them to inhabit places very different from their homelands.

Since the early nineteenth century in New Zealand, settlers from Polynesia and Europe (and elsewhere) have clashed and forged alliances with one another. In this remote, beautiful archipelago, debates over what is real, and good, and what matters in people's lives have been fiercely contested.[7] In these exchanges across the middle ground, ancestral Māori conceptions have been mobilised, usually but not always by Māori, and Western frame-works deployed, mostly but not invariably by Europeans. In the process, deep-seated assumptions and forms of order (so often invisible, or natural-ised as 'common sense') have been brought to light, and challenged. At times – when the Treaty of Waitangi was signed between Māori and the British Crown; or New Zealand became the first country in the world to give the vote to women; or the Treaty settlement process was established; or the Whanganui River was recognised as a legal person – these exchanges have helped to provoke new ways of thinking.

Here, I want to explore the likelihood that like bio-diversity, cosmo-diversity (in the sense of multiple 'worlds') may be a force for adaptation and survival. For the old Cartesian dualisms and their fragmented dreams are no longer working – in science, in material matters, or in human affairs.[8] In order to find more adaptive ways of being, exchanges across different realities may be helpful, allowing new forms of order to emerge.[9] In New Zealand, and elsewhere in the Pacific where ancestral insights remain vital, this can happen. The first part of this book examines such 'experiments across worlds' through a fine-grained inquiry into the early period of encounters between Māori and Europeans in New Zealand (1769–1840), when collisions and exchanges between people holding different assumptions about 'how the world works' were particularly stark and vivid. The second part of the book investigates such engagements in particular areas of life – waterways, land, the sea, and people; and asks whether these might help to open up new pathways to the future.

Whakapapa (genealogy), for instance, a way of being based on complex networks that encompass all forms of life, interlinked and co-emergent, might assist in exploring relational ways of understanding the interactions between people and the land, other life forms, waterways and the ocean.[10] The idea of the hau, the wind of life that activates human and non-human networks alike, animated by reciprocal exchanges; or the spiral of space-time in Māori might help in devising non-linear, recursive ways of investigating the dynamic interactions among different life-forms (including people). This is fitting, because in Māori ways of thinking, knowledge itself is a taonga (ancestral treasure). As knowledge is given or received, hau passes back and forth across the pae – the horizon or threshold between sky and earth, light and dark, local people and visitors, life and death, past and present – reshaping realities and shifting the way that things happen. The pae is a volatile, emergent space, now and then flashing out insights that create new kinds of order.

As my mentor Eruera Stirling once said, 'Knowledge is a blessing on your mind, it makes everything clear and guides you to do things in the right way . . .'[11] This book about experiments across worlds is written in that hope, and spirit.

PART ONE

Early Encounters, 1769–1840

Tupaia's 1769 sketch of Joseph Banks bartering white cloth for a crayfish in Uawa.

CHAPTER ONE

Hau: The Wind of Life

He iwi kē, he iwi kē   One strange people and another
Titiro atu, titiro mai   Looking at each other
– CHANT BY MERIMERI PENFOLD

IN OCTOBER 1769 IN UAWA, ON THE EAST COAST OF THE NORTH ISLAND OF New Zealand, the star navigator and high priest Tupaia sketched Joseph Banks, a wealthy young botanist, exchanging white cloth for a crayfish with a local man. Tupaia and Banks had arrived on board the *Endeavour*, commanded by James Cook, and sent into the Pacific by the Royal Society of London and the British Admiralty to observe the transit of Venus, and to search for Terra Australis Incognita (the Unknown Southern Continent).

The ship had sailed from Ra'iatea, Tupaia's home island and one of the homelands of Māori. After a three-month stay in Tahiti, where Tupaia joined the expedition, the high priest escorted his *Endeavour* shipmates to the great voyaging marae Taputapuatea, where he had trained as a priest of 'Oro, the god of fertility and war in the Society Islands. Afterwards they headed south across the Pacific, arriving on the east coast of New Zealand in spring, when the kōwhai trees were flowering.

Although Tupaia died in Batavia during the *Endeavour*'s return journey to England, Joseph Banks preserved the sketch made by the high priest in Uawa, along with others he had drawn in Tahiti and Australia. These were lodged in the British Museum, where many years later, art historians guessed that since many of these 'naïve' images were painted in watercolours,[1] the artist might have been none other than Joseph Banks himself.[2] It was not until 1997 that these drawings were attributed to Tupaia. During his

Capt. James Cook
of the Endeavour.

*Captain James Cook,
by William Hodges,
1775–1776.*

research into the life of Joseph Banks (later friend of George III, President of the Royal Society and impresario of British imperial exploration), Banks's biographer Harold Carter noticed a passage in one of his letters that mentioned this drawing. In 1812, Banks wrote to a friend:

> Tupia the Indian who came with me from Otaheite Learnd to draw in a way not Quite unintelligible. The genius for Caricature which all wild People Possess Led him to Caricature me and he drew me with a nail in my hand delivering it to an Indian who sold me a Lobster but with my other hand I had a firm fist on the Lobster determind not to Quit the nail until I had Livery and Seizin of the article purchasd.[3]

While the Uawa sketch shows Joseph Banks holding a piece of white cloth (almost certainly Tahitian bark cloth, highly sought after by Māori), rather than a nail, the description in his letter almost certainly refers to the image that Banks lodged (with others by the same artist) in the British Museum.[4]

Joseph Banks cross-dressing in a Māori cloak with a magnificent tāniko border, with painted paddle and a taiaha in the background, by Benjamin West, 1773.

Far from being a 'wild man', however, Tupaia was a brilliant and charismatic leader in the Society Islands. When he joined the *Endeavour*, he was seeking to enlist Cook and his men in seeking to avenge the conquest of his home island, Ra'iatea. As a high priest and star navigator, Tupaia was a leading figure in the 'arioi cult dedicated to 'Oro, the god of fertility and war, famed for its lovers, artists, dancers, actors, scholars, warriors and star navigators.[5] After their departure from Tahiti, Tupaia piloted the ship through the surrounding islands, and worked with Captain Cook on a remarkable chart of the Pacific, centred upon Tahiti and based on relative bearings and distances in space-time (elapsed nights) between different islands. Later, the young naturalist Georg Forster would describe Tupaia as 'an extraordinary genius'.[6]

Like his charts, Tupaia's sketches were revolutionary. During his time with the Royal Society party, he often sat with the ship's artists, drawing the same subjects but creating new kinds of art works, using European techniques with a quintessentially Polynesian vision. Painted in the colours of bark cloth

– black, brown and red-brown – his image portrays two men, one European (Joseph Banks) and one Māori, standing face to face, offering gifts to each other. In New Zealand, as in the Society Islands at that time, life was ordered by relational networks, and driven by exchange. If a taonga (treasured item) was handed over, it carried part of the vital force, or hau,[7] of the donor and his or her kin group, tangling the lives of donor and recipient together.

In 1907, when Elsdon Best, a New Zealand ethnologist who had spent a lifetime studying Māori customs, wrote to an elder called Tamati Ranapiri, asking him to explain the concept of the hau, Ranapiri replied:

> As for the *hau*, it isn't the wind that blows, not at all. Let me explain it to you carefully. Now, you have an ancestral item (*taonga*) that you give to me, without the two of us putting a price on it, and I give it to someone else. Perhaps after a long while, this person remembers that he has this *taonga*, and that he should give me a return gift, and he does so.
>
> This is the *hau* of the *taonga* that was previously given to me. I must pass on that treasure to you. It would not be right for me to keep it for myself. Whether it is a very good *taonga* or a bad one, I must give to you, because it is the *hau* of your *taonga*, and if I hold on to it for myself, I will die. This is the *hau*. That's enough.[8]

The hau is at the heart of life itself. As Ranapiri explained to Best, if a person fails to uphold their obligations in these transactions, their own life force is threatened. As good or bad taonga and gifts or insults pass back and forth, embodying the power of the hau, patterns of relations are transformed, for better or for worse.

When Elsdon Best wrote about Ranapiri's account of the hau, it captured the imagination of a French sociologist, Marcel Mauss. In 1925, Mauss published *The Gift*, a classic work exploring gift exchange in a range of societies, including his own. Quoting Ranapiri, he contrasted the Māori concept of the hau of the gift with the assumption in contemporary capitalism that all transactions are driven by self-interest, arguing that this gives an impoverished view of how relations among people generate social life.[9] For Mauss, the hau, or the 'spirit of the thing given', impels a gift in return, creating solidarity. His discussion of the concept is perceptive, but in fact, it only scratches the surface. In Māori ways of thinking, hau drives the whole world, not just human relations. It goes far beyond the exchange of gifts among people.

According to the tohunga (experts) in the ancestral whare wānanga (schools of learning), hau emerged at the very beginning of the cosmos. In a chant recorded by Te Kohuora of Rongoroa for the missionary Richard Taylor in 1854, for example, the world begins with a burst of energy that generates thought, memory and desire. Next comes the Pō, long aeons of darkness. Out of the Pō comes the Kore, unbound, unpossessed Nothing, the seedbed of the cosmos, described by an early ethnologist as 'the Void or negation, yet containing the potentiality of all things afterwards to come'.[10] In the Kore, hau ora and hau tupu, the winds of life and growth, begin to stir. As hau flows through the world, the sky emerges, and the moon and stars, light, the earth and sky and ocean:[11]

Na te kune te pupuke	From the source of growth the rising
Na te pupuke te hihiri	From rising the thought
Na te hihiri te mahara	From rising thought the memory
Na te mahara te hinengaro	From memory the mind-heart
Na te hinengaro te manako	From the mind-heart, desire
Ka hua te wananga	Knowledge becomes conscious
Ka noho i a rikoriko	It dwells in dim light
Ka puta ki waho ko te po . . .	And Pō (darkness) emerges . . .
Na te kore i ai	From nothingness came the first cause
Te kore te whiwhia	Unpossessed nothingness
Te kore te rawea	Unbound nothingness
Ko hau tupu, ko hau ora	The hau tupu (wind of growth), the hau ora (wind of life)
Ka noho i te atea	Stay in clear space
Ka puta ki waho ko te rangi e tu nei	And the sky emerges that stands here
Te ata rapa, te ata ka mahina	The early dawn, the early day, the mid-day
Ka mahina te ata i hikurangi!	The blaze of day from the sky!

Through these exchanges, new forms of life emerge. As a Te Arawa scribe, Te Rangikaheke, told Sir George Grey, an early governor of New Zealand, at the beginning of the world when life first appears, '*kotahi anō te tupuna o te tangata Māori – ko Ranginui te tū nei, ko Papatūanuku e takoto nei*' – 'there is just one Maori ancestor, Ranginui standing here and Papatuanuku lying here'.[12] Male sky and female earth are a single being, locked together. From their union the ancestors of agricultural crops, sea and waterways, the winds, fern-root and people emerge, crushed in darkness between their parents.

Cramped and frustrated, the older brothers decide to separate earth and sky, letting light into the world. After a series of unsuccessful attempts, Tane-nui-a-Rangi, the ancestor of forests, takes an axe known as Hauhautu (make hau and hau stand)[13] and cuts them apart. Stricken with grief, they cry out, 'Why has this crime been committed? Why have we been separated?' As Rangi's tears fall down to earth, forming lakes and rivers, Papa's mists rise up to greet him. Enraged by this assault on their parents, Tawhirimatea, Space-twister, the ancestor of winds (hau), attacks his older brothers, smashing and splitting Tane's trees, assailing land and sea with whirlwinds and hurricanes, and driving the ancestors of root crops underground. In the midst of this chaos, the offspring of these founding ancestors quarrel with each other and go their separate ways, finding new places to live in and becoming new kinds of creatures – the ancestors of fish diving into the sea, for instance, while the ancestors of lizards hide under rocks on the land.

Only Tu, the ancestor of people, stands tall against Tawhiri's onslaught, earning the right for his descendants to consume those of his brothers – birds, trees, fish, shellfish, fern-root, yams, taro and sweet potatoes, destroying their tapu (ancestral presence) and making them noa (ordinary, free from ancestral constraints).[14] Through the separation of Rangi and Papa, te ao mārama – the everyday world of light – emerges. Light is separated from (but still linked with) darkness; life from death; sky from earth; male from female; up from down and left from right, oriented by the bodies of the founding ancestors.[15] Different ancestral beings are generated and take their places, linked by their quarrels and ongoing exchanges. Later, Tu's descendants – tangata (people) – sometimes also quarrel and separate, migrating to new places and forging new kin networks. Many of the stories about exploring Polynesia, including New Zealand, tell of disputes followed by journeys to distant places. In this viral kinship system, driven by the exchange of gifts (that bind people together) or insults (that divide them), ancestral networks are readily replicated and transported, allowing the exploration and settlement of new places and forging new groups of people, as well as maintaining relationships over time.

Māori kin groups are contextual and dynamic, with some relations forged by insult and fighting; others by adoption, friendship and marriage, accompanied by gift exchange; while others, of lesser value, are allowed to wither away.[16]

Rather than bounded groups, these are open-ended networks springing from 'root ancestors' planted in the ground. People can activate different links under different circumstances, constantly changing through space and time. On the marae (ceremonial centre for kin groups), with its carved meeting house, its marae ātea, or forecourt for orators, where hosts and visitors sit facing each other, and its dining hall, ancestors are present as their descendants debate the questions of the day, recount ancestral deeds, forge new alliances, and are married or farewelled back to the Pō, the ancestral realm.[17] This is captured in a haka (war chant) composed by Merimeri Penfold:

He iwi kē, he iwi kē	One strange people and another
Titiro atu, titiro mai	Looking at each other

This chant evokes an exchange of gazes across the marae. Iwi means 'a group of people' and kē invokes the strangeness of one group to another. Titiro atu is one's glance directed at another, while titiro mai is the others' glance in reply. In these recursive exchanges, identity takes shape, and shifts. All of the action – for better or for worse – happens across the pae, the middle ground. In this liminal space, male sky and female earth, living and the dead, local people and their visitors meet, intermingle and change places. Ancestors appear in genealogies and stories, in photographs, and in the carvings that line the inside walls of the meeting house, support its roof, and decorate the exterior gable and porch.

As the Tainui expert Pei Te Hurinui Jones explained, in Māori ancestral thinking, space-time is a spiral, a vortex.[18] Standing in the present, one can spin back to the Kore, the Void, where the first burst of energy unleashed the winds of growth and life – and out into the future. At the University of Auckland marae, for example, Tāne-nui-a-Rangi, the carved meeting house, embodies the ancestor who first ascended the layered heavens on a whirlwind to fetch the three baskets of knowledge for his descendants.

Inside the meeting house, the ridgepole and its carved posts tell the story of Tane separating his parents, Rangi and Papa, while carved ancestors stand around the walls, the priestly experts and navigators who guided their canoes across the Pacific from Hawaiki to New Zealand. Sitting inside Tāne-nui-a-Rangi, the belly of the ancestor, one is literally transported into te ao Māori, the ancestral Māori 'world'. At the centre of the back wall of the house stands a carving of Hinenuitepo, the ancestress of death. During

The house Tane-nui-a-rangi at Waipapa marae, the University of Auckland.

a tangi (funeral), the body of a deceased person lies at her feet. Towards the back of the house, the kōwhaiwhai (rafter paintings) shade off into darkness, while towards the front, the door and window open into te ao mārama (the world of light) where the colours of the kōwhaiwhai become bright.[19]

The waiata (chant) sung at the opening of the marae, composed by Merimeri Penfold, incorporates Te Kohuora's creation chant.[20] According to Viveiros de Castro, such cosmological chants do not reflect a 'world view' but rather, express 'a world *objectively from inside it*'.[21] As Marshall Sahlins remarks, 'The [Māori] universe is a gigantic kin, a genealogy . . . a veritable ontology'[22] – a way of being that patterns the world, based on whakapapa – vast, intricate networks of relations in which all forms of life are linked, generated by exchanges between complementary pairs, animated by hau.

Thus when Māori greet each other by pressing noses, their hau (breath, wind of life) intermingles.[23] If a person presses noses with a carved ancestor, the same thing happens. When rangatira, or chiefs, speak of an ancestor in the first person as ahau, or 'I', it is because they are the 'living face' of that ancestor, and if they speak of their descent groups in the same way, it is because they share ancestral hau together. A refusal to enter into reciprocal exchanges, on the other hand, is known as hau whitia, or hau turned aside. Hauhauaitu (or 'harm to the hau') is manifested as illness or ill fortune, a breakdown in the balance of exchanges. The life force has been harmed, showing signs of collapse and failure.

In early times, the hau of an enemy might be extinguished by rituals including awhe i te hau (gathering in the hau),[24] while the hau of a kin group might be destroyed by ceremonies that included whāngai hau (feed the hau), in which the hau of their leader was fed to an enemy atua (ancestor god).[25] Equally, the hau might be revitalised by a successful act of retribution – for instance, in the kai hau kai (eating the hau as food) ceremony, in which the hau of the enemy and his or her atua was consumed. In this way, the original insult is wiped out, restoring ora – life, health, prosperity and abundance – to the victors. Utu, the principle of reciprocity, drives the exchanges between individuals and groups and all other life forms, past and present, working towards (an always fragile) equilibrium.[26]

Because hau animates all phenomena, in this way of being there are no Cartesian gulfs between mind and matter, animate and inanimate beings, people and environment, Culture and Nature. As the nineteenth-century thinker Nepia Pohuhu remarked: 'All things unfold their nature (tupu), live (ora), have form (ahua), whether trees, stones, birds, reptiles, fish, quadrupeds or human beings.'[27] Hau flows through all things, whether rivers, mountains, forests, reefs, fishing grounds, plants, animals or people. If their hau is in a state of ora (hau ora: health, well-being, prosperity), they will flourish; but if it is in a state of mate (hau mate: sickness, ill-being, misfortune), they will decline and perish. As Tamati Ranapiri explained to Elsdon Best, in catching birds, for example, one must offer the first bird captured to the hau of the forest, to ensure its ongoing ora – its well-being,[28] and protect one's own health and good fortune. This also applies to catching eels in a river, or fish in the ocean. The fundamental kinship between people and other life forms is never forgotten.

Indeed, kin networks are often spoken of as plants – the gourd plant for instance, branching and sprawling across the land.[29] A Māori person might refer to themselves as *he kākano i ruia mai i Rangiatea* (a seed sown from Rangiatea – Ra'iatea, Tupaia's birthplace). Some branches in these ramifying forms grow vigorously, while others wither and die – an image of rhizomatic growth echoed in the kōwhaiwhai paintings on the blades of paddles or the rafters of meeting houses – or as the anthropologist Marilyn Strathern has noted, in modernist talk about knowledge itself.[30]

In ancestral Māori thinking, then, exchange is the stuff of life. As beings engage with each other in these relational networks, new forms of life are generated, along with efforts at domination, control or liberation. In many

ways these whakapapa networks resonate with the complex systems of contemporary science, including ideas of symbiotic exchanges, the World Wide
Web and neural networks.[31] As Mattei and Capra remark:

> We have discovered that the material world, ultimately, is a network of
> inseparable patterns of relationships; that the planet as a whole is a living,
> self-regulating system. The view of the human body as a machine and of the
> mind as a separate entity is being replaced by one that sees not only the brain
> but also the immune system, the bodily tissues, and even each cell as a living,
> cognitive system.[32]

In te ao Māori, people are constituted by their relationships, and identity
is recursively generated. Each group (or individual) creates its identity by
engaging with the other, and recognising that they are different. In each
case, difference is differently understood, however.

Before the first Europeans arrived in New Zealand, for example, there
were no Māori 'people', just different kin networks based in different places.
According to the East Coast tribal expert Mohi Turei, māori (a term that
simply means 'ordinary, usual, normal, everyday') was used to describe
people and phenomena in te ao mārama, the everyday world of light and
life, in contrast with those in te pō, the dark, invisible ancestral world.[33]
In exchanges with the new arrivals (as recorded in Tupaia's sketch of Joseph
Banks and the Māori warrior, for instance), local people came to see themselves as māori (ordinary, normal) in contrast with pākehā, or Europeans
– beings so strange that they might have arrived from the ancestral realm.
Until that time, Māori had no need to distinguish themselves as a group
from others, or their archipelago as a country in comparison with others.

Likewise, in these early encounters with Europeans, Māori began to refer
to their own ancestral ways as te ao māori (the familiar, everyday world) in
contrast to te ao pākehā (the world of the strangers). If one uses the term
'world' in English as the best translation for ao in Māori (as is often done;
in the subtitle of this book, for instance), it can be misleading, however.
In Māori, ao is a state of existence or a dimension of reality, usually translated as 'world', but without the implication of a bounded, self-contained,
singular entity that underpins that term in English.[34] Rather, the whakapapa
networks that structure te ao māori, shaping its patterns, are intrinsically
dynamic and open-ended. Strangers can be bound into these living webs

by acts of generosity and alliance, often marked by gifts of taonga (ancestral treasures) including names, knowledge, artefacts, sexual partners or children, or severed from them by acts of aggression and humiliation – both of which require utu, equal (or greater) return over time.

Thus in Māori a hoa is a friend or companion; a hoa rangatira (chiefly friend) is a husband or wife; while a hoa riri (angry friend) is an enemy. The key term here is hoa, a relation of some kind. In Māori, it is the relation itself (not its quality; or the parties involved) that is ontologically prior. In this way of being, a person is constituted by their place in the relational networks, and in speaking Māori, the state and nature of one's relationships are constantly being negotiated. In addressing other people, for instance, you must decide whether your relationship with them is close (in which case, the inclusive pronoun is used) or distant (when the exclusive pronoun applies), and whether it is dual or plural – for example, tāua (us two) or māua (me and someone else, excluding you); tātou (us, including you) or mātou (us, excluding you).[35] Thus the pronouns māua and mātou encompass not only the speaker and the person or group they are including, but also the person or group they are excluding. Even the recipient of an insult as radical as kai tangata (being eaten) is still part of the relational matrix – in this case, a hoa riri (angry friend) whose mana has been destroyed.

At the same time, as Mauss pointed out in *The Gift*, notions of reciprocity and gift exchange are not unique to 'exotic' societies, but are also present in Europe.[36] This allowed early European visitors to New Zealand to make some sense of their exchanges with Māori. As Captain Cook observed: 'I have allways found them of a Brave, Noble, Open and benevolent disposition, but they are a people that will never put up with an insult if they have an oppertunity to resent it.'[37] While such 'rough intelligibility' allowed relationships to be forged, efforts at engagement between Māori and Europeans often backfired, thwarted by differing assumptions about how the world works.[38] At the same time in these encounters – titiro atu, titiro mai – hidden premises sometimes come to light, making it possible for new ideas and practices to emerge as taken-for-granted forms of order are challenged.[39] The element of surprise in such meetings was (and still is) at once disruptive, and creative.[40]

In the first part of this book, such exchanges are explored during the early contact period in New Zealand (roughly, 1769–1840) – during the first meetings between Māori and European explorers; in the debates between

Māori and the first missionaries, where notions of the real were tested to their limits; and in the signing of the Declaration of Independence and the Treaty of Waitangi, when ground rules were laid down for the relationships between Māori and the British Crown. Throughout this period, Māori were dominant. As relationships were forged with the incoming settlers and visitors from Europe and other places, despite their own assumptions of superiority, the new arrivals were forced to deal with Māori realities. The clashes, debates and improvisations that took place provide rich, vivid ways of exploring what happens when people with different taken-for-granted ideas about what is real and what matters in life come together, and try to negotiate shared ways of living.

Inevitably, as an exercise in historical ethnography, this investigation of early 'experiments across worlds' in New Zealand draws upon modernist assumptions, as well as a lifetime of exploring te ao Māori (Māori ways of being). The term 'ontology', for instance, which crops up in this work, may puzzle some readers. It refers to the study of the nature of reality, along with the basic categories of being and their relations. As for the 'ontological turn' in anthropology, this assumes that reality and its underlying patterns may differ across different groups of people, and that these differences may be investigated. For some practitioners, the realities of different groups of people can be observed, described and classified, producing taxonomies of different ways of being.[41] For others, anthropology itself is based on particular propositions about the nature of existence, which are themselves historically and culturally specific. The shocks and surprises that arise when anthropologists engage with people who work with very different assumptions about what is real may provoke philosophical creativity, and new kinds of understandings.[42]

For my part, I think that such shocks and surprises are not peculiar to anthropology – nor the clashes and innovations that arise in encounters between people who understand the nature of being differently. While seeking to investigate such processes of encounter and transformation between Māori and Europeans (and others) in New Zealand, I know that as an anthropologist and a person, I am a part of and shaped by the histories of these exchanges. In what follows, I try to acknowledge this by placing myself in the narrative every now and then, entangled in these networks of relations, spinning in the spirals of space-time.

CHAPTER TWO

Tupaia's Cave

URING A STORM IN 2007, AS WAVES SURGED INTO COOK'S COVE in Uawa, on the east coast of New Zealand, the banks of this small inlet collapsed, revealing bands of dark soil with fish, bird and dog bones, charcoal, shell fragments and artefacts. Archaeologists from the New Zealand Historic Places Trust and the local people, Te Aitanga-a-Hauiti, decided to carry out a rescue excavation. To their delight they found that as well as being the scene of very early exchanges between Māori and Europeans, this was one of very few sites in New Zealand with occupation layers from the first Polynesian arrival to the present.

In November of that year, my husband Jeremy and I joined a group from the Trust to visit the excavation, walking down a long, steep trail through bush-clad slopes to the back of the inlet.[1] To the north, high white cliffs dropped steeply into the sea. To the south, lower cliffs sheltered the entrance to the cove, where a stream runs down a fertile basin into the ocean. At the edge of the bush the sun lit up the bay, with its green hills, grey sand and a blue, glittering sea.[2] At the site, the archaeologists and local people showed us fragments of moa and seal bone in the lower layers, along with oven stones, post-holes, stone flakes and several small moa-bone and shell fish-hooks. Starch grains later proved to include both kūmara (sweet potato) and taro, indicating that the first settlers had brought these root crops with them from the islands.

According to the archaeologists, when the first Polynesian travellers landed in New Zealand around the fourteenth century, a small group settled at Opoutama. Moa, a great flightless bird, still lived in the hills, and it was easy to drive these birds down to this little valley and trap them. The stream and a spring provided the settlers with fresh water, seals basked on the rocks, fish shoaled out at sea and shellfish flourished on the rocky coastline.[3] After millennia of living in small tropical islands, the new arrivals had to work out new ways of living in this large, temperate archipelago. Pigs and chickens from their homelands did not survive the journey, and many of their ancestral crops, including banana, coconut and breadfruit, either died at sea or failed to grow when they were transplanted.

Nevertheless, these early settlers learned to plant, harvest and store other crops from the Pacific – sweet potato, yam and taro – in this much cooler climate, and aute (bark cloth, which struggled to survive in New Zealand) and sennit were replaced by various varieties of harakeke (New Zealand flax, or *Phormium tenax*). Moa and seals provided an early source of protein, but as the bush was fired for fern-root plantations and gardens, and the moa were vigorously hunted, these big birds became scarce, and died out altogether. The ancestors of Māori also had to master coastal navigation in the absence of sheltering coral reefs, shape new types of stone into tools and weapons, and design new kinds of buildings and watercraft. Over time, Uawa became the home of a famous school of learning, Te Rawheoro, established by the ancestor Hingangaroa, a priest, carver, star navigator and canoe-builder whose son Hauiti gave his name to the local people.[4]

As one can see from the chant quoted earlier, in Māori accounts of the creation of the world, thought, memory, knowledge and desire are highly prized. In the East Coast schools of learning, tohunga (experts) passed on ancestral stories that included accounts of the separation of the earth mother and the sky father by their son Tāne-nui-a-Rangi, allowing light into the world; the feats of the trickster ancestor Maui, who snared the sun and fished up the land, leaving his canoe on top of Hikurangi mountain; disputes involving various ancestors in the island homeland, Hawaiki; and ancestral voyages to New Zealand. Prominent among these narratives is the tale of Uenuku's illegitimate son Ruatapu, who in a fit of jealousy caused a canoe to sink, drowning 70 young men except his elder brother Paikea, who chanted a powerful incantation, either becoming a whale or summoning up a whale that carried him safely to the east coast of the North Island. There were also stories about the voyages of various ancestral canoes and their arrival in New Zealand, including the *Horouta* canoe and its commander Pawa.[5]

The genealogical lines from Maui, Paikea and the later voyagers, traced through male and female links to the founders of local kin groups, were embellished with tales about ancestral travels, quarrels, friendships, love affairs and battles, leaving an intricate scatter of place names across the land. At Te Rawheoro, the school of learning founded by Hingangaroa eight generations after Paikea's landing, songs and incantations, tattoo, carving and fine weaving were also taught, and this whare wānanga produced skilled carvers, tattooists and weavers who travelled around the country, practising their arts.

In October 1769, when Captain James Cook and his *Endeavour* companions arrived at Uawa (which they named 'Tolaga Bay'), they described it as a second Paradise. They spent seven peaceful, happy days at Uawa, going ashore at Opoutama (now named 'Cook's Cove') to fill the ship's water barrels, gather fresh food, and collect botanical and zoological specimens. Tupaia, the high priest and star navigator who joined the expedition in Tahiti, slept in a rock shelter above Cook's Cove, where he talked with the tohunga (leading expert) from Te Rawheoro. Havai'i, the ancient name of Ra'iatea, Tupaia's home island, was one of the homelands of Māori. These conversations must have been extraordinary. No doubt Tupaia and the local priests shared stories of their voyaging ancestors, traced their genealogical links, and talked about what had happened since the departure of the Māori ancestors from Hawaiki. The local people, who were deeply impressed by the high priest, named the rock shelter after him, Te Ana-o-Tupaia (Tupaia's Cave).[6]

At the same time, Tupaia acted as an interpreter for his European shipmates, including Joseph Banks, the wealthy young botanist who headed the Royal Society party, and his scientific companion, Dr Daniel Solander. A number of images survive from the *Endeavour*'s visit, including charts of Uawa, a sketch of the sailors filling water barrels in Cook's Cove, drawings of the artefacts and plants that they collected, along with Tupaia's sketch of a local man exchanging a crayfish for white bark cloth with Joseph Banks. According to Hauiti people who later described his visit to an early trader, Joel Polack, Tupaia also sketched a ship and some boats on the walls of the rock shelter in the cove.[7]

During our trip to Cook's Cove, Jeremy and I were keen to see whether any traces of Tupaia's cave drawings remained. When we climbed up to the rock shelter, however, we found that it had largely collapsed. All we could see were large smears of red ochre on the walls, a fragment of a charcoal sketch of a whale or a dolphin, and a word or two (apparently in Tahitian) written beside it. Perhaps Tupaia had slept in this cave because it was close to Te Kararoa, a fortified village that stood on the ridgeline. At the time, it was often used as a shelter by visiting fishermen. In any case, the view out to sea is spectacular, a perfect place to sit and talk about ancestors who had sailed across Te Moana-nui-a-Kiwa (the Great Sea of Kiwa). Up there on the hillside, it was easy to imagine Tupaia sitting and talking with local people beside a fire, as shadows flickered across the walls of the cave.[8]

First encounters: *He iwi kē, he iwi kē*
[One strange people, and another]

As we have seen, the *Endeavour* was on a scientific voyage of exploration, sponsored by the Admiralty and the Royal Society of London. Before they sailed from England, the Earl of Morton, President of the Royal Society and a Scottish astronomer, had given Cook a set of 'Hints' about how he and his men should conduct themselves in encounters with any 'natives' they might meet in the Pacific, urging him:

> To check the petulance of the Sailors, and restrain the wanton use of Fire Arms.
>
> To have it still in view that sheding the blood of those people is a crime of the highest nature:– They are human creatures, the work of the same omnipotent Author, equally under his care with the most polished European; perhaps being less offensive, more entitled to his favor.
>
> They are the natural, and in the strictest sense of the word, the legal possessors of the several Regions they inhabit.
>
> No European Nation has a right to occupy any part of their country, or settle among them without their voluntary consent . . .
>
> Therefore should they in a hostile manner oppose a landing, and kill some men in the attempt, even this would hardly justify firing among them, 'till every other gentle method had been tried.[9]

In his 'Hints', the Earl of Morton also suggested how Cook and the Royal Society party of scientists and artists might determine whether or not any land they discovered was part of a large continent, describe the 'appearance and natural dispositions' of its inhabitants, including their 'progress in Arts or Science', especially astronomy, and observe and describe the animal, vegetable and mineral kingdoms (including fossils) in the places that they visited.

In addition, the Admiralty gave James Cook a set of secret instructions, ordering him to search for and claim Terra Australis Incognita, a mythical continent thought to lie in the far southern ocean,[10] and:

> . . . with the Consent of the Natives to take possession of Convenient Situations in the Country in the Name of the King of Great Britain; or, if you find the Country uninhabited take Possession for His Majesty by setting up Proper Marks and Inscriptions, as first discoverers and possessors.[11]

On 3 October 1769, almost a month after sailing south from the Society Islands, when a sudden squall hit the ship, Joseph Banks was jubilant, certain that at last they were about to discover Terra Australis:

> This [is] a sure sign of land as such squalls are rarely (if ever) met with at any considerable distance from it . . . Now do I wish that our freinds in England could by the assistance of some magical spying glass take a peep at our situation:
>
> Dr Solander setts at the Cabbin table describing, myself at my Bureau Journalizing, between us hangs a large bunch of sea weed, upon the table lays the wood and barnacles; they would see that notwithstanding our different occupations our lips move very often, and without being conjurors might guess that we were talking about what we should see upon the land which there is now no doubt we shall see very soon.[12]

Three days later, when the surgeon's boy Nicholas Young sighted land from the masthead, he was rewarded with a gallon of rum. The following day as ranges of high mountains appeared above the horizon, Banks exclaimed, 'Many conjectures about Islands, rivers, inlets &c, but all hands seem to agree that this is certainly the Continent we are in search of.'[13]

According to early tribal accounts, when they saw the *Endeavour* sailing into their harbour at Turanga-nui-a-Kiwa (now Gisborne), the local people thought that this might be a floating island, driven by ancestral power, or perhaps a great bird, like the bird of Ruakapanga that had brought the sweet potato from their island homeland. Fires of warning were lit in the hills, and local warriors placed on the alert.

On 8 October 1769 when Cook and his scientific companions came ashore on the east bank of the Turanganui River, the first Europeans to land in New Zealand, they were accompanied by a party of marines.[14] After crossing the river to inspect a fishing hamlet, Joseph Banks and Dr Solander went botanising, leaving four young boys from the *Endeavour* in charge of the yawl. As the boys wandered down to the beach, four warriors were sent down from Titirangi hill to challenge the strangers. Seeing one of these men lift his spear (almost certainly in a wero, or ritual challenge), the coxswain shot him dead. This set the scene for the tense, uneasy meetings that followed.

The next day when Cook's party, accompanied by Tupaia, returned to the east bank of the river, the body of this man, a rangatira named Te Maro, still lay on the beach. Warriors lined up on the opposite bank of the Turanganui, defying the strangers with a fiery haka (war dance). When these men reproached them for the shooting, Tupaia found he could understand what they were saying. He told them that his companions only wanted fresh food and water, and offered them iron in exchange.

Sketch of Te Maro, the rangatira shot by the coxswain during the first landing in Turanga-nui-a-Kiwa (Gisborne), by Sydney Parkinson, October 1769.

Eventually, one of the warriors swam across the river and stood on Te Toka-a-Taiau, a sacred rock near the river's edge, a famous tribal boundary marker.[15] Putting down his musket, Cook went to meet him, and they greeted each other with a hongi (pressing noses), mingling their hau together.[16] When the other men swam across the river and tried to exchange weapons with the strangers, however, this ended in a scuffle and further shootings that left a warrior named Te Rakau lying dead beside the river. Later that day, when Cook attempted to capture some young men from a fishing canoe in an attempt to take them on board the *Endeavour*, treat them kindly and gain their trust, they resisted, hurling their paddles, anchor stones and fish at the strangers. Cook's men fired, shooting four of these fishermen, two of whom fell into the sea and drowned. That night Banks wrote in his journal: 'Thus ended the most disagreable day My life has yet seen, black be the mark for it and heaven send that such may never return to embitter future reflection.'[17] The memory of the killings in Turanga has not faded, however. The shots fired by the *Endeavour*'s men still echo across the bay.

Despairing of being able to befriend these people, Captain Cook decided to head south to discover whether or not this land was Terra Australis Incognita. As the *Endeavour* sailed from the bay, the wind died and the ship was becalmed off Te Kuri-a-Paoa (Young Nick's Head), where canoes came out, but stayed at a distance. When a small canoe from Turanganui arrived, bringing the man who had greeted Cook on Te Toka-a-Taiau, he invited Cook, Tupaia and their companions to return to the bay. Seeing this, the crews of the other canoes also boarded the ship. During this encounter, a set of paddles, their blades vividly painted with swirling scarlet kōwhai-whai patterns, was presented to the strangers, which the ship's artist Sydney Parkinson later sketched.[18] The owners of these paddles also offered their canoe, perhaps hoping to entice the visitors ashore.[19]

Cook sailed off, however, heading south. After coasting Hawke's Bay, where canoe-borne priests and warriors vigorously challenged the ship and its crew, the *Endeavour* was caught in contrary winds. Deciding to retrace his track, Cook headed north at Cape Turnagain, sailing past the Mahia Peninsula and Turanganui until they arrived at Anaura Bay, 85 kilometres north of Gisborne, where they experienced their first peaceful exchanges with Māori people.

Te Whakatatare-o-te-rangi – the ariki, or paramount chief, of this district – who had already heard about the strangers, was eager to learn more

Hoe, or paddles, collected on board Endeavour *off Te Kuri-a-Paoa (Young Nick's Head), by Sydney Parkinson, 1769.*

about them. Te Whakatatare had trained at Te Rawheoro, the nearby school of learning at Uawa, where students learned about the ancestral voyages from Hawaiki, how to build canoes, and the arts of tattoo, carving and star navigation. Intensely curious about these bizarre visitors, their strange vessel and the star navigator who had arrived from Ra'iatea, the ancestral homeland, he sent envoys out to the ship to meet them, who invited Tupaia and his companions ashore. As the *Endeavour's* anchors splashed down in Anaura Bay, the high chief donned his ceremonial cloak and, accompanied by another senior leader, went out to the ship. As these two venerable men, one wearing a dog-skin cape and the other dressed in a cloak covered with tufts of red feathers, came alongside, Tupaia invited them on board, where Captain Cook presented each of them with four yards of linen and a spike nail. As always, Tupaia conducted the rituals of greeting with local people.

When Te Whakatatare and Tupaia met, this was an encounter between Polynesian aristocrats. Tupaia, a high-born Ra'iatean priest and star navigator who had trained at Taputapuatea, one of the greatest voyaging marae

Sketch of warriors on a waka taua (war canoe) visiting the Endeavour
in Te Matau-a-Maui (Hawke's Bay), by Sydney Parkinson, 1769.

in the Pacific, was reputed to be one of the most intelligent and knowledge-able men in the Society Islands. When warriors from Borabora, a nearby island, conquered his homeland, Tupaia had fled to Tahiti where he became the lover and high priest of Purea, the 'queen' of that island. In June 1769, shortly after a failed attempt to install Purea's son as the paramount chief of the island, the *Endeavour* expedition arrived at Matavai Bay in Tahiti, where the Royal Society party set up a shore camp. Intrigued by the strangers and fascinated by their scientific instruments and rituals, Tupaia spent a great deal of time with them. When they left Tahiti the high priest decided to go with them, hoping to persuade Captain Cook to help him drive the Borabora invaders from his homeland. During their voyage through the Society Islands, he piloted the *Endeavour* and guided his companions through the rituals of landing and exchanges with local people, including those in Turanganui and Hawke's Bay.

By the time the *Endeavour* anchored off Anaura Bay, the ship's supplies of fresh food, water and firewood were running low, and Cook was delighted by the friendly welcome they received from Te Whakatatare and his people. Still convinced that they had found Terra Australis, Joseph Banks was eager to explore Anaura and discover what exotic plants and animals this fabled continent had to offer. That afternoon, after dining in the Great Cabin with

Cook and Banks, Te Whakatatare escorted Cook, Banks, Solander, William Monkhouse (the ship's surgeon) and Tupaia ashore to a village where his people sat quietly beside their houses. The high chief showed them large hillside gardens, which Banks and Monkhouse described as meticulously weeded, planted with kūmara and yams in mounds laid out in rows or a quincunx pattern, taro in circular concaves to keep them moist, a few bark-cloth plants, and flowering gourd plants sprawling over the houses. Walking into the hills on the south side of Anaura Bay, they visited a single dwelling inhabited by a man and his wife, who showed them all their possessions; and the man presented them with the body of a mummified newborn baby. As visitors (perhaps ancestors) from Ra'iatea, perhaps they seemed fitting guardians for this dead child.

Back at the beach, however, the waves were running high, and the sailors struggled to load the water barrels into the boats. When Banks borrowed a canoe to go out to the *Endeavour*, it capsized, unceremoniously tossing him and his companions into the surf. After this mishap, Te Whakatatare decided to guide the ship to Uawa, 10 kilometres to the south, where the inlet of Opoutama provided a more sheltered harbour. At that time Uawa was the headquarters for two senior descent groups, one led by Te Whakatatare and the other by his daughter-in-law Hinematioro. In 1769 Hinematioro (a high-born woman later described by the early missionaries as a 'queen') was still very young, and Te Whakatatare led the East Coast people.[20]

When the ship anchored off Uawa, Cook and Charles Green, the expedition's astronomer, carried out a series of instrumental observations. By now Tupaia was used to this kind of performance, but Te Whakatatare must have been fascinated. The tohunga (experts) at Te Rawheoro also studied the sun, moon and stars, using their movements in the sky to predict the weather, anticipate seasonal rhythms, and guide their canoes across the ocean.

In order to estimate the longitude of Uawa, Cook and Green used their sextants to measure the angular distance from the moon to the sun, and the tables in the *Nautical Almanac* to calculate their position. When this did not agree with their previous estimates, they worked out an average, recording this in the ship's log. At noon when Cook used the astronomical quadrant to observe the altitude of the sun, he was able to estimate the latitude of the bay with much greater precision.

While Captain Cook and Green were making these observations, Lieutenant Gore with a guard of marines and sailors landed at Opoutama

Sketch of Opoutama (Cook's Cove) in Tolaga Bay, by Herman Diedrich Spöring, 1769.

inlet/'Cook's Cove' where the sailors set to work, filling barrels with fresh water, felling trees for firewood and collecting greens that the ship's cook mixed with oatmeal as a remedy for scurvy. As canoes flocked around the ship, their crews exchanged fish and 'curiosities' (artefacts) for Tahitian bark cloth and European beads, nails, trinkets and glass bottles. The local people put a high value on their sweet potatoes, however, and refused to exchange their greenstone ornaments and weapons for anything that the strangers could offer.

Meanwhile, Joseph Banks and Dr Solander were impatient to go ashore. When Cook finally landed them and their assistants in Cook's Cove, they were enthralled by what they found. According to the artist Sydney Parkinson:

> The country about the bay is agreeable beyond description, and, with proper cultivation, might be rendered a kind of second Paradise. The hills are covered with beautiful flowering shrubs, intermingled with a great number of tall and stately palms, which fill the air with a most grateful fragrant perfume.[21]

Everywhere they looked, Banks and Solander discovered plants unknown to European science. Wandering around the cove, they collected specimens from a bewildering variety of new species of trees, palms, bushes, creepers and ferns. They also found many beautiful kinds of birds, including parrots, pigeons and quail, and Polynesian rats and dogs like those in Tahiti. Blazing away with their guns, they shot birds whose skins were later preserved on board the *Endeavour*.

When they returned to the ship, Banks and his companions sat in the Great Cabin, Sydney Parkinson sketching samples of plants while Banks and Solander classified them using the Linnaean method, and Herman Spöring (Banks's Finnish draughtsman) wrote down the botanical descriptions. Afterwards, the plants were pressed between pages torn from a commentary on Milton's *Paradise Lost*, ripped apart for the purpose. In all, Parkinson drew 32 different species of plants collected in Te Oneroa (Gisborne), 24 species collected in Anaura Bay and 37 species in Uawa, jotting down notes and swathes of colour on the sketches that were later engraved for Banks's magnificent *Florilegium* from the voyage.[22]

The next day, when Banks came across a natural rock arch north of the watering place, he exclaimed: 'It was certainly the most magnificent surprize I have ever met with, so much is pure nature superior to art in these cases.'[23] Back in England, rock arches and grottos were all the rage, and Banks instructed his artists to sketch this picturesque formation, not realising that it was known as 'Te Kotore-o-te-whenua' (The Anus of the Land) – a cosmographic version of a whakapohane, a graphic insult featuring the exposure of a naked backside. That evening, an old man at the watering place, armed with a spear and a stone club, put up a pole and vigorously attacked it, giving them a demonstration of hand-to-hand fighting.

On 25 October, Tupaia spent most of the day immersed in conversation with the head priest from Te Rawheoro, comparing accounts of the creation, tracing genealogies back to common ancestors, and discussing local beliefs and customs. According to Banks, 'they seemd to agree very well in their notions of religion only Tupia was much more learned than the other and all his discourse was heard with much attention'.[24] In his rough notes, Cook recorded snippets from these exchanges, which show his liking and respect for the local people.

1. The Religion of the Natives bear some resemblance to the George Islanders –
2. they have god of war, of husbandry &c but there is one suprem god whom the[y] call . . . he made the world and all that therein is – by Copolation

3. they have many Priests
4. The Old men are much respected –
5. they have King who lives inland his name is . . . we heard of him in Poverty Bay
6. They eat their enimies Slane in Battell – this seems to come from custom and not from a Savage disposission this they cannot be charged with – they appear to have but few Vices . . .
7. Their beheavour was Uniform free from treachery
8. The Women may be know by their Voices they paint their faces red
9. the Womens faces are not tattoued[25]

While talking with the local priest, Tupaia was told that at the beginning of the world, Tane, the son of Rangi and Papa, created many new forms of life by having sex with different kinds of beings. This story was later recounted by the East Coast tohunga Mohi Ruatapu, who explained how Tane shaped the first woman, thrusting his penis into different parts of her body to create sweat, saliva and mucus.[26] In the Society Islands, on the other hand, Tane was the god of beauty and peace, and the guardian of blue-water sailors. In the rituals at Taputapuatea in Ra'iatea, dedicated to 'Oro, the god of fertility and war, the priests (including Tupaia) offered slain enemies as sacrifices, with their jawbones, skulls and hair kept as trophies on his marae. Despite this, Tupaia was scandalised by the Māori custom of kai tangata (eating people), the ritual sacrifice of their enemies.

According to Banks, when the Ra'iatean high priest asked the local people 'whether or no they realy eat men, which he was very loth to believe; they answerd in the affirmative saying that they eat the bodys only of their enemies who were killd in war'. Although they 'put themselves into a heat by defending the Custom', Tupaia took 'every Occasion to speak ill of [it], exhorting them to leave it off'.[27] His reaction may seem odd, given the prevalence of human sacrifice in his homeland. In the Society Islands, however, it was the ancestors who consumed the bodies of enemy warriors, not the priests, and Tupaia may have considered the local custom sacrilegious.[28] Although many of the Europeans, including the sailors, were also horrified by kai tangata (for very different reasons), James Cook was phlegmatic – in his words from above, attributing it to 'custom and not . . . a Savage disposission'.[29]

The day after Tupaia talked with the high priest from Te Rawhero, it pelted with rain. As the *Endeavour* lay shrouded in mist, Banks and Solander sat in the Great Cabin, working on their collections. On 27 October when they returned to Cook's Cove, a group of boys demonstrated the art of whipping tops (one of which Banks acquired) while some men and women performed a haka (war dance), rolling down their eyes, poking out their tongues and heaving loud sighs. Climbing up to the northern ridgeline to inspect Kararoa pā, Banks found the fortified village in ruins. He measured the palisades at 14 to 16 feet high, standing in two rows six feet apart along a ditch that curved around the end of the peninsula.

Later that day, Captain Cook took a boat and sounded the bay, his men using a lead and line to measure the depth of the water. After landing on the point at the northern side of the harbour, they rowed up the Uawa River and climbed a high hill, where he recorded the bearings of headlands and islands with an azimuth compass. Many of the observations taken by Cook and Green (including latitude, longitude, bearings, soundings, islands, rocks and the coastline) are recorded in Cook's charts of the East Coast and Uawa. From this high vantage point, Cook saw 'the Vallies and sides of many of the Hills . . . luxuriously clothed with Woods and Verdure and little Plantations of the Natives lying dispers'd up and down the Country'.[30] These gardens were each several acres in size, surrounded by low windbreaks with traps set on the ground to catch kiore (Polynesian rats). Like the gardens in Anaura Bay, the cultivations were finely tilled. It was spring, and the tips of the plants were just appearing above the ground. Although there were houses in the valleys, these were empty, with the inhabitants living in light shelters on the ridges.

On October 28, while Lieutenant Gore and his men were getting the ship ready for sea, Captain Cook, Banks, Solander, Parkinson and Spöring visited Pourewa Island, the home of the young chieftainess Hinematioro. When they landed, they saw a very large canoe lying on the beach, 68 feet 6 inches long with carved gunwale planks and a finely carved prow.[31] While Spöring sat sketching this canoe, he thought he saw a bird with a very long tail flying overhead. Very likely, however, this was a kite. At that time, bird-shaped kites made with bark cloth were often flown into the heavens to carry messages to the ancestors. Close to the beach, the Royal Society party found a house about 30 feet long, filled with chips and shavings. Inside, a number of squared posts and intricately carved wall panels were stacked against the walls. This chief's house seemed to be abandoned. According to local oral histories, during his visit to the bay, and perhaps on this occasion, Captain

Cook met Hinematioro, and presented her with blue beads that she later handed down to her descendants.

That afternoon, a group of officers and gentlemen were invited inland to another house where a number of chiefs were meeting. At the end of this gathering, some of the visitors were offered sexual hospitality. Returning to the watering place after dark, one of these men was carried on a man's back over channels filled with running water, probably irrigation ditches for the local gardens.

Until that afternoon, the Europeans had found the local women elusive. On the East Coast, where high-ranking women were often the leaders and founders of kin groups, the women were confident and assertive. As Parkinson remarked ruefully, 'They seem to be proud of their sex, and expect you should give them every thing they desire, because they are women; but they take care to grant no favours in return, being very different from the women in the islands who were so free with our men.'[32] According to Banks, 'They were as great coquetts as any Europaeans could be and the young ones as skittish as unbroke fillies.'[33]

On 29 October, as the *Endeavour* sailed from Uawa, heading north, Joseph Banks commented with pleasure on his visit to this district, writing in his journal that the communities on the East Coast were 'in a state of Profound Peace; their Cultivations were far more numerous and larger than we saw them anywhere else and they had a far greater quantity of Fine boats, Fine cloaths, Fine carvd work; in short the people were far more numerous, and lived in much greater affluence than any others we saw'.[34]

The wooden world of the *Endeavour*

If one examines the *Endeavour* records and Māori oral histories of these meetings, it is clear that these were complex encounters, characterised by intense curiosity and empirical inquiry. Tupaia, the 'arioi high priest and star navigator from Ra'iatea, was on his own voyage of discovery, adding new islands to the lists of those known to Society Island navigators while studying their inhabitants and landscapes. At the same time, he served as an interpreter and mediator for his European companions, initiating new kinds of exchanges. As a leading expert from the ancestral whare 'aira'a-upu (schools of learning) in the Society Islands, an ancestral homeland of Māori, Tupaia had a great deal to offer the tohunga in New Zealand. In most places (except for Uawa and Queen Charlotte Sound), however, their conversations were fleeting, and only vestigial traces of these exchanges survive in the records from the voyage.

At the same time, the *Endeavour* expedition was a travelling sideshow of the Enlightenment, lavishly provided with scientific equipment to scan the heavens, collect and examine plants and animals, and explore the remote corners of the planet. Just as the *Endeavour* arrived in New Zealand, modernity was taking shape in Europe. As Frängsmyr, Heilbron and Rider have noted, in mid-eighteenth-century Europe, a mechanistic, quantitative vision of reality was going viral. Many aspects of life were transformed – from science (with the use of instruments and measurement, the division of the disciplines and the increased specialisation of knowledge) to administration (with the invention of censuses, surveys, archives and bureaucratic systems) and industry (with manufacturing based on mechanisation, the replication of parts and processes), for instance.[35]

This particular strand of Enlightenment thought traces at least as far back as the seventeenth century, when the philosopher René Descartes had a new vision of reality, at once powerful and intoxicating. In his dream, the Cogito – the thinking self – became the eye of the world, which in turn became an object for inspection.[36] As the mind's eye replaced the Eye of God, people were separated from Nature, and eventually from each other. As mind (*res cogitans*) and matter (*res extensa*), subject and object and Culture and Nature were split, different realms of reality were set apart and subdivided, producing arrays of bounded objects that could be classified, counted and examined.[37] This 'Order of Things', as Michel Foucault has called it, lay at the heart of Enlightenment science.[38] Here, the cosmos was understood as a singular, bounded, law-governed entity (or uni-verse) – a view of reality sometimes described as a 'one world ontology'.[39] In modernist science, the aim was to examine, analyse, count, classify and record everything that exists, and discover the laws that govern these phenomena.[40] In France, for example, the *Encyclopédie*, or 'Systematic Dictionary of the Arts, Crafts and Sciences', edited by Denis Diderot, which sought to collect and summarise all human knowledge, appeared from 1751 onwards, while the *Encyclopaedia Britannica* was published in three volumes, at the same time as the *Endeavour* sailed around the world.

In this way of knowing, one of the iconic patterns was the grid, used to abstract, divide up and measure space, time and life forms, bringing them

*A hierarchical cosmos:
The Great Chain of
Being, from* Rhetorica
Christiana *by Diego
Valades, 1579.*

under control for practical purposes.[41] In this way, the world was transformed
into bounded entities at different scales, whether units of time, blocks of
land, areas of ocean or different types of living beings, that can be classified
and counted in various ways. On board the *Endeavour*, this form of order was
reflected in cartography and Linnaean taxonomy, for example.

Often, the grid was hierarchical – based on the old European vision of
the Great Chain of Being, with God at the apex followed by archangels and
angels, divine kings, the aristocracy and successive ranks of human beings,
from 'civilised' to 'savage', followed by animals, plants and minerals and the
earth in descending order.[42] Those at the top of the Great Chain exercised
power and authority over those lower down, who in turn were required to
offer up deference and tribute. In this cosmic model, men ruled over women

and children, free men over slaves, and 'civilised' people over 'barbarians' and 'savages'. Another iconic model was the idea of the cosmos as a machine, made up of distinct, divisible working parts. Coupled with notions of 'progress' and 'improvement', the 'Order of Things' gave an air of virtue to imperial expansion, the industrial revolution, global capitalism and models of technocratic control. With its focus on discovery, instrumental recording, mathematical and taxonomic description, the *Endeavour* voyage epitomised this way of understanding the world.[43]

At the same time, however, as Peter Hans Reill and others have argued, another strand in Enlightenment thinking explored relational forms of order. Here, one of the iconic motifs was the network (or web).[44] Thinkers including Count Buffon in France, many of those involved in the Scottish Enlightenment and later Joseph Priestley and Erasmus Darwin in England and the Humboldt brothers in Germany understood the world as a living system patterned by networks of relations among (and within) different life forms, animated by interactions among complementary forces – the 'Order of Relations', one might call it. These forms of order underpinned ideas of transformation, in both the cosmos and social life. In many ways, they resonate with Māori and Pacific ways of thinking.

Relational ideas in the Enlightenment, based on Greco-Roman precedents and notions of equilibrium and exchange, provided an alternative to the old top-down models, underpinning arguments for freedom from the rule of the merchants (Adam Smith's *The Wealth of Nations*, 1776); and the rights of ordinary people (Tom Paine's *The Rights of Man*, 1791), women (Mary Wollstonecraft, *a Vindication of the Rights of Women*, 1792), slaves and indigenous people. In this 'web of life', people were just one life form among many, and the world was constantly changing. Ancestral ideas such as justice, truth, equality and honour helped to determine how exchanges among people should be handled. Here one can find the origins of participatory democracy, the emancipation of women and slaves, earth sciences, environmental theory, anthropology, the World Wide Web and the science of complex systems, for example.[45] On board the *Endeavour*, this kind of thinking was reflected in the Earl of Morton's 'Hints', with its emphasis on the legal rights of Pacific peoples to control their own lands, and in the scientists' journals written during the voyage, with their interest in the interactions among people, plants, animals, landscapes and seascapes in the Pacific.

European science at this time was exciting, provocative and paradoxical. This was the era of scientific agriculture (including enclosure), the noble savage (alongside imperial domination and exploitation), arguments in favour of peace (in the midst of almost incessant fighting), and the rights of consumers (at a time of frequent food riots) and commoners, just before the French Revolution and the American War of Independence. Together, these and other strands in Enlightenment thought[46] produced passionate debates about topics as varied as land use, slavery, taxation, education and the rights of ordinary people (including the rights of those living in colonies, commoners, women and indigenous people) – debates that in many ways we are still having.

Not surprisingly, these divergent views were also echoed on board the *Endeavour*. As a member of the landed gentry, Joseph Banks found hierarchies and gridded models congenial. Like the great Swedish naturalist Linnaeus, he invoked the Great Chain of Being, and took it for granted that he and his fellow Europeans (especially the gentry) occupied a higher place on the cosmic ladder than the people he met in the Pacific. In his musings upon Māori cannibalism, for instance, Banks remarked that 'Nature recoils at the thought of any species preying upon itself', adding, 'Anyone who considers the admirable chain of nature in which Man, alone endowd with reason, justly claims the higher rank, will easily see that no Conclusion in favour of such a practise can be drawn from the actions of a race of beings placd so infinitely below us in the order of Nature.'[47] Although Banks was fascinated by Tupaia, enjoyed his company and learned a great deal from him, he found no difficulty in comparing the high priest with the lions and tigers kept and displayed by his aristocratic friends in their zoological parks back in England.[48] A keen Linnaean botanist and scientific farmer, this future president of the Royal Society was also quick to identify and classify plants, resources and places that might serve Britain's economic interests.

James Cook, on the other hand, was less certain about the virtues of a stratified world. A farm labourer's son, he had served his apprenticeship with Captain John Walker, a Quaker ship owner in Whitby who became his lifelong guide and mentor. The Society of Friends was at the radical edge of relational thinking in Britain, with beliefs in spiritual equality for all (including women), freedom for slaves and fair treatment for indigenous peoples. As we have seen, Cook regarded Māori cannibalism as an ancestral custom, not a mark of savage depravity, and was perturbed by the impacts

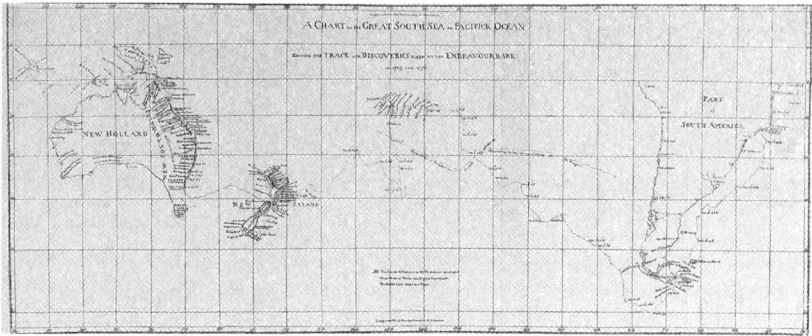

Gridding the world: James Cook's 'A chart of the great South Sea or Pacifick Ocean shewing the track and discoveries made by the Endeavour Bark in 1769 and 1770'.

of venereal diseases and European goods on Pacific islanders. As he later remarked of his encounters in New Zealand:

> What is still more to our shame as civilized Christians, we debauch their morals . . . and we interduce among them wants and perhaps diseases which they never before knew, and which serves only to disturb that happy tranquility which they and their forefathers had injoyed. If anyone denies the truth of this assertion let him tell me what the natives of the whole extent of America have gained by the commerce they have had with Europeans.[49]

No doubt Cook's attitudes were shaped by the Earl of Morton's 'Hints', as well as by his own upbringing. Like him, each member of the Royal Society party (and the crew) had their own views about imperial expansion and the nobility of 'savages' (a concept that infuriated many of the sailors).

Despite Cook's humanitarian impulses, however, there is no doubt that on board his ship (and in his instructions from the Admiralty) the 'Order of Things' was dominant. In Cook's surveys and charts, the ship's track and coastlines were traced on sheets of paper gridded with latitude and longitude, fixed by surveying and astronomical observation, with orientation indicated by compass bearings.[50] In the alchemy of hydrography, the land was reduced to a coastline, stripped of most of its features and emptied of people – a *terra nullius*. With its inhabitants erased, the sea was similarly abstracted into a blank, two-dimensional watery wasteland – a *mare nullius*, waiting to be discovered and claimed by European powers.[51]

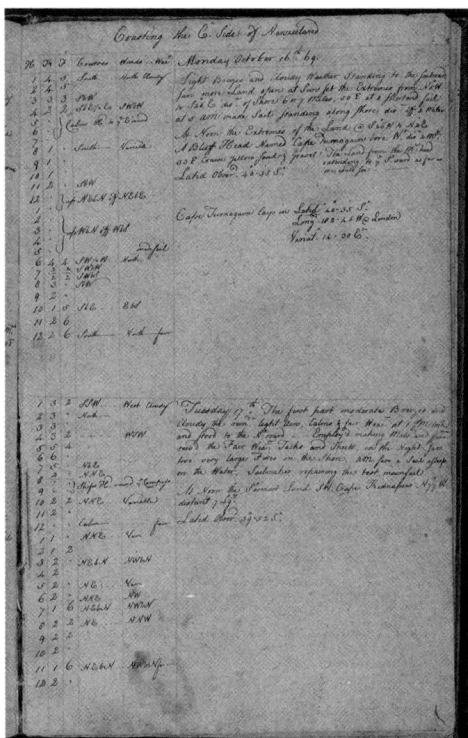

A page from Zachary Hicks's Endeavour *log, off the coast of Hawkes Bay.*

In the ship's logs, time was gridded into years, months, days and hours, with columns showing the direction of the wind, the location of the vessel and its speed measured by knots across the ocean. Instruments such as telescopes, quadrants, sextants and chronometers gave increased precision and scope to these measurements, although older technologies continued to be used. The depth of the coastal seabed was measured with the lead, for instance, especially near harbours or lagoons, and these soundings were recorded on the charts.

While the officers drafted these records, the naturalists collected specimens of plants and animals and sorted these into genera, classes and orders, each with its own definition and (binomial) descriptor. Joseph Banks used the taxonomic system devised by Dr Solander's mentor Carl Linnaeus, sorting plants into genera and species by counting and describing their sexual organs. Like the ship's charts and journals, this gridded system of classification was abstract and highly 'artificial' (and criticised as such by the

Sophora tetraptera *(kowhai)*
J. S. Millar. Hand coloured line
engraving by G. Sibelius, after
Sydney Parkinson, 1769.

French naturalist Buffon, for example).[52] It was based on a few distinctive features that allowed specimens to be placed in mutually exclusive categories whose contents could be easily sorted and compared – invaluable in its simplicity for describing the extravagant profusion of exotic animals and plants that travelling Europeans encountered in their voyages around the world.[53] In addition, the Royal Society party gathered numerous 'type specimens'. In the case of plants, these were pressed, while animals were skinned or bottled, and labelled, ready to be taken home to Britain, and artefacts (artificial curiosities) were collected as exemplars of local ways of living.

The same taxonomic approach is reflected in Sydney Parkinson's sketches. He was a botanical draughtsman, disciplined to accurately trace the outlines of different species of plants on paper. The first image of a plant was usually a simple pencil sketch, with notes or splashes of colour to guide a later, more finished portrait, usually in watercolour.

Flowers, stamens and pistils were important for the purposes of botanical classification, and for this reason the scale of these parts is often exaggerated, or colours made more vivid, or parts that were never present at the same time are depicted in a single drawing. 'Realist' art, then, was not a mirror of the world but strategically shaped by scientific and aesthetic purposes, as the art historian Bernard Smith has argued in his brilliant studies of the artists who sailed with Captain Cook.[54]

Likewise, Banks's observations of landscapes, people and artefacts were organised according to a taxonomic system that Cook copied, allowing the different places they visited to be compared under headings such as 'Terrain', 'Climate', 'Minerals', 'Population', 'Forts and Leaders', 'Religion', 'Burial and Mourning'. Here, Banks drew upon methods for describing new countries that had been devised by members of the Royal Society during the early years of Enlightenment science.[55] Under these gridded headings, the accounts of what the explorers saw and experienced often seem curiously inanimate and inert. The ship's journals, on the other hand, especially those by Joseph Banks and William Brougham Monkhouse, the ship's surgeon (who according to Cook was given to 'intemperance'), are vivid and lively, demonstrating the wide-ranging, detailed style of observation cultivated during an eighteenth-century scientific education.

At this time in Europe, relational thinking dominated the medical schools, and medical students in London, Edinburgh, Montpellier and Leyden were taught to observe and meticulously describe plants, landscapes and climates as well as people and their diseases, and reflect upon the complex interactions among (and within) these living beings.[56] In many of these centres, Cartesian dualism and mechanistic, quantitative models of Nature were vigorously contested. Buffon, for example, argued that the mathematical 'truths' claimed for these kinds of accounts were artificial, abstract, and self-certifying in nature:

> [These are] only truths of definition. They depend on simple, but abstract suppositions, and all truths of this kind are abstract consequences compounded from these definitions . . . thus mathematical truths are only the exact repetitions of the definitions or suppositions. . . . They reduce to the identity of ideas, and have no reality.[57]

Instead, Buffon advocated the close empirical observation and testing of the patterns of relations among (and within) different kinds of phenomena.

On board the *Endeavour*, the ship's surgeon William Monkhouse, Dr Solander and his clerk Herman Spöring all had medical training.

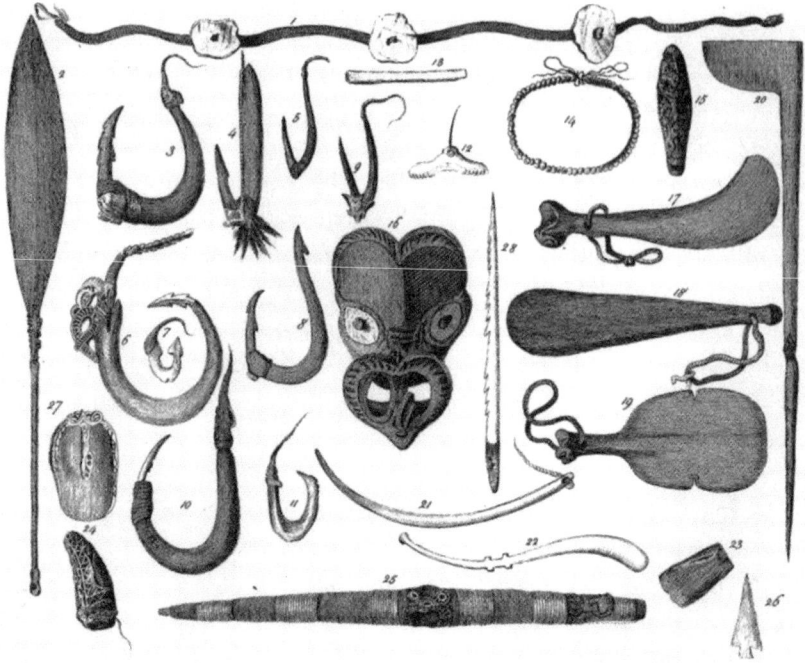

*Classifying artefacts: 'Musical Instruments and other Objects
from New Zealand', by John Frederick Miller, 1771.*

Monkhouse's journal in particular is finely crafted, combining a wealth of
detail with an omnivorous curiosity about everything that could be seen
(especially of human life) in the localities that they visited. Unfortunately,
however, it survives only in a fragment, beginning in Poverty Bay and ending
with the *Endeavour*'s visit to Anaura Bay.[58]

At the end of the voyage, the officers' journals, logs and charts were
handed in to the Admiralty, where they were classified and stored, while
Joseph Banks either owned, could claim or procured the 'gentlemen's' written accounts, and many of the sketches, paintings, 'artificial curiosities' and
botanical and zoological objects collected by both scientists and sailors.

The artefacts were later sketched, listed and classified in London using
a functional typology ('paddle', 'spear', 'club', and so forth), along with the
location in which they were collected, and kept and exhibited in Banks's
private collection. The charts with their linked records – logs, journals and
sketches – placed New Zealand and its coastlines on the maps of the world,

while the artefacts and specimens became part of collections that exhibited the cultural and natural orders of the world, displayed in museums back in Britain.

In many ways, the 'wooden world' of the *Endeavour*, with its instruments, scientists and artists, was a travelling laboratory, capturing and recording new phenomena. In the process, Māori and their territories came under 'imperial eyes', a top-down inspection linked with global expansion and colonial control.[59] At the same time, there was also a willingness to engage with Māori and a curiosity about different ways of living that derived from relational thinking, suggesting a more open-minded approach to these encounters 'across the pae' (horizon or threshold between sky and earth).

Voyaging taonga

If one examines the records from the Māori or Polynesian sides of the meetings that took place when the *Endeavour* visited Anaura and Uawa, on the other hand, few eyewitness accounts remain, compared with those that survive in European archives. This asymmetry in lines of evidence is not accidental, but arises from very different ways of preserving significant objects and information.

When Tupaia died in Batavia, his memories of his extraordinary adventures on board the *Endeavour* died with him, and the gifts that he had been given during the voyage were dispersed (or claimed by Joseph Banks, as his sponsor). Among Hauiti people, memories of the *Endeavour*'s visit were kept alive in oral traditions and songs. The people of this region were famed as composers, acclaimed as 'the bards of their country'.[60] They passed Tupaia's name down to their children, transformed nails into carving chisels, and handed down the blue beads given to them by Captain Cook to their descendants.

Like Cook and his Royal Society companions, local Māori were intensely curious about the strangers they met during the encounters in Uawa. The local whare wānanga Te Rawheoro was a magnet for tohunga from other regions, a centre for exchanges about oral knowledge, voyaging and the arts. Carvers and tattooists from Te Rawheoro travelled widely, carrying out commissions in other parts of the country. During their meetings with their *Endeavour* visitors, Māori, Polynesian and European goods and technologies were exchanged, and tested. Even the conversations that occurred were highly experimental, based on borrowings and innovations. Tupaia, Te Whakatatare, the priest from Te Rawheoro and other Hauitians must have spoken with each other in a mixture of Tahitian and Māori. Tupaia, an experienced traveller who had mastered the sound shifts between different Polynesian languages, quickly learned to communicate with Māori. He had also acquired a little English, while some of the scientists, artists and sailors had a smattering of Tahitian, which they tried out on the local inhabitants.

Like these dialogues, Tupaia's charts and sketches were created across the pae, the middle ground, reflecting the history of exchanges between the high priest and the ship's navigators (Cook and Molyneux) and the expedition's artists, Sydney Parkinson and Herman Spöring, as well as his own navigational and artistic expertise and what he witnessed during his travels. In Tahiti, Tupaia had given his shipmates (including Parkinson and Banks) 'arioi tattoos, while they taught him to sketch and paint in watercolour in a 'realist' style (although in his sketch of Banks in an exchange with a Māori warrior, he depicted both men with eyes based on an ancient Pacific motif, also found on the 'Lapita' pottery made by the ancestors of Polynesians).

Unfortunately, we know almost nothing about Tupaia's reactions to Māori art. During his visit to Uawa, however, the young Quaker artist Sydney Parkinson was struck by the rioting spirals that embellished everyday objects:

> The men have a particular taste for carving: their boats, paddles, boards to put on their houses, tops of walking sticks, and even their boats valens, are carved in a variety of flourishes, turnings and windings, that are unbroken; but their favourite figure seems to be a volute, or spiral, which they vary many ways, single, double, and triple, and with as much truth as if done from mathematical draughts: yet the only instruments we have seen are a chizzel, and an axe made of stone. Their fancy, indeed, is very wild and extravagant.[61]

Disciplined as he was by a Quaker upbringing and the conventions of botanical draughting, Parkinson was bemused by Māori art forms. Here, the emphasis is not on distinct entities and their outlines, but on the spaces between them. In many carvings, ancestors emerge from each other or are locked in sexual congress. Although Parkinson was taken aback, it is likely that Joseph Banks, a member of the 'Hellfire Club' back at home who had a libertine streak, found these images titillating. In their own context, however, they are neither provocative nor shocking. They celebrate fertility through the union of complementary forces, and the passage of the hau (life force) from one generation to another.

In Māori art, the power of life and growth (hau ora and hau tipu) is often expressed in exuberant, sprawling spirals incised on bodies, faces and objects. Etched with chisels and stained with dye, these transform people and carvings into living ancestors. According to Pei Te Hurinui Jones, a twentieth-century expert from the Tainui whare wānanga, the double spiral in Māori carving and tattoo depicts the emergence of the cosmos, impelled by the breath of life.[62] In a South Island chant, the atua (god) sings the universe into life.[63] A person might likewise sing their desire into the wind (hau), sending it to a distant lover.[64] Spirals are song lines in ink or wood, unfurling the world. Unlike the arrow of time in modernity, which flies in one direction, calibrated by the mechanically measured standardised units that were then being defined in Europe, life in Māori spirals in and out with the rhythms of the hau – the seasons, the tides, the ebb and flow of breath, life and death, exchanges between the present, past and future.

In the whare wānanga, or schools of learning, cosmological chants were recited in the dark, imprinted in the mind-hearts of the tauira (students) and passed on from one generation to another. The hau, or breath, of the tohunga (priestly experts) animated the chant, summoning up ancestors. This is also true of Māori music, which features song or wind instruments, powered by the hau of the player. As they chanted, the tohunga took alternate breaths so that the flow of hau joining them to the ancestral source was not broken. At times, these matakite (literally 'those with eyes that can see') looked into the future, anticipating the arrival of white-skinned strangers, for example.

In the chant quoted at the beginning of this book, the messenger bird (or tūī) urges his listeners to bind the lines of people coming down from Hawaiki. In Māori, the word kāwai (used in the chant) refers at once to a strand of fibre used in weaving; a line of descent; the twining shoots of a creeper; the plaited handles on a flax basket; and the breeze that blows across the land. In this one word, the hau of descent lines, weaving, wind and a range of valuable plants are fused.

The life of these plants echoes the patterns of human existence. The harakeke, or flax plant, with its array of named varieties, for instance, sends up fans of tall, wide green leaves with flowers that provide nectar for

tūī and kōmako, or bellbirds. In each fan, the outer leaves or tipuna (ancestors) are harvested for basketry, lashing, plaiting or weaving, while at the
heart of the fan, two mātua, or parent leaves, protect the rito, the inner leaf
that is the source of ongoing life. In harvesting, these three leaves are left
intact, protecting the mauri (life force) of the plant, its source of hau ora.
As the saying goes:

Hutia te rito o te harakeke	If the rito is plucked from the flax plant
Kei hea te kōmako e kō	Where will the bellbird sing?
Kī mai ki ahau	Ask me
He aha te mea nui o te ao	What is the most important thing in the world
Māku e kī atu,	And I will tell you
He tangata, he tangata, he tangata.	It is people, people, people.

Other plants grow rhizomatically, putting down roots as they sprawl across
the ground, or withering and dying. These evoke the growth or decline of
kin groups, and the link between tangata (people) and whenua (land). They
include the kūmara, or sweet potato, a chiefly crop, with its rampaging vines,
and the hue, or gourd, the only domestic plant grown from seed (and carried
as seeds on long oceanic voyages), which grew over houses and other structures as well as gardens. In referring to their ancestral origins, for instance,
a person might say He kākano i ruia mai i Ra'iatea, I am a seed sown from
Hawaiki.

In all of these sayings, word and world fuse in ways that reflect Māori,
rather than Western, onto-logic. These patterns also animate toi Māori
(Māori art), with motifs that later became national icons. The koru, or
double spiral, for instance, which evokes the unfurling frond of a ponga,
or silver fern, flies around the world on the tail of Air New Zealand planes,
while the silver fern leaf has become the emblem for New Zealand sports
teams including the All Blacks, the national rugby team, and the Silver
Ferns, the national netball team.

In his video work *Takarangi Loop*, displayed in the Museum of New
Zealand Te Papa Tongarewa in 2012, the Māori artist Brett Graham animated these ancestral devices, taking a number of Pei Jones's sketches of
double spirals and making the lines spin like gyres, flash like nebulae, twine
like double helixes or rotate like vortices – whirlpools or whirlwinds.

'Nebula 11', by Brett Graham, 2011.

In these spirals, the double lines are often joined by chevrons of affinity and alliance, a relational form of order based on exchange between complementary pairs. Like the Uawa carvings, the vines of life in these sketches explode and sprawl from curling stems, impelled by hau tipu and hau ora (the winds of growth and life).[65] This is more than symbolism, however. In Māori ways of being, hau spirals through space and time, linking people with their ancestors. Just as a meeting house or a fine canoe or a carved wall panel can *be* an ancestor, the same can be true of a photograph, for example. Once when I found a photograph of my mentor Eruera Stirling's chiefly grandfather, Maaka Te Ehutu, and brought it to him, Eruera wept and talked with the photograph, stroking his grandfather's face.

Equally, paramount chiefs such as Te Whakatatare-o-te-rangi and Hinematioro, in whom many powerful lines of descent converge, carry the hau of many ancestors, making them tapu (sacred) and endowing them with mana, the ability to act powerfully in the world. They act as portals across the pae (or threshold) between te pō and te ao, allowing ancestors to be active and visible in the kanohi ora (living face) of their direct descendants.[66] It is this hau that gives identity, rather than its āhua (its form or material expression). Thus, a person might press noses with a carved ancestor or their photographic image, mingling their hau together. An ancestor can *be*

Carved canoe prow, in Uawa (Tolaga Bay), by Herman Diedrich Spöring, 1769.

a mountain, or a river. In Māori oratory, a speaker often begins by reciting the names of the main mountain, river and ancestor in their home territory, binding people together with land, ancestors, mountains and rivers as tāngata whenua (people of the land).

In the same way, the art works – Tahitian, European and Māori – that survive from the *Endeavour*'s visits to Te Oneroa and Uawa have the capacity to travel through space/time (or wā). In their trajectories of exchange, new relations are forged. Through these voyaging taonga, the story of the encounters between Cook and his men, Tupaia and East Coast people is still unfolding. During their visit to Pourewa Island, for instance, Spöring measured and sketched a canoe with a carved stern and prow.[67] In this carving, serpentine shapes decorated with spirals curl and tangle, carved in openwork right through the wood so that the light shines through, casting shadows on the ground.[68] During the same visit, it seems that a poupou (wall panel) was taken from among the carvings stacked up against the wall in a house on the island that seemed to be abandoned (or perhaps unfinished, still in a state of tapu, or ancestral presence and power). The island was the home of the young chieftainess Hinematioro, and this carved ancestor may have been presented as a gift to Banks or Tupaia. This poupou is also embellished with double spirals, etched in openwork beside the face and carved into shoulders and knees, the major joints in the body. The ancestor's mouth is incised with

'*Carved Plank from New Zeland*'. *Pen and wash sketch by John Frederick Miller in London,* 1771 *(poupou almost certainly collected in Uawa during the* Endeavour's *visit in October* 1769*), with the original carved poupou alongside.*

openwork, exposing the tongue and allowing the hau, the wind of life, to flow around it.

As we have seen, in the exchange of gifts, relationships are created as hau intermingles, binding different individuals and their descent lines together; and in the etiquette of Polynesian gift exchange, an object that is admired must be handed over. It is possible that Banks admired the carved poupou, or perhaps it represented an ancestor linked with Tupaia. It may also have happened that Banks or one of his companions took the carving without permission, although since it is an ancestor, the local people would have reacted strongly to such an affront. What we do know is that the poupou was carried on board the *Endeavour* and taken back to London, where it was sketched in 1771 in Joseph Banks's collection – a pen-and-wash drawing that still survives in the British Museum.[69]

In his writings about taonga (ancestral treasures), Paul Tapsell likens these objects to the tūī, a bird with an iridescent blue-green body and a white puff of feathers at its throat – another link with the chant at the beginning of this book, which features this bird.[70] In both New Zealand and Tahiti, birds were messengers of the gods. The tūī is a special bird, a song bird that can be taught to speak. As it flies across the bush, a tūī sometimes swoops down into the darkness and then soars up into the light, where everyone can see it. Like the tūī, some of these treasures disappear into the Pō (the dark realm of ancestors) for a period, before reappearing in the world of light.

Just in this way, this carved ancestor alternately soared into light and disappeared into darkness. After being exhibited in Banks's collection in London, it passed out of his possession, either as a gift during his lifetime or when his collection was sold and dispersed after his death. Eventually, the carving was acquired by Ferdinand von Hochstetter, a German geologist who visited New Zealand. After his death, his daughter presented it to Tuebingen University, where it is now housed in their museum. In 1996, when a collection of artefacts from Captain Cook's voyages held in Goettingen was being catalogued for an exhibition, Dr Volker Harms, an ethnologist from Tuebingen University, recognised the ancestral figure from the 1771 drawing of this carving, made in London.[71] When the identification of the carved wall panel in Germany was announced, the New Zealand press picked up the story.

In my book *Two Worlds: First Meetings between Maori and Europeans* (1991), I'd described the *Endeavour*'s visit to Uawa, illustrating the account with the 1771 sketch of the poupou and speculating that this carving had been collected on Pourewa Island.[72] When the story broke,[73] Te Aitanga-a-Hauiti people who were attending a land case at the High Court in Auckland invited me to a gathering at the marae at Auckland Teachers' Training College, where they were staying. Elated that an ancestral taonga from Uawa had come to light, the Hauiti people asked whether during a forthcoming research trip to Europe, I might visit the carving. I sent an email to Dr Harms, who replied that the poupou had just been sent to Dresden, where it was going to be restored.[74] Since its departure from Uawa, it seems that parts of the head and arms of the ancestor had been cut off, perhaps so that the carving could be built into a piece of European furniture.[75]

Just before I left New Zealand, the conservator Dr Anke Sharres, a specialist in restoring painted wall panels, sent a message asking whether

I could find some tōtara wood, and bring it to Dresden for the restoration. The slabs of tōtara had to be old and dry, cut in a certain way, with particular dimensions. After an unsuccessful hunt among various Māori carvers, my husband Jeremy (a conservation architect) found suitable lengths of old tōtara in a cabinetmaker's workshop. These were cut to the right sizes, and packed in our bags as we set off on our travels. When we finally arrived at the conservator's studio in Dresden, the ancestral carving was lying on a table with a copy of the 1771 sketch beside it, and a Plasticine maquette that Anke had made to ensure that the restoration was as faithful as possible. She was concerned about the damage to the carving, how best to repair it, and whether or not to renew the red ochre and oil that had been discovered in the interstices of the spirals.

The final restoration is magnificent. Now displayed in a special cabinet in Tuebingen Museum, the carving has been visited by a series of Te Aitanga-a-Hauiti groups, who travel around the world to greet their ancestor with chants, songs and tears. The first of these encounters was reported in Germany on television and in the press, and in New Zealand in a documentary broadcast by Māori TV.

Even before the re-emergence of this carving, Te Aitanga-a-Hauiti had unfurled a remarkable series of projects based on the legacy of Te Rawheoro, their ancestral school of learning, in projects of economic, social and cultural renewal. In 2003, for example, led by Dr Pat Ngata, the 'Hauitians' set up a temporary exhibition called 'Te Pou o Te Kani', curated to a high professional standard and installed in Dr Ngata's house on the main street of Tolaga Bay, with its low wooden buildings. Inspired by a phrase in an ancestral chant – *kia tipu anō te whaihanga e hika ki roto o Uawa* (let creative knowledge flourish and grow again in Uawa) – the exhibition was a stunning success, visited by many people including curators from a number of international museums. That same year, when Dr Ngata died, according to his wish, Hauiti held the world's first 'tele-tangi', a traditional tangi (mourning ritual), broadcast live on the internet so that widely dispersed members of his kin group could participate, using mobile text-messaging to link up with their families and farewell the dead.

Soon afterwards, the Hauiti people began to develop a digital repository for their tribal taonga, real and virtual, in collaboration with Te Papa Tongarewa. This developed into a project called Te Ataakura, driven by Hauiti and using the internet to reconnect members of the kin group with ancestral stories, songs, landscapes and taonga. This project included engagement with a research programme called 'Artefacts of Encounter', initiated by our daughter Amiria, then a fellow at Caius and Gonville College and a senior curator at the Museum of Archaeology and Anthropology at the University of Cambridge. With her colleagues, Amiria had co-edited a book, *Thinking Through Things* (2007), that helped to spark off an 'ontological turn' in anthropology.[76] In this text, they explored the relations between people and the artefacts and ideas they create and exchange across a range of societies. The Artefacts of Encounter project, funded by the Economic and Social Research Council in Britain, aimed to locate artefacts collected across the Pacific during the early years of European exploration and now held in European and other collections, link them with oral histories as well as con-temporary manuscripts (including sketches and paintings) produced by the explorers, and build virtual collections of these taonga in collaboration with communities whose ancestors had created them.

In the course of this project, based on the idea of reciprocity, Wayne Ngata, Hera Ngata-Gibson and other members of Te Aitanga-a-Hauiti worked with the Artefacts of Encounter team, including a software devel-oper from Cambridge and another from Gisborne, to build a database for Te Ataakura, based on whakapapa and housed in Tolaga Bay. While the database in Cambridge and the Te Rauata database in Tolaga Bay each have their own structures, they can be linked in ways that allow for reciprocal exchanges between them. As part of the project, Hauiti and the Artefacts of Encounter team explored software 'ontologies' and 'relational' databases to link images, texts, video and sound tracks online, in an effort to discover whether the patterns of whakapapa can generate virtual worlds that do jus-tice to tikanga, ancestral Māori ways of being.[77] Was it possible for databases and whakapapa to be 'relational' in the same way?

In Māori cosmo-logic, beings are generated by the constellations of rela-tions that constitute their identity, whereas in modernity, entities are often understood as isolates, linked by relations that are external to the boundaries that define them. In these databases, tribal stories, manuscript accounts and images are gathered together with accounts of recent events and visits to see these ancestral objects, wherever they might be in the world – in Germany, Italy, or the United States, for example. Over the past few years, Hauiti and its leaders have also worked with Kew Gardens and the Natural History Museum in London to bring back plants of the same species collected in

Uawa by Dr Solander and Joseph Banks in a project to restore the banks of the Uawa River. In 2012 they hosted a spectacular gathering of scientists, local people and others at Tolaga Bay to witness the transit of Venus, which could be seen from sites in the southern hemisphere. Although the sky was covered with cloud, as the national anthem was sung in Māori the sun came out and the clouds vanished, giving a thousand people a clear view of the transit, as Venus passed across the sun.

Afterwards, the visitors helped the Hauiti people to plant the Uawa River bank with native plants grown from the seed provided by Kew Gardens, and students at the local high school performed a play that they had written themselves about the 1769 encounters, featuring their ancestors Te Whakatatare-o-te-rangi and Hinematioro, along with Tupaia, James Cook, Joseph Banks and Sydney Parkinson. These students had just won a national contest for their production of a Shakespearean play, and the performance of their own script was superb, earning a standing ovation. At the end of the play, it was poignant to hear each of the young actors (including the young Māori woman who played Mrs Cook) explain why they had chosen their particular character, and what they admired or liked about them.

Dr Wayne Ngata, Hera Ngata-Gibson and others of Te Aitanga-a-Hauiti also participated in the Waka Tapu (Sacred Canoe) project, which aims to reconnect Māori with their voyaging ancestors by sailing double-hulled sailing canoes across the Pacific, using traditional navigation techniques. In late 2012, two of these canoes sailed from New Zealand to Rapa-nui (Easter Island), sailing by the stars and battling storms and contrary winds to reach this small, remote outpost of Polynesia. The following year, Ngata led a party of Hauiti people to attend an international workshop in Vancouver to discuss their Digital Repatriation project, and on the way back to New Zealand the group stopped in New York to visit another ancestor. This time it was Paikea himself, the whale rider, in the form of a tekoteko, or carved figurehead, that once stood on the gable of the house named for the ancestor Te Kani-a-Takirau, the grandson of Hine Matioro, the chieftainess who had met Tupaia, Banks and Captain Cook.

When this house was dismantled during the early twentieth century and the carvings dispersed, Paikea was sent to London and then purchased by the American Museum of Natural History in New York, where the Hauiti people went to visit him. As Ngata, Billie Lythberg and Jenny Newell have recounted, meeting Paikea face to face after more than a century, the Hauiti people saluted their ancestor with a hongi (pressing noses) and greeted him with a haka and the action song 'Paikea', composed to celebrate the whale rider and Te Kani-a-Takirau, the house on which the carved ancestor once stood.[78] Te Kani-a-Takirau, the ancestor embodied in that meeting house, was an ariki (paramount chief) so powerful that in the 1860s he was invited to become the first Māori King. He refused, saying 'My mountain does not move' (Ehara taku maunga he maunga nekeneke). One day, Te Aitanga-a-Hauiti hope to rebuild this ancestral house in digital form, with its carvings and their repository of stories, further unfurling the legacy of Te Rawheoro, the great school of learning at Uawa.

In addition to the taonga from Uawa, the Artefacts of Encounter team have identified an array of hoe (canoe paddles), their grips carved and blades painted with swirling red ochre kōwhaiwhai patterns, now held in museums in Europe and New Zealand. From the evidence, these paddles were among those handed over to Cook, Tupaia and their companions in Turanganui (Poverty Bay) as the *Endeavour* sailed out of that harbour in October 1769. During a 2015 visit to Linden Museum in Stuttgart with the team, including Amiria Salmond, Billie Lythberg and Steve Gibbs from Ngai Tamanuhiri, we found a carved and painted hoe almost identical to one sketched by Sydney Parkinson on board the *Endeavour*. Again, people in Turanganui are eager that these paddles, or some of them, should return home, reconnecting them with their seafaring ancestors.[79]

In 2019, the two hundred and fiftieth anniversary of the first exchanges between Māori and Europeans will be commemorated in the Tai Rawhiti (East Coast), at Gisborne, Anaura and Uawa. The event is being referred to as Te Ha, an allusion to the mingling of breath (or hā, another term for hau) between Captain Cook and the unarmed warrior by Te Toka-a-Taiau, the sacred rock in the river at Turanganui.[80] It is possible that some of the taonga collected by Captain Cook's companions during the voyage may return to New Zealand on this occasion. In October 2019 the *Endeavour* replica may sail across the horizon, accompanied by naval ships and descendants of Cook's men, voyaging waka and descendants of Tupaia. Certainly, other new, visionary initiatives will spring out of these commemorations.

In all of these experiments, the expansive spirit of whakapapa is unfurling. The spirals of history are still spinning, impelled by the hau as they surge in and out of ancestral sources, reaching out to bind new lines of people around the world.

CHAPTER THREE

Ruatara's Dying

Lo! Where the chieftain on his matted bed,
Leans the faint form, and hangs the feverish head,
The turf on which he lies is hallowed ground;
The sullen Priest stalks gloomily around;
And shuddering friends, that dare not soothe or save,
Hear the last groan, and dig the destined grave.

– W.M. PRAED, 'AUSTRALASIA', PRIZE POEM,
CAMBRIDGE UNIVERSITY, 1823: ON THE DEATH OF RUATARA[1]

O N 21 DECEMBER 2014, TWO HUNDRED YEARS AFTER THE ARRIVAL of the first missionaries and their families in the Bay of Islands, the contemporary sailing ship *R. Tucker Thompson* brought a party descended from these people to Hohi,[2] a small, landlocked cove in the Bay where their ancestors had disembarked. Although it was a hot summer's day, some of the missionaries' descendants were dressed in period costume. As the ship headed towards the cove, they talked about their forebears Thomas Kendall, William Hall, John King and their wives and children, and why they had travelled halfway around the world to New Zealand.[3]

After landing on the gravel beach, we headed for Marsden's Cross, near the site of the first Christian sermon preached in New Zealand by the Church Missionary Society chaplain at Port Jackson, Samuel Marsden, and then climbed up the hill track to a ceremony commemorating the arrival of the first missionary settlers in New Zealand.[4] On 22 December 1814, Marsden had landed on this beach with Kendall, Hall and King and their families, escorted by local rangatira (chiefs) Ruatara and Hongi Hika. Two hundred years later, the site of the first mission house below Rangihoua pā looked cramped and barren, although the view out to sea was spectacular.

I had visited Hohi once before, during a conference on death held in the Bay of Islands in January 1996. A group of international and local philosophers (and one anthropologist) had gathered at Purerua, a nearby bay in Te Puna Inlet, to discuss this sombre topic. Over four sunlit days, the participants presented papers, talked and thought about what death might mean. In my paper I spoke about the death of Ruatara, which had happened shortly after the arrival of the first missionary settlers, as a quarrel between worlds in which this young rangatira was entangled, and torn in different directions.[5] Later, we boarded a helicopter and flew to Rangihoua, the remains of Ruatara's fortified village overlooking Hohi and Te Puna. Standing on the hillside, it was easy to imagine the enclosure in which Ruatara lay dying in March 1815 as his kinsfolk and the missionaries fought it out over his sweating, increasingly emaciated body. According to Thomas Kendall, in his suffering, the young chief complained about a 'want of breath' and pain.[6]

Because of his illness, Ruatara was drawing close to te pō, the dark realm of ancestors, and his hau was waning. Cooked food, which is noa, or common, clashes with the tapu of the ancestral world, and had to be kept away from the sick man. When Kendall tried to persuade Ruatara to take some food, he replied, 'When breath comes, I shall eat.'[7]

With his kinsman Hongi Hika, Ruatara had been responsible for bringing Kendall and his fellow missionaries to the Bay of Islands. Then in his twenties, Ruatara was a rangatira from the kin group Te Hikutu, the commander of 400 warriors.[8] His illness was an ill omen for the mission, the first to be established in New Zealand.

For almost a decade, Samuel Marsden, the chaplain who headed the missionary party, had hoped to visit New Zealand, but he had been thwarted – first by a lack of resources, and then in 1809 by a spectacular attack upon a European vessel just north of the Bay of Islands, when the ship *Boyd* was burned to the waterline in Whangaroa Harbour, and almost all of the passengers and crew killed and eaten. This episode gave Māori a terrifying reputation, inspiring Gothic horror stories in Britain and Australia about man-eating savages in New Zealand, and delaying the establishment of the mission.[9]

Since Captain Cook's arrival at New Zealand in 1769, relationships between Māori and visiting Europeans had been marked by sporadic fighting. There were also powerful forces that drew them together – mutual curiosity; a desire for European goods and experience of a wider world on the Māori side; and among Europeans, for local resources including timber, flax, pigs and potatoes, seals and whales. Like the arrival of Captain Cook and his companions in New Zealand, the landing of Marsden and his party of missionaries at the Bay of Islands was a world-shifting event. A number of Māori leaders, especially from the north of New Zealand, had already visited Port Jackson and Norfolk Island and experienced life in these harsh Antipodean 'thief colonies'. They despatched young men to these places, and to the Pacific, China, India, the Americas and England on timber and whaling vessels.

Some of these travellers returned home with riveting tales of their adventures. At the same time, increasing numbers of European ships were arriving in New Zealand, and their sailors kidnapped and abused young men and women, stole food from plantations and storehouses, and quarrelled with local people. Often, the crews of these ships, who came from many different nations, breached the tapu rules that governed the relations between Māori kin groups and their ancestors. The burning of the *Boyd*, for example, had been partly provoked by an epidemic that broke out after the captain of a European ship had dropped his watch (which the local people regarded as an atua [ancestral power]) into the waters of Whangaroa Harbour. To make matters worse, the captain of the *Boyd* had flogged their rangatira, who boarded the ship in Port Jackson, for refusing to work his passage.[10] The ancestral power of a Māori aristocrat was concentrated in his or her head, back and spine, and a flogging attacked the hau of their ancestors and kin group, a dreadful insult that had to be requited.[11]

By the same token, for Māori, Europeans and their things alike – ships, muskets, animals, plants and other paraphernalia, including watches – were imbued with the power of their ancestors. The arrival of the missionaries, who brought their atua (gods) ashore in the Bay of Islands, focused their mana, or power, at the missionary settlement at Hohi with its associated rituals and taonga (treasured items), for good or for ill. When Ruatara complained of a 'lack of breath', then, this was ominous. As his hau was affected, so was that of his land and people. As we have seen, in Māori ways of thinking, hauhauaitu (harm to the hau) manifested itself as illness or ill fortune in the kin network, caused by a breakdown in the balance of reciprocal exchanges. Ruatara's life force had been affected, and was showing signs of failure. A rangatira was a kind of human knot (or here tangata) binding key descent lines together (indeed, the term ranga-tira literally means 'weaver of people'),[12] and the loss of his hau affected all of his kin networks.

Ruatara's illness, just weeks after he had welcomed Samuel Marsden and his companions to Rangihoua, was a sign of mate, or existential danger. Convinced that Ruatara's hau was being assailed by atua (powerful ancestors), perhaps those of the Europeans, the tohunga (priest) isolated the young chief from all but his closest relatives, and tried to prevent the missionaries from visiting the tapu enclosure. The Europeans, on the other hand, understood Ruatara's affliction to be a 'violent cold . . . attended with inflammatory symptoms'.[13] Accordingly, they visited him, and tried to assist his recovery with gifts of food, drink and medicines. The scene was set for an ontological collision, with Ruatara's life in the balance. Competing cosmologies swirled around his sickbed. Ideas of ora and life, mate and death, tapu and the Christian God, atua and Satan, hau and the immortal soul battled it out over his wracked, tormented body.

The signs of approaching death provoked a struggle over the meaning of life and death, which in fact the missionaries had come to initiate with Māori. In these arguments over how best to handle his affliction, each side was determined to win. In the midst of it all was Ruatara, too weak to say much, but unwilling to die. On the one side of this tug of war stood the tohunga, headed by Te Rakau, the chief priest of Rangihoua pā and Ruatara's father-in-law, who were trying to revive his hau ora. On the other side were Marsden and his missionary companions, including Thomas Kendall, who wanted to heal his body and save his soul so that he could go to heaven. They hoped to bring Ruatara into the light of God, and free him from the Prince of Darkness.

The cosmogonic account that inspired their hopes was expressed in the Bible, for example in Genesis:

In the beginning God created the Heaven and the Earth
And the earth was without form, and void; and darkness was upon the face of
    the deep
And the Spirit of God moved upon the face of the waters.
And God said, let there be light: and there was light.

And God saw the light, that it was good; and God divided the light from the
darkness.

And God called the light Day, and the darkness he called Night. And the
evening and the morning were the first day.

And God said, Let there be a firmament in the midst of the waters, and let it
divide the waters from the waters.

And God called the firmament Heaven. And the evening and the morning
were the second day.

On the third day, God made dry land, and covered it with grass, herbs and
trees. On the fourth day, He made the sun and moon; on the fifth day, fish
and birds; and on the sixth day, He created animals, and man and woman in
His own image. God blessed them, saying to them, 'Be fruitful, and multiply
and replenish the earth, and subdue it: and have dominion over the fish of
the sea, and over the fowl of the air, and over every living thing that moveth
upon the earth.' On the seventh day, He ended his work, and rested, and
made that day sacred, 'because that in it he had rested from all his worke,
which God created and made'.[14]

While in the Māori account, the cosmos began with a burst of primal
energy, in the Christian creation story the spirit of God moved in the Void,
calling up the elements of creation. God summoned the light, and divided it
from darkness; and called up the firmament, dividing the waters above and
below Heaven. He divided the land from the sea, and made the Earth productive. He set lights in the Heaven, to divide and rule over day and night;
and made fish, birds and animals, and man and woman. God commanded
man and woman to subdue the Earth, giving them dominion over all other
living creatures. In this way people were divided from 'Nature', which God
gave them to command for human purposes (the origin of modernist ideas
of 'resource management' and 'ecosystem services', for instance). While in
the Māori creation story, each form of life engaged with its complement,
generating something new from their union, in the Christian account God
ordered the world by splitting its parts into binary opposites. The deity was
an analytical logician.

Marsden and his companions were inspired by the biblical account of
creation. It is fascinating to see how it resonated with other contemporary
ideas that influenced them. The old idea of the Great Chain of Being, for
instance, often echoed in their writings, took the notion of dominion from

the Genesis story and turned it into a cosmic hierarchy. The upper end of the Great Chain of Being (with God at its apex, followed by the ranks of 'civilized people') was lit by the light of knowledge and understanding; the lower ranks (which descended from 'barbarians', including the Scots and Irish, to 'savages', apes and other sentient animals, down to lesser animals, plants and minerals) was sunk in primeval darkness. The missionary enterprise was understood as taking the Gospel of God to savages lost in an epistemic murk, and raising them up to enlightenment.

The idea of a divided world was also commonplace in missionary thinking. Marsden and his Church Missionary Society missionaries took it for granted that mind should rule over matter and spirit over the body; just as God controlled the Earth, civilised men should command barbarians and savages, and men should rule over women and children. They were preoccupied with saving souls, which they saw as separable from the body. If a world split into isolable, controllable, calculable parts was characteristic of early modern science, ideas of property and persons, and European imperial practice, it also had much in common with early nineteenth-century missionary thinking. The ideas of 'progress' and 'improvement', widespread in Britain at this time, were also rooted in the biblical story. Like the wild Earth and its creatures, barbarians and savages were in a 'state of Nature', to be improved by cultivation.[15] It was part of God's plan that they should be civilised and saved by the Gospel message, just as sinners could save themselves by purifying their lives and souls.

While evangelical Christianity had much in common with the Order of Things and the utilitarian thinking and stadial theories that emerged from it in the late eighteenth century, Marsden and his colleagues were not rationalists. Here, life was a Manichean struggle between God and Satan, light and darkness, salvation and the Fall, with the outcomes ruled over by Providence. Men and women were fallible, tainted by original sin and susceptible to the wiles of Satan, and could be saved only by the grace of God. The only way to seek redemption was to live a life of virtue, inspired by Christ. By taking light to the heathen, a man could have his sins forgiven, a belief that inspired many to join the mission. First he should marry, however, to avoid temptation from native women. He and his wife should model a virtuous Christian household in the wilderness, keeping the Sabbath, practising purity and piety, and leading the heathens away from their rude, barbaric customs.

In his proposals to the Church Missionary Society in London for a mission in New Zealand, Samuel Marsden echoed many of these ideas – a ranked cosmos, the mind-body split, and the division between Nature and Culture, 'improvement' by civilisation and 'progress' through religion, the imperial ambitions of Satan in contest with those of the Kingdom of God, and the redemptive power of Christ on the Cross.

Samuel Marsden and Ruatara

[T]he rituals of meeting after a long separation, the act of embrace, the greeting made in tears . . . the exchange of presents . . . . In short, this represents an intermingling. Lives are mingled together, and this is how, among persons and things so intermingled, each emerges from their own sphere and mixes together.
– MARCEL MAUSS, *THE GIFT*, 1990, 20

The relationship between Ruatara and Samuel Marsden was a turning point in early exchanges between Māori and Europeans. Soon after meeting Ruatara and other Māori at Port Jackson, Marsden wrote:

Their minds appeared like a rich soil that had never been cultivated, and only wanted the proper means of improvement to render them fit to rank with civilized nations. I knew that they were cannibals – that they were a savage race, full of superstition, and wholly under the power and influence of the Prince of Darkness – and that there was only one remedy which could effectually free them from their cruel spiritual bondage and misery, and that was the Gospel of a Crucified Saviour.[16]

Ruatara, a young rangatira from Rangihoua, had enlisted as a sailor as soon as whaling and sealing ships arrived at the Bay of Islands. His first voyage was on the *Argo*, which went whaling off the New Zealand and Australian coasts during 1805 and 1806. At the end of the cruise, Ruatara left the ship at Sydney, where he met Samuel Marsden.

Marsden, a former blacksmith's apprentice from Yorkshire, was a formidable individual – robust, energetic, blunt and outspoken. In the 1780s, after being selected as a potential cleric by the Elland Society, he was tutored

Samuel Marsden, by
Richard Read, 1833.

and sent for training to Hull Grammar School and Magdalene College in Cambridge. After gaining an appointment as an assistant chaplain at Port Jackson, he became a wealthy farmer and magistrate, infamous for the floggings he ordered as punishments, and well known as the principal chaplain and sponsor of the London Missionary Society's Tahitian mission.

When Marsden met Te Pahi, a senior chief closely related to Ruatara, at Port Jackson in 1805, and Ruatara himself the following year, these men struck him as intelligent and enterprising. As he wrote later, 'A finer race of men has seldom, if ever, been found in any country, than the New Zealanders . . . I am fully convinced that they would soon become a great nation, if the Arts could be introduced among them, without the ruinous vices and prevalent diseases of Civilized Society.'[17] Once Marsden was seized by the idea of establishing a mission station in New Zealand, he invited Māori to stay with him at his farm in Parramatta, on the outskirts of Port Jackson. They worked for him as labourers, learning agriculture, carpentry and brickmaking. According to Marsden, 'Commerce promotes industry – industry civilization and civilization opens a way for the Gospel.'[18] At the same time, he equated civilisation with Christian virtues, rather than with European customs. Like other evangelical Christians, he was sharply critical of aspects of his own society, whose 'ruinous vices' included sexual licence, drunkenness, gambling and riotous living under the sway of Satan, the Prince of Darkness.

Indeed, Marsden and many of his colleagues were wary of the 'Order of Relations' associated with the *philosophes* in France, and men like Erasmus Darwin, Tom Paine, Joseph Priestley, William Blake and the key players in the Scottish Enlightenment in Britain. They associated this kind of thinking with religious dissent, secularism, ideas of sexual freedom and other challenges to the status quo, including the American and French revolutions. For this reason, they urged that the Church of England (rather than Dissenters such as the Methodists or Wesleyans) should lead the missionary enterprise in the Pacific. As one of his colleagues urged in a letter to Marsden, the Dissenters were a threat to Church and State alike:

> Their places of worship are seminaries of infidelity. They seem to us now to
> be exactly of the same sentiments with the French philosophers or Jacobins
> & have for many years past been laboring to propagate their sentiments
> in England & to bring us into the same state that France Ireland & other
> countries have been from these principles.
>
> These men I mean Voltaire & his co-adjutors of those principles were
> doubtless the cause of all these wars & horrible scenes of bloodshed &
> ravishment which have so dreadfully overrun Europe of late . . . . I have
> one Hope left that God may baffle their Designs, which is that the faithful
> Ministers in the Establishment are daily increasing.[19]

Missionaries from these 'infidel' cults could only lead islanders in the Pacific astray. Marsden agreed, and in February 1807 he sailed to England to recruit Church of England missionaries for the New Zealand mission.

Meanwhile, Ruatara was exploring European life and society. He joined the *Albion*, which went whaling in New Zealand waters for about six months before dropping him off at the Bay of Islands. The captain of this vessel treated the young man kindly, giving him European articles in exchange for his services. Next he sailed on a sealer, the *Santa Anna*, which dropped off its gang on Bounty Island. There, three of Ruatara's companions died of thirst and hunger before the ship returned five months later. Nevertheless,

Ruatara decided to stay on board for the return voyage to England, determined to see King George III in London. Such encounters (he kanohi kitea – a face that is seen) are important to Māori, because without them hau cannot be exchanged between groups, tangling descent lines together through face-to-face greetings between their leaders.

When the *Santa Anna* arrived in London in June 1809, Ruatara's ambitions were foiled. He was forced to stay on board and work without pay, and was beaten and abused by the captain, who told him that the king's house was too hard to find, and that the king did not receive visitors.[20] When he fell ill and could not work, Ruatara was transferred, almost naked and coughing up blood, to the *Ann*, a convict ship bound for New South Wales. As it happened, Samuel Marsden, his family and the two artisan missionaries he had recruited for the New Zealand mission, John King and William Hall and his wife, joined the *Ann* for the voyage to Port Jackson. Marsden fed and clothed Ruatara, and with the help of the ship's surgeon, restored him to health.

When Marsden wrote to Dr Good, a physician, linguist and friend of Sir Joseph Banks (now the president of the Royal Society in London, and a close friend of King George), Good replied:

> Poor Duaterra! How sincerely do I pity him that he should have fallen into the hands of a wretch so unworthy of the British name, and so careless about its reputation! But [there are] yet savages among Englishmen, and philosophers among savages.
>
> I rejoice most ardently . . . that he at length fell so marvellously into your care; whose kindness, and moral and religious instruction have already, I doubt not, atoned for the brutal treatment of his first master. [If he is not] yet too much discouraged to repeat his voyage, we will take care that he shall not again quit England, without feasting his eyes upon King George, and obtaining a full insight into the chief productions and curiosities that King George's country has to boast of.[21]

During his travels on European ships, Ruatara had learned to speak some English.[22] In jocular style, Good urged Samuel Marsden to master Māori, saying, 'I feel confident that by this time you have become a proficient in the New Zealand tongue and ought to have a patent from His Majesty to assume the professorial chair in this new department of literature.'[23] Like many medical men at this time, Good was intensely curious about life in other places, urging Marsden to collect Māori oral literature and history and draw up a detailed vocabulary of the language, while offering a strikingly modern account of Māori origins. According to Good, Māori were descended from the 'restless and roving' Malayan boundary tribes of Asia:

> [people] who were restless and intrepid, [and] by their peninsular site accustomed to navigation, and bade defiance even to the ocean itself, migrating from shore to shore, from island to island; a few of them perhaps remaining behind as the rest advanced, still passing forward and only settling in the remotest regions and on the farthest shores they could explore, viz in New Zealand . . .[24]

During their voyage on the *Ann*, Marsden wrote an account of Ruatara's life and career, describing him as 'a very fine young man, about two and twenty years of age, five feet ten inches high. He possesses a most amiable disposition; is kind, grateful, and affectionate: his understanding strong and clear. He is married to one of the daughters of a great Chief, called Wanakee [Waraki, a rangatira near the Kerikeri Falls].'[25] As Ruatara's knowledge of English improved, Marsden began to study Māori. Using a mixture of these two languages, Ruatara told him about Maui, a trickster ancestor who had hauled up the islands of New Zealand from the ocean. As far as Marsden understood it, Maui made the first woman out of one of his own ribs, but no doubt this story came from the Bible, and very likely Ruatara heard it from Marsden himself during one of their nightly conversations. Ruatara also told him the story of Rona, a man who was carried up to the moon; and about the quarrel between the sharks, who wanted to live on land, and the 'serpent' (in fact, lizards) who refused their consent, saying that if the sharks did this, men would eat them. A series of such cosmogonic tales, which always involve heated arguments, describe how after earth and sky were set apart, different beings went their separate ways to occupy different parts of the cosmos.

After telling Marsden about Te Reinga, the sacred site at the northern tip of the North Island where at the point of death, spirits dived down into te pō, Ruatara explained that tohunga could divine the identity of a thief by projecting their ata, or shadow, on a wall. He described the great ceremonies that were held after a rangatira died and when the kūmara was

harvested, attended by thousands of people, and reported that although
'simple fornication does not appear a great evil', married women who committed adultery were punished by powerful ancestors. During these sessions
Ruatara also gave Marsden the names of the principal chiefs in Northland,
his first glimpse into the intricate kinship politics in the region. Marsden
sent this account of Māori life to the Church Missionary Society in London,
who published it in their *Proceedings*.[26]

From a Māori point of view, by caring for Ruatara during his illness,
Marsden's hau and that of the young chief had become entangled. When
the *Ann* arrived at Port Jackson, Ruatara travelled with Marsden to his farm
at Parramatta, where Marsden (known as Te Matenga in Māori) gave him
some land where he learned to cultivate beans, peas and cereals, especially
wheat, as an alternative to the root crops (sweet potato, taro, yam and fern-
root) grown in New Zealand. Part of what was once Marsden's farm at
Parramatta, known as 'Rangihou Reserve', is still regarded by some northern Māori living in Sydney as Māori land. By now Ruatara had learned a
good deal about European ways, which he was keen to share with his people.

After some time in Parramatta, Ruatara and three Māori companions
took passage on the *Frederick*, whose master promised that if they worked
on board during a whaling cruise around the New Zealand coast, he would
drop them off in the Bay of Islands. After six months at sea, however, when
the ship called into the Bay for provisions, the master refused to allow them
to go ashore. The vessel sailed to Norfolk Island instead, where they were
abandoned naked and without payment. Ruatara lived in this harsh penal
colony for some months until the *Ann* arrived, whose captain gave him a passage back to Port Jackson, where he lived once again with Samuel Marsden,
studying agriculture and attending Divine Service.

When Ruatara finally returned to the Bay of Islands in 1811, his people
received him with joy. According to Marsden, they made him their 'king'
(which may simply mean that he had adopted the name 'Kingi', in honour of
King George).[27] When Dr Good heard this news, he replied, 'I rejoice most
cordially at Duaterra's assumption of the imperial purple in New Zealand.'[28]

Marsden sent gifts of agricultural tools and seed wheat to the Bay of
Islands, which Ruatara distributed among his aristocratic kinsmen, including
his uncle, the fighting chief Hongi Hika. He told them that this was the plant
from which Europeans made their biscuits and bread, but when the seeds
sprouted and the plants grew tall, his relatives pulled them up, expecting

to find wheat on their roots, and scolded Ruatara for telling them such far-fetched stories. In response, the young rangatira sent a message by a whaler to Samuel Marsden, asking for a hand mill so that he could make flour as proof of his assertions.[29]

At the same time, Marsden worked hard to persuade Governor Lachlan Macquarie to offer greater protection to islanders who worked in British-registered ships, given the abuses that Ruatara and many other young men were suffering at the hands of their masters. In December 1813, Macquarie issued a proclamation requiring masters of British ships sailing from New South Wales to sign a bond of good behaviour, and stating that 'the Natives of the said Islands are under the Protection of His Majesty, and entitled to the good Offices of his Subjects', and that any offences against 'the Law of Nature and of Nations . . . would be further punished with the utmost rigour of the Law'.[30]

The first missionary reconnaissance

In early 1814, Marsden purchased the brig *Active* as a missionary ship and sent her via the Derwent to the Bay of Islands, bringing an advance party of two missionaries, Thomas Kendall and William Hall, with gifts of wheat, a steel mill, a frying pan, a cock and some clothing, and a letter for Ruatara:

Duaterra King,
I have sent the Brig Active to the Bay of Islands to see what you are doing; and Mr Hall and Mr Kendall from England. Mr Kendall will teach the Boys and Girls to read and write. I told you when you was at Parramatta I would send you a Gentleman to teach your Tamoneekee's [tamariki – children] and Coeteedo'es [kōtiro – girls] to read.

You will be very good to Mr Hall and Mr Kendall. They will come to live in New Zealand if you will not hurt them; and teach you how to grow corn Wheat and make Houses. Charles has sent you a cock and Mrs Marsden has sent you a shirt and jacket.

I have sent you some wheat for seeds, and you must put it into the ground as soon as you can. I have sent you a Mill to grind your corn. If you will come in the Active to Parramatta, I will send you back again . . . .
I am, Your friend
Samuel Marsden[31]

In this letter, Marsden addressed Ruatara as his friend, reminding Ruatara that he had promised to send him and his people a teacher, and of the relationship that the young rangatira had forged with Marsden's family. These reminders were reinforced with presents, and in return Marsden asked him to treat the missionaries kindly – a classic gift exchange.

Thomas Kendall, a schoolmaster from Lincolnshire,[32] and William Hall, a carpenter, had been recruited in England for the New Zealand mission, along with John King, a shoemaker and flax-dresser.[33] Hall, a stubborn, independent man, often clashed with Marsden, who regarded him as worldly and self-interested (although Hall thought the same about Samuel Marsden).[34] When Hall and King began to express doubts about going to New Zealand, Rev. J. Pratt, the Secretary of the CMS, wrote them a stern rebuke: 'We all profess to serve one Master. You have the higher honour of laying the heavier burden on your shoulders; but if you cast if off, or take your hand from the plough, better would it be if you had never been born.'[35] Marsden, whose style of management was uncompromising, remarked tersely that 'Hall will require to be held in with Bit and bridle until he understands his situation.'[36] He instructed the two missionaries to bring back any of the chiefs or their children who wished to visit Port Jackson, and to fill the *Active* with spars, flax, Māori artefacts and baskets of potatoes in the Bay of Islands, to help defray the expenses of the voyage.[37]

Eager to persuade local people of the blessings of literacy,[38] Kendall took with him a library of books donated by the Church Missionary Society, along with 50 copies of the *Missionary Register* to distribute to Ruatara and his friends, while Hall carried iron tools and fruit trees from the Derwent. Acutely aware that he was not ordained, but would arrive in New Zealand as a lay missionary, Kendall wrote to his friend Rev. Basil Woodd: 'it is very painful to the feelings of every sincere lover of the Church of England that no persons can be admitted into Deacon & Priests orders except such as have received a Classical education'.[39]

Before they set sail, Kendall's wife Jane, who had lost a baby shortly after their arrival in Port Jackson but still had five young children at home, wrote him an affectionate letter: 'My dearest love, I did not think that I could bear your absence from me so long as we have lived ten years together so very happy. God grant we may meet again and spend many more years together as happy. I do not care where I am if we are together. I cannot bear the thought of being parted. I think the time very long.'[40]

On this first journey to New Zealand, Kendall and Hall were accompanied by Tui, the younger brother of Korokoro, a Ngare Raumati rangatira from the south-east Bay of Islands, as their guide and interpreter,[41] and Mura, a young sailor from the Bay of Islands who joined the ship at Hobart.[42] Mura had previously lived with Hall and his family in Port Jackson while Tui had spent time at Parramatta, where he forged a close relationship with the Kendalls' convict manservant Richard Stockwell, whom he called his 'brother'.[43] During his time at Parramatta and on the voyage to New Zealand, Tui worked with Kendall on the first book in Māori, *A korao no New Zealand, or, the New Zealander's first book: being an attempt to compose some lessons for the instruction of the natives*, which included a vocabulary, some phrases and an attempt at translating the Genesis story into Māori.[44] Impressed, Kendall remarked that 'the New Zealanders are certainly a fine race of men and much superior in point of mental capacity to any Savages which I have hitherto seen'.[45]

This booklet illustrates the perils of trying to communicate in a previously unrecorded language, made more difficult by the fact that Tui spoke little English.[46] The phrase 'Kapi ta Hara no God. Kakeno ta Hara no Tungata' (*Ka pai te hara nō God. Ka kino te hara nō Tangata*, sounded phonetically), for instance, which Kendall understood to mean, 'The way of God is good. The way of Man is bad', in fact says 'God's wrongdoing is good; Man's wrongdoing is bad'; while 'Kedunga ra ta Iehovah, ke te Ranghee a kahingha' (*Kei runga rā tā Jehovah, kei te Rangi a ka hinga*), which Kendall translated, 'Jehovah is above, his seat is in heaven', would have been heard as 'Jehovah is above, in the heaven, and falls down'. As for the Genesis story of creation, judging from the way in which the Māori words were transcribed, Māori must have struggled to make sense of what the missionaries were saying. Although Hall claimed that 'we are able to make them understand us almost upon any common subject',[47] this overstates their linguistic competence. These difficulties in communication led to fundamental confusions.

In New Zealand, the missionaries hoped to 'sow to [God's] praise on Earth, and reap with him in Heaven'. During the voyage, Kendall prayed for their efforts among the 'perishing Heathen' to be successful:

Unmoved by hardships or persecutions, let thy servants count not their lives dear to themselves . . . Prepare the hearts of multitudes to welcome their message. Arm them with faith and patience; clothe them with humility;

endue them with the meekness of wisdom: and make them of one heart and
one soul.

   Pour out Thy Spirit upon them from on high. Let mountains before
them become plains. Let barren deserts blossom with the rose. Cause thy
holy name to be adored by tens of thousands, where now Satan reigns with
destructive sway over benighted idolators.[48]

On 10 June 1814 when the *Active* anchored at Te Puna, Ruatara welcomed
Kendall and Hall to his principal settlement at Rangihoua.[49] Using their
limited Māori and with Ruatara as their interpreter, the missionaries told
his people that if they were kindly treated, they would bring their wives and
families and live with them in the Bay of Islands.[50] Kendall promised that
he would teach their children to read and write, while Hall said he would
build them large houses and fine canoes, and teach them to grow wheat,
corn and potatoes.[51] Te Rakau, the high priest at Rangihoua, paid particular attention to William Hall, while the children clustered around Thomas
Kendall.[52]

   After these first exchanges, tea, sugar, flour, cheese and two chests of
European clothing were brought ashore from the *Active* and placed in
Ruatara's storehouse.[53] Kendall and Hall presented the rangatira with the
steel mill that Marsden had sent him, two cocks and two hens from Charles,
Marsden's son, the shirt and jacket from Mrs Marsden and three bushels of
wheat, one hundredweight of potatoes and two boxes of young fruit trees,
including peaches, apples and quinces, which he immediately planted.
Ruatara and his relatives were delighted by these gifts, exclaiming, 'Nuee
nuee rangateeda pakehaa' (nui nui rangatira pākehā – great pākehā chiefs)[54]
(showing that by 1814, the term pākehā for Europeans was already in use in
the Bay of Islands).

   When Ruatara escorted them to his lands at Te Puna, they were surprised
to see meticulous gardens planted with European crops, including wheat,
potatoes, cabbages, turnips, carrot and onions; and pigs in a pig sty. Several
days later when Ruatara took them to visit his inland cultivations, where he
had planted wheat and was planning to grow potatoes,[55] he decided to prove
to his people that it was possible to make bread from wheat. Taking some
wheat, he ground it into flour with the steel mill that Marsden had sent him,
and made damper in a frypan, when 'they burst out in expressions of surprise
and admiration'.[56]

During a visit to Rangihoua pā on 15 June, they met Ruatara's uncle, the fighting chief Hongi Hika (who commanded 600 warriors, and had 10 muskets), and other leading chiefs.[57] Kendall was impressed by Hongi Hika:

He is a Warrior but apparently a man of a very mild disposition. And altho, this is the first time he has had any intercourse with Europeans he is remarkably steady and decent in his outward behaviour and has little appearance of the savage about him. He is chief over the People of seventeen places: is a man of a very ingenious turn and is very desirous to learn the European Arts. He shewed us a Musket which had been stocked and mounted by his own hands, and the performance does him much credit, since he had no man to instruct him.[58]

According to Kendall, the local people often spoke about Samuel Marsden, and included his name in their songs. When the high chief Tara, Hongi Hika's rival from the southern alliance, visited the *Active* the following day, Kendall gave him a letter from Marsden inviting him to travel to Port Jackson. Tara, an elderly man about seventy years old (who also 'presides over the people of Seventeen Places') invited them to anchor the ship off Kororareka on the south side of the Bay, and presented them with five baskets of potatoes. He took them to see his people who were tilling gardens for kūmara and potatoes, clearing the ground of weeds and rubbish that they piled up in heaps and burned.[59]

Afterwards they visited Pomare, a leading chief from the northern side of the Bay who took them to inspect a kauri forest at Kawakawa where they could procure spars as a cargo for the *Active*. During this excursion Pomare remarked with disapproval on the bad language used by the *Active*'s sailors: 'Europa tangata said D---n your Blood. D---n your England and G-d D---n you you Bugger. These expressions were no good.'[60] Māori, who did not like to drink alcohol at this time, regarded swearing as insults that required utu, fundamentally disrupting relations. That night Kendall slept under the stars, unarmed and surrounded by Pomare's people. As he wrote to Pratt, he felt happy in their company: 'The stars shone with peculiar lustre on my head; it was a season for contemplation, prayer and praise! [If they had] the least inclination to have done me an injury they had it in their power.'[61]

On 19 June, when Kendall conducted Divine Service on the deck of the *Active*, where the Union Jack had been hoisted, Tara flew his own flag at

Kororareka. Over the days that followed, Ruatara collected a cargo of flax
for the *Active* while Pomare and his people delivered spars to the ship. Hongi
Hika often visited the missionaries, attending Divine Service on board on a
number of occasions. Tara and Pomare also spent time with them, kneeling
down while Kendall and Hall conducted their morning prayers. On 5 July,
Kendall attended a tangi (funeral) where the women wept and slashed their
breasts and arms with stone flakes while the men sang a funeral chant and
performed a sham fight, followed by a feast. Kendall was impressed by the
people in the Bay of Islands, describing the men as intelligent, and 'many of
them industrious and full of ingenuity'. The women were skilled in weaving
flax, while the children were 'lively, active and witty':

> When they saw me they usually said, 'How do you do Mr. Kendarro?' They
> then offered me their little parcels of Millo [miro] or thread which they had
> made with their own hands, and asked for fish Hooks, nails and buttons in
> return.[62]

Towards the end of their stay, Hongi decided to travel with the missionaries to Port Jackson, accompanied by his son Ripiro and several attendants.
Korokoro, the chief of Paroa in the southern alliance, and his younger
brother Tui also decided to make the journey. At Hongi's invitation the
Active sailed back to the north side of the Bay, and anchored off Te Puna
Inlet. When Hongi asked Ruatara to accompany them as their interpreter,
his three wives begged him to stay, but Hongi's mana was greater. When
he heard that Ruatara had decided to accompany his uncle, Te Rakau, the
priestly father of his senior wife Rahu, who was pregnant, warned him if he
left her, she would die. Turikatuku, Hongi's senior wife, camped on shore
with their children until the *Active* sailed from New Zealand.

Hongi Hika, Ruatara and Korokoro visit Port Jackson

On 25 July 1814 as the *Active* set sail, Turikatuku and Rahu both wailed
loudly, echoed by their female companions. While the ship was tacking out
of the Bay, Thomas Kendall, who had been sitting on a water closet on the
quarterdeck, talking to some of Korokoro's men alongside in a canoe, was
ignominiously knocked overboard by the main boom. Although he could not
swim, the crew of this canoe swiftly rescued him from a 'Watery Grave'.[63]

By this time Kendall had heard a great deal about the attack on the *Boyd*, and in his report on this expedition he defended Te Pahi and his people at Te Puna against the accusation that they had been the ringleaders: 'When the New Zealanders are provoked by insult and ill treatment they will undoubtedly retaliate with the utmost fury, but I cannot learn that they have generally, if at any time, been the first aggressors.'[64] Like Captain Cook, Kendall understood the practice of kai tangata (eating people) as an ancestral habit:

> In giving a fair account of a Savage Nation some allowance ought to be made for Ancient Customs and Usages which have been handed down from one generation to another for many ages. Because there are practices amongst the New Zealanders which are . . . abhorrent to the tender feelings of humanity they have been condemned as the most dangerous and degraded of the human race.
>
> That the condition of these fallen sons and Daughters of our first Offending Parents 'is very low' it is too true; but I trust I can with strict adherence to truth notice to my Christian friends many favorable appearances which may induce them to attempt their improvement . . . .
>
> It has been truly said of the New Zealanders that they are a Noble Race of men. They stand in need of our friendship; and if proper steps were taken for their instruction in the Arts, attention paid to their wants and they were dealt with upon just and good principles they would by the Divine Blessing soon be brought over to a state of civilization.[65]

During their journey to Port Jackson, Hongi tried to teach Kendall and Hall to speak Māori. At the same time, he and his older son Ripiro and Korokoro studied the English alphabet and learned to write, covering page after page with letters in fine copperplate script, while Kendall gave them a fishhook for every page they copied correctly.[66] Hongi Hika was a skilled carver, and a sure, firm hand is evident in the four pages of his handwriting that survive. While Hongi enjoyed the voyage, Ruatara was subdued and morose, telling his missionary companions that he feared his wife might be dead or dying.

On 5 August 1814 as the *Active* approached Port Jackson, they were hailed by the brig *Campbell*, whose captain invited Captain Dillon, Kendall and Hall on board. He plied them with liquor until Kendall got drunk, insulted Dillon with foul language and was punched for his pains. Afterwards

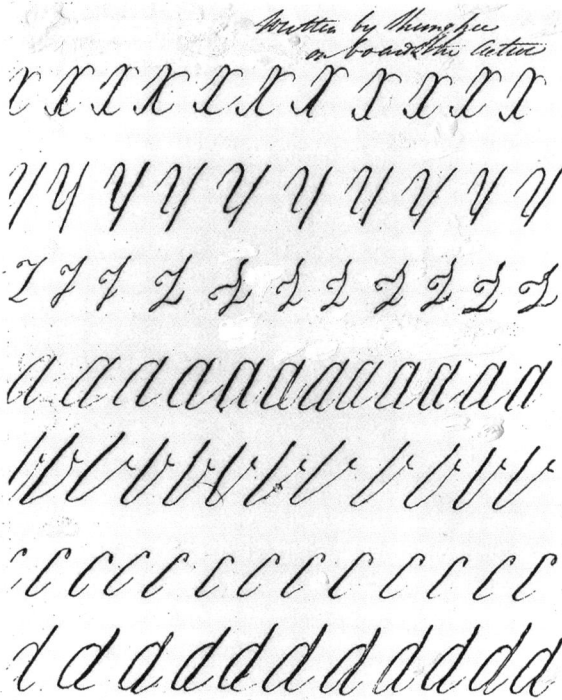

Hongi Hika's handwriting on board the Active *in 1814.*

Kendall apologised to Dillon and prayed to God for forgiveness for this sinful behaviour.[67]

Back in Port Jackson, a letter had arrived for Marsden from Josiah Pratt, the Secretary of the Church Missionary Society, thanking him for a fishing net that he had sent earlier, a gift from Ruatara. Pratt added, 'the Committee will be very glad to receive any curiosities that they may be placed in the Museum. Whatever tends to illustrate the superstition and moral state of the Heathen will be particularly acceptable, as such things – images of Deities &c &c speak in forcible language to the pity and the conscience of those to whom they are shewn.'[68]

When the *Active* arrived in Port Jackson, Kendall despatched a list of words and phrases in Māori that he had compiled to the CMS in England (although many of these are very strangely transcribed).[69] He also sent a case packed with Māori artefacts on board the *Seringapatam* as gifts for his CMS sponsors and associates, including a 'curious box' (probably a wakahuia, or

Hongi Hika's carved self-portrait, 1814.

carved feather box) and a cloak for Rev. Pratt, a flute and a hei tiki (greenstone ornament) for his mentor Rev. Woodd, and a small flute, upper garments, a belt, flax thread and a war club for other friends.[70] For his part, Marsden sent several cloaks to Rev. Pratt, and in his letter praised Hongi Hika, whom he described as 'a very fine Character; very polite, and well-behaved at all times'. During this visit to Port Jackson, Hongi Hika carved a self-portrait from an old post, adorned with his moko (facial tattoo), which Kendall included in his consignment to the CMS, who proudly displayed this effigy in their headquarters in Salisbury Square.[71]

It was almost certainly during this visit that Hongi's son Ripiro took the name 'Charley' or 'Hare' (Charley transliterated into Māori), a sign of the friendship that he and Marsden's son Charles had forged.

Marsden was also very impressed by Tui, his ability to learn English and to repeat the Lord's Prayer, telling him that just as his father had been a New Zealand priest, he could be an English one, teach his people the true religion and become a great man.[72] On the basis of his own experiences with Māori and Kendall's reports, Marsden decided to proceed with the mission to New Zealand:

> From my first knowledge of these people, I have always considered them the finest, and noblest race of Heathens known to the civilized world, and have ever been persuaded that they only wanted the introduction of the arts of civilization and the knowledge of the Christian religion to make them a great Nation.[73]

During their visit to Port Jackson, Marsden took the rangatira to visit farms where they watched the farmers and their convict servants ploughing and threshing, and the women spinning and weaving.[74] They observed black-smiths, bricklayers and carpenters at work, and the Sunday musters of convicts as they were marched to church. Marsden remarked:

> They tell me that when they return, they shall sit up whole nights, telling their People what they have seen, and that their men will stop their Ears with their Fingers – We have heard enough, they will say, of your incredible Accounts, and we will hear no more – they are impossible to be true.[75]

The first European settlement in New Zealand

On 28 November 1814 when Samuel Marsden boarded the *Active* and set off from Port Jackson, he had instructions from Governor Macquarie to explore the northern part of New Zealand. In the event of a favourable report, Macquarie thought that the British government might 'form a permanent establishment on those islands'[76] – the first hint that an official British presence might be established in New Zealand.[77] From the outset, evangelism and colonisation were linked together.

On this journey, Marsden was accompanied by Thomas and Jane Kendall and their three sons (they had decided to leave their two daughters at the Female Orphan School in Port Jackson);[78] John King with his son and wife Hannah, who was heavily pregnant; and William and Dinah Hall (who was also pregnant), with their son. After his previous visit to the Bay of Islands, Hall had asked the CMS for a firearm and some duckshot, 'as a kind of defence as there is nothing the Natives so much dread as the sight of a

Gun'.[79] This time the *Active* was commanded by Thomas Hansen, Hannah's father, while her mother Hannah and her eldest brother Thomas were also on board. They were joined by the free settler John Liddiard Nicholas,[80] two sawyers, a blacksmith and a runaway convict. In all, there were 25 Europeans on board the ship, along with two Tahitians and eight Māori including Ruatara, his uncle Hongi Hika and his sons, Korokoro and Tui, and several other men from Northland.[81]

In an effort to protect local Māori from marauding sailors off visiting ships, before they set sail Governor Macquarie appointed Kendall a resident magistrate, supported by Hongi Hika, Ruatara and Korokoro, each of whom was given a military uniform, a sword and a cow in honour of their new status, along with a bull.[82] In addition, Marsden had loaded a stallion and two mares for the new mission.[83] During his visit to Port Jackson, Ruatara also asked for a flag, a drum and a bell so that he could muster the Rangihoua people, and establish a day of rest in the Bay of Islands.

According to Nicholas, Ruatara was a man 'in the full bloom of youth, of tall and commanding stature, great muscular strength, and marked expression of countenance: his deportment, which I will not hesitate to call dignified and noble, appeared well calculated to give sanction to his authority, while the fire and animation of his eye might betray even to the ordinary beholder, the elevated rank he held among his countrymen'.[84] During their passage to the Bay of Islands, however, Ruatara often seemed downcast. Eventually, he confessed that at Port Jackson, he had been warned not to take the missionaries to New Zealand. According to Marsden:

> Some Person or Persons with the most dark and diabolical design, [told] Duaterra not to trust us,– that our only object was to deprive the New Zealanders of their Country, and that as soon as we had gained any Footing there we should pour into New Zealand an armed Force, and take the Country to ourselves.
>
> To make the impression more deep, they called his Attention to the miserable State of the Natives of New South Wales, who are going perfectly naked about our Streets; and from whom the English had taken their Country and reduced them to their present wretchedness.
>
> – This Suggestion darted into his mind like a poisoned Arrow destroyed his Confidence in the Europeans, and alarmed his Fears and Jealosey for the Safety of his Country, for which he had the most unbounded Love.[85]

Although the missionaries tried to set Ruatara's mind at rest, assuring him
that they had no intention of taking over his country, they could not undo
the damage. As Marsden remarked disconsolately, 'The Poison infused into
his mind was too subtle and infectious ever to be removed.'[86] As he later
reported to Governor Macquarie, 'I am of opinion that they would not quietly submit to have any part of their Country wrested from them by any
other nation, but would resist to the utmost of their power, any attempt of
this nature.'[87]

During the voyage, Hongi made a cartridge box, while Korokoro insisted
on being addressed as 'Makoare', in memory of his meeting with Governor
Macquarie. Marsden and Kendall were both prostrated by seasickness.
Ruatara and Nicholas played draughts and talked about Māori beliefs, and
the ancestor gods who controlled the visible world. Although Nicholas
enjoyed these conversations, he took it for granted that Māori cosmological
ideas were mistaken:

> Though the savage does possess all the passions of Nature, pure and
> unadulterated, and though he may in many instances feel stronger and more
> acutely than the man of civilized habits; still is he inferior to him in every
> other respect: the former is a slave to the impulse of his will, the latter has
> learned to restrain his desires; the former stands enveloped in the dark clouds
> of ignorance, the latter goes forth in the bright sunshine of knowledge;
> the former views the works of his Creator through the medium of a blind
> superstition, the latter through the light of reason and of truth; the one
> beholds Nature and is bewildered, the other clearly 'Looks through Nature
> up to Nature's God.'[88]

This passage, riddled with pre-judgement, was written even before he had
arrived in New Zealand.

Like Marsden, Nicholas upheld the claims of European 'common sense',
which linked reason and truth with Enlightenment, Christianity and civilisation, and ignorance and superstition with savagery and the rule of the
'Prince of Darkness'. For the missionaries and many of their contemporaries
in Europe, the technological efficacy of secular Western knowledge offered
decisive proof of the hierarchical order of the 'Great Chain of Being', and
the superiority of rational, restrained Europeans over passionate, ignorant
savages. Most Māori, on the other hand, adopted a more open-minded

Rangihoa [Rangihoua],
New Zealand, by unknown
artist, W E & F Newton,
London, 1852-1857.

attitude. In te ao Māori, beliefs, statements or action were judged to be tika (right, correct) if they were fitting in the context of different relationships and circumstances. The term pono (true, truth), which refers to a context-free kind of truth, was (and is) much less commonly used. This approach allowed Māori to consider that there might be merit in some European ideas and practices. Certainly, they were quick to pick up European customs that seemed intriguing. Ruatara, for example, had three wives, including his head wife Rahu, the daughter of Te Rakau, the high priest of Rangihoua. Upon his return to New Zealand, he learned that during his absence, his youngest wife had had an affair. In New Zealand adultery was usually punished by death, but on this occasion Ruatara fashioned a cat-o'-nine-tails and had his wife's lover captured and put in chains, flogged with 30 lashes and exiled on board the *Active*.[89]

On 22 December when the *Active* sailed into the Bay of Islands, anchoring off Rangihoua, they were greeted by Korokoro's son. Hongi and Ruatara went ashore, where their people wept over them and slashed their bodies. According to Nicholas, the following day when the livestock were landed, the local inhabitants were astounded:

Cows or horses they had never seen before, and diverted now from every
thing else, they regarded them as stupendous prodigies. However, their
astonishment was soon turned into alarm and confusion; for one of
the cows that was wild and unmanageable rushed in among them, and
caused such violent terror through the whole assemblage, that imagining
some preternatural monster had been let loose to destroy them, they all
immediately betook themselves to flight.[90]

When Marsden mounted one of the horses and rode it on the beach,
local Māori watched in disbelief. After this performance, Ruatara took his
European companions to Rangihoua and introduced them to his family,
including his senior wife Rahu with their new baby son and her father
Te Rakau. Soon afterwards, Marsden's party began to clear the terraced site
at Hohi, the small cove below the pā that local leaders had set apart as the
site for their mission station.

On 24 December 1814, Ruatara and his fellow rangatira gave the *Active*
a formal welcome. As Korokoro approached the ship at the head of a fleet
of canoes, packed with warriors accompanied by some women and children,
paddling in strict unison and performing a haka, Captain Hansen answered
the challenge by firing thirteen guns. Korokoro came on board with some
other chiefs, introducing them to Marsden and his companions. After a
meal, they went on shore where one of Ruatara's warriors, stark naked, challenged Korokoro's canoe, backed by a contingent of warriors lined up on
the beach, also naked and painted with red ochre, the tapu colour. During
the spectacular sham fight that followed, Te Pahi's widow, about seventy
years old, and Ruatara's senior wife Rahu, dressed in a red gown, armed
with a horse pistol and wielding a hoeroa (a long chiefly weapon made from
whalebone), took leading roles.[91] At this time in the North, a number of
high-born women were accomplished warriors.[92] This performance, with its
naked warriors and militant female leaders, must have startled the missionary wives, who were supposed to be quiet and submissive, staying at home
and avoiding public affairs.

On Christmas morning, which fell on a Sunday (the Sabbath), Marsden
wrote in his journal:

When I went upon deck I saw the English flag flying. I considered it the
signal and the dawn of Civilization, Liberty and Religion in that dark and

benighted land. I never viewed the British Colors with more gratification, and flattered myself that they would never be removed till the Natives of that island enjoyed all the happyness of British subjects.[93]

On shore, Ruatara and his men had erected a flagstaff on the summit of Rangihoua pa, flying the British flag. Below on the beach, a pulpit and reading desk covered with black cloth had been set up, with rows of upturned canoe hulls as seats for Divine Service.

About 400 local people attended the service, including Ruatara and Hongi Hika, dressed in their military uniforms, wearing their swords and carrying switches. While the Europeans carried out their ritual, the congregation stood up and down as Korokoro raised and lowered his switch. They listened attentively while Marsden, wearing a surplice, preached his sermon – 'Behold I bring you tidings of great joy.'[94] When his people asked him what Marsden was saying, Ruatara replied that 'they were not to mind that now for they would understand by and bye'.[95] No doubt the local people grasped very little of what Marsden said. Rather than interpreting his sermon, it seems likely that Ruatara delivered his own speech on this occasion.[96] As a finale, the first Christmas service in New Zealand ended with a rousing haka.

Despite his admiration for Māori, Marsden shared with Nicholas a Manichean vision of likely futures for New Zealand. Along one fork in the path lay progress and improvement – British sovereignty, civilisation, freedom, commerce and Christianity, lit by 'the bright sunshine of knowledge'; down the other fork lay barbarism, enslavement, misery and savage error, benighted by ignorance and darkness. Marsden hoped that Ruatara's interest in European agriculture and technology (including building, flax-work and iron-work) would help to make the mission self-sufficient, and persuade Māori of the advantages of European civilisation. He had chosen artisan missionaries for this first settlement, intending through their technical skills (which in Kendall's case included reading and writing) to demonstrate the virtues of a Christian way of living.

Their Māori hosts, however, took a different view of the matter. Although Hongi, Korokoro and Ruatara were intrigued by Western technologies such as writing, iron-work, agriculture, military techniques and weapons, and were eager to adapt these to Māori purposes, after seeing the soldiers and their weapons in Port Jackson, they were anxious that the British might try to take over their country and dispossess them, like the Aboriginals in New South

Wales. No doubt for this reason, Hongi and Ruatara decided to locate the
mission on the small, confined site at Hohi, overlooked by Rangihoua pā,
where the missionaries would be constantly under surveillance, vulnerable to
raids by canoe and unable to grow their own food. As a result, the missionaries
were forced to rely on these rangatira for their safety and survival, allowing
the chiefs to control the relationship largely on their own terms.[97]

Although Kendall, Hall and King were eager to locate the mission at
Te Puna, where the land was more extensive and fertile and they could support their families by growing their own food, Marsden refused, saying
that the population at Rangihoua was much larger and they would be living
among friends, who would protect them from being attacked by strangers.[98]
This decision shaped the early years of European settlement in New
Zealand. Forced to barter with Māori for food, and with visiting ships for
muskets and powder to meet the demands of their Māori hosts; and often
desperate for clothing and supplies to feed their families, the missionaries
were set at each other's throats. They found their dependency galling, along
with Marsden's refusal to see what it meant for their everyday lives.

The local people, on the other hand, were intrigued by the new
arrivals. Several days after the Christmas Day service, it was pouring with
rain. Because Māori houses were tapu (imbued with ancestral presence)
and cooked food was noa (free from ancestral power), people did not eat
inside, and Nicholas was forced to eat his dinner sheltering under the eaves
of a chief's house with water dripping down his neck. In his discomfort,
he snapped at Tui that 'the taboo taboo [is] all gammon'. Turning sharply
around, Tui retorted,

> "[I]t was no gammon at all; New Zealand man . . . say that Mr. Marsden's
> *crackee crackee* [karakia – prayers] (preaching) of a Sunday, is all gammon."
> "No, no," I rejoined, "that is *miti* [maitai]" (good). "Well then," retorted the
> tenacious reasoner, "if your *crackee crackee* is no gammon, our taboo taboo is
> no gammon;" and thus he brought the matter to a conclusion; allowing us to
> prize our own system, and himself and his countrymen to venerate theirs.[99]

This idea that what was right for Europeans might not be right for Māori,
and vice versa, and that each might happily go their own way was engrained
in Māori thinking. Here, something is considered tika (right, correct,
appropriate, proper) if it is true to its own nature. For Tui, while Christianity

might be tika for Europeans, tapu was tika for Māori; but as the world keeps on turning, tika and tikanga (right ways of being) might also adapt and change over time.[100] This led to an experimental approach to ways of living. Ruatara was keen to lay out a European-style town at Te Puna, with a flagpole on a nearby hill, a site for a church and open streets.[101] When Marsden, Nicholas, Kendall and Hall went to Kawakawa to fetch timber for the mission station, he was organising his people to prepare land for cropping wheat in an area 40 miles from Rangihoua (probably at Taiamai),[102] planning to send the surplus grain to Port Jackson, the first export industry in New Zealand.

Before Nicholas and Marsden went to visit the timber district at Kawakawa, which belonged to the ariki Tara, the head of the southern tribes in the Bay, they went to visit the old chief, who gave them a meal of kūmara and urged Marsden to set up the mission in his district. He gave them permission to fell trees. When they went to Kawakawa, they met an old man who remembered Captain Cook's 1769 visit to the Bay of Islands, and showed them where the *Endeavour* crew had set up their camp site.[103] After they returned to Rangihoua, Hongi and Ruatara invited them to visit a fortified settlement inland near Lake Omapere, which had already been adapted for musket fighting.

Okuratope pā, which had about 200 houses, was set on a steep hill, defended by three trenches with palisades about 20 feet high. In the village, a carved stage had been erected on a post 6 feet high where Hongi's older half-brother Kaingaroa, the ariki, or high chief, of the district, used to sit, high above his people. Another seat stood nearby for his mother Waitohirangi, the senior wife of their deceased father Te Hotete, alongside a small elevated storehouse for her tapu (sacred) provisions.[104] Kaingaroa and his mother were both so tapu that on ceremonial occasions they had to be carried on litters so that their feet did not touch the ground, making it tapu (the original meaning of the term waewae tapu – sacred feet).

During this visit, Marsden and Nicholas walked to Lake Omapere through acres of wheat, European flax, turnips, kūmara and potatoes in high cultivation, without any weeds. Gazing around him, Nicholas imagined a European-style capital city built on the banks of this beautiful lake, which reminded him of the 'pleasure grounds' in England:

> A spirit of civilized industry would be diffused all over the country, and they would be gradually initiated into all our pursuits; while being protected

in their persons and property by the wholesome laws of our inestimable constitution, they would have nothing to apprehend; their physical comforts would always keep pace with their moral improvement.[105]

According to Nicholas, at this time there were three ariki in this part of New Zealand – Kaingaroa, the high chief from the Cavalli Islands to the north-west side of the Bay of Islands, with his pā at Lake Omapere, who led the northern alliance; Tara at the south-east side of the Bay, with his headquarters at Kororareka, who led the southern alliance; and Te Haupa from the south to the Hauraki Gulf, who led the Hauraki tribes, each supported by a 'fighting chief', usually a younger brother.

Nicholas was told that in the interior, as in the Society Islands and like Kaingaroa and his mother, the paramount chiefs were so tapu that they were carried on a litter.[106] While ariki (both male and female) were physically raised above their people as an expression of their tapu, or ancestral presence, this did not necessarily translate into secular authority, which was often delegated to their tēina (junior brothers and sisters). Indeed, the relationships between ariki and rangatira and their kinfolk in the Bay of Islands and Thames seemed remarkably democratic. As Marsden remarked, the people were 'all either Chiefs, or, in a certain degree Slaves; the Chiefs neither give their commands indiscriminately to their people, like Masters do to their servants in civil society, nor do their dependents feel themselves bound to obey them'.[107] Except when punishing a theft, in battle or commanding their taurekareka or slaves (almost invariably war captives), the authority of Māori leaders was limited. Rather, they or their representatives had to use the art of oratory to persuade their people to adopt particular lines of action.

According to Marsden, the chiefs were surprised to learn that there was only one king in England, and were very interested in British ideas of justice. They were astonished when Marsden told them that in England, when a person was accused of a crime, twelve gentlemen had to examine the case, and King George had no power to execute them; observing that these laws were very good. When one man asked what governor the British would send to New Zealand, Marsden replied that 'we had no intention of sending them any but wished them to govern themselves'.[108] Another rangatira remarked that 'there were too many Kings in New Zealand, and that if they were fewer they would have less wars and live more happy'.[109]

While Marsden and Nicholas were exploring around the Bay of Islands, Ruatara's people were working with the European sawyers to build a temporary house for the missionary families at Hohi. This was an adapted chief's house 60 feet long by 14 feet wide and subdivided into four sections, one for each family, an innovative structure. From ancestral times, a chief's house was understood as the body of an ancestor (or even the rangatira him- or herself), with the ridgepole as the spine and main line of descent, the carved wall panels as more recent ancestors, and the ancestor's arms spread wide at the gable, welcoming descendants and their visitors inside. The idea of internal partitions was new to Māori architecture, but during his time at Parramatta, Ruatara had learned something about European ideas of privacy, and wanted to make his manuhiri, or visitors, as comfortable as possible.

Like other Māori houses, however, this temporary dwelling had no chimney or window, or raised timber floor. When the missionary families moved in, they found their new home dark, damp and smoky. John King grumbled:

> On Sunday it rained very much. The water came through upon our wheat, rice, bed, clothing and the water was half over my shoes in our bedroom from the wetness of the dirt floor our clothing damp we have no fire to dry them. It is uncomfortable indeed for my Wife and Child in the state she is in, it will be a great blessing indeed if it does not make her suffer exceedingly as she has taken a serious cold already.[110]

They were very cramped in their small apartments – especially, no doubt, Thomas Kendall and his wife and three sons. For these first European settlers, and for their hosts, life in this small settlement was extremely challenging, and these domestic discomforts gave an existential edge to their unease. For the local people, on the other hand, the presence of the missionaries was a source of amusement and curiosity, and they often breached their privacy. Kendall had brought an organ with him, for instance, and when he played on this instrument and the other missionaries sang, the local people, 'astonished at the sound',[111] clustered around the house to listen.

Undeterred by these challenges (which he did not share), Nicholas saw this dwelling as the first signs of improvement in a heathen land:

> Many interesting ideas occurred to me while I beheld the missionaries thus seated in their new residence, and preparing for the work of civilization in

a land where never before was the least gleam of knowledge, except what nature instinctively supplied, and where man, roving about as a lawless denizen, acknowledged no authority except that of an individual barbarous as himself, who constantly led him on to deeds of carnage against his fellows, and taught him not only to satisfy his revenge with their destruction, but to crown it with a bloody banquet.

In such a land it was that a few civilized beings were now going to reclaim a whole race to subdued and regular habits; and afford, at the same time, another proof of the immense superiority of mind over matter.[112]

For Nicholas, it was simple. Māori lived in a state of nature, and were barbarous by definition. The sooner they were civilized, the better.

Samuel Marsden, on the other hand, who did not believe that Māori were barbarians, harshly criticised many of the European sailors who visited Northland. Warning his colleagues in Port Jackson and Britain that visiting seamen were committing many outrages, and in the case of the *Boyd* were responsible for the 'massacre' of its crew and passengers, he echoed Kendall's judgement (and Captain Cook's before him):

[T]he New Zealand Chiefs are a Warlike race, and very proud of their dignity and rank, they seem to be Men who never forget a favor nor a wrong, but retain a greatful [*sic*] remembrance of those Europeans who have been kind to them, and to have the most sovereign contempt for any who have injured them . . .[113]

At the same time, Marsden observed, among their own families Māori were mild and good-humoured:

[T]hey appear to live in amity and peace amongst themselves when under the Government of one Chief. I saw no quarrelling while I was there. They are kind to their Women and Children; I never observed either with a mark of violence upon them, nor did I ever see a Woman struck.[114]

This was in marked contrast to everyday life in Britain and Port Jackson at the same time, where women and children were often physically chastised, and those who broke the law were brutally punished with floggings or hanging.

Even Nicholas engaged in such comparisons. During a brief excursion with Ruatara to Hauraki where they met Te Haupa, the dignified, impressive old paramount chief of that district, Nicholas compared Te Haupa's attack on the East Cape with Napoleon's abortive expedition to Moscow in 1812:

> The only difference between the expedition that passed the Duieper, never to return, and the noteless horde that proceeded to the East Cape, is the number and attributes of the respective forces, the principle and motives being exactly the same.[115]

In these passages, one can see the struggle between prejudgement and experience that characterised early European reactions to Māori life. While the sharp-edged categories and gridded hierarchies of the Order of Things and the Great Chain of Being shaped (and still shape) the relations between Māori and Europeans, its rigid assumptions of European superiority were challenged by direct experience with Māori, and subverted by Western relational thinking, with its echoes of many of the patterns (complementary pairs, living networks and rhizomes, for example) that shaped Māori habits of mind. Among Māori, a similar tension marked their experiences with Europeans, although their ways of thinking, influenced as they were by the shifting, expansive networks of whakapapa and relational ideas of truth, were often more accommodating.

Ruatara's dying

> '[A human being] is an existence carving itself out in space, shattering in chaos, exploding in pandemonium, netting itself, a scarcely breathing animal, in the webs of death.'
> – MICHEL FOUCAULT, *LE RÊVE ET L'EXISTENCE*[116]

The story of Ruatara's illness and death illustrates these clashes. Towards the end of Marsden's stay in the Bay of Islands, the young rangatira fell ill again, reminding his people that despite its attractions, contact with Europeans had its dangers. Before the first arrival of white men, there had been no venereal or epidemic diseases in New Zealand. Since that time, there had been a number of devastating outbreaks of these maladies. Ruatara's illness testified to the power of the European gods and their emissaries, while undermining faith in the ability of the local tohunga (priests) to deal with these afflictions.

At the same time, although Marsden and the ship's surgeon had healed Ruatara of a serious illness on board the *Ann*, and he regularly attended Divine Service, according to Marsden 'the superstitious notions of the religion he had imbibed from his infancy in New Zealand were deeply rooted in his ideas. He had great confidence in what the native priests asserted and in the effects of their prayers.'[117] During his last visit to Parramatta, Ruatara was plagued by doubts. Although he had invited the missionaries to come to New Zealand, some Europeans at Port Jackson had warned him that the British intended to take over his country. Now that the missionaries had arrived to settle at Hohi, his illness returned and he struggled to breathe. His hau ora (breath of life) was waning.

As soon as they heard that he was ill, on 12 February, Nicholas and Kendall visited the young chief, bringing him medicines, food and drink. He was not permitted visitors, cooked food or any drink except fresh water, however. Because of his illness, he had drawn close to te pō, the night of death, and was in a state of tapu. Cooked food was inimical to tapu, and could destroy his hau. After conducting some rituals, Te Rakau, Ruatara's father-in-law and the high priest of Rangihoua, finally allowed the missionaries into the tapu enclosure. They found Ruatara perspiring profusely and running a high fever, and Nicholas gave him a dose of rhubarb. Over the next few days, they went to see him several times, giving him food and herbal doses, but as the young chief's condition worsened, his relatives decided that these breaches of tapu by the Europeans were to blame. When Nicholas tried to force the issue, Te Rakau forbade him to enter the enclosure.

On the following day, when Marsden returned to Rangihoua, he insisted on going to see Ruatara. As he wrote in his journal:

> Duaterra was laid on his dying bed. I could not but look on him with wonder and astonishment, as he lay languishing under his affliction, and scarcely bring myself to believe that the Divine goodness would remove from earth a man whose life was of such infinite importance to his country, which was just emerging from barbarism, gross darkness, and Superstition. No doubt he had done his work, and finished his appointed course, although I had fondly imagined that he had only begun his race.[118]

Likewise, Ruatara's family were dismayed and disconcerted by Marsden's unauthorised entry into the tapu enclosure. As Nicholas reported:

> [They said] that the Etua [atua] would not yet have fixed himself in the stomach of the chief, had they not in their unhallowed temerity suffered us to see him while he was tabooed against such visitors.
>
> I remonstrated with them in urgent terms, and thought to prevail on them to admit me; but it was of no use, they all cried out with one voice 'nuee nuee taboo taboo' [the tapu is very intense], and forbidding me to approach the shed, they would, as I believe, have killed me on the spot, had I presumed to disobey.[119]

Ruatara's family told Kendall that on the night of the missionaries' first visit to the invalid, a shooting star had streaked across the sky over Rangihoua, a fearful omen.[120] The next day Ruatara became delirious, and Te Rakau told his family that an atua (ancestral power) in the form of a lizard had entered his body, where it was eating his hau and vital organs.[121]

The missionaries regarded this explanation as foolish, a heathenish superstition. They were horrified that Ruatara had been forbidden food and drink, believing that this would weaken his resistance to the illness. As soon as Marsden left on another excursion, however, Te Rakau reinstated the tapu. When he returned again to Rangihoua, Marsden was furious, telling the high priest that if he refused to let him see Ruatara, he would order the *Active*'s cannons to fire on Rangihoua, and 'blow it about their ears'.[122]

Although Ruatara's family begged him to respect the power of their ancestor gods, and warned of the harm they would inflict if the tapu was breached, Marsden would not listen. Finally, Te Uri-o-Kanae, Te Rakau's younger son and Ruatara's heir who had spent a great deal of time with the Europeans, addressed his people, telling them to forget about tapu restrictions:

> Gunna now spoke in a bold strain of sarcastic eloquence, not only against the impropriety of refusing free access to Duaterra, but against the taboo itself, which, as he expressed it, was 'no good in New Zealand, but only henerecka [deceit];' and he told them openly, that it ought not ever again to be feared or revered.
>
> The other natives looked upon Gunna as a blasphemous sceptic for making this declaration, yet his consequence as a rungateeda [rangatira] had

'*A Hoodee o Gunna [Te Uri-o-Kanae], chief of*
Ranghee Hoo', *by John Lewin, 1815–1819.*

some weight with them; but Mr. Marsden's threat was more efficacious than
all, and their fearful scruples being at length obliged to yield to it, they found
themselves under the necessity of consenting to his ingress.[123]

When Marsden finally entered the enclosure, Ruatara seemed glad to see
him, although he was weak and running a high fever, with sharp pains in
his bowels. Perhaps he remembered how Marsden and the ship's surgeon
had cured his illness on board the *Ann*. Several days earlier, when Te Rakau
ordered his people to take the young chief to an island where his people were
customarily buried, Ruatara picked up a pair of pistols that the Europeans
had loaned him, and threatened to shoot anyone who laid hands on him.
When Marsden asked Ruatara whether he had had anything to eat or drink,
he replied that he had had nothing except potatoes and water. Marsden
ordered him some tea, sugar, rice and wine, but when Ruatara told his family

to hand over a quantity of iron that he had been keeping in trust for the missionary party, they refused, saying that it was tapu.

On 25 February 1815 when Marsden and Nicholas went to visit Ruatara for the last time, they found him in a high fever, racked with convulsions and lying in the arms of his head wife Rahu, who was hollow-eyed and grief-stricken. Upon hearing that they were about to return to Port Jackson, Ruatara instructed his wives to present Marsden and Nicholas with fine mats and a pig, and to hand back various things that they given him, including the pair of pistols that he had beside him in the enclosure. Down at the beach when Nicholas fired off one of these pistols as a signal for the *Active*'s captain to send off the boat, it exploded in his hand, flying up and hitting him in the forehead, knocking him unconscious. Far from expressing any sympathy for Nicholas, the local people 'upbraided me with my impiety for meddling with a pistol that was tabooed, and considered me justly punished by the indignant wrath of the Etua [atua]'[124] – an example of utu (balanced exchange) at work. That afternoon, while Ruatara was on his deathbed, Marsden and Te Uri-o-Kanae negotiated the first 'land sale' in New Zealand.

This was a revolutionary step. The idea of land – Papatuanuku, the earth mother – as property that might be bought and sold was entirely new to Māori. In order to ensure a 'secure title' for the mission site, Marsden approached Te Uri-o-Kanae and his brother Wharemokaikai (Weree),[125] whom he understood were the 'proprietors' of the land on which the mission was sited, and asked them to 'sell' an area of about 200 acres for twelve axes. Because Marsden spoke little Māori and they spoke little English, it is very unlikely that Kanae and his kinsman understood what was intended by this transaction. No doubt sign language was used to indicate the extent of the site. As Marsden later reported to Governor Macquarie: 'The boundaries of their estates appear to be all accurately ascertained by land marks, to show who is the proprietor, and particularly on their fishing grounds.'[126]

Nor would Te Uri-o-Kanae have been able to read the deed that he signed, which was in English:

I, Ahoodee o Gunna [Uri-o-Kanae], King of Rangheehoo [Rangihoua], in the Island of New Zealand, have in consideration of twelve axes to me in hand now paid and delivered by the Rev. Samuel Marsden, do give, grant, bargain, and sell unto the Committee of the Church Missionary Society . . . all that piece and parcel of land situate in the district of Hoshee [Hohi] . . . together

with all the rights, members, privileges and opportunities thereunto belonging . . . for their own absolute and proper estate forever.'[127]

In Māori, there was no term for 'sell', let alone 'absolute and proper
estate'. The closest equivalent is the term hoko (to barter), but in 1815 this
applied only to items that were noa, devoid of ancestral presence. This was
never the case with land, or Papatuanuku, where use rights to different
resources were inherited from ancestors who were buried in the ground.
The Māori term used to explain this transaction was almost certainly tuku
– to release or give – the word used in chiefly gift exchange and, indeed, in
many early land deeds in Māori.[128] Nor was there any idea that land could be
divided into bounded units and all rights in these sold as a bundle in perpetuity, by one individual to another individual or group, who might be strangers
to each other. In te ao Māori, when land was gifted to recognise a marriage
or alliance, or as compensation for a hara, or offence, this was a taonga that
strengthened the bonds between the groups concerned.

In the presence of a number of local chiefs, who had gathered to farewell
the *Active*, Te Uri-o-Kanae declared that 'the land was no longer theirs,
but the sole property of the white people and was tabooed for their use',
and signed the deed with his moko (facial tattoo).[129] Most likely Kanae was
placing a rāhui (ancestral prohibition) on the land, setting it aside for the
Europeans to use while cloaking it with ancestral power – quite literally,
by erecting a pole with a strand from the rangatira's cloak, reserving it for
particular purposes, or in this case, by placing his moko on the parchment.

After the signing, the axes, or toki, were distributed to different kin groups,
and one of these survives as a taonga – Ringakaha (mighty hand), a long-
handled axe imbued with mana (ancestral power).[130] Marsden announced
that while the land now belonged to the Europeans, local people would be
able to come there to purchase axes or hoes or other tools, but not weapons
or muskets. This gift exchange forged an alliance between the two groups,
giving the missionaries rights to occupation and protection, but also imposing an ongoing obligation to contribute to the local kin group's security and
well-being.

Shortly afterwards Marsden and Nicholas boarded the *Active* with three
escaped convicts as prisoners, the rangatira Te Morenga and a number of
other northern Māori, and sailed for Port Jackson, taking with them an
array of Māori artefacts, including garments, a stone adze, a tiki or neck

ornament, a wood funnel for oil and some spears, to give to their friends in England.[131]

Back in the Bay of Islands, Thomas Kendall, Hall, King and their families visited Ruatara every day. Often, Kendall brought him rice wine, but on one occasion when he tried to take the decanter away to refill it, Ruatara reproached him, saying:

> 'You are very unkind Mr Kendall, if the Decanter is taken away Atua will kill me this very day.' I told him the Atua must be very cruel, and reminded him of the God whom we worshipped, who was infinitely kind; and as he had heard, had given his own Son, who had suffered, bled and died for the Sin of Man, in order that man might live and die happy. He made no reply to my observation.[132]

It is likely that Ruatara's friends understood these gifts of food and drink from the missionaries as ō matenga, food for the death journey. Just before dying, a person might ask for the flesh of the Polynesian dog or rat, or human flesh, or earthworms of a special sweet kind, or water from a particular stream from their family land, to sustain them on their journey to Te Rerenga Wairua (the point at the northern tip of the North Island where spirits leaped off a tree into the underworld). A man who had lived with Europeans might well ask for wine and rice water. Whether foreign or local, such foods were in the shadow of the ancestral realm, and intensely tapu.

On 2 March 1815, Ruatara was carried on a litter to a hill at Te Puna, where he had planned to build his European-style town.[133] He gave his cow and her calf to Te Pahi's widow, and his military uniform to his baby son, asking that he should be sent to Sydney when he was old enough, to be brought up at the Orphan School among Europeans. Early the next morning, he died.[134]

After his death, Ruatara's body was trussed in a sitting position and wrapped up in his garments. His relatives decorated his head with a coronet of feathers and covered his face with a small piece of scarlet English cloth, the tapu colour. His head wife Rahu sat to his right, weeping bitterly and slashing herself with an obsidian knife in the haehae, a ritual of mourning, while his sister and other female relatives sat on his left side, also weeping and cutting themselves. When Kaingaroa and Hongi Hika, his senior relatives, arrived, Hongi wept over Ruatara's body, uncovering his face, taking a blade of green flax in one hand and occasionally taking hold of Ruatara's hair, thus creating a pathway for the wairua (spirit, or immaterial self) to leave his body and begin its journey to Te Rerenga Wairua. He told Kendall that this departure would not finally happen until three days after Ruatara's death, and until that time, his spirit could hear everything that they said.

The following day, while the rituals of mourning were still under way, Rahu, an aristocratic, vivacious woman – expert weaver, canoe paddler and warrior – left the enclosure and hanged herself. Her mother wept for her daughter, but her father, the high priest Te Rakau, and her brothers seemed proud that she had decided to accompany her husband on his journey to Te Reinga. Their bodies were placed together on a high stage, surrounded by their possessions. The chiefs who took part in the rituals of mourning also became tapu, and had to be fed by others for some days.[135]

His people now referred to Ruatara as an atua (powerful ancestor), and as Kendall noted, 'Whenever we come near a piece of Taboo'd ground and ask the reason why it has been taboo'd, if a person has been buried in it, we always receive for an Answer, "Atua lies there."'[136] He was told that the right eyes of Ruatara and his wife Rahu were now living spirits on earth, and their left eyes had become stars in the sky. According to Kendall, the bones of a chief were taken up four or five times before they were polished, oiled and put in a basket as a sacred relic with the skull, which was referred to as an atua.[137]

When Marsden heard about Ruatara's death, he remarked mournfully that it 'appeared to be a very dark and mysterious dispensation'.[138] For Marsden and his fellow missionaries, Ruatara had been destined to lead his country out of 'barbarism, gross darkness, and superstition', and yet these terms described beliefs that Ruatara himself cherished. The myth-model of the Great Chain of Being, in which 'civilised' people were intrinsically superior to 'barbarians' and 'savages', was fundamentally inimical to Māori ideas of utu, which relied on reciprocity and balanced exchange. In the Great Chain, on the other hand, those at the lower levels were expected to offer up tribute to those higher on the cosmic ladder, and to be grateful for whatever they received – an ethic of *noblesse oblige*.

By the early nineteenth century, while some Europeans (including Marsden himself, and his friend Dr Good, for instance) held fast to Enlightenment ideas about justice and equality, insisting that there could be 'savages among Englishmen, and philosophers among savages', stadial theories ranking human societies from 'primitive' to 'advanced' were also commonplace – as one can see from the writings of John Liddiard Nicholas. Stadial thinking was at the heart of the evangelical enterprise, with its ideas about benighted savages who had to be redeemed by Christianity, and 'raised up' to civilisation.

The constant, often deliberate breaches of tapu that resulted from these habits of mind were not just offensive, but dangerous. While in modernist accounts, an abrupt increase in mortality among 'natives' after the arrival of European settlers is generally explained by the onset of infectious diseases, among Māori, this was seen as an increase in hauhauaitu – failed exchanges in which the flow of hau ora (the breath of life) was stifled, leading to a state of mate (illness and often death). Such lapses could endanger Europeans as well as Māori. Failures in utu, or reciprocity, were potentially damaging or fatal for all concerned.

From the outset, the relationship between the missionaries and northern Māori was fraught, since the missionaries had come to try to displace many Māori ancestral practices and understandings of the world. Ultimately, however, the missionaries were dependent on the rangatira, and forced to accommodate many local ways of living. The intimate relationship between the missionary Thomas Kendall, the tohunga Te Rakau and the fighting chief Hongi Hika, forged around Ruatara's deathbed, illustrates the explosive nature of relational lines thrown across worlds, especially when such relationships were regarded (certainly by many Europeans at the time, and no doubt by some Māori) as a betrayal of their own land and people.

CHAPTER FOUR

Hongi Hika and Thomas Kendall

D
URING THE HEARINGS FOR THE NGA PUHI CLAIM TO THE WAITANGI
Tribunal in 2010, northern kaumātua (elders) often spoke about
Hongi Hika, the great fighting chief, and his visit to England with
Thomas Kendall in 1820, when he met King George IV. As Erima Henare
from Ngati Hine remarked, during this first face-to-face encounter between
a northern rangatira and a British monarch, they met as equals:

> What is the underlying meaning of the stories about Hongi Hika? The great
> thing was his meeting with the King of England. Like to like, mana to mana,
> rangatira to rangatira, ariki to ariki.[1]

This was significant, because the affable exchanges between Hongi and the
King of England opened the way for other northern rangatira to forge relationships with successive monarchs and sign the Treaty of Waitangi in 1840,
strengthening their relationship with the British Crown.

When the first missionaries arrived in the Bay of Islands in 1814,
Hongi Hika was about 40 years old, a tall, imposing man who served as
the fighting chief for his half-brother Kaingaroa, the ariki, or paramount
chief, for the northern alliance in the Bay, to whom he was devoted. As we
have seen, Kaingaroa, a quiet, good-natured, slightly corpulent man, was
so intensely tapu that on ritual occasions he was carried around on a hurdle
so that his feet (or waewae tapu, literally 'sacred feet') did not touch the
ground. According to J.L. Nicholas, although Hongi 'had the reputation of
being one of the greatest warriors in his country, yet his natural disposition
was mild and inoffensive, and would appear to the attentive observer more

inclined to peaceful habits than strife or enterprise'.[2] Hongi was close to the women in his family, including his mother, Tuhikura, a high-born Ngati Kahu woman from Whangaroa; and his senior wife Turikatuku, a prophetess and a powerful warrior in her own right, also from Whangaroa, who often accompanied him into battle.[3]

As a young man, Hongi had fought in the disastrous battle of Moremonui near Maunganui Bluff in 1807 or 1808, during which Nga Puhi were overrun by Ngati Whatua and two of his brothers were killed, along with his sister Waitapu, a noted warrior who suffered a horrific death while urging Hongi to escape.[4] He never forgot this calamitous defeat, nor the utu that had to be taken to avenge his relatives and restore his family's mana.

When Kendall and Hongi Hika first met, Thomas Kendall was in his mid-thirties, a married man with five children. Unlike Hongi, he was not an aristocrat. Born to a farming family in Lincolnshire, Kendall worked as a teacher and farmer before marrying his wife Jane and setting himself up as a draper. During a visit to London, he had been transfixed when he heard the charismatic evangelical cleric Rev. Basil Woodd preach at Bentinck Chapel. After Kendall joined the congregation and became a Sunday-school teacher, Woodd's sermons inspired him to join the Church Missionary Society. He decided to go to New Zealand to save 'the perishing heathen'.[5] Reputed to have a gift for languages and with some teaching experience, Kendall was appointed as the schoolmaster for the New Zealand mission. When he arrived at the Bay of Islands on an exploratory visit, Kendall was laden with books, which fascinated Hongi Hika and other Māori. During the voyage back to Port Jackson, Kendall began to teach Hongi and his favourite son Ripiro how to write. This was not a one-way exchange, however. From the beginning, Kendall was intrigued by Māori cosmology, and determined to learn to speak Māori.

When Ruatara died, Kendall and the other missionaries attended the tangi for Hongi's young kinsman. By now Kendall had learned some Māori, and at the tangi he asked Kaingaroa, Hongi and Te Rakau, Ruatara's father-in-law and the tohunga at Rangihoua, to explain Māori beliefs relating to death and dying. After the tangi, these rangatira assured the missionaries that despite his death they would take over the young chief's role and protect the mission. Not long afterwards, however, Kaingaroa also died. Devastated by the loss of his older half-brother, Hongi tried to hang himself, but was prevented by some of his people.[6] Hongi's survival was fortunate for Kendall and the other missionaries, because without his protection they would have been forced to return to Port Jackson. Since they could not grow their own food and were not allowed to use weapons, they had to rely on the rangatira for provisions and protection, and were defenceless against Māori incursions.

Confident about their own tikanga (ancestral ways), at first Māori gave the missionaries little choice at about observing local customs. As John King, the shoemaker who accompanied Kendall to the Bay of Islands, remarked grumpily, 'If we are under them we can do them no good; they want to teach us how to treat our children, and many things we must do which we ought not to do; besides, they steal all we have and laugh at us.'[7] While they were curious about Europeans, the Rangihoua people were uncertain about the virtues of having the missionaries among them. According to King:

> They are very jealous of our God, saying Mr. Hall and Mr. Kendall and myself praying so much makes our God destroy them. At about this time a great number has died here. Some say it is our God kills them, others the New Zealand god. They drop off very fast, the weather being wet and cold and having no kind of nourishment.[8]

In September 1815, when news came that the *Trial* and the *Brothers* had been attacked near Thames, and two European sailors and many local people had been killed,[9] their hosts blamed the sailors for ill-treating the iwi (tribe) from Thames. They feared that the Thames people would attack the missionaries, and take utu on them for inviting Europeans to live in New Zealand. After hearing about the attack on the *Trial*, for instance, Te Rakau's young son Tama, who had been living with the King family at Hohi, left their house, saying, 'it was very good to kill and eat white people, but no good to kill New Zealand men'. At the same time, Hura, Ruatara's little daughter, who had been living with the Kings to learn European domestic skills, became afraid to stay with them at night, saying that 'by and by all our children will be roasted and eaten'.[10] Despite this, Kendall reported that he and the others were not afraid to live among the people at Rangihoua, adding that the captain of the *Trial* 'was an unfit man to go amongst Natives.'[11] To protect themselves, the missionaries appealed to the power of King George, telling the local people how many soldiers he had in his army, and to the mana of Hongi Hika.

Although Kendall tried to defend local Māori against many of the visiting sailors, who stole their crops, violated Māori women and insulted their chiefs, the captains treated him with contempt when he tried to exercise his powers as a magistrate, and restrain their abuses.[12] Back in Port Jackson, Marsden did not fare much better when he tried to bring the master of the *Jefferson* to justice for theft and violent conduct towards Māori.[13] Again, the assumption of European superiority over 'savages' was entrenched. In defiance of these difficulties, Hongi was staunch in defence of the missionaries. As Kendall reported to the CMS in London:

> Our friend Shunghee [Hongi] is strongly attached to our interests. Whenever he hears of strong parties paying us a visit, he is sure to bring his men for our protection. His residence is about thirty miles from us, but he says as soon as my house is built he will come to live near me and resume his former studies. He will put his sons under my care.[14]

The tohunga Te Rakau also stayed close to the missionaries, keeping an eye on them, attending their services, and trying to learn how to write and read.[15]

While Hongi Hika was in the Bay, the missionaries and their families felt quite safe, but when he went away, their sense of security vanished. Their access to supplies dried up, and they began to argue with each other. John King quarrelled with both Kendall and William Hall,[16] who by then had built two houses and a smithy at Rangihoua, and a small ship, the *Experiment*, using a canoe as its keel.[17] Tired of these dissensions, in late 1815 Hall moved to Waitangi with his wife, son and baby daughter, where there was plenty of timber and good soils.[18] He built a house, planted a vegetable garden, and began to grow wheat with the help of the local people. Apprehensive that the Europeans intended to take their land, however, some of the rangatira there remarked that 'it was very good for a few white people to live at New Zealand, but not for many'.[19]

Four months after arriving at Waitangi, Hall was raided by a group of Korokoro's warriors, who were angry with their host iwi for desecrating a tapu site.[20] A muru (or ritual plundering party) was a customary way of taking utu for an affront by raiding the families, friends and allies of the offenders, without killing them. In this muru raid, they struck Hall down, tore off his clothes, ransacked his house and his gardens, and took his bedding, clothing, his axe and tools, and two muskets. When his wife Dinah tried to stop them, she was struck in the face with a hand club, and almost lost an eye. As he told Rev. Pratt, 'I beheld my dear partner laying moaning, and I could not see a feature in her face for blood.'[21] After the attack, Captain Graham of the *Phoenix* rescued them and carried them to Hohi, where John King and his family took care of them.[22] As Hall wrote to Rev. Pratt, 'I hope I shall never forget the kindness of that man and his family towards us when we were distressed.'[23]

At this time in Northland, utu balances were radically out of kilter, causing instability and chaos. There were many reasons for this – the presence of European visitors who often breached tapu restrictions, whether accidentally or on purpose; the arrival of epidemic diseases, which caused illness and deaths often blamed on these derelictions; the introduction of firearms, that bypassed ancestral protocols of hand-to-hand combat by allowing warriors to kill at a distance, giving those who possessed muskets a huge advantage and greatly increasing the numbers of those wounded or killed in battle; and unequal access to other European goods including domestic plants and animals and iron tools, increasing the mana of those who controlled places where Europeans visited or lived, and allowing a rapid expansion of agriculture and a demand for war captives to take care of pigs and cultivate the fields.

Visiting ships were attracted to the Bay by the presence of the missionaries, and as Hongi Hika's people and other kin groups in the Bay acquired more muskets, these tensions spiralled out of control. In 1816, Hongi led a taua (war party) to the north armed with muskets obtained by trade with the missionaries and with visiting ships. During that time the missionary families almost ran out of food, and their ticket-of-leave convict workers abandoned the mission.[24]

The following year, Hongi took a taua of 30 canoes and 800 warriors to make peace with his enemies at North Cape. On the way, however, his men quarrelled and fought with some Whangaroa people (the home district of his mother and his senior wife Turikatuku).[25] As Kendall remarked, 'War is all their glory. They travel to the south and kill great numbers. Almost the whole of the native men belonging to this Bay are now gone to battle.'[26]

During Hongi's long absences on these expeditions, Kendall, who had been appointed as a magistrate to protect Māori interests with Hongi's support, found himself isolated. Although the missionaries were supposed to hold their property in common, William Hall traded privately from the outset, raising prices in the Bay, and forcing his colleagues to do the same.[27]

War dance, New Zealand, by Joseph Jenner Merrett, 1845.

Unable to grow their own food at Hohi and without adequate supplies of shoes or clothing,[28] Kendall and his fellow missionaries found themselves having to barter muskets and gunpowder to feed and dress their families, although this was strongly discouraged by the Church Missionary Society.[29] Tormented by fears for himself, his family and the mission, frustrated by Hall's obstinacy and reluctance to build a schoolhouse, and by an irregular supply of paper, slates and pencils, clothing and provisions for his pupils,[30] Kendall found his efforts to act as a magistrate mocked by visiting sailors[31] and resented by Hall and King. They accused him of getting drunk, setting himself up like Governor Macquarie at Port Jackson, and telling local Māori that his fellow missionaries were only servants, while he was a great gentleman.[32]

At the same time, thwarted by his lack of linguistic training, Kendall was struggling to master the Māori language. He felt increasingly lonely; and when his wife Jane had an affair with their convict servant Richard Stockwell and bore him a child,[33] life in New Zealand became intolerable.[34] At about that time, to the great entertainment of the local people, Kendall and Walter Hall, the convict blacksmith, brawled over the ownership of a chisel. When the blacksmith pointed a horse pistol at him, Kendall wrestled him to the ground, striking him furiously with the chisel until the pistol went off, wounding Hall's wife in the arm. That night, he set Hall's hut on fire.[35]

In his misery, Kendall turned to his Māori friends for companionship, and went on board visiting whalers, trading and drinking with their captains. He became increasingly unrestrained, and when his servant Stockwell, who had a fine singing voice[36] (which would have endeared him to Māori), was accused of 'having imprudent connections with the girls' and threatened to kill himself in front of the missionaries, Kendall knocked him down.

During this time, Kendall wrote 'The New Zealander's First Book', which he sent to his friend Rev. Basil Woodd for the Church Missionary Society to examine.[37] In August 1816, when the schoolhouse at Hohi finally opened, a building 30 feet long by 18 feet wide, with a raised mezzanine at one end for the teacher and the European children, Kendall threw himself into trying to teach his pupils,[38] assisted by Te Pahi's seventeen-year-old son. This venture was also fraught with difficulty, however.

The school began with 33 pupils, peaking at 70 in April 1817. When supplies of provisions for his students failed to arrive from Port Jackson, Kendall had to wake them at daybreak to teach them the alphabet before sending them off to the rivers or into the bush to find fern-root, fish or cockles to eat. At night he tried to teach his pupils the catechism in Māori, before they went to sleep. As he remarked ruefully:

> They are so very lively and playful that it is not easy to gain their atten-
> tion. . . . When a teacher amongst the heathen (for it could not be endured in
> civilized society) is surrounded by a number of children, and perhaps while
> one is repeating his lesson, another will be playing with his feet, another
> taking away his hat, and another, his book, and all this in a friendly manner,
> he cannot be angry at them, yet it requires some study how to introduce a
> salutary discipline; and this is what we want here.[39]

Attendance was irregular, and Kendall pleaded with the Church Missionary Society to send him writing paper, quills and copy books, scarlet and yellow worsted binding, earrings and rings, knitting needles, thimbles, hair combs, knives, fishhooks, boys' whistles, bird calls and small iron toys (including a miniature cannon later found in archaeological excavations of the site)[40] as rewards for his pupils – gifts that would enable him to uphold his relationships with them and their families.

In British schools at this time, children were expected to sit still in gridded arrays of desks, separated by gender, listening quietly to their teacher,[41] but this kind of physical constraint was alien to Māori. Used as they were to freedom of movement and governing their own activities, both children and adults found this kind of 'discipline' almost intolerable. As John King found when he tried to teach Māori men to spin rope: 'The most labour I have with them is to prevail upon them to stay constantly and persevere, at times it is needful to reprove or scold them, this they can hardly bear, while they can find a place of more liberty and less control.'[42]

Like the other missionaries, Kendall was frustrated by his limited command of Māori: 'I shall, as soon as I can arrange the school to my satisfaction, be considerably relieved. But this I do not expect to be able to do until I am better acquainted with the New Zealand language and my books of instruction are more suitable to our purpose.'[43] The more fond he became of his pupils and entered into the world of the Māori language, however, the more he found his own values and standards slipping away.

Although Kendall tried to keep the female scholars away from visiting ships, he was not always successful.[44] Sexual chastity before marriage was not highly valued among Māori, and these young women would have been bare-breasted much of the time, and prone to tease their schoolmaster. In addition, the rangatira were eager to try to bring Europeans they valued into their whakapapa networks by promoting sexual liaisons between them and local girls. Back in Britain at this time, on the other hand, increasing restraints were being placed on sexual relations. If a missionary had sex with a Māori girl, this was a terrible affront – a flagrant breach of marital fidelity, conventions about keeping sexual alliances within the same group,[45] and evangelical expectations about personal purity. Plagued by temptation, Kendall was in turmoil. In a letter to Josiah Pratt, the Secretary of the CMS, he lamented, 'I am not perfect. Alas I am an heavy laden Sinner.'[46]

In early 1817, although Hongi sent his son Ripiro (also known as 'Hare' Hongi, or Charles or 'Charley' in English, after Marsden's son) to the school, attended by a servant, the sons of Korokoro and Tareha attended only for a couple of days. When some supplies and small rewards such as fishhooks finally arrived, the children returned to school rejoicing, singing and dancing. Kendall reported: 'I can now command their attention. They will learn to read and write, work at their raiment, make fences, and fetch water and firewood, very cheerfully. They rise at daylight, and repeat their lessons to me. After breakfast, several of the boys write a copy. The girls are employed in making their raiment the whole of the day.'[47] Perhaps to help him with the female scholars, in June 1817 Kendall summoned his daughters from Port Jackson to stay with him at the Bay of Islands.[48]

In July when one of his students fell ill, the boy's father cursed the atua (or powerful ancestor) responsible (although it's not clear whether this being was European or Māori), trying to drive the malevolent spirit away from his son. Kendall lamented:

> Pride and ignorance, cruelty and licentiousness are some of the principal
> ingredients in a New Zealanders religion. He does not, as far as I can learn,
> bow to a stork or a stone but he magnifies himself into a god. The chiefs and
> elders of the people are called Atuas even whilst they are living. . . . The head
> of a New Zealander being the seat of the Atua is sacred . . . . To the carved or
> graven head of a friend or enemy after death the same ode is sung.[49]

Nevertheless, he praised local Māori for their kindness and friendship.[50]

In February 1818, about a thousand warriors with 50 war canoes gathered in the Bay,[51] and Hongi led a large taua south to Maketu and the East Coast at the request of Te Haupa, the ariki at Thames.[52] In early 1819 when this expedition returned home with the heads of many enemy warriors and prisoners of war (300 according to Kendall, or 2000 according to Samuel Marsden), many of these captives were enslaved while others were sacrificed and eaten in the kai tangata (eating people) ritual by the grieving relatives of northern warriors who had been killed in the fighting, horrifying the missionaries.[53]

Perhaps because of Hongi's absence, by mid-1818, supplies for the school had dried up and Kendall's pupils returned to their homes.[54] In an effort to win them back, he asked the CMS to send him writing paper; fabric, needles and thread for the girls; and portraits of King George III in his robes, William Wilberforce the anti-slavery campaigner, Lord Gambier, the president of the CMS, and images of Adam and Eve, and the birth, death and resurrection of Jesus Christ for the schoolhouse. Kendall also requested a Greek dictionary and testament for himself, an English grammar and six dictionaries, an *Encyclopaedia Britannica* and a copy of his friend J.L. Nicholas's book *Narrative of a Voyage to New Zealand*.[55] In return he sent Pratt a preparatory catechism in English and Māori, some flax cloaks made by the female scholars, copy books written by his male pupils, a model war canoe for the missionary museum and, later, a war trumpet.[56] By the end of 1818, Kendall had acquired copies of the catechism in Tahitian from a

Hongi returns from East Cape and the Bay of Plenty in 1819, by unknown artist.

visiting ship. There, the missionaries transcribed the vowels as in Italian or Spanish. When Kendall used the Tahitian orthography as a model to translate the catechism into Māori, noting the similarity between the two languages, Māori found it much easier to follow, although his fellow missionaries found it difficult to use the text.[57]

The cause of Christianity was not helped by the bitter quarrels among the missionaries. When King complained about Kendall, he earned a rebuke from the CMS Secretary Pratt for his unchristian conduct: 'Mr. Kendall has not complained of you, as you evidently do of him';[58] while King's mentor Daniel Wilson exhorted King to follow Marsden's instructions, accusing him of being 'at ease with worldly security'.[59] When Kendall apologised for his role in these dissensions,[60] Pratt assured him that the CMS was delighted with 'The New Zealander's First Book', and his plan to instruct the children in Māori. He added:

> Respecting our opinion of your character & usefulness, your mind may be quite easy. We are well convinced of the singleness of your heart in this cause: Nor have we heard any thing from any one, that would lead us to doubt your steady & judicious pursuit of the great object of the Society. Go on! & may the Lord prosper you![61]

Letters from London took a long time to reach New Zealand, however, and while he was waiting to hear back from Pratt, Kendall lost heart. At the end of December 1818, he wrote a poignant letter to the Secretary, saying that it was now nearly six years since he had been in England and worshipped with a Christian congregation:

> [D]uring the last four years my eyes have been constantly fixed on scenes of human depravity and woe, and my ears have listened to, and have partly been infected with the profane and obscene rubbish contained in heathen songs. The latter I am under the necessity of attending to: For it greatly assists me in learning the Language, by writing down the themes of the Natives, and studying their true meaning. The study is painful, and like the Study of the Metamorphoses of Ovid tends to injure the mind. O how it would refresh me to enjoy a little repose – in a Christian land, to be again united . . . under a pious minister of the Gospel. But I must check these feelings. I trust I am in the Service of the Same Heavenly Master with you: that he will bless me still . . . It is not my own work I am called to. It is his own. I am a sinful, polluted, worm.[62]

The more Kendall studied Māori and worked with experts in the language (including the tohunga Te Rakau), the more he felt his own world collapsing. He was increasingly desperate to return to England to refresh his Christian beliefs, and escape the temptations of sexual freedom. In Māori ideas of the world, sex is a creative, generative force, not a source of sin and pollution, and there must have been many times when Kendall envied the relaxed attitudes of his Māori friends, and the sexual freedom enjoyed by the missionaries' convict servants and visiting sailors.

By early 1819, too, there were still no signs that Māori were ready to receive the Gospel. Although many of the chiefs' sons embarked on the *Active* to visit Samuel Marsden at Parramatta,[63] they were mainly interested in his orchards and vineyards, and stoutly denied that there was only one God. In their view of reality, Māori and European ways of living and atua could co-exist, each within their own spheres – a 'multi-verse' (rather than a uni-verse) approach that echoed the existence of multiple ao (ontological dimensions) in Māori. As Marsden reported:

> When I told them there was but one God, and our God was theirs, they asked me if our God had given us any sweet potatoes. I replied, 'No.' They answered, 'Our God has given us sweet potatoes, and if He had been your

God also He would have given you some.' I told them our climate was too cold, they would not grow, and therefore He knew it would be no use to give us any. They said, 'Your God has given you cattle and sheep and horses and many other things, which He has not given us. Were He our God as well as yours, He would not have acted so partially. He would have given us cattle &c as well as you.' This brought us to the creation of the world and to Noah's flood, from which I showed them how the different animals came to be spread over the world, and told them that England was for a long time without cattle &c, but in due time God had given them to England and now He was going to give all these things which we had to them . . . They then replied, 'But we are of a different colour to you, and if one God made us both, He would not have made such a mistake as to make us of different colours.' This I endeavoured to explain also . . . Many other arguments they used to prove that there must be more than one God. Their reasoning faculties are strong and clear and their comprehension quick.[64]

The missionaries in the Bay of Islands agreed:

The natives of New Zealand are men of strong intellects & in general possess a Spirit of enterprise & enquiry. When they return to this Island they will spend many hours & sometimes whole nights, in telling their Countrymen what the customs of Englishmen are . . . There appears to be no particular impediment to the introduction of the Gospel any further than the powerful effect of traditionary Superstitions – Principles implanted in their minds by their Ancestors.[65]

Visits by the rangatira to Port Jackson had alerted local leaders to the danger that, backed by British soldiers, European settlers might take over their country. As Kendall warned: 'They cannot endure the thought that they should lose the property which is descended to them from their forefathers and be driven into the bush, as they say is the case of the natives of New South Wales.'[66] The rangatira also deplored the frequent quarrels among the missionaries, and in March 1819 the missionary settlers tried to end these by signing a written agreement that none of them would engage in private trade.[67] This accord was quickly broken, however.

Worse, when William Hall preached hellfire and damnation, threatening local Māori who had been cursing in English with 'the eternal miseries of all the wicked in hell after death',[68] this seemed like a promise of being eternally cooked, a terrible insult in Māori. Hongi had recently heard that the Whangaroa people had desecrated the sepulchre of his wife's father, taking his bones to make fishhooks and putting his skull on a pole, an act that demanded utu;[69] and the threat of being cooked after death was an extreme provocation.

As he became more intimate with the local people, Thomas Kendall found working with Hall increasingly intolerable. As he reported to Marsden: 'Mr Hall and myself can act no longer in concert together. We are like unto the Iron Pot and the earthern Pot carried on by the same current; We must not come near each other in haste lest one of us be dashed to pieces.'[70]

Marsden's second visit to New Zealand

Troubled by reports of incessant squabbling among the missionaries, in August 1819 Samuel Marsden boarded an American brig, the *General Gates*, in Port Jackson, intent on refreshing the New Zealand mission and settling their dissensions. On this occasion he was accompanied by Rev. John Butler and his family; James Kemp, a blacksmith, and his wife; the carpenters William Fairburn and William Bean and their families; Francis Hall, a new schoolmaster; and Tui (Korokoro's brother) and Titere, who had recently returned from England.[71] Butler, a former clerk in a carrying company in London who had been ordained before he left England, had just been appointed superintendent of the New Zealand mission, supplanting Thomas Kendall as its de facto leader.

During his first visit to the Bay of Islands, Marsden had noted the rich soils at Kerikeri. Shortly after his arrival on this occasion, when Hongi Hika offered him land for a new mission station beside Kororipo pā in the Kerikeri basin, impressed by the fertility of the land, Marsden decided to accept this offer. He remarked: 'Shunghee is a man of the mildest manners, and disposition, and appears to possess a very superior mind.'[72] As soon as the chiefs from other districts in the Bay of Islands heard about this deal, however, they were enraged – especially Te Morenga, the rangatira of Taiamai, and Korokoro, the Ngare Raumati chief from the southern alliance in the Bay who had accompanied Hongi on his journey to Port Jackson with Kendall and Hall, and whose younger brother Tui had visited Port Jackson and England.

When he saw Marsden, Korokoro castigated him, saying that 'his Brother Tooi had been been long absent from him, and his friends; had gone to England; had brought out the white people with him, and after all, he was not to have the advantage of any of them to reside with him. That this was an act of great injustice . . .'[73] He said that Hongi 'would now cut him and his people off'. When Marsden tried to console him by saying that Hongi had promised to stop fighting, Korokoro retorted bitterly that 'Shunghee would make fair promises but we could not see into Shunghee's heart'.[74] If Hongi controlled all the resident Europeans, any balance of power among the tribes in the Bay would be upset.[75] In private, Tui advised Marsden to locate the mission at Kerikeri, since Hongi was the most powerful rangatira in the north, and under his protection the missionaries would be safe.

The people at Rangihoua were also furious with Marsden and the missionaries, feeling that their hospitality had been slighted. When Kendall turned Te Uri-o-Kanae out of his house one day, without giving any reason, the chief was bitterly offended. The mission at Rangihoua had been built on his ancestral land, which the Rangihoua people had placed under a tapu for the missionaries, forging an alliance with them. In local eyes, they were Kanae's guests. In recompense for this insult and by way of demanding an explanation, Kanae's brother took two earthen pots from William Hall, which Hall regarded as 'theft'. When Marsden scolded Kanae, saying that he had no reason to be offended and Hall should not be punished for what Kendall had done, his brother demanded an axe as utu for the return of the pots. In reply, Marsden told him that he could keep them, 'for we would not purchase them because they were stolen' – a dreadful insult. While muru, or ritual plunder, was the proper way to avenge an offence,[76] a theft that was detected was the act of a person without mana.

Later that day some tools were taken from the missionaries, no doubt as utu for this insult, and Marsden summoned the local people. He told them that 'King George and the Gentlemen in England would be ashamed of them, when they heard of their thefts, and that I could allow no thief to go in the *Active* to Parramatta, and if they were there, and stole there, Governor Macquarie would hang them'.[77] Covered with whakamā (humiliation and shame) by these insults, Kanae burned down his house at Rangihoua, saying that he would never live there again. When Marsden reproached Hongi for allowing the 'theft' of their tools, however, Hongi said with a smile that if the

Rangihoua people had taken only one axe, he would not have thought much about it.

Ten days later when Kanae returned to mourn over the embers of his house, slashing his body and weeping with his kinfolk, he told the missionaries that he had gone to Kawakawa to live with a relative. To comfort him, Marsden presented him with some gifts and he seemed overjoyed, no doubt because these could be seen as utu for the things that Marsden had said, restoring some of the mana he had lost at the hands of the missionaries.[78]

At the same time as Kanae and his family were being humiliated, the mana of Hongi Hika was in the ascendant. As a result of his relationship with the missionaries, especially Kendall, who handled trade with the ships, Hongi was acquiring a large armoury of firearms, giving him and his men a formidable advantage in conflicts with opponents without muskets. This made him tolerant of the missionaries, and willing to deal with them.

On 15 September Marsden met a young woman at Rangihoua, a niece of Hinematioro ('a great queen' on the East Coast), whom Hongi had captured as a prisoner of war during a surprise attack on her settlement, and given to a young local rangatira as a war captive. During this visit, too, Marsden often questioned Hongi and other chiefs about Māori warfare, especially their practice of kai tangata, which had become notorious in Europe, using Kendall as an interpreter. When he asked them whether they ate those killed in battle, the rangatira explained that when an enemy ariki was killed, the victors demanded his body and his wife from the conquered kin group. If the defeated party refused to deliver them up, the battle was immediately resumed. If they agreed, the enemy ariki's wife was killed, and laid beside the body of her husband. The victorious ariki then ordered the rangatira to cook his enemy's body as an offering for his atua (senior ancestor), while the female ariki ordered the chief's wives to prepare the body of his wife for her atua. No commoners were allowed to touch these bodies, because they were so intensely tapu. When the bodies were cooked, the male and female ariki each took a piece of flesh from the body of their defeated counterpart and put it in a small basket as an offering, while carrying out a divination ritual to predict the outcome of the battle. These ceremonies were conducted in absolute silence, those present covering their faces with their cloaks or their hands.

Only ariki could eat from the bodies of such sacrifices. If their offerings were accepted, the battle was renewed, and afterwards all who were slain could be eaten, their heads taken as trophies and parts of their bodies, including flesh and bones, distributed to friends and allies.[79] The bones were often turned into fishhooks, musical instruments or ornaments as a further way of destroying their mana.[80] Although this custom was regarded with horror in Europe, Marsden's report of his discussion with the rangatira about kai tangata was matter-of-fact. As he had supposed, the purpose of this practice was to destroy the mana and tapu of the enemy kin group by destroying the mana and tapu of their aristocratic leaders, and that of their ancestors. In the north, these rituals had to be carried out for male and female leaders alike, destroying the mana of both the male and female senior descent lines of their enemies.

When questioned about the origins of this custom, Hongi remarked that as 'large fish eat small ones – small fish eat insects. Dogs will eat men and men will eat dogs, and dogs devour each other. The louse that sucks the blood of man, that man will eat as a just retaliation.'[81] Marsden commented:

> I should not have understood how the gods [atua] could eat each other, unless Shunghee had informed me, when he was to the Southward and had killed a number of People, he was afraid their God would kill him in retaliation – esteeming himself a God; but he caught their God, being a reptile, and eat part of it, and reserved the other part for his friends; and by that means he rested satisfied that they were all secure from his resentment.[82]

As Marsden learned, upon the death of Kaingaroa in 1815, Hongi Hika had succeeded his elder brother as ariki of the northern alliance, and was now regarded as an atua himself. On occasion, people would greet Hongi by saying, 'Haere mai, haere mai Atua! [Welcome, welcome, Atua!]',[83] while a flash of sunlight on a hill was described as the wairua (immaterial presence) of Hongi's father. This was, however, very different from a 'god' in the European sense. Although the missionaries translated atua as 'god', those Europeans who later became more fluent in Māori insisted that this term referred to powerful ancestors, no more and no less.[84] As the kanohi ora (living face) of his warrior ancestors, embodying their tapu (presence) and mana (power), Hongi was properly described by this term.

Warriors who ate human flesh, thus consuming the hau of a chiefly enemy and his ancestors, were also referred to as atua. From a Christian point of view, this was blasphemous. Among men, only Christ could be God incarnate.

While some of the missionaries regarded cannibalism with horror, however, others recognised that in te ao Māori, rangatira could be the 'living face' of their ancestors, and the act of consuming the flesh of a dead enemy destroyed their mana. Like Captain Cook, both Kendall and Marsden were relatively unmoved by this practice. As a fighting sailor, Cook was used to naval punishments such as keel-hauling and flogging around the fleet, which would be regarded as barbaric today; while Marsden as a magistrate was in the habit of handing out punishments including hanging, and floggings, which even at that time were seen as harsh for the offences committed.

From early missionary times onwards, words referring to Māori cosmological ideas were translated with English words that refer to Western religious beliefs and practices – atua as 'god' (rather than powerful ancestor) and wairua as 'spirit' (rather than a person's immaterial being); tapu as 'sacred', rather than ancestral presence; noa as 'profane', instead of ancestral absence; tohunga as 'priest' rather than expert; karakia as 'prayer', instead of chant; and Tangaroa, Tane and Tawhiri as the 'gods' of the sea, forest and winds, instead of these ancestral beings in all of their power. This interpretive approach cast Māori understandings as a direct challenge to Christianity, which had to be cast out and replaced by Christian doctrine. Far from being mystical in the European sense, however, these ideas are matter-of-fact in Māori, reflecting taken-for-granted ontological assumptions. Indeed, as we have seen, there are striking resonances between aspects of Māori onto-logic and relational scientific thinking in the Enlightenment, which also explored ideas of the world as a living system, often described as the 'web of life' or the 'tree of life' – forms of order, as noted earlier, that are resurgent in contemporary science.[85]

Assuming that Māori thinking was fundamentally wrong-headed, however, the missionaries described Māori ideas as 'superstition' or 'idolatry', dismissing them out of hand. Another strategy was to displace Māori customs to the remote past, comparing them with ancestral Western practices – for example, those of the Greeks, Hebrews or Anglo-Saxons – although it might have been more pertinent to compare Māori practices such as cannibalism, warfare, infanticide and slavery with contemporary European punishments such as hanging, flogging and keel-hauling, and warfare, infanticide and slavery in Europe during the early nineteenth century.

In an effort to make sense of Māori martial practice, for instance, Marsden drew upon biblical precedents to suggest that Māori might be descendants of the lost tribes of Israel. Just as the high priest of the Jews addressed the warriors before battle in Deuteronomy, he noted, Māori priests spoke to their armies; and as David cut off Goliath's head and took it to Jerusalem as a trophy, so conquering chiefs in New Zealand brought home heads of their enemies to be exhibited, as proof that 'justice had been obtained'.[86] Marsden also reported that in New Zealand, if the victors wanted to make peace, they might meet with their opponents and display the preserved heads of their dead chiefs. If the defeated wept over the heads of their leaders, peace was made. If not, the fighting resumed. On the other hand, if the victors were still angry, they might humiliate their enemies by selling their chiefs' heads to visiting ships,[87] or desecrate them in other ways.

The head of a rangatira was referred to as an atua, and treated with great veneration by their kinsfolk.[88] At a tangi, or funeral, the heads or skulls and bones of ancestors were placed on the left side of the dead person (a custom still practised, although photographic portraits of forebears are now used instead).[89] When a strong wind blew, people said that they could hear voices of their dead kinfolk, whistling in the hau (wind).[90]

While in general, Marsden was immune to the appeal of Māori understandings of reality, quite remarkably, he compared kai tangata with Christian sacraments:

> The New Zealanders believe that the Soul of a Chief when departed from the body becomes a God, and has the power of life and death. They also believe that by eating the flesh, and drinking the blood of the departed Chief his System becomes incorporated into their System and by that means they are secured from all danger from the departed ghost of the dead Chief, and that his Spirit will then take up its residence in their bodies . . . This is a singular idea, and one would be led to think that it had been derived from divine revelation. Our Saviour told the Jews 'He that eateth my flesh and drinketh my blood dwelleth in me and I in him'.[91]

During this second visit to New Zealand, much of Marsden's time was spent debating with the chiefs about this and other matters. Fascinated by Western ideas and technologies, they lost little time in trying to understand how these worked, and how they might serve their own interests. Marsden was intrigued by this, and by the way that rangatira children often participated in these discussions:

The Chiefs are in general very sensible men, and wish for information upon all subjects. They are accustomed to public discussions from their infancy. The Chiefs take their Children from their Mothers breast, to all their public Assemblies. They hear all that is said upon Politics, Religion, War &c by the oldest men. Children will frequently ask questions in public Conversation, and are answered by the Chiefs. I have often been surprised, to see the Sons of the Chiefs at the age of 4 or 5 years sitting amongst the Chiefs, and paying such close attention to what was said. . . . In every Village, the Children, as soon as they learned any of our names, came up to us, and spake to us with the greatest familiarity.[92]

Marsden found Māori children engaging, saying that they 'are generally very easy, open and familiar at the first interview, and show an anxiety to pay every little attention in their power to strangers. There can be no finer children than [those of] the New Zealanders in any part of the world. Their parents are very indulgent, and they appear always happy and play-ful, and very active.'[93] He failed to connect their happiness, however, with the absence of contemporary British child-rearing practices which included harsh physical punishment. Marsden also enjoyed his nightly discussions with the rangatira:

We [often] spent the evening . . . conversing upon various subjects, and in gaining all the information we could relative to the Rivers in New Zealand, the number of Inhabitants on their banks, upon what they lived, and the mode of communication they had with distant parts of the Island. . . . If we asked how far any mountain or river was off, they would say, 'What do you want to know for? Are you going there?[94]

Sometimes, the chiefs amused themselves by teasing him. When Marsden urged them to treat the new missionaries kindly, saying that the Society had feared to send Europeans among them for fear that they might be eaten, they replied that:

as we had done them no injury, they had no satisfaction to demand from us, and no just feelings to gratify: and observed with a smile, if they naturally craved after human flesh, we might make ourselves easy on that head, as the flesh of New Zealanders was much sweeter than an European, in conse-quence of the white people eating so much salt.[95]

When Marsden (using Kendall as his interpreter) told the chiefs that in England, gentlemen did not expect their wives to work on the land, and that they had only one wife, while some rangatira had ten, who often argued with each other, they replied that 'what we said was very true, that such a number of wives caused great disputes amongst them, that it often happened that the women in these quarrels would go and hang themselves'. They needed many wives, however, they said, because they had no money to pay anyone else to cultivate their land.[96] At that time, northern rangatira were engaged in a dramatic expansion in agriculture, in an effort to acquire muskets and after the introduction of potatoes and other European crops, and iron hoes, spades, axes and other tools Marsden estimated that compared with his 1814–15 visit to New Zealand, there had been a tenfold increase in the area of land under cultivation in the Bay.

During this visit, Marsden also travelled to Hokianga, where he spent many days with Te Manene, the high priest of the Hokianga heads, discussing matters including the movements of the Earth, the relationship of New Zealand to other countries, the productions of different lands, and debating the origins of the cosmos. He also met the rangatira Patuone, a friend and ally of Hongi's who would later play a major role in the debates over the Treaty of Waitangi, whom he described as 'one of the most pleasant Chiefs I had met with. He has a fine open countenance, in which the greatest kindness, and good nature is expressed.'[97] Marsden remarked that the chiefs were great travellers, often leaving their homes for ten or twelve months at a time, and that they told him about the Waikato River, with its innumerable inhabitants.[98] When he explored the Hokianga Harbour in a canoe, the tohunga Te Manene came with him, chanting to still the wind and the waves. As they landed near one of the sacred rocks at the heads, his chiefly companion urgently warned him not to touch it, or he would die. Although Marsden scoffed at Te Manene's powers and often challenged him to prove the existence of his god, he listened to him on this occasion. Clearly, he enjoyed the company of the high priest, and the debates they had about such matters.[99]

When Marsden tried to convince the chiefs that there was no need to observe various tapu, saying that 'tabooing their provisions, the Vessels they eat out of, their Houses &c were all a delusion – that there was no such thing in Europe', they retorted that if they did not listen to their priests, they would die;[100] and when he assured them that in Tahiti the paramount chief Pomare had given up tabooing his houses and provisions, and yet was alive and well, they replied that if the missionaries could convince them that their religion was wrong, they might do likewise.[101] Later, when Marsden tried out these same arguments on the great warrior Murupaenga and his people at Kaipara, they told him firmly, 'Our God and theirs were different. They said that I might violate their taboos, eat in their houses or dress my provisions upon their fires – their god would not punish me, but he would kill them for my Crimes.'[102]

Once again, Māori insisted on the existence of parallel ontological dimensions, in which different atua and ways of living could co-exist side by side. This approach, which echoed Māori conceptions of te pō, te kore and te ao, was radically different from the 'universe' of early modernist science, which recognised only one Nature with its God-given laws; and of evangelical Christianity, in which there could be only one true God and one good way of life, which Māori had to adopt or suffer eternal hellfire. To many Māori, the missionaries seemed arrogant or whakahīhī (raising oneself above others) in their ardent conviction of the superiority of their own beliefs (with Thomas Kendall as a striking exception).

When Marsden returned to Kerikeri after his excursion to Hokianga, he was glad to find new buildings already rising at the mission station. He had earlier planted 100 grapevines, hoping to establish a wine industry in the Bay of Islands, and the vines were now in leaf. The other missionaries had established a garden with fruit trees, along with large fields of maize. Before he sailed back to Port Jackson on 9 November 1819, Hongi and a number of other chiefs 'sold' him 13,000 acres at Kerikeri for 48 felling axes, although the deed was written in English. It stated that Hongi Hika did 'give and grant to the Directors of the said Church Missionary Society and their successors for ever that Parcel of Land now called Pookay Kohay Ta Weedingha Tou [*Puke Kowhai tā Whiringatau* – Kowhai Hill belonging to Whiringatau] with all the Timbers Minerals Waters Rights and Appurtenances to the same'.[103] Hongi and Rewa signed the deed with their moko (facial tattoos), and afterwards, Marsden gave Hongi a personal gift of a cask of gunpowder.[104]

As had been the case with the Hohi mission and Rangihoua pā, the Kerikeri mission station was located below Kororipo pā, Hongi's fortified village where important gatherings were held, taua (war parties) gathered and were farewelled and welcomed back to the Bay. Once again, the missionaries were under constant surveillance, and the cloak of Hongi's protection.

Disputes between missionaries and Māori

Two weeks after Marsden's departure, Te Morenga's people attacked the new buildings at Kerikeri, breaking down the pigsties and taking the pigs and some iron tools. When Hongi's warriors shot some of the marauders, Te Morenga burned Hongi's fleet of war canoes. The ostensible take, or reason, for this dispute was that some of Hongi's war captives had taken cockles from Te Morenga's shellfish beds without his consent, but it probably also involved a quarrel over gift exchanges for the use of the land.

Several days after this raid, John Butler summoned a meeting at Kerikeri and lectured the assembled rangatira, including Hongi, about the evils of theft (although he did not yet speak Māori, and used a Māori brickmaker as his interpreter). He told them that 'the great God of the Christians was very angry with them and white people considered it a very bad thing, and that those who were known to do such things were severely punished'.[105] Not surprisingly, since his people had just been attacked by Te Morenga's warriors, Hongi supported Butler on this occasion, saying that at Port Jackson he had seen thieves confined in irons or tied to a post and flogged, and one man hanged for this crime. Other speakers at the gathering said that it would be good if Butler would build a house in which thieves could be locked up and starved, or put irons on their legs and send them out into the bush, where people would mock them so much that they would die crying with shame.

The next day, the chiefs summoned their people and mustered them in kin groups, where they sat in profound silence as each rangatira harangued his own people, threatening them with the severest of punishments if they were found guilty of theft.[106] These speeches may have been satirical in part, and in any case they made no practical difference, although the rangatira were gratified when Butler gave them 1000 fishhooks to distribute among their people. Three weeks later when Butler and Kemp shifted their possessions to Kerikeri, the Rangihoua people threw down their boxes and smashed the casks, taking many of their hoes and axes.[107]

Like William Hall, John Butler was a firm believer in European superiority. Although he shared Marsden's admiration for Māori, Butler thought that the sooner they adopted a European way of life and learned to speak English, the better: 'The New Zealanders are a robust, athletic and noble race of men, of lively dispositions, amazing quick in perception, and generally speaking, they are a kind and affectionate people. Many of them speak a great deal of broken English, and are very fond of our language.'[108]

In mentioning Māori cannibalism, he lamented, 'Oh! The dreadful chains of darkness with which Satan has bound these people.'[109] Far from supporting Kendall's study of Māori language and cosmology, Butler looked forward to the assimilation of Māori into European ways of life. Those Māori who spent time at Port Jackson, he declared:

> do not appear like the same persons; when they return back their natural ferocity seems very much softened, their minds enlightened, and themselves more than ever attached to the white people, and especially to the missionaries. They also relate to their own people all the things which they see and hear. This will have a great tendency to [open] their eyes to see our real intention of coming among them, viz. to do them good, both in body and soul.[110]

When Butler tried to force his own beliefs on Māori by appealing to the power of God, however, the chiefs told him that his god had no authority in New Zealand. When a rangatira offered him a woman to sleep with, he replied:

> I was tabooed, and also a priest, and if I committed such wickedness my God would destroy me. I further explained to him . . . the wickedness of having more than one wife, and that the great God was angry with all men that had many wives. I asked him if he was not afraid of God's anger. He replied, 'No, our God is not angry with us, and your God does not live in New Zealand.' I answered, 'Our God is a Spirit, and lives in New Zealand as well as Europe, and that he understands all that we are saying, and I was very much afraid He would be angry at such bad discourse.' He said, 'If you are afraid of His anger, I will say no more.'[111]

Like others in the CMS, Butler saw the introduction of European beliefs and customs as 'improvement' and 'progress'. At the Kerikeri mission station, Māori brickmakers, wood-cutters, sawyers and farmers were helping to erect buildings and cultivate the land. Butler often used agricultural metaphors for the process of conversion:

> I humbly trust that the barren deserts of New Zealand and the valleys (which are now covered with noxious weeds) will ere long stand so thick with corn that they may be said to laugh and sing, and the inhabitants thereof made to

rejoice, because of the loving kindness of the Lord, and for His great mercy and goodness, which He will pour upon them.[112]

Six months later, he wrote:

> Let us all pray that the same good God, who giveth seed to the sower, may soon cause the seed of His holy word to be received into the hearts of the people, so that the mind of the New Zealander, which is at present so wild and uncultivated, may by the dew and the seeds of the Holy Spirit become like a tree planted by the watercourses, and like a watered garden whose waters fail not.[113]

In addition to lecturing the rangatira, Butler was determined to assert his authority over the other missionaries, especially Thomas Kendall, the former head of the mission. Rev. Basil Woodd, who knew both Butler and Kendall, later told Rev. Pratt, the Secretary of the CMS, that it had been a mistake to appoint Butler as the superintendent of the mission: 'Mr. B is not a man to be entrusted with such power; he is far too hasty & injudicious'.[114] In late January 1820, Butler found an opportunity to put Kendall in his place.

When the whaler *Catherine* arrived in the Bay, Kendall went on board and bartered local goods for eight blunderbusses, a fowling piece and some gunpowder, advising Hongi to send his pigs on board another ship, the *Echo*, where he told him he could get excellent muskets. As soon as he heard about these transactions, Butler summoned a council, telling the missionaries to meet in the schoolroom. When Butler read out charges against Kendall and King for trading in muskets, Kendall 'flew into a most violent rage, and stamped and stormed about the school-room for half an hour'. When King was accused, he also flew into a fury.[115] Kendall, who had been appointed a magistrate by Governor Macquarie and was formerly regarded as head of the mission, had now spent six years in New Zealand, while Butler had just arrived and had very little understanding of local customs and conditions.

Butler's assertion of authority was too much for Thomas Kendall. During his last visit, Samuel Marsden had told Hongi that he could accompany Kendall when he returned to England, and within a week the missionary had organised a passage for them both on board a whaler, the *New Zealander*. Hongi Hika was eager to visit King George in England, and procure muskets and soldiers, while Kendall hoped to work with Hongi and Professor

Samuel Lee at Cambridge University on a grammar of Māori, and to be
ordained as a minister, so that Butler would no longer outrank him.

Marsden's third visit to New Zealand

On 27 February 1820, Samuel Marsden arrived back in the Bay of Islands
for his third visit to New Zealand, this time on a government ship, HMS
Dromedary, which had been sent to collect a cargo of spars and investigate the wisdom of establishing a settlement in New Zealand under the
auspices of the British Crown,[116] accompanied by the 84th Regiment.
Tui, Korokoro's younger brother who had visited England before Hongi
Hika, and Hongi's favourite son Ripiro, who had spent three months with
Marsden in Parramatta, were also on board. Marsden found the mission in
turmoil, and Kendall and their key protector, Hongi Hika, about to set off
for England. As Marsden remarked with chagrin:

> Shunghee has been very kind to the Settlers since they have been there. . . .
> Mr. Kendall has gained very considerable knowledge of the language, as well
> as the confidence of the natives. I wish much he had obtained the permission
> of the Society and the approbation of his Colleagues to visit England before
> he attempted to leave his Station.[117]

Marsden had other reasons to be angry with Kendall. A month earlier,
Kendall had warned Marsden that some of the chiefs (including Ruatara,
Tui and Titere) had been making disrespectful comments about Marsden's
daughter Maria, suggesting that she had had an affair with one of his Māori
guests at Parramatta.[118] Incensed, Marsden accused him of making up these
stories. To make matters worse, when Marsden arrived in the Bay and
supplies were being unloaded from the *Dromedary*, a parcel addressed to
Kendall and labelled as containing leather dropped on the deck, and two
muskets fell out in full view of the officers.[119] As Marsden anticipated,
Governor Macquarie later reprimanded him for allowing the CMS missionaries to trade in firearms (although as Butler later pointed out, Marsden
himself had been involved in the exchange of muskets and gunpowder with
Māori), and Marsden never forgave Kendall for these offences. By this
time, Macquarie and Marsden were at loggerheads. Their violent disputes over the New Zealand mission and other matters had led to a Select

Committee of the House of Commons under Commissioner John Bigge being established to inquire into the state of the country, and the despatch of the *Dromedary* to New Zealand with the 84th Regiment, whose officers were later interviewed by Bigge.

As Ensign McRae of the 84th Regiment eventually testified to the Committee, during their visit to New Zealand they heard that there were about 500 stands of firearms (with bullet moulds) in the Bay of Islands, while axes, billhooks, bayonets and iron-pointed spears were also being used as weapons. He confirmed that the whalers freely traded in muskets and gunpowder, forcing the missionaries into the same trade to acquire provisions for themselves and their families, and that Māori were extremely eager to acquire muskets, paying 15 pigs or 200 baskets of potatoes for a gun, and often prostituting women on board the ships to obtain firearms. McRae also cited cases of great cruelty towards local people by the crews of visiting ships, including severe floggings and kidnappings, and confirmed the existence of cannibalism, saying that during their visit to the Bay a female slave had been killed and eaten on a nearby island. He described Māori people as extremely healthy, although venereal diseases had been introduced, which were controlled by keeping the victims in strict isolation. Māori disliked alcohol, had great faith in European medicine, and lived to a great age, and he said he had met several people who remembered Captain Cook's arrival at the Bay 50 years earlier, when they were already adults.

McRae also testified that northern Māori had both priests and priestesses. They had not acquired Christian ideas, but held fast to their own beliefs. They were impressed by the British soldiers on board the *Dromedary*, but suspicious of their intentions. Some of them had learned a little English. They held convicts in great contempt, and did not greatly esteem the missionaries, who lived behind wicket gates and high palisades, although Marsden was more respected than the others. McRae added that Thomas Hansen, the son of the former captain of the *Active*,[120] lived in the Bay and worked as a trader, buying mats and curiosities that were bartered to the whalers – which helps to explain the large number of Māori artefacts that arrived in Port Jackson, the United States and the United Kingdom at about this time, some of which still survive in museum and family collections.[121] Although Māori were willing to sell land, and would welcome European settlers, McRae thought that it would be dangerous to settle among them, since they quickly took offence and never forgot an injury.

In his testimony to the Committee, Dr Fairfowl, the *Dromedary's* surgeon, added that Māori called venereal diseases, which had been introduced along with consumption and dysentery, the 'Europe god'. They also suffered from inflammation of the bowels, rheumatism and ulcers. According to Fairfowl, Kendall and Butler (both missionaries appointed as magistrates) did not investigate the outrages committed by visiting seamen against local people, and made no secret of trading in muskets and gunpowder themselves. He thought that the pitched battles among Māori were not particularly bloody, however, since fighting ended when a few people had been killed (although evidently this began to change after the introduction of firearms).[122]

Soon after the *Dromedary's* arrival, hoping to impress Samuel Marsden, Butler wrote Kendall a stiff letter of rebuke:

> Dear Sir,
> I think your journey to England is very ill-timed on many accounts. Several of us are just arrived in the country, and our settlement is in its very infancy, and we, of course, can have no knowledge of the language, and, therefore, require every assistance. Moreover, there is no object can justify you, in leaving your family unprotected in a heathen land. I should have thought you had suffered enough in your family to prevent you from ever leaving them.
>
> By taking away Shunghee, you take from us all our protection; the natives are exceeding rude now, but how much more after his departure. . . . I have no doubt but they will abuse us, and steal everything they can lay their hands on.
>
> . . . The Lexicon and Grammar I cannot spare, as I want them for my own use. . . .[123]

This letter only made Kendall more determined to leave New Zealand. He wanted to spend time at Cambridge, where he knew that Professor Lee, a distinguished orientalist, had been working on a Māori grammar with Titere and Korokoro's younger brother Tui.[124] He hoped to complete his draft lexicon and grammar of Māori with Lee's assistance,[125] and to seek ordination, so that he could perform Divine Service. No doubt he also hoped to ease his spiritual turmoil and seek support by talking with his mentor, Rev. Basil Woodd.

Although he was still estranged from his wife Jane, before his departure Kendall wrote her an affectionate letter, urging her to look after their eight children during his absence:

I cannot doubt but, after having lived so many years in your society and the many returns of sweet conversation, that I have possessed some share in your reflections, and I now thank you for all your offices of kindness which you have invariably performed towards my person. If I live to see you again, I hope it will be the means of between us, particularly if there should be on your part no obstacle in the way.[126]

As for Hongi Hika, he was furious with Butler for trying to block his supply of muskets and powder, and for humiliating his friend Thomas Kendall. After his recent campaigns, he had a formidable array of utu accounts to settle across the North Island. As Kendall later explained, Hongi was eager to go to England to meet King George IV, and to establish a military settlement in the Bay of Islands as a source of European skills and control over other Māori and resident and visiting Europeans:

Shungee and Whykato [Waikato] are come with a view to see King George, the multitude of his people, what they are doing, and the goodness of the land. Their desire is to stay in England only one moon; and they wish to take with them at least one hundred men as settlers. They are in want of a party of men to dig up the ground in search of iron.

An additional number of Blacksmiths: an additional number of carpenters; and an additional number of preachers who will try to speak to them in the New Zealand Tongue in order that they may understand them. Also 20 soldiers and 3 officers over them. The above settlers are to take cattle with them in order to assist in cultivating the land. Land will be readily granted to the settlers.[127]

Hongi and his people were deeply impressed by the *Dromedary*'s size and armaments, and by the manoeuvres performed by the 84th Regiment when the soldiers went ashore and fired a salute in honour of King George's birthday. According to Lieutenant Richard Cruise:

The deference that discipline obliged the soldiers to pay to their officers, and the costly dress of the latter, gave the islanders a very exalted idea of our rank, and they frequently asked us if we were not the sons of the King of England, and if we did not live in the same house with him, when we were in our own country.[128]

Cruise described Hongi as a fine-looking man, dressed in the uniform coat of a British officer. Although he was one of the most powerful chiefs in the Bay of Islands, and its bravest and most enterprising warrior, he seemed by far the least assuming of those who had been permitted to come on board. According to Cruise, Hongi was certain that if he went to England, he would obtain twelve muskets and a double-barrelled gun.[129] Ensign McRae added that he hoped to obtain a large dog in England, and that when Marsden promised to buy him a double-barrelled musket from William Hall if he would stay in New Zealand, Hongi turned down this offer.[130]

Hongi had much more than a dog and a double-barrelled gun in mind, however. He wanted to meet King George IV face to face, explore England and study English society and ways of living, accompanied by Thomas Kendall as his interpreter and guide. A formidable leader in his own country, secure in his own mana, Hongi Hika intended to investigate European technology, agriculture and ideas, and use them selectively for Māori purposes. In particular, he was intent on avenging the deaths of his kinsfolk at Moremonui and in other battles. Like Captain Cook and his companions, when they were guided around the coast of New Zealand by the high priest navigator Tupaia, Hongi and Waikato were off on a voyage of discovery, exploring and evaluating new worlds.

CHAPTER FIVE

How D'ye Do, Mr King Shunghee?

O N 13 NOVEMBER 1820, TWO TALL, TATTOOED MĀORI CHIEFS, escorted by their host, Sir John Montague, a successful banker and nine times Mayor of Cambridge, arrived at Carlton House in London to meet King George IV. Passing through the portico of Ionic columns in the front of this large, opulent townhouse, they entered the central hall with its double staircase and octagonal skylight, and a series of gilded, lavishly decorated state apartments.[1]

When Hongi Hika and Waikato, dressed in court costume with flax cloaks across their shoulders, were introduced to the king, they bowed gracefully, presenting their cloaks to him and saying 'How do you do, Mr King George?' He replied, 'How do you do, Mr King Shunghee?' and 'How do you do, Mr King Waikato?' Although Hongi could understand English, he did not speak it, so it must have been Waikato, his junior kinsman, who greeted the king.[2] Intrigued by these exotic visitors, George accepted their gifts and, arm in arm, escorted them around Carlton House, showing them its magnificent art collection, conservatory and gardens. As they walked, he quizzed them about their home country and customs, 'how many wives and children each of them had? How did they rule them &c. &c., and was highly pleased with their answers.'[3]

During his time as Prince Regent, George had been notorious for his mistresses and his extravagant, libertine lifestyle. Recently ascended to the throne, he was in the throes of trying to divorce his wife, Caroline of Brunswick, whom he had exiled to the continent where she was rumoured to have taken an Italian lover. To his chagrin, she had returned to England, demanding to be recognised as the new queen of Britain, winning strong

The Throne Room, Carlton House, by Charles Wild, c. 1818.

public sympathy and support.[4] At the time of Hongi and Waikato's visit, evidence of her infidelity was being presented to Parliament, making the king's marital affairs a public scandal. During this conversation, Hongi described his domestic arrangements back in the Bay of Islands, assuring the king that his five wives gave him no trouble. (Indeed, Samuel Marsden had recently met three of these women, including Turikatuku, his blind senior wife and trusted advisor, who smiled when she remarked that Hongi had been neglecting her for these two new wives, both aristocratic war captives.[5])

Enjoying these affable exchanges, George IV decided to show the chiefs the armoury in his private quarters, usually closed to visitors. At the top of the grand staircase, five rooms housed his military collection, one with swords from around the world, another displaying plate armour, helmets and firearms, while a third featured an effigy of a famous Indian warrior on horseback and weapons from many countries, including Hawai'i and other Pacific islands, arrayed around the walls and on the ceiling.[6] Hongi, a noted warrior, was riveted by this collection. Seeing his fascination, King George presented him with a coat of chain mail, along with a helmet and two muskets. When he asked Hongi how British subjects behaved in New Zealand, Hongi answered judiciously, and asked the king whether he had told the missionaries who had been sent to his country not to supply him with muskets and powder. In reply, George assured him that he did not know these men, and had given no such order. As they left Carlton House, the king allowed the two rangatira to kiss his hand.[7]

These exchanges were a turning point in relations between Māori and Europeans. In his efforts to persuade Hongi and other rangatira to give up fighting, Marsden had often invoked King George's authority, and recently forbidden the missionaries in New Zealand to trade muskets and powder with Hongi and other Māori. Not only had Marsden given a false impression of the king's views, he had also suggested that he knew King George well and had his backing. Hongi now knew that this was untrue, and that George IV had never heard of Samuel Marsden. From this time onwards, Māori in Northland had a vivid impression of what kīngitanga (kingship or sovereignty) might mean, in relation to their own ideas of rangatiratanga or chieftainship. King George had greeted Hongi and Waikato warmly, exchanging gifts and mingling their hau together, a relationship that passed down the descent lines. He was hospitable and generous, treating the northern leaders with genial kindness.

As the Te Arawa tribal expert Te Rangikaheke later wrote, a good rangatira should be a man of his word, a leader in battle and a skilled sailor. He should summon the people, speak in gatherings and extend hospitality to visitors.[8] This visit led to an expectation that British monarchs could be trusted to uphold their alliances with Māori leaders, and that ariki (high chiefs) and kīngi (kings) would honour their promises, and treat each other as equals. The face-to-face exchange between George IV and Hongi Hika set the seal on an alliance between northern Māori and the British Crown, although in fact this had been initiated much earlier, through exchanges between Māori rangatira and particular governors (kāwana) in Port Jackson and Norfolk Island.

The first exchange between aristocratic Māori and a representative of the British Crown had been involuntary on the part of the two Māori involved in this episode. In 1793, Hurukokoti, a high-born young rangatira from the southern Bay of Islands, and Tukitahua, a priest's son from Oruru, had been kidnapped by a British government supply ship off the Cavalli Islands, where

*Philip Gidley King and Anna Josepha King, and their children Elizabeth,
Anna Maria and Phillip Parker, by Robert Dighton, 1799.*

they were on a fishing expedition, and taken to Norfolk Island, to the north-
west of New Zealand.

Since his arrival at that bleak, brutal penal colony, the commandant of
Norfolk Island, Lieutenant-Governor Philip Gidley King, had been writing
to Sir Joseph Banks and the British authorities, urging them to send some
Māori to the island to teach his convicts how to work flax, so they could
make their own clothing from the local flax plants. Orders had been despatched, and in 1793 when the *Daedalus* visited Matauri Bay, Tuki and Huru
were enticed on board and offered a meal. While they were eating below
deck, the ship sailed off to Port Jackson.

When Tuki and Huru arrived at Norfolk Island, they told Governor King
that they could not greatly assist the flax workers, because as he remarked
ruefully, 'this operation is the peculiar Occupation of the Women, & as
Woodoo is a Warrior, & Tookee a Priest, they gave us to understand, that
Dressing of Flax, never made any part of their studies'.[9] Nevertheless, King
liked these young men, especially Tukitahua. For the next six months they
lived with him and his family in Government House, learning some English
and teaching King about Māori customs. Tuki told him, for instance, that
when a person dies, a gentle wind (or hau) carries their spirit along a pathway
to Te Reinga, the north-west tip of the North Island, where it plunges from

a tree into the ocean. In explanation, Tuki sketched a remarkable map of the northern half of the North Island on the floor of King's study, showing the spirit's pathway to Te Reinga and the sacred tree, marking the main districts, giving the numbers of warriors in each, naming the principal chiefs and showing the carved houses of the two rangatira of his own district.[10]

In fact, the relationship between Tuki's family and the British dated back to a meeting between his father and Captain Cook off Matauri Bay in 1769. On that occasion Tuki's father, who was on a fishing expedition, was given a red jacket, forging a link between his family and the British. Red was the tapu colour, a sign of ancestral presence, and such a chiefly gift tied ancestral lines together. King always regarded Tuki as the more friendly and open-minded of the two chiefs, remarking that 'Hoo-doo, like a true patriot, thinks there is no country, people nor customs equal to his own, on which account he is much less curious as to what he sees about him'.[11]

Upon their arrival at Norfolk Island, King had promised Tuki and Huru that he would return them to New Zealand. In the end he commandeered a ship from Port Jackson, taking them to North Cape, or Muriwhenua, where he landed them with many gifts, including two green suits faced with orange, three swords, carpentry and agricultural tools, and pigs and potatoes – gifts that transformed the northern economy. When they arrived off North Cape, the high chief of Muriwhenua boarded the ship and greeted Governor King with a hongi, repeating his name. After pressing noses with Tuki and Huru, he promised to take them home, and they agreed to go with him, assuring King that 'a high chief never lies'.[12] At some time during these exchanges, King was presented with two stone patu (hand weapons). In later years, Tuki and Huru always spoke highly of 'Kawana Kingi' and how kind he and his family had been to them. Indeed, when Huru met Marsden in the Bay of Islands in 1819, he spoke warmly about Governor King and asked after his eldest daughter, Maria, with great affection.[13]

Like various taonga collected by Captain Cook and his *Endeavour* companions, the patu given to Governor King have travelled through space and time. During the early 1990s, while I was researching Tuki and Huru's adventures in Port Jackson and Norfolk for a book, *Between Worlds*, I visited Norfolk Island. The islanders decided to commemorate the two hundredth anniversary of Tuki and Huru's stay on the island in 1993 by inviting their descendants to visit their island. When Norfolk leaders asked me to assist them in organising this trip, I asked my friend Merimeri Penfold (from

Ngati Kuri in Muriwhenua) to take charge of the arrangements. She gathered together a party that included a group of Muriwhenua elders led by herself, Dame Mira Szazy and Selwyn Muru, accompanied by a netball team, a rugby league team and a film crew from a Māori television programme to travel to Norfolk Island.

The Norfolk Islanders are descended from the *Bounty* mutineers and their Tahitian wives. When the convict colony on Norfolk was evacuated, these people were relocated there from Pitcairn Island, where the surviving *Bounty* mutineers had settled. In honour of their shared ancestry with Māori, the islanders arranged for a stamp to be issued to commemorate the anniversary of Tuki and Huru's visit, and for the two patu presented to Governor King to be returned to them from the National Museum of Australia so that they could be presented back to Tuki and Huru's descendants – a classic Polynesian gift exchange.

Before setting off on this journey, the Muriwhenua elders met in Tane-nui-a-Rangi meeting house at the University of Auckland marae to discuss their visit to Norfolk, and what to do when the ancestral patu were handed over. After much discussion they decided that upon receiving the taonga (ancestral treasures), they would hand them back to the Norfolk people in honour of the ancestral links that they shared with the Society Islands.

Soon after arriving on Norfolk, we were formally welcomed in a dawn ceremony at Kingston, beside a group of Georgian stone buildings built during the penal era. In the eerie half-light, with waves crashing on the beach behind us, Ernie Christian, a descendant of the *Bounty* mutineer Fletcher Christian, greeted the Muriwhenua contingent. Afterwards, a descendant of Philip Gidley King gave a speech, before handing the two patu to Dame Mira Szazy. She held these weapons for a time, stroking them, before giving them to other members of the visiting party, who wept over these taonga. When the patu were handed back to Dame Mira, she placed them in a woven kit brought from New Zealand and presented them to Ernie Christian, saying that the Muriwhenua people had decided that the taonga should stay on Norfolk Island in memory of this visit, and the kinship between their Tahitian ancestors and Māori. It was a spine-chilling moment as, once again, ancestral taonga transcended distance in space/time, binding descent lines together.

On the Māori side of this transaction, 200 years earlier, the gifts presented by Governor King to northern people had generated a similar sense of chiefly obligation. Wharerau, the principal chief of Te Puna and

Rangihoua in the northern Bay of Islands, was a kinsman of Tukitahua's, and before he died, he asked his son Te Pahi to go to Port Jackson and thank Governor King for the gift of pigs and potatoes that he had presented to the northern people. By 1800, King had become the third governor of New South Wales, and was eager to establish a British colony in New Zealand. In 1805 he issued a Government Order in an effort to ensure that Māori, Tahitians and Hawai'ians crewing on whaling ships were fairly treated, stating that 'they are protected in their properties, claims for wages and the same redress as any of His Majesty's subjects',[14] and drew up plans for a British settlement in Northland.

In honour of his father's wishes, Te Pahi always welcomed Europeans to his district. Shortly after King's proclamation arrived in New Zealand, he sent his son Matara to Port Jackson as an emissary to thank the governor. Matara was entertained at Government House, returning home with gifts of pigs and goats for his father. Upon receiving these gifts, Te Pahi decided to thank Governor King in person and, with four of his sons (one of whom was named Tuki), set off for Port Jackson. In November 1805 when he arrived at Government House, dressed in a fine cloak and accompanied by his sons, Te Pahi laid his cloak and a stone patu at Governor King's feet, thanking him for taking care of Matara and for his gifts of pigs and potatoes. As Tapsell has noted, in such ritual presentations, taonga are 'laid out on the marae – symbolising past and present, connecting land and sky upon the sacred courtyard, representing ancestors and descendants as one identity standing before their hosts or distinguished visitors'.[15]

Te Pahi also told King about his promise to his father that he would visit 'Kawana Kingi' and thank him for his gifts to the people of the north, adding that 'If I wished him to remain here, go to Europe, or return to his own country, he was resigned to either, and with the most manly confidence submitted himself and his sons to my directions. All this was said in such an imposing manner that no doubt could be entertained of his sincerity.'[16] Impressed and disarmed, Governor King showed Te Pahi around Government House, inviting him and his sons to stay there during their visit. According to the *Sydney Gazette*, Te Pahi was a tall, heavily tattooed man with an imposing demeanour: 'Every action shows an uncommon attention to the rules of decency and propriety, and [he] has much of the airs and manners of a man conversant in the world he lives in. As he never reflected on any person, so Tip-a-he was alive to the least appearance of

Te Pahi, by George Harris, 1827.

slight or inattention.'¹⁷ When Samuel Marsden was introduced to Te Pahi, the chaplain was equally impressed with the chief, praising his 'Clear, Strong and Comprehensive mind'. After this meeting, Marsden decided to establish a mission in New Zealand.

During their three-month stay in Port Jackson, Te Pahi and his sons studied European agriculture and carpentry, spinning and weaving, and gathered seeds and fruit trees to take home to the Bay of Islands. Te Pahi took a close interest in local customs, watching an Aboriginal mortuary ritual for a man who'd been speared, reacting dismissively when the killer was allowed to fend off flights of spears with a bark shield, and expressing his horror when a convict who had stolen pork from the Kings' storehouse was sentenced to death. Begging Governor King not to kill this man, Te Pahi offered to take him to New Zealand, weeping and throwing himself on the ground, exclaiming that while 'a man might very justly be put to death for stealing a piece of iron, but stealing a piece of pork, which to use his own expression, was eat and passed off, he considered as sanguine in the extreme'.¹⁸

While he was fascinated by life in New South Wales, Te Pahi's own mana was threatened at times. When one of the Europeans mocked his tattoos, for instance, he retorted that putting grease and powder in one's hair was much more absurd; and when an officer's wife, seeing him present some earrings that she had given him to another young woman, took the jewellery back, Te Pahi was furious, packing up all her gifts, sending them back to her and refusing to speak to her again. According to the etiquette of Māori gift exchange, a gift is intended to keep circulating through networks, carrying hau from one person to another to forge new relationships, and it is for the recipient, not the donor, to praise any act of generosity. Te Pahi always reacted with disgust when people spoke of the gifts they had given him, although he was quick to acknowledge any kindly gesture.

When Te Pahi and his sons left Port Jackson, Governor King gave them iron utensils and tools, a box of fruit trees, and bricks and the framework of a prefabricated house to be erected on his land at Te Puna. He hung a silver medal around his neck, engraved on one side, 'Presented by Governor King to Tip-a-he, a chief of New Zeland, during his visit at Port Jackson, in January 1806', and on the other with the name of King George III. In New Zealand, the gift of a name was another way of mingling hau, binding descent lines together.

Perhaps in honour of this gift, later that year Te Pahi sent his son Matara on a whaler to London to meet King George III, 'and to obtain from His Majesty and the English nation axes, Iron and Musquets in order that they may be enabled to build houses and live as English men do'.[19] Upon his arrival in England, Matara was taken to see Sir Joseph Banks, now the president of the Royal Society, and a close friend of George III. As a young man, Banks had visited New Zealand during his voyage with Captain Cook on the *Endeavour*, and was the first to report the potential value of New Zealand flax and timber. Banks ensured that Matara was fed and lodged, introduced him to the royal family and arranged for him to have a passage back home to New Zealand. In this way, Matara became the first Māori to meet a British monarch.

During the return voyage to New Zealand, when the young chief met the Russian explorer Vasily Golovnin at the Cape of Good Hope, he proudly showed him an 'Order of Friendship' that the king had given him, a medal with a blue ribbon and a silver star decorated with two golden clasped hands. Matara told Golovnin that his father had 15 wives and many children; that he himself had two wives; that King George spoke very fast, and one of his daughters had a squint.[20] He added that when they met, George III had saluted him by doffing his hat.[21] At this time, such medals were presented to 'Indian chiefs' as a sign of alliance with the British Crown. Gifts such as fine mats and cloaks, greenstone ornaments and weapons, and medals, red jackets, swords and armour tied a here, or knot, in the descent lines, binding them together. No doubt Matara had also taken gifts with him for the British monarch, including cloaks or fine mats.

As we have seen, Māori words relating to kinship and alliance often refer to flax work. In addition to the word kāwai, which refers at once to the hau, or breeze, that blows across the land, a line of descent, a strand of fibre used in weaving, the plaited handles on a flax basket, and the twining shoots of a creeper, terms such as kaha (a line of ancestry, strength, a navel cord, a boundary rope, a line of rods in a ritual of divination and a rope), aho (a line of descent, radiant light, the medium for an ancestor in a divination and the woof of a cloak),[22] and kanoi (to trace one's descent, authority, the strand of a rope, and to weave the aho tāhuhu, or main thread, in a cloak) bind together ideas of descent lines and weaving and plaiting in single words.

While Captain Cook, Philip Gidley King, Joseph Banks and the British royal family grasped the Māori ethic of chiefly gift exchange, resonating as it did (at least in part) with ideas of aristocratic *noblesse oblige*, by the turn of the nineteenth century the Enlightenment ideal of the Noble Savage was being displaced by the notion of the ignoble savage, benighted, brutal and in need of salvation. Increasingly, many other Europeans began to treat Māori as inferior beings. During this time, the old idea of the Great Chain of Being – a cosmic hierarchy with God at the top followed by archangels and angels, a divine monarch, the serried ranks of the aristocracy and commoners, barbarians and savages, animals, insects, plants and minerals – was being transformed into stadial theories that ranked societies from primitive to civilised, introducing the idea of 'progress' from one state to another.

As mentioned earlier, in the Genesis creation story, God told Adam and Eve to 'be fruitful, and multiply, and replenish the earth, and subdue it: and have dominion over the fish of the sea, and over the fowl of the air, and over every living thing that moveth upon the earth.' For many Englishmen at this time, these living things included 'barbarians' and 'savages' (including Highland Scots and Irish) living in a 'state of nature', who could only be raised to a 'higher state' by contact with 'civilised' people. In New Zealand, the notion of the 'ignoble savage' provided a perfect excuse for Euro-American whalers, sealers and traders to raid Māori communities, stealing their crops, kidnapping young men as crew, refusing to pay them, and beating and abusing Māori men and women. Tragically, this included Te Pahi and his family.

In October 1807, Te Pahi was punched during a dispute with the pilot of a trading ship, the *General Wellesley*, who stole his patu (hand weapon). Later that year, Te Pahi's daughter Atahoe and her English husband George Bruce were kidnapped at sea by a visiting whaler, who carried them to Penang where he sold Atahoe into slavery. Although Bruce managed to rescue his wife, she died of dysentery upon their return to Port Jackson. In March 1808, Te Pahi was tied to the rigging of the *Elizabeth* during a dispute over a trade of potatoes in the Bay of Islands. Later that year, he decided to visit Port Jackson with three of his sons, to complain about the disreputable behaviour of visiting European sailors. When they arrived in Australia, William Bligh, who had been appointed governor of New South Wales, was under house arrest after a mutiny by the NSW Corps, and Te Pahi and his sons received no welcome. Shortly after Te Pahi returned home, his son Matara arrived from London in March 1809, suffering from consumption, and died shortly afterwards. While Te Pahi was still in mourning for his heir, the ship that had brought Matara back from England returned to the Bay, and when an axe went missing the captain gave Te Pahi a flogging.

In December 1809, after a Whangaroa chief, Te Ara (or George), had been grossly insulted and flogged on board the *Boyd*, his kinsfolk attacked and burned the ship in Whangaroa Harbour as utu, and most of the crew were killed and eaten. When a rival chief accused Te Pahi of leading the attack, a party of whalers raided his settlement in the Bay of Islands, shot and wounded the rangatira and killed many of his people, including women and children, burning all the houses at Te Puna and plundering his property.[23]

The plunder must have included the medal that Governor King had presented to Te Pahi, because in mid-2014 this appeared in a Sotheby's auction at Sydney, having been held for many years in a private collection in Australia. When Te Pahi's descendants, including Hugh Rihari from the Bay of Islands and Dr Deidre Brown, an Associate Professor in Architecture at the University of Auckland, learned about the forthcoming sale, they sought legal advice about the ownership of the medal. In the end, understanding the significance of this taonga and supported by Te Pahi's descendants, Te Papa Tongarewa and Auckland Museum made a successful combined bid, making sure that this chiefly gift would return to New Zealand.

Medal presented to Te Pahi by Governor King to commemorate
Te Pahi's visit to Sydney, New South Wales in 1806.

Before Te Atahoe was kidnapped and Matara arrived home, Ruatara, another young relative of Te Pahi's, made his own determined but futile effort to visit the king. The story of how he met Samuel Marsden in London, and how the first mission to New Zealand was established under Ruatara's protection, has already been told. It was also at this time that Thomas Kendall, one of the founding missionaries, first met Hongi Hika, Ruatara's uncle, in the Bay of Islands. Very likely, however, Hongi had decided to travel to England a decade earlier, as he listened to Matara talking about his adventures, and his meeting with King George III.

Hongi and Kendall's expedition to England
On 2 March 1820, when Hongi, Waikato and Thomas Kendall set sail from the Bay of Islands on the *New Zealander*, the harbour was bustling with vessels. The *New Zealander*, a whaler commanded by Captain Munroe,

had been fishing off New Zealand for the past eighteen months, making a visit to Port Jackson before anchoring at Paroa Bay alongside three other whale ships, the *Indian, Echo* and *Anne*.[24] HMS *Dromedary*, a naval storeship, accompanied by the schooner *Prince Regent*, had arrived in the bay five days earlier with Samuel Marsden on board, accompanied by Tui, and Hongi's favourite son Ripiro, who had returned from Port Jackson just in time to farewell his father on his journey to England.

When Samuel Marsden came out to the *New Zealander* to say goodbye to Hongi Hika and Kendall that morning, he found Hongi's wife Turikatuku and his children already on board. Many of their people had come out in their canoes to farewell Hongi and his junior kinsman Waikato, and no doubt Kendall's family were also present. As the *New Zealander* weighed anchor, the *Prince Regent* sailed into Paroa Bay, returning from an excursion to inspect timber at Kawakawa. From the deck of the schooner, Ensign McRae saw a cross that had been erected to hang the bodies of local people who had been killed for theft (a new practice), standing on a hill near the bay. At the same time, a large fleet of canoes, which had just returned from a tangi at North Cape, carrying the preserved body of Korokoro's cousin, was heading towards a pā on an island, while another large fleet of about 40 fighting canoes, commanded by another of Hongi's rivals, Te Morenga, entered the bay from the south, returning from a war expedition to Thames. As the *New Zealander* tacked out of the bay, a canoe caught in its wake almost capsized, tossing a little boy about two years old overboard. He paddled about confidently in the sea until he was rescued. As the ship sailed off, Hongi's people cried out in farewell, and in response the whale ship fired a gun and its crew saluted them with three cheers.[25]

As a whaler, the *New Zealander* was packed with barrels for whale oil, leaving little room for passengers. Unfortunately, no records survive from this voyage, which took the long, difficult route around Cape Horn. Apprehensive about how the Committee of the Church Missionary Society might view his impetuous decision to leave the Bay of Islands, in June 1820, when they encountered another whaler at sea, Kendall sent a message to the CMS to tell them that he and the two chiefs would shortly be arriving in London. In this letter, Kendall said that he hoped to undergo an examination in the Māori language, publish a guide to the study of Māori, and discuss his future prospects as a missionary. By way of justification, he added:

Shunghee was promised by Mr. Marsden when he was at New Zealand last year that he should come to England with me when I came. The natives will live with me as I know what diet will suit them best. You will have the goodness to instruct me where we are to go. I shall want to reside in some house where I can attend to my writing.[26]

When the *New Zealander* arrived in London on 6 August, Kendall hastily presented himself to the CMS Committee. In their written report of this meeting, the Committee formally rebuked him for leaving New Zealand and bringing the chiefs to England, contrary to the Society's regulations, saying that 'with much regret, from the value which they feel for his former service and character, [they] highly disapprove his conduct in returning'. Nevertheless, they resolved to welcome Hongi and Waikato, and to treat them kindly, adding that while Kendall's visit was irregular, they would allow him or his wife to draw on his salary during his absence from New Zealand.[27] When Kendall received this reprimand, he was mortified, writing an abject letter of apology:

My mind was in such a state of affliction and disorder at the time of my embarkation for this country that I did not sufficiently consider the evil tendency of such a step. I entreat the Honourable Committee to forgive me . . . I know I often do wrong, sometimes in consequence of the wickedness of my own heart, at other times in consequence of the want of a clear judgement as to the path of duty.[28]

During the voyage to London, Kendall had spent time with Hongi and Waikato trying to complete an outline of 'A Guide to the Study of the New Zealand Language', which included a Māori dictionary and grammar, while tutoring his Māori companions in English. As he tried to explain to Rev. Pratt, writing the grammar was a difficult task:

The New Zealand Language is formed upon the principles of natural philosophy, including medicine, anatomy, optics &c. A student unacquainted with these sciences might therefore labour long and in vain before he could arrive at any degree of proficiency in it. I can already see many things in the Language which are far above my comprehension.[29]

Although they disapproved of Kendall's decision to leave New Zealand, the Committee could see the value of his linguistic work, and arrangements were made for him to escort Hongi and Waikato to the University of Cambridge, where they would work with Professor Lee at Queen's College to finish the guide.

Their visit was announced in the *Missionary Register*, which had earlier published a number of stories about Ruatara and Hongi and the support they had given the mission – including an engraving of Hongi's carving of his own head that he made for Samuel Marsden during his 1814 visit to Port Jackson. According to the *Register*, Hongi had been born shortly after Captain Cook's visit to the Bay of Islands, and was now about 50 years old. His sister had been the mother of the late Ruatara; while Ruatara and Waikato had married two sisters. The author added: '[W]e hope, through Mr. Kendall, to obtain such an acquaintance as will enable us to place the affecting condition of this noble race in its true light – the finest natural dispositions, abused and held in bondage, under the dark and cruel tyranny of the God of this World!'[30]

Although it was late summer, the English weather was chilly and wet. When Hongi fell ill (probably with pneumonia), Kendall asked the Society to provide him and Waikato with thick blankets, flannel caps, pantaloons and heavy shoes, and escorted them to Cambridge where Samuel Lee, the professor of Arabic, had arranged accommodation in a small house near his own, on Auckland Street, in a part of the town afterwards known as 'New Zealand'.[31] It was the university summer holidays, and Professor Lee, a former carpenter's apprentice and brilliant self-taught linguist, had time to work with Kendall, Hongi and Waikato, recording Māori texts and vocabulary and analysing the grammar.[32] Having mastered Malay along with Latin, Greek, Chaldaic, Syriac, Hebrew, Hindustani, Persian and Arabic, Lee was interested in comparing structures of thought, and the problems of translatability across very different languages.

During their visit, Professor Lee introduced Kendall and the chiefs to the Vice-Chancellor, various ministers including Rev. Simeon, one of the founders of the Church Missionary Society, and Farish, a professor of natural and experimental philosophy and an expert on gunpowder. When they dined in Old Hall at Queen's College, with its vaulted, decorated roof and ancestral portraits, this ornate building may have reminded Hongi and Waikato of the carved chiefs' houses back in New Zealand. On 'scarlet days' in this college, festive gowns were worn, and the dons' scarlet robes (the tapu colour) no doubt suggested that this was a kind of whare wānanga (school of learning) where tohunga (knowledgeable experts) gathered.[33] During a sabbatical year I spent at King's College in Cambridge during 1980–81, the colleges often reminded me of marae back at home, with their grass court-yards, carved and painted halls, stately ceremonies and dignified elders, like my mentor Eruera Stirling and his peers.

During their visit to Cambridge, Hongi, Waikato and Kendall also met Charles de Thierry, a young commoner at Queen's College who had served in the French army during the Napoleonic Wars, and as an attaché to the French ambassador in London. After marrying the daughter of the arch-deacon of Gloucester, de Thierry had been sent to study at Oxford, and then Cambridge. The young man was fascinated by the chiefs, presenting each of them with a gun engraved with his name and theirs on the barrel, and decided to purchase land in New Zealand to set up a model European settlement, just as Hongi intended.

When they met Rev. Samuel Leigh of the Wesleyan Missionary Society, who was eager to establish a Wesleyan mission in New Zealand, Leigh invited the rangatira to come to London at his expense. During this visit, a number of people were asked to meet Hongi and Waikato at an evening party held at the house of a 'highly respectable gentleman'. When a lady visitor traced the lines of Hongi's facial moko, smiling as she did so, Hongi 'instantly rose up in a state of excitement, threw himself across three chairs, and, covering his face in his hands, remained in that posture until the company retired'.[34] Female tapu was inimical to male tapu, which was concentrated in the head; and for a woman to touch Hongi's moko, or facial tattoo, in this way was a violent attack on the mana of his ancestors. This was probably why he and Waikato returned to Cambridge after just a week in London, with gifts of a box of carpenter's tools each and a dress for Hongi's wife.

Kendall had stayed behind in Cambridge to work with Lee on a revised version of his guide, now called *A Grammar and Vocabulary of the Language of New Zealand*.[35] When it was finished, the *Grammar* was an impressive work 240 pages long, including a 100-page dictionary. Lee encouraged Kendall and closely supervised his efforts,[36] greatly improving the orthography of Māori, which is very similar to that now used, although the sound 'h', which must have been softly aspirated (and usually written as 'sh' by the missionar-ies), is often missing. 'Wh', which was also softly aspirated, is written as 'h';

while 'r', which is flapped in Māori, was often written as 'd'; and 'p' as 'b', showing the different ranges between these phonemes in Māori and English. This work also includes an analysis of key grammatical elements in Māori, written by Lee, lists of phrases and seven songs, including a chant of longing for a European named 'Taiwa' (translated as 'Stivers'), who is said to have visited the Bay of Islands before Captain Cook; a song recording Kendall's visit to Hokianga, where he is referred to by his Māori name 'Te Kini'; and chants for a tūī bird and a paper kite. It also records some fascinating dialogues, including those between missionaries and Māori, and a teacher and his Māori pupils.

In Port Jackson and the Bay of Islands, his colleagues were already troubled by Kendall's behaviour, and the CMS Committee in London doubted his suitability as a candidate for ordination. Impressed by Kendall's industry and dedication, however, Professor Lee urged the CMS Committee to support his candidature by arguing that his deep study of the Māori language meant that he was uniquely placed to communicate the Gospel to Māori. Pratt, Woodd and Bickersteth all supported Lee's proposal, and the Bishop of Norwich agreed, on the understanding that Kendall would spend the rest of his life in New Zealand.[37] On 15 October, Kendall was ordained a deacon in Norwich Cathedral, while Hongi watched benevolently from the Bishop's own family pew, asking whether the Bishop's wig was a sign of wisdom.[38] Lee's advocacy must have been persuasive, because on 13 November, Kendall was ordained as a priest by the Bishop of Ely.

By this time Kendall, Hongi and Waikato were staying with Sir John Mortlock at 29 Montague Square in London, a splendid new Georgian brick townhouse where Mortlock's wife and daughter Mary hosted a stream of visitors, eager to meet the two Māori chiefs. Later, Waikato named one of his sons Tamati Mokaraka (Thomas Mortlock), as a tribute to the relationship he had forged with the Mortlock family.[39] Their visitors included the Dukes of York and Clarence; the Earls of Yarmouth, Winchelsea and Harcourt; various bishops; the Lord Mayor of London; the Chancellor of the Exchequer; John Liddiard Nicholas, who had visited New Zealand with Marsden in 1814; and some of Kendall's former students. In the midst of this social whirl, the artist James Barry painted a portrait of Waikato, Kendall and Hongi, although he was unable to arrange a live sitting with his subjects.

Sir John, who cut an elegant figure in English society, had commanded the Cambridge Volunteers during the Napoleonic Wars. According to oral

*John Mortlock of Cambridge,
by John Downman, c. 1790.*

histories from the Bay of Islands, Hongi was fascinated by his accounts of these campaigns, and the tactics adopted, including a wedge-shaped formation that he later used in battle in New Zealand. Sir John also arranged for them to attend the House of Lords, fashionably dressed, where the peers clustered around to meet them.[40]

Because Sir Joseph Banks had died two months before Hongi and Waikato's arrival in England, they did not meet Captain Cook's companion on his first voyage around the world. The meeting with King George IV at Clarence House was the highlight of their visit. According to one of Hongi's contemporaries, the King told them that 'they must not kill any of his subjects who visited New Zealand, & they promised to obey the king's commands'. In a letter to Queen Victoria in 1849, the Bay of Islands rangatira Hone Heke reminded her of Hongi's visit:

> King George asked him, 'what was your reason for coming here;' he said
> 'I had two objects in doing so – muskets and 60 soldiers.' To which King

George answered, 'I will not consent to send soldiers to New Zealand lest you should be deprived of your country, which I wish should be left for your children and your people, for they would not act properly.' They continued arguing on the subject for a long time, and then King George said to Hongi, 'it is better that I should send some missionaries to you, as friends for you, for they are good people; should they act wrongly, send them back; but if they act properly, befriend them.'[41]

After their audience with the king, the two chiefs were taken to the Woolwich Arsenal, which Hongi enjoyed, the Tower of London, and to the Menagerie, where the elephant amazed him. While Hongi was mainly interested in military matters during this visit to England, Waikato enjoyed almost everything he saw. Hongi, who had fallen ill with a lung infection, was now eager to return home. In late November, the Committee of the CMS finally arranged a passage and presented them with gifts that Hongi angrily rejected, since these were much less lavish than the gifts that they had showered on Tui, Korokoro's younger brother, and his companion Titere, during their visit to England two years earlier, when they had also worked with Professor Lee on a study of Māori.[42] Given the relatively junior status of Tui and Titere, and the fact that they belonged to Hongi's rivals, the southern alliance in the Bay of Islands, this was a bitter insult. Kendall, who understood about mana and the hau of the gift, urgently appealed to his mentor Rev. Basil Woodd, who wrote to the Committee asking them to make amends. More gifts were presented, but it was too late. The damage had been done. John Liddiard Nicholas, on the other hand, was generous with his gifts, as Hongi later gratefully acknowledged.

Unlike the king and the dukes, earls and bishops he met in England, Hongi now knew that Samuel Marsden, John Butler and the other missionaries, and most of the CMS Committee, stood relatively low in the English social hierarchy. From his vantage point, this explained their uncouth behaviour. As Te Rangikaheke later explained, a failure in generosity was he ritenga tūtūā (a low-born custom),[43] and unlike King George IV, the missionaries had no notion of chiefly largesse. In addition, rangatira should always tell the truth, and Hongi concluded that Samuel Marsden had deceived him. While Marsden often rebuked the rangatira for having more than one wife, Hongi now knew that King George IV was notorious for his extramarital affairs. While the missionaries had urged him and other

rangatira to give up fighting, Hongi had heard about the many bloody battles fought by the English against their enemies on sea and on land, before
and during the Napoleonic Wars, especially from his London host Sir John
Mortlock. The fact that the CMS missionaries did not fight, and that they
had appealed to the authority of King George to stop him from obtaining
muskets, when King George did not even know them, undermined their
mana in Hongi's eyes. Their niggardly gifts, so paltry compared with those
that they had given Korokoro's younger brother, were the last straw. In early
December 1820, Kendall, Hongi and Waikato boarded the *Speke*, a convict
transport crammed with prisoners and guards, and set off on the long journey back to Port Jackson. During the passage they had a heated cabin, sat at
the table with the other passengers, and occasionally drank wine.[44]

By this time, while the members of the CMS Committee were convinced
of Kendall's integrity and devotion to the cause, they were worried about
his stability. Rev. Pratt wrote to Marsden that he 'appears to have acquired
a sort of wildness and absence of self-restraint, probably arising from his
long residence among a barbarous people, which renders it difficult to control him, and to induce him to come cordially into measures which oppose
his own feelings and opinions'.[45] For Kendall's missionary colleagues, his
close relationship with Hongi and Te Rakau, his dedication to the Māori
language and fascination with Māori ideas hinted at a regression to savagery,
a surrender to Satanic habits of mind. He had 'gone native'. For his Māori
friends, on the other hand, to become 'māori' was simply to become normal
or ordinary, a person like themselves.

One can see this in a poignant dialogue in the *Grammar*, apparently based
on a discussion between Professor Lee and Waikato about relationships at
the mission station back at Rangihoua:

T: *Ko wai koia te pa o Waikato?*
P: *Ko Rangi Houa ra oki [hoki]*
T: *E noho ana oti te pakeha ki kona?*
P: *E noho ana ra oki [hoki] ki Hoyi [Hohi]*
T: *He iwi ata wai [atawhai] te tangata Maori ki te pakeha?*
P: *He iwi ata wai ra oki [hoki], e pai ana; ka ore [kāhore] ra oki [hoki] te didinga
     [riringa], ka ore e tutu, ka ore e mea*
T: *Ka maoditia [māoritia] te pakeha?*
P: *K'wai oki au ka kite?*

T: What is the name of Waikato's pa [fortified village]?

P: It is Rangi Houa

T: Do Europeans live there?

P: They live at Hoyi [Hohi]

T: Do the Maori people [te tangata Māori] take care of the Europeans [te pākehā]?

P: They take care of them: it is good: there is no quarrelling, or teazing, or any thing

T: Has the European [pākehā] become naturalised [māoritia]?

P: Who can tell?[46]

By 1820 in the Bay of Islands, it seems, while a contrast between te tangata pākehā (European people) and te tangata māori (Māori or normal people) had been firmly established, these identities were not hermetically sealed. In te ao Māori, Cartesian dualism with its binary oppositions and the idea of the autonomous individual did not apply. For Māori at that time, it was possible for a pākehā to become māori – i.e. a normal, ordinary person, bound into the whakapapa networks by acts of friendship and alliance. As for Thomas Kendall, the last question in the dialogue precisely captured his dilemma – was he becoming māori, and if so, who could tell, and what would that mean? Despite the missionaries' concerted attempts to convert Māori to Christian ways of thinking and living, at times the impacts went the other way.

During Hongi's absence, back in Northland, Māori were holding fast to their own tikanga (ways of doing things), despite the missionaries' best efforts. After Hongi and Kendall's departure from the Bay of Islands, while the *Dromedary* was still in the north of New Zealand, Samuel Marsden spent three months travelling around the northern and western coastlines, often in terrible weather, visiting Hokianga, Whangarei, Thames, Mercury Bay, Waitemata, Manukau and Kaipara, among other places. For most of this journey, he was accompanied by Te Morenga, the rangatira from the Bay of Islands who acted as his interpreter and guide.[47] According to Ensign McRae, Marsden's efforts to convert the Hokianga people during this visit were futile. They slept during his services, and when he tried to tell them about the Genesis creation story, told him that he was mistaken, referring him instead to the story of Maui fishing up the land, and the power of their tohunga, or priestly experts, to command the winds and waves:

Mr. Marsden assured them [that] the story of the Creation had been handed down to him through Centuries by his ancestors. They then remarked that that might be the way amongst the Pakeha (or white men) but with them the belief was that their God had fished up New Zealand from the bottom of the Sea with three fish hooks made of Poenaniamiou [*pounamu*, or greenstone], a green serpentine, and that some of their people had seen one of them a long way to the Southward.

The Priest joined in the conversation and told us that the winds and waves which he had power over were confined in a great cave on the shore which he afterwards showed us. He said that his father had given him this power at his death and that his son should have the same when he died.[48]

Once again, while they were prepared to accept that pākehā might think differently, Māori held fast to their own conceptions of reality.

Nevertheless, these people were eager for a European settlement to be established in their district. When Marsden visited Thames on the *Coromandel*, another government vessel that had been sent to collect spars, their leaders were keen to recruit European settlers to protect them from the northern taua armed with muskets that raided them every year. Many of these men told Marsden how weary they were with these one-sided conflicts, and the chaos and devastation they caused. During a visit to Mercury Bay, Marsden arranged a truce between Te Morenga and Awiri, a local rangatira whose people had been decimated as utu for killing and eating one of Te Morenga's kinswomen,[49] and made peace between Hinaki and Tepuhi, two warring chiefs from the Coromandel.[50] Hinaki was an impressive man, tall and handsome, with many battle scars, including 50 spear wounds and two teeth knocked out by patu.[51] When Marsden arrived on the west coast, where the people had never seen Europeans before, they marvelled when he conducted a service. According to one of the oral histories, they said:

'E mea ma! Ka tu ki runga!' 'O friends, he stands up!' When he commenced singing a hymn they exclaimed to one another, *'E mea ma! Ka hamama te waha!'* 'O friends, he opens his mouth!' [the mouth opens] And when he knelt to pray, they called out, *'E mea ma! Ka tuturi nga turi, a ka komekome nga ngutu!'* 'O friends, he kneels on his knees! his lips move!' [the knees kneel, the lips move] We were all entire strangers to *pakehas* at that time. The things that Mr. Marsden brought with him were pipes, Jew's harps, and a she goat.

The Maoris were delighted at the Jew's harp, for their own *roria* were made of supplejack bark.[52]

At Kaipara, Marsden met Murupaenga, the great Ngati Whatua warrior who had crushed Hongi's people at the battle of Moremonui, killing two of his brothers and his sister. Murupaenga told Marsden that he was tired of fighting but was forced to defend his people. Hongi had sent yet another taua to the Kaipara, and he was eager for some kind of protection against the marauders. During this discussion, Te Morenga told Murupaenga and his people that at Port Jackson there was only one king, Governor Macquarie, just as there was only one king in England, King George; and that while there were so many kings in New Zealand, there would be endless wars. He thought that if a man-of-war were sent to New Zealand, it would help to keep the peace.[53] Marsden was struck by Murupaenga's astute intelligence, and during this visit they had many long conversations about 'their Ideas of God their Tabooing and various Superstitions under which they suffer many privations'.[54] When Marsden assured Murupaenga and his people that there was only one God, however, they did not believe him. They told him that when they died, their spirits went into a cave at North Cape, and then descended into the sea to the next world. In reply, Marsden told them the creation story from Genesis, which 'struck their minds with great force'.[55]

After leaving Murupaenga's settlement, Marsden and his companions visited other villages on the Kaipara Harbour, where they witnessed the devastation caused by Hongi's warriors. He promised local leaders that he would try to persuade Hongi and his people to stop fighting, and 'pressed upon all the Chiefs wherever I have gone the necessity of some regular Government being established in New Zealand for the general Benefit and protection of the whole; and that until something of this nature was established, the powerful would always murder and oppress the weak'.[56]

When he returned to Port Jackson in December 1820, Marsden was in despair over the state of the New Zealand mission. In his report to the Church Missionary Society, he deplored the missionaries' endless squabbling, and self-interest:

All the difficulties in New Zealand that I have met with have been in governing the Europeans. They will not do what is right. They will not live in unity and brotherly love. The love of money, the thirst for pre-eminence,

the want of industry, and zeal for the good of the heathens, have greatly
mitigated against the success of the Mission. I had used every persuasion and
every means in my power to put a stop to the abominable traffic in muskets
and powder. I had obtained their solemn pledges, signed with their own
signatures, that they would put away this accursed thing. I relied upon their
promises. Before I left New Zealand I found these promises broken.[57]

Marsden also sent a detailed report about the powers of the rangatira to
the Bigge Commission, established after Hongi's departure from Britain
to inquire into the state of New Zealand. In this report, 'The Authority
which the Chiefs possess in New Zealand', Marsden noted that in times of
peace the authority of the chiefs was very limited, restricted to their own
families, servants and war captives. A rangatira could not command free
people to labour or fight, but had to 'ensure their obedience more by cour-
tesy and kindness than by command, knowing that he has no authority to
command them'. He judged that the ariki and rangatira were 'too proud and
jealous to invest their authority in the hands of any individual of their own
country'. Although those kin groups with few muskets were afraid of those
with many guns, and most chiefs were tired of fighting, Marsden thought
that they would hesitate before putting themselves under the control of a
foreign power: 'They will never wish to be commanded if they can possibly
avoid this.' For these reasons, he favoured the idea of a protectorate under
a 'civilised nation' that would allow Māori to focus on agriculture and other
civil arts, noting that Te Morenga had asked for a British man-of-war to be
sent to New Zealand.[58] He thought that a small timber settlement serviced
by well-armed ships would suffice. At the same time, according to Marsden,
Hongi Hika had no idea of placing his country under British protection.

While he prized the armour and the guns that King George IV had given
him, when the *Speke* arrived in Port Jackson, Hongi immediately set about
trading the other gifts he had received in England for muskets and powder.
It seems likely that de Thierry also had sent a large consignment of muskets
to Port Jackson for Hongi as payment for an estate in New Zealand.[59]

When Hongi and Waikato went to visit Samuel Marsden at Parramatta,
the meeting did not go well. Adding insult to the injury of the miserly gifts
that the CMS had given him in England, Marsden deplored Hongi's efforts
to acquire firearms, and refused to give him anything at all. Infuriated by this
slight, Hongi told Marsden not to return to New Zealand. In Port Jackson,

Hongi also met Te Hinaki and Te Horeta, two important Hauraki chiefs who had arrived on board another timber ship, the *Coromandel*. There are two very different versions of what happened during this encounter.

According to Hauraki tribal accounts, Hongi stood in front of the Hauraki chiefs and chanted a song of revenge, showing them the muskets that he had acquired, and naming some of these guns after battles in which his people had been defeated or his relatives had been killed, indicating that he intended to take utu with these weapons.[60] According to an account given by a northern chief to Samuel Marsden, on the other hand, during Hongi's absence in England, his rival Te Morenga had taken a taua south to avenge the deaths of his sister and his niece, who had been kidnapped by a whaler, the *Venus*, along with a kinswoman of Hongi's. The sailors had left Te Morenga's niece at Tauranga, and his sister at East Cape, where they were abused and killed by local people.[61] En route to Tauranga, Te Morenga's taua visited Thames, where some of his people raided Te Hinaki's potato gardens, and one of Te Morenga's relatives was killed as utu. In turn, some of this man's kin group travelled from the Bay of Islands to Thames, where they killed some of Te Haupa's people, allies of Te Hinaki's. According to this Nga Puhi account, when they met in Port Jackson and Te Hinaki told Hongi about these quarrels, Hongi asked Te Hinaki whether he wanted to make peace. Although the Hauraki rangatira replied that he intended to take utu for these attacks, Hongi advised him against it, presenting Te Hinaki with a billhook, a red shawl and a pair of pistols, which he accepted, promising to give Hongi a war canoe when they returned to New Zealand. Later, Hongi confirmed this story, saying that he understood this gift exchange with Te Hinaki as a promise of alliance.[62]

Whatever the truth of these stories, Hongi Hika was in no mood to listen to Marsden's admonitions. During his visit to England, he had learned that King George IV and his people were formidable warriors. Almost as soon as he returned to the Bay of Islands with the King's chain mail and helmet, an arsenal of muskets and vivid memories of Sir John Mortlock's tales of the Napoleonic Wars, Hongi set off on a series of taua that threw the country into turmoil. In this way, the first detailed European accounts of life in New Zealand, which gave Māori a bloodthirsty reputation, were written at a time when unequal access to European guns led to fighting that was unprecedented in its scale and destructive power.

The New Zealander, engraving by Gustav Doré, 1872.

CHAPTER SIX

Decline and Fall

DURING HIS TIME IN ENGLAND, HONGI HIKA IMPRESSED MANY people, including King George IV, with his acute intelligence and dignified demeanour, confounding their ideas about cannibals and savages. In 1840, Thomas Macaulay, the author of a monumental five-volume *History of England*, imagined a future in which London would lie in ruins, and 'some traveller from New Zealand, shall in the midst of a vast solitude, take his stand on a broken arch of London Bridge to sketch the ruins of St. Paul's'[1] – a distant echo of Hongi's visit. This vivid image, which prophesied that like Rome, the British Empire would 'decline and fall', posed an alternative to those stadial theories that described human evolution as an inevitable progress from 'savagery' to 'civilisation'.

When Hongi arrived back in the Bay of Islands in July 1821, he was disenchanted with the missionaries. In England he had learned that despite their pretensions to superiority, Marsden and his fellow missionaries were commoners, or tūtūā, not rangatira; and that some of the things that they had told him were untrue. When he learned about a quarrel during his absence between his adult daughter Taieke and William Puckey's eleven-year-old daughter Elizabeth, Hongi was incensed. During this quarrel, Taieke had called Puckey a kuki, or slave, saying that her father would kill and eat him when he came back from England. In response Elizabeth retorted that when Hongi returned, she would cut off his head and boil it in an iron pot – a terrible insult.[2] According to Butler:

> [Hongi] remained sullenly at his hut about half a mile distant from the Settlement for several days, without coming to see us. He represented among the

Hannah King, sketched by
Thomas Hutton, 1844.

Tribe that we were only poor people (Cooks) that King George whom he had
seen knew nothing at all about us nor Mr Marsden either. In consequence of
this, we have had to bear with many hard speeches and cruel mockings not
worth repeating.[3]

Those who had been helping the missionaries in their houses and fields
stopped work, while others plundered their crops, confiscating their potatoes and kūmara. When Butler's loyal foreman Taiwhanga tried to stop
them, he was wounded with a bayonet, and Butler's wife and son were given a
thrashing. In a muru raid on Puckey's house, their cutlery, china and kitchen
goods were confiscated, and a warrior seized his son by the hair, threatening
to cut off his head. The other missionaries were also cursed at and threatened, and their domestic animals, tools and household items were seized.

The missionaries' families were terrified, and Mrs King was so trauma-
tised by an attack on their house that she had a breakdown. When Butler
reproached Hongi for these outrages, saying that he and his fellow missionaries had been kind to his family during his absence, Hongi accused him of
trying to stop him from making the journey to England.

Butler admitted that he had not wanted Hongi to go to England, saying that it was because he loved him and it was too dangerous. In reply, Hongi snapped that this was not true, and that he was only trying to stop him from acquiring muskets and gunpowder. Although Butler and Marsden both told him that the king had forbidden them to trade muskets with Māori, Hongi said, when he had asked King George about this, the king replied that he had given no such order, and that he did not know these people.

Hongi also accused Marsden of writing a 'bad letter' about him and Kendall to the Church Missionary Society, so that the Secretary and the Committee in London insulted him with niggardly gifts. When they returned to Port Jackson, Marsden had refused to give him anything at all, despite the debt of gratitude he owed to Hongi and his people for protecting the mission. He told Butler that if he would not barter muskets and gunpowder for his provisions, he should leave the country. Finally, he said that he no longer wanted his children to learn to read and write, and that 'the people at the Warre Karrakeeah [whare karakia – church] are bad, and the Karrakeeah [karakia – Christian worship] itself was no good for the New Zealand man'.[4]

After his experiences in Britain and Port Jackson, Hongi had largely rejected European beliefs and customs, and for the rest of his life he held fast to tikanga Māori (Māori ideas of proper behaviour). During their voyage to England, Kendall and Hongi had become good friends, and Kendall backed Hongi in these disputes. He told Butler that he was willing to trade muskets and gunpowder to Hongi and his people, and wrote to Samuel Marsden, saying that he had no right to try to forbid Māori from trading with Europeans as they wished in their own country:

> They consider themselves free, whatever we may think to the contrary. They have too much pride and independence of spirit to take in good part any restraints that we may think necessary to lay upon them. . . .
>
> Reflect for a moment that we are the subjects of a heathen government. Consider the absolute control which the natives have over us directly and over our property and proceedings indirectly, having it in their power to increase or diminish our supplies, and that the passion of the natives for war and arms is ungovernable.

Kendall also reproached Marsden for exaggerating the successes of the New Zealand mission in his reports to Britain; for investing its resources in agriculture rather than in schools and churches; for sending out former convicts who cursed and slept with local women; for being too harsh and judgemental; and for condemning the missionaries for trading in muskets when he himself had done the same:

> Commend the poor missionaries for the little that they are able to do, and do not crush them with reproach for the much they cannot do. Treat them not as servants but as brethren.
>
> Let them feel an equal share of your regard and do not distress them by preferring one before another. . . . The feelings of the whole of the missionaries are wounded at your unreasonable expectations, and they are of opinion it is both in your place and in your power to heal them.[5]

At this time Butler was also angry with Marsden, accusing him of hypocrisy for forbidding the missionaries to barter in guns and gunpowder, and for dishonouring a bill of Butler's, when he had engaged in the same trade.[6] After sailing to Port Jackson to confront Marsden, Butler had moved into a fine new house at Kerikeri (known today as Kemp House). Kendall and Butler had very different attitudes towards Māori. Butler called them 'a proud, savage, obstinate and cruel race of cannibals',[7] and was highly censorious of the Europeans who slept with local women, castigating these men for 'the dreadful evil of such conduct'.[8] Kendall, on the other hand, had become close to the Rangihoua people, and since his return to New Zealand, spent most of his time 'itinerating' among Māori communities, praying with them in Māori, studying their 'language, Customs and Manners'[9] and urging his colleagues to respect their independence.

In addition to his resentment against the missionaries, upon his return to the Bay of Islands, Hongi learned that the son of Te Haupa, whom he had met at Port Jackson, had brought a taua north and killed his friend, the chief of Tutukaka. Regarding this as an act of betrayal, he decided to take a party south to seek satisfaction from Te Haupa and his ally Te Hinaki.[10]

Soon after his angry meeting with Butler, Hongi left the Bay of Islands with a very large taua of about 2000 warriors in more than 60 canoes, armed with 1000 muskets, intent on seeking utu for his friend from Tutukaka, and restoring the mana lost in former defeats. These included the ancient battle of Waiwhariki at Puketona in the inland Bay of Islands; the battle of Moremonui near Kaipara, during which his brothers and sister had been

Nga Puhi war fleet, by Louis Auguste de Sainson, 1839.

killed; and other battles near Thames. If his enemies had been worried about his intentions, this new onslaught would be even more devastating than they had feared.

When his war fleet arrived in Tamaki (now Auckland), Hongi looked through his telescope and saw Te Hinaki's flag flying at Mauinaina pā (at Panmure). Te Hinaki himself, dressed in regimental uniform, was parading among his warriors as the war trumpet blared in warning. Donning his regimental jacket and King George's chain mail and helmet, Hongi stood at the head of his war party, took up his sword and ordered one of his men to blow a war trumpet in reply. Deciding to test the pact of friendship he had forged with Te Hinaki in Port Jackson, Hongi sent his son Hare (or 'Charley'), who was about seventeen years old, accompanied by a rangatira with a handkerchief on a long spear, requesting a parley. In response, Te Hinaki sent out his eldest son armed with a spear and a tomahawk and shot Hongi's envoy through the head, leaving Hongi's warriors wailing in anger and grief.

Despite this hostile gesture, Hongi waited for several days, and then sent a message to Te Hinaki, offering to make peace by exchanging their sons as hostages. When they met at the head of their armies, Hongi took off his helmet, showing Te Hinaki his face, and bowed, saying that it would be wise to make peace, since he had met King George in England, as Te Hinaki could see from the helmet, chain mail and sword that the king had given him. Te Hinaki retorted that he had met Governor Macquarie in Port Jackson, and that he was determined to fight. Hongi replied that in that case, the next time that Te Hinaki would see his face, it would be on the battlefield.

In the battle that followed, Hongi used a wedge-shaped formation, evidently based on tactics used by Napoleon and explained to him by Sir John Mortlock. When Te Hinaki took aim with his musket and shot Hongi in the side, the bullet was deflected by the chain mail given to him by King George. As Hongi staggered, one of Te Hinaki's men hit him on the back of the head with a mere (hand club), but he turned and shot his assailant from the ground with his pistol. When Te Hinaki went to bayonet Hongi Hika, he was shot and killed by two of Hongi's warriors.

Later, during an attack on Mauinaina pā, Hongi's foot became entangled in a vine as he tried to climb the palisade, and once again, he was almost killed but miraculously escaped. Taking these near misses as a sign that his ancestors had abandoned him, he was about to retreat when his friend and ally Patuone, the rangatira from Hokianga who was acting as a tohunga for the taua, assured him that on the contrary, these were signs that he was under the protection of the atua, and must renew the attack.

After the defenders at Mauinaina retreated to an interior fortification, Hongi had a high platform built for his marksmen and shot almost everyone inside the pā, including three Europeans, although Wharepoaka (Te Rakau's son) ushered many of the chiefly children to safety, ensuring that negotiations for peace would later be possible. In the bloody aftermath of this battle, the pā was burned to the ground, hundreds of Te Hinaki's people were killed, and Hongi cut off the rangatira's head as a trophy, drinking his blood and consuming his mana.[11]

Afterwards, Hongi and his warriors sacked Mokoia pā, a little inland at Tamaki, and carried on to the Waihou River in Thames where they besieged Te Totara pā, where the defenders had only one musket. During the attack, Hongi's son-in-law Tete and his brother were killed. When the fortified village proved unassailable, Hongi sent in his allies to make peace. After accepting two prized heirlooms as peace offerings, they withdrew from the

*Hone Heke and
Patuone, by George
French Angas, 1847.*

battlefield. Urged on by his wife Turikatuku, famed as a matakite (seer), the
following night Hongi and his warriors gained covert entry to the pā, killing
many more people as utu for the death of his son-in-law and his brother.[12]
By then Patuone, who regarded this stratagem as treacherous and unworthy
of a rangatira, had left the taua and returned to Hokianga.

According to an account collected by John White, the people in
Te Totara pā knew nothing about guns. When their companions began to
drop dead around them, they were terrified:

> These people, who were ignorant in regard to the thunder of guns, went to
> see what the noise was caused by, and what the lightning of the strange god
> was that had been brought there; but the guns were used on these stupids,
> and many of them fell dead.

These stupids saw that many of those who were gazing at the lightning
and hearing the thunder were being killed with what they did not know; but
soon the idea occurred to the minds of those of the pa which caused them to
utter this remark: 'Ah! it is the Nga-puhi who have come back, and are now
breaking the peace they have made.'

There was one gun in Te Totara; and the man in the pa who had this
gun took it and pointed it at the Nga-puhi people, as he thought that by the
mere fact of pointing it at any one the gun would speak. Ah! how you do act,
O stupid![13]

When three of Hongi's canoes returned to Kerikeri in the Bay of Islands
in December 1821, the people were devastated to hear that Tete and his
brother had been killed at Te Totara pā. The heads of their enemies were
paraded, including that of Te Hinaki, and in a fury of grief, the women beat
a number of war captives to death, right outside the mission. Afterwards
Hongi's daughter Aku tried to kill herself for the loss of her husband and,
when she was restrained, shot herself in the arm.[14] Because the missionaries
had failed to support Hongi Hika by procuring muskets to trade with him,
relationships between them and the Bay of Islands people hit rock bottom.
As Francis Hall, the new schoolmaster – a gentle, kindly man whom
Marsden had brought to the Bay during his last visit – lamented:

> They look upon us with contempt: they disregard what we say, have no
> respect to our feelings, but disgust us with acts of cannibalism before our eyes
> from day to day. They break our fences, steal our things, withhold all the food
> they can & their behaviour generally speaking is mischievous, threatening,
> insolent, sullen and mysterious.[15]

Despite this hostility towards the Europeans, however, Kendall and Hongi
remained steadfast friends. In September 1821, Kendall, who had been
unable to forgive his wife for her affair with their servant Stockwell, began
an affair with Te Rakau's daughter Tungaroa, who lived in his house, helping
his wife with her domestic duties. Very likely Hongi encouraged this relationship as a way of consoling Kendall, and making him part of his extended
family. Although he managed to keep this relationship secret for a time,
Kendall's close relationship with Te Rakau and his family was already provoking adverse comment. James Shepherd, for instance, who had recently

joined the mission, wrote that the missionaries 'seem to have fallen into the mire of this place, and instead of Evangelising the Heathen, are themselves becoming Heathen'.[16] At the same time, Kendall's affair with Tungaroa was well known among Māori. A high-born young woman, she had been set apart as a wife for Towhi, now regarded as the rangatira of Rangihoua. In January 1822 Kendall's house was subjected to a muru, or plundering raid, by Towhi's relatives, and chickens and two donkeys were taken as utu; while in February another larger taua from Hokianga broke into his house, and one of the warriors struck at Kendall with a hatchet and would have killed him, if his friend Waikato had not parried the blow.[17]

Later that month, Marsden replied to Kendall's earlier letter with its excuses for trading in muskets, saying that these 'Carnal Weapons' would bring a curse rather than a blessing on the warriors who used them, and expressing his anger at the discovery of muskets consigned to Kendall on board the *Dromedary* just before his departure for England. He added:

[A]s a Christian, you [possess] very valuable qualifications for a Missionary, but these only shine forth occasionally like the Sun in a Winters day, but as a Man I would say you were under the dominion of very strong angry passions, and obstinately bent upon following your own opinion upon all occasions, regardless of future consequences . . . This has been the rock upon which you have often struck, and upon which I fear you will continue to strike against all remonstrance . . .[18]

Kendall replied defiantly that Māori were also using the hatchets they had acquired from the missionaries to kill their enemies, and that as weapons, muskets were relatively civilised. He added: '[W]e are <u>fallen men</u>, living in a <u>fallen world</u>: and we well know that men, as they are compelled by the Devil . . . take delight in tormenting and destroying each other. . . . The people at or near the Bay of Islands are bent upon subduing the Natives of the whole northern island.'[19]

In March 1822 Hongi left the Bay of Islands with another huge fleet of canoes and 3000 warriors to seek utu from the Waikato people, hauling his canoes across the Tamaki portage, sailing down the west coast and heading up the Awaroa River to attack Matakitaki pā at Pirongia, where the Waikato forces commanded by Te Wherowhero, later the first Māori King, had gathered.[20]

Te Wherowhero, or Potatau, by George French Angas, 1847.

Like the people at Te Totara pā, these warriors had never experienced musket fire, and when they heard rumours about this new weapon they were terrified:

> If a gun were pointed at a man it would speak, and not any one could see the thing that would fly which would kill the man. Whenever the mouth of a gun was heard to speak it told the death of a man, and, though a man might be at a distance, if a gun opened its mouth and spoke to him, he would die.[21]

Like a man's mouth, it seems, the mouth of a musket could speak of its own volition. When Matakitaki pā was attacked by Hongi's taua, the warriors panicked and fled. In a merciless pursuit, many were slaughtered. Later, Te Wherowhero took utu when he managed to attack and kill a group of about 70 Nga Puhi warriors at night while they were sleeping, and take their muskets, having sent a message to tell their female captives to exhaust them with sex before the raid.[22]

During Hongi's absence, Kendall, who was increasingly guilt-stricken about his affair with Tungaroa, sent a note to Rev. Pratt in London, confessing his sin, although his wife and children still knew nothing about it. When he heard about this confession, Butler was horrified, and deputed Francis Hall to confront Kendall about it. Hall wrote Kendall an impassioned letter, acknowledging that without God's help he might have fallen in the same way, and begging him to end his relationship with Te Rakau's daughter:

> O consider Sir what the Society has expected from you as the Head of the Advance Guard of their little Army in this land – and shall you, who fill so distinguished a Post, and are so well qualified to Lead them on to Victory, turn Traitor to King Jesus – desert your Colours, fly from the Standard of the Cross, and engage on the side of the Prince of Darkness – Mingle with the Heathen and learn their ways? I humbly beseech you!
>
> O let the sighs and tears of your penitent heart broken wife, prevail in turning you from the crooked path in which you are entangled to the path of virtue & honour and Happiness.
>
> O let the tears and Solicitude of your promising Children speak as so many Angels Trumpet tongued proclaiming, 'O Father proceed no further on the road which leadeth to destruction.'
>
> O take my advice Sir, and all may yet be well. Cherish your wife and children, and put away that Wicked heathen Woman from your dwelling, and shun her embraces as you would avoid the Gates of Hell. God is gracious and full of Compassion. He alone can enable you to do this.[23]

William Hall, on the other hand, rejoiced in Kendall's downfall. He wrote to Pratt, telling him that since 1816, Kendall's wife had been unfaithful to him:

> R. Stockwell that Convict that Mr Kendall brought to N. Zealand with him was cohabiting with Mrs. Kendall well known to all the Settlement except Mr K., self and she actually brought forth a son by Stockwell nothing like any other part of Mr Ks family and when she was charged with it she confessed the whole of her shameful conduct and the child remains a spurious brood in Mr Kendalls family until this day . . .

If you had had the faintest Idea of the real character and conduct of
Mr. Kendall since he came to N. Zealand, you would no more have Ordained
him than you would have Ordained his Shoe Black. If I were but one hour
in your company, I could tell you absolute facts respecting the conduct of
Mr Kendall that would make your hair lift your hat.[24]

Likewise, Samuel Leigh, the Wesleyan missionary who had recently arrived
in the Bay of Islands, began to collect evidence against Kendall, saying that
he had slept with Tungaroa immediately after Divine Service on Sundays,
going to Rangihoua pā to be with her, and that he had confessed to the
captain of the *Active* 'that he loved the person and hated his wife. . . . His
brethren have forsaken him, and he is dispised by the heathen – Such a mis-
erable man I never before saw!'[25]

By now Kendall was at loggerheads with all of his colleagues. As Francis
Hall reported to Marsden:

> Things are going on badly amongst us in a way which is enough to make a
> Christians Heart bleed – The Conduct of Mr Kendall has of late been very
> wicked, and outrageous, he has insulted that pious and worthy Mr Leigh
> with as much cause as he might have found to insult a New born babe –
> He endeavoured to stir up the Natives to break down Mr Halls fence and
> take away his property – but they would not obey him – he is living in open
> Sin with a Native women, and despises reproof – and seems in danger of
> mingling with the Heathen and learning their ways – I wrote a letter to him
> yesterday, but am afraid it will have no effect.[26]

Condemned by his fellow missionaries, Kendall took Tungaroa and several
boxes of his possessions to a friend's pā, and then fled alone to Whangaroa
and took passage on a visiting ship to Hokianga. At the end of May 1822,
he travelled back briefly to the Bay to baptise his last child with Jane, a boy.
Meanwhile, the Rangihoua people exclaimed: 'Mr. Kendall no more a missionary he is now one of us a New Zealand tungata [tangata, or person].'
As the dialogue in his *Grammar* had anticipated, Kendall had become māori.[27]

When Marsden heard about Kendall's affair with Tungaroa, there was
no question of forgiveness. When Kendall wrote to ask him for timber to
build a church at Rangihoua, Marsden lashed out furiously, dismissing his
request and saying that 'you have ruined yourself in this life, and lost your

honourable and sacred rank in society, which you can never regain to the day of your death'. Suspending Kendall from the mission, he ordered him to surrender any property belonging to the Society and told him that he would receive no further support until instructions were received from the CMS Committee in London.[28] By then, however, Kendall had already built a church which he called Bethel at Kaihiki in the Te Puna Inlet.[29]

Kendall and his wife were now both in disgrace, and when Marsden's angry letter arrived, Kendall wrote Jane another affectionate note, trying to comfort her for being ostracised by their fellow missionaries.[30] Although Kendall had stopped sleeping with Tungaroa, Marsden was incensed with him for trading muskets for Hongi, for telling him about his daughter's dubious reputation among the northern chiefs, and for reproaching him for being too high-handed with both missionaries and Māori.[31] At the same time, Marsden was also furious with John Butler, who had travelled to Port Jackson to confront him about trading in muskets and gunpowder (and at least one preserved head) while chastising the missionaries in the Bay of Islands for doing the same.[32] To make matters worse, Butler had sent a letter repeating these accusations to the Secretary of the Church Missionary Society in London.

In New Zealand, Butler was pursuing his own interests in trade, affronting his colleagues. As Francis Hall wrote to Marsden about Butler:

> He is unstable as water in all his ways except one – and that is, his own interests, and in this particular he is as steady and as faithful as the Needle to the North – One cannot 'keep the unity of the spirit in the bond of peace' with him – I believe he has never been at peace with me in his heart since you gave me charge of the Stores. He has vexed & tricked me so, from time to time, with his crooked, perverse, selfish, proud, vain-glorious, overbearing, contemptible conduct that I shall be happy, very happy, when the day arrives that I shall be removed at a great distance from him.[33]

In late July 1822 when Hongi's fleet returned home from the Waikato, laden with yet another cargo of war captives and preserved heads, it was too much for Francis Hall, who decided to leave New Zealand. Although Kendall tried to dissuade him, he failed.

At this point Kendall decided to leave the Bay of Islands and go to the Hokianga, where his son was building a house but Hongi would not allow him to leave. In September 1822 he wrote to his fellow missionaries, pleading for kindly treatment and saying that while he was 'a very unworthy servant of the Society . . . we are fallen men and liable to sin'. He added:

> I was one of the first missionaries who ventured to embark with my family
> for New Zealand. I was the first missionary who slept on shore among the
> natives, the first missionary who attempted to fix the native language, and to
> introduce into print the first rudiments of the Christian religion, and also the
> first missionary to introduce prayer in a language which the New Zealanders
> could understand. I have made the New Zealand language my study both by
> day and night.[34]

While some of the missionaries were inclined to be sympathetic, the next day when Butler arrived at Rangihoua to preach and Kendall came up to take communion, Butler was outraged, almost refusing him the sacrament and saying afterwards that 'without repentance, he will perish everlastingly'.[35]

For a time, Kendall stayed at Rangihoua. In November that year, he threw himself again on the mercy of his fellow missionaries, asking them to judge whether or not he and his family should return to England. John King and William Hall said he should go, while his other colleagues thought that he could stay, as long as he could keep away from local women and abstain from the arms trade.[36] When Francis Hall finally left New Zealand, Butler castigated Kendall, and in response Kendall showed Hongi a letter from Butler that John Liddiard Nicholas had given to him, criticising both Kendall and Hongi Hika for destabilising the mission.[37] Hongi never forgave Butler for his treachery, although in May 1823 when his son Hare Hongi was badly burned in a gunpowder explosion, he was cared for at the Kerikeri mission for some time.

During this period, while Hongi Hika held fast to his hoa (friend) Thomas Kendall, he also decided to take the muskets he had acquired in the Bay of Islands, England and Port Jackson and head south to pursue further mana and utu for past defeats and insults. Kendall, on the other hand, vacillated between respect and admiration for his Māori friends, and horror at the way he had 'fallen into sin', dishonouring his vocation as a missionary. Perhaps because Hongi and other Māori took the existence of parallel ao (dimensions of reality) for granted, they found it easier to move between te ao Māori and the pākehā world. For Kendall, however, trained as he was to believe in one Christian set of values and a one, true God, the more he adopted Māori ways of being, the more he felt that his own world was imploding. As he wrote to a colleague in New South Wales:

> I am now after a long, anxious and painful study, arriving at the very foundation and Ground work of the Cannibalism & Superstitions of these Islanders. All their notions are metaphysical and I have been so poisoned with the apparent sublimity of their ideas, that I have been almost completely turned from a Christian to a Heathen.[38]

For Thomas Kendall, his immersion in tikanga Māori (Māori ways of living) had undermined his own deepest assumptions and beliefs. He felt that he was falling under the sway of Satan – for a missionary, a terrifying fate.

In February 1823 Hongi left the Bay of Islands and set off on another taua, this time to Mercury Bay and Waihi with 100 war canoes. After paddling up a stream, the warriors hauled their canoes to Lake Rotoehu and Lake Rotoiti, and then to Lake Rotorua, where Te Arawa had retreated to Mokoia Island. When Te Aokapurangi, a chiefly war captive from Mokoia who had married one of Hongi's lieutenants, pleaded with Hongi to spare her people, he grudgingly promised that all those who 'passed between her thighs' would be spared – a ritual that raised the tapu of battle. Her husband landed Te Aokapurangi on the island, and she warned her people that Hongi Hika was at the head of the taua, they cried out in fear: 'There is the God of New Zealand, we shall be all killed.'[39] As Hongi's canoe paddled towards the island, a local marksman fired at him, hitting his helmet and knocking him down. Once again, King George's armour had saved his life.[40] While he was still stunned, the canoe grounded, and Te Aokapurangi ran to the carved meeting house, climbing up on the ridgepole where she straddled the apex, urging her people to enter the house 'between her thighs'. In the slaughter that followed, all those who had crammed inside the house were saved.[41]

While Hongi was away on this expedition to the south, Kendall had shifted with his family to Matauwhi at Kororareka, which he called 'Paternoster Valley'. Asserting his status as an ordained priest, he began to hold Divine Service among local Māori, redoubling his efforts to become fluent in Māori and to understand Māori ways of thinking. Although Marsden argued that Māori were descended from the lost tribes of Israel, Kendall disagreed, thinking that they had more in common with the ancient Egyptians.[42]

In April, Kendall reached out to Rev. Pratt at the Church Missionary
Society in London, sending him a case containing six carvings from the Bay
of Islands, on board the *Mariner*, and trying to excuse his actions. No doubt
these taonga had been acquired through his friendships with Te Rakau and
Hongi. As he wrote to Pratt, the carvings had been made 'for the purpose
of commemorating, preserving and handing down the traditions of their
forefathers to posterity', and would illustrate his remarks on Māori ideas,
which he said derived from 'very impure sources' connected with midwifery
and anatomy. One of the six carvings, he said, showed 'a Trinity in perfection
or in the first state', which he described as 'a state of death or a universe,
a field of skulls' (te pō?). Another showed 'a Trinity in creation or the second
state' (perhaps illustrating the story of Rangi and Papa being separated by
Tane); while the others were 'the Covenant of a New Zealanders Espousals'
(the sexual act?), 'two New Zealand crowns for a house' (tekoteko, or carvings for the apex of the bargeboards?) and 'the statue of a chief'.[43]

Some of these carvings must have been sexually graphic, because when
Marsden wrote to Pratt, he caustically dismissed this letter (which Kendall
had copied to Marsden's son-in-law, Rev. Hassall)[44] as Kendall's attempt to
excuse himself for living in adultery with a Māori woman:

> He means to say in plain language that by prying into the obscure mysteries
> of the natives in order to ascertain their notions of the Supreme Being, his
> own mind was polluted, his natural corruptions excited, and his vile passions
> inflamed, by means of which he fell into their vices. . . . The whole that he
> has stated, in my view, may be summed up in the words of Eve – The Serpent
> beguiled me, and I did eat.[45]

Kendall also sent four more carvings with his letter to Hassall, intending
that these would also be forwarded to the CMS, although Hassall kept them
for a time to allow Marsden to inspect them. When these carvings were
finally sent to London on board the *Mariner*, the ship failed to round Cape
Horn and was wrecked off Chile, where its cargo was lost at sea.[46]

In June 1823 Kendall sent eight more carvings to Rev. Pratt, this time by
the *Marianna*. The first carving, he said, showed a Creator making a human
being, using light which was hung on his chest, comprised of a serpent
cut in pieces in the form of a fishing line (representing the 'breath of life'
[or hau ora]), the 'likeness' (or fishhook) and 'knowledge' (or bait) – perhaps

a reference to the story of Maui fishing up New Zealand. The second carving, the 'crown' (tekoteko, or apical carving) of a storehouse, showed 'a Trinity opening the firmament and supporting the light of day', no doubt a reference to the story of Tane separating Rangi and Papa, allowing light into the world. The third carving depicted the 'crown' of a man's bedroom (probably a tekoteko, or apical carving from the roof of a chief's house); the fourth the stern of a war canoe, showing the 'Dual or Mystic rib held together at the extreme points or toes by a bird, and defended at the lower part by a narara [ngārara] or "reptile"'; the fifth another canoe sternpost; and the sixth a canoe prow showing 'the Pitao or Mystic Tongues or Spear', indicating that for Māori, to enter a war canoe was to enter 'a state of death' – te pō. Canoe prows often featured a head with an extended tongue, a motif also found on the arero, or 'tongue', of a taiaha, or fighting club, a gesture of courage and defiance. Finally, according to Kendall, the seventh carving illustrated 'the seven first principles constituting man in his second state in this world', with a beast representing the sun and the moon on each side of him, dragging and pushing the human being along, who had one lame leg, the past, and one sound leg, the present. The eighth carving was a variation on the same theme.[47]

None of these carvings has been located in Britain, although the *Marianna* arrived safely in London. They are unique examples of Māori art works from the time of first European settlement, accompanied by a commentary that illustrates the intensity of Kendall's efforts to comprehend Māori realities. If his explanations are incoherent and largely unintelligible, it was partly due to his distress of mind, but also because there was no adequate way to describe Māori conceptions in English, certainly not at this early stage in Māori–European relationships, and least of all to an audience like the Church Missionary Society. It seems that in certain respects at least, and at that time, Kendall's world and Hongi's were incommensurable.

To the Church Missionary Society, no doubt Kendall's writings seemed deranged, a Gothic horror story of a missionary under the sway of Satan. In his letters to the Society, Marsden condemned Kendall without mercy, saying that his fall had not been sudden, and he was too fond of alcohol. He wrote scathingly: 'His vows and promises are only like a spider's web when they have to oppose the power of unsubdued lusts.'[48] Tungaroa had been set aside to marry a chief, and he was surprised that this man had not taken revenge on Kendall. On the other hand, Marsden praised Kemp and Shepherd, a young man whom he had recently sent out as a gardener to the mission.

Marsden's fourth visit to New Zealand

On 22 July 1823 Marsden boarded the *Brampton* in Port Jackson for his fourth visit to New Zealand, determined to expel Thomas Kendall from the Bay of Islands and restore order to the mission. On this voyage he was accompanied by the CMS missionary Henry Williams and his wife Marianne with their three children and two servants,[49] the missionary carpenter William Fairburn with his wife and two children, Rev. Nathaniel Turner and his wife, and John Hobbs, who were joining the Wesleyan mission at Whangaroa, where Rev. Samuel Leigh had fallen very ill.[50] Henry Williams, a former naval lieutenant, was physically courageous and untiring. With his cheerful, resilient wife Marianne, he would bring new life to the CMS mission in New Zealand.

As the *Brampton* entered the Bay of Islands on 3 August, the ship struck a rock at the entrance to the harbour;[51] and when the missionaries landed, they found that many of the key rangatira were away on a war expedition.

Rev. Henry Williams, by Charles Baugniet, 1854.

Canoes came alongside, their crews greeting Marsden with a shout of joy. When Te Uri-o-Kanae and his wife came on board, Marsden took their little naked son and put him in the cabin with the Williams children.[52] He burst out crying, however, and had to be returned to his parents. Rev. Butler's boat crew, dressed in European clothing, sang a hymn in Māori written by Shepherd, and recited some prayers, delighting the new arrivals; and young Edward Williams (Henry's son) pressed noses with several tattooed warriors, and handed out raisins to various Māori children.[53]

Three days later Marsden summoned the local CMS missionaries, and berated them for wrecking the mission with their selfishness, envy, greed and pride. On 8 August he went to see Kendall at Matauwhi, and told him that he had been dismissed from the mission. Kendall, who had not expected this, was shattered, telling Marsden that he did not intend to leave New Zealand. Marsden was infuriated by his refusal to do as he was told: 'He appears to have been wholly under the dominion of ungovernable Lusts pride and passion with all their attendant Evils. I am convinced he will never recover himself out of the snare of the Devil while he remains in New Zealand . . .'[54]

After this meeting, Kendall wrote to Marsden, protesting that he had been dismissed before he knew any charges had been laid against him, and without any chance to defend himself; and that his salary was being stopped while he was still in New Zealand, giving him no chance to return with his family to Britain. He mentioned the hard work he had done in instructing the local people, learning their language and studying their religion, customs and manners; the incessant toil of his wife, and the contributions of his nine children, about whom he spoke with pride.[55]

On 12 August, when Marsden met Kendall again, he gave him a letter enclosing a copy of the resolution by the Committee and their order of dismissal.[56] When Kendall refused to open it, Marsden told him that he had been authorised to take him and his family back to Port Jackson on the *Brampton*. Kendall retorted that he and his family did not want to leave New Zealand. Marsden asked him, what would happen to his children? Would they be forced to marry Māori young men and women? After challenging Kendall to explain his ideas about Māori religious beliefs, he remarked contemptuously that Kendall could not find English words for these concepts, and that he could make no sense of what he was saying.[57] This is not surprising, however, because in fact there are no words in English to translate words like tapu, mana, utu and hau, which were (and are) ontological terms, premised on the taken-for-granted presence and power of ancestors in everyday life, and different states of being in te ao mārama, te kore and te pō. Such words presuppose a reality that is, in many respects, fundamentally at odds with Western ideas about the world.

While condemning Kendall for adopting Māori ways of thinking, Marsden expressed warm admiration for Māori:

> They are a noble race of men; they are very religious in their way – they are men of the first capacity of mind, men of great perseverance and enterprize; who never lose sight of an object that they set their mind upon until they attain it. They are powerful reasoners upon every subject that has come within their knowledge, possess a quick conception, and are well acquainted with human nature.

If only they would give up fighting, he said, they would be a great nation.[58]

When he finally read Rev. Pratt's letter dismissing him from the Church Missionary Society, Kendall was desolate. In bitter distress he wrote to Pratt:

> I grieve to think that I have sinned so greatly against the Lord, and against the Society. After long and sore temptations, I myself fell. From December 1821 until April 1822, I was completely under the influence of Satan. I was reduced to such a dreadful state of mind that I had no thought whatever as to what might happen to me in this world. I was both a fool and a madman.[59]

He said that he and his wife realised that they had brought their troubles on themselves, and thanked Rev. Pratt for his past kindnesses.

Kendall also wrote to Marsden, saying that he and his wife had decided to separate themselves from the other missionaries, and to devote themselves a little longer to their work among Māori before saying goodbye to New Zealand. While he had learned a great deal about the Māori language, his youngest sons were now fluent speakers, and could help him to translate texts into Māori. He gave Marsden advice about how to run the school successfully, and expressed his intention of living at peace with his former colleagues.[60] These are heartbroken letters. In Māori, one would say that Kendall had suffered a patu wairua – a cataclysmic blow to the spirit.

After a brief trip to Whangaroa, where he helped the Wesleyan missionaries to purchase some land, Marsden returned to the Bay of Islands. When a number of chiefs came out to the *Brampton*, anxious to know why Kendall was being punished, Marsden explained that because Kendall had taken the daughter of a chief to live with him, contrary to English customs, he could no longer serve as a missionary. They admitted that he had done wrong, but said that since he was no longer living with Tungaroa, he should be forgiven.[61] Unmoved by their arguments, Marsden wrote that night: 'His mind has been greatly polluted by studying the abominations of the Heathen and his ideas are very Heathenish. No change will ever be produced in his sentiments & feelings while he remains here.'[62]

When Taua, one of the sons of the late Te Pahi who had visited Marsden at Parramatta, asked whether Kendall had been dismissed for selling muskets and gunpowder to Māori, Marsden replied that the Society in England had ordered the missionaries not to sell firearms, and that as Taua had seen for himself, they did not sell them in Port Jackson. Taua said that this was true, but at present, Māori were like the Tahitians a few years earlier, mad for muskets, although before long they would tire of fighting. He added that for his own part, he had decided not to go to war again, and many of his companions agreed.[63] Marsden was glad to hear this, remarking that once they had given up fighting, Māori would prosper like the Tahitians, who owned the *Queen Charlotte*, a brig that had just sailed from the Bay of Islands. The Tahitians were now trading whale oil and many other articles to Port Jackson, receiving in exchange sugar, tea, flour and clothing; and with sperm oil and spars, Māori could do the same.

While most of the chiefs seemed willing that Kendall and his family should return to Port Jackson, the tohunga Te Rakau and his family were very angry with Marsden, and kept out of his way. Although they had sent messages that they were too ashamed [whakamā] to meet him, on 27 August Marsden went to see them at Rangihoua. At first Te Rakau and his relatives averted their eyes, refusing to look at Marsden; but finally Tungaroa's sister-in-law remarked that she understood that Kendall would receive no more sugar, tea, axes, hoes or spades, and while it was true that he and Tungaroa had lived together for a time, they did so no longer and Kendall should be forgiven. They named other missionaries who had behaved in the same way, and told Marsden that Hongi would be furious if he returned to the Bay of Islands and found that Kendall was gone. Marsden replied that in that case, he would take the missionaries back to Port Jackson, but that he did not believe that Hongi would be angry.[64]

In the days that followed, Marsden worked hard to persuade Kendall to
leave New Zealand, saying that while he remained there, he would never
'recover from his fall'. Finally, Kendall agreed, and Marsden arranged a passage for him and his family on the *Brampton*, along with Rev. and Mrs Samuel
Leigh (so that Leigh could get medical treatment at Port Jackson) and John
Cowell, a European workman who had been a close friend of Kendall's, with
his family. Marsden also had long conversations with the local chiefs, trying
to persuade them that it was proper that Kendall should be removed from
the Bay of Islands. During these exchanges, the rangatira told Marsden about
large plains in the interior to the south, with high mountains covered with
snow, lakes and hot springs, and a dense population. All of their fine mats and
carvings, they said, came from the south.[65] Indeed, there were war captives
from the East Coast in the Bay, including a niece of Hinematioro's. Ensign
McRae from the *Dromedary* had seen at least one house carved by a tohunga
from the land of Hinematioro, which he accurately guessed was near East
Cape – in fact, Uawa (Tolaga Bay), the home of Te Rawheoro whare wānanga
(school of learning), visited by Captain Cook in October 1769.[66]

Soon after his visit to Te Rakau, Marsden spoke at length with Wharepoaka, the son of the tohunga Te Rakau, who had fought with Hongi Hika in
the battle at Mauinaina pā. Wharepoaka told him about the recent wreck of
an American schooner, the *Cossack*, at the Hokianga heads. As Marsden had
discovered during his visit to Hokianga, there were two sacred rocks beside
the harbour, inhabited by the atua of the winds and the waves. According to
Wharepoaka, the sailors of the *Cossack* had disrespectfully struck these tapu
rocks with a hammer. When the priests reproached them, saying that the
missionaries had treated this sacred site with care, they mocked them, ignoring their warnings. As the *Cossack* was sailing out of the harbour, the wind
had died and waves drove the ship onto the rocks, smashing her to pieces.
According to Wharepoaka: 'The god of the rocks got under her Bottom,
and, in great Anger, danced under her and threw her up and down like a
Ball. The Master let go his Anchors to hold her, but the angry God cut the
Anchors – not the cables – at the Bottom of the Sea, and threw the Vessel up
until he dashed her to Pieces.'[67] When the crew was rescued, the local people
remarked that the taniwha was more merciful to white people than to Māori,
who would surely have been drowned for such a terrible breach of tapu.[68]

By telling Marsden the tale about the *Cossack*, it is likely that Wharepoaka
was warning him not to take Thomas Kendall away from the Bay, hinting

at his own likely fate if he persisted. Marsden was now eager to leave New Zealand, however. He also bought some sawn timber from Kendall for Henry Williams's new house, and ordered Kendall to return any of the Society's goods still in his possession to the public store. On 4 September, Marsden had a final meeting with Te Rakau, who was extremely agitated, telling him again not to take Kendall away. Waikato, a son-in-law of Te Rakau,[69] was also present, and told Marsden that they were all 'ashamed' (whakamā, or humiliated) because of the way that Kendall and his adoptive family were being treated.

After farewelling Hall and King at Rangihoua, Marsden went out to the *Brampton*, accompanied by Waikato. Thomas Kendall and his family, the Leighs and the Cowells were already on board. Waikato told Marsden that although he had fought alongside Hongi Hika at the battle of Mauinaina pā, he was tired of fighting, and wanted to work on his farm and live peacefully with his wife and children. He said that 'he wished the English would come and take Possession of the Country, as he was sure there would be no end to their public Calamities until there was a Power sufficient to prevent these evils of War'.[70]

As a final act before leaving the Bay, Marsden wrote a letter of condemnation to the missionaries, accusing them of backsliding:

I feel justified in saying some have mingled amongst the heathen and have learned their ways – Such abominations have been committed as decency forbids me to mention –. When fleshly lusts have obtained the dominion by which the body is defiled, spiritual sins will obtain very easily dominion over the soul. Envy, pride, hatred, malice, evil surmisings and every devilish disposition will reign in the heart and will break for on every occasion in bitterness, in evil speaking, in slandering and backbiting. . . . [Y]ou become unhappy in your own minds, and bite and devour one another, and expose the whole body of the Mission to the reproaches of the heathen amongst whom you dwell, instead of constraining them like the primitive Christians to say, 'See how these Christians love!'[71]

Shipwreck: The loss of the *Brampton*

Early in the morning of 7 September, while the *Brampton*'s anchors were being weighed, Marsden went to Rev. Leigh's cabin, where he read the first chapter of *Romans* to the sick man. It was dark and stormy, and the ship was lightly laden. As they headed out of Kororareka Bay, the ship was caught by a gust of wind and did not answer the helm. Although the captain ordered the anchors to be lowered, as the tide dropped, the wind rose to a howling gale, and the *Brampton* was driven onto the rocks. Fearing that the ship was about to break up, Marsden asked the captain to lend him the boat so he could take Rev. Leigh and his wife to Moturoa Island, where they landed in driving rain, leaving behind Thomas Kendall and his family, the Cowells, and several of the *Cossack*'s sailors, who were returning to Port Jackson. Although two women and a number of children were still on board the *Brampton*, perhaps Marsden thought that only he and the Leighs were worthy of being saved.

A small group of Māori who were camping on the island sheltered the bedraggled missionaries in their small reed house and took care of them. As Leigh reported later:

> For several days we were in their power and they might have taken all we had with the greatest ease; but instead of oppressing and robbing us, they actually sympathized with us in our trials and afflictions. Mr Marsden, myself and Mrs Leigh were at a Native Village for several days, and nights without any food but what the poor natives brought us, and what they had they gave us willingly and said 'Poor Creatures you have nothing to eat, and you have not been accustomed to our kind of food.' I shall never forget the sympathy, and kindness of these poor Heathens.[72]

At Marsden's urging, some of these people braved the storm to tell William Hall at Rangihoua about the shipwreck, and asked him to rescue those who were still on board the *Brampton*. Later that afternoon, Hall, King and Hansen arrived in Hall's boat and rescued them, leaving Marsden and the Leighs on Moturoa Island. They were rescued the next day and taken to the Butlers' house at Kerikeri. As James Kemp remarked: 'Mr. Leigh also very ill. Poor man.'[73] Shocked and startled by this calamity, Marsden wrote in his journal:

> The loss of the *Brampton* appears to me very mysterious. No Ship was ever lost in the Bay of Islands before – the Harbours are so commodious and fine. I censure no one for her loss, although I think – and always shall – that it is a very extraordinary Circumstance.[74]

It is unlikely, however, that the local people in the Bay of Islands were surprised by the loss of the *Brampton*. Hongi Hika was known to be the 'living face' of the atua of the ocean, and Te Rakau was a well-known tohunga. Marsden was trying to remove Thomas Kendall and his family from Rangihoua without Hongi's knowledge, and against Te Rakau's wishes. Like the loss of the *Cossack* in Hokianga Harbour, the wreck of the *Brampton* was no doubt seen as the work of their atua, punishing Marsden for his temerity and preventing Kendall and his family from leaving the Bay. As an expression of their mana over the area, local people stripped the ship, which they 'considered their own when stranded on the rocks'.[75]

For Marsden, the existence of sea ancestors with the power to wreck a ship was a fundamental challenge to his ideas about the world. Indeed, the reality of taniwha is still a cause of ontological clashes in New Zealand. In 2002, for instance, a major motorway project near Meremere in the Waikato was halted when local Māori warned that a swamp that was about to be filled was inhabited by several taniwha, whose anger had already caused a number of fatal crashes on the highway. Television New Zealand reported the story under the headline 'Maori spirits in motorway':

> The demands of the modern world have collided head-on with those
> from the past as talks with Maori leaders failed on Thursday night. Maori
> believe Taniwha, or spiritual guardians, reside in the area where work has
> already started upgrading State Highway 1. Maori mythology says the three
> Taniwha: Karutahi, Waiwai, and Te Iaroa, have a reputation for good deeds
> but can turn nasty if they are not respected.[76]

When the BBC picked up the story, reporting that 'construction on a major highway in New Zealand has been halted because a local Maori tribe says it is infringing on the habitat of a mythical swamp-dwelling monster', a writer in the *New Zealand Herald* remarked that 'you could hear the sniggering all the way around the globe'.[77] In the end, a compromise was reached between Transit New Zealand and local elders. Saving face all round, the road design was modified on ecological grounds to preserve the wetland, which was associated with a grove of kahikatea trees, and the taniwha were saved.[78]

That same year, when local Māori warned against building a prison on the site of a swamp in Northland on the grounds that it would disturb Takauere, their resident taniwha, these protests were dismissed by the

Environment Court. When the building began to sink and crack, requiring expensive repairs, Māori blamed this on the wrath of the taniwha.[79] In 2011 an underground train route in Auckland, New Zealand's largest city, was proposed for a disused tunnel now occupied by a stream that once flowed above ground in Queen Street. When a member of the Independent Māori Statutory Board warned against disturbing Horotiu, the taniwha who lives in the stream, his protest was also treated with derision – despite a provision in the Resource Management Act that the principle of kaitiakitanga (roughly, guardianship) should be respected.[80]

Like his contemporary successors, Marsden found the idea of a taniwha fantastic, and struggled to make sense of the wreck of the *Brampton*. Kendall, on the other hand, took the warning seriously. Gathering up their sodden possessions, he and his family returned to 'Paternoster Valley' near Kororareka, and decided to stay in the Bay of Islands. Dismayed by what had happened, Marsden occupied himself by reading Lee's *Grammar*, concluding that the orthography was faulty, making it too difficult for the missionaries to learn to speak Māori. Since Māori were so good at learning English, he reasoned, it would be easier to use the English vowel system when writing Māori, making it simpler for the missionaries to pronounce the words. Once the local people had mastered the English pronunciation of vowels in Māori, Māori people and missionaries would be able to communicate with each other. Having resolved this linguistic conundrum to his own satisfaction, Marsden also decided that in speaking about new objects and animals in Māori, their original names in English should be kept, so that a sheep would be a 'sheep', a cow a 'cow', and so on. He went to visit Kendall, who was now at Kororareka, put these arguments to him and asked him to rewrite the *Grammar* according to this new system.[81] What Professor Lee at Cambridge would have thought of this ingenious scheme, which required Māori to speak their own language using English vowel sounds and words, is anybody's guess.

On 29 September 1823, Hongi Hika returned to the Bay of Islands after an absence of seven months, fighting in Tauranga, Rotorua and the East Coast. He stayed away from Marsden, and so did Kendall. Five days later, when Kendall came to see Marsden, he brought a list of 500 words written in the new orthography; but despite this conciliatory gesture, the meeting soon became heated. Upset by the way he and his family had been treated, Kendall raged against his fellow missionaries, the Committee of the Church

Missionary Society and Marsden himself, saying that he was determined not to leave New Zealand, but would live at Kerikeri with Hongi. According to Marsden:

> Mr Kendall appeared to me to be as full of Pride, Wrath and Bitterness, as if he had never known anything of Christianity. He manifested all the Violent Passions of a Heathen. When Professors of Religion fall into the Snare of the Devil, how dreadfully does the Prince of Darkness work in their Hearts! . . . He seems to be wholly under Satanical Influence and his last state is worse than his first.[82]

While Marsden and Kendall were still arguing, Hongi walked into the house. He was civil but reserved, and when Kendall asked whether he could come and live with him at Kerikeri, Hongi said that he would come to see him soon. As Marsden commented, Māori detested this kind of row: 'A rude and violent man is very offensive to them. Amongst themselves they live in great peace and harmony. I have not seen either man, woman or boy struck since I have been in the Island.'[83] Marsden evidently had no idea of how often he himself provoked such altercations.

Two days later, Marsden invited Hongi to breakfast. Hongi came, but reminded Marsden that he had told him not to return to New Zealand. Later that day, Marsden was shown some plans for a house that was being built for Butler's son Samuel at Te Tii in the Mangonui Inlet, under the mana of Tareha.[84] Considering it too large and extravagant, he ordered the house to be reduced in size. He and Butler quarrelled angrily, and afterwards Marsden wrote letters of formal reprimand to both Kendall and Butler.

In an effort to conciliate Hongi, Marsden promised to have a small house built for him at Kerikeri, urging him to settle down and become a great farmer. When Hongi expressed his concern that the English would send soldiers to New Zealand and take over the country, Marsden produced a chart of the Pacific, showing him how small New Zealand was compared with Australia, and reassuring him that the English had plenty of land in that country. Taking for granted the superiority of European political arrangements, he added that it would be best if the other chiefs made Hongi their king, so that he could put an end to their incessant wars. Hongi replied that they would never do this. While they were fighting the rangatira feared and respected him, but in times of peace they would not listen to anything he said. Changing the subject, Hongi told Marsden about his recent campaign in Rotorua, during which he had been hit four times by bullets, once in his helmet, once on his coat of mail, and once each in the thigh and the arm. He had gone to a hot spring and stayed there all night, soaking his wounds, which soon healed.[85]

When Marsden, who had supported the installation of Pomare as the king of Tahiti, talked with Waikato, again suggesting that Hongi should become the king of New Zealand, Waikato was reserved and said little. When Marsden tried out this suggestion on Rewa, another of the Nga Puhi chiefs who had fought alongside Hongi, he dismissed it out of hand, saying that the rangatira would never agree: 'They would think this would degrade them to have any Superior.'[86] Likewise, when Marsden suggested that the chiefs in the Bay should get together and buy a ship, so that they could come to Port Jackson whenever they liked, Rewa replied that this would never work, because they would all want to be the captain. Top-down, hierarchical styles of leadership were far from popular among Māori.

A European ship, the *Dragon*, had finally arrived in the Bay of Islands, and on 23 October Marsden began to negotiate a passage for himself and the Kendall family back to Port Jackson. There were no other ships in the Bay, and Marsden was furious when the captain tried to take advantage of his predicament by charging a fee of £1000 for their passage. Kendall had gone to stay with Hongi at Kerikeri, avoiding his fellow missionaries at the mission station nearby. When Marsden, accompanied by Henry Williams, spoke to Kendall again, trying to order him to leave the Bay of Islands, Kendall flew into a rage and walked out of the house.

Butler and his son Samuel were also angry with Marsden, and after a bitter quarrel with Marsden, Butler went on board the *Dragon* and (it was said) got drunk with the captain. Marsden had already decided that it was too dangerous to leave Kendall and Butler together at Kerikeri (Butler at the mission and Kendall at the pā, where he wanted to live with his family),[87] fearing that they would quarrel, and the missionaries would be wiped out by local Māori when they finally lost patience with their endless altercations. Seizing the opportunity to remove Butler from the mission, Marsden accused him of drunkenness, and of being too hot-tempered and violent with the local people, saying that he and his family would have to leave the Bay of Islands. Butler, who denied that he had been drinking on board the *Dragon*, demanded a formal inquiry. Butler's Māori friends were very

The Beehive, the first home of Henry and Marianne Williams
at Paihia, by Henry Williams.

upset when they heard that Marsden wanted to take Butler and his wife and children back to Port Jackson, saying that there was no need for such drastic action.

Harassed and dismayed, Marsden went to stay with Henry and Marianne Williams at Paihia, where they had decided to settle. The local people had built them a raupō (bulrush, *Typha orientalis*) house, which they called the 'Beehive', and a store surrounded by a palisade; and they had stocked the place with vines, fruit trees (including orange trees) and vegetables, and poultry, cows, goats and rabbits.[88]

As Marianne wrote home: 'We are in a little romantic Paradise in a barbarous land with every prospect of usefulness, every comfort, every blessing. My heart is overflowing.'[89] Marsden shared her pleasure, remarking gratefully that 'the situation of Mr. Williams' Station is most beautiful, and the Natives very well behaved. They are as quiet and feel themselves as secure as if they were in any part of England. I have no doubt but they will be blessed in their work.'[90] A few days later, when Marianne gave birth to a little boy, Henry, Marsden remarked with admiration that 'Mrs Williams is a woman of strong Faith and sound Piety and has no idea of fear, and she is well suited for her present Situation – happy and content at all times.'[91] Marsden, who got on well with Henry Williams, authorised him to build a schooner to carry the Gospel to other parts of the country. They also discussed building a vessel of about 100 tons that could sail back and forth between the Bay and Port Jackson.[92]

When Marsden spoke again with Butler, Butler enumerated the ways in which Marsden had ill-treated him, but also spoke about the need for forgiveness. According to Butler, Marsden told him that if any man tried to 'wound his moral character, he would never forgive that man; "No!" said he again, "I would never forgive him!" and he illustrated his assertion with an example, saying "There is a man at Port Jackson now, who endeavoured to injure me sixteen years ago, and I have not forgiven him, and I will never forgive him. When I meet him, I pass him, but I never speak to him, and I never will." Well, thinks I to myself, "this is a pretty good hint for me."'93

By this time Hongi Hika had left the Bay of Islands for Hokianga to attend the hahunga (burial of bones) of his mother, his son-in-law who had died at Te Totara, and two other great chiefs. Such ceremonies involved scraping the bones, coating them with red ochre and storing them in a wāhi tapu, or burial ground, a ritual that took place about a year after death. Before leaving the Bay, Hongi talked with James Kemp, one of the missionaries at Kerikeri, saying that Thomas Kendall was his friend who had done a great deal for him, and that Kemp should give Kendall and his family supplies from the mission store, or he would be very angry. He remarked that among Māori, if a chief took another man's wife, 'they had one fight and there was an end of it, but we continued our anger'.94 Hongi also asked Butler to take his youngest son to Port Jackson, but as soon as Turikatuku heard this, she stormed into Butler's house, telling Hongi that if their son went to Sydney he would die, and insisting that he take their son home again, which he did.95

When the other missionaries held an inquiry into Butler's behaviour, it was resolved that he and his family should return to Port Jackson. When he heard their verdict, Butler exclaimed 'my heart is fairly broken, and my strength gone', and went outside to weep.96 His little daughter Hannah was very ill, and eventually Butler and his wife decided that they would accompany Marsden on board the *Dragon* to New South Wales, where she could receive medical treatment. Before sailing from the Bay of Islands on the *Dragon*, Marsden tried to buy Moturoa Island for a new mission station. The rangatira refused to sell the island for axes, hoes or spades, saying that these articles would all soon be bartered away, but if Marsden would send him a missionary, he could have the island for nothing. Marsden also wrote a letter to Hongi Hika, saying: 'You were amongst the first of my New Zealand friends, and I hope my friendship for you will continue until one or both of us die.' He promised to send him a good man to help him with the farm, some wheat and a plough and a team of bullocks as soon as he was able, and urged Hongi to stop fighting and spend his time on agriculture instead.97

In his report to the Secretary after this fourth visit to New Zealand, Marsden quoted Hongi on the subject of kai tangata, or ritual cannibalism: 'We have made no new laws, we have established no new customs, we are only following the institutions of our forefathers, which we cannot as yet relinquish. Our forefathers ate human flesh, and taught us to do so.' In his account of this custom for the Church Missionary Society, Marsden agreed. Like the British custom of hanging criminals, Māori cannibalism was simply an ancestral practice:

> We do not abhor their cannibalism more than they abhor our custom of hanging felons. They think it is much better to kill a man with one blow than to hang him. We do not see the New Zealanders drinking and swearing and fighting and murdering one another, as is the case in civil society. I never saw a woman struck by a man in New Zealand, nor two men fighting together.[98]

Far from cannibalism being a feature of everyday life, he said:

> Some of the missionaries never saw them eat human flesh. Mr. Kendall never did, and I could not learn that any of the missionaries at Rangheehoo [Rangihoua] ever did. At Kiddee Kiddee [Kerikeri], on Shunghee's [Hongi's] return from war, some slaves were killed and eaten. The missionaries saw some human flesh dressed for eating.[99]

Marsden also wrote a letter to Rev. Pratt, roundly condemning the conduct of Kendall, Hall, King and Butler. Kendall was 'proud, perverse and obstinate', he wrote, and his 'whoredoms and drunkenness' so notorious that he had 'given him up as a lost man'. Likewise, Jane Kendall's affair with their manservant had placed her 'in the lowest state of degradation, in the opinion even of the poor Heathens. They expected Mr. Kendall would have put her to death for her Adultery.' During Kendall's affair with Tungaroa, 'from Pride, and Lust, and Guilt & Rage he became a terror to his Colleagues, and kept them in constant fear, and alarm, while he was squandering away the Property of the Society to ensure his Influence, and Authority with the Natives'. As for William Hall, while he was industrious and an excellent mechanic, he lacked piety and compassion. 'The love of money appears to have been, and still is, his besetting Sin.' Although John King was pious, he had little knowledge and 'very feeble Abilities'. He was also ignorant,

proud and obstinate. Marsden also condemned John Butler, 'always a man
of violent overbearing temper. His conduct to the natives was rude and
unchristian-like.' Although he praised Mr and Mrs Kemp and Mr Shepherd,
he concluded that as a result of his recent actions, 'the natives will see that
the Conduct of the Adulterer, the Violent man, the idle, the drunkard will
not pass unpunished by the Society'. This letter was a remarkable outburst
from Marsden, who also suffered from obstinacy and pride, a love of material
prosperity and an explosive temper.[100]

As the *Dragon* sailed away from the Bay of Islands on 14 November 1823
with Marsden and the Butler family on board, Kendall asked to be able to
stay in the Butlers' empty house at Kerikeri. Kemp refused, and when Hongi
protested, Kemp told him that he knew Kendall could not return to the
mission station, which belonged to the Church Missionary Society. Kerikeri
was under the mana of Hongi Hika, however, and this refusal made him very
angry. According to Kemp, Hongi retorted that 'Mr Kendall was his friend,
and had been ever since he had been at New Zealand, and that the people with
whom he lived with now were not his friend, and that Mr Kendall did not
like to live with them'.[101] In response, Kemp told him that if Kendall came to
the mission, Marsden and the CMS officials in England would be very angry
and perhaps take all the missionaries away from the Bay of Islands.

Two days later, when Hongi arrived with a letter from Kendall, saying
that Hongi had decided he should have the house, Kemp replied that the
house belonged to the Society, and that if he and Kendall wanted to enter
it, they would have to force their way in. Discomfited by this quarrel with
Hongi, Kemp concluded that 'this is the work of the wicked one to over-
throw the work in this land'.[102] Finally, however, Jane Kendall and their
eldest son resolved the dispute by telling Thomas that they did not want
to live in Kerikeri, but would rather stay at Kororareka, where they were
now living under Hongi's protection. Some months later, Kendall's empty
house was stripped, the chapel and the school at Rangihoua were ransacked,
weatherboards pulled off and all the windows broken by a taua allied with
Hongi. He had taken Kendall as his hoa, or friend, and remained loyal to
him, through all their trials and tribulations.

Hongi often clashed with James Kemp, who was dismissive of Māori
beliefs. Hongi responded by declaring his hatred of the English religion:
'We New Zealanders in our hearts hate your worship to your God because
it is so opposite to our own.'[103] The missionaries' sermons were long and

tedious, he said, the children were bored by having to sit so long, and they did not enjoy school. The missionaries worshipped in places where food was eaten (a profound breach of tapu). While the Europeans might remain and follow their own religion, Māori must be allowed to follow theirs without interference.

Hongi was now acting as a tohunga among his people, presiding over hahunga (bone-scraping ceremonies) and inviting several of the missionaries to a séance at Kerikeri by the sickbed of his elder kinsman Wairua, to hear the atua speak. When they arrived, they found all the people lying on the ground at a respectful distance from the tohunga and the invalid, scarcely moving lest they offend the atua. After a long wait, the tohunga performed a karakia (incantation), and then they heard a whistling sound. When the missionaries were permitted to speak, they asked where the New Zealand god was, 'because we had not yet heard him?' In reply, the people assured them that the whistling was the atua speaking to the priest. When the missionaries accused the tohunga of making the whistling sound instead, Hongi and the priest were furious, saying that if they did not show more respect, the atua of the water would capsize their canoe next time they crossed the Kerikeri River. In his journal that night, George Clarke, one of the missionaries, wrote in disgust: 'The New Zealanders are deceived, deceivers and deceiving one another.'[104]

In February 1824 Hongi decided to take a taua against Ngati Whatua to avenge the deaths of his two brothers and sister at Moremonui, but was deeply upset when he found that some runaway slaves had stolen his helmet and chain mail. The taua headed south, and when the priest Tohitapu prophesied that they would be defeated, the attack was abandoned.

Meanwhile, Kendall and his family were making a living by trading with the ships that anchored off Kororareka. From his home in 'Paternoster Valley', Kendall was still studying the Māori language, and writing an account of Māori 'manners and customs'. According to Dumont d'Urville, who visited the Bay in the Coquille in April 1824, Kendall was the most sensible of the missionaries, who had gained the affection of Māori by living with them and learning their language.[105] D'Urville reported that Kendall was very attached to Hongi Hika, always praising him and insisting that when he was not fighting, 'he was the best of men'.

D'Urville's praise, and that of René Lesson, the naturalist on board the Coquille, encouraged Kendall to make another attempt to share with the

Church Missionary Society what he had learned about Māori cosmological ideas. In July 1824 he sent Rev. Bickersteth and Rev. Pratt each a fascinating letter, trying to explain more about Māori philosophy, and the three 'states of existence' mentioned in his earlier letters – almost certainly te kore, te pō and te ao mārama.[106] Kendall described the 'first state' as a state of union, the 'First and Last' in the union of the 'Eternal Word of Wisdom [wānanga]' and the 'Eternal Word of Life [ora]'. In this state, he said, the Eternal Word was shut up, secret, unrevealed – a state known as tapu. 'Koro-matua', the thumb or big toe, according to Kendall, was the First, while the 'Koro-iti', or little toe or finger, was the Last, and he related this to carving motifs. When the thumb and the little finger are shut in the first state, he said, they are a tapu. As we have seen, in some Māori cosmological accounts, knowledge, or wānanga, emerges very early in the creation of the world, hidden in the darkness of the te pō and te kore, and before the winds of life and growth begin to stir, generating various forms of life. While the word koromatua refers to the thumb or big toe, it also means the penis, or a chief; while toinui (big toi), another word for thumb or big toe, also means the origin or source of mankind, or summit. As Elsdon Best later recorded, one way for a man to acquire his father's knowledge and mana as he lay dying was to bite his big toe, or his penis, connecting with the ancestral source.[107] The thumb, big toe and penis were evidently portals of some kind, linking a person with his ancestors in te pō.

According to Kendall, the word ū, the breast, or union, also corresponded to the 'first state', which had no gender. He linked this state with the dual pronouns in Māori, tāua (I and thou), māua (we two), kōrua (ye two) and rāua (they two), adding that these dual pronouns, which embodied two in one, were related to the First and Last. This brings to mind Te Rangikaheke's account of Rangi and Papa, before they were separated by Tāne – '*Kōtahi anō te tupuna o te iwi Māori, ko Rangi rāua ko Papa*' (There is but one ancestor of the Māori people, Rangi and Papa). In Māori, the dual pronouns, which describe two people as one, have no gender, along with many personal names.

In relation to the universe, Kendall said, the first state was a state of union in which the upper or external waters, the wai mangu, or dark waters, were united with the lower or central waters, the wai mā, or white waters. When these waters were unified, they were known as wai ū, waters of the breast (i.e. breast milk), and there was no ū-ā – ua, or rain. When the thumb and little finger of the First and Last are closed, they shut up all the waters as one ocean, a state of ū and tapu. This may explain why various experts from the whare wānanga, or schools of learning, are quoted as saying that 'everything comes from the water'. In this state, the universe was one pure, white, virgin womb, or chaos, in which was held all the seed from which creation sprang, creation in pure embryo. In this first state, Kendall added, the wisdom and presence of the Deity was as much in the minutest grain or particle of the universe as in the whole body. In this state there is no time, the eternal word is always present. This 'first state' sounds very like te kore, the state of nothingness, darkness, chaos and pure potential, the Void.

In relation to people, Kendall remarked, human beings in the first state were originally without distinctions of gender or person, and tapu. Here Kendall referred to Nukutawhiti, the founding ancestor of Nga Puhi, and made a sketch of a carving of this ancestor to send with his letter, in which the middle three fingers and middle three toes on each hand and foot are missing, a sign that the ancestor was in the 'first state'. In the sketch, the left hand of this ancestor lies on the belly, the puku, or seat of the emotions and the place where memories were stored, while the ngā rara, or dual ribs, are depicted, one on each side. Nukutawhiti's genitals are not clearly marked, so this ancestor was androgynous. This evokes the cosmological account in which Rangi and Papa, sky father and earth mother, were said to be one ancestor at first, undivided, male and female at once.

In Kendall's sketch of the carving, Nukutawhiti's son, described in early northern manuscripts as Ranginui, the sky father, emerges from his/her loins. This ancestor is male, holding his erect penis (often called Tiki) in his left hand, which has three fingers, a sign of active power, while holding up a layer (perhaps the heavens) with his right. Kendall identified the spiral motifs on either side of this figure as the serpent's eye, tooth and tail. Below Ranginui was 'The Door of the World' (probably Te Tatau o te Pō, which opened into te pō, the ancestral realm), a portal, with guardians on either side. It seems that this carving was taken from the entrance to a tapu store-house. As for beasts, birds, fish, insects, trees, fruit, vegetables and plants, Kendall added, they were also originally in a state of union, and tapu, spring-ing from virgin seed or semen. Before a seed was planted, it was covered with a garment or shut up between the thumb and little finger. The serpent, or ngārara (two ribs), was another emblem of the First and Last, with his tail in his mouth, closed up, in a state of tapu (perhaps a reference to the motif

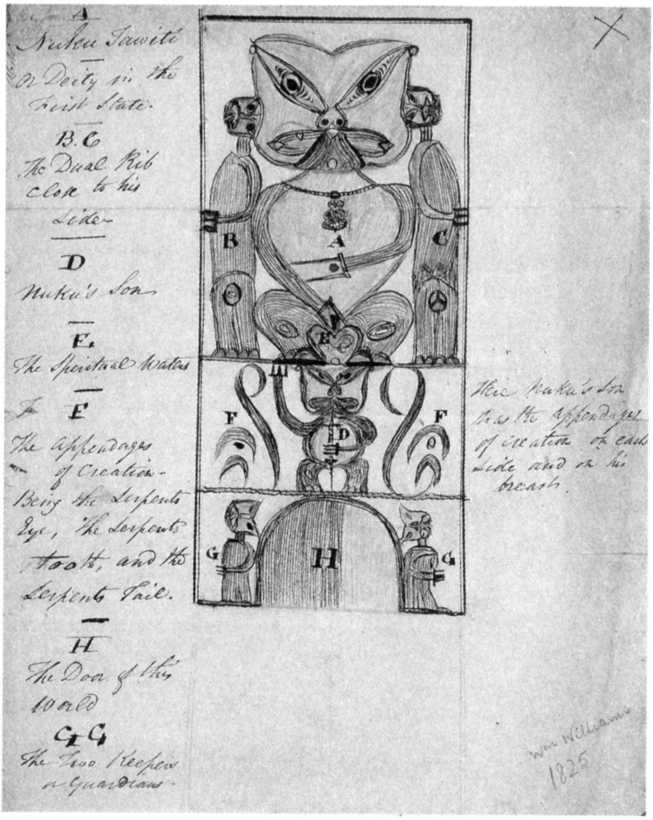
A
Nuku Tawiti
or Deity in the
First State.
B.C
The Dual Rib
close to his
side
D
Nuku's Son
E.
The Spiritual Waters
F
The Appendages
of Creation –
Being the Serpents
Eye, the Serpents
tooth, and the
Serpents Tail.
H
The Door of this
World
G G
The Two Keepers
or Guardians
A
B
C
D
E
F
F
G
G
H
Here Nuku's Son
has the appendages
of creation on each
side and on his
breast.
Wm Williams
1825

'Nuku Tawiti, a deity in the first state', by Thomas Kendall, 1824.

of the double spiral). Kendall added that he had taken the idea of the First and Last from the Apocalypse, which seemed to him to correspond closely to Māori ideas about the cosmos. This may explain why his account of this particular concept is so confused, and difficult to follow.

In the 'second state', which was equal and dual, the waters were open and divided, constituting a wairua (two waters, or spirit in Māori) in their ascent and descent, as in the clouds. This evokes the story of the separation of Rangi and Papa, when Rangi wept for his wife, and Papa sent up mists to greet him. The second state suggests life in the everyday world of light, te ao mārama, in which the genders and different beings were separated and distinguished, along with the being of a person, which now has two wai, or waters – its wairua, or immaterial self, with one wai from the earth (mist, and pure spring water) and the other from the sky (rain). The third state was Triune, although Kendall says no more about it in this letter.

In addition, Kendall mentioned a number of other traditions, including Rona, the god in the moon; Mauimua and Mauipotiki, Maui the first and last; Hina, the first mother, a virgin; the waters of the great deep; Kae with his coat on, and his teeth whole; and Kae without his canoe: the sperm whale, originally a tree known as a kauri; stories that are all readily identified with northern cosmological accounts.

Hongi's decline

While Kendall was delving into the mysteries of Māori cosmology, Hongi's world was unravelling. At this time, his elderly kinsman Wairua was ill, and being treated by a tohunga. When George Clarke asked to feel his pulse, Wairua reluctantly agreed, but said that he only listened to his atua, who spoke to him in a whistling sound. The next day the old man said that because Clarke had taken his pulse, he had lost the use of his arm.

Soon afterwards, when Hongi was chopping down a tree, it fell on him and hit him on the shoulder. Clarke let his blood, despite Turikatuku's adamant opposition, but afterwards had to submit to a rigorous tapu-raising ritual. The blood that had splattered on him was carefully washed off and buried in a deep hole, then Hongi took a plant, chanted a karakia over it, got them to touch it and then buried it in a wāhi tapu (sacred place), performing a similar ritual with a kūmara to remove the tapu. Turikatuku urged Clarke not to eat with his hands, and when he refused, was very angry.[108] The local people wept, and when Henry Williams asked them what had happened to Hongi's spirit, they answered that it had gone below, to join their ancestors. Afterwards Hongi was ritually plundered of his cloaks and potatoes to requite this mate (hurt, ill fortune), which had damaged his wairua (immaterial self).[109]

In October 1824 one of Hongi's daughters died of consumption, and two of his sons-in-law shot a man from Waimate, whom they thought had bewitched her.[110] Hongi, however, blamed the Kemps, with whom she had been living when she contracted the disease, holding the missionaries and their atua responsible for the deaths of so many of his relatives. In early November when a rangatira tried to enter the Shepherds' house at Kerikeri, Mrs Shepherd tried to stop him, hitting his hand. When Shepherd intervened, the rangatira took up a knife and was about to stab him but changed his mind and grabbed a spar, hitting Shepherd on the arm instead. The missionaries appealed to Hongi, who seemed quite unconcerned about what had happened (no doubt an act of utu for the death of his daughter) and refused to intervene. When the missionaries threatened to leave the Bay, according to James Kemp, Hongi retorted that 'if we liked we might go or if we liked we might stay',[111] and Shepherd and his family decided to return to Port Jackson.

Now that Thomas Kendall had been dismissed by the Church Missionary Society, and Hongi was becoming increasingly distant, Kendall's mana was waning. With the help of his Māori friends, he built a small schooner, and while he was in Hauraki with the Wesleyan missionary William White, met the captain of the *St Patrick*, bound for Chile, who told him that the British merchant colony at Valparaiso was looking for a clergyman. On 3 February 1825, while Hongi and his people were away planting winter potatoes inland, Kendall and his family boarded the *St Patrick* and slipped away from the Bay of Islands. Thomas Kendall never returned to New Zealand, serving as a clergyman for a time in Chile before taking his family back to Port Jackson. He continued to work on the Māori language, however, every now and then sending a message to the Committee of the Church Missionary Society, full of sorrow for the trouble he had caused.[112] In 1831 he made one last attempt to explain the religious ideas of Māori, 'that noble race of human beings', in a letter to the editor of the *Sydney Gazette*.[113]

According to Kendall, Māori came from Hawaiki (which he translated as a 'fertile field', identifying this country as Egypt) in search of a long-haired garment (perhaps a dog-skin cloak?) that made its wearer immortal, which their priests identified as one of the Magellanic Clouds. As they sailed up into the sky to find it, their canoe was turned into the constellation Argos, an account that Kendall linked with the story of Jason and the Argonauts. Māori worship their dead ancestors, he wrote, whose left eyes became stars in the sky, and their cannibal feasts are sacramental rituals. Their prophets can foresee future events, and anyone can assume that role; but the power of the priests is hereditary. Kendall added that for Māori, the hair on their head is sacred, the seat of the atua who whispers knowledge into their ears, while their back between the shoulders is the seat of ancestral power. The term for a chief (rangatira) was derived from a commander giving orders in a loud voice (ranga) to a group of his people (tira). When he first arrived in New Zealand, the people had been wild and barbarous, and when the first schoolhouse had opened, parents, children and slaves rushed in, filling the room and covering the roof. There was shouting, singing and dancing, but eventually the missionaries managed to bring their pupils to order, 'correcting their wild habits, training them up to habits of industry and giving them a Christian education'. Kendall also quoted from Isaiah, a reference to vessels of bulrushes, and Revelation, a story about the Euphrates being dried up, as prophecies of the movement of missionaries across the Pacific from island to island. He referred to several Māori who were then living in Port Jackson, and others who regularly visited the colony, as a reason for trying to illuminate their traditions. He signed himself 'Solicitus', 'One who cares'.[114] In that same year, Kendall also took up a subscription to have his *Grammar* republished, an initiative that was blocked by Samuel Marsden.

In 1832, when Kendall was drowned in a shipwreck, Marsden was implacable. Perhaps recalling the wreck of the *Brampton* in the Bay of Islands, he sent a vindictive epitaph to the Secretary of the Church Missionary Society: 'The Revd. T. Kendall came to an awful death lately – He was drownd and the Boats crew with him, none of their bodies have been found – He was much given to indulge in Spirits.'[115]

Upon Hongi's return to the Bay of Islands in mid-February 1825, his reaction to Kendall's desertion is not recorded. Soon afterwards he mustered a taua of 600 warriors and went south to fight Ngati Whatua, determined to take utu for the battle of Moremonui in which his brothers and sister had been killed. Before the battle, Hongi's allies (who included Patuone and his brother Waka Nene from Hokianga) gathered at Mangawhai. Rituals were performed to place the warriors under the war tapu, and his wife Turikatuku exhorted them to be brave, so that they could return in honour to their wives and children. As they hauled their war canoes across to Kaipara, Hongi's enemy Murupaenga launched a night raid, killing many of their warriors and burning or holing most of their canoes.

Several days later, while they were still repairing the fleet, Ngati Whatua attacked again unexpectedly, and some of Hongi's allies fled in panic. Despite her blindness, Turikatuku cried out in warning. Supported by Patuone, his friend and ally from Hokianga who had fought alongside him at Mauinaina pā, Hongi charged his enemies, and together they turned the tide. In the counter-attack during this battle (known as Te Ika-a-Ranganui), however, Hongi's favourite son and heir Hare Hongi (Ripiro), then about 21 years old, was shot in the chest. Although Hongi extracted the bullet, Ripiro (or Charley, as he was known in English, named after Charles Marsden) died three days later. Crazed with grief, Hongi pursued Ngati Whatua relentlessly, not stopping until he had taken 100 heads as utu for the loss of his son.[116]

In July 1825 Hongi presided at his son's tangi (funeral) in the Bay of Islands, which the missionaries attended. At first when they greeted him, he was so overcome that he could not speak.[117] When Kemp challenged the worth of these rituals, threatening Charley with hellfire and damnation, Hongi was furious. He told Kemp: 'It is what New Zealand man considers to be right, and our forefathers believe the same.' After these ceremonies, Charley's youngest brother took his wives as his own, following chiefly custom.[118]

Some months later when Hongi talked with Kemp about a flourishing wheat crop that Kemp had grown with manure, he observed that, according to the missionaries, God made the wheat grow, but that from what he could see, it was the manure. Kemp asked him who sent the rain and the sun but God, and 'if those blessings were withheld, we might manure for ever but nothing would grow'. This made Hongi very thoughtful, and he remarked that he thought perhaps he and his people should give up their customs and accept the missionaries' ideas.[119]

Later that year, however, when the missionaries summoned a gathering of chiefs at Kerikeri, and tried to persuade them to give up fighting, Hongi would not agree, although he acknowledged that the missionaries had spoken out of aroha (fellow feeling, compassion, love):

> *Hongi:* I suppose you are come to try to stop us from going to fight.
> *Missionaries:* Our friends feel very much for you, their love is great and they are glad to hear of your improvement in agriculture. Once we were as you are, living in houses similar to yours. But you see now – we possess all things. Our friends seeing you had nothing – no axes, no blankets, no corn, no pigs, no potatoes etc., sent a ship to visit you – Captain Cook, and since that time several others have come, and within these ten years missionaries have resided on shore amongst you at the hazard of our lives.
> *Rewa:* What?
> *Missionaries:* Why, we knew that the *Boyd* had been taken by the natives of Whangaroa and the whole of her crew murdered by them, and were it not for the missionaries living on the shore amongst you, the shipping would not visit the Island as they do.

Chiefs: True! True!

Missionaries: The missionaries have already been sufficiently long on shore for many of you to have learnt the civil arts of life such as carpentering, black-smithing, shipbuilding, reading and writing etc.

Chiefs: The children are the best to learn those things.

Missionaries: Those that understand the book best in England are the greatest and most useful men.

Hongi (addressing his countrymen): The gentlemanship [rangatiratanga] of the English is not altogether derived from their forefathers, but from their great learning.

Pakira: If we had the same desire to learn the European arts that we have to learn our own nonsense, we should have understood many things by now.

Missionaries: You have received vast quantities of tools. But where are they? You have had vast quantities of potatoes. But where are they? You have had vast quantities of pigs. But where are they? Your potatoes and pigs have all been sold for muskets and powder to the shipping. The powder is gone to smoke and your muskets are continually breaking, and the reason that you have not learnt the useful arts of life from us is every season you have all gone away to the southward to war. We are exceedingly sorry on account of the death of those who were killed and for those who were wounded in your last fight. Should you proceed to the war you will be very sorry yourselves when you again find many of your relatives are killed that you did not take our advice.

Hongi: Yes we shall be sorry.

Hihi: Your words press ours down. You do not give us time to speak for ourselves.

Missionaries: Well, we can but speak to you and express our great love. Is it not from love that we have thus addressed you?

Hongi: Yes, truly, the white people have spoken to us from love.

Missionaries: We are afraid some of you will be killed. In the last fight, Charley was killed. Toutiri was killed also, with many others. If you go to kill your enemies, are you not likely to be killed yourselves?

Chiefs: Yes, indeed.

Hongi: Can you tell which of us will be killed?

Missionaries: No! But in going to war, do you not rush, as it were into the arms of death as from a frightful precipice?

Hongi: A man that hath a large and loving heart for his friends who have been killed will bid the world farewell and jump from the precipice.

Missionaries: Where is the satisfaction to you in thus going to fight as some of you will be killed?

Hongi: When we fight there are but few of us killed and many of our enemies, and that is a satisfaction.

Missionaries: Our forefathers were like you. They fought till they had nearly killed each other, and the people of an adjacent island seeing their weakness came over and took the country from them, and if you proceed in this way it may be the same with you.

Hongi: Yes, it may.

Missionaries: If you go to the fight and are all killed, that would be of little consequence were it not for the anger of God. Those of you that are killed will go to the place of fire and be slaves to the devil. This we know to be true, as it is written in the book of God. We have now concluded. Is it not from love that we have thus spoken to you?

Chiefs: Yes, it is love indeed.

Missionaries: We pray for you every day that God may bless you with new hearts and give you grace to leave off fighting.

Hongi: My heart is as hard as a piece of wood. I cannot stop. I must go. I must kill that one man Toko, the principal chief of Kaipara. But I believe that you have spoken to us out of love.[120]

Before leaving to fight once more with the Kaipara people, Hongi visited Clarke's house and asked him if he still had the red jacket that Charley used to wear. When Clarke fetched it, Hongi held on to it and wept bitterly, and then went off into another room and cried for a long time, while Kemp harangued him about the folly of war. Despite their differences of opinion, Kemp remarked: 'I do not know another chief so favourably disposed to Europeans as Shunghee is. His behaviour when at our house is far superior to any other chief I have yet seen.'[121] When Hongi and his comrades went off to take utu for Ripiro's death, his enemies fled before him and there was no conclusive battle.

After the loss of his son, Hongi's life fell apart. In October 1826 he felt a sharp pain in his knee that left him lame, an affliction that many blamed on a curse by a chief from Thames. His senior wife Turikatuku was now very ill, dying of tuberculosis, the same disease that had killed their daughter. When Hongi discovered that one of his favourite younger wives was having an affair with his bereaved son-in-law, he was so distraught that he tried to shoot himself, but once again, was prevented from committing suicide. When his unfaithful wife and former son-in-law fled from his anger, Hongi ordered them to be pursued, but his wife hung herself and his son-in-law shot himself before they could be captured. As utu for these attacks upon his mana, Hongi was subjected to a muru (ceremonial raiding party) and lost most of his property,[122] and his dead wife's relatives ordered him to leave the Bay of Islands. His betrayal by these close family members, along with Turikatuku's illness and his lameness, showed that his life force was ebbing.

Fearing that his father's ancestors had turned against him, Hongi decided to leave Kerikeri, the scene of these humiliations, and take his dying wife Turikatuku back to her family land at Whangaroa, where his mother had also been born. Upon his return to his mother's land, he took on the responsibility for avenging an insult to his maternal grandfather, whose grave had been desecrated by Ngati Pou.

After Hongi's departure from Kerikeri, the Wesleyan mission station at Whangaroa was plundered, and the missionaries fled to the Bay of Islands.[123] On 10 January 1827 Hongi and his warriors attacked the Ngati Pou pā at Tauranga Bay in Whangaroa, capturing two of the cannon taken by Ngati Pou in the attack on the *Boyd* in 1809.[124] As they pursued Ngati Pou towards Mangamuka, Hongi was not wearing his coat of mail, which was still missing. When he was shot in the chest, the bullet passed through his right lung and exited by his spine. As his Ngati Pou enemies ran up, eager to kill him, he shouted out, ordering a party of 200 chiefs who lay concealed in the bush to attack. This was a subterfuge, and as Ngati Pou retreated, Hongi was rescued.

Upon hearing that Hongi had been seriously wounded, the missionaries, terrified that if he died they would be driven out of the Bay, loaded much of their property onto a ship and buried their valuables. Shortly afterwards, in early April 1827, Marsden arrived on the *Rainbow* for a very short visit to check on the status of the mission, his fifth expedition to New Zealand. Hongi had rallied, however. When he visited Kerikeri and Waimate in May, he was very thin and had lost the use of his right arm, and the wind whistled through his lung as he breathed, a sign that his hau was waning. Finding that his people no longer welcomed him, he burned his house at Kerikeri and vowed never to return, and went to Kororareka. Soon afterwards, the artist Augustus Earle paid a visit to Hongi's camp at Kororareka where the wounded ariki lay in state, surrounded by his family:

Shunghie, not only from his high rank, (but in consequence of his wound being taboo'd, or rendered holy,) sat apart from the rest. Their richly ornamented war canoes were drawn up on the strand; some of the slaves were unlading stores, others were kindling fires. To me it almost seemed to realize some of the passages of Homer, where he describes the wanderer Ulysses and his gallant band of warriors. We approached the chief, and paid our respects to him. He received us kindly, and with a dignified composure, as one accustomed to receive homage. His look was emaciated; but so mild was the expression of his features, that he would have been the last man I should have imagined accustomed to scenes of bloodshed and cruelty. But I soon remarked, that when he became animated in conversation, his eyes sparkled with fire, and their expression changed, demonstrating that it only required his passions to be roused, to exhibit him under a very different aspect. His wife and daughter were permitted to sit close to him, to administer to his wants; no others being allowed so to do, on account of his taboo.[125]

During this visit Earle presented Hongi with a glass of wine, and gave him a razor (at his request) so that he could shave his beard. While Earle was there, Hongi paid a formal visit to 'King George', Te Whareumu of Ngati Manu. His mother Turoro, a high-born woman regarded as a 'queen', saluted Hongi with a long chant. In this song, she mourned the wound that had brought him close to death, recounted his many deeds and battles, naming his friends who had died and lamenting that their enemies still lived, while everyone wept bitterly for this great warrior.[126]

Despite the severity of his wound, Hongi lingered on for more than a year, cared for by his family. Many of the local people thought that he had been makutu'd, or cursed, by Pango, a chief from south of Thames who was visiting the Bay of Islands.[127] While his tapu (presence of ancestors) remained strong, his mana (ancestral efficacy) had almost gone. As some of the chiefs told the missionaries, 'what cared they for Hongi now? He was an old woman and could do nothing'.[128]

In March 1828 the Hokianga rangatira Patuone paid Hongi a farewell visit. As friends, he and Hongi had fought side by side at the battles of Mauinaina and Te Totara at Thames, and at Te Ika-a-Ranganui, where his favourite son Ripiro had been killed. Patuone was shocked to see Hongi's body so emaciated, although his face was clear and his spirit was strong.

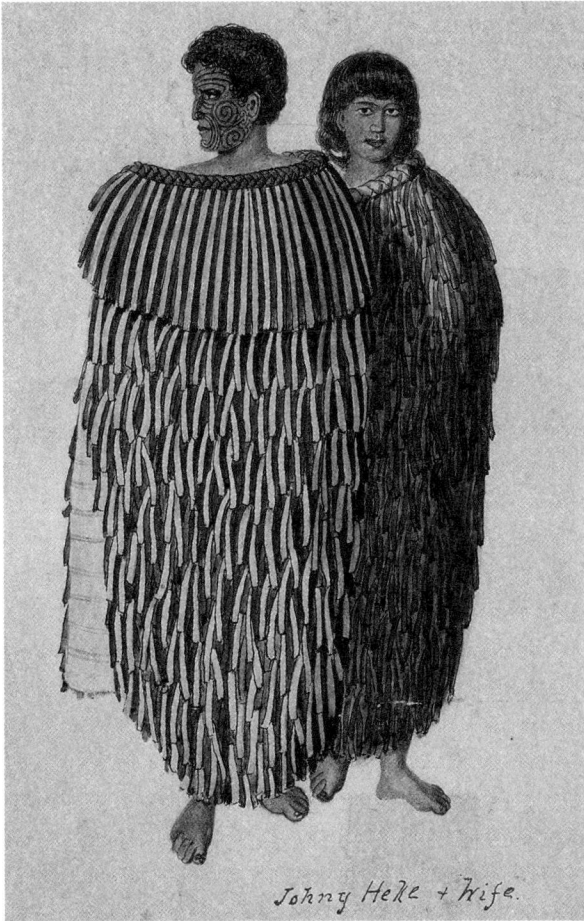

Hone Heke and his wife Hariata, by Joseph Jenner Merrett, c. 1845.

According to oral histories in the Bay, Kawiti (another leading chief who had visited Port Jackson)[129] also came to see Hongi, and they discussed how the people of the north might be unified.[130] As he lay dying, Hongi bequeathed his muskets and ancestral weapons to his sons, and asked that no utu should be taken for his death.[131]

As Hongi Hika breathed his last breath on 6 March 1828, Patuone presided over the tangi. Although the missionaries had been terrified that when Hongi, the 'friend of the English',[132] died, they would be driven out of the Bay of Islands, they were not molested. Hongi's daughter Harriet (also known as Hariata, or Rongo) went to live with the Kemp family at Kerikeri, while her cousin and future husband Hone Heke stayed with the Williams family at Paihia, learning European skills, although 'they never forgot their high birth'.[133] Hongi's ohākī, or farewell message, heralded a new era in which the rangatira might work together and with the missionaries, and utu (the principle of balance) might be handled in new and different ways.

Different worlds, different lives, different selves

Did Thomas Kendall and Hongi Hika inhabit a shared reality – an idea sometimes described as a 'one world ontology', based on the notion of a singular world and shared humanity – although different people might 'see' this world differently (i.e. have different 'world views')? Or were Māori and European ways of being in some sense different 'worlds' (or ao), based on distinct, even incommensurable, underlying forms of order and assumptions about what is real (as Māori themselves at this time often insisted)?[134] How difficult is it for people to understand each other's realities, and how is intelligibility across different ways of living crafted and accomplished?

Certainly, for Marsden and many of his contemporaries, there was just one world, ruled by one true God, with one set of standards for virtuous or sinful behaviour. If Māori standards deviated from these taken-for-granted realities – for instance, in relation to the existence of taniwha or te pō, or the powers of tohunga – such differences were dismissed as 'superstition', or worse. At the same time, among the missionaries, the existence of beings such as Satan or angels or places such as Hell was taken for granted. As they urged when exhorting Hongi and his fellow rangatira to leave off fighting: 'Those of you that are killed will go to the place of fire and be slaves to the devil. This we know to be true, as it is written in the book of God.'

Kendall's heresy was that for a time, at least, he lost that kind of certainty, entertaining Māori arguments and assumptions about the validity and advantages of their own realities and ways of living. At a time when few 'bridges of intelligibility' between te ao Māori and te ao pākehā had been built, he and Hongi Hika had made extraordinary efforts to understand each other's worlds. According to Hongi, he and Kendall became friends, or hoa, when the missionary arrived in the Bay of Islands in 1814, and this relationship made it possible for him to visit England. Thomas Kendall, likewise, enjoyed his friendship with Hongi Hika, proclaiming him the 'best of men', and his relationships with Hongi and Te Rakau allowed him to immerse himself in Māori ways of living. For a time at least, Kendall became māori – normal, ordinary, 'one of us' (tātou – we, including you). If Hongi thought his own tikanga (right ways of doing things) superior to those in England, and was determined to defend them, Thomas Kendall came to agree with him, at least for a while.

During their unauthorised expedition to England, there is no doubt that their friendship deepened. Upon returning to New Zealand, there was trust and loyalty between them. After Kendall's marriage to his wife Jane broke down, it is likely that Hongi Hika made sure he had another woman to sleep with, a high-ranking unmarried girl from within his own kin network – an ancestral form of manaakitanga, hospitality and kindness. After learning about King George's numerous infidelities, no doubt Hongi also thought that this was acceptable behaviour among Europeans. His affair with Tungaroa, however, helped to precipitate Kendall's demise as a missionary. Later, he condemned himself as 'a fool and a madman' who had succumbed to the power of Satan. In this case, travel 'across worlds' was a form of torment.[135] The more Kendall adopted Māori ways, the more he was castigated as a sinner, in the thrall of Satan. In the end, the paradox tore him apart. As for Hongi, clad in King George IV's gift of armour, he led a charmed life on the battlefield until his chain mail was stolen. After that, his mana deserted him, and he blamed the English atua for the deaths of his favourite son Charley, his senior wife Turikatuku and his daughter, who died of tuberculosis.

Despite their anguish at their personal losses, however, a bond of loyalty remained between them. Although he did not agree with the missionaries, Hongi still described himself as their hoa, or friend. As he said to the missionaries when they tried to persuade him and the other chiefs to stop fighting: 'I cannot stop. I must go. But I believe that you have spoken to us out of love.' Likewise, until the day of his death, Kendall was fascinated by Māori language and cosmology. If he and Hongi found it impossible to grasp each other's conceptions, an intimate relationship had been built, for all its fragility and uncertainties, and relational ropes flung across the gulf.[136]

During these early encounters, as Māori and missionaries forged relationships with each other, learning each other's languages and trying to negotiate shared ways of living, different individuals handled the clashes between incommensurable forms of order and different understandings of reality in different ways. In his relationship with Ruatara and other rangatira, for instance, Samuel Marsden learned some Māori, and studied and described Māori beliefs and customs with a degree of sympathy. During his visits to New Zealand, he often acted as a kind of proto-ethnographer, hiding in the bush to write up detailed notes on his exchanges with Māori, sending reports on his journeys and Māori customs to the CMS Committee.[137]

Although he often visited Māori communities, however, Marsden did not join them. He never wavered in his belief in the superiority of his own beliefs, nor did he learn to speak much Māori, and nor was he ever tempted to adopt Māori ways of living. This served as a kind of ontological armour, protecting his deepest assumptions about reality and right ways of living from critical scrutiny. In this respect he was like Hongi Hika, who never joined a European community, learned to speak English, or seriously doubted the validity of Māori beliefs – with the difference that Hongi showed little interest in trying to convert Europeans to his way of thinking.

Ruatara and Thomas Kendall, on the other hand, were each transformed by their experiences with different ways of living. Ruatara, who had spent long periods on board European ships and with Samuel Marsden at Parramatta, and learned some English, decided to adopt many European practices when he returned home to Rangihoua. Although he offered to host the missionaries, he was also tormented by doubt about the wisdom of bringing Europeans to live in New Zealand. As the first of the missionaries to learn to speak Māori, Kendall acted as a mediator in their exchanges with local people, including the taking of property (which the missionaries invariably regarded as 'theft', but which Māori often saw as utu), warfare, cannibalism, polygamy and sexual freedom – all of which were understood quite differently in te ao Māori and Christian Britain. As he explored tikanga Māori (Māori ways of being), Kendall found many of the Māori alternatives appealing. The more he succumbed to local habits of mind, however, the more he castigated himself as a 'sinful polluted worm'. Like Ruatara, Kendall was often tormented by his immersion in another way of living. As he had written to the Secretary of the Church Missionary Society in 1818:

> During the last four years mine eyes have been constantly fixed on scenes of depravity and woe, and my ears have listened to and been partly infected with the profane and obscene rubbish contained in heathen songs.
>   The latter I am under the necessity of attending to, for it greatly assists me in learning the language to write down the themes of the natives and

study their true meaning. The study is painful, and like the study of the Metamorphoses of Ovid tends to injure the mind.[138]

Part of the difficulty for Kendall and other European missionaries was that in Māori philosophy, sex, conception and birth embodied cosmological processes. In a universe ordered by whakapapa and driven by exchanges of hau between complementary pairs of beings, the creation chants, carvings, dance and everyday talk were often sexually graphic. Phallic displays in carvings or as statements of anger and defiance, for instance, shocked and sometimes terrified the missionaries and their wives. To make matters worse for a missionary who was supposed to model Christian fidelity, sex was often used among Māori to forge and strengthen relationships. One way of welcoming outsiders was to give them a lover, entangling their hau with that of their adoptive kin group. For nineteenth-century evangelical missionaries, this custom provoked a headlong collision with Christian ideas about purity, sin and sex outside marriage. After many CMS missionaries, especially in Tahiti and then New Zealand, 'fell from grace', the Society tried to ensure that their missionaries were married before they 'went into the field', and that they sent their children to school in Port Jackson or England before they, too, were 'polluted'.

Later, when Kendall tried to explain these aspects of Māori life to the Secretary of the Church Missionary Society, he wrote:

It may be proper to notice that the language, idolatry, theology, mythology, traditions etc of the New Zealanders are inextricably blended together. . . .
If I am correct in my judgement, to study their ideas is to study the science of metaphysics from nature itself.

This is a very difficult task for me who am entirely unacquainted with such intricate and abstruse notions. . . . As they in all respects draw their spiritual and metaphysical notions from the study of nature, they are of course obtained from very impure sources.

A public relation of them could not be endured amongst Christians or only those whose professional office lends them to study midwifery, anatomy etc.

With them to study the different members and appendages of the human body with their uses, and the origin, progress and end of nature, is to study the Supreme Being, the work of his creation, and what he is carrying on and accomplishing in the world. It is in fact to study the universe.[139]

A sketch by John White, the nephew of another early missionary in Northland, the Wesleyan William White, casts some light on these ideas. In a layered cosmos, ten heavens (or space-time realms) stand above the everyday world of light, and ten underworlds below, each with its own atua.[140] Tumatauenga, the atua of war, is shown standing in the realm between earth and sky, in which he creates Tiki, the first human, a male, with different atua inhabiting each part of his body.[141] As Agathe Thornton has noted, in early Māori manuscripts, body parts are often spoken about as agents in their own right, alongside the person themselves – for example, '*Tahuri mai kōrua ko tō kanohi*' (Turn and look at me, you and your eyes), or '*Whakarongo ana māua ko taringa*' (My ears and I listen). The penis, sometimes referred to as Tiki, was a source of male mana and power, as in the war chant, '*A whea tō ure ka riri? Awhea tō uri ka tora?*' (When will your penis become angry? i.e. When will your penis become erect?),[142] while the vagina is a source of female potency, associated with darkness, life and death, and Hine-nui-te-po, Great Daughter of the ancestral realm. In Māori, one might say, '*Kawenga waha mate ia māua ko taku tinana*', 'I and my body will be carried into death', with the immaterial self and the visible body being taken into te pō side by side.[143]

Powerful ancestors dwelled in the bodies of senior chiefs – for instance, Hongi Hika told Thomas Kendall that the atua of the ocean lived inside him, while the ariki Tara had the atua of thunder in his forehead.[144] As Kendall remarked, to study 'the different members and appendages of the human body with their uses' was to examine 'the origin, progress and end of nature', the science of the universe. The body was at once a micro-cosmos and a living community, a conception very different from the modernist idea of the autonomous, bounded, rights- and property-owning self, or the twentieth-century neo-liberal conception of the cost-benefit calculating individual. As one can see, in te ao Māori it was not just the structure of the cosmos that differed from the 'universe' of the missionaries, but the nature of the person. These were truly different ways of being, and different bodies in which to dwell.[145]

CHAPTER SEVEN

The Spring of the World

I N THE TE PAPARAHI O TE RAKI CLAIM TO THE WAITANGI TRIBUNAL,
lodged by northern leaders in 1990, the question of different realities was
tackled head on. In their statement of claim, the rangatira challenged the
Tribunal to understand and respect the intentions of their ancestors when
they signed He Whakaputanga (the Declaration of Independence) in 1835,
and Te Tiriti (the Māori text of the Treaty of Waitangi) in 1840. In pursuing
this claim, northern leaders returned in spirit to the time of their ancestors,
and the relationships they forged with key Europeans – the missionaries
Samuel Marsden, Thomas Kendall and Henry Williams, for instance, who
translated both the Declaration and the Treaty into Māori; government officials including James Busby, the first British Resident in New Zealand; and
various governors of New South Wales.

In May 2010, when the Tribunal members arrived at Waitangi for the
first hearing of the Te Paparahi o te Raki claim, they were met with a fiery
challenge. Members of northern kin groups held up flags and portraits of
chiefs who had signed Te Tiriti, brandishing ancestral weapons including
muskets, taiaha (fighting staffs) and long-handled tomahawks. In their opening speeches, their leaders vehemently denied that their ancestors had ever
ceded sovereignty to the British Crown. Rather, they had forged a covenant
with Queen Victoria. As Erima Henare declared:

> Ngāpuhi do not and have never seen Te Tiriti as a cession of sovereignty.
> By Te Tiriti our tūpuna [ancestors] bound themselves to the Queen, and
> agreed to the Queen's Governor remaining here to look after her sub-
> jects. In Pākehā legal terms, this seems to present something of a paradox.

Ancestral portraits, musket and taonga at the Northland
Treaty hearing, by Malcolm Pullman.

> Sovereignty is seen as all or nothing. For Ngāpuhi Te Tiriti was a solemn
> commitment, a kawenata [covenant] to a relationship with the Queen.[1]

When Rima Edwards, a leading elder from Hokianga, spoke to the Tribunal,
he recited a chant describing the creation of the cosmos, tracing his own line
of descent from the beginnings of the world to the present. In this way and
by speaking Māori, holding up ancestral portraits and brandishing ancient
weapons, he and other elders sought to shift the Tribunal into te ao Māori,
where dominant understandings based on the English draft of the Treaty
could be challenged, although some were doubtful that their efforts would
succeed. As another elder, Kingi Taurua, remarked:

> [The Tribunal] looks at both Treaties, the Pākehā and the Māori, which is
> totally wrong. We did not sign the Pākehā. We signed the Māori version.
> We are here to talk about the Treaty that we in Ngāpuhi did not sign,
> and they are here to judge in English what our tūpuna [ancestors] signed
> in Māori.[2]

Like a number of other colleagues (including Hone Sadler, Dr Patu Hohepa, Dr Manuka Henare and Dr Merata Kawharu), I was invited to prepare a report for this northern claim. This was intended to update an earlier report, commissioned by the Tribunal during the Muriwhenua Land Claim in 1992 to investigate Māori understandings of the Treaty at the time when it was signed.[3] For the 1992 report, I had worked with two friends and colleagues in Māori Studies, Dr Merimeri Penfold and Dr Cleve Barlow, both native speakers of Māori. Drawing on early Māori texts, Barlow's concordance of the Māori Bible and other translations, and their deep knowledge of the language, we sought to interpret the text of Te Tiriti, and place the document in historical context by examining an array of contemporary accounts of the northern Treaty transactions in English, written by European officials or observers. We concluded that in 1840 their ancestors did not cede sovereignty to the British Crown; and in 2009 the Tribunal asked me to revisit that earlier submission.

In August 2010 when I appeared to speak to the new version of the report in front of the Tribunal at Waipuna marae beside the Hokianga Harbour, Taurua's comments at Waitangi seemed prescient. Inside the meeting house, the space was set up like a court, with members of the Tribunal, chaired by a judge of the Māori Land Court, sitting at a table as a long line-up of lawyers (many of them also Māori) conducted cross-examinations of a series of 'expert witnesses'. Although Nga Puhi elders had opened the Waitangi hearings by presenting their own accounts of the Treaty transactions and by challenging the sovereignty of the Crown, this was being reasserted by the use of legal protocols, just as the Crown's understandings of the Treaty were reinforced by frequent references to the English draft, often by non-Māori-speaking historians and lawyers. Even the Māori expert witnesses, some fluent native speakers and tribal authorities, were expected to present their evidence in writing – although Hone Sadler and other elders, steeped in the whare wānanga tradition, refused to do this, presenting their evidence in Māori oratorical style. As the lawyers and expert witnesses battled it out, the elders and other tribal members sat as spectators. Sometimes they interjected, calling out 'Kia ora!' (Thank you, be well!) in support, or 'Teka!' (Lies!) if an 'expert' seemed wilfully mistaken. As much as a debate about what had happened in the past, this was an ontological struggle. Different worlds were at stake, along with cash settlements and political influence; and these were mutually implicated.[4]

At the same time, the hearing was held in the meeting house, which made its own existential statements. This house, Te Puna o te Ao Marama (The Spring of the World of Light), is named after the spring where the voyaging ancestor Kupe placed his son Tuputupuwhenua as a taniwha, leaving him as a guardian for the Hokianga Harbour. From this source, Tuputupuwhenua would dive into the harbour, and swim along underground channels to Kerikeri and the Bay of Islands. Kupe also left behind his dogs, petrified as stone guardians, naming the harbour Hokianga-nui-a-Kupe, the great final return of Kupe, before sailing back to Hawaiki (possibly Ra'iatea in the Society Islands).[5]

In his subterranean forays, Kupe's taniwha son linked together the west and east coasts of Northland. The west coast of Northland, with its roaring westerlies and rough seas, is known as te tai tama tāne (the male child coast), while the east coast is called te tai tama wahine (the female child coast), with its sheltered harbours and calm waters, safer for canoe travel. These complementary pairs (west–east; rough–calm; male–female) and the exchanges between them shape the northern landscapes. Between the east and west coasts, the underground channels ebb and flow, so that it is said, '*Ka mimiti te puna i Taumārere, ka totō te puna i Hokianga. Ka totō te puna o Taumārere, ka mimiti te puna i Hokianga*' (When the spring at Taumarere is empty, the spring at Hokianga is full. When the spring at Taumarere is full, the spring at Hokianga is empty).[6] According to Erima Henare, these springs also refer to the inhabitants of those districts – when the Hokianga people are in trouble, their kinfolk in the Bay of Islands will go to their aid, and vice versa.[7]

The headlands of the Hokianga Harbour stand in memory of Araiteuru and Niua, two taniwha who escorted the voyaging canoe of Nukutawhiti and Ruanui, descendants of Kupe, on their sea path from Hawaiki to Hokianga. After landing in the harbour, Nukutawhiti and Ruanui built sacred houses for their atua (powerful ancestors), one on the south headland and the other on the north side, with its high, pure white sand hills. As a whale swam into the harbour, these two priestly experts stood on opposite headlands, each chanting incantations to try to attract it ashore as an offering for his atua. When they had used up their repertoire of chants, the whale swam back out to sea, and the harbour was named 'Hokianga whakapau karakia' – 'Hokianga, which exhausts incantations'.[8]

At Panguru, the meeting house is set inside the great 'house' of Nga Puhi, the landscapes of central Northland, with Papatuanuku as its floor, the sky its roof, supported by the poupou, or side posts, the mountains of each of the northern kin groups, sheltering them all. From these pillars, rivers and aquifers flow to the sea, linking the male and female coastlines.[9] At the centre of this territory stands Whiria, the flat-topped mountain at Pakanae where the great Nga Puhi ancestor Rahiri grew up, a fortified site named after the resolution of a quarrel between his two sons. Fearing that they would hurt each other, Rahiri sent them off to plait (whiria) the string of a kite, used to communicate with ancestors, and when it flew, the kite landed near Kaikohe, establishing a boundary that divided the land between them, keeping the peace.[10]

For all the assertion of sovereign power inside the meeting house, the surrounding landscape proclaimed its own mana. As is often said in Māori, '*Toi tū te whenua, whatungarongaro te tangata*' – 'While human beings come and go, the land always stands'. At the same time, the land itself is an ancestor, and in the Māori world, ancestral precedents are definitive. Many participants in the Paparahi-o-te-Raki Tribunal located themselves in the living networks linking land, people, ancestors and taonga (ancestral treasures) in Northland. During the hearings, it was taken for granted that one cannot understand He Whakaputanga and Te Tiriti without exploring the ancestral relationships – both Māori and European – involved in drafting, debating and signing these documents, and the contexts in which they were negotiated and signed.

Henry and Marianne Williams

In the evidence presented to the Tribunal (including my own) about the exchanges that led to the signing of He Whakaputanga (the Declaration of Independence) in 1835 and Te Tiriti in 1840, the CMS missionary Henry Williams emerges as a pivotal figure. In early contact times in Northland, while some high-born individuals (like Hongi Hika) acted as fighting leaders, others devoted themselves to the task of settling disputes, and were greatly respected among their people. Henry Williams, the former naval lieutenant turned missionary, was gradually drawn into this role, assisting some of these rangatira in their efforts to make peace. In their attempts at improvising new forms of governance, Māori and European leaders alike at that time drew on both Māori and Western conventions.

Like most rangatira at that time, and unlike many of his fellow missionaries, Henry Williams was battle-hardened, physically strong and fearless.

From the age of 14, when he joined the Navy, he had fought in a series of
battles during the Napoleonic Wars and the War of 1812, including the
Battle of Copenhagen and the capture of the US ship *President*, where he
was one of a small prize crew that had sailed the badly damaged vessel back
to port, surviving a terrible storm and a mutiny by the American prisoners.
When peace was declared in 1815, Henry Williams retired on half-pay and
married his wife Marianne, the daughter of the Mayor of Nottingham, and
a spirited, active young woman. After taking a job as a drawing master, he
eventually decided to join the Church Missionary Society and serve in the
New Zealand mission. To prepare himself, Williams was ordained by the
Bishop of London and learned about carpentry, boat-building and medicine, while Marianne studied nursing, midwifery, teaching and cooking.[11]
As he told the CMS Committee, Marianne would be his indispensable
partner in the New Zealand mission: 'With regard to Mrs Williams, I beg
to say, that she does not accompany me merely as my wife, but as a fellow
helper in the work.'[12]

When they arrived in the Bay with Samuel Marsden in 1823, Marianne
was heavily pregnant. She and her children were taken by boat to the
Kerikeri mission, along a winding river to a small lake with a fall of water
near where Hongi's pā with his 'rude palace' stood on the hill. Below, the
white wooden houses of the Butler and Kemp families had been built beside
the beach, surrounded by a high palisade with a flag flying. Mrs Kemp gave
her a warm welcome, and when Marianne greeted her three Māori maidser-
vants, who were dressed in English bedgowns and aprons, saying to them,
'Tina raka kue [Tēnā rā ko koe]', they replied politely in English, 'How
d'ye do Madam.'[13] That night, Marianne was wakeful: 'The tall and muscular forms of the New Zealanders flitted before my mind's eye whenever I
endeavoured to go to sleep.' She added:

> At present this noble though cannibal race of men, are fast bound in the cruel
> chains of Satan; and what can be a nobler ambition than to enlist beneath
> the banners of the King of Kings and in his strength rescue them from their
> deadly foe. Often had I in the course of the day pictured in idea our ancestors
> at the time of the conquest. Mr Marsden had the same idea and many a noble
> Caracatus might we fancy we beheld amidst these warlike, yet kindly looking
> savages.[14]

Henry was also impressed by the Māori people. As he wrote to Rev. Pratt shortly after arriving in the Bay:

> When I consider the Natives, their noble and dignified appearance, their pertinent remarks and questions, their obliging disposition, with the high sense of honour which they possess, I cannot but view them as a people of great interest, and one which our Almighty Father will ere long adopt for his own.

It seemed to him that many of the difficulties experienced by the missionaries had been caused by their own unruly behaviour. He added:

> It is very usual now, when a Chief expresses a desire that a Missionary should be established at his district, he will say, he wants a man who is not fond of fighting, who does not scold and make a noise, for though the New Zealander in war is as ferocious as a human being can be, yet at home he is another man.[15]

From the time of his arrival in New Zealand, Henry Williams became the new leader of the mission – resolute, energetic, organised and single-minded. He took vigorous action to stop the trade in muskets between missionaries and Māori, set up schools for Māori, and worked to make the mission farms self-supporting, while Marianne ran the station during his frequent absences. In her work, Marianne was supported by the Māori men and women who lived in their household. While she called the young women 'girls', they addressed her as 'Mata' (Mother).[16] She wrote to her family, 'You can have little idea of the fatigue of being shut up all day with four little fidgety things [her children] in small close rooms, attended by native girls. For savages I think they do wonders, but still they are savages.'[17] If she scolded them, she lamented, the young rangatira women would 'run away in a pet' while the war captives laughed at her, and told her that she had 'too much of the mouth'.[18] Eager to impose British ideas of decorum on her household, Marianne was horrified when her 'girls' went to the ships, or participated in the utu meted out to war captives:

> As an instance of their savage nature, we were told that Jane, the native girl in this house, upon the return of the fight from the river Thames, killed two prisoners herself, the instance the canoes landed at Hongi's Point.[19]

As Henry Williams had anticipated, in the mission he and Marianne worked closely together, united in their determination to uphold their independence in a new land. After establishing the mission station at Paihia, an area under the mana of Hamu, the wife of Te Koki, the rangatira of the timber district at Kawakawa, Henry resolved to remain neutral in tribal quarrels, and beyond the control of any particular kin group. This was evident, for instance, in a dispute with the Te Roroa tohunga Tohitapu in early 1824. The mission store was surrounded by a paling fence, and when Tohitapu, who had been troubling the missionaries, arrived outside, his colleague William Fairburn (who spoke good Māori)[20] told the people to shut the gate. Insulted, Tohitapu jumped over the fence and threatened Fairburn with his mere (hand-club) and a long spear. When Williams appeared, reproaching Tohitapu for this behaviour, the tohunga brandished his weapons. Pretending to ignore him, Williams walked quietly with his fellow missionary down to the beach, followed by the tohunga, who stripped off his upper garments and threw a couple of cloaks on the ground before leaving the mission, placing the site under his personal tapu.

When Williams returned, he picked up these garments, put them outside and shut the gate. Soon afterwards, Tohitapu banged on the gate with his spear, and upon being refused entry again, leaped over the fence and caught his heel on it, then furiously demanded utu for having hurt his foot. When Williams refused, Tohitapu aimed his spear at him, and then seized an iron pot as payment. Wresting it from him, Williams barred the gate, saying, 'Kati e mara. Heoi ano!' (Stop it, friend. That's enough!) According to Marianne:

> [T]he blacksmith now came forward and snatched up the pot. Tohitapu still flourished about, and then began to prepare for fight in a way which I can scarcely describe. The agility of this huge man astonished me. He ran to and fro with his spear in his hand, something like a boy playing at cricket, except that the New Zealander dances sideways, slapping his sides, and stamping with a measured pace and horrid gestures, every now and then stooping or crouching down, beating his breast and panting and panting as if trying to excite his own rage to the utmost.[21]

As Tohitapu stamped and grimaced, performing a wero (ritual challenge) and demanding utu, Henry still refused to give him the iron pot, so Tohitapu threatened to burn down his house. As his allies began to arrive, along with some rangatira friendly to the missionaries, the tohunga stood outside the compound in the dusk and chanted a karakia, summoning his atua to destroy the missionary. While this was going on, Henry told Marianne to take the children inside and put them to bed. As dark fell and the family retired, their Māori friends warned them: 'Come, tomorrow you see a great fire in the house. Oh yes, the children all dead, all dead. Plenty of muskets, a great fight!'[22]

In the morning, the Williams family found their house surrounded by Tohitapu's allies, still brandishing their muskets and threatening to shoot the missionaries. Marianne, who was heavily pregnant, brewed tea and sent some out to Tohitapu, who drank it. While he was distracted, she handed two of her children out through the window to a friendly chief, who had promised to take them to safety, but was terrified to hear heavy blows striking the wall of their dwelling. When Williams went outside, placing himself between the armed warriors and his family, his wife and children wept and prayed. At the suggestion of the friendly rangatira, he gave Tohitapu the iron pot that he had been demanding. Having received utu from Williams at last, the tohunga left the mission. Afterwards, when Marianne told their eldest son Edward not to be afraid because the local people were their friends, the boy exclaimed, 'Oh mama, what frightful creatures our friends are!'[23] When neither Henry nor any of his family became ill as a result of Tohitapu's incantations, however, he and his atua gained considerable mana, and Tohitapu became much friendlier towards the mission.

Williams's determination to uphold his mana was tested again later that year when the old carpenter at the mission cursed Te Koki, the local rangatira, for upsetting his tool chest. Soon afterwards a raiding party arrived at the mission to seek utu for this insult, grabbing clothes from the washing line and assaulting a visiting Englishman, wounding him in the heel. During the muru (plundering raid), one of the Māori men attached to the mission stood in front of the station, brandishing a cooking pot (which would have destroyed the mana of anyone he hit with it) and threatening to spear anyone who stepped forward. Afterwards, Williams demanded utu from the raiders, saying to Te Koki, 'My heart is very sick, and I will not make peace till all the stolen property is returned and an utu for this attack and the wounded man.'[24]

In the end, peace was made. As utu for the raid, Te Koki threw two fine mats at Marianne, hitting her in the chest (a customary way of making such offerings), while the raiders arrived with gifts of pigs and baskets of potatoes. After an exchange of speeches, the two sides pressed noses in the hongi, mingling their hau, followed by a lavish feast. Afterwards, Henry told Te Koki and his people that although he knew how to fight, he had not come to fight with them: 'He would sit in peace and deliver his message to them, or he would go to another place. "Stop here," they would answer. . . .'[25] From now on, it was agreed, the Williams family would be placed beyond the law of utu, and their station would suffer no more plundering raids.[26]

One day when Henry told Te Koki that although he might struggle to understand Christian ideas, when they were both dead and buried, his sons Edward, Samuel and Henry would teach Te Koki's children, and they would become missionaries and preach to their people, Te Koki flew into a rage, exclaiming, 'The *taurekareka* (slaves)! The children! Must they have all the good things, and I nothing? Am I to be dead, laid down, not to see anything, not to speak, and the children, the *taurekareka*, they to have all?' Trying to calm him, Henry assured him that if he were to know God, Te Koki's spirit would never die.[27]

In response to Henry's arguments, however, local Māori once again adopted a relativistic position. 'It is very well for [the missionaries] to observe the orders of our God, and for themselves to remain under the jurisdiction of their own God . . . [but] should they serve our God and not observe the customs of their fathers, the New Zealand God will get into their inside and eat them up.'[28] Adopting an empirical attitude, one of the local rangatira, Rangi, planted some kūmara without observing the tapu rituals and restrictions, telling Henry that if they grew well, he would know that the white people were telling the truth.[29] Frustrated by this resistance, Henry Williams and Fairburn persisted, telling the local people the stories of the creation of the world, the fall of man, the flood, Noah and the Ark, the building of the Tower of Babel and the confusion of tongues, and saying that the Tahitians now accepted the Christian God:

> The people of Tahiti a short time since were as you are now – they are of
> a strange language, had tapoos [tapu] amongst them – and wooden Gods
> which they worshipped, but after the Missionaries went amongst them they
> attended to their instruction and believed in the Great God, and he gave
> them His Holy Spirit and they split up their wooden Gods and cooked their
> food by them, and now they have become Missionaries themselves and

The launch of the Herald, *Paihia, January 1826,*
by Philip Walsh, based on a sketch by Marianne Williams.

teach their countrymen in the neighbouring Islands and build large houses for prayer.[30]

Unlike his younger brother William, however, who joined the Bay of Islands mission with his wife Jane in March 1826, Henry Williams was not a natural linguist, and found it difficult to hold his own in debates with Māori orators. William Williams, a scholarly man who had studied medicine before acquiring a BA in Classics from Oxford and attending the CMS training college at Islington, soon mastered Māori. As Henry marvelled, he 'appears not to learn it, but it seems to flow naturally from him'.[31] Henry's children, especially Edward, also became fluent in the language. After William's arrival, Henry redoubled his efforts to learn Māori, acquiring a growing influence among the local rangatira. With Marsden's approval, he built a small ship, the *Herald*, which was launched in European style, greeted with haka by about 4000 Māori.[32] Using his seafaring skills, he began to visit other parts of the North Island on this vessel, although it was wrecked in the Hokianga two years later. Increasingly, Henry Williams doubted the wisdom of Marsden's approach to bringing Māori to Christianity, arguing that this could only be achieved by mastering the Māori language and teaching them Christian ideas.[33]

Echoing Thomas Kendall's frustrations with Marsden's obstinacy, he wrote:

> I cannot but think our opinions ought to have some weight although they may not accord with Mr. Marsden's. We are in the field, he is not. We have to endure the burden and heat of the day, he has not. [Maori] are perishing for lack of knowledge, but not the knowledge of making nails or planting corn.[34]

Sobered by his experiences in the Royal Navy, Henry had become a dedicated peace-maker. In March 1828, shortly after Hongi's death, he and Shepherd were asked by the local people to help make peace in the Hokianga, where Pomare's son had been killed during a quarrel. They went, leaving their families at the Paihia mission station. As Marianne wrote in fear and trembling:

> Henry has thus left me for an unlimited time, to go with a little heroic band amidst a savage host, in the strength of the Lord, to endeavour to stay the slaughter of thousands. They have hitherto formed one warlike band against the Southern tribes with whom they have yearly gone to war; and now they are stirred up by the enemy of souls to butcher one another.[35]

At Hokianga, the missionaries joined Rewa and Tohitapu among their people in a beautiful valley packed with visiting warriors, organised into separate camps. When Tohitapu sent the missionaries into the enemy pā to speak to Patuone (the great Hokianga rangatira) and his people, they seemed glad to see them. The next day the missionaries accompanied Tohitapu into the enemy pā, preceded by a white flag. After a sham fight performed by 700 men carrying 500 muskets, followed by thunderous haka and volleys of musket fire, Patuone, Rewa and other leading rangatira spoke, urging reconciliation. Peace was made, and the missionaries returned thankfully to their homes.[36]

At the end of that year, a great huihuinga, or gathering, was held at Paihia for the missionaries, their families and Māori followers from Rangihoua, Kerikeri and Paihia. As the canoes converged at Paihia, their crews, dressed in different uniforms (with white shirts and Scotch caps for the Paihia crew), chanted as they paddled. A service was held, and the male students were examined in the catechism, reading, writing and accounts while the girls were examined in sewing, followed by a lavish feast. To mark the occasion, Henry Williams fired four carronades from the hill above Paihia, giving the students a terrible fright.[37] In mid-February 1830, the missionaries celebrated again when David Taiwhanga, formerly a leading warrior with Hongi Hika, was baptised, his four children having been baptised six months earlier.[38]

On 6 March 1830, however, the 'Girls' War' broke out at Kororareka in the Bay of Islands, shattering the peace. When the daughter of Kiwikiwi, the local rangatira (from the southern alliance in the Bay), who had been attached to the whaler Captain Brind, insulted the daughters of Hongi Hika and his ally Rewa (from the northern alliance), who had succeeded her in Brind's affections, angry passions flared. During a fracas at Kororareka, Kiwikiwi's wife, a high-born woman from Thames, tore hair from the head of Hongi's daughter and later burned it, a dreadful insult accompanied by a curse.[39] As warriors gathered at Kororareka, Captain Brind supported the daughters of Hongi Hika and Rewa, urging their kinsmen to kill Kiwikiwi. He sent a message to several other whaling captains in the bay to fire on Kiwikiwi's settlement. When they refused, he set sail on his ship the *Conway* and left the Bay. Williams had almost managed to persuade the parties to make peace when one of Kiwikiwi's men shot a woman from the other side, and furious fighting broke out between the opposing groups.

During the battle Kiwikiwi's wife and daughter took over a whale-boat and fled to the *Elizabeth*, leaving her master in danger on the beach. As they were rowed away, Kiwikiwi's daughter was shot and killed, although her mother got safely to the ship.[40] In this skirmish about 70 people were wounded and 30 were killed, including six rangatira.[41] These included Hongi's brother and Hengi, a chief from Whangaroa who had come to support Rewa and his daughter. Henry Williams showed great courage, walking alone into the middle of the battle with bullets flying around him, waving a white handkerchief tied to the end of a stick in an effort to stop the fighting. Many of the wounded were carried on board the *Royal Sovereign*, which was anchored 200 yards off Kororareka; while others were taken to Paihia, where they were treated by William Williams. In the aftermath of the battle, a rangatira from Kororareka ran to the beach with a hatchet and cut a piece of liver from the body of an enemy rangatira who was lying there, an offering to his atua. Everyone prepared for further outbreaks of hostilities. It was rumoured that thousands of warriors were about to descend on the Bay.

In the midst of the uproar, Samuel Marsden arrived on 8 March with his daughter Mary, making his sixth visit to the Bay of Islands. When a local man shouted out that Marsden was on board a brig sailing into the Bay, a warrior who had been making a speech on the beach at Paihia stopped in his tracks, dropping his weapon.[42] After landing on the beach, Marsden boarded a boat flying a white flag, and joined Henry Williams in his efforts to make peace.[43] Kiwikiwi had left Kororareka with 1000 warriors from Kawakawa and Taiamai and headed for an inland pā at the junction of the Kawakawa and Waikare rivers, while the allies of Hongi and Rewa (from Whangaroa, Waimate and Rangihoua) were gathering on Moturoa Island.[44]

After days of travelling back and forth between the warring parties, flying a white flag and supported by a number of powerful rangatira including Tareha, Titore and Marsden's friend Te Morenga, a group of four 'commissioners' was appointed to negotiate a settlement – Marsden and a principal chief on Kiwikiwi's side, and Henry Williams with a leading Whangaroa tohunga for Rewa's party. During his visits to the opposing groups, Henry Williams conducted Christian services among them, telling them that 'they were urged to this madness by Satan'.[45] Finally, the two sides agreed to hold a parlay at a bay near Kiwikiwi's encampment. As the canoes set off from Moturoa, Tohitapu informed the missionaries, who rushed in their boats to meet them.

When Rewa's allies landed on the beach where Kiwikiwi's party was assembled, their 'commissioner', the tohunga from Whangaroa, delivered an impressive speech, pacing back and forth in the midst of the crowd. Striding with great dignity towards his counterpart on Kiwikiwi's side, he declared that the sun was beginning to shine upon them. Only two paces from their faces, he stamped his foot, spun around and retraced his steps before striding towards them again, uttering another few sentences urging peace. During this long speech, the Whangaroa tohunga was heard with great attention. He held a short stick in his hand, and finally he chanted a song, snapped the stick in two and cast the pieces at the feet of his counterpart, the 'commissioner' from Kiwikiwi's people, as a sign that their anger was ended.

A rangatira from the other side stood and spoke in reply, and the exchange of speeches went on for hours before it was finally agreed that Kiwikiwi would surrender the district of Kororareka to Rewa's allies as utu for the death of Hengi. The 'commissoner' from Kiwikiwi's side now stood, holding a stick and chanting a song of his own as he snapped the stick in half, throwing the pieces at the feet of the priest from Whangaroa as a sign that peace had been agreed.[46] At this signal the rangatira mustered their warriors, and about a thousand men performed a deafening haka, stripped naked except for their war belts, yelling and firing their muskets in the air. Unable to seek utu in Northland, Hengi's sons felt compelled to find vengeance elsewhere, and organised an expedition to Tauranga where they suffered a severe defeat at the hands of Ngai Te Rangi.[47]

Letter to King William IV from the northern rangatira

While this southern expedition was under way, the CMS missionary William Yate, who was based at the inland mission station at Waimate, visited Port Jackson with Rewa, one of the rangatira at Kerikeri. When the French corvette *La Favorite* arrived in Sydney harbour, Rewa met her captain. Back in the Bay, rumours began to circulate that *La Favorite* was on its way to New Zealand to seize the country for France; and when Rewa and Yate arrived back in the Bay of Islands in September 1831, this gossip spread like wildfire.

From the outset, relationships between the northern rangatira and the French had been turbulent. In 1769, for instance, when the French commander Jean de Surville arrived in Tokerau, just a month after James Cook's visit to the Bay of Islands, his men had kidnapped a young rangatira named Ranginui and carried him off to South America, where he drowned off the coast. Three years later when Marion du Fresne arrived in the Bay of Islands from the French East Indies, despite his romantic view of Māori as 'noble savages', his men broke various tapu, and along with many of his sailors du Fresne was captured, killed and eaten.[48] In the aftermath, du Fresne's men killed many local people.

By contrast, relationships between northern Māori and the British had generally been cordial. When the *Endeavour* arrived off the northern coast in 1769, for instance, Tapua, the father of Patuone and Waka Nene, had met the ship at sea and presented the strangers with a gift of fish. In return, Captain Cook gave him a red garment, a chiefly gift that established a relationship between his kin group and the British.[49] When he landed in the Bay of Islands, Cook had escaped an attempt to ambush him and some of his officers on Motuarohia Island, and his mana remained intact. Neither he nor local Māori sought to avenge themselves for this skirmish.

Given this history, northern Māori found it easy to believe that the 'tribe of Marion' intended to seek utu for his death, and turned to the British for help. After hearing about the imminent arrival of the French corvette, several rangatira visited Henry Williams to ask him how they could seek protection from King William IV. On 3 October 1831, when *La Favorite* sailed into the Bay, David Taiwhanga, the Nga Puhi warrior turned farmer who had recently been baptised by Henry Williams, came running to tell Marianne that the French corvette had arrived with 400 men on board, and that these people were enemies of King William, who had come to spy out the land. He urgently asked her for a British flag to fly from the flagpole, to show that the Bay of Islands leaders were allies of the British. When she told him that the halyard was broken, he borrowed her new washing line to hoist the flag. Soon afterwards when Cyrille La Place, the French commander, and several officers came ashore at Paihia, Marianne gave them tea. According to her account, they expressed great contempt for Māori, and when David Taiwhanga knelt down to talk with John Williams, a toddler, La Place exclaimed 'Diable!' (Devil!)[50]

The following day when a hui (gathering) was held at Kerikeri to draft a letter to King William IV, the missionary William Yate acted as the scribe. Thirteen rangatira including Patuone, Waka Nene, Rewa and Titore (mostly from Hokianga or the northern alliance in the Bay of Islands), who had sought advice from Henry Williams,[51] signed the letter with their moko, or facial tattoos, although Kawiti, Pomare and Tareha did not join them. In this letter, the rangatira addressed King William as the 'Rangatira atawhai o Ingarangi' (the caring Chief of England), saying that they had heard he was the great rangatira across the water whose ships had been visiting their country. While they were poor people, with nothing but timber, flax, pigs, pork and potatoes to barter (hoko) with his people, they saw that Europeans had many treasures, and that only his people were kind to them, and the missionaries, who taught them to believe in Jehovah and his son Jesus Christ.

They also told King William that they had heard that the tribe of Marion was coming to take away their lands, and begged him to be their hoa (friend) and take care of these islands, so foreigners (tau iwi) could not harass them and take away their country. If any of the king's people who had escaped on the ships were troublesome, they asked him to be angry with them, so that Māori people did not have to deal with them instead.[52] They signed themselves '*ko matou ko nga Rangatira o te Iwi Maori o Niu Tireni*' (We [excluding the addressees], the Chiefs of the Māori people of New Zealand), signalling an emerging sense of collective identity, and calling their country Niu Tireni, the transliterated form of New Zealand. At that time, it seems, there was no Māori term for the whole country – although in more recent years the name 'Aotearoa' has been used in this way.

In this letter, the northern rangatira asked King William to be their friend and protector. Clearly, some northern rangatira had concluded that the best way to defend their lands and people against foreign incursions was to forge a closer alliance with the British. No doubt Samuel Marsden, Henry Williams and the other missionaries were actively encouraging such a move. After fighting against France in the Napoleonic Wars, for example, it is very unlikely that Henry Williams would have welcomed a strong French presence in New Zealand, and the CMS missionaries were virulently opposed to Roman Catholicism. By this time, too, the missionaries were making inroads in converting local people, who were increasingly adopting British ideas and customs.[53]

When the acting governor of New South Wales, Patrick Lindesay, sent a sloop to the Bay of Islands with a warning to any Frenchmen who tried to claim New Zealand that the country was under British protection, the *Zebra* returned to Port Jackson with the chiefs' letter, which was forwarded to England. As the *Sydney Gazette* reported, this request by the chiefs would 'greatly facilitate that formal occupancy on the part of our nation, which we have so frequently and so strongly urged, and on which the future peace and welfare of these colonies will so materially depend'.[54] At this time, however, Henry Williams and his fellow missionaries doubted whether it was in the interests of Māori for their country to be brought under British control. As we have seen, Williams disagreed with Marsden's approach to the missionary enterprise, which relied upon European technology and skills to open a way for the Gospel, urging instead 'the importance of first seeking the spiritual good of these people. . . . In speaking upon the unsearchable riches of Christ, the study of the language [is] the main object, until every one [can] declare to those around in his own tongue the glad tidings of the gospel of peace.'[55]

To the missionaries' joy, some Māori were converting to Christianity at last, and there was enthusiasm for learning to read and write and study the Scriptures, which William Williams was translating into Māori. Local Māori were giving up stone tools and weapons, bartering these to the missionaries, who sent them back to their families and friends in England. According to Henry Williams, 'quietness and good order has succeeded to their native wildness, and now we never hear anything of their songs or witness their dances'.[56] Carving and tattooing, which the missionaries abhorred, had been largely abandoned, although tohunga from Hauraki sometimes visited for this purpose,[57] for as local Māori told the missionaries, 'We really must just have a few lines on our lips; else when we grow old our lips will shrivel, and we will be so very ugly.'[58]

In October 1831, when Henry Williams visited Rotorua, many of the people asked him to teach them the catechism and to read and write; and the rangatira asked him to tell them about British laws, expressing 'great wonder that chiefs were as amenable to the law as a poor man, and said it would not be so with them'.[59] Some strangers who arrived gazed at him in amazement 'at hearing things so entirely opposed to their ideas'.[60] As Māori heard the word of God, Williams hoped they would soon give up fighting and adopt other ways of resolving disputes, without the imposition of British control.

Inter-tribal fighting

During this period, Henry Williams and his fellow missionaries veered between delight as increasing numbers of Māori began to listen to their preaching, and despair as many powerful rangatira resolutely ignored what they had to say, holding fast to tapu practices, and continuing to seek utu for deaths and insults. According to Williams, Māori often told them that the Europeans would soon take the land, 'for we increase while they decrease'.[61] Although the missionaries were greatly relieved when the warring parties made peace after the Girls' War at Kororareka, the defeat of Hengi's sons by Ngai Te Rangi at Tauranga gave a new cause for utu against the southern tribes.

In January 1832 a taua led by the Nga Puhi rangatira Titore, Tareha, Wharepoaka, Rewa and his brother Moka, and the tohunga Tohitapu headed south in a fleet of eleven war canoes to seek utu for the deaths of Hengi's sons.[62] The missionary ship *Active*, and Henry Williams with his fellow missionaries William Fairburn and James Kemp in the little schooner *Karere* (Messenger), sailed with them, hoping to persuade them to make peace. They stopped at Waikare, where Henry asked Titore why the canoes did not travel as a fleet. Titore answered that 'it was their usual way for each

The mission ship accompanying a war fleet to the south, by William Yate, 1835.

party to go where they liked, that everyone was his own chief'. That night Williams exclaimed in his journal, 'What want of wisdom, even in a worldly point of view!'[63] The travelling party set up camp at Waikare, cooking their food on shore, since cooked food (which is noa, or common) was not allowed in tapu war canoes. The following morning, Titore conducted a ceremony of propitiation, taking a clump of seaweed from the sea, dipping it in the ocean and then tying it to a tree with karakia to ensure that the sea would be calm and safe.[64]

When the fleet landed at Tutukaka, Tohitapu communed with his atua, his eyes rolling in his head. On 13 January, Titore and Rewa decided to hold a general muster. Williams vividly described how 400 warriors prepared for this occasion, polishing the brass on their muskets and donning waistcloths, fine cloaks or scarlet mantles decorated with dogs' hair before parading in groups, muskets or sabres held upright, to the beach. There they gathered in two opposing parties, rushing at each other before joining in an uproarious haka, rolling back their eyes, poking out their tongues and leaping in the air. Afterwards, the warriors sat on the beach, leaving a space in the centre where the orators ran back and forth, speaking about the forthcoming conflict with Ngai Te Rangi.[65]

Several days later, when the fleet arrived off the Coromandel Peninsula, they saw the great fighting chief Tareha (a huge, imposing man who later played a prominent role in the Treaty of Waitangi debates) pass by in a tapu

'Tareha to the life', by William Bambridge, 1844.

canoe with his three wives, carrying the body of Hengi who had been killed during the Girls' War. They were heading for the place where Hengi's sons had been killed during their expedition to the south. A son of Tareha's, who had died long ago and turned into a taniwha, accompanied this waka mamae (canoe of pain). The war fleet was also under a tapu, and the warriors could not eat or spit or smoke their pipes on board their canoes, or the taniwha would punish these infractions.

When the taniwha appeared to Tohitapu, he complained that some members of the taua had broken the tapu, and threatened to raise a storm to punish them. Hearing about this, Williams told his companions that the English were the masters of the ocean, and went everywhere in their large vessels without worrying about such fantastic creatures, but they ignored him.[66] Dismayed by their failure to take any notice of what he said, he decided to return to the Bay of Islands.

Meanwhile, Fairburn and Kemp had been taken by some local rangatira to Mokoia, the former stronghold of Hinaki, the rangatira from Thames who had been killed by Hongi Hika. Since Hinaki's death the place had been abandoned, and their companions conducted a tapu-raising ceremony with a piece of beef on the end of a stick, reciting karakia to render the place noa (unrestricted). When Fairburn reproached them, saying that they were talking to 'the god of this world who had blinded their eyes, their reply was that it was the New Zealand custom'. These men hoped to restore the mana of the place (which they expressed as whakarangatira – make chiefly) by bringing the missionaries to live there.[67]

In late February, Henry Williams decided to make another attempt to stop the Nga Puhi taua from attacking Tauranga. Arriving at Moehau on the *Karere*, where he and his companions found no signs of the expedition, he exclaimed, 'Very apprehensive they have all passed on and probably commenced their murderous and wicked proceedings unless restrained by the mighty hand of God. Poor creatures how greatly they need all we can do for them. Every man's hand is against his brother, surely the land is polluted with blood.'[68] On 3 March when he met Titore, Rewa and their warriors at Whangamata, Henry redoubled his efforts to persuade them to abandon the taua against Ngai Te Rangi.

The following day, a Sunday, Williams attended a divination ritual conducted by two tohunga, one very old, emaciated man and Tohitapu, the elderly northern priest. All those who attended were placed under a strict tapu, and forbidden to eat or drink.[69] The two tohunga were accompanied by eight rangatira, all naked, who set up sticks (called hau, according to some authorities) in rows,[70] each about a foot long and representing the life force of a canoe of one of the contending parties. After asking Tohitapu about his dreams and talking about his own, the other priest moved in a trance among the sticks, knocking about a third of them over, a sign that these canoes would be destroyed in the forthcoming campaign; although the sticks representing the missionaries' vessels remained upright, indicating that they would be safe. That evening, Williams held a service attended by about a hundred members of the war expedition.

When they arrived at Tauranga Harbour, they found Rewa already attacking Otumoetai pā. Although Williams implored Titore, Tohitapu and Rewa to stop the fighting, they ignored him. On 8 March when Fairburn and Kemp went ashore, they found that the fighting was desultory, with no deaths on either side. They visited Kiharoa, the principal rangatira at Otumoetai pā, who told them, 'Go, in the name of us all to Ngapuhi and tell them we wish for peace. They gave the first anger and now they make war upon us for a requital of their own aggression.'[71] When they delivered this message to Henry Williams, however, he told them that Nga Puhi were in no mood to settle the quarrel.

On 10 March Williams watched an attack on the pā, horrified as he saw women and little children running out to pick up spent shot and bullets, taking them back to the defenders. At the same time, his accounts of these battles describe fighting that was not particularly deadly, with attackers sheltering behind rocks, and light casualties being inflicted on either side. Even during these musket wars, the clashes were not always fatal. Once again, Williams drew on his naval experience to deplore the tactics adopted by the defenders, remarking: 'Had the enemy acted with any thought, and with that courage known to Europeans, they might have planted themselves within two hundred yards of the canoes, and thrown all into confusion; but they were savages, and consequently their movements less destructive.'[72]

During the skirmishes that followed, his efforts to persuade the rangatira to stop fighting were futile. Rewa declared, 'As long as there is fern root for digging and fish for catching, we'll remain from one month up to twelve, till we ultimately sit down as conquerors in their Pa.'[73] On 12 March three men were wounded in the pā, and one warrior from Nga Puhi was killed. The next day, four men were killed in the pā and four more mortally wounded, while Nga Puhi lost only one of their contingent. That afternoon a cutter commanded by Hans Tapsell, a European who lived at Maketu and had married the sister of a powerful Bay of Islands rangatira, arrived with a supply of several cannons and ammunition for the northern taua.[74] Realising once again that his efforts were futile, Henry Williams decided to return to the Bay of Islands, writing despondently:

> Felt very weary in body, and much distress of mind at the present state of things in this land. All is dark, dreary and dire confusion. By vessels from the Southward we hear of nothing but war and blood shed, of the assemblies of large bodies of natives armed with muskets gone forth utterly to annihilate all whom they may meet, but we have this assurance – the Lord is faithful. It is a season which demands earnest and constant prayer of the church on behalf of the nations of the earth, that they may be delivered from the chains of darkness.[75]

After a week's rest, Williams decided to make yet another attempt to stop the war, sailing back to Tauranga with Fairburn on the *Active*. At a meeting with Tohitapu, Tareha, Titore and Rewa, some of the warriors confessed that they were sick of fighting. They had almost run out of food, and their repeated attacks on Otumoetai had failed to breach the defences, even when they lined up six cannons and fired them at the pā. All of the cannonballs flew over the palisades, and the northern taua had been repulsed.[76] As Moka remarked bitterly, 'The Atua of the Pakeha had altogether enfeebled all their efforts.'[77] Nevertheless, the northern rangatira declined to make peace. Depressed and frustrated, Williams decided to sail back once again to the Bay of Islands. Off the east coast of Coromandel the *Active* was hit by a violent storm and almost wrecked on the rocks.[78]

When they returned home, Williams found that a plague of English rats was attacking the food stores, which the local people attributed to their neglect of their ancestors. There was also a great deal of sickness in the Bay, and 'the natives spoke of their having been makutud, bewitched by us and consequently they were all dying'.[79] According to Fairburn, the local people believed that the atua of the missionaries was attacking their hau, or life force, and would turn the land upside down, killing them all while leaving the missionaries unharmed.[80] In late July, when canoes from the southward expedition began to straggle back to the Bay of Islands, having failed to win a victory against Ngai Te Rangi, some of the warriors complained that their guns had failed to shoot straight, which they also blamed on the missionaries.[81]

Soon afterwards, the Hokianga rangatira Patuone came to see Williams, saying that he had decided to go and live in the south, where he would try to make peace between the northern and southern tribes. Williams was glad to hear this because he admired Patuone, the high-born tohunga and warrior from Hokianga, although he had refused to convert to Christianity:

> He is certainly a first rate native, tho as yet no signs of changed nature. Blind to spiritual wants, he knows no Heaven he fears no Hell, and is daily led captive of the wicked one. He stated that he was going to the Southd. to live which was truly gratifying intelligence, as it may tend much to the preservation of peace.[82]

In February 1833, when Titore and Tareha resumed their attacks on the Tauranga tribes, the missionary ships followed them south once again. After spending a month with the northern war expedition in Tauranga on this occasion, trying to negotiate a peace settlement, Henry Williams finally acknowledged that his efforts with these 'overgrown, self-willed perverse children' had failed.[83]

Upon his return to the Bay of Islands, Tohitapu came to see Williams, saying that he had heard on board the European ships that the missionaries intended 'to take the land, and make slaves of the Chiefs, and that we were to receive a number of dollars for each person who became a believer'.[84] Over the following days, Williams was often asked how much money the missionaries had been paid for the people they had converted.[85] When he visited Kororareka, he saw the sailors thronging the grog shops, which were decked with flags. The local people called these shops the whare karakia o Hatana, the churches of Satan, where his followers worshipped the Devil.[86]

James Busby, British Resident

In the midst of these events, on 6 May 1833, news came that a British Resident, James Busby, had arrived in the Bay of Islands. Since the Bigge Commission's deliberations, there had been much debate in Britain about how best to handle the relationship with New Zealand, where increasing numbers of European ships were arriving and many offences were being committed by their crews, against both Māori and Europeans. Bigge had concluded that while the jurisdiction of the governors of New South Wales legally extended as far as New Zealand, it did not support a criminal authority being established; and recommended this should be done.[87]

In 1823 an Act had been passed by the British Parliament giving the New South Wales legal system the power to prosecute, try and punish British subjects who committed offences in New Zealand. Since New Zealand 'was not subject to His Majesty', however, they had to be returned to Australia for this purpose; but as the new British Resident in New Zealand, Busby was given no effective powers for this purpose.[88]

In Britain, representatives of the Church Missionary Society made much of the disreputable conduct of many visiting sailors and runaway convicts in New Zealand, and the thefts, assaults, kidnappings, rapes and murders they committed. In New South Wales, there was also a concern that these offences, along with musket fighting among Māori groups, were threatening the trade with New Zealand, a rich source of flax, timber, seals, whale oil, pork and other supplies. In 1832, James Busby, a Scottish settler in New

*James Busby, by
Richard Read, 1832.*

South Wales, had sent a *Brief Memoir Relative to the Islands of New Zealand*
to the Secretary of State for the Colonies in Britain. Although at that time
he had never visited the country, Busby described the rich variety of commodities available in New Zealand and the difficulties caused by runaway
convicts, citing the case of Captain Stewart of the *Elizabeth*, who in 1830
had given a passage to Te Rauparaha and a taua of 100 warriors to Banks
Peninsula. Here Te Rauparaha had lured his enemy Tamaiharanui and his
wife, eight-year-old daughter and his niece on board, on the pretext of trading muskets for flax.

After seizing Tamaiharanui and his family, Te Rauparaha and his warriors
had attacked his settlement, killing several hundred people and enslaving
dozens. Tamaiharanui strangled his daughter to save her from the fate that
awaited him and his wife and niece at Kapiti Island, where they were slowly
tortured to death by the widows of men killed by his relatives. Although
Stewart's role in this affair led to him being placed on trial in Port Jackson as

Te Rauparaha,
by Edward Abbot,
June 1845.

an accomplice to murder, the evidence of Tamaiharanui's people was disallowed on the grounds that they were 'heathens' and the New South Wales courts had no jurisdiction over New Zealand, and Stewart went unpunished.

In his *Memoir*, Busby hinted that the French and Russian governments were interested in New Zealand, and the French wanted to take over the country. While deploring the custom of kai tangata (eating people) among Māori, he attributed this to 'a nice feeling of honour on points that concern his dignity, that leads him to perceive and resent any slight or insult offered to his person. But he is not distinguished for ferocity and cruelty to the enemy, than for a strength of attachment to his kindred.' He spoke with admiration about the Māori who had visited Port Jackson, who 'evinced a curiosity and penetration which would have been considered as the characteristics of an educated foreigner, rather than of an unenlightened savage'.[89] In this document, Busby proposed that an 'authorised agent or resident' invested with the authority of a magistrate should be sent to New Zealand. Such a resident would be able to enter into a separate treaty with each chief to protect the mutual safety of British subjects and their people in their 'commercial intercourse', in part by delivering up runaway convicts. He suggested that with the help of the missionaries, 'some of whom are very enlightened men', the resident could persuade Māori to 'abandon the ferocious character of the savage and the cannibal, for the principles of a milder religion, and the habits of a more civilized people'.[90]

At Edinburgh University, Busby had learned about the stadial theories developed by Adam Ferguson and others during the Scottish Enlightenment. In these models, the static hierarchies of the Great Chain of Being were mobilised with the addition of 'the arrow of time', and human history became an inevitable progress from 'savagery', characterised by tight communal bonds, to 'barbarism', transformed by the introduction of private property and governed by military leadership, to commercial or 'polite society' featuring an extensive division of labour. With the assistance of his patron Lord Haddington, who lived close to his family home in Britain, Busby put himself forward as a candidate for the position of British Resident in New Zealand, eager to assist Māori in making these steps towards 'civilisation'. After sending 40 pint bottles of wine (made at his vineyard in New South Wales) and a pamphlet he had written about viticulture to Lord Goderich, the Secretary of State for War and the Colonies,[91] in March 1832 he was awarded the post.

By this time Lord Goderich had received the letter written to King William by the northern chiefs. In an attachment, Sir Richard Bourke, the governor of New South Wales, had suggested that a British Resident should be appointed in New Zealand, backed by a contingent of soldiers. In his reply to Bourke, Lord Goderich wrote that a resident should be sent, but without the powers of a magistrate or any troops to support him:

> After the Resident shall have conciliated the good will of the native Chiefs and in some measure restored that confidence between them and British Subjects, which the bad faith of the latter has so unhappily interrupted, you will be better able to judge in what manner it will be practicable to support the authority of the Resident without exciting the jealousy or illwill of the Natives.[92]

Nevertheless, the government strongly supported the need to punish offenders and punish atrocities:

The unfortunate natives of New Zealand, unless some decisive measures of prevention be adopted, will I fear, be shortly added to the number of those barbarous tribes, who, in different parts of the Globe, have fallen a sacrifice to their intercourse with civilised men, who bear and disgrace the name of Christians.[93]

He assured Bourke that a 'South Seas Bill' would soon be passed which aimed to make it possible to prevent and punish crimes committed by British subjects in the islands in the Pacific Ocean, allowing the New South Wales legislature to pass laws and regulations on such matters. In fact, the Bill failed when members of the British Parliament pointed out that they could not legislate for a foreign country like New Zealand.

In his instructions to James Busby, Bourke echoed Goderich's sentiments, making it plain that his duty as resident was 'to endeavour, by every possible method, to rescue the natives from the evils to which their intercourse with Europeans had exposed them'. His task was to encourage them to move towards 'a settled form of government', by 'the skilful use of those powers which educated men possesses over the wild or half civilized savage'.[94] The fact that these 'powers' were illusory is no doubt why in his role as resident, Busby would long be referred to as a 'man-of-war without guns'.

Busby finally set sail for New Zealand on HMS *Imogene*, arriving in the Bay of Islands on 6 May 1833. Henry Williams reacted to the new resident's arrival with scepticism, grumbling about being forced to vacate his study, since there was no 'other place in the neighbourhood where we can deposit so great a personage', and serving Busby a meal of a few slices of bacon and pipi (shellfish, *Paphies australis*) during one rain-soaked visit, as 'a good introduction to our table, as many run away with the idea that we have little else to do than to attend to our personal comfort and convenience'.[95]

Busby brought with him a reply from Lord Goderich to the rangatira's letter to King William IV, which he asked Henry Williams to translate into Māori. In Williams' translation, Lord Goderich addressed the rangatira as 'E hoa mā' (Friends), saying that the king had instructed him to tell them that he had received their letter, and was glad to hear that the cause of their apprehension had passed (i.e. the threat of a French invasion), and that he hoped they would have no further trouble that might disturb the trade (hokohoko) between them and his people of England. He added:

The King is unhappy to hear about the bad deeds of his people towards the inhabitants of Nu Tirani, and if they suffer further injuries, the King will be angry and seek utu from those bad people according to the customs [tikanga] of their own country, whenever they can be seized and tried. The King says that you should have peaceful thoughts [kia pai marie nga wakaro] towards his people, one to the other.

And the King has sent Te Puhipi [Busby], the man on board this ship, to stay among you as the King's man, as a mediator [kai wakarite] between the maori people of Nu Tirani and King William's people living with them as traders. It will be his task to judge all bad deeds that you bring before him, and to prevent the arrival of those who have committed bad deeds in their own countries or escaped from confinement, and to seize such people who have arrived among you.

The King's man will seek to protect the people of Nu Tirani from the bad deeds of the people from England, and in return, the King suggests you repay [utua] this thought by being his friend and protector, so that he can accomplish these aims and achieve good things for you, because you have decided to become friends with the King of England.[96]

Goderich signed himself, 'Your friend [hoa], Te Koreriha.'

As in the rangatira's letter, New Zealand was described as Nu Tirani, and its inhabitants as 'maori' – i.e. ordinary or indigenous people – without this term being capitalised and treated as a proper name. In this translation, there is no element of hierarchy. Rather, Henry Williams's translation of Lord Goderich's letter suggests an alliance between King William and the rangatira as hoa, or friends, with the new British Resident as a kaiwhakarite, or mediator, who would aim to prevent Māori from being harmed by British subjects. The rangatira are urged to protect James Busby, so that he can carry out this role, and to be peaceful towards the British, knowing that the king will do his best to seek utu for any injuries to them, according to the laws of his country.

On 17 May 1833, as canoes landed at daybreak at Paihia from around the Bay of Islands for the meeting with Busby, the sky looked dark and menacing, and their crews began to build shelters for the principal rangatira who had come to greet the resident.[97] According to Henry Williams, they were anxious to know whether the warship would be staying in the bay, and if the soldiers would be coming ashore. The rangatira instructed their warriors to polish their muskets to ensure that the new resident received an impressive challenge. As the boats were lowered from HMS *Imogene*, seven guns were fired in honour of the new resident, and Busby landed, accompanied by Captain Blackwood and his officers and Henry Williams and his fellow missionaries.

They were greeted by three white-haired orators, and then a host of crouching warriors yelled out in unison, leaped up and rushed to within a few paces of the visiting party, where they performed an impassioned haka, brandishing their muskets, 'to the no small astonishment of the strangers'.[98] Other rangatira followed with their speeches of welcome, one group advancing with one of Tohitapu's wives at their head, performing a 'kind of dance'.[99] Finally, the visitors, about 600 in number, moved into the chapel yard, where seats had been provided for the Europeans, and a table, on which Lord Goderich's letter was laid in a sealed envelope. Busby broke the seal and read out the letter in English, followed by Henry Williams who read out his translation in Māori. Afterwards Busby made a speech in reply to the chiefs, which William Williams fluently translated.

Like Lord Goderich's letter, the text of Busby's speech has survived in both languages. In his remarks, Busby assured the rangatira that the king wanted them to be his hoa pūmau, his lasting friends, and for the hokohoko, or trade, between Māori people and pākehā to be tika, or proper. If someone troubled them, he remarked, 'you will see that I am the friend for Māori people'. He told them that it was the custom of the king of England to send one of his people to distant lands, those places inhabited by his friends, and that he was the person sent to live in their country. They would see that this would be good for them, a bond of trade between the English people and themselves, and an act by the king of England upholding their chiefly status (wakarangatiratanga), because he had made them his friends. Busby added that representatives of the king such as himself should not be interfered with, or their children or prized possessions. They were sent to do good, to take care of others (atawai), and keep the peace (maunga rongo). If such a person was harmed, all pākehā would be angry. He had heard that the rangatira and people of New Zealand were good to those pākehā who were kind to them, and he had no fear of living among them.

Having assured them of his wish to befriend them, Busby gave the rangatira a lesson in stadial theory. He said that in past times, the people of Great Britain had been very like themselves, lacking good houses, clothing and food. They painted their bodies, and wore the skins of wild beasts. Every village fought against the other, and many people perished, as they did now in New Zealand. Then God (Atua) sent his child to the world, to teach all people not to hate or destroy, but to love and treat each other kindly. Once the people of England listened, they stopped going to war, and all the tribes were united. These good people began to build large houses, because no one came to destroy them, they cultivated the land and had plenty of food, and their animals multiplied, and they became wealthy. Finally, Busby asked the chiefs, did they want to be like the people of England? If so, they should listen to the word of God, which he had given to his missionaries. Instead of eating fern-root, they could eat bread (taro); and once they had plenty of food, they could gather flax, and timber and foodstuffs to trade with the ships, and acquire clothing and everything they wanted, and become rich. If they did not work, there would be no taonga, however. It was from work, and peace, and living quietly that these things would come.[100]

When the chiefs spoke in reply, about ten in number, one of them assured Busby that he should have brought soldiers to protect him, since the local people were 'very wicked'. Another quoted gossip in the Bay which claimed that the missionaries and the resident would be paid a certain number of dollars for every Māori who converted to Christianity, adding, 'You are welcome – *even if you are the man who has come to sell us!*'[101] Busby presented about forty leading rangatira with a gift of a blanket and six pounds of tobacco each, and Williams invited the European officers, local residents and some of the missionaries to dine in his house, about fifty guests in all. Soon afterwards, the rangatira and their people were fed outside with beef, potatoes and 'stir-about' (a paste of flour and water), served in 800 flax baskets. The European guests were served a separate meal, which no doubt sent its own message. Henry Williams was affronted when the commander of the *Imogene*, Captain Blackwood, insisted that he had to leave the Bay on Sunday, breaking the Sabbath. When Williams crossed the Bay to Kororareka to hold the Sunday service, he met the local rangatira Moka and his older brother Wharerahi, who remarked that it was beneath their dignity to attend the service, 'because they were chiefs'.

The next day Henry Williams escorted Busby to Kororareka, the scene of the Girls' War, where they were served a feast of pigeons, shellfish and kūmara. The tohunga Tohitapu, who was now very ill, refused to discuss the afterlife with Williams, preferring to talk about the Tauranga campaigns.

Williams was still trying to negotiate with the Waitangi people to purchase
land where the frame of Busby's prefabricated house could be erected, but
they were reluctant to enter into a sale; and on 20 June when they met
Pomare, a former chief of Kororareka who had been forced to cede the
town after the Girls' War, Busby refused to meet him because he had seized
a small vessel from a European who had not paid his debts. Pomare was furious, and Williams had to reassure him that he did not share Busby's view on
this matter.

During June 1833 when Busby tried to identify runaway convicts to be
sent back to Port Jackson on the *Governor Phillip*, the rangatira frustrated
him by saying that they could not be sure which Europeans in their districts were former prisoners, and which were free men. He wrote to his
brother Alexander that he had ordered a passport in Māori to be printed,
so that British subjects without a passport could be removed from New
Zealand. He also spoke about his plans to build a parliament house where
the rangatira could meet to discuss their collective affairs:

> With them I expect to establish an influence which will give me almost entire
> authority over the Northern part of the Island. . . . I have no fear but I shall
> be able to bring them forward in the formation of political Institutions –
> when I have once got them to assemble and taught them to decide questions
> affecting them all by the will of the Majority, the foundation of a Government
> is laid.[102]

Busby's grandiose conception of his own status and influence was not supported by other observers. Māori were demographically and politically
dominant, and according to most accounts Busby was not greatly respected,
either by the missionaries or settlers, or by the rangatira.

On 14 July 1833, Tohitapu died.[103] Visiting the tūpāpaku (corpse) of the
old tohunga, Henry Williams sketched him sitting up dressed in a cloak, his
head decorated with feathers. When Tohitapu's relatives asked whether they
could mourn him in the old way, crying and slashing themselves, Williams
refused; and when they began to fire their muskets as a sign of grief, he confiscated their guns.

Later that year, Williams began to negotiate with Marsden's friend
Te Morenga to purchase land at Taiamai as a 'family estate' for his eleven
children (eight of whom had been born in New Zealand),[104] and for a

Tohitapu, by Henry Williams, (n.d).

township for local Māori. The people in that district had long been asking for a missionary, and Williams promised that his eldest son Edward would join them once he had trained as a doctor in England. Henry had written to the CMS three years earlier, seeking permission to purchase land for the missionaries' children,[105] and this transaction was finally settled in February 1834.[106] This was the first of Williams's land purchases in the Bay, which later returned to haunt him – during the debates over the Treaty of Waitangi, for instance, and many years after when Bishop Augustus Selwyn and Sir George Grey tried to check his influence among Māori by attacking his land dealings, and having him dismissed from the mission.[107]

In January 1834 the hahunga ritual for Tohitapu was held, his bones laid out in state for the mourning rituals, along with the preserved heads of about twenty of his relatives (in the same way as today, photographs of deceased relatives are placed at the end of the coffin). Several days later, when HMS

Alligator arrived in the Bay of Islands, Busby spoke with its captain about seizing the small vessel that Pomare had confiscated from a European for non-payment of a debt. Williams did not approve of this plan, saying that it would be provocative and hazardous. Although Busby persuaded the *Alligator*'s commander to anchor off Pomare's pā in preparation for shelling the town, the commander took the precaution of asking Williams to make further inquiries. When he interviewed Pomare, Williams discovered that the European concerned was at fault, having taken a cargo of timber without payment. Busby's efforts to assert his authority were often ill-judged, and the controversies over the land he was occupying at Waitangi were an ongoing source of dissension.

In March 1834 Busby called a number of leading rangatira to meet at Waitangi and choose an official flag for New Zealand. In 1830, when a Hokianga-built barque *Sir George Murray* had been seized in Port Jackson on the grounds that it was not officially registered, the powerful Hokianga chiefs Patuone and Taonui were on board. Māori were trading to Australia and further afield, and needed the ships they owned or hired to be respected outside New Zealand. Since that time the Hokianga ship-building business had been sold to a local trader, Thomas McDonnell, a former naval officer, who was anxious to get his vessels registered. Soon after Busby's arrival in New Zealand, he proposed to the secretary of state that the northern rangatira should be asked to choose a flag for New Zealand, to fly on these ships; and if two-thirds of them agreed on the design and petitioned King William to approve it, this would be a good first step towards some kind of British governance. Governor Bourke approved of Busby's proposal, sending him a draft design for a flag that included four horizontal blue bars on a white background and the Union Jack in the top left-hand corner. Busby reported that the missionaries (and presumably the rangatira) did not like it because it did not feature the tapu colour red, a sign among Māori that an object or person was imbued with ancestral power. Three new designs were sent on board the *Alligator*, one of which was the mission's own flag, that had been flown on the *Active*.

On 20 March, a gathering was held at Waitangi attended by 26 principal rangatira, including Waikato (Hongi's companion on his visit to King George IV) and Hone Heke. A tent was erected, divided by a rope, and as the leading chiefs were called by name they crawled under the rope, joining the group that was permitted to vote on the design of the new flag, leaving those rangatira who were left on the other side of the rope feeling insulted and disgruntled. For Māori at that time, flags and flagpoles acted as a means of communication between people and their atua or ancestor 'gods', evoking the rāhui poles erected to declare a tapu on a particular area, often decorated with part of a rangatira's cloak, and the hau, or rods, used in divination rituals. This custom traced back to the Society Islands, where carved posts were erected on stone ahu (altars) on marae as a perch for sacred birds (or manu tahi) which delivered messages to and from the ancestors. In parts of New Zealand, similar carved posts were sometimes seen outside chiefs' houses, or in the palisades guarding a fortified village.

In the Society Islands, too, white flags were used as a sign of peace, and when the first Europeans arrived in New Zealand, flags from the ships had been brought ashore and flown. As we have seen, when the French frigate *La Favorite* arrived in the Bay of Islands, a local chief had insisted that the Union Jack should be flown at Paihia to announce their alliance with the British. By this time, many rangatira had their own flags which they flew from the sterns of their canoes, or from flagpoles above their villages, as a sign of mana or ancestral power; and when Hongi was on his deathbed, the missionaries had arranged for a canoe flying a red flag to be sent to the Bay of Islands as a sign that he had expired.

By now, Busby had learned some Māori, and on this occasion he addressed the rangatira without an interpreter. After speaking, he allowed the chiefs inside the roped-off enclosure to vote on the three flags on display. According to his own account, twelve of these rangatira voted for the mission flag, ten for another design, and two for the third option, although according to other eyewitnesses, many of the chiefs were baffled by the proceedings. When Busby declared the mission flag the winner, it was hoisted on a flagstaff next to a taller staff that flew the Union Jack, and the crew on board the *Alligator* fired a 21-gun salute in its honour. Once the flag (known as Te Kara) had been adopted, it was regarded as an emblem of the mana of the rangatira.[108]

Afterwards, Busby invited the 50 Europeans who attended this gathering to a meal in the residency, while his Māori guests were given a meal of stirabout. This was an insult, because in Māori etiquette, lavish gifts of food were a sign of mana, both for the giver and the recipient. Nor would the rangatira have missed the fact that their flag was flown on a pole that was lower than that on which the Union Jack fluttered. As the Europeans were

enjoying their meal inside the residency, rangatira strode up and down outside, delivering fiery speeches. One of them, Kiwikiwi, asked:

> How have we come into this situation of having to hoist a flag on our boats
> to ensure our own safety? It is through our own fault that we have to do
> it, if we had been more united among ourselves, if we had had no enmity
> of one horde against another, we would have been able to oppose their
> landing.

Marsden's friend Te Morenga answered:

> I will tell you why we had to bow down before the will of the strangers.
> Would any of us really urge other New Zealanders to drive strangers away
> from the landing-place? . . . Our fault was not in allowing the strangers to
> land, it was in our setting upon them and murdering them. Now the ships are
> afraid to approach our coasts, and yet what things we have received through
> the strangers! Whence came the blankets we wear, the tobacco we smoke, the
> pigs and potatoes? It all came from the strangers . . .[109]

Afterwards, when Busby sent the design of the new flag back to Britain,
King William signalled his approval and the Royal Navy was instructed to
respect it.

No doubt many of the rangatira were troubled by the proceedings at
Waitangi, the arrival of British warships, and a sense that the Europeans
were acquiring too much land and power. Six weeks later, Williams was
woken after midnight by a European messenger sent by Busby, who reported
that some local Māori had broken into the residency, where they were firing
guns, and that his household was in an uproar. Williams dressed hastily,
fetched the surgeon from a ship in the Bay, and went with his wife Marianne
to check on Mrs Busby, who had just given birth two days earlier. They
found Busby slightly wounded in the cheek, and his wife in a state of shock.

Soon afterwards, heavily armed boats arrived from three ships, led
by their captains, armed with muskets, pistols, lances and harpoons, and
the sailors roamed around the house, brandishing their guns and swearing vengeance. By then, the attackers had vanished, and it was with some
difficulty that Williams persuaded the sailors to return to their vessels.
At daybreak they found a trail of paper, rags and feathers leading away from

the house, and musket balls embedded in the outer walls. One of these bullets had struck the doorpost in line with where Busby had been standing, sending out a spray of splinters that hit him in the face.[110]

During his first speech to the rangatira upon arriving in the Bay, Busby had insisted that as the king's representative, his person, household, family and possessions were sacrosanct. Incensed by this attack on his family, he wanted to avenge himself on his assailants. Williams sent messengers to the chiefs at Waimate, Kerikeri and Whangaroa to tell them what had happened, perhaps supposing that the culprits were from the southern alliance. As the other missionaries gathered, Rewa, Wharerahi and Titore all arrived to express their concern, followed by Hone Heke.

After calling a meeting of the ships in the Bay, their captains decided to ask the New South Wales governor to send a military contingent to support the British Resident. Governor Bourke ignored their request, however, and would not allow Busby increased protection. On 6 May when Kawiti arrived at Paihia with 400 men, infuriated because he thought that the missionaries were blaming him for the raid on Busby's house, Williams calmed him down. The Waitangi people were still refusing to hand over the land on which Busby's house stood, the attack was almost certainly a muru raid related to this transaction, and Williams was feeling weary and beleaguered.

In the aftermath of the attack on the residency, when the missionary William Yate was about to leave on a visit to England, Titore and Patuone decided to send their own message to King William IV, aiming to strengthen their alliance with the British Crown. Yate was sailing on HMS *Buffalo*, which had been sent to New Zealand to collect spars for the Royal Navy, and these two rangatira had helped Captain Sadler to obtain his cargo. In addition, each of them gave Sadler a greenstone mere and some cloaks as gifts for the king.

On 24 June 1834, Titore sat with Yate and dictated a letter to King William, telling him that the *Buffalo* was fully laden, and hinting that he would like a small ship of his own. He added, 'I have put on board the *Buffalo* a meri ponamu [greenstone mere] and two Garments for you: these are all the things which New Zealanders possess. If I had anything better, I would give it to Captain Sadler for you.'[111] In the Māori text of this letter, Titore gave the name of the mere as Te Puwaro, indicating to the king that this was a significant ancestral taonga, although Yate did not include this name in his translation.

When Titore's letter and these gifts arrived in London, it was delivered to King William IV, whose private secretary wrote to Lord Aberdeen, Secretary of State, instructing that a suit of armour from the Tower of London should be sent as a return gift. After arranging this, Lord Aberdeen wrote to Titore in January 1835, addressing him as 'His Highness Titore' and saluting him as 'Friend and Brother'. He went on to say:

> King William will not forget this proof of your Friendship and he trusts that such mutual good offices will continue to be interchanged between His Majesty's Subjects and the Chiefs and People of New Zealand as may cement the Friendship already so happily existing between the two countries, and advance the commercial interests and wealth of Both.
>
> The King, my Master, further commands me to thank you for your Present, and in return, he desires you will accept a Suit of Armour, such as was worn in former times by His Warriors, but which are now only used by His own Body Guard.
>
> This letter, as well as His Majesty's Royal Present will be conveyed to you through James Busby Esquire, His Majesty's authorised Resident at the Bay of Islands, whose Esteem and Friendship you will do well to cultivate, and who in his turn, will do all in his power to promote your Welfare and that of your Countrymen.[112]

Once again, it is plain that the British authorities were treating New Zealand as a friendly sovereign country; and greeting Titore as an equal of the king. This armour (which still survives, and is kept in the Museum of New Zealand Te Papa Tongarewa) arrived in the Bay of Islands in late November 1835, when Busby delivered it to Titore, who was extremely gratified.[113] Patuone was chagrined that his own presents to the king had not been recognised, although a suit of 'bright armour' was sent to him a year later.

In the meantime, the inquiries into the raid on Busby's house had not been resolved. Hone Heke had been showing a strong interest in Christianity, and as Henry Williams marvelled:

> It is wonderful to see the effect of the Gospel on this man. He has always been regarded as an ill disposed person, perpetually engaged in mischief, whereas now he is quiet, respectful and attentive, and embraces every opportunity to receive instruction himself, and also to impart to others of that little he may

himself possess. He ranks high as a bold daring fellow, a *ware* soldier. I trust by the grace of God he may become an eminent Soldier of the Lord Jesus amongst his benighted country men.[114]

Finally, on 22 October 1834, Hone Heke came to tell Henry Williams that a man named Rete had confessed to the raid on Busby's house. When they informed James Busby, he demanded that Rete and his two accomplices should be executed, on the grounds that his raid had been an attack on the British Crown. Williams refused, saying that as the 'Guardian and Father' of these people, he could not support such bloody measures. After much debate, it was decided that Rete's land at Puketona should be confiscated and handed over to the British government. When Titore arrived with 70 warriors, fully armed, he supported this verdict, and Kawiti also agreed. The HMS *Hyacinth*, which had fortuitously arrived in the Bay of Islands, sailed on 30 October, shortly after the rangatira had decided to ratify Rete's punishment. Naming Rete's land 'Ingarangi' (England), Busby claimed it as a farm for the king of Great Britain.

Although Busby had no real power as British Resident, and no military support, he often attempted to mediate in disputes between Māori and Europeans. At about this time, when Pomare appealed to him over a theft by a European, he showed some respect for Busby by referring to him as the 'Tahuhu', or ridgepole, that bridged the gap between his people and pākehā,[115] while Waka Nene and Taonui in the Hokianga and others pledged their support for the king's whakarite (mediator – literally making things equal).[116]

While Henry Williams was grateful that the crisis over the attack on the residency had apparently been resolved, he was much distressed at the same time by his discussions with Titore and Tareha, who had become intrigued by the teachings of Papahurihia (land turned over), a young tohunga from Rangihoua who combined ancestral beliefs with passages from the Scriptures, and was preaching this new faith in the Bay of Islands and Hokianga. According to Papahurihia, the arrival of the missionaries and their God was causing the land to turn over, killing many people, as had happened in various versions of the creation story when Papatuanuku was separated from Ranginui, and her sons turned her over on her belly. He spoke of a Heaven for Māori, with plenty of flour, sugar, guns and ships, while Hell was reserved for the missionaries.[117] Perhaps inspired by these teachings, Rete remained defiant, and in the end the rangatira failed to drive him off his land, unwilling to provoke further conflicts in the Bay of Islands.

At the end of 1834, when the missionary printer William Colenso arrived in the Bay, he began to print religious texts translated by William Williams and others on a press that he had brought with him. Māori were eager to learn to read and write, and the circulation of these texts increased the mana of the missionaries, and those who mastered these new powers. As Henry Williams remarked:

> Our boys seemed to read over their letters with us with as much pleasure as we did ours to the delight of all around; they repeated them aloud, to the admiration of their auditors, who were struck with wonder at hearing, as they described it, 'a book speak.' – for though they expect that a European can perform any extraordinary thing, yet they cannot understand how it is that a New Zealand youth can possess the same power.[118]

In early 1835, Henry headed south yet again. After landing at Tamaki, where he remarked upon the fertile land watered by many rivers, and the portage where canoes were hauled across the isthmus between the Waitemata and Manukau harbours, he visited two new mission stations that had been established to the south, one at Puriri, near Thames, and the other at Mangapouri, near Te Awamutu. From there, he went on a peace-making mission to Te Horo, a pā on the Waikato River under the command of the brother of Te Wherowhero, the high chief of Tainui, whose people were fighting with Te Kanawa and his people.

During his visit to Te Horo, Williams described the chiefs assembled 'in parliament – a large circle. Three speakers frequently on their legs at once, with several voices joining occasionally.'[119] That night in thick fog, Williams woke up to hear a great squealing sound. It proved to be the atua, speaking in a woman's voice and telling the warriors that there would be a battle, and if they acquitted themselves like men, victory would be theirs.[120]

At this time, debates were conducted outdoors, with the participants sitting on the ground in a circle, listening to the orators who ran back and forth in their midst (except in times of war, such as the Girls' War for instance, when the orators from the opposing parties sat opposite each other as they tried to sort out their differences). Unlike today, where only one orator speaks at once, and the people are often seated in rows on benches with the local people and visitors facing each other across the marae ātea, or speaking ground, there might be more than one orator speaking at one time, and there was no paepae (speakers' benches). Since the arrival of Europeans, the seating arrangements on marae have been transformed, featuring rows of seats (like Victorian schoolrooms). In that early period, however, anyone could speak (although this was usually reserved for the rangatira), and the orators rose up from the gathering, announcing themselves with a chant.

Back in the Bay of Islands, drunkenness was a growing problem among Māori and a major cause of strife and disorder among Europeans, especially visiting sailors. In September 1835 when Henry Williams visited Busby to propose a ban on liquor imports, Busby declined, saying that he would have to get permission from Governor Bourke. To Busby's annoyance, less than two weeks later, Thomas McDonnell, the Hokianga trader who had been appointed an 'Additional British Resident' the previous year without any reference to the resident, declared a ban on the import of spirits to that district, backed by the leading rangatira Patuone, Taonui and Mohi Tawhai, the missionaries and the trader James Clendon.[121] Seeing this as an affront to his authority, Busby complained to Bourke, who showed him scant sympathy. The new resident was gaining a reputation for being self-important and hasty; and from that time on, McDonnell became his ardent enemy, while Williams mistrusted his judgement.

The Declaration of Independence – He Whakaputanga o te Rangatiratanga o Nu Tirene[122]

Several weeks later, Busby was alarmed to receive a letter from Baron de Thierry, the young Frenchman who had met Hongi and Waikato at Cambridge University in 1820, claiming that they had sold him a vast estate in the Hokianga. De Thierry had kept in touch with Thomas Kendall while the missionary was still in New Zealand, asking him to pursue his claim, and after a time in the United States, had decided to come out to New Zealand, visiting Panama en route where he applied for a concession to cut a canal across the isthmus.

When he and his family arrived in the Society Islands in June 1835, de Thierry recruited a fighting force, declared himself the 'king of Nukuhiva' (in the Marquesas), and sent a letter to James Busby, saying that he was on his way to New Zealand to establish a sovereign government under his own leadership. In fact, de Thierry designed the first New Zealand Coat of Arms, featuring two Māori warriors and the motto 'Tenax' – 'tenacity' – also part of the species name for New Zealand flax (*Phormium tenax*).

As always, any hint of a challenge galvanised Busby. Although he thought that de Thierry was probably mad, he decided to speed up his plans to set up a kind of parliament in New Zealand. After his experiences with Rete, he was well aware of the difficulties of getting the chiefs to act in concert, but nevertheless, wrote to Bourke:

> I have resolved to call as early a day as possible a meeting of the Chiefs in order that they may declare the independence of their Country, and assert as a collective body their entire and exclusive right to its Sovereignty, and their determination to maintain that right in its integrity, and treat as a public enemy any person who professes to assume a right of sovereignty within their territories.[123]

Busby also fired off an indignant letter to de Thierry, dismissing his claims, and drafted a message to the European settlers in the Bay, which he had printed as a circular, warning them that he had received a letter from 'a person styling himself Charles, Baron de Thierry, Sovereign Chief of New Zealand, and King of Nukahiva, an Island of the Marquesas', who 'might acquire such an influence over the Simpleminded Natives as would produce effects which cannot be too Anxiously Deprecated', and asking them to exert their influence over local Māori.[124] In his invitation asking the rangatira to meet with him at the residency at Waitangi on 29 October 1835, he asked, 'What should be done with this interfering person? Shall the land be handed over to him, and all you be slaves, or not?'[125]

In the midst of this frenetic activity, Busby drafted a 'Declaration of the Independence of New Zealand', a document which has been analysed in detail by witnesses to Te Paparahi o te Raki Tribunal, and by the Tribunal itself in its massive report on the Declaration and the Treaty. As northern leaders argued in front of the Tribunal, it is likely that the key points in this draft in English had been discussed with key rangatira to ensure that it had their support.[126] In this text, Busby declared their land to be an independent state, claiming all sovereign power and authority within the territories of 'the United Tribes of New Zealand' for the hereditary chiefs and heads of tribes 'in their collective capacity'. In their name, he stated that they would not permit any legislative authority separate from themselves to exist, or any function of government in their territories to be exercised, unless by persons appointed by them, and acting under their authority.

Just how Busby's own role as British Resident could be reconciled with this clause in the Declaration is not clear. Untroubled by this, however, in the English draft he declared that in autumn each year, the hereditary chiefs would meet in Congress at Waitangi to frame laws for the dispensation of justice and the preservation of peace and good order. Autumn was the customary time for large inter-tribal gatherings, when the harvest had been gathered and large-scale feasting, rituals and celebrations were common. He added that the chiefs cordially invited the southern tribes to 'lay aside their private animosities' and join the Confederation – a call that must have seemed ironic, given the frequency with which the northern tribes had gone raiding to the south. In addition, Busby stated in this document that the chiefs agreed to send a copy of the Declaration to the king of England, to thank him for his acknowledgement of their flag, and in return for their friendship and protection for his subjects who had settled in New Zealand, asked the king to 'continue to be the parent of their infant State . . . and its Protector from all attempts upon its independence'.

After drafting this document, Busby sent it to Henry Williams, asking him to translate it into Māori. One of the two Māori texts of the Declaration that survive is in Williams's handwriting with a number of corrections, also in his hand. Some time after that, a young Māori scribe named Eruera Pare made a fair copy.

The Māori version of the Declaration, titled 'He Whakaputanga o te Rangatiratanga o Nu Tirene', has many interesting features. Like all of the letters and addresses in Māori exchanged between rangatira and the British authorities at this time, the Declaration refers to New Zealand by its transliterated name, 'Nu Tirene'. The word 'Independence' is translated as 'Rangatiratanga', and the chiefs themselves described as 'Tino Rangatira' – 'Great Chiefs'. Likewise, their land is described as 'Whenua Rangatira' – a 'Chiefly Land', often used in Māori to describe a land which is prosperous and at peace, and their collectivity was named 'Ko te Wakaminenga o nga Hapu o Nu Tirene' – 'the Gathering of the Hapu of New Zealand'.

Hapū were kin groups, networks of people descended from a common ancestor, and bound together by shared use and occupation of networks of gardens, stretches of forest, eel pools, birding trees, fishing grounds and reefs, and shared activities such as fighting and feasting. Rather than bounded units, as the term 'group' might imply, they were open-ended networks, based on whakapapa (genealogy). As Maori Marsden puts it, a hapū was 'an organism, rather than an organisation'.[127] They were led by rangatira, and elders, or kaumātua. At this time, hapū were the dominant kin groups in the country, along with whānau, or extended families, although larger alliances known as iwi, or tribes – linked networks of hapū loosely bound together by descent and sometimes acknowledging a paramount chief, or ariki – also came together for very large-scale activities.

The Wakaminenga was modelled on these loose alliances, but on a larger scale. In He Whakaputanga, the Declaration of Independence, the British monarch is greeted as a 'matua', a senior relative or parent, playing a similar ritual role to a paramount chief, or ariki, an apical here, or knot, in the kin networks that ties different kin groups together. In reserving sovereignty to the rangatira, however, Williams treated them and the king as equals, translating sovereignty as 'ko te Kingitanga ko te mana i te whenua' – 'the Kingship and mana arising from the land', reserving these for the 'Tino Rangatira', or 'Leading Chiefs'; and saying that they would not allow (tuku) any other people, or any other form of governance (kawanatanga) to lay down laws (wakarite ture) for them, here using the missionary term ture for law, taken from 'torah' in the Bible; whakarite literally means 'making things equal' or 'the same'.

Throughout, the rangatira were referred to by the exclusive pronoun mātou – us rangatira Māori, excluding you foreigners, whether English or French; another sign of an emerging sense of a unified Māori identity. They sent the king their warm affection (aroha) for recognising their flag, promised to welcome (atawai) and take care of (tiaki) the pākehā or white people living ashore, and asked him to be their senior relative or 'parent' (matua) in their immaturity (tamarikitanga, or childhood), lest their Independence (Rangatiratanga) be destroyed.

As Busby wrote to his brother Alexander: 'We had a great meeting of the Chiefs on 29th October, when the Magna Charta of New Zealand was signed.'[128] The only account of this meeting at Waitangi that survives is Busby's official report, although Henry Williams and James Clendon were also present. According to Busby, the 35 leading chiefs who attended this gathering included Titore, Tareha, Pomare, Kawiti, Te Kemara and Kiwikiwi, who universally declared that Baron de Thierry was not welcome in New Zealand, and unanimously supported the Declaration. The rangatira Patuone and his brother Waka Nene, who were delayed by flooding in Hokianga, signed later, as did Te Hapuku from Hawke's' Bay and a signatory for Te Wherowhero in the Waikato – two leading chiefs from the south. The signatories thus included a wide range of rangatira from the northern and southern alliances in the Bay of Islands, from Hokianga and elsewhere in the north, as well as the two ariki from the south.

He Whakaputanga was a major new step in bringing different hapū together, although there was much scepticism among the rangatira as to whether Busby's idea of a parliament to make laws could succeed. As Busby himself remarked to his patron the Earl of Haddington a year later:

> They rightly observed that though eleven of their number should regulate their conduct by the law if the 12th were disposed to break it, they had no resource but to let crime go unpunished or levy war. Tribe against Tribe as at present.[129]

The complex networks of whakapapa, in which an individual could claim descent from all four grandparents and ally themselves at different times with different descent networks, were remarkably flexible and fluid. In te ao Māori, just as parents hesitated to punish their children, so rangatira found it difficult to assert absolute authority over their people, except in times of war (and sometimes not even then). Unlike the hierarchical class systems in Europe, there were no structural mechanisms (such as policemen, prisons or the army, punishments like flogging, or the physical discipline exerted in schools) to allow lasting impositions of power. Mana among the rangatira ebbed and flowed, according to their feats in battle, feasting and oratorical contests.

As many of the witnesses reminded the Tribunal during its Te Paparahi o te Raki hearings in 2010, furthermore, Northland is still famed for the independence of its kin groups. This is expressed in the proverb 'Ngā puhi ko whao rau' – 'Ngā puhi of a hundred holes'. As this suggests, you can never be sure when or whether a northern kin group will pop up from the ground, or what action they will take.

As Patu Hohepa remarks, however, the saying 'Ngā puhi ko whao rau' also evokes a fishing net, its many holes interconnected by woven strands of flax; and in this sense, the proverb also evokes the shifting alliances that frequently gave Nga Puhi success in battle.[130] A number of witnesses to the 2010 Tribunal hearings gave evidence about major inter-hapū gatherings that were held in Northland from 1808 onwards to discuss how best to manage their relations with Europeans, and there are also many references to such large meetings in the missionary records.[131]

Now, as then, success in navigating the intricate, ever-shifting networks of whakapapa requires an ability to speak eloquently, and to galvanise ideas and relationships rooted in the ancestral past. In te ao Māori, the study of whakapapa and associated forms of knowledge – carving, karakia (incantations), waiata (chants), boundaries and place names in landscapes and seascapes, ancestral stories – was a prerequisite for effective leadership, and a lifelong pursuit, as I learned during travels with my mentor and tipuna Eruera Stirling, and from experts such as Patu Hohepa, Hone Sadler, Rima Edwards and Manuka Henare, who appeared before Te Paparahi o te Raki Tribunal.

In many ways, the 2010–11 Waitangi Tribunal hearings in Northland echoed the gathering to discuss the Declaration of Independence at Waitangi in 1835, where rangatira and tribal experts met with European officials to declare their kīngitanga (sovereignty) and their mana to a wider world; and many of the same paradoxes and contradictions are still in play. This was the first formal attempt to negotiate a lasting pattern of relations between Māori and Europeans in New Zealand, and between Māori and the wider world.

CHAPTER EIGHT

Our Words Will Sink Like a Stone

IN HIS SUBMISSION TO TE PAPARAHI O TE RAKI TRIBUNAL, THE EMINENT
linguist and Hokianga leader Dr Patu Hohepa quoted the lament of the
rangatira Mohi Tawhai during the Treaty debate at Mangungu in 1840:
'Our sayings will sink to the bottom like a stone, but your sayings will float
light, like the wood of the whau-tree, and always remain to be seen. Am I
telling lies?' Hohepa added, 'The stones have now come up and they want
to talk.'[1] Indeed, during the 2010–11 Tribunal hearings about Te Tiriti o
Waitangi, it was fascinating to see how often contemporary power relations
were projected back into the past, and then challenged, and how 'evidence'
about what had happened in 1840 was constructed, authorised, presented
and contested, often on the basis of modernist assumptions.

By 1840, while about 600 Europeans lived in the Bay of Islands,[2] they
were outnumbered by about twenty to one by Māori, Māori was the dominant language and tikanga Māori, or Māori ways of living, largely prevailed.
At that time, Europeans were forced to accommodate Māori practices, even
those that they found intrusive or abhorrent, and accept Māori assertions of
authority, usually associated with tapu, or ancestral presence, and mana, or
ancestral powers. In front of the Waitangi Tribunal 170 years later, however,
witnesses with little knowledge of the Māori language, ancestral practices or
habits of mind often spoke confidently about life in the Bay of Islands and
Māori negotiations over the Treaty in 1840, without realising how far their
understandings were shaped by a reliance on documents written in English
and underpinned by modernist habits of mind.

In such settings, where power and ontological assumptions engage,
fundamental presuppositions about how the world works rarely surface for

conscious inspection, except where people who understand reality very differently have to deal directly with one another. Even then, they may operate at cross purposes, not realising why, or even that their interpretations do not converge. Dominant assumptions embedded in familiar settings and routines, and continuous with ancestral habits of mind, are difficult to discern, let alone to challenge.

At the same time, in the Te Paparahi o te Raki claim, a number of the members of the Tribunal, the lawyers and the witnesses were Māori, with deep understandings of te ao Māori. Throughout these hearings, the mana of Māori understandings and knowledge of He Whakaputanga and Te Tiriti were powerfully upheld, and quite often, ontological issues were tackled head on. The Hokianga elder Rima Edwards, for instance, quoted the prediction of the prophet Papahurihia after the signing of Te Tiriti: '*Kua mau tātou ki te ripo. Kāti ka taka ki tua o te rua rau tau ka tū mai te pono ki te whakatika i nga mea katoa*' – 'We have been caught in a whirlpool. Alas, it will last for beyond two hundred years when the truth [pono] will stand to put everything right'.[3] By sharing the oral knowledge taught to him in the whare wānanga established by Papahurihia, Edwards sought to bring that truth to light.

In their exchanges with the Tribunal, many of the other northern witnesses challenged a long-standing asymmetry between ancestral Māori conceptions and modernist modes of knowledge.[4] Ultimately, this asymmetry traces back to a disjunction between two very different forms of order – the rhizomatic, ramifying networks of whakapapa, powered by exchange and ideas of mana and tapu; and the stadial, hierarchical theories that dominated British thinking about 'natives' and 'savages' at the time of the Declaration of Independence and the Treaty of Waitangi, and for many generations since. As we have seen, stadial ideas in modernity trace back to sources including the creation story in Genesis and the Great Chain of Being, with their assumptions that when God created the world, He made human beings in his likeness, told them to subdue the earth and gave them dominion over the fish of the sea, the fowl of the air and all living creatures.

During the Scottish Enlightenment in particular, thinkers including Adam Ferguson, Adam Smith, Lord Kames, Lord Monboddo and David Hume[5] added linear time to this tiered structure in a schema covering all of human history (a 'one world' or 'universal' account). In their stadial narratives, world history began with the Age of Hunters, when people moved across the land but did not subdue it. These hunters and gatherers had no written language, no laws and no authority apart from that which could be imposed by brute force. This was an era of great personal freedom, but little security or safety. After the Age of the Hunters came the Herders, who domesticated their animals and roamed across the land; followed by the Age of Agriculture, where people tilled the soil and had permanent dwellings; and finally the Age of Commerce, as exemplified by Europe, at the apex of human development. Hunters and herders alike were often described as 'savages', agriculturalists as 'barbarians', and commercial societies as 'civilised'. These myth models were powerful, and pivotal in shaping British debates about sovereignty, property and the future of governance in New Zealand.

According to William Blackstone in his famous *Commentaries on the Laws of England*, for instance, in the state of savagery, there was no private property – 'all was common among them, and everyone took from the public stock to his own use such things as his immediate necessities required'.[6] As populations increased, animals were domesticated, houses were built and fields were cultivated, and the idea of property emerged – 'that sole and despotic dominion which one man claims and exercises over the external things of the world, in total exclusion of the right of any other individual in the universe'.[7] This was necessary, said Blackstone, so that a man could enjoy the fruits of his labours. As Moloney has pointed, along with 'property', the idea of the 'savage' lay at the heart of Victorian identity, because without the 'savage' as a reference point, it was not possible to claim one's own society as 'civilised' or 'advanced'.[8] At the same time, British people also occupied different rungs on the cosmic ladder. Ancient Britons as well as Māori might be described as 'savages', while Scottish Highlanders and other Celts could be regarded as 'savage' or 'barbarians'.

In the North Island of New Zealand, where Māori built permanent houses and agriculture was practised, it was supposed that most kin groups had emerged from savagery into barbarism, on their way to 'civilisation', although there were still traces of savagery in their way of life – most spectacularly, the practice of cannibalism. In the South Island, however, where small nomadic bands of hunters and gatherers were common, according to stadial theorists, a state of 'savagery' still applied. At the same time, many of the European residents in New Zealand in the 1830s – escaped convicts, reprobate sailors and ruthless land-jobbers – were seen as being as 'savage' and 'barbaric' as their Māori counterparts. They, as well as Māori, had to be raised into 'civil society'.

Like the idea of 'property', the concept of 'sovereignty' also traces back
to the Great Chain of Being. Here, divine sovereigns were given the power
by God to rule over earthly kingdoms. According to Blackstone, just as the
idea of property emerged in 'civilised' societies, this required the emergence
of the state, laws and punishment. Sovereignty thus rested on the need to
protect private property. In his *Commentaries*, Blackstone defined sovereignty
as 'a supreme, irresistible, absolute, uncontrolled authority . . . placed in those
hands in which goodness, wisdom and power are most likely to be found'.[9]
In the past, while this power had flowed from God through a divine monarch to his and her subjects, since the signing of the Magna Carta in Britain,
the power of the king or queen was constrained by Parliament. Apart from
the power to declare war and make treaties, sovereignty had passed to the
lawmakers.[10] Under the Declaration of Independence in New Zealand, since
the capacity to make laws was exercised by the Confederation of the United
Tribes (although with the British Resident acting as the power behind the
throne), they held sovereignty over the country. Many of the British authorities and those interested in New Zealand, however, did not think that the
rangatira were capable of exercising such powers, even with British guidance.

At this time, capitalist ideas of commerce were radiating out from
European outposts in New Zealand. When they worked for Europeans,
Māori were increasingly paid in cash as well as kind, and large areas of Māori
land were being alienated to various missionaries (including Henry Williams
and Richard Taylor), James Busby[11] and others. In Sydney, land speculators
were turning their eyes to New Zealand, and in Britain, the New Zealand
Company, inspired by the ideas of Edward Gibbon Wakefield, proposed to
form commercial settlements in the country. On every side, the rangatira
were assailed by Europeans eager to buy their land, and treat it as private
property as soon as the purchase was finalised. Back in Britain, a war of
pamphlets broke out, with those interested in the future of New Zealand
arguing about the rights and wrongs of British settlement, and how this
should be managed. These were serious, searching debates, involving a
series of inquiries into what was happening in the country, and marked differences of opinion about how to deal with these challenges.[12]

Some British writers regarded the missionaries as the salvation of the
Māori people. In December 1835, for instance, when the young naturalist
Charles Darwin arrived in the Bay of Islands on board the *Beagle*, he gave
a glowing account of the missionary settlers and their influence upon local

Māori. During a visit to Rev. William Williams at the inland mission farm at Waimate, Darwin was delighted by the 'sudden appearance of an English farm-house and its well-dressed fields, placed there as if by an enchanter's wand'.[13] At the Waimate station, three large houses, a blacksmith's forge, stables and a barn stood amidst fields of wheat, barley, potatoes and clover, and gardens with 'asparagus, kidney beans, cucumbers, rhubarb, apples, pears, figs, peaches, apricots, grapes, olives, gooseberries, currants, hops, gorse for fences and English oaks', along with many flowers: 'All this is very surprising', Darwin remarked, 'when it is considered that five years ago, nothing but the fern here flourished. Moreover, native workmanship, taught by the missionaries, has effected this change – the lesson of the missionary is the enchanter's wand.'[14]

Although he was struck by the large, terraced and palisaded fortifications in the Bay, some abandoned and others adapted for musket-fighting, Darwin rejoiced that Māori warfare was being displaced by 'the progress of civilisation'. Witnessing an animated debate between James Busby and some local people over his land purchase at Waitangi, during which one old man, 'a perfect genealogist', indicated those who had successively occupied the site by putting sticks in the ground, he did not question the virtue of missionary land purchases in New Zealand. Like John Liddiard Nicholas before him, Darwin saw the missionaries as a shining beacon of civilisation in a savage land:

> In the evening I went to Mr. Williams's house, where I passed the night.
> I found there a very large party of children, collected together for Christmas-day, and all sitting round a table at tea. I never saw a nicer or more merry group, and to think this was in the centre of the land of cannibalism, murder, and all atrocious crimes![15]

When the Parliamentary Select Committee on Aboriginal Tribes, established in Britain in 1833, reported four years later, however, its members were less sanguine about the impact of European settlement, observing that in countries where Europeans lived among 'aborigines', or indigenous people, the consequences had been generally dire:

> Too often, their territory has been usurped; their property seized; their numbers diminished; their character debased; the spread of civilization impeded.

European vices and diseases have been introduced amongst them, and . . .
our most potent instruments for the destruction of human life, viz. brandy
and gunpowder.[16]

The committee argued that the British government itself, or governors in
the colonies, had the duty to protect indigenous peoples, since 'this is not
a trust which could conveniently be confided to the local Legislatures'.[17]
In response, the New Zealand Association published a book, *The British
Colonization of New Zealand*, largely written by Edward Wakefield, advo-
cating 'a deliberate and methodical scheme for leading a savage people
to embrace the religion, language, laws and social habits of an advanced
country . . . instead of exterminating . . . the natives of the country to be
settled'.[18] This provoked the Aboriginal Protection Society to produce a
pamphlet in response, arguing that colonisation invariably injured the interests of indigenous people.[19]

Indeed, by the late 1830s, life in Northland was increasingly volatile and
uncertain. Shortly after the signing of He Whakaputanga, a dispute broke
out between some local rangatira including Waikato, who had visited King
George IV with Hongi, and a Ngati Manu rangatira over cutting rights in a
kauri forest. When Henry Williams became involved, warning off European
traders who were trying to buy the logs, Waikato was infuriated, delivering
a letter to Williams that declared 'I will never give up my claim to my own
lawful property', and handing back the musket that King George had given
him. In January 1836 when the opposing sides gathered at Waitangi to try
to settle the dispute, while Ngati Manu orators were reciting their ancestral
rights to the land a scuffle broke out, and a number of their people were shot,
while the rest crowded into the residency, where 'the floors were covered
with the blood of wounded men'. Without military backing, Busby could not
retaliate for this fracas, and he wrote to Governor Bourke, asking for assistance so that he could punish those responsible. Over the next few months,
he wrote several more times about this dispute, urging British intervention
to keep the peace.[20]

At the same time, Bay of Islands Māori were experimenting with practices abhorred by the British, especially the missionaries. In August 1836, for
instance, Busby accompanied a young Māori man to a meeting in the bush
where about thirty men (including four or five white men) were being taught
voodoo rituals by four or five black sailors from a visiting American whaler.

Two of the white men had drunk rum mixed with tutu juice (*Coriara arborea*), and one was rigid with paralysis while the other had died.[21]

In March 1837, when Samuel Marsden, now 72 years old and very frail, arrived for his seventh and last visit to the Bay of Islands, he reported to the CMS in London that warfare had broken out between Pomare's people and Nga Puhi.[22] Busby sent the same news to Governor Bourke, presenting a petition from European settlers in the Bay asking for British protection, and arguing that since inter-tribal fighting was putting British subjects at risk, a 'paramount authority, supported by a force adequate to secure the efficiency of its measures', was now needed in New Zealand. Otherwise, he could not see any prospect of peace 'whilst there remains a stronger man to murder his weaker neighbour'.[23] Under the Confederation, Busby suggested, each of the leading chiefs could be given a small salary, and a medal with his name and the name of his district, and a school established in each district:

> In theory and ostensibility the government would be that of the confeder-
> ated chiefs, but in reality it must necessarily be that of the protecting power.
> The chiefs would meet annually or oftener, and nominally enact the laws pro-
> posed to them; but in truth the present race of chiefs could not be intrusted
> with any discretion whatever in the adoption or rejection of any measure that
> might be submitted to them . . . The congress would, in fact, be a school in
> which the chiefs would be instructed in the duties required of them . . .[24]

For James Busby, like many of his British contemporaries, Māori were chil-
dren to be raised by caring parents to adulthood, as they progressed through the 'Ages of Man' from infancy to manhood or 'civilisation'.[25]

Likewise, Captain William Hobson (described by Henry Williams as a 'thin, pleasing man'), who arrived in the Bay of Islands on the *Rattlesnake* in May 1837,[26] expressed his regret that 'so fine and intelligent a race of human beings should be found in barbarism, for there is not on earth a people more susceptible of high intellectual attainments, or more capable of becoming a useful and industrious race under a wise government'.[27] As an alternative to Busby's scheme, Hobson suggested a system of 'factories' or commercial settlements (like those in India) as a way of managing the peaceful British settlement of New Zealand. These settlements would be headed by magistrates, with a chief factor accredited as a political agent and consul

Captain William Hobson, by James Ingram McDonald, 1913.

to the united chiefs of New Zealand, who would sign a treaty recognising the factories, and the protection of British subjects and property.[28] By this time Governor Bourke had lost faith in Busby, and threw his weight behind Hobson, whom he described as an 'experienced and judicious officer'.[29]

When the despatches from Busby and Hobson were laid before Parliament, the supporters of the Church Missionary Society rose up in arms at any suggestion that commercial settlement (whether by the New Zealand Association or in Hobson's factory scheme) could accomplish 'the arduous task of raising the New Zealanders to the enjoyment of the blessings of a Christian and civilized state'.[30] Rather, they argued, such proposals seemed likely to make matters worse, by bringing more British settlers to New Zealand and creating endless conflicts over land. In response to these concerns, Rev. Samuel Hinds, an advocate for the New Zealand Association, wrote a pamphlet arguing that the New Zealand Association's plan for colonising New Zealand would check the evils plaguing New Zealand. Although land would be purchased from the natives, New Zealand was thinly inhabited, and colonisation would increase the value of the land that remained in Māori hands:

> Civilized man is the guardian of the savage. God and nature appoint that it should be so; and if civilized man deprives the savage of his real or supposed inheritance, by disposing of it to those who will cultivate it and settle in it, this not only raises the value of the land disposed of, but of the land which remains. . . . It [also] teaches them to make their property more and more valuable, and to assume a sovereignty over their portion of the earth, in some other sense than that in which the lion and tiger are sovereigns of their jungles, and the buffalo of his pasture grounds.[31]

Hinds also roundly attacked the CMS missionaries (especially Henry Williams) for their land purchases, which he outlined in scathing detail.

Although Williams had earlier opposed British government intervention in New Zealand, by 1838 he had changed his mind. After fighting in the Bay of Plenty, three new mission stations at Matamata, Tauranga and Rotorua had to be closed, lawless Europeans were creating havoc in the Bay of Islands, and the land sharks were circling. Later that year, James Clendon, a local settler, was appointed US Consul to New Zealand, and the following year 80 American vessels visited the Bay. There was also the risk of French intervention. As Williams wrote to the CMS in London after reading the New Zealand Association pamphlets: 'I do not hesitate to say that unless some protection be given by the British Government, the country will be bought up, and the people pass into a kind of slavery, or be utterly destroyed.'[32] He argued for a kind of protectorate, with the chiefs forming a general assembly guided by officers and headed by an English governor, protected by a military force, saying that the rangatira had been requesting such an arrangement for some time.[33]

In these and other British debates about a shared future, however, Māori had little say. The contest was not so much about the rights of Māori, but about which Europeans could do the best job of looking after them in their 'infant state'. Such notions of intellectual superiority have proved enduring. As Henare [Salmond], Holbraad and Wastell have observed:

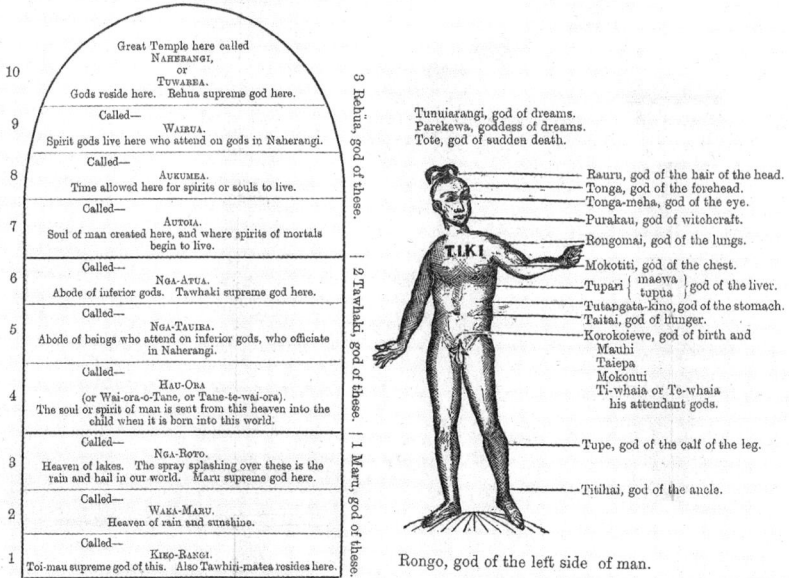

Tiers of Rangi: a tiered cosmos, with Tiki, the first human being and his atua.

> In keeping with its monotheistic origins . . . ours is an ontology of *one* ontology . . . For if cultures render different appearances of reality, it follows that one of them is special and better than all the others, namely the one that best *reflects* reality. And since science – the search for representations that reflect reality as transparently and faithfully as possible – happens to be a modern Western project, that special culture is, well, ours . . .[34]

Now, as then, Māori ways of living and thinking are rarely thought of as being on the same footing as modernity and Western 'civilisation', govern-ance and science.

Such hierarchical forms of order, and the power relations they expressed, were not utterly unknown among Māori, however. Ariki, or paramount chiefs (not unlike British kings and queens), for instance, might be placed on a stage, raised up above their people or be carried on a litter so that their feet did not touch the ground, such was the intensity of their tapu (ancestral presence). Such high-born people were surrounded by tapu restrictions and played a key role in the seasonal rituals and those associated with warfare.

In te ao Māori, hierarchical conceptions were also expressed in a layered universe, with its tiered heavens above the earth and tiered underworlds below it. The link between height and power was echoed in the poles and rods used in ritual contexts, and in the mountains that held up the sky, often associated with high-born leaders, with tapu and mana derived from proximity to powerful ancestors.

Unlike the Great Chain of Being, such hierarchies did not carry with them the power of top-down control, however. Descent traced through many lines created multiple opportunities for the strategic use of whakapapa, and in a descent system where a person could trace from all four grandparents, male and female (although with an emphasis on tuakana [senior sibling] and male lines), most people could lay a legitimate claim to some kind of ancestral mana (or power). The only exceptions were taurekareka, or war captives, and the descendants of those whose mana had been destroyed by acts of kai tangata (ritual cannibalism), for example. Otherwise, mana ebbed and flowed, won or lost in battle, oratory, lavish feasting and gifting, and in taking care of the people. In this way, tēina (younger brothers or sisters) might acquire greater influence and power than their tuākana (elder brothers and sisters). From the stories of Maui the trickster ancestor onwards, Māori oral histories feature the adventures of younger siblings who reshaped the world.

As European observers noted from the time of Captain Cook onwards, Māori (and particularly rangatira) were very protective of their mana. A gift enhanced, and an insult diminished; the hau ora, the wind of life that flowed through them, and from them to their people and land, leading to health, prosperity and success, or illness, poverty and failure. For these reasons, they were quick to acknowledge a generous gesture, and equally quick to avenge an insult. As Rewa wrote to McDonnell during the conflict with Pomare in 1837:

> Are the things (letters) which you sent to Pomare to make him a chief over us? Perhaps not – No – we will not have him for our chief . . . We are not like the King of England – we are all chiefs here.[35]

When a European leader – a missionary, a governor or a king, for example – treated a rangatira with respect, exchanging gifts with them, addressing them as hoa (friend) and offering them hospitality, the entanglement of hau forged a bond that was rarely forgotten. Conversely, a belittling gesture or verbal insult was a patu wairua (a blow to the spirit), deeply resented and bound to be revenged. This included the breaking of tapu restrictions associated with a rangatira and their family, as Marion du Fresne and his sailors and many of the early missionaries and their families discovered to their cost.

It is easy to see, then, how a way of living based on reciprocity and exchange might collide with stadial assumptions. While in the beginning, high-born Māori leaders took it for granted that they were on an equal footing with British monarchs and other European aristocrats, given stadial thinking, astute and dignified people like Hongi Hika, Patuone and their peers could be treated as children, mocked as savages and reprimanded for their ancestral customs, especially during their visits to New South Wales and other European places, including mission stations and ships. Given Māori ideas of mana, such insults demanded some kind of utu, or reparation. At the time of the Treaty, European settlers in New Zealand (including people like Samuel Marsden and Henry Williams) were greatly outnumbered by Māori, and had to contend with the force of mana as a reality. At the same time, Māori leaders exercised considerable restraint, given the interest they had in acquiring European goods, and the threat of reprisals from visiting ships if utu was taken.

Trade with Europeans had brought considerable prosperity to some rangatira and their people. Because of this, and a growing desire for peace, by 1840 perhaps half of the population of the Bay of Islands had become mihinare – affiliated with the missionaries.[36] Kai tangata had largely come to an end, along with hahunga (ceremonies surrounding exhumation), and those who converted to Christianity observed Sunday, went to church, gave up polygamy and released their war captives. While the mihinare included a number of powerful rangatira (including David Taiwhanga and Waka Nene), others (who included Titore, Tareha, Rewa, Pomare, Kawiti and Taonui) held fast to ancestral tikanga, and resented the growing influence of the missionaries. When Henry Williams preached in a sermon that all men, without distinction of rank, were condemned if they did not believe in Christ, for instance, Tareha 'roared like a bull' and told Williams that such beliefs 'might do for Slaves and Europeans but not for a free and noble people like the Ngapuhi'.[37]

A Tale of Two Treaties

At the same time in Britain, in the midst of furious arguments over future relations with New Zealand, the New Zealand Association decided to defy Parliament and go ahead with its plans to set up settlements in New Zealand. Finally, the British Government had to act. In July 1839 Lord Normanby, the Secretary of State, drafted instructions for William Hobson to proceed to New Zealand and 'treat with the Aborigines . . . for the recognition of Her Majesty's sovereign authority over the whole or any parts of those islands which they may be willing to place under Her Majesty's dominion'. While he recognised the dangers of these proceedings for Māori, Normanby argued that action had to be taken, because they were at imminent risk from land speculators and unauthorised settlement. At the same time, he deplored:

> the injury which must be inflicted on this kingdom itself, by embarking in a measure essentially unjust, and but too certainly fraught with calamity for a numerous and inoffensive people, whose title to the soil and the sovereignty of New Zealand is indisputable, and has been solemnly recognised by the British Government. . . .
>
> I have already stated that we acknowledge New Zealand as a sovereign and independent state so far at least as is possible to make that acknowledgement in favour of a people composed of numerous dispersed and petty tribes, who possess few political relations to each other, and are incompetent to act or even deliberate in concert. But the admission of their rights, though inevitably qualified by this consideration, is binding on the faith of the British Crown.
>
> The Queen disclaims for herself and for her subjects, every pretention to seize on the islands of New Zealand, or to govern them as a part of the dominion of Great Britain, unless the free and intelligent consent of the natives, expressed according to their established usages, shall first be obtained.
>
> The natives may probably regard with distrust a proposal which may carry on the face of it the appearance of humiliation on their side and of a formidable encroachment on ours: and their ignorance even of the technical terms in which that proposal must be conveyed, may enhance their aversion to an arrangement of which they may be unable to comprehend the exact meaning or probable results.
>
> These, however, are impediments to be gradually overcome by the exercise on your part of mildness, justice and perfect sincerity in your intercourse

with them. . . . If it should be necessary to propitiate their consent by presents
or other pecuniary arrangements, you will be authorised to advance at once
to a certain extent in meeting such demands, and beyond those limits you will
reserve and refer them for the decision of Her Majesty's Government.[38]

Back in New Zealand, when James Busby was approached by one of the local
rangatira, who invited him to become their 'king', he hastily declined this
invitation. Although other rangatira were asked to take up the role, nothing
came of it.[39]

Soon afterwards, the famous warrior Te Rauparaha sent a letter to Henry
Williams, asking him to send a missionary to his people, and following this
up with the arrival of two of his sons as emissaries to the Bay of Islands
to 'fetch' him. Williams decided to head south along the east coast of the
North Island, taking Octavius Hadfield to establish a new mission at Otaki.[40]
After stopping at Maketu, where Williams tried unsuccessfully to broker a
peace between the local people and a taua from the Waikato, they arrived
in Wellington Harbour, 'a perfectly sheltered place, with sufficient room
for all the fleets of England'.[41] When local people came out in their canoes,
they told Henry that the New Zealand Association ship *Tory* had been there,
buying up all the land. Although they had wanted to reserve some land for
themselves, the Europeans would not agree, and fighting had broken out
among the local kin groups over the transactions, and 70 people were shot.
The Europeans on board the *Tory* had now gone to Queen Charlotte Sound
to buy land, and intended to do the same in Taranaki.

After sailing to Kapiti Island, where he was told that the *Tory* had been
'buying all right and title over the land from the natives for a considerable
extent', Williams and Hadfield met Te Rauparaha, who promised to give up
fighting.[42] They went ashore at Waikanae, where 1200 people gathered for
a Christian service, singing hymns in Māori, and Williams arranged to purchase the Wairarapa as 'a sitting place for the natives',[43] hoping to frustrate
any New Zealand Company purchase in this district. After travelling over-
land through Taupo and Rotorua to Tauranga, where Henry Williams met
his brother William and his family, on their way to establish a new mission
in Poverty Bay, Henry returned to the Bay of Islands by sea, accompanied by
several rangatira from Rotorua and Taupo, including the younger brother of
the ariki Te Heuheu. After being reunited with his own family, overjoyed by
'the unspeakable pleasure of finding myself at home and all my family well

after an absence of thirteen weeks',[44] Williams briefed his fellow missionaries on what he had learned about the New Zealand Association's activities in the south. When Patuone and his wife expressed a wish to be baptised, Williams was delighted that so respected and distinguished a rangatira wished to join the church, and Patuone and his wife were baptised on 26 January 1840.

Three days later, a mounted messenger arrived from Captain William Hobson, who had just arrived in the Bay of Islands on board the *Herald*, asking to meet Henry Williams as soon as possible. Hobson also met with James Busby, giving him a letter from the British government announcing that the role of resident had been terminated. On 30 January, Williams went out to the ship and met Hobson, who gave him a letter from the Bishop of Australia instructing him to do everything he could to assist Hobson with his mission,[45] although there were no letters with instructions from the Church Missionary Society in Britain. Soon afterwards, Hobson went ashore, and at a gathering at the Kororareka church proclaimed that he was taking up his duties as lieutenant-governor, that the boundaries of New South Wales had been extended to include those parts of New Zealand to which British sovereignty might be extended, and that from that time on, land sales must be backed by a Crown grant to be recognised as valid.

A treaty with the rangatira still had to be negotiated, however, and Busby circulated an invitation in Māori for the northern chiefs to meet on 5 February at Waitangi. Although Hobson had instructions from the British government, he had not been provided with a draft. In the event, Hobson drafted the first English version of the Treaty of Waitangi on board the *Herald* (evidently based on British treaties with tribal rulers in West Africa),[46] which was then revised as a result of suggestions by James Busby, who insisted that the rangatira would never sign it unless their rights over their lands and taonga (ancestral treasures) were formally guaranteed. This draft was refined again by Hobson and his officials, while some of the European settlers in the Bay were warning Māori that the country had been taken over by Queen Victoria, and they were now taurekareka, or slaves.[47]

On 4 February 1840, as Henry Williams later recalled, Hobson brought the draft Treaty in English to him and asked him to translate it into Māori:

On February 4, about four o'clock p.m., Captain Hobson came to me with the Treaty of Waitangi in English, for me to translate into Maori, saying

*Queen Victoria, by
Sir George Hayter,
c. 1838–1840.*

that he would meet me in the morning at the house of the British Resident,
Mr. Busby, when it must be read to the chiefs assembled at ten o'clock.

    In this translation, it was necessary to avoid all expressions of the English
for which there was no expressive term in the Maori, preserving entire the
spirit and tenor of the treaty, which, though severely tested, has never yet
been disturbed, notwithstanding that many in power have endeavoured
to do so.[48]

With his 21-year-old son Edward, a fluent speaker of northern Māori,
Henry worked overnight to translate the document into Māori. Among the
missionaries, his brother William was regarded as the better speaker of the
language, but he had recently left the Bay of Islands for the East Coast.[49]
In any case, Henry was the head of the mission, entrusted to handle dip-
lomatic matters, and five years earlier he had translated the Declaration of
Independence into Māori.

The English draft of the Treaty of Waitangi is quite short, with a Preamble and three Articles. In various reports to Te Paparahi o te Raki Tribunal (including mine with Merimeri Penfold), the fidelity of Williams's Māori translation has been questioned in depth and detail – with reference to Williams's earlier translation of the Declaration of Independence into Māori; the likely understandings of those who heard Te Tiriti (the Māori Treaty) read out in Māori at Waitangi; and by examining a number of 'back translations' (from Māori to English) that were made soon after the signing, when it became clear that the English draft of the Treaty and Te Tiriti in Māori were significantly different.

As is now almost universally agreed, the two treaties – the English draft and the Māori translation – express very different understandings of future relations between Māori and Europeans. The Preamble to the English draft, for example, states that Her Majesty Queen Victoria, anxious to protect the 'just Rights and Property' of the chiefs and tribes of New Zealand, has decided to 'constitute and appoint a functionary authorised to treat with the Aborigines of New Zealand for the recognition of Her Majesty's Sovereign authority over the whole or any part of those islands'. In Article One of the English draft, the chiefs cede to 'Her Majesty the Queen of England absolutely and without reservation all the rights and powers of Sovereignty'. In Article Two, the queen confirms and guarantees to the chiefs 'the full exclusive and undisturbed possession of their Lands and Estates Forests Fisheries and other properties'. In turn, they yield to her the 'exclusive right of pre-emption' in land sales. In Article Three, the queen confirms and guarantees to the 'Natives of New Zealand' her royal protection and 'all the rights and duties of British subjects'.

If the English draft of the Treaty had been the version that the rangatira debated and signed at Waitangi and elsewhere, it would be safe to conclude that they made a clear cession of sovereignty to Queen Victoria, along with the right to control land sales, although their property rights were protected, and in return they and their people received the rights and duties of British citizens. In the hierarchy of power, the rangatira would have been placed below Queen Victoria, who became their protector, and probably below the governor as well. This is not what happened, however. Rather, it was Te Tiriti, the translation into Māori, that was debated and signed by the rangatira. In this Māori text, the relationship between the rangatira and the queen is very differently defined.

In the Preamble of Te Tiriti, for instance, the queen gives (tuku) to the Māori people of New Zealand a rangatira as a kaiwakarite (mediator or adjudicator, perhaps administrator). Tuku is the term used in chiefly gift exchange for handing over a taonga of some kind. In Article One, the chiefs tuku rawa atu (completely give) to the queen the kāwanatanga of their lands – variously translated as 'government', 'governance' or more literally, the right to have a kāwana, or governor, although his powers are not defined. In Article Two, the queen agrees to uphold the tino rangatiratanga, or absolute powers, of the rangatira as chiefs over their lands, dwelling places and all of their taonga (ancestral treasures) – a very different thing from 'properties'. In return, they give (tuku) her the right to control the barter (hoko – the term used in contrast with tuku for mundane exchanges in which the ancestors are not involved) of land through her trading agent. In Article Three, the queen promises to care for (tiaki) all the māori (ordinary) people of New Zealand and give (tuku) them tikanga (rights, or customs) exactly equal to (rite tahi) those of her people of England.

In their Statement of Generic Issues to the Waitangi Tribunal, the northern leaders argued that since Te Tiriti was the document that their ancestors debated and signed at Waitangi and elsewhere, this was the only valid record of their agreements with the British Crown. They vehemently denied that by signing the Māori Treaty, their ancestors had ceded sovereignty to Queen Victoria:

> Te Tiriti was not a treaty of cession, and Te Raki rangatira did not cede
> sovereignty to the Crown. . . . Te Raki rangatira agreed to and signed only
> Te Tiriti. The Treaty of Waitangi is an unknown and meaningless document
> to them. . . .

By relying on the English draft of the Treaty and taking control of the country, they argued, the Crown had breached its guarantee of their tino rangatiratanga in Article Two:

> The fundamental breach, from which all other breaches emanate, is the usur
> pation by the Crown of the Māori mana. . . . Wrongfully and in fundamental
> breach of Article 2 of Te Tiriti the Crown has assumed unto itself supreme
> authority within Aotearoa–New Zealand even over the terms of Te Tiriti
> itself. This is the original and fundamental breach.[50]

PLATE 1 *Marsden's mill and cottage, Parramatta, NSW by J. Lycett, 1820.*

PLATE 2 *The missionary settlement Rangihoua on the north side of the Bay of Islands, New Zealand, by unknown artist, c. 1832.*

PLATE 3　*The Armoury in Carlton House, by Augustus Charles Pugin, 1814.*

PLATE 4　*The artist Augustus Earle meeting Hongi Hika at
the Bay of Islands, by the artist, November 1827.*

PLATE 5 *Tukopoto at Kaitoke, Te Wherowhero's pā, by George French Angas, 1844.*

Jeune fille de 18 ans   *Schongée*   *Tooi.*   *chef*

Naturels de la nouvelle Zélande.

PLATE 6 *Tui in European costume, by Jules LeJeune, 1824.*

PLATE 7 *The Rev. Thomas Kendall and the Māori chiefs Hongi and Waikato, by James Barry, 1820.*

PLATE 8 *The mission station at Kerikeri, by Jules Lejeune, 1824.*

PLATE 9 *Te Kara, the United Tribes ensign, Waitangi. Edward Markham, 1834.*

PLATE 10 *A hākari, or feast, in the Bay of Islands, by Cuthbert Clarke, 1849.*

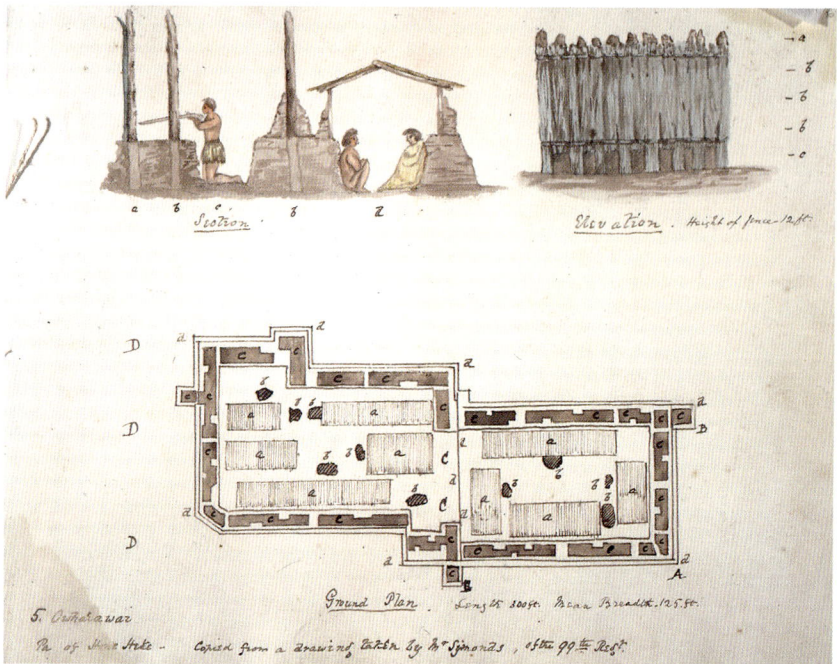

PLATE 11 *'Owharawai. Pa of Hone Heke', copied from a drawing taken by Mr Symonds of the 99th Regt by Thomas Biddulph Hutton, 1845.*

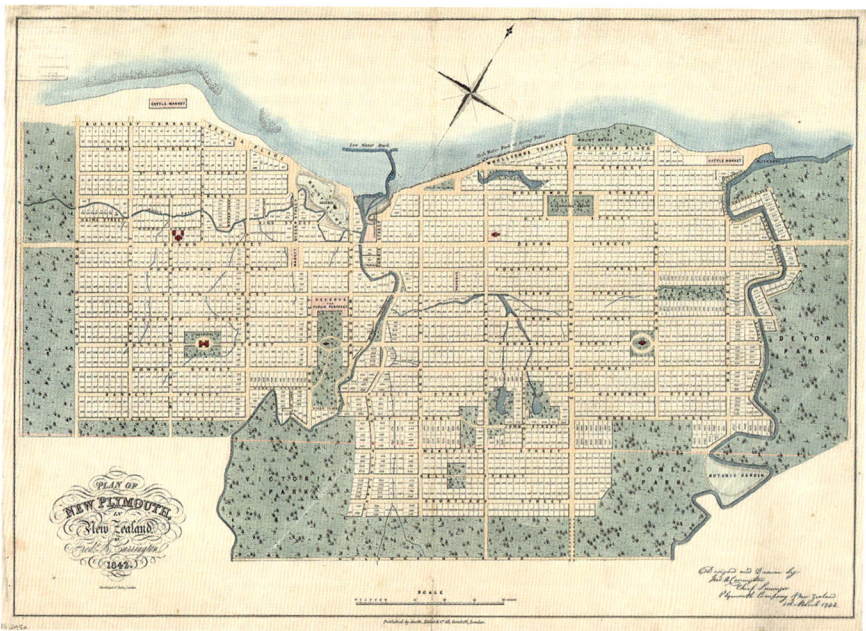

PLATE 12 *Plan of New Plymouth in New Zealand, by Frederick A. Carrington, 1842.*

PLATE 13 *Children on the banks of the Waipa, lithograph by Louisa Hawkins after George French Angas, 1847.*

PLATE 14 *'He that chastiseth one, amendeth many', by H. Heath, 1831.*

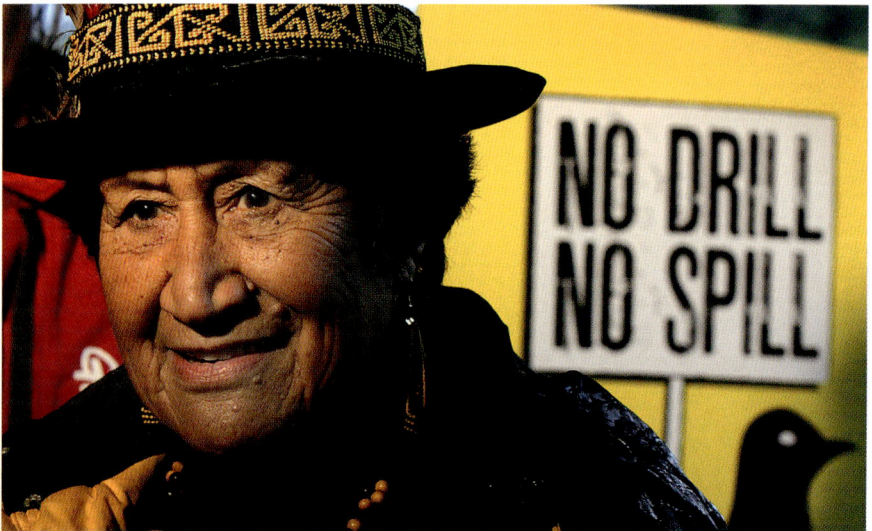

PLATE 15 'No Drill No Spill' — protests against oil drilling in Whanau-a-Apanui waters.

PLATE 16 Foreshore and seabed hīkoi at Parliament, 5 May 2004.

As one might expect, given the high stakes involved, the differences between each section of the two treaties were examined in minute detail in front of the Tribunal. A number of the claimants and witnesses argued, for example, that in Article One of Te Tiriti, where the rangatira of the hapū absolutely give kāwanatanga (governance, governorship) to the queen, they were giving her the right to appoint a governor (or kāwana) in New Zealand – no more and no less. According to some of the claimants, the role of the governor was to mediate between Māori and Europeans, while others argued that his powers were to be restricted to dealing with Europeans. While various Crown witnesses argued that, in 1840, kāwanatanga was a fair translation for 'sovereignty', other reports to the Tribunal (including my own with Merimeri Penfold) argued that at that time in Northland, kāwanatanga was understood to be a lesser and delegated power.

A great deal of evidence was given to this effect, including references in the Bible to various kāwana, or governors; the many encounters between northern rangatira and British governors in Port Jackson and Norfolk Island, where they became well aware of the subordinate role of kāwana in relation to ruling monarchs; and Henry Williams's translation of the Declaration of Independence in 1835, in which kāwanatanga is used to translate a 'function of government' that the rangatira might choose to delegate to someone whom they themselves appointed. At the same time, it was noted, in the Declaration, that Williams had translated 'sovereignty' with the phrase te kīngitanga me te mana (the kingship and mana), powers which the rangatira reserved for themselves in the Declaration, clearly distinguishing this as superior to kāwanatanga, or 'function of government'. According to many of the claimants, if Williams had used the phrase te kīngitanga me te mana to translate 'sovereignty' in Article One of Te Tiriti, their ancestors would never have signed.

In examining Article Two of Te Tiriti, in which Queen Victoria agrees to uphold te tino rangatiratanga, or absolute chieftainship of the rangatira over their lands, dwelling places and all of their taonga, various Crown witnesses argued that tino rangatiratanga falls under the mantle of kāwanatanga, or 'sovereignty'. A number of northern claimants and witnesses vehemently disagreed, arguing that this Article would have been understood by the rangatira as a further guarantee by the queen of their independence and freedom. Again, evidence was cited from translations of the Bible and the Lord's Prayer, in which rangatiratanga is used to translate 'kingdom', and

from the Declaration of Independence, where Henry Williams used rangatiratanga to translate 'independence', for example. Surprisingly, the use
of the term taonga (prized ancestral goods) in Article Two as a translation
equivalent for 'properties' was not debated. This raises questions about the
role of 'property rights' under Te Tiriti, a modernist conception based on
very different relations between people, land and other prized goods from
those that applied in te ao Māori at the time – a matter pertinent to contemporary debates about the 'ownership' of fresh water, for example.

In most of the evidence, it was agreed that Article Three of Te Tiriti
was fairly close to the English draft, establishing a bond between the Māori
people and the queen, who agrees to tiaki, or take care of them. In Māori,
a kaitiaki, or guardian, has very particular obligations to take care of those
they protect, based on the exercise of mana or ancestral power. However,
another key matter that was not debated in front of the Tribunal is how the
use of *ngā tikanga katoa rite tahi ki āna mea, ki ngā tāngata o Ingarangi* in Article
Three as a translation equivalent for 'all the Rights and Privileges of British
subjects' would have been understood by the rangatira. While tikanga means
'right ways of doing things', rite tahi in this context would almost certainly
have been understood as 'exactly equal', placing ancestral Māori tikanga on
an equal footing with those of the queen's people in Britain.

In working out ways to run a shared society, it follows from this understanding of Article Three of the Treaty that the governor and the rangatira
would do this together, and that tikanga Māori – Māori notions of justice and
fair play, ways of organising collective life, and people's relationships with
land, waterways and the ocean, for instance – would be drawn upon in equal
measure with habits of mind and customs from Britain and Europe. This
helps to explain why in Northland, Te Tiriti is often described as a kawenata
(covenant) with the British Crown. As we have seen, a close inspection of
the text of Te Tiriti shows a series of tuku, or gifts, passing back and forth
between the queen and the northern rangatira. In this way, as many of the
northern witnesses pointed out, Te Tiriti can be seen as another, very significant step in the sequence of chiefly gift exchanges between royalty and
senior northern rangatira that began with the meetings between Matara
and George III, and Hongi Hika and George IV, forging alliances with the
British royal family and tangling their descent lines together.

Perhaps the most vivid glimpses into the thoughts of the rangatira about
Te Tiriti, and the power plays among various Europeans, however, can be

gained from the eyewitness account of the gathering at Waitangi on 5–6 February 1840 written by William Colenso, the CMS missionary printer, based on notes he jotted down in English at the time. Colenso's account is one of the best we have of an early debate at a huihuinga, or gathering, with its exchange of speeches – a vital element in Māori decision-making, although many of the rhetorical flourishes that must have embellished the oratory (chants, proverbs and songs) are missing. During the Tribunal proceedings, Colenso's description of the debate at Waitangi was enriched by much research into other eyewitness accounts and background information about the participants, often provided to the Tribunal by their descendants, some of whom offered insights based on oral histories about their ancestors.

According to Colenso's notes, the transactions around the signing of the Treaty of Waitangi began on 4 February 1840, when the *Herald*'s officers and sailors came ashore and improvised a large tent from the ship's spars and sails (100 feet by 30, according to Captain Robertson of the *Samuel Winter*), its side ropes and poles fluttering with flags, erecting this in front of James Busby's house at Waitangi. A platform was set up inside the tent, with a table decorated with a Union Jack. At 9 a.m. the next morning, Lieutenant-Governor Hobson and Captain Nias of the *Herald* arrived at Busby's house, where Busby, Hobson and Henry Williams worked together on the final draft of Te Tiriti in Māori. While they were doing this, troopers from the New South Wales police paraded in full uniform as flotillas of canoes and boats converged on the harbour, heading towards Busby's house, where a large crowd was gathering, and various individuals went inside to greet the new Governor.

At about 10.30 a.m., Bishop Jean-Baptiste Pompallier, who had arrived in New Zealand two years earlier to establish a Roman Catholic mission, much to the consternation of the CMS missionaries, strode into Busby's house with Father Catherin Servant, both dressed in full canonicals. According to Richard Taylor, another of the CMS missionaries who was present, Pompallier, 'a mild good-looking man', wore a purple gown buttoned down the centre with purple stockings and an order suspended from his waist, with a large ruby ring on his hand.[51]

At this impressive spectacle a buzz went around the Māori spectators – '*Ko ia ano te tino Rangatira! Ko Pikopo anake te hoa mo te Kawana!*' (He is the real chief! Only Pompallier is the Governor's friend!) According to William Colenso, he now urged the other missionaries to follow Pompallier inside the house, 'for the sake of our position among the Natives'.[52]

*Bishop Pompallier, by
Tito Marzocchi, 1848.*

At about 11 a.m., William Hobson and Captain Nias in full dress uniform and accompanied by Pompallier, left the house and walked arm in arm in a procession behind the mounted police to the tent. Exclaiming, 'I'll never follow Rome!', Richard Taylor tried to get in between the lieutenant-governor and the French bishop, but Pompallier stayed so close to Hobson that this was impossible, and Taylor was forced to walk beside them. As he wrote furiously in his journal, 'The popish bishop . . . professed much pleasure in giving his aid but I feel assured he came either as a spy or to get himself acknowledged as an important personage before the natives which I think he succeeded in doing.'[53] At the table on the dais, Henry Williams sat on the governor's right-hand side, beside Captain Nias; while Pompallier and Servant sat to the left of James Busby. Willoughby Shortland, the superintendent of police-designate, came to the CMS missionaries and told them to line up behind Williams – 'Go to that end and support your cloth.'[54] The assembled chiefs, who sat in a semicircle in front of the dais, leaving a space for the orators, no doubt took careful note of these manoeuvres, as mana was won and lost.

In his account, Colenso describes the striking scene – Bishop Pompallier with his gold chain and crucifix shining on his dark purple habit; the *Herald*'s officers in their uniforms and the dark-suited missionaries on the dais; and the male and female chiefs seated on the ground in front of them, many of them wearing dogskin or kaitaka (flax fibre) cloaks, others dressed in crimson, blue, brown or plaid blankets. During the Tribunal hearings on the Treaty of Waitangi 170 years later, the seating echoed these arrangements, with the Tribunal members seated at a table in front of the gathering. Instead of William Hobson, however, the Tribunal was chaired by a Māori judge of the Māori Land Court, and a number of members of the Tribunal and the lawyers were also Māori. While there were historical echoes, some things had fundamentally changed.

Once William Hobson and his party were seated, he opened the meeting by speaking briefly to the Europeans in English, telling them that 'the meeting was convened for the purpose of informing the Native chiefs of Her Majesty's intentions towards them, and of gaining their public consent to a treaty now proposed to them'. According to Colenso's account, Hobson now addressed the chiefs in English (with Henry Williams acting as his interpreter):

Her Majesty Victoria, Queen of Great Britain, wishing to do good to the Chiefs and people of New Zealand, and for the welfare of Her Subjects living among you, has sent me to this place as Governor. But as the Law of England, gives no Civil power to Her Majesty, out of her Dominions, her Efforts to do you good will be futile unless you consent –

Her Majesty has commanded me to Explain these matters to you, that you may understand them –

The people of Great Britain, are, thank God, free; and, so long as they do not transgress the Laws, they can go where they please, and their Sovereign has not power to restrain them. You have sold them lands here, and Encouraged them to come here. Her Majesty, always ready to protect Her Subjects, is, also, always ready to restrain them.

Her Majesty, the Queen, asks you to sign this Treaty, and so give Her that power which shall Enable Her to restrain them. – I ask you for this publicly: I don't go from one chief to another. –

I'll give you time to consider of the proposal I shall now offer you. What I wish you to do is Expressly for your own good, as you will soon see by the Treaty.

You, yourselves, have often asked the King to extend His Protection unto you. Her Majesty now offers you that Protection in this Treaty. I think it not necessary to say any more about it. I'll therefore read the Treaty.[55]

Instead of acting as a literal translator of these remarks, according to his own account, Henry Williams read out Te Tiriti, the Treaty in Māori, explaining it clause by clause and telling them:

not to be in a hurry, but telling them that we, the missionaries, fully approved of the treaty; that it was an act of love towards them on the part of the Queen, who desired to secure to them their property, rights and privileges; that this treaty was as a fortress for them against any foreign power which might desire to take posession of their country, as the French had taken possession of Otaiti (Tahiti).[56]

This part of the proceedings was surprising, because at a Māori gathering it was the custom for the tāngata whenua, or local people, to open the exchange of speeches. Having just arrived in the Bay of Islands, Hobson was a waewae-tapu (sacred feet) who had yet not been formally welcomed by Māori, and it was odd that a manuhiri (visitor) should stand to speak before the local people had opened the way. Already, it was clear that the British were assuming control of the proceedings, and conducting them according to their own protocols. After the chiefs shook hands with Hobson, Busby stood to assure them that Hobson had come to secure them in the possession of their lands, and that any land not properly acquired by Europeans would be returned.

At this point, according to Colenso, Te Kemara of Ngati Rahiri suddenly rose to his feet.[57] A visionary tohunga who could control the waters and fore-tell the outcome of battles, Te Kemara was the original owner of the Treaty site at Waitangi, the subject of a controversial purchase, who represented the tāngata whenua. He had fought alongside Hongi Hika in various battles, including the attack on Te Totara pā in the Hauraki in 1822, on Mokoia Island in Rotorua in 1823, and at Te Ika-a-Ranganui in Tamaki in 1825.[58] Te Kemara was also a signatory to the 1835 Declaration of Independence. Perhaps he found Hobson's speech presumptuous. In any case, he spoke strongly against the governor, against the English, and against the loss of his lands to Busby and Williams, among others:

> Health to thee, O Govr., this is *mine* to thee o Govr. – I am not pleased
> – towards you – I dont wish for you – I will not consent to your rem.g.
> [remaining] here – If you stay as Govr. perhaps Kamera will be judged and
> condd. [condemned] – Yes, indeed, more than that, Even hung by the neck –
> no, no, no, I shall never agree to your staying. Were all to be on an Equality,
> then perhaps Kamera would say yes – but for the Govr to be up and Kamera
> down! Govr high – up, up, up and Kamera, down, low, small, – a worm
> – a crawler! No, no, no – O Govr this *is mine* to thee, O Govr.
>
> My land is gone – gone – all gone, – the inheritances of my ancestors,
> fathers, relatives, all gone, stolen, – gone, with the Missionaries – Yes, they
> have it, all, all, all – that man there *the Busby and that, there*, the Wiremu,
> they *have* my land *the land on which we stand this day, this even this under my feet
> return it to me* – O Govr.
>
> Return me my lands – say to W. [Williams] return K [Kemara] his land
> – you (pointing to H.W. [Henry Williams]) you, you bald head man, you
> . . . have got my lands . . . O Govr I *do not* wish you to stay – you English are
> not kind like other foreigners – You do not give us good things – I say go
> back, – go back Govr. – we do not want you here – and Kamera says to thee
> Go back.[59]

Te Kemara's opening speech at Waitangi raised a number of key questions. What would happen to the mana of the chiefs if the governor stayed in New Zealand – would the governor be higher than the chiefs? Could he have a chief hanged? Would the governor and the chiefs be equal? What would happen about the loss of lands which had been stolen by the missionaries and Busby? Would the governor return them? He ended with a jibe comparing the English unfavourably with other foreigners – probably a sly reference to Bishop Pompallier and the French. His tone was angry and sceptical of the benefits of having a governor in New Zealand.

When Te Kemara sat down, he was followed by Rewa of Ngai Tawake, Hongi Hika's successor.[60] With Hongi, Rewa had been involved in the release of lands at Kerikeri to the Church Missionary Society in 1819,[61] and with his brothers Wharerahi and Moka, along with Titore and Tareha, in the release of Waimate to the CMS in 1830.[62] In 1826 Rewa had fought

Hakiro (Tareha's son), Waka Nene and Rewa, by William Charles Cotton, 1845.

alongside Te Kemara and Titore (Tareha's nephew) against Ngare Raumati
at Te Rawhiti in the Bay of Islands, and defeated them.

In 1827 Rewa had prepared a cargo of flax with the view of going to
Sydney to get a ship;[63] and in 1831 he visited Sydney with the CMS missionary William Yate, bringing home a rumour that a French warship was about
to come to the Bay of Islands to annex New Zealand and to avenge the
killing of Marion du Fresne in the Bay in 1772. It was this report that had
provoked a letter to King William IV, signed by thirteen major northern
rangatira, including Rewa himself. In 1835 Rewa signed the Declaration of
Independence. By 1840 he was living at Kororareka (which he and Titore
had taken during the 'Girls' War' of 1830) and had forged close links with
Bishop Pompallier.[64] As a past ally of Te Kemara's, he spoke after him and
in a similar vein, but beginning with a jovial greeting in English:

> *How d'ye do Mr. Govr. This is mine to thee O Govr. – go back.* Let the Govr.
> return to his own country. Let my lands be returned to me which have been
> taken by the Missionaries, *by D.* [Davis] *and Clarke, and who and who*, I have
> now no lands – only a name. Foreigners know Mr. Rewa, but this is all I have
> left – a name.

> What do native men want of a Govr. – *we are not whites nor foreigners –*
> *this land is ours – but the land is gone – but we are the Govr. – we the chiefs of this*
> *our fathers land.* I won't consent to the Govr's rem.g. [remaining] *No, return:*
> *What! This land being like Port Jackson, and other lands seen by the English?*[65]

Like Te Kemara, Rewa focused on the governor – should he go or should he
stay? – and asked for his lands to be returned. He stated categorically that
the chiefs were the governors of their own lands, and needed no governor;
drawing a parallel between New Zealand and Port Jackson which as we have
seen, he had visited in 1831.

In his despatch to Sir George Gipps, governor of New South Wales,
that evening, Hobson wrote that Rewa had said, 'Send the man away; do not
sign the paper; if you do you will be reduced to the condition of slaves, and
be obliged to break stones for the roads. Your land will be taken from you,
and your dignity as chiefs will be destroyed.'[66] Hobson added that Rewa was
a follower of the Catholic bishop, who had been prompted to speak in this
way by 'ill-disposed whites'. It is more likely, however, that after seeing the
treatment of the Aborigines in the penal colony at Port Jackson, Rewa had
come to his own conclusions about the benefits of having a governor.

Rewa was followed by his younger brother Moka, with whom Henry
Williams had often clashed. Like Rewa, Moka had signed the Declaration
of Independence, and he now also lived at Kororareka. During the Waitangi
deliberations, he took a similar line to his older brother:

> Let the Govr. return – let us remain as we were. Let my lands be returned
> – all of them. Those with Mr. Baker – *don't say they will be retd. Who'll obey?*
> Where is Clendon. Where is Mair? gone to buy our lands; notwithstanding
> the book of the Govr.

When Moka's words were translated to the governor, Hobson interjected,
'All lands unjustly held wd. be returned – that all lands however purchased
after the date of the Proclamn. wod. not be held to be lawful.'[67] Upon hearing this, Moka retorted:

> That's right Govr., that's straight – but stop, let me see, yes – yes indeed –
> Where is Baker? Where is the fellow? There he is – Come, return me my
> lands?

Moka's challenge was directed at Rev. Charles Baker of the Church Missionary Society, who responded in a way that cannot have inspired much faith in Hobson's assurances. According to Colenso, Baker came forward on the platform and said laconically, 'E hoki koia?' (Will it return?). This provoked Moka to retort:

> There Yes that's as I said – *No, no, no, all false, all false alike*, they wont return.[68]

Like Te Kemara and Rewa, Moka was protesting about land transactions with the CMS missionaries and settlers, and asking for lands to be returned, although the precise grounds for their protests are not made clear in their remarks.

After Moka's speech, a white man stepped forward and complained that Williams was not interpreting all that the rangatira were saying, or translating all of the governor's remarks. He suggested that a Mr Johnson (who Colenso identified as 'an old resident, [dealer in spirits] of Kororareka') should act as an interpreter instead. When Hobson called him forward, however, Johnson demurred; asking only that Williams should speak so that everyone could hear what he was saying, and that he should interpret the chiefs' orations in full: 'They say a great deal about land and missionaries which Mr. Williams does not translate to you, Sir.'[69] Williams and Busby then stood to justify their land transactions, Williams saying that he had purchased land to support his 11 children, most of whom were born in New Zealand, and that the missionaries had come to live with Māori when other Europeans were afraid to do so; and Busby saying that he had only bought land when pressed to do so by Māori, and in order to provide for his family after his office was suspended.

Now that the local rangatira, Te Kemara, and two of the rangatira from Kororareka – all from the northern alliance in the Bay – had spoken against the governor, three rangatira from the southern alliance stood to support him. First Tamati Pukututu, another signatory of the Declaration of Independence, told the governor to stay, jibing at Te Kemara, Moka and Rewa for having sold their lands to the white people:

> *This is mine to thee O Govr.* Sit, Govr., sit a Govr. for us – for me –for all – that our lands may remain – that those fellows and creatures who sneak

about looking for our lands [here the words piritoka, piriawaawa, translated
in Colenso's published account as 'sticking to rocks and the sides of brooks
and gullies' are jotted in the margin] may not have it all –

Sit Govr. sit for me, for us, a father for us . . . these chiefs say, don't sit,
because they have sold all their possessions – and they are filled – and have
no more to sell. Sit Govr., sit – *you and Mr. Busby.*[70]

Pukututu was followed by Matiu, probably a Christian convert, who spoke
to similar effect.

At this point the great warrior Kawiti of Ngati Hine, who had also signed
the Declaration of Independence, and a resolute opponent of land sales,
stood up and spoke strongly against the governor:

No, no, go back, go back. What do you want here, we don't want to be tied
up, & trodden down, we are free; Let the Misss. [missionaries] remain, you
return. I wont consent – to yr. remg [remaining]. What! To be fired at in
our boats by night? What, to be fired at in our Canoes by night? No, no,
go back – there's no place here for you.[71]

Kawiti assumed that the governor would be accompanied by soldiers who
would attack the rangatira, and curtail their freedom.

After Kawiti, Wai of Ngai Tawake spoke, yet another signatory of the
Declaration of Independence. Wai complained that he had just been cursed
by a pākehā, and that white people routinely cheated Māori:

Will you remedy the selling, the cheating, the Stealing of the Whites,
Governor? Yesterday I was cursed by a white man, is that straight?
The White gives us a pound for a Pig, but he gives a white Four pounds
for such a pig – is that straight? he gives us 1/- for a basket of potatoes
but to a white he gives 4/- is that straight? No, no, they won't listen to
you; go back – go back. *Have they listened to the Busby? Will they listen to
you – a newly – arrvd. man?* Sit, indeed, what for? Will you make dealing
straight?[72]

In his speech, Wai claimed that whites gave other whites more for the same
goods than they gave to Māori, and that they would not listen to the governor any more than they had listened to James Busby. The fact that a white

man had just cursed him inspired a desire for utu. Not surprisingly, of all the rangatira who spoke at Waitangi on 5 February 1840, Wai was the only one who never signed Te Tiriti.

The next rangatira to speak in favour of the governor was Pumuka of Te Roroa, who later signed Te Tiriti with his mark. He, too, had been among the signatories to the 1835 Declaration of Independence:

> Stay, Govr. rem [remain] for me. Hear all of you; I'll have this man, a foster-father for me – Stay, sit, listen to my words. Govr., don't go, remain.[73]

Pumuka was followed by Wharerahi, the older brother of Rewa and Moka, who had previously spoken in opposition to the governor. It is interesting that in this debate, Wharerahi took a different position from his younger brothers. Like Pumuka, he spoke in favour of Busby:

> Yes, stay, what else? Is it not good to be at peace? We will have this Govr. – what turn away? No, no –[74]

Wharerahi was a senior figure, and his speech provoked Tareha, a leading rangatira of Ngati Rehia, and his son Hakiro to try to turn the tide of the debate against the governor. After clearing a space in front of the tent, they delivered fiery speeches in ancestral style, running to and fro and gesturing to dramatic effect.

Hakiro had succeeded Titore, his cousin who had visited Sydney in 1819 and signed the 1831 letter to King William IV and the 1835 Declaration of Independence. In 1834 Titore had sent his own letter and some gifts to King William, receiving a suit of armour in return, but he had recently died. In Titore's name, Hakiro spoke against the governor:

> Indeed! I say No, no, go back don't sit – What sit here for, we are not your people; we are free, we wont have a Govr. – return, return, leave us; – the Misss. [missionaries] and Mr. B [Busby] are our Matuas [parents].

When Hakiro sat down, he was followed by his father Tareha, a powerful, imposing rangatira who lived at Te Tii on the Mangonui Inlet, and another signatory of He Whakaputanga. In order to satirise the supposed poverty of his people, Tareha had donned 'a filthy mat, used only as a floor mat, but evidently dressed in this manner for the occasion', and carried a bundle of dried fern-root as a statement of economic self-sufficiency.

According to Colenso, '[Tareha's] habit, his immense size – tall and very robust (being by far the biggest Native of the whole district) – and his deep sepulchral voice, conspired to give him peculiar prominence, and his words striking effect: this last was unmistakeably visible on the whole audience of Natives.'[75] In this debate, Tareha added his weight (which was considerable) to the anti-Governor party:

> No Governor for me – for us – we are the chiefs – we won't be ruled. What, you up, and I down – you high, and I *Tareha*, the great chief, low? *I am jealous of you, go back, you shant stay*. No, no, I wont assent. *What for? Why? What is there here for you?* Our lands are gone – our names remain, *never mind*. Yes we are the chiefs – Go back – return – make haste away. We dont want you return, return –[76]

Tareha's speech focused on the question of mana – would the governor rule the rangatira? Would he be high, and Tareha low? His answer to these questions was a resounding rejection of the kāwana.

In response to Tareha, Rawiri Taiwhanga now stood and spoke. One of the first rangatira who had converted to Christianity, he was a keen student of European agriculture and a literate man who signed the Treaty with his own name – 'Ko Rawiri Taiwanga'. Colenso gave Taiwhanga's hapū as Ngati Tautahi. Taiwhanga had fought with Hongi Hika on the East Coast in 1818, and at the battle of Te Ika-a-Ranganui in 1825. His son Hirini was named after Sydney, the town that his father had visited in the early 1820s. With Taiwhanga's speech, the balance of the debate began to shift in the governor's favour. Like Rewa before him, he began with several phrases in English:

> Good morning Mr. Govr. – very good you – our Govr. Stay – sit – that we may be in peace – a good thing this for us – yes, for us my friends – stay, sit – remain, Govr.[77]

By urging the governor to 'sit' (presumably noho), Rawiri raised an issue to which Wharerahi had earlier referred – that it would be good to be at peace. At least some of the speakers at Waitangi could see advantages in having a governor as a means of ending inter-hapū fighting (although equally, Rawiri may have been referring to disputes with Europeans).

After Taiwhanga, Hone Heke rose to his feet. A rangatira of Te Mahurehure, he had married Hongi Hika's daughter as his second wife. Like Taiwhanga, Heke was literate, signing Te Tiriti with his own name, and also had a close relationship with Henry Williams at this time. According to most accounts, he crystallised the doubts that many of the rangatira were feeling, but was persuasive in the governor's favour:

> To raise up or to bring down? To raise up or to bring down? which? which? Sit Govr. If you return we are gone – ruined – what shall we do? Who are we? We dont know? Remain, a father for us – this is a good thing – Even as the W. [word] of God. –
>
> You go, no, no, then the French, or the rum sellers, will have us. Remain, remain. But we are children; its not for us, but for you, Fathers, Missionaries, for you to say, to choose, we are children. – we don't know do you choose for us – you our Fathers – Missionaries.[78]

After a brief, almost inaudible, speech by a Te Rarawa rangatira in favour of the governor, Tamati Waka Nene from Ngati Hao at Hokianga now stood to address the assembly, further swinging the debate in favour of the governor. A leading rangatira, he was the younger brother of Patuone and son of Tapua, a renowned tohunga and rangatira in the Bay of Islands, and Kawehau, a rangatira woman from Ngati Hao in the Hokianga. As mentioned earlier, when Tapua met Captain James Cook off the Bay in 1769, Cook had given him a red cloak. It seems likely that he and his sons regarded this gift as establishing a chiefly alliance with the British, which they later extended to other British visitors (just as the Pomare lineage did in Tahiti, after Pomare I forged a bond friendship with Captain Cook). Nene had fought in the great northern taua to the south in the late 1810s, and later became a major force in the Hokianga, extending his protection to European missionaries and traders. In 1831, he, Patuone, Wharerahi, Rewa, Titore and others had signed the letter to King William IV, the day before the French ship *La Favorite* anchored in the Bay of Islands. When Nene was baptised in 1839, he took the name Tamati Waka (Thomas Walker) after an English merchant patron of the Church Missionary Society.

In the Waitangi deliberations, Nene spoke strongly in favour of the governor:

I shall speak to us – to ourselves – what do you say? The Govr. return – what *then* shall we do? – Is not the land gone? Is it not covered all covd with men, with strangers, over whom we have no power, we are down, they are up: – what! do you say? the Governor to go back! I am sick with you! Had you sd. so in old time – when the traders, & grog-sellers came – had you turned them back, then you cod. say to the Govr. go back – and it wod. have been correct – and I would also have sd. go back – but now? No, no (turning to ye Govr.) O Govr. sit – I say sit, dont you go away – remain, for us, a father – a judge – a peacemaker – Yes – it is good – straight – remain – dont go away – *Heed not what Ngapuhi say – you stay – our friend & father O Governor.*[79]

In his speech, Nene argued that the Europeans had already covered the land – 'strangers, over whom we have no power, we are down, they are up' – and the land was already gone. Those who spoke against the governor should have opposed the Europeans from their first arrival, but now it was too late. While urging the governor to remain, Nene described his proper role as 'father, judge, peacemaker' – very close to contemporary understandings of kaiwakarite – a judgement he later felt inclined to retract after customs duties and restrictions placed on the felling of kauri were imposed by the governor's fiat in Northland; acts which Nene as well as other rangatira regarded as illegitimate infringements on their tino rangatiratanga, or unfettered chiefly rights.

Perhaps the decisive intervention on this occasion, however, was the speech by Patuone, Waka Nene's elder brother. For some years, Patuone had been living on Waiheke Island in the Hauraki Gulf, where he had located himself as a peacemaker, and he had only returned north several weeks before the governor's arrival. Like his brother, Patuone was a noted warrior who had taken part in the musket wars during the 1820s, fighting alongside Hongi Hika. In Hokianga he had extended his protection to European traders, and in 1826 travelled to Sydney with Captain J.R. Kent, to negotiate for ships to sail to the Hokianga to collect spars. In 1827 Rev. John Hobbs of the Wesleyan mission in Hokianga had reported:

I find that Patuone is not the greatest man in the river. A person by the name of Muriwai is considered by the natives as the father or head, and his cousin Taonui is considered the next, and perhaps Patuone may be the next. Muriwai's elder brother is still living, but as he is a man of slender talent he does not command any more respect than any other person.[80]

During the early 1830s Patuone had fought in the Thames district as an ally of Ngati Paoa, and married a young Ngati Paoa woman. For the rest of the decade he spent much of his time in the Hauraki Gulf, living in different places and returning periodically to Hokianga. In 1831, he and Nene signed the letter to King William IV; four years later, he signed the Declaration of Independence; and in 1837 Patuone received a suit of armour and a suit of green clothes from the Crown for supplying naval ships with timber and other necessities.[81] Just days before, when Henry Williams returned to the Bay of Islands, Patuone and his wife had been baptised.

Patuone was the first speaker to express antipathy towards 'Pikopo' (Bishop Pompallier) and the French, a hostility that may also have derived from the killing of Marion du Fresne and the subsequent punitive killings of Māori – also mentioned in the letter to King George IV in 1831.

> What shall I say? This is to thee, o Govr. sit – stay – you and the Misss. [missionaries] – and the Word of God – remain – that the French have us not, that Pikopo, that bad man, have us not. – Remain, Governor, sit, stay.[82]

As the most senior, Patuone was the last of the manuhiri, or visitors, to speak. According to Pompallier, he 'spoke at length in favour of Mr. Hobson, and explained, by bringing his two index fingers side by side, that they would be perfectly equal, and that each chief would be similarly equal with Mr. Hobson'.[83]

As Claudia Orange pointed out, neither the rangatira Pomare nor Waikato, both powerful leaders who were staunch advocates of Māori independence, attended the Waitangi meeting. Had they done so, they might have answered Nene's arguments and swung the debate against the governor, but this did not happen.[84] In the event, Te Kemara, the rangatira of the land at Waitangi, stood to round off the day's proceedings. As the representative of the tāngata whenua, he had the last word:

> No, no, who says stay? go away – I want my lands – Let us all be alike then remain, but the Govr. up, the Kamera down – no, no.

Running up to Hobson, he crossed his wrists as though handcuffed – no doubt a riposte to Patuone's gesture – and according to Colenso, asked:

Shall I be like this? Like this? Eh! Say! Like this? He then caught hold of the Govr.'s hand, *shaking it lustily* & roaring out, How d'ye do – then again, & again and again – the whole assembly being convulsed with laughter.[85]

Although Te Kemara had not retreated from his earlier opposition to the governor, or his concerns about mana and the implications of the introduction of European laws, he ended the debate on a hilarious note, shaking the governor's hand over and over again in burlesque style, and calling out 'How d'ye do? How d'ye do?'

According to Colenso, this session ended with a roar of laughter. The governor announced that the gathering would reconvene on Friday 7 February, and after three cheers from the crowd, they dispersed. According to Felton Mathew, who arrived with Hobson in New Zealand as the first surveyor-general:

[At the end of the speeches on February 5] one of the chiefs said, 'Give us time to consider this matter – we will talk it over amongst ourselves, we will ask questions, and then decide whether we will sign the treaty.' The speeches lasted about six hours, and the whole scene was one I would not have missed for worlds, and which I will never forget.[86]

Those rangatira who remained behind at Waitangi that day received gifts of tobacco, a botched distribution that aroused much dissatisfaction. After staring fixedly at Hobson as he was about to board the boat to return to the *Herald*, an old rangatira from the interior exclaimed '*Auē! He koroheke! E kore e roa kua mate!*' – 'Alas! An old man! He will soon be dead!'[87]

That night, many of the rangatira sat with Henry Williams and the other missionaries, questioning them about Hobson's arrival and what it might mean. Some of the Europeans who did not want land sales placed under British control were telling the rangatira that 'their country was gone, and they were now only taurekareka (slaves)'.[88] According to Williams, he and his colleagues went through the Treaty:

clause by clause, showing the advantage to them of being taken under the fostering care of the British Government, by which act they would become one people with the English, in the suppression of wars, and of every lawless act; under one Sovereign, and one Law, human and divine.[89]

These explanations must have been reassuring, and there is no indication that the rangatira realised that they were about to cede sovereignty over New Zealand. As was often the case with gatherings organised by James Busby, the food offered to his guests was inadequate (a mark of a tūtūā, or commoner), and a number of the rangatira decided to return to their homes.

The next morning when the missionaries realised that the rangatira were about to disperse, they sent an urgent message to the *Herald*, asking William Hobson to come ashore to collect signatures for the Treaty. He arrived in civilian dress, except for his hat, and told the remaining rangatira that although no more speeches would be permitted, he was willing to receive signatures on the parchment. Pompallier had also arrived with Father Servant, and when he asked for a guarantee of religious freedom to be added to the Treaty, Hobson agreed.

At first, none of the rangatira came forward to sign the document. As soon as Henry Williams began to call out their names, beginning with Hone Heke, Colenso intervened, asking the governor whether he thought that the rangatira understood the articles that they were being asked to sign. Hobson replied testily:

> If the Native chiefs do not know the contents of this treaty it is no fault of mine. I wish them fully to understand it. I have done all that I could do to make them understand the same, and I really don't know how I shall be enabled to get them to do so. They have heard the treaty read by Mr. Williams.[90]

Colenso answered:

> True, your Excellency; but the Natives are quite children in their ideas. It is no easy matter, I well know, to get them to understand – fully to comprehend a document of this kind; still, I think they ought to know somewhat of it to constitute its legality. I speak under correction, your Excellency. I have spoken to some chiefs concerning it, who had no idea whatever as to the purport of the treaty.

In that case, Busby retorted, they should follow the advice of the missionaries, and Hobson agreed.

Presumably Colenso was speaking here about the English text of the Treaty, rather than Te Tiriti. While few of the rangatira spoke or understood English, the suggestion that they were children who knew nothing about

the world, and did not understand what they were signing, still rankles with
many of their descendants. As Hone Sadler remarked:

> As the rangatira prepared themselves for signing Te Tiriti, they knew that
> there were benefits in the signing because they had seen the world, the wider
> world and all it had to offer. For over 20 years, they had observed Pakeha.
> Their ancestors had travelled overseas, they had seen with their own eyes,
> heard with their own ears what is beyond what they can see within their
> whenua (land) of Nu Tireni.[91]

When Henry Williams called out Heke's name again, he came forward
and signed the Treaty. Almost all of the other rangatira also signed, some
with their written names but most with their marks, and shook hands with
the governor, who said 'He iwi tahi tātou' (We are one people).[92] As Erima
Henare explained to the Tribunal, when they signed the Treaty, many of the
rangatira used their nose tattoos as signatures, in effect pressing their noses
to the document – an exchange of hau that tangled their mana together with
that of Queen Victoria. For that reason, too, the parchment of Te Tiriti is
regarded as intensely tapu.

After the signings, Patuone presented a greenstone mere to Hobson for
Queen Victoria, as a way of sealing the alliance. In response, Hobson invited
him to dinner on board the *Herald*, and each of the signatories was given
two blankets with some tobacco and potatoes. As Rima Edwards said in his
evidence to the Tribunal: '*[H]orekau i tukua e nga Rangatira o nga hapu to
ratou mana ki a Kuini Wikitoria. . . .[I] whakaae nga Rangatira o nga hapu kia
whakatungia he hononga tapu waenganui nga mana o Aotearoa me Ingarangi.*'
– 'The rangatira of the hapu did not give their mana to Queen Victoria. . . .
They agreed to establish a sacred bond between the mana of Aotearoa and
England.'[93] When the English draft of the Treaty was sent to England,
however, it was certified as the official version of what had been agreed at
Waitangi and elsewhere, and the promises by which the Crown and rangatira
alike would be bound. This led to a fundamental European misunderstanding
about the nature of the Treaty, which is above all expressed in its Māori text.

The debate and signing at Waitangi was followed by signings at Waimate,
Mangungu and Kaitaia in Northland, and around the country, although
Hobson claimed sovereignty over the South Island by right of discovery,
regarding this part of New Zealand as *terra nullius*, land not claimed by others

(since most of the South Island was occupied by kin groups who made a living as hunters and gatherers, and under stadial legal theory they could not claim sovereignty over their lands). This hasty, rather chaotic proceeding has been subjected to intricate analysis in recent years. Rather surprisingly, however, it was not until the central Northland tribes asked the Tribunal to examine Te Tiriti itself, that the wider context in which He Whakaputanga (the Declaration of Independence) and Te Tiriti were conceived, drafted, debated and signed in the Bay of Islands and Hokianga was formally investigated, almost forty years after the establishment of the Waitangi Tribunal.

In the Te Paparahi o te Raki claim, oral histories, written documents, claimant statements in Māori and expert reports in English were called for and commissioned by the northern kin groups, the Crown and the Tribunal, weighed against both Māori and modernist scholarly and legal conventions and standards, and assessed in the light of their constitutional implications. The result of this extraordinary effort is a tour de force, a 600-page report by the Tribunal that summarises and judiciously weighs a mountain of evidence and arguments. From the outset, the claimants urged the Tribunal to tell 'the truth' about Te Tiriti and He Whakaputanga, and the status of Māori in New Zealand:

> The role of the Tribunal is to delve into 'our' understandings of Te Tiriti and He Whakaputanga and the reasons for which they were signed. Importantly we seek to have the untruths that exist within the myths that are perpetuated about us thrown off. In this light we ask you to listen to us, to question us, and to actively seek our understanding of what our tupuna tried to achieve.[94]

As counsel for the claimants said to the Tribunal:

> [H]aving finally had the courage to launch this waka [you] must not now take fright at the depth or size of the ocean. The Crown must now wade out beyond the shallow waters of de facto power and what Erima Henare has called 'squinty legalism'.[95]

In the end, after summarising the main lines of evidence and recapitulating the key arguments, the Tribunal came to a conclusion that overturned long-standing official understandings about constitutional arrangements in New Zealand. In their final report, they wrote:

Our essential conclusion . . . is that the rangatira did not cede their sovereignty in 1840; that is, they did not cede their authority to make and enforce law over their people and within their territories. Rather, they agreed to share power and authority with the Governor. They and Hobson were to be equal, although of course they had different roles and different spheres of influence. The detail of how this relationship would work in practice, especially where the Māori and European populations intermingled, remained to be worked out over time on a case-by-case basis.[96]

Having drawn a line under stadial interpretations of the Treaty and declaring them invalid, they sought to reassure their readers:

This conclusion may seem radical. It is not. A number of New Zealand's leading scholars who have studied the Treaty – Māori and Pākehā – have been expressing similar views for a generation. . . . Moreover, the conclusion that Māori did not cede sovereignty in February 1840 is nothing new to the claimants. Indeed, there is a long history of their tūpuna protesting about the Crown's interpretation of the treaty.[97]

Despite the Tribunal's exhaustive inquiries and their judicious balancing of different lines of evidence, the question of whether sovereignty was ceded in the Treaty may not yet be settled. Just as the Tribunal's report was released, a PhD thesis on the import of the English text of the Treaty was submitted which argued that at the time the Treaty of Waitangi was signed:

The [intent of] British intervention in New Zealand in 1840 was to establish government over British settlers, for the protection of Maori. British settlement was to be promoted only to the extent that Maori protection was not compromised. Maori tribal government and custom were to be maintained. British sovereignty was not seen as inconsistent with plurality in government and law.[98]

This more limited definition of 'sovereignty' as understood in Britain in 1840 may well be correct. It does not explain, however, why Williams used such different terms to translate this key concept into Māori in He Whakaputanga and Te Tiriti. In Māori, at least, the difference between te mana me te kīngitanga (the mana and kingship) and kāwanatanga (governorship) was (and still is) profound. In any case, almost as soon as Te Tiriti was signed, a much less restricted understanding of British sovereignty was adopted by governors in Port Jackson and in New Zealand, and by some secretaries of state in Britain, breaching the promises in Te Tiriti. It was these failures to protect their tino rangatiratanga over their lands and taonga that led to Māori resistance and complaints, and eventually to two successive wars in New Zealand, first in Northland, and then across much of the North Island.

All of this begs the question of what the rangatira agreed to when they signed Te Tiriti. By forging an alliance with Queen Victoria, the young queen who married her cousin Prince Albert just days after the Treaty was signed; by fixing their tattoos or names to the parchment; and by the gift of a patu (hand club) from Patuone to the queen, they made a commitment to work together towards a shared future, in which the mana of both rangatira and the queen would be upheld. Just as Māori had long imagined that their own atua and the Christian God could co-exist, each in their own sphere, Te Tiriti applied a similar logic. Queen Victoria and her governor would control te ao pākehā (the British sphere of action), while the rangatira would control te ao Māori (the Māori realm), each looking after their own people. At the same time, as allies, they acquired mutual responsibilities and obligations to uphold each other's mana – their fates were intertwined. For this reason, northern leaders have persistently described Te Tiriti as a kawenata, or covenant, a sacred agreement with the British Crown in which rangatira and the Crown alike would work out ways of living together.

The public reaction to the Tribunal's 2014 report on the Treaty of Waitangi, and its conclusion that in Te Tiriti sovereignty was not ceded was curiously muted. The Minister of Treaty Settlements, Chris Finlayson, chose not to argue with its fundamental findings, saying that the Tribunal understood that its report recognised 'continuity, rather than dramatic change' in Treaty scholarship. He stated that the report did not change the fact that the Crown held sovereignty over New Zealand, which had been acquired in ways other than cession in the Treaty. According to the Minister, the Crown is now focused on the future, on developing the Māori–Crown relationship as Treaty partners and achieving just, durable settlements of Treaty claims.[99] Across the pae (threshold) between Māori and the Crown, it seems, space is being left for constitutional innovation.

After 175 years of talking at cross purposes about the Treaty of Waitangi, it is formally accepted that when they signed this agreement the rangatira thought they were forging an aristocratic alliance with Queen Victoria, who had promised to uphold their mana; while the Crown's representatives assumed that it gave them the right to govern the country – a right that the New Zealand government still maintains.[100] In this way, an ontological impasse lies at the heart of the New Zealand state. It will be fascinating to see how these negotiations proceed.

PART TWO

Rivers, Land,
Sea and People

At Pipiriki on our trip down the Whanganui River in 2010.

CHAPTER NINE

Tears of Rangi
Awa / Rivers

IT WAS WINTER, 10 AUGUST 2010, A COLD, STILL DAY. TWO DAYS EARLIER, the Whanganui – a river that runs to the west coast from the centre of the North Island – had been in flood. When we parked outside Pipiriki marae, mist drifted across the hills behind the little red-and-white meeting house, its red ensign flag fluttering in the breeze. After the local people formally welcomed us onto the marae, we shared a meal in the dining hall and then joined them inside the meeting house.[1]

Our team, led by Libby Hakaraia and Tainui Stephens, was filming a documentary about my great-grandfather, James McDonald, a film-maker and photographer who had travelled down the river in 1923 with a Dominion Museum expedition, recording ancestral tikanga. Lying around on mattresses, we watched as Libby showed a silent movie and photographs shot by my great-grandfather, including footage of local people working eel weirs from elegant river canoes, displaying weaving, and playing skipping games in the village.

The local people were fascinated, recognising places and ancestors, calling out their names and telling stories about them, although the meeting house went quiet when the film showed a tohunga, or priest, performing a divination ritual, chanting and shaking his finger as sticks jerked weirdly across the ground towards some standing wands. Afterwards, Libby, who had brought a portable printer with her, printed copies of some of these ancestral images.

Eel weirs on the Whanganui River, by James Ingram McDonald, 1921.

The next morning, our party, led by Libby and Tainui with two cameramen and a sound technician, my husband Jeremy and me with our daughter
Amiria (also an anthropologist) and her son Tom, boarded a replica ancestral
canoe that had been built for the Hollywood movie *River Queen*. As we paddled down the river, sliding past sheer cliffs green with ferns, the cameramen
filmed our progress from a boat. At one bend on the river the canoe came
to a standstill, caught on an underwater snag. Saying that the local taniwha
(river ancestor) was obstructing our passage, our guide Ned Tapa stripped
to his wetsuit, dived under the canoe and set it free. When we arrived at
Hiruharama, the next settlement downriver, we landed beside a steep, slip-
pery mud bank, climbing it by jamming our paddles as footholds into its face.

That night at Hiruharama, Libby showed more of McDonald's films and
photographs, projecting them onto a sheet hung across a corner of the meeting house. One local man spoke about his ancestress, Mere Pakeha, shown
in one of the portraits, a European girl raised by a Māori family after being
abandoned at Moutoa Gardens in Whanganui township. In those days, he
said, young girls who got 'into trouble' would sometimes leave their babies
at Moutoa, knowing that Māori visiting from upriver would pick them up,

Meeting with elders at Koroniti during our trip down the Whanganui River in 2010.

take them home and raise them. Other locals described how some of the settlements filmed by McDonald had been shifted across the river when the road was built, so that the people could drive into town.

The next day when we visited Ranana marae, further down the river, a kuia (elderly woman) talked about how her grandmother used to work flax, stripping the muka, or fibres, and dyeing them in living mud, scenes that had been shot by McDonald during the 1923 Whanganui expedition. In 1994 when the Whanganui River claim was argued in front of the Waitangi Tribunal, McDonald's film and photographs had been used to demonstrate the intimacy of ancestral relationships between local kin groups and the river. As we visited each marae, the river was a powerful presence, linking their communities together.

Four years later, on 5 August 2014, a large crowd including leading Māori chiefs, mayors, ambassadors and local residents gathered at Ranana marae. Whanganui leaders signed a deed of settlement with the New Zealand government over their Treaty claims to the river, legally recognising the Whanganui as a living being, the first waterway in the world to gain this status.[2] In many ways, this was a revolutionary step. By recognising the river, Te Awa Tupua (River with Ancestral Power),[3] as a legal person with its own rights, the Whanganui River was placed in a new relation with human beings. Key parts of the settlement deed are in Māori. In the opening section, the Whanganui River is described as the source of ora (life, health and well-being), a living whole that runs from the mountains to the sea, made up of many tributaries and binding its people together, expressed in a saying often used by Whanganui people, '*Ko au te awa, ko te awa ko au*' (I am the river, the river is me).

In the deed of settlement, two people, mutually chosen by the Crown and the Whanganui tribes, are established as Te Pou Tupua, 'the human face' of the river, acting in its name and in its interests and administering Te Korotete (literally a storage basket for food from the river), a fund of $30 million dedicated to enhancing the health and well-being of the river. These two individuals are supported by Te Kopuka,[4] a group representing people with interests in the river; and Te Heke Ngahuru,[5] a strategy that brings these people together to advance the 'environmental, social, cultural and economic health and well-being' of the river. In the settlement, a payment of $80 million is also made to the Whanganui tribes as redress for breaches of their rights in relation to the river under the Treaty of Waitangi.

In the Māori text of the Treaty, as we have seen, the version debated in 1840 and signed around the country, Queen Victoria had agreed to uphold 'the full chieftainship of the rangatira, the tribes and all the people of New Zealand over their lands, their dwelling-places and all of their prized possessions'.[6] In the English draft, the queen guaranteed to their ancestors the 'full, exclusive, undisturbed possession of their Lands and Estates Forests Fisheries and other properties . . . so long as it is their wish and desire to retain the same in their possession' – in both cases including freshwater fisheries and their ancestral rivers, lakes, springs, wetlands and estuaries.

Since 1975 the Waitangi Tribunal, established to inquire into breaches of Treaty promises by the Crown, has investigated many complaints by Māori kin groups relating to the loss and/or degradation of their ancestral waterways, holding hearings around the country to address these grievances. The Tribunal has issued reports and made recommendations about particular waterways, generally upholding these complaints (e.g. Waitangi Tribunal 1992, 1993, 1999). Where these kin groups voluntarily shared their ancestral rivers with the incoming settlers or sold the land around them, however, the Tribunal has ruled that these rights have been qualified. In response to these findings, successive governments have offered apologies to many kin groups around the country, and settlements in cash and kind, including co-management arrangements for lakes and rivers.

In the case of the Whanganui River, for instance, the tribes complained to the Tribunal that since 1840 and without their consent, their tino rangatiratanga, or absolute authority, over the river had been usurped by the Crown. Despite their resistance, by fighting, petitions and legal action, eel weirs had been destroyed, gravel removed, customary practices forbidden, fishing rights denied, water-use laws imposed, the river polluted and water diverted for a huge hydro-electric project. As a result, their ancestral river and their way of life had been damaged and degraded. In the Whanganui deed of settlement, ancestral Māori conceptions of the relations between the Whanganui River and its people were recognised,[7] and reparation was made, but with a number of significant caveats – that the agreement does not interfere with existing private property rights in the river; and that Te Pou Tupua's consent is not required for the use of water from the river or its tributaries, for instance. Instead, the use of water is subject to a review process that is intended to resolve the issues of rights and interests in water, in which the Crown's position is that 'no one owns water'[8] – although it may be quantified and rights to its use may be licensed, and bought and sold. In this way water is divided from Te Awa Tupua, although as Whanganui iwi members argued before the Tribunal, the river is precisely fresh water (wai māori) flowing through space and time, the 'lifeblood' of the land.[9]

Freshwater debates

At the beginning of the twenty-first century when the Treaty claims of Whanganui tribes were being negotiated with the government, the control of fresh water was a topic of passionate debate in New Zealand. In part, this was provoked by the degradation of rivers, springs and aquifers in many parts of the country, and in part by Māori claims to waterways in the face of the imminent privatisation of local power companies. During the 2011 election campaign, the centre-right National Party announced that if it were elected, it would partially privatise a number of state-owned assets, including three power companies. After it was elected, National decided to proceed with the asset sales, despite strong public opposition to this policy.

Recognising that if they proceeded unilaterally, legal challenges from Māori kin groups were almost certain to succeed in the courts, government representatives began to negotiate with the Freshwater Iwi Leaders Group, representing those iwi (tribes) with major ancestral lakes and rivers that would be affected by the asset sales, including Whanganui, although the question of ownership was excluded. The exact terms of these discussions have not been made public, but they do involve various kinds of co-management of these waterways between regional bodies and iwi. In February 2012, these delicate negotiations were disrupted when the New Zealand Māori Council, a statutory body representing all Māori, submitted a claim to the Tribunal, asking for an urgent hearing of a nationwide claim that the asset sales were detrimental to Māori interests in fresh water. Once the power companies were partially privatised, the Māori Council argued, private owners who were not bound by the Treaty would resist remedies for the loss of Māori rights in water, such as shares in the power companies, a say in their governance or water royalties.

Sir Eddie Taihakurei Durie, a former justice of the High Court and chairman of the Waitangi Tribunal, was the spokesman for the council's freshwater claim. During his time as chairman of the Tribunal, he had heard many complaints about ancestral waterways, and indeed had written one of the most eloquent and influential reports on this subject, the report on the Whanganui River.[10] In their claim, the Māori Council asked for the asset sales to be delayed until the government had made a formal commitment to uphold Māori rights in fresh water. The prime minister, John Key, opposed this request, as did the Freshwater Iwi Leaders Group, saying that they were already in tribe-by-tribe discussions with the Crown, and that on this matter, negotiations were preferable to a hearing in front of the Waitangi Tribunal or litigation in the courts. Despite their opposition, however, the Waitangi Tribunal decided to hold an urgent hearing on the claim, which began in July 2012. Soon afterwards, the Tribunal ordered that the asset sales should be delayed until after the first stage of the inquiry had been completed.

When the prime minister expressed frustration, asking the Tribunal to issue an early report on its findings, the Freshwater Iwi Leaders Group supported him at first. Along with Whanganui and other iwi, this included Waikato-Tainui, a confederation of kin groups based on the Waikato River, at the heart of the Māori King movement led by Tuheitia, the present Māori King.[11] The Waikato River is also a major source of water for Auckland, the largest city in New Zealand, and for Mighty River Power, the first power company that the government intended to privatise. This great river, famed in tribal history, is celebrated in the proverb, '*Waikato taniwha rau, he piko he taniwha, he piko he taniwha*' – 'Waikato of a hundred taniwha, at every bend, a taniwha', celebrating the powerful chiefs who live on its banks. As we have seen, taniwha are awesome beings who act as guardians of rivers, harbours and other significant places. Tuwharetoa, a confederation of kin groups around Lake Taupo and another powerful member of the Freshwater Iwi Leaders Group, also supported the government's position. Tuwharetoa and Waikato have been allies for many generations, since the founding of the Māori King movement and beyond.

While the Tribunal was sitting, the prime minister declared that 'no one owns the water' – the position adopted by the Crown's lawyers during the hearing. When the Tribunal issued its first report, however, it dismissed the Crown's arguments and found that Māori kin groups hold property rights in fresh water.[12] The Tribunal recommended that the government should hold a national hui (gathering) to discuss these issues, and delay the asset sales until they were settled. In addition, it suggested that in recognition of Māori rights to fresh water, the kin groups should be awarded shares and some governance rights in the partially privatised power companies. As soon as the Tribunal's findings were released, there was a furore. In letters to the editor, articles, blogs and in private, many New Zealanders expressed incredulity that Māori should claim to own fresh water (although some were sympathetic).

Buoyed by these expressions of public support, the prime minister contested the Tribunal's findings, reiterating that 'no one owns the water, no one owns the wind, no one owns sunlight, no one owns the sea'.[13] For this reason, he argued, there was no need for a national hui to discuss the matter. When, in defiance of this admonition, King Tuheitia summoned such a gathering, the prime minister announced that he would not attend and forbade members of his government (including the Māori MPs) to go there. This put the Māori Party in a difficult position. Along with two other small parties, the Māori Party (which seeks to advance the interests of Māori people) was in coalition with the National-led government, holding the balance of power. When the co-leaders of the Māori Party announced that they would not attend the hui, their former colleague Hone Harawira abused them, using an offensive term implying that they were slaves.

Despite widespread popular opposition to the partial sales of the power companies, public anger was now diverted towards Māori claims to the ownership of fresh water. Rodney Hide, a former right-wing politician, wrote in the *New Zealand Herald*:

> Who would have believed it? Singing a song can make a river yours. Plus give you a chunk of a power company and a say over how that company's run. Well, that's what the Waitangi Tribunal says. It's not quite enough to just sing a song. You should also know the river's taniwha and use the river to wash away spells and curses. But the clincher is to recognise the river's life force. Then it's yours.[14]

At the same time, the idea that Māori kin groups enjoy special relationships with particular waterways is quite widely accepted. When the *Herald* reported that the Whanganui River would be granted legal status in its own right, for instance, there was little controversy. Indeed, many New Zealanders who are concerned about the state of the country's waterways support the idea that a river can be a legal person.

In the event, the national gathering to discuss Māori water rights was held, attended by leaders from across Māoridom, including the leaders of the Māori Party. Towards the end of the gathering, King Tuheitia went head to head with the prime minister, declaring, 'We have always owned the water.' In his speech, the king said that his tribe intended to take back control of the Waikato River. 'We have never ceded our mana [ancestral prestige] over the river to anyone,' he added. 'In the eyes of our people, Pakeha law was set up to minimise our mana and maximise their own.'[15] After many of the key tribal leaders had left the gathering, resolutions were moved that all negotiations between Māori kin groups and the government over ancestral waterways should cease. These recommendations were adopted, but later disavowed by a number of key leaders who were absent when they were passed.

During the weeks that followed, public controversy about Māori water rights died down. Although Waikato boycotted a subsequent meeting with the government, most other members of the Freshwater Iwi Leaders Group decided to continue their negotiations with the Crown. Subsequently, the government decided to press ahead with the sale of Mighty River Power, while the New Zealand Māori Council appealed to the Supreme Court to seek a review of the asset sales process. In its decision, the Supreme Court ruled that despite the partial sale of the hydro companies, the government would be able to compensate Māori for any losses of their rights to fresh water, and that the asset sales process should not be halted as a result of the appeal.[16] Accordingly, the asset sales went ahead. It was these disputes that set the scene for the Whanganui River settlement.

'I am the river, the river is me'

In these clashes and debates, deep-seated assumptions are being contested. As the New Zealand law professor Alex Frame has noted, in front of the Waitangi Tribunal, Māori witnesses involved in freshwater claims often deploy modernist conceptions of private property and ownership to buttress their arguments.[17] At other times, however, they appeal to ancestral cosmological ideas. In the process of these shifts and juxtapositions, deep-seated, taken-for-granted presuppositions are sometimes brought to light, and negotiated. When explaining ancestral approaches to particular waterways, for instance, elders often speak of fresh water as the 'lifeblood of the land',[18] reciting chants that re-enact the origins of the cosmos. As Viveiros de Castro has argued for Yanonami cosmological accounts, such accounts do not reflect a Māori 'world view' but rather, 'express the [Māori] world *objectively from inside it*'.[19]

In the creation process described by Māori cosmological accounts, as we have seen, water appears early. In one of these chants, for example, water emerges while Ranginui the sky and Papatuanuku the earth are locked together:

> The Earth trembles, the Sky trembles, the Ground trembles, the Source trembles
> The numerous trembles, the resounding tremble, the ebbing
> The Waters of the Earth, the Waters of the Sky, the Waters of the Ground
> The Source of Waters, the ebbing.[20]

When Rangi and Papa are separated by Tane, they weep bitterly for each other. The tears of Rangi fall down to earth, forming rivers and lakes including Whanganui, Tongariro and Lake Taupo.[21] Mists rise up from Papa's body, exhaling sorrow and loss. While the rain is known as wai mangu (dark waters), the springs, groundwater and aquifers that bubble up from the earth are known as wai mā (pure, clear waters), used in tapu-raising rituals.[22] Together these comprise the wai rua (two waters, or spirit) that animate all forms of life. As the relations between these male and female ancestors alternate between union and intimacy, and quarrelling and separation, their descendants care for or attack the hau ora (the 'breath of life' or energy) of other life forms, including land and water bodies. An attack on the hau of a river is an attack on the life force of its people, since they share ancestral hau together.

In evidence presented to the Whanganui River Tribunal, this co-mingling was evoked in many ways. In ancestral times, for instance, it was necessary to offer the first catch of the season to a river ancestor to ensure the ora (health, well-being) of the river and its people. If these and other gestures of respect were not made, the hau of the river and its people alike would suffer. This hauhauaitu (or harm to the hau) was manifested as illness or ill fortune, a breakdown in the balance of reciprocal exchanges. The life force had been affected, showing signs of collapse and failure. As an elder lamented:

> It was with huge sadness that we observed dead tuna [eels] and trout along the banks of our awa tupua [ancestral river]. The only thing that is in a state of growth is the algae and slime. Our river is stagnant and dying.
>
> 'E rere kau mai te awa nui mai i Te Kahui Maunga ki Tangaroa. Ko au te awa, ko te awa ko au.' [The great river flows from the Mountains to the Sea. I am the river, the river is me.] If I am the river and the river is me – then, emphatically, I am dying.[23]

Witnesses also described particular taniwha (ancestral water guardians with uncanny powers), the places where they live and their idiosyncratic habits. They discussed the practice of rāhui, where a leader places a stretch of water under a prohibition because someone has drowned there, or fish and eels are becoming scarce.

Such associations between people and waterways are deep and intimate. In formal speeches, Māori orators identify themselves by naming their key ancestor, their mountain and their river, and these landmarks and their paramount chiefs and ancestors are regarded as one. After the Land Wars, for example, when many of his territories were confiscated in 1865, Tawhiao, the second Māori King, sang a lament, bidding farewell to his ancestral land as a beloved woman, the Waikato River springing from her breasts:

'*Tawhiao, Maori King*' *n.d.*

I look down on the valley of Waikato,
As though to hold it in the hollow of my hand . . .
See how it bursts through
The full bosoms of Maungatautari and Mangakawa,
Hills of my inheritance:
The river of life, each curve
More beautiful than the last,
Across the smooth belly of Kirikiriroa,
Its gardens bursting with the fullness of good things,
Towards the meeting place at Ngaruawahia
There on the fertile mound I would rest my head
And look through the thighs of Taupiri.
There at the place of all creation
Let the King come forth.[24]

In this cosmo-logic, people, land, waterways and ancestors are literally
tied together – thus the term tāngata whenua (land people), the people

Waka near the Whanganui River, by James Ingram McDonald, 1921.

who belong in a particular place. In this form of order, rivers bind land and people together. They may be spoken about as plaited ropes composed of different genealogical lines, entangling land, people and ancestors.

In the Whanganui River hearings, for instance, the river was described as a 'three-stranded rope', binding together the upper, middle and lower river iwi (tribes) – a motif expressed in carvings in Whanganui meeting houses, assisting the different kin groups to join forces in advancing their claims about the river. As Whanganui elders told the Tribunal, the river was the heartbeat of their communities, and the pulse of their everyday lives. In ancestral times, the river had been a highway, linking them together. In each of the villages that lined its banks, there was a marae (ceremonial centre) where they greeted and fed their guests. In spring the Whanganui people planted their gardens, in summer they fished at the mouth of the river, and in autumn they fished for eels, lamprey and other native fish, gathered berries and harvested the gardens. They went to the river for healing, and rituals of renewal. The rhythm of life was decided by the agricultural cycle, and the movement of fish and people up and down the river.

Another way of speaking about the binding power of rivers is by reference to vortices – whirlpools and eddies – formed as the flows and currents

James Ingram McDonald and Johannes Andersen, n.d.

from different streams and springs spiral together. In Māori carving, as we have seen, the double spiral enacts the recursive emergence of the cosmos as a vortex, with whakapapa lines swirling in and out of an ancestral source. In this way, James McDonald's photographs and films of the Whanganui River were used in the Whanganui River claim, allowing Tribunal members to spiral back in space-time to see the state of the river in 1923 for themselves, and to see the intimacy of the links between Whanganui iwi and their river. Because they depict ancestral lives, McDonald's films and photographs are regarded as taonga by local iwi.

At the same time, these images emerged from long-standing relations between Māori and non-Māori. The Dominion Museum expeditions, initiated by Sir Apirana Ngata and supported by his secretary Raumoa Balneavis, aimed to record historic events and tikanga that were in danger of being lost. The team included the ethnologist Elsdon Best and my great-grandfather James McDonald, artist, photographer and film-maker. They visited Gisborne (1919), Rotorua (1920), Whanganui (1921) and the East Coast (1923), and on the last two expeditions were accompanied by Te Rangihiroa/ Peter Buck, a Māori medical doctor and former MP who was about to embark on a distinguished international career in anthropology.

The team used cutting-edge technology, including wax-cylinder sound recordings and moving pictures. During the Whanganui expedition, McDonald shot silent-film footage and hundreds of glass-plate photographs on and beside the river, while Best and Te Rangihiroa interviewed local people and studied weaving, chants and other tikanga.

On our journey down the Whanganui River in 2010, we met descendants of those who had welcomed the Dominion Museum Expedition almost 90 years earlier. In the world of whakapapa, such intergenerational exchanges are common, binding descent lines together. As Matiu Mareikura told the Whanganui River Tribunal, our ancestors cast long shadows into the present: 'We have been given the task to hold and preserve these things for our mokopuna [grandchildren, descendants] – not for us, but for the generations yet to come. . . . [T]ime is like this shadow. It starts to spread out, and spread out, and when our shadow is long, we are in line with the old people . . .'[25]

'No one owns the water': modernist views of rivers

In their recent article 'The Politics of Ontology', Holbraad, Pedersen and Viveiros de Castro have written about anthropologists having the ability to 'pass through' what they study, like an artist 'releasing shapes and forces that offer access to what may be called the dark side of things', and 'leaving a way out for the people you are describing' while 'giving the ontological back to "the people"' – as though this was in the anthropologist's gift.[26] There are other possibilities for anthropological engagement with 'others', however, although these may be less heroic. It is not unthinkable, for instance, that anthropologists might learn from the approaches of these 'others' to relationships – as exchange partners, friends and allies in shaping 'how things could be' – working together to confront current challenges and dilemmas, generating new kinds of insights and outcomes on the way.[27]

For anthropologists and citizens alike, this might involve experiments in philosophical reciprocity, in which assumptions about what is real, ways of describing and ideas about desirable purposes are genuinely up for grabs. In the process, a field of play may emerge that opens up the possibility of ontological creativity, as well as collisions and clashes. Indeed, something of this kind seems to have happened in the Whanganui deed of settlement. At the same time, different forms of order may rely upon incompatible assumptions about how the world works (e.g. that ancestors and descendants may, or may not, be co-present; or that a person can, or cannot, move between the everyday world and the ancestral realm; or that a river is, or is not, a living being), and such clashes may prove to be recurrent and resilient.

Just as Māori ancestral ideas are deployed in front of the Waitangi Tribunal, for instance, the position adopted by the prime minister and the government in the freshwater debates – that while water rights can be sold to private owners, 'no one owns the water' – derives from ideas that arrived with the first European settlers in New Zealand. The habits of mind involved here are so deeply entrenched as to be almost invisible, until they collide with competing realities. As we have seen, they include the Cartesian division between Nature and Culture, reflected in the idea of the 'state of Nature', including the 'untamed wilderness' with its mountains, forests, waterways, plants and animals, and 'wild' and 'barbaric' peoples (including Māori).[28] According to key Enlightenment thinkers, things in a state of Nature could not be owned as property and bought or sold – for instance, air, the ocean and fresh water.[29]

While the 'wilderness' was often celebrated, by the Romantics in Europe, for instance, there was also a powerful impetus to bring it under human control, often described as 'progress' and 'improvement'. Unless people applied their labour to the land, through cultivation for instance, it was thought to remain in 'a state of Nature' and they could not lay claim to it – the doctrine of *terra nullius*, which was applied to the South Island of New Zealand, inhabited largely by hunters and gatherers when it was claimed in 1840 by the British Crown. Under stadial thinking, a shift from a 'state of Nature' to one of 'civilisation' and 'progress' was both inevitable, and virtuous – with 'civilisation' assumed to equate with 'modernist' conventions. Since the European settlement of New Zealand, for instance, different dimensions of existence – land, forests and fish; time and knowledge; airwaves, the ocean and fresh water – have been progressively transformed into distinct, quantifiable units, commodities for sale in the market. Even before the first parties of European settlers arrived, surveyors began to map out the land, drawing grids based on latitude and longitude to define and divide up settlements and sections.[30] In the process, the islands – including rivers, springs and lakes – were partitioned into 'blocks', bounded units that could be bought and sold on the market.[31] As soon as the Treaty of Waitangi was signed in 1840, British agents assumed that all land in New Zealand was vested in the Crown, and subject to British law.

From the outset, however, Māori contested the imposition of this kind of logic. The queen's promise to Māori in the English draft of the Treaty, for instance, that she would uphold the undisturbed possession of their lands, forests, fisheries and other property (including waterways), as long as they wished to retain them in their possession, recognised a powerful determination among Māori to maintain control over their own country. In Te Tiriti, the queen's formal acknowledgement of their tino rangatiratanga over their lands, forests, fishing grounds and all of their taonga, and the promise that the queen would ensure that their tikanga (right ways of doing things) would be equal to those of her people in Britain, made it possible for the rangatira to sign the agreement, allowing Governor Hobson to represent Queen Victoria in New Zealand.

At first, the challenge that tino rangatiratanga posed to the inevitability and virtue of European settlement was resolved by legally defining Māori rights (including rights to fresh water) as a 'burden' on the Crown's title until they were extinguished. This was achieved by voluntary sales in the first instance, although many of these early transactions were later repudiated. Later, when Māori began to refuse to release land and waterways, their rights were extinguished by military action, followed by confiscation, forced sales and freehold titles generated by the Native Land Court. This process has been closely documented,[32] although some Europeans at the time, including the first Chief Justice of New Zealand, Sir William Martin, railed against the injustice of these proceedings as violations of the Treaty of Waitangi.[33]

With respect to fresh water, where land blocks were adjacent to non-tidal rivers and lakes, it was assumed that under English common law, title to the land ran to the centre line of the waterway (or the centre point, in the case of lakes) – the maxim of *ad medium filum aquae*.[34] At the same time, it was assumed that fresh water itself could not be owned. As Sir William Blackstone argued in his *Commentaries* (1765–1769), because 'water is a moveable, wandering thing, and must remain common by the law of nature, . . . I can only have a temporary property therein'.[35] Since it was 'wild' and 'untamed', fresh water was held to exist in a state of nature, where property rights did not apply. As European settlement intensified, however, the Crown claimed the control of all navigable rivers and lakes in New Zealand, on the grounds that this was necessary to protect the 'national interest' in drainage, flood control and town water supplies. Nevertheless, it did not claim to own the water itself, which was still regarded as part of the commons. In the recent debates over Māori claims to fresh water, the Crown has continued to uphold this position.

At the same time, in New Zealand as elsewhere, the idea that fresh water is part of the commons is under siege. From Brazilian rainforests to the Arctic and Antarctic ice caps to 'wild' waterways, the last refuges of 'untouched nature' are being redefined as 'resources' for human uses. In this anthropocentric framing, even those who seek to protect these places talk about the 'services' that they perform for humanity (in talk of 'ecosystem services', for example),[36] fostering the idea (based on ancient myth-models that include the Genesis story and the Great Chain of Being) that people are in charge of the planet. Once these services are quantified and a price is put on them, they too become commodities, available for sale on the market. Within such a logic, it makes sense to charge for the use of fresh water; and to suppose that a river, even one which is a 'legal person', needs humans to speak on its behalf.

In the first draft agreement between Whanganui iwi and the Crown, for instance, the two people appointed to speak for the river were described as guardians, one appointed by local kin groups and one by the Crown. Under this arrangement, the river is placed in the same legal category as children, or adults who are incapacitated, who have guardians to make decisions for them.[37] In this draft version, the river's 'independent voice' is a kind of ven-triloquism. For Whanganui Māori, as we have seen, this marked a radical shift from ancestral conceptions, in which earth and sky, mountains and rivers are powerful beings upon whom people depend, and where river taniwha act as kaitiaki (guardians) for people, not the other way around. It is possible, however, that this inversion has been avoided in the final ver-sion of the Whanganui deed of settlement, which describes Te Pou Tupua – two guardians appointed by the Whanganui iwi and the Crown – as 'the human face' of the river, echoing the Māori idea of kanohi ora, people as living faces of their ancestors. How this works out in practice is yet to be seen.

'Bind the lines'

Ancestral Māori relations with rivers and other waterways remain powerful in New Zealand. Nevertheless, as we have seen, this is not the only logic adopted by Māori, whether in front of the Waitangi Tribunal or in the wider

debates about fresh water. As Alex Frame has observed, one way in which
Māori contest the Crown's claims to control rivers and other waterways is to
claim them as property themselves:

> The 'commodification' of the 'common heritage' has provoked novel claims
> [to the Waitangi Tribunal] and awakened dormant ones. . . . Claims to water
> flows, electricity dams, airwaves, forests, flora and fauna, fish quota, geother-
> mal resources, seabed, foreshore, minerals, have followed the tendency to
> treat these resources, previously viewed as common property, as commodities
> for sale to private purchasers. Not surprisingly, the Māori reaction has been:
> if it *is* property, then it is *our* property![38]

While elders or young people who are immersed in te ao Māori make unself-
conscious, matter-of-fact statements about taniwha and river ancestors, for
instance, others use such concepts strategically, or with 'scare quotes' around
them. Indeed, outside of the context of these debates, many Māori regard
rivers in ways that differ little or not at all from other New Zealanders.

This is not surprising, because as we have seen, since the early contact
period in New Zealand, Māori have engaged with a range of modernist ontological styles, often very successfully, and sometimes exclusively. While some
of these styles are difficult to reconcile with ancestral Māori ways of doing
things, others resonate across 'worlds', making some kind of sense-making
possible. In the claims presented to Tribunal hearings, ancestral Māori
and modernist propositions are often strategically interwoven, forming a
single complex kaupapa, or argument.[39] The Māori participants typically
include not just elders and tribal experts, but also historians, lawyers, scientists, priests, administrators and Tribunal members (who may be the same
people). Many of these individuals are highly educated, well-travelled and
cosmopolitan. As the anthropologist Marilyn Strathern has written about
the process of reasoning: 'I take a thread [of thought] to be something that
can be caught, both caught hold of and getting itself caught onto what is in
its vicinity. . . . Any particular thread of thought might appear as a singular
twist, might seemingly take the form of a genealogy or archaeology, but in
truth was never unknotted from innumerable others.'[40] This idea of weaving
an argument from diverse strands echoes the way in which ancestral Māori
and modernist ideas entangle in debates about fresh water in New Zealand.
They do not exist in immutable, binary boxes – far from it.

Some of the most interesting scholarship on fresh water in New Zealand is carried out in this mode, with environmental scientists (e.g. Hikuroa, Slade and Gravley 2011, Tipa 2013, Morgan 2011, 2014), anthropologists (e.g. Muru-Lanning 2010, 2016) and sociologists (Douglas 1984), many of whom are Māori, weaving Māori conceptions with global frameworks in exploring river systems. In a 'singular twist', for instance, Muru-Lanning points out, in te ao Māori, the relation between a person and a river is defined by their genealogical relationship. In laying claim to one's ancestral river, one must say tōku awa – 'my river', using the subordinate possessive tōku which indicates that the speaker is junior (teina – from a junior line) to the river, which is tuakana, or from a senior line, and dominant. Instead of translating tōku awa as 'my river', then, it would be more accurate to say, 'I belong to this river', thus turning the modernist idea of ownership on its head.[41]

The same kind of creative rethinking is also happening in the law, with ideas from global discussions (e.g. Christopher Stone's suggestion that natural resources might be given legal personality[42]) being strategically combined with ancestral conceptions by lawyers involved in the Treaty process in New Zealand,[43] including Māori environmental lawyers (e.g. Morris and Ruru 2010[44]), and tribal claimants in relation to waterways. In their 2010 article, for instance, Morris and Ruru were the first to suggest that rivers might be recognised as legal persons in New Zealand. They outlined Stone's arguments, examined a series of Waitangi claims around rivers and offered a draft Rivers Bill, which they then critically analysed. As they remarked:

> The beauty of the concept is that it takes a western legal precedent and gives life to a river that better aligns with a Maori worldview that has always regarded rivers as containing their own distinct life forces. Furthermore, the legal personality concept recognises the holistic nature of a river and may signal a move away from the western legal notion of fragmenting a river on the basis of its bed, flowing water, and banks.[45]

This danger of fragmentation has not entirely been avoided in the final Whanganui River agreement, however. Nor did Morris and Ruru think that this path is without its dangers, including overgeneralising the state of rivers in relation to particular iwi.

In front of the Tribunal, too, this kind of weaving of different lines of argument with distinct, yet entangled, genealogies or archaeologies is ubiquitous. As discussed, the Treaty of Waitangi itself exists in two different versions, the original draft in English and the Māori translation that was debated in 1840 at Waitangi and other places, and signed by almost all of the English witnesses and the rangatira. Contemporary discussions about the Treaty typically shift, almost imperceptibly, from Māori to English and from one text to the other, often juxtaposing rather than interrogating or even noticing their differences.[46] This ontological braiding is easy to do in whakapapa, a multi-dimensional, open-ended and intricate field of action, where a single ancestral link suffices for membership, although this link has to be activated and kept alive by participation. In different contexts, a person may call upon different arrays of relations, turning from one taha, or 'side', of themselves to another (for instance, different kin groups or ethnic identities) in the networks, shifting states of being in the process.[47] While at one moment, a person may stand in te ao Māori, where river ancestors are real and co-present, at another they may speak and think as a physicist, or a historian, or a highly trained lawyer, with no evident sense of contradiction. Place in the relational field and modes of being are mutually implicated.

In ancestral Māori ways of being, there is nothing new about shifting between different dimensions of reality (for instance te pō, the realm of ancestors, and te ao, the everyday world of light), or between different papa, or levels, in the relational field – hence whakapapa, to move between papa, different dimensions of being. At certain strategic points, these dimensions intersect, and the sites at which this happens are particularly potent. These sites, which act as pae (or portals between different dimensions of reality), may be taonga (or ancestral treasures); toi Māori (ancestral art forms); people – for instance, tohunga (priests) or ariki (high chiefs); or places and events in which Māori 'ways' are dominant – for instance, marae (kin group ceremonial centres), kapa haka (action song) groups, waka ama (outrigger canoe) paddling groups, and so on. In these people, practices and places, ancestral Māori concepts are active and alive, adapting to changing conditions, including various modernist assumptions about reality. The process of juxtaposition and exchange has generative effects. It makes it possible to deal creatively with competing and shifting universalisms without feeling the need for a 'theory of everything' in which only one set of assumptions about the world can prevail.[48]

This is just as well, because throughout the Tribunal hearings and public debates over fresh water, it was evident that the Freshwater Iwi Leaders

Group and the claimants were being placed in a series of double binds.[49] On the one hand, as the Tribunal observed in its Interim Report, if Māori kin groups do not claim 'ownership' of ancestral freshwater bodies, and rights to fresh water are privatised, they may be left with nothing. As a claimant from one tribe, Te Arawa, exclaimed at the Freshwater Tribunal hearing, while his people had been comfortable with the Crown managing their rivers for the good of the nation, they did not agree that these waterways should be handed over to partially privatised power companies. 'Te Arawa begins to wake up,' he said. 'Blame the Government for us claiming ownership.'[50] In consequence, claimants and their counsel in that particular claim drew on British common law and New Zealand case law to argue that, at the time of the Treaty, they were in undisturbed possession of their ancestral waterways, and that in 1840 the rights guaranteed to them under the English text of the Treaty equated to absolute ownership. Since then, those rights may have been modified, but have never been extinguished.

On the other hand, various witnesses expressed frustration about being forced into a language based on possessive individualism (property, ownership and rights) to speak about their relations with ancestral water bodies. Toni Waho, for example, exclaimed, 'It's not an ownership issue . . . it's kaitiakitanga [guardianship], it's mana. My Māori heart says let it cease; but my western mind says perhaps we can find a solution.'[51] In his closing remarks, however, the Crown Counsel quoted these words back at the claimants, arguing that, in their own terms, Māori could not properly claim to 'own' waterways in New Zealand. In its findings, the Tribunal identified the nub of the problem (without offering any real solution):

> We agree with the Whanganui River Tribunal, which found in respect of that river: . . . *it does not matter that Maori did not think in terms of ownership in the same way as Europeans.* What they possessed is equated with ownership for the purposes of English or New Zealand law.[52]

In other words, if Māori claimants wish to uphold their relations with ancestral waterways, they must acquiesce in having these redefined as property interests 'for the purposes of the law' – a kind of ontological submission. If they refuse, their claims will have no legal force.

If they do agree, however, they may appear opportunistic and insincere. Statements such as '*Ko au te awa, ko te awa, ko au*' – 'I am the river, and the river is me' – are turned against them, framing their position as self-betrayal if they allow ancestral springs, streams and rivers to be turned into resources for sale. At the same time, the Māori claimants could be seen as betraying a wider public interest in retaining fresh water as part of the commons, bargaining for shares and cash when they might have stopped the asset sales. To make matters worse, if different Māori groups deal with this paradox differently (as in the case of the Freshwater Iwi Leaders Group and the New Zealand Māori Council), they can be accused of inconsistency, undermining the overall legitimacy of kin group claims to special relationships with ancestral waterways. No matter which way they turn, they risk losing mana and public support.

In front of the Tribunal, Māori claimants in the Freshwater claim were acutely aware of these dilemmas. Toni Waho remarked, posing the ontological question:

> But here's the problem. There is no place where things can be graded with proper legal form in our world [te ao Māori], here in our land [New Zealand], which . . . is able to resolve the conflict of the two worlds [te ao Māori, te ao pākehā – the Maori and Western 'worlds'].[53]

In such a situation, is there any way out? There may be.

In Gregory Bateson's formulation of the double bind, it is suggested that one way to escape such 'lose-lose' situations is to shift to another logical level. This is most likely to happen when current attempts at constructing intelligibility and workable solutions are being thwarted.[54] The struggles between Māori kin groups and the Crown over claims to fresh water present such an opportunity. A space opens up in which resonances as well as contradictions between different assumptions about reality can be recognised, and new forms of order explored.

Since the beginning of New Zealand's shared history, echoes between ideas of the commons and other relational thinking from Europe and ancestral Māori conceptions and their inheritors have allowed a kind of 'rough intelligibility' to emerge between Māori projects and those of the incoming settlers. Arguably, this led to the signing of the Treaty of Waitangi and, more recently, to the establishment of the Waitangi Tribunal and the claims process. Backed by Māori and other advocacy, such resonances help to open up zones for experiment. In many spheres of life in New Zealand, Māori ancestral conceptions are being deployed, often without translation. Some non-Maori New Zealanders, for instance, have begun to think of themselves as kaitiaki, or guardians, for rivers, beaches and endangered species, and talk about these as taonga, ancestral treasures. As Māori terms increasingly shift into New Zealand English,[55] and vice versa, European and Māori ways of thinking alike are being transformed.

This is having a major impact on the law in New Zealand. In the Local Government Act, for instance, in making their decisions, councils are required to take into account the relationship of Māori and their culture and traditions with their ancestral land, water, sites, wāhi tapu (ancestral sites), and other taonga. Similar Māori terms are used in the Resource Management Act, and elsewhere. As Amiria Salmond has argued, when terms such as this are used in New Zealand law, the legal process is being transformed by the irruption of ancestral conceptions, thus acknowledging 'the persistence and creativity of a distinctively Māori register of value'.[56] This is very evident in the recent agreement between Whanganui iwi and the Crown over the Whanganui River, which speaks about the awa tupua and is prefaced with a statement in Māori:

> *Ngā wai inuinu o Ruatipua ēnā*
> *Ngā manga iti, ngā manga nui e honohono kau ana*
> *Ka hono, ka tupu, hei awa*
> *Hei Awa Tupua*

> *Those are the drinking fonts of Ruatipua*
> *The small and large streams which flow into one another*
> *and continue to link, and swell, until a river is formed*
> *Te Awa Tupua*[57]

In this hydrological account of identity, distinct streams of people with their different histories swirl together to form a river that in turn flows out to sea, a conception that dates back to ancestral times.

At the outbreak of the Land Wars, for instance, Wiremu Tamihana, a Christian rangatira who had helped to establish the King movement, drew upon this idea when he accused the governor of being 'double-hearted', with his 'lips given to this side [taha] and [his] heart to the other side':

This is my thought with regard to the inland rivers that flow into their deep channels from their sources with their mouths open, until they reach the point where they terminate. I thought that the currents of every river flowed together into the mouth of Te Parata [a great taniwha in the ocean, whose breathing caused the tides], where no distinction is made.

It is not said there that 'you are salt water and that is fresh water', nor that you should prefer only salt water, since they all intermingle. Just as the currents from the different islands flow into the mouth of Te Parata, so the kingdoms of the different nations rest on God as the waters rest in the mouth of Te Parata.[58]

At the heart of the Pacific, Tamihana argued, fresh water (wai māori, associated with Māori people) and salt water (associated with Europeans, since they had arrived by sea) intermingle with the currents from the different islands as they flow into Te Parata, a great vortex leading to te pō, the ancestral realm, from which people are born and to which they return. Likewise, Europeans and Māori alike rest on God, and for this reason, the governor was wrong to prefer one people above the other.

At the same time, as Tamihana recognised, the law has been a powerful force for domination and control in New Zealand. The agreement between Whanganui iwi and the Crown is still constrained in many ways by power relations, and legislative frameworks based on modernist assumptions about how the world works. Nevertheless, the agreement shows that creative jurisprudence and experimental practice are possible. Rather than defining waterways, forests and fisheries as 'common pool resources' (an anthropocentric conception that is still wedded to notions of property, albeit held in common), for example, as the Nobel Prize-winning economist Elinor Orstrom has suggested,[59] it is evidently not unthinkable in New Zealand to pursue the idea that lakes, harbours and forests may have their own life and rights, alongside those of people.

As the anthropologist Elizabeth Povinelli has argued, it might be possible to experiment 'across worlds', shaping 'how things could be' – drawing upon divergent strands from different philosophical legacies to confront current challenges and dilemmas, generating new kinds of insights and outcomes on the way.[60] Such approaches, according to the sociologist John Law, should be 'contingent, modest, practical, and thoroughly down-to-earth; ways of proceeding that acknowledge and respect *difference* as something that cannot be included'.[61] Like the Treaty of Waitangi itself, with its two texts in Māori and English, such approaches might juxtapose rather than try to assimilate different ways of being different, contributing to a 'planetary conversation on human possibilities'.[62]

Waterways in New Zealand, for instance, might be recognised as awa tipua, more ancient than people, and as taonga to be cherished. They might have their own identity and rights, including the right to remain in a state of ora – with sustainable flows and healthy ecosystems – so that in their relations with people, they are not degraded or destroyed.[63] This might be linked with the science of complex networks to understand waterways as living systems (or communities) of water, earth, plants, animals and people, in which our fates are tied together. Once the 'rights of the river' are legally recognised, cutting-edge environmental science might be used to define 'ecological bottom lines' that ensure their ongoing flourishing. After that, the use rights of different groups of people can be negotiated and defined.

In New Zealand, as elsewhere, it is likely that the most intransigent obstacles to solving environmental (and other) challenges lie at the level of presupposition. For waterways, the assumption that they were created to serve human purposes drives towards their degradation and destruction. As Jane Bennett has argued, 'the image of dead or thoroughly instrumentalised matter feeds . . . our earth-destroying fantasies of conquest and consumption'.[64]

Fundamental presuppositions will have to shift if more sustainable styles of living are to be found. Weaving together different, even incommensurable, vocabularies in legal frameworks, as in the case of the Whanganui River agreement, will have unpredictable outcomes, but they may prove enlivening. Listen to the cry of Papatuanuku, the earth mother, calling out for the water of life:

Piki mai, kake mai	Climb here, draw near
Hōmai te wai ora ki ahau	Give me the water of life
E tūtehu ana	The sleep of this old woman has been troubled
Te moe a te kuia i te pō	In the night
Ka pō, ka ao, ka awatea!	But now it is dusk, it is dawn, it is day!

CHAPTER TEN

Like a Bird on a Sandbank
Whenua / Land

I N THE AFTERMATH OF THE LAND WARS, SOME TIME DURING THE 1870s, tribal experts from various parts of the North Island engaged in a debate about the origins of the kūmara (sweet potato). This prized crop, brought to New Zealand from Pacific homelands, was a source of mana, especially in the lavish feasts staged on ceremonial occasions. During this debate, which was conducted in Māori (and later translated into English by John White),[1] proverbs, chants and songs were recited – devices used by orators to illustrate their eloquence, demonstrate their learning, and demolish their opponents.

This debate began with Major Ropata Wahawaha, a leading warrior and rangatira from Ngati Porou on the East Coast, recounting how his ancestral canoe *Horouta* had been sent from New Zealand back to Hawaiki to fetch the kūmara. Before the canoe, commanded by Kahukura, set sail, the priests appealed to their atua (ancestral gods) to stop up the pits of the winds, calm the waves and bring the canoe safely back to their homeland. When *Horouta* made the return voyage with the kūmara, it landed at Ahuahu (Great Mercury Island), Whakatane, Whangaparaoa near East Cape, Waiapu on the East Coast and Turanga (or Gisborne), Nukutaurua at Mahia and Heretaunga (now Hastings), leaving the prized plant at each of these places – a journey recalled by Wahawaha in a chant.[2]

In response to Wahawaha, an elder named Iraia Tutanga Waionui from Whanganui contested his account, upholding the mana of his own people. In fact, Iraia said, the first kūmara had been brought to New Zealand on his own ancestral canoe, the *Aotea* commanded by Turi, and was planted at Hekeheke-i-papa in the Patea district. In dismissing Wahawaha's narrative, Iraia retorted that 'his assertions are all a myth [tito – lie], invented while sitting in the porch of his own house'. He added: 'Friends of the Nga-ti-porou tribe, do not believe, or state, that the kumara came on *Horouta*, or that your ancestors fetched the kumara from Hawaiki, lest your children be deceived and live in ignorance [kūwaretanga]!'[3]

Provoked by Iraia's acerbic comments, Rev. Mohi Turei, a Ngati Porou tribal expert and Anglican priest, retorted:

> Oh friend! The man who contradicts Major Wahawaha, you are the man who utters myths [tangata tino tito]. If you think that we [Ngati Porou] are descended from Turi, you are lying. If you say that we came on *Aotea* canoe, that is false. You are correct that in the days of Turi, the kumara was planted in the gardens at Hekeheke-i-papa, but does it still grow there today?
>
> I say to you, you have your kumara, and your ancestor, and your garden, and I have mine. The hold of *Horouta* was baled out at Waiapu, and thus the proverb 'Ka mahi te tainga o te riu o Horouta, to taea te opeope' [When the hold of *Horouta* was baled out, there was a great abundance (of kūmara)].
>
> When the *Horouta* landed at Waiapu the kumara was at once planted to produce a crop, and the name of this plantation was Whakararanui, where today the offspring of this kumara may still be seen growing, and where I, the Ngati Porou tribe, go and take up the crop in the tenth month of the year.[4]

As further evidence of the truth of his claims, Mohi Turei described the pōhutukawa tree that marked this garden, and a māpau (*Myrsine australis*) that sprang from the sacred rod used by the tohunga during the planting rituals.

At this point in the debate, Hoani Nahe of Hauraki intervened, giving a long, detailed account of the origin of the kūmara and trying to put the two previous speakers in their places:

> Now all the tribes of these islands, south and north, listen to me. These men are both confused, and appear to think that their *iwi* are the most knowledgeable of all the tribes, and that of all men, they are most able to rehearse the whakapapa and histories all of the tribes that inhabit these islands.

Iraia Tutanga Waionui is trying to take the mote from his friend's eye, while ignoring the mote in his own. In fact, each iwi has its own kumara, brought in its own waka. I have my own kumara, brought over to these islands on board the canoe *Tainui*, the canoe of Hotunui and Hoturoa, and the women Marama and Whakaotirangi, who brought the kumara and the hue [gourd], aute [bark-cloth] and the karaka tree in that canoe from Hawaiki.

According to Nahe, after arriving in New Zealand, the *Tainui* canoe had been dragged across the Tamaki isthmus between the Waitemata and Manukau harbours, and sailed down to Kawhia, where it was turned into stone. The aristocratic women Marama and Whakaotirangi had each planted seeds in her own garden, except that Marama's seeds turned into other, less useful plants, because she slept with her slave while crossing the Tamaki isthmus. 'Now, Major Ropata and Iraia Tutanga!' said Nahe. 'You say that the canoes *Horouta* and *Aotea* brought the kumara to these islands of New Zealand. You, of all men, repeat the most absurd myth, falsehood and invention.' Singing a song about the arrival of the kūmara on the *Tainui* canoe, he concluded: 'What saddens me is that these lies told by my friends might be thought to be true. Truth is always truth [he pono anō te pono], and here we are telling lies.'

As other orators from Whanganui, Hauraki and the East Coast joined the fray, invoking the names of their ancestors and gardens, reciting proverbs and chanting songs, the nature of knowledge as a taonga, or ancestral gift, was illuminated. Far from having 'closed' minds, ossified by ancestral precedent, for these orators the vigorous testing of accounts was at the heart of the wānanga tradition – wānanga atu, wānanga mai (my ancestral knowledge in exchange for yours, back and forth). As Tamati Tautuhi from Ngati Porou remarked, rebutting Hoani Nahe, this kind of knowledge is handed down from one generation to the next:

The old men of the most remote times related the past history to those of a later age, and thus each generation related the past history to the next generation, giving the history from the first days of man even down to the generation in which we now live.

It is not asserted that Major Ropata saw Kahukura depart in his canoe for Hawaiki. No, but he heard the ancient men relating the history of that voyage, and this history is still repeated in these days. It would not be correct to say that Major Ropata obtained his knowledge from his own self, but he derived his knowledge from the teaching of the very old men. Nor was his knowledge a myth concocted in front of his own house.

Now o friend! Ponder this matter, lest you take for granted and for truth what you have been taught by your ancestors, and think what our ancestors have taught us is all fiction, lest your similes turn on you and condemn you, and lest you believe all that you have been told, but which you have not actually witnessed, and lest you persist in upholding the statements of others relative to history of which you have not been an eyewitness, so that your insanity may be known by all people.

As you say, you merely state what has been told to you by your ancestors: then why do you contradict the statements of Major Ropata? He merely states what we have been told by our ancestors.

As Tamati Tautuhi explained, Māori knowledge is contextual and relative, handed down from generation to generation, resisting ultimate forms of authority and the construction of monolithic accounts. He added: 'Ponder this matter, lest you take for granted and for truth what you have been taught by your ancestors, and think what our ancestors have taught us is all fiction, lest your similes turn on you and condemn you.' This cautionary remark could apply equally to the relations between modernist and Māori forms of knowledge, each with their own histories, hidden forms of order and assumptions, and entanglements with power.

Māori conceptions of whenua (land)

The debate about the coming of the kūmara also illustrates the existential interlock in Māori thinking between ancestors, kin groups and land. Just as the sprouts (tipu) of the kūmara were planted in mounds of earth, so Tane mounded up the first woman, Hineahuone (woman heaped up) from the body of his mother, Papatuanuku, and impregnated this woman with his seed. Children were born (whānau) from their union, hence the terms whānau (extended family, or birth) and hapū (sub-tribe, or pregnant). As Tane and Hineahuone had children, they became the ancestors (tipuna – literally 'grown') of people. The place where a person was born is known as te ū kai pō, the night-feeding breast, where they were nurtured by Papatuanuku. The ancestor who first occupied and cultivated a particular territory was known as the take, or root ancestor, and the whenua (placenta) or umbilical cords of their children and their own iwi (bones) are buried in the whenua (land), hence the term tāngata whenua (people of the land).

In ancestral times as the descendants of 'root' ancestors who first explored, settled or conquered the land flourished and flowered, the ariki (paramount chief) or rangatira (chief) of particular kin groups would summon their people to harvest and defend their territories. The great seasonal rituals and feasts (hākari), marked by towering tiered stages piled high with food, celebrated fertility and abundance. As Te Rangikaheke explains in his manuscript on rangatiratanga (chieftainship), one of the most important characteristics of a rangatira was their ability to provide food and to take care of guests: 'Food cultivation, harvesting, inviting guests, welcoming guests, speaking in assembly, showing hospitality. So when that [knowledge] was acquired it is proclaimed throughout the land, "So and So is the rangatira."'5 Tino rangatiratanga was not about private possession, but about relational wealth – giving and receiving gifts through networks of kinship and alliance, planting new relationships and cultivating old ones, enabling them to thrive.

This ability to take care of land, waterways, sea and people depended on complex patterns of exchange. Networks of whakapapa, with their named ancestors, entangled with networks of place names, sprawled across the land. These names triggered ancestral stories, chants and proverbs. Eruera Stirling once explained to me how, as a small child, he was taken into the bush to live with his 'grandparents' Hiria Te Rangihaeata and Pera Kaongahau (relatives of his grandparents' generation) who had trained at Kirieke, the local whare wānanga, and how they taught him to live on the land:

> I liked staying with the old people because I got plenty to eat, they gave me the best of food. We ate berries – taraire, tawa, karaka and miro cooked in the hangi; pigeons, tui and parrots cooked in their own fat and kept in calabashes; wild pigs and fish, but one of the special delicacies my grandparents liked to eat was the kiore, the Polynesian rat – that was their special. When it's cut up and cooked it's something like the bird, eh, it tastes very sweet.
>
> When my grandfather [great-uncle] took me eeling to the deep pools of the river he'd catch just one or two of the big black ones and carry them home to hang in the sun to dry – we'd be eating eels for weeks after that! Sometimes we went to the sea and fished with a baited net; we'd let our net down into the water and when the fish were feeding we pulled it up and dragged the fish to shore.

Pera taught me how to snare pigeons in the trees, and the parrot too, he'd
call the parrot and it would hop right into the snare! He knew the songs of all
the birds in the bush, and he could call a pigeon down into the tree and catch
it with his hand. Sometimes we set up a waikaha net in a taraire tree while the
berries were ripe, and when the birds flew down to the branches to feed, my
grandfather pulled on a rope that closed the net and caught them all.

We have plenty of kumara and that was one thing about the old people,
they always like you to eat; if they saw you weren't eating they'd get worried
and try to find something that you wanted.

[Pera] told me about the mana on the land, how each ancestor came
to own the land and how it was passed on in history right down to now.
He showed me the places where the ancestors collected food, cultivated the
ground and where they built their pa. He taught me the days of the month,
the good days of planting and the bad days, the good days for fishing and the
days to go out and catch eels, because the old people had a proper day for
every kind of work in their calendar, following the stars and the moon.[6]

These seasonal migrations, following the movements of the stars and the
moon, were another key feature in relations between land and people.
People travelled across the land at different times of the year, following
the pathways of their forebears, guided by constellations of place names.
Their links with key ancestors allowed people to harvest particular animals
and plants in particular places at particular times of the year, indicated by
the flowering of particular plants and signs in the sky – at named eel pools,
birding trees, fern-root diggings, gardens, eel weirs, channels in reefs or
deep-sea fishing grounds, each in its season.

Given the ambilateral tracing of descent and the fact that girls might
inherit use rights and plants from their mothers, while boys often inherited
use rights from their fathers, many extended families had complex patterns
of seasonal dispersal. Ancestral rights had to be activated by occupation,
a practice known as ahi kā (keeping one's fires alight on the land), or they
would go cold – ahi mātaotao (cold, extinguished fires). When Captain Cook
visited Mercury Bay in 1769, for instance, he found a group of people from
the west side of the Coromandel Peninsula camped out in the bay, harvesting shellfish and keeping their ancestral fires alight on the land.[7]

In the 1970s, the archaeologist Agnes Sullivan carried out an intricate
study of such trajectories of movement across the Tamaki isthmus in about

1820, based on evidence from Native Land Court records.[8] Those who gave evidence in the 1860s to the Land Court about their earlier lives in Tamaki described a pattern of occupation that they described as he whenua rangatira – a chiefly land – a state of peace and prosperity in which they moved freely around their territories. In the Declaration of Independence, the northern chiefs also referred to New Zealand as a whenua rangatira, a free and independent country. This casts new light on our understanding of te tino rangatiratanga (the unfettered chieftainship) guaranteed in Article Two of Te Tiriti, as a state of freedom, abundance and prosperity for people and land alike.

In about 1820, before Europeans arrived in Tamaki, the Taou people had permanent settlements at Mangere and Onehunga, linked with a circuit of sites around the isthmus that they visited each year – hokihoki mai (always returning). In winter, between about May and July, they gathered at Mangere and Onehunga, living on stored foods, tilling their gardens and fishing for winter snapper. In early spring, in August and September, small working parties dispersed to small outlying fishing camps, where they planted potatoes, first on the Manukau Harbour and then on the Waitemata, areas they shared with their Ngati Paoa relatives. In spring, from October to November, agricultural work at Mangere and Onehunga intensified. People returned to clear new gardens, dig fern-root, plant kūmara and potato, and tend pigs, while others went fishing at scattered sites in both the Manukau and Waitemata harbours.

Over summer, from December to January, the people went fishing, migrating around each of Taou's fishing grounds in turn, eating food from gardens planted earlier at the sequence of fishing camps. Along the Waitakere shore of the Manukau Harbour, they harvested pipi (*Paphies australis*) and cockles from the coastal bays, mussels, oysters, pāua (abalone, *Haliotis* spp.), kina (sea urchins, *Evechinus chloroticus*) and crayfish from rocky shorelines, and caught hāpuku and trevally out at sea. Moving to the opposite side of the Manukau, they collected flounder and sole, mussels and cockles, mud oysters and scallops, and went fishing for shark. Hauling their canoes across the Otahuhu and Whau portages, they caught shark and other fish in the lower Waitemata and then the upper Waitemata harbour, while a small caretaker population remained at their main settlements, weeding gardens and tending pigs. In late summer, Taou people returned to their main settlements where they carried out part-time fishing near their gardens, dried fish, harvested karaka berries and snared birds in the Waitakere Ranges. In autumn, from March to May, they went eeling and harvested their crops of kūmara and potatoes, putting them carefully in underground stores. Afterwards they went visiting or received visitors at their main settlements, feasting, singing, dancing and enjoying themselves, before the winter work of preparing their gardens began again in June.[9]

Such seasonal patterns of migration happened all over New Zealand, adapted to different landscapes and seascapes, and these carried on well into historic times. When I interviewed my friend and colleague Merimeri Penfold for the Muriwhenua Land Claim to the Waitangi Tribunal in 1986, for instance, she told me how her family used to visit their gardens at Kapowairua (Spirits Bay), where her father grew many different varieties of the main crops, especially kūmara; the excitement of fishing for dog-fish in the Parengarenga Harbour; and the joys of collecting toheroa (large shellfish, *Paphies ventricosa*) and going fishing on the Ninety Mile Beach. (Indeed, the migration of New Zealanders to temporary dwellings [or 'baches'] on the coastline and lakes in summer each year reflects a similar seasonal rhythm.)[10]

The interlock between land, sea and people was intimate and foundational. During the Tribunal hearings for the Muriwhenua Land Claim, the relations between kin groups and land provoked an impassioned debate among scholars (anthropologists, historians and linguists) about the nature of early land transactions with Europeans in that region. This was essentially an argument about northern Māori understandings of land, and how quickly these had shifted towards Western ideas of land as property and a commodity during the early contact period. The debate turned on two terms used in early land deeds in Muriwhenua, tuku and hoko (both also used in Te Tiriti), and the question of how closely these equated to the European notion of 'sale'.

According to a thesis by Philippa Wyatt that investigated the 'Old Land Claims' in the Bay of Islands before 1840, submitted to the Muriwhenua Tribunal, at that time kin groups often regarded Europeans as valuable sources of goods, trade, knowledge and technologies, and sought to recruit them as allies and settlers by offering them land, women and protection. A transaction of this kind did not amount to a 'sale' in the European sense of the word. Rather, incoming Europeans were treated as settler guests and allies, who were expected to give loyalty, long-term gifts and practical support to their co-occupant hosts. If the service was not forthcoming, if they did not occupy land or if their loyalties shifted, the arrangement was regarded as null and void, and the host group reoccupied the land.[11] At first in Northland, according to Wyatt, land could only be tuku, or 'released', to Europeans, forging a relationship between them and their host group. The idea that land could be bought and sold as a commodity for a consideration, with no lasting relationship established between buyer and seller, was so alien that it was only slowly and imperfectly grasped by local people. When the term tuku used in a land deed was translated as 'sold' or 'sell', this was very misleading. Such a transaction was not a 'sale' in the sense that both parties understood all the implications of the deal.

In 1991, when I was invited by the Tribunal to inquire into likely Māori understandings of the terms tuku and hoko used in land deeds in the North in this period,[12] I agreed with Wyatt's main conclusions. After examining about a thousand occurrences of these terms in Dr Cleve Barlow's database of early texts in Māori, including *Nga Mahi a nga Tupuna*, edited by Sir George Grey, and *Te Paipera Tapu* (the Holy Bible, whose language seemed likely to be similar to the early missionary-drafted land deeds in Northland), I found that tuku was never used in these texts as a translation equivalent for 'sell', and only once in connection with land. Rather, tuku was used in these texts as a translation equivalent for words such as 'give, send, deliver, let go, offer, allow, release' – as in Te Tiriti. Hoko, on the other hand, was used in the Bible to refer to exchanges of people (bondsmen or women), animals, foodstuffs including wheat and, very infrequently, to land, but in the negative (e.g. *Kaua e hokona te whenua, he mea oti tonu atu, noku hoki te whenua* – The land shall not be sold forever, for the land is mine – Leviticus 25:23).

In early Māori land deeds in Northland, on the other hand, tuku was routinely translated as 'sold' or 'sell', although in some of the later deeds it was coupled with hoko as well. A number of these deeds also included provisions that those who were 'releasing' the land would continue to occupy it, and that the relationship with the incoming Europeans would carry on down the generations. In my report to the Tribunal, I concluded:

> In the case of the term tuku, I do not believe that it has ever carried anything like the referential values of the English word 'sell'. While it seems to me that Maori people who signed deeds in which tuku was a key term often intended those transactions to be binding, I do not believe that they intended to permanently extinguish all their rights in the land in question.

Of all of the early types of tribal transfers of land with which I am familiar, the case of 'tribes who wished to settle' provide the nearest parallel with early land transactions with incoming Europeans. Tribes who wished to settle were allocated places for houses and gardens, were expected to give loyalty, assistance and regular offerings of food to host groups, were protected from outside attack, and could be evicted if they abused or neglected the obligations inherent in the arrangement. If they ceased to occupy the land, it reverted to the host group.

In the case of the word hoko, on the other hand, in Muriwhenua [the Far North], this seems eventually to have adopted most of the referential values of the English word 'sell'. This must, however, have been a slow and uneven process of semantic shift, with some implications being grasped later than others. Until there was a system of titles, laws of trespass and agencies for enforcing property rights established in New Zealand, it must have been extremely difficult for Maori people to grasp the full, practical implications of 'sales' of land.[13]

Such conditions did not apply in New Zealand until after the Land Wars of the 1860s, which were largely fought to impose them, and the establishment of the Native Land Court in 1865 – and later in some parts of the country (the Urewera and the Rohe Potae [King Country], for example). When Professor Joan Metge and Dr Margaret Mutu delivered longer, more detailed and in-depth analyses of early land deeds in Muriwhenua,[14] and in the Tribunal's final report,[15] similar conclusions were drawn. While various of the Crown witnesses and Dr Lindsay Head for the Tribunal[16] sought to argue that, by the 1830s, Muriwhenua Māori had adopted the concept of 'sale' as applied to land – as the permanent, total alienation of rights in a bounded area of land for a consideration – this argument was not upheld by the Tribunal.

As we have seen, during the pre-Treaty period in Northland, different Europeans forged different kinds of relations with their host kin groups. Although some missionaries (Thomas Kendall, for example) did their best to comply with the expectations of their hosts, others (Henry and Marianne Williams, for instance) sought to establish their independence from local rangatira from the outset, fencing off their mission stations with high fences and trying to establish these as European enclaves beyond the reach of the rules of tapu, mana and utu. Even so, Henry and Marianne were expected to assist their hosts in many ways, Henry giving access to agricultural technologies and advice about how to deal with other Europeans, and helping his hosts to make peace with their enemies, while Marianne passed on valuable skills to their children. These relationships were long-lasting and intimate, and the autonomy of these Europeans remained strictly constrained.

Again, the fundamental clash – both in this early period, and in arguments 150 years later before the Tribunal – lay at the level of taken-for-granted understandings, in this case about the nature of land and rights to occupy, control and alienate it. For Māori, complex networks of whakapapa and use rights were intertwined; their ancestors' bones, and their own umbilical cords and placentas, were literally 'planted' in the land from which their descendants sprang; and the use rights of tāngata whenua 'kept alight' by seasonal occupation. In early modern Europe, however, new ideas about sovereignty, property and land were taking shape in which these relations were differently articulated, and in the wake of European settlement, many of these ideas were imported to New Zealand.

Modernist ideas about land

In his *Two Treatises of Government* (1689), John Locke delivered a devastating critique of *Patriarcha*, a work by Sir Robert Filmer that argued for the absolute power, sovereignty and divine right of fathers and kings by drawing upon the Genesis story about Adam, and the injunction given by God to Noah and his sons after the Flood:

> Be fruitful and increase in number and fill the earth. The fear and dread of you will fall on all the beasts of the earth, and on all the birds in the sky, on every creature that moves along the ground, and on all the fish in the sea; they are given into your hands. Everything that lives and moves about will be food for you.[17]

According to Filmer, the dominion given by God to Adam over all other living beings (which included Eve and their children) was passed down to Noah, and then to the biblical patriarchs, and a succession of divine kings in Europe. Such a doctrine underpinned the Great Chain of Being, ideas about absolute monarchy, slavery, aristocratic and patriarchal power.

In disputing Filmer's account, Locke pointed out that in the biblical account God's gift to Adam of 'dominion over the fish of the sea, the fowl of the air, and every living thing that moveth upon the earth' was not absolute, but shared with Eve,[18] and Noah's control over 'everything that lives and moves about' was shared with his sons.[19] As far as John Locke was concerned, this dominion over the 'inferior creatures' was given by God to all people in common.[20] Human beings were born free and equal (although because of Eve's sin in the Garden of Eden, women had to live in subjection to their husbands).[21] He was also scathing about slavery. In its vigorous rhetorical style and its rigorous scrutiny of ancestral accounts, *The Two Treatises* often reminds me of the debate among Māori orators about the coming of the kūmara quoted at the beginning of this chapter.

According to Locke, in a 'state of Nature' (for instance, in the Garden of Eden; or a state of savagery, for instance in the Americas), all people were equal, free and independent.[22] Each person could take what they needed from the 'common', as long as they harmed no other person. If harm was caused to another, each person had the right to punish this transgression against the law of Nature. The one thing that every person could claim as their property was their own body, and the work it performed:

> Though the earth and all inferior creatures be common to all men, yet every man has a *Property* in his own *Person*. This no one has any right to but himself. The *Labour* of his body and the *Work* of his hands, we may say, are properly his. Whatsoever, then, he removes out of the state that Nature hath provided and left it in, he hath mixed his *Labour* with it, and joined it to something that is his own, and thereby makes it his *Property*. . . . He by his labour does, as it were, enclose it from the common. . . . As much land as a man tills, plants, improves, cultivates and can use the product of, so much is his property.[23]

At first, according to Locke, in the state of Nature, when 'All was America', there was plenty to share without impinging upon the rights of others. People could claim as property only what they could consume, while the rest became 'waste' and could be claimed by others.[24] Over time, however, the surplus production was converted into money, which could be stored. In this way, people were given the incentive to produce more than they needed. As the population increased and land became scarce, he argued, people settled the boundaries of distinct territories, dividing them up, and passed laws to protect the property thus created. This 'property' included lives and liberty as well as land, and the laws to protect these became the foundation of the modern state. In this way, 'civilised' societies emerged. Nevertheless:

> There are still great tracts of ground to be found, which the inhabitants thereof, not having joined with the rest of mankind in the consent of the use of their common money, lie waste and are more than the people who dwell on it do, or can make use of, and so still lie in common.[25]

Since the common lands of these people were 'waste', their occupants could not claim them as private property. For this reason, 'civilised' people were justified in taking them over, and making them productive. Although these arguments were built on mythic foundations, in particular the Genesis story, it is easy to understand their attraction for early European settlers in New Zealand, and commercial agencies such as the New Zealand Company.

During the Enlightenment, it seems, most European theorists agreed with Locke about the right of 'civilised' peoples to dispossess those who did not cultivate the soil. In 1758, before Cook's circumnavigation of New Zealand, for instance, the jurist de Vattel published his work *The Law of Nations, or the Principles of Natural Law*, which adopted an extreme Lockean view on the rights of non-agricultural nations:

> Every nation is then obliged by the law of nature to cultivate the land that has fallen to its share; and it has no right to enlarge its boundaries or have its share, but in proportion as the land in its possession is incapable of furnishing it with necessaries. Those nations . . . who inhabit fertile countries, but disdain to cultivate their lands . . . are injurious to all their neighbours, and deserve to be extirpated as savage and pernicious beasts.[26]

Fortunately for Māori, given de Vattel's ideas, they were agriculturalists who cultivated land in most parts of the country, although not in much of the South Island.

Under these conventions, the process of transforming land from 'a state of nature' into private property by investing labour and money in it transformed land into a commodity that could be owned, and bought and sold. In Britain and British colonies during this period, land was being surveyed, measured and fenced into bounded units, a process known as 'enclosure', in which almost all use rights in these bounded sections were bundled together. Between 1750 and 1850 in Britain, some 4000 Enclosure Acts were passed, dividing up commons and waste lands that had formerly been collectively held, and accelerating a process that had been under way since the Tudors, transforming shared spaces into private places.[27] Today in New Zealand and elsewhere, the ideas of 'property', 'person' and 'labour', and the conventions for partitioning and counting these, are so far taken for granted that their mythic foundations have become invisible, as they have passed into 'common sense'.

Struggles over land

Because Māori kin networks held their lands in a kind of symbiosis with ancestral landscapes, waterways and seascapes, with ariki or rangatira overseeing the allocation of use rights, it seemed to many European settlers that Māori were living in a 'state of nature'. Under Article Two in Te Tiriti, however, the tino rangatiratanga of the rangatira over their lands and all their taonga had been guaranteed by the queen, but in the English draft of Article Two their use rights to their taonga (including land) were translated as 'property', with all its implications – a fundamental transformation. Equally, under Article Three in Te Tiriti, while the queen promised to tiaki, or care for and protect, Māori people, a kaitiaki relationship, and give them ngā tikanga rite (tikanga, or rights, equal to those of her people of England), in the English draft this became 'the Rights and Privileges of British subjects', a very different matter. As we have seen, for John Locke, the purpose of the state was to protect property, which included lives, land and liberty, and this in turn led to the idea of the rights-bearing, property-owning citizen (often termed 'possessive individualism'). The English draft of Article Three echoed this modernist logic.

Once the English draft of the Treaty of Waitangi was accepted by the British government as the official version of the agreement, the transformation of Māori land, lives and liberty into 'property' had already been accomplished, at least in British eyes. Many of the incoming European settlers (some of who had been forced to leave Britain as a result of the enclosures) were eager to buy land for themselves. They wanted to establish secure title to the land that they occupied, and to require Māori to submit to processes that had taken centuries of theorising and enforcement to bring about in Britain. In order to achieve this, however, a number of fundamental shifts had to be enacted.

First, members of Māori kin groups had to be detached from the land on which they had been born, lived and worked. Since people and land were tangled together as tāngata whenua, and whakapapa networks of people literally grew from the land, this shift was profound. Second, Māori had to come to see themselves as dominating and controlling the land, rather than being born from Papatuanuku, the earth mother, and returning to her in death, if a sense of 'ownership' was to become possible. Again, this was a fundamental transformation. Third, the land had to be abstracted into a commodity that could be measured, bought and sold. In te ao Māori, the nearest precedent for this kind of transaction – hoko, or barter – applied only to goods that lacked ancestral presence, while land was itself an ancestor, the earth mother. Fourth, the land had to be divided from the sea, surveyed, and split into blocks in which almost all use rights were transacted together. This process separated ancestral land from its inhabitants and transformed it into a series of bounded, abstracted, static entities, cutting across the complex rhythms and patterns of seasonal occupation.

Fifth, the 'owners' of blocks had to be determined and listed, cutting up the kin networks and turning them into bounded entities – in parallel with the land, severing and fragmenting the complex, shifting networks of whakapapa, and transforming them according to a logic that also turned kin groups into objects. Sixth, property in land had to be recorded in written deeds and protected by laws of trespass, backed by the impersonal powers of the state; and land could be owned without being occupied. This cut across the ancestral principle of ahi kā, in which only those use rights that were actively upheld could be claimed.

As these conventions were progressively introduced to New Zealand, the land – the body of Papatuanuku, with her mountains, rivers and people – was divided up, and each block became a commodity that could be owned, bought and sold. Until that time, the land had been a living being, Papatuanuku, the earth mother, with her own independent existence and freedom. As the great fighting chief Renata Kawepo told Thomas Fitzgerald, the superintendent of Hawke's Bay, in 1863, in the colonial process the land itself, formerly a rangatira, was being enslaved:

E ta – he rangatira to matou whenua katahi nei ka taurekareka ka hokona hoki ki te moni. I mua kahore e hokona ana.

Sir, our land is a *rangatira*, but now it is being enslaved, inasmuch as it is being sold for money. In the old days it was not sold.[28]

Not surprisingly, while the incoming European settlers took modernist ideas of sovereignty, property and liberty for granted, and their right as 'civilised' people to acquire Māori lands, many Māori regarded these assumptions as whakahīhī (arrogant, presumptuous).

As we have seen, for instance, in the very first land transaction with Europeans, the young rangatira Te Uri-o-Kanae, Ruatara's heir, was enthusiastic about the 'sale' of Rangihoua to the Church Missionary Society. Later, however, he came to regret it, when he realised that the missionaries were oblivious to his ongoing mana as their host. Likewise, Hongi was eager to 'sell' land at Kerikeri to Samuel Marsden, although he was furious when his right as a rangatira to determine who could occupy houses on the land was ignored by the missionaries, in the case of Thomas Kendall, for example. By the time of the debates over the Treaty of Waitangi, most rangatira regretted earlier 'sales' of land to the missionaries and other Europeans, although many of them had entered into such transactions. It has been estimated that, by 1840, over 160,000 acres in the Bay of Islands had been 'sold' to Europeans, including the missionaries and James Busby.[29] The arrival of land sharks from Sydney, many of whom had no intention of settling in New Zealand, and the New Zealand Company, which in a very short time claimed to have purchased 20 million acres on either side of Cook Strait,[30] quickly taught Māori that their ancestral ways of dealing with land held little sway with most Europeans.

In an effort to control these transactions, in January 1840 the governor in New South Wales issued a proclamation declaring that no title to land in New Zealand would be regarded as valid unless it was derived from, or issued by, a Crown grant.[31] After the signing of the Treaty, however, the clause in the English draft that gave the Crown the pre-emptive right to purchase land meant that in the case of all further land transactions with Māori, this restriction would apply. Many rangatira felt betrayed, since Te Tiriti had guaranteed their tino rangatiratanga, or absolute chieftainship, over their lands and other taonga, while European investors associated with the New

Zealand Company were infuriated, railing at 'the Treaty's tangled web of imbecility', and this 'blanket-bought missionary Magna Carta'.[32] Just two months after the signing of the Treaty, some northern chiefs told Governor Hobson: 'Our hearts are dark and gloomy from what the Pakeha have told us, they say that the missionaries first came to pave the way for the English who have sent the governor here, that soldiers will follow and then he will take away our lands.'[33] Although Hobson assured them that Britain would protect, rather than destroy or dispossess them, in April 1840 an army contingent arrived in the Bay of Islands.[34]

Two months later a New Zealand Claims to Land Bill was introduced in the New South Wales Legislature to enquire into land purchases before 1840. This Bill included a clause that all claims over 2560 acres would be disallowed, and that these 'surplus lands' would become the property of the Crown.[35] Although Hobson had personally promised the chiefs at Waitangi that all lands unjustly held would be returned to them, this provision suggested that the governor could not be trusted. At about that time, various rangatira announced that no more land transactions would be permitted in their districts.

In 1841 when two Land Claims commissioners began sitting in Kororareka, this process was also fundamentally flawed. The surveys of the original transactions were inaccurate; the commissioners' recognition of payment values in almost all cases was inflated; while the network of overlapping rights in many areas was not properly investigated. The lands declared surplus for the Crown were maximised, and reserves were not allocated in most cases. Over the protests of many rangatira, the commissioners awarded absolute titles to the 'purchasers'. Even Governor George Grey later argued that in these early land transactions, 'it is by no means clear that [Māori] understood that they gave an absolute title to the land'.[36]

Late in 1841, when Hobson issued a regulation forbidding the felling of kauri, Tamati Waka Nene, the Hokianga chief who had helped to persuade his fellow rangatira to sign the Treaty at Waitangi, was furious at this denial of his tino rangatiratanga. A few months later, on the other hand, when a youth named Maketu was put on trial and hanged for killing a European woman, her son and daughter, her manservant and Rewa's granddaughter, who was in her care, the rangatira went along with this, partly because his own grandchild had been killed.[37]

As the Crown took control of all new land transactions, buying cheaply from Māori and selling at a high price to the settlers to fund the new government, Māori became even more disaffected. The pre-emptive right to handle land transactions had been promoted as a protective measure against land speculators; but now the Crown itself was making profits at the expense of Māori. When settlers began reselling land, furthermore, Māori were puzzled and affronted, since at first they regarded the original transactions as forging personal relationships with lasting mutual obligations. As the new government began to claim customs duties, instead of the chiefs, and the new capital was shifted from the Bay of Islands to Auckland, the chiefs felt that their prosperity was at risk and their tino rangatiratanga – absolute chieftainship – was being undermined.

Hone Heke, Hongi Hika's nephew and a former pupil at the CMS mission school at Kerikeri who had been the first to sign the Treaty, led the northern resistance to these measures. At first he was not opposed to the presence of European settlers, but that of the soldiers, who undermined chiefly authority: 'To the soldiers only, who are enemies to our power, to our authority over the land, also to our authority over our people, let our hearts be dark.'[38] In support of tino rangatiratanga, Heke erected a flagpole at Kororareka to fly the flag of the United Tribes. When the settlers flew a British flag from it instead, he chopped it down. In ancestral times, a rangatira had the power to place a tapu over land or sea by erecting a rāhui pole, often with a piece of his clothing attached, channelling the mana of his ancestors; and if a usurper did this instead, the rangatira knocked it down. When he heard that Gilbert Mair, a trader with whom he had been friendly, was planning to erect a pole at Whangarei to fly the British flag, Heke wrote him a letter, urging him not to take this provocative action. He also scolded Mair for selling land that he had been given by Heke's people to another European:

> Friend, your action is wrong [hē], and I urge you to correct [tika] it. We gave [tuku] you the land, but now you have called a strange European to occupy it, this is not right.[39]

At gatherings in the Bay, when the chiefs challenged Henry Williams about his role in the Treaty signings, the missionary spoke in defence of the Treaty, persuading some of the chiefs that the Treaty promises were genuine. When Robert FitzRoy, the governor who followed Hobson, lifted the Crown's right to control land transactions and its imposition of customs duties, some chiefs including Waka Nene, who had spoken in favour of the Treaty at Waitangi, began to think that their fears were unfounded. In any case, they regarded Heke as an upstart, and had tried to dissuade him from confronting the governor. In January 1845 when Heke cut down the pole again, he wrote to FitzRoy:

> The Europeans taunt us. They say, 'Look at Port Jackson, look at China and all the islands; they are but a precedent for this country. That flag of England which takes your country is the beginning. . . . Well, I assented to those speeches, and in the fifth year of hearing this we interfered with the flagstaff for the first time.
>
> We cut it down, and it fell. It was re-erected, and we said, 'We will die for our country that God has given us.' If you demand our land, where are we to go? To Port Jackson? To England? If you say we are to fight, I agree. If you say you will make peace, I agree. Peace must be decided by you, the Governor.[40]

Nene and other chiefs put a guard on the flagpole, although they did not use force when Heke chopped it down for the third time. Afterwards, though, they joined the British and attacked Heke and his ally Kawiti, who had spoken against the governor during the Treaty debate at Waitangi; and a civil war broke out in Northland.

In late 1845 when George Grey was appointed to replace FitzRoy as governor, Kawiti sent him a letter warning him that Nene was not fighting for the British cause, but to avenge ancestors who had been killed in ancient battles. He added: 'Sir the Governor. Do not be hasty about the land. Land is heavy [enduring], but man is light [perishable]. Sir if you say that we do fight, it is well. If you say 'Cease,' it is well; but do not say that you will not yield some portion of your thoughts.'[41] Heke was more impetuous, sending a letter to Grey telling him to go back to England:

> Friend the new Governor. You are a stranger. God made this Country for us, it cannot be sliced – if it were a Whale it might be sliced – but as for this, do you return to your own Country, to England which was made by God for you. God has made this land for us, and not for any stranger or foreign Nation to touch this sacred Country.

He ended with a haka (challenge): 'Ah, let us fight, fight, fight, aha! Let us fight, fight for the land which lies open before us; let us fight, fight. You have not taken it away to your land, to Europe.[42] Infuriated by Heke's defiance, Governor Grey did his best to defeat him and his allies. Although Heke was seriously wounded in one of the battles that followed, he and Kawiti fought bravely, adapting their pā and military tactics to deal with artillery as well as musket fire, and the conflict ended in a stalemate.[43]

In 1846 when Earl Grey became the secretary of state in Britain, he lost no time in telling Governor Grey that he did not believe 'that the aboriginal inhabitants of any country are the proprietors of every part of its soil of which they have been accustomed to make any use or to which they have been accustomed to assert any title'.[44] Rather, in keeping with the doctrines of Locke and de Vattel, he argued, the queen was entitled to claim all waste lands in the colony – i.e. those areas that Māori did not occupy. In response, the Chief Justice William Martin, Bishop Selwyn and many others signed and sent a petition declaring that such a policy would be a disaster, and urging that the letter and spirit of the Treaty should be upheld.[45] Te Wherowhero, the ariki of the Tainui tribes, also wrote to the queen, saying that his people had heard that her councillors were considering taking their lands without cause, although successive governors had assured them that this would never happen. On 3 May 1848 when Earl Grey answered this letter on behalf of the queen, he assured Te Wherowhero that:

> there is not the slightest foundation for rumours to which they allude, and it never was intended that the Treaty of Waitangi should be violated by dispossessing the tribes which are parties to it, of any portion of the land secured to them by the Treaty without their consent. On the contrary, Her Majesty has always directed that the Treaty should be most scrupulously and religiously observed.[46]

In the event, instead of seizing 'waste lands' for the Crown, Governor Grey accelerated the Crown's land purchases to meet the demands of the settlers who were flooding into the country. As Hone Heke observed in a waiata (chant) composed in 1849, only Grey's fine words arrived in the North, while the storms he unleashed blew on the land.[47] Heke also wrote to Queen Victoria, reminding her of various assurances given to Hongi Hika by King George IV.[48] Not surprisingly, many Māori were devastated by the loss of their ancestral territories, and angry about the unscrupulous way in which contested lands were often acquired. In 1850, for instance, a number of Taranaki rangatira wrote to Donald McLean, then a police inspector in Taranaki, protesting against the government's attempt to claim lands that had been released (tuku) and not bartered (hoko) to European settlers:

> This land was given to you for cultivation, and you should assent to that agreement, and not listen to what another says. I myself have the say for my land, and it is right to say that my land is my own. It is not as if you can divide up my stomach, that is, the middle of the land.[49]

In 1852, when the Constitution Act was passed, six Provincial Councils were set up, and a national Parliament with an appointed Upper House and an elected Lower House. All males over 21 years old with a freehold estate above a certain value were given the right to vote, but since almost all Māori men held their land in tribal estates, they were disenfranchised. Instead of being a fundamental guarantee of their tino rangatiratanga, their collective rights to land left Māori without a say in the governance of their own country. As McHugh has noted, 'the land-hungry settler community was an unruly mob whom even the most skilful and canny Governor could never rein in'.[50] As the numbers of European settlers increased, reaching parity with the Māori population, disillusionment among Māori with the settler government accelerated. In 1854, at a great meeting in Taranaki, the gathering decided that the sale of land to Europeans should end, or at least be radically curtailed.

In order to achieve this, in 1856 Iwikau Te Heuheu, the younger brother of Mananaui, the ariki of Tuwharetoa in the central North Island who had refused to sign the Treaty, convened a gathering of rangatira from around the country to appoint a Māori King, in an attempt to safeguard their lands and uphold their mana. After much debate the choice fell upon Te Wherowhero, the ariki of the Tainui tribes who had written to Queen Victoria. At Pukawa, his headquarters beside Lake Taupo, Te Heuheu (a signatory of the Declaration of Independence) set up a high flagpole to represent Tongariro, his ancestral mountain, supported by flax ropes attached at intervals, and raised the flag of the United Tribes. When the tribes had gathered around the pole, the ariki picked up one of the flax ropes and said:

'This is Ngongo-taha' – the mountain near Rotorua Lake – 'Where is the
man of Ngongo-taha to attach this mountain to Tongariro?' The leading
chief of Te Arawa tribe rose, and taking the end of a rope fastened it to
a manuka peg which he drove into the ground in front of his company.
The next rope symbolized Pu-tauaki (Mt. Edgecombe [*sic*]) the sacred
mountain of Ngati-Awa of the Bay of Plenty. The next was Tawhiuau,
the mountain belonging to Ngati-Manawa on the western borders of the
Ure-wera country. Every tribe giving its adherence to the King movement
had its rope allotted to it, representing a mountain dear to the tribe.[51]

When all of the iwi had driven their pegs into the ground, bracing the flagpole, Te Heuheu handed over the combined mana of their mountains and
descent lines (represented by the ropes) to Te Wherowhero (also known
as Potatau, or doorway to te pō, the ancestral realm) from Tainui, the new
Māori King. As in the case of Hone Heke, a flagpole and a flag had been
chosen to epitomise tino rangatiratanga.

In this ritual proceeding, the Māori King (holding the mana of the land)
was set up in parallel to the British Queen. In an intriguing inversion of
the relationship between Ranginui, the sky father, and Papatuanuku, the
earth mother, the king embodied tino rangatiratanga over the land, while
the queen embodied the sovereignty of the Crown. While this arrangement,
with its relational, complementary forms of order, made perfect sense in
te ao Māori, it ran contrary to ancient Western mythic ideas such as the
Great Chain of Being, in which a nation-state could have only one God, one
monarch, and one form of governance, in which it was proper for 'civilised'
people to rule over 'savages'. Affronted by what he saw as a challenge to
the queen's authority, and ignoring the protests of Wiremu Kingi, a leading rangatira, Governor Thomas Gore Browne purchased the district of
Waitara in Taranaki from a dissident chief. When the Executive Council
resolved that the land should be surveyed and the military forces 'shall . . .
keep possession, by force if necessary, of the said land, so as to prevent the
occupation of, or any act of trespass upon it by any natives',[52] this gesture
sparked off the Land Wars.

Shortly after this purchase, Gore Browne, concerned about the growing influence of the Māori King, convened a conference at Kohimarama
in Auckland to try and persuade as many rangatira as possible to remain
loyal to Queen Victoria. In his opening speech, Gore Browne congratulated

the rangatira on having given up many of their ancestral practices, instead adopting 'enlightened ways of being' (ngā tikanga o te māramatanga, literally the ways of light):

> Cannibalism has been exchanged for Christianity; Slavery has been abolished; War has become more rare; Prisoners taken in war are not slain; European habits are gradually replacing those of your ancestors of which all Christians are necessarily ashamed.
>
> The old have reason to be thankful that their sunset is brighter than their dawn, and the young may be grateful that their life did not begin until the darkness of the heathen night had been dispelled by that light which is the glory of all civilized Nations.[53]

The governor also argued that since the differences between the Māori and English languages were a major source of difficulty, leading to strife and confusion, the chiefs should ensure that their children learned English. Paora Tuhaere, a leading local rangatira, disagreed, proposing instead a complementary arrangement in which the governor would allow (tuku) the chiefs to join his council, so that matters such as murder or land disputes could be handled by joint discussion and decision:

> The Governor says that there is a difference of language. In my opinion this does not matter, inasmuch as there are plenty of European friends who would make matters clear to us, as they know our language.
>
> I am desirous that the minds [whakaaro] of the Europeans and the Maories should be brought into unison with each other. Then if a Maori killed another Maori his crime would be tried and adjudicated on by the understandings of both Pakeha and Maori.
>
> And if one man should interfere with the land of another, then let the same council try him. When a woman has been violated, let the same course obtain. Murders and 'Makutu' (sorcery) would come before the same tribunal, because there would then be but one law for both Pakehas and Maories, and the understandings of both people would be exercised in the council.[54]

Similarly, when Makarini Te Uhiniko spoke against a government policy of denying land rights to 'half-castes' (using a transliteration – 'hawhe-kahe' – for the term, because there was no parallel in Māori), he offered a relational solution. Since in relation to their Māori kinfolk, they were Māori, he argued, these people should enjoy the same rights to land as others through their Māori taha, or 'side' (for in te ao Māori, children inherited use rights from both parents):

> Now about the 'half-castes,' they are in the middle between Maori and Pakeha. They are like a bird on a sand-bank: the tide flows over it and he [or she] is obliged to take wing. Let us put this matter right, because they have a side [taha] that links to us, the Maori; let us show our regard for the side that turns towards us. Let us show him [or her] a piece of land from their mother's ancestors, lest someone else take it and their descendants are left wandering aimlessly.[55]

At Kohimarama, although the rangatira were eager to try to handle different understandings by co-existence and collaboration across parallel realms of action, the governor had already told them that they must be 'faithful children' (tamariki piri pono) to the queen, and that there could be only one head for her people in New Zealand. He was adamantly opposed to any recognition of the Māori King, or any support for those who fought to defend their lands. While some rangatira accepted this approach, most did not. Renata Tamakihikurangi, for instance, a rangatira from Hawke's Bay, wrote a brilliant series of letters (in Māori) to the local superintendent, defending Wiremu Kingi, the 'rebel' leader in Taranaki:

> You say, 'That man must let down his bristles, and pay obeisance to his Sovereign the Queen.' Sir, what then is the Maori doing? For years he has been listening to that teaching of the Queen's. But the Governor has made it all go wrong. Perhaps you think that he is not a man, that you say he should not raise his bristles when his land is taken from him? If your land were taken by a Maori, would your bristles not rise? Give him back his land, and then we will see if his bristles are still sticking up.
>
> [And when you speak of the Māori King], Sir, cease to cite this as a cause of quarrelling. For behold, the Treaty of Waitangi has been broken. It was said that the treaty was to protect the Maoris from foreign invasion. But those bad nations never came to attack us; the blow fell from you, the nation who made that same treaty. *Sir, it is you alone who have broken your numerous promises.*[56]

At the outbreak of the Land Wars, Sir William Martin, now retired as the Chief Justice, wrote a pamphlet assailing Governor Gore Browne for his decision to uphold the contested sale at Waitara by force, and outlining key principles of Māori land tenure and the rights of Māori under the Treaty of Waitangi. Martin concluded:

> Here in New Zealand our nation has engaged in an enterprise most difficult, yet also most noble and worthy of England. We have undertaken to acquire these islands for the Crown and for our race, without violence and without fraud, and so that the Native people, instead of being destroyed, should be protected and civilized.
>
> We have covenanted with these people, and assured to them the full privileges of subjects of the Crown. To this undertaking the faith of the nation is pledged. By these means we secured a peaceable entrance for the Queen's authority into the country, and have in consequence gradually gained a firm hold upon it. The compact is binding irrevocably. We cannot repudiate it so long as we retain the benefit which we obtained by it.[57]

New Zealand's civil war was thus a contest over land and mana, not strictly an inter-racial conflict.[58] Some Europeans (usually those who spoke Māori and had close relations with Māori people) argued in sympathy with Māori grievances, although they were always in a minority. Some Māori kin groups held fast to their covenant with the queen, fighting with the Crown against former enemies, while others fought against the Crown; and still others split, with some members fighting with and others against the European forces at different times. As James Belich has argued, rather than military conquest, the Land Wars ended in a stalemate.[59] After some years, unable to maintain a full-time military presence to combat the imperial and colonial troops (who greatly outnumbered them), those Māori who had fought against the Crown withdrew, and more than three million acres of land were confiscated by the settler government, from 'friendly' as well as 'hostile' kin groups across the North Island.

Afterwards, when the Native Land Court was established and survey teams and buyers went out across the country, the further loss of land through sale became almost impossible to resist, as innumerable reports to the Waitangi Tribunal have attested. The land was divided into blocks with boundaries and lists of owners, survey costs were awarded against them, the shares of individuals were sold, and millions more acres passed out of Māori hands.[60] As Hone Mohi Tawhai wrote in a bitter parody of a whakapapa (genealogical) recital:

> Aotearoa slept with the mana of England, and Governor Hobson was born.
> He slept with the rangatira Maori of the North and South Islands, and begat
>   the Treaty; and with Parliament and the laws of New Zealand were born.
> The Chief Judge slept with the Surveyor and Government Grants were born.
>   All these things have been sent to suppress us.
> The Maori Land Court slept with lawyers and begat first Leases, and then
>   Wills and Mortgages. And all the debts that go with them.
> Deceit slept with Alcohol and first Let's Sign it Away was born, and then Sell
>   It and finally Drunkenness.
> Landlessness slept with the Saddened Heart, and begat Sudden Death.[61]

Ironically, the tactics used to enact this dispossession were almost identical to those used in Britain to carry out the enclosure of the commons, and the clearances in the Scottish Highlands and islands, whose inhabitants were also often described as 'barbarians'. In Te Puke, for instance, in the wake of the depopulation of the district by epidemic diseases and the Land Wars when the Crown acquisition of the Māori land in that district was being promoted, the local newspaper declared in 1874:

> [T]he whole of that country . . . lays waste – as it has lain for centuries
> under the nominal control of contending tribes – unproductive and unoc-
> cupied, save by a handful of dusky savages. . . . [W]hen we . . . consider the
> Cornucopia of blessings which the occupation of such a wide district, by an
> industrious and energetic population would confer upon the community, we
> begin to realize . . . the heavy loss we are now sustaining, and must endure so
> long as it remains 'Native Land.'[62]

A very long tale could also be told about the way that, over the generations, Māori kinship networks have been cut up into bounded units, their members treated as autonomous individuals voting for management boards, register- ing their interests in land blocks, and often living at a distance from their ancestral territories. The expectation that in order to retain use rights, active occupation (or ahi kā) must be upheld was annulled by legislation, and as a result, land titles became so fragmented that they were almost impossible to manage for practical purposes, and much of the land lay idle.

As the links between people and land became attenuated, ancestral land was increasingly treated as private property and sold, or aggregated under the control of influential individuals and families, causing bitter rifts within kin groups. This still happens on a regular basis. Kin groups are also treated as corporate units for the purposes of Treaty settlements, in accord with the protocols of global capitalism. In the process, however, the checks and balances and values that encourage kin-group leaders to distribute and share wealth as well as accumulate it, and to take care of the land rather than exploit it, are often eroded, leading to inequities and bitter internal divisions as cash and property are handed over to settle Treaty grievances.[63] Some Māori kin groups handle these tensions better than others; but in every case, the clashes between kin-based expectations and those characteristic of contemporary capitalism are profound.

Even cutting-edge scholarship on indigenous land rights, aimed at emancipation, may contribute to these difficulties. International experts sometimes speak as though land has always been 'property' for Māori and other indigenous peoples, and their relationship defined as 'rights' and 'title', erasing a history of bitter resistance to these conceptions. As McHugh writes, for instance, 'Common law aboriginal title is concerned with the effect of Crown *sovereignty* upon the pre-existing *property rights* of the tribal inhabitants'[64] – and yet these ideas were not pre-existing and ancestral, but imposed by imperial fiat. Alternative indigenous approaches to land are obliterated by the very language in which reparation is made possible. Perhaps this is why, as McHugh observes, the fight to recognise aboriginal title in settler societies has so often backfired, leaving many indigenous peoples still marginalised and disempowered.[65]

While people come and go, the land still stands

Two hundred years after the first European settlement in New Zealand, the land itself has been transformed. The 'Order of Things' is now inscribed in the landscape – in gridded patterns of cultivation and occupation, fences, and the placement of houses and communities; in ownership regimes based on ideas of property and laws of trespass; in mono-purpose urban zones (e.g. industrial, commercial, retail and residential), and mono-cultural styles of forestry and farming. Its characteristic forms of order are also ubiquitous in virtual space – gridded maps, organisational structures, time sheets, Outlook calendars, balance sheets and the like – making it seem that this is the nature of reality itself, displacing other, alternative ways of seeing and organising relations among people, and between people and the land.

The Cartesian split between mind and matter (*res cogitans* and *res extensa*), 'Culture' and 'Nature' has led to the creation of parks and reserves as 'wild' spaces, the preservation of endangered species behind high, prison-like fences, human lives that are largely lived inside, and a sense that people are detached from the ecosystems that make their lives possible. The idea that the earth was created to serve human purposes underpins talk of 'ecosystem services' that should be paid for, which defines the planet as a servant or contractor; while the imperative to 'subdue the earth' as a sign of 'progress' and 'improvement' is evident in regimented rows of crops and trees, and industrial forms of cultivation. 'Dominion over every living thing' has been accompanied by losses of bio-diversity, the degradation of freshwater and marine ecosystems, the acidification of the ocean and climate change. The notion that we are now in the 'Age of the Anthropocene', in which 'natural' processes are dominated by human action, is another reflex of this style of reasoning.[66]

At the same time, however, Cartesian reasoning, with its divisions between mind and matter, subject and object, nature and culture, and an anthropocentric model of the cosmos is being confounded by the findings of contemporary science, from brain science and quantum physics to ecology and the biological and social sciences. Relational forms of order are resurgent, with the spread of the World Wide Web, ideas about complexity, and systems theory. In everyday life, these are expressed in networks of various kinds – the use of social media, collaborative decision-making, trans-disciplinary inquiry, and insights into the ways that human forms of life and environmental transformations are entangled. In relation to land, it is increasingly understood that in towns and cities, mono-purpose urban zones (industrial, residential, commercial, and so on) that require people to live, work and play in different places help to generate extra pollution, congestion and fragmented styles of living. Small-scale, internally diverse urban villages are being contemplated, each with its own distinctive character, and urban forests, gardens and waterways, linked by networks of public transport. In the countryside, industrial agriculture and forestry based

*Apirana Ngata taking the lead in a haka on Waitangi Day at the centennial
celebrations at Waitangi, by James Robert Snowden, 1940.*

on mono-crops – more classic Cartesian spaces – are being challenged by
approaches including agro-ecology, mixed-species forests and restorative
farming, closely adapted to particular landscapes and bio-regions.

In New Zealand, Māori ideas are often drawn upon in these debates,
and many Māori landholders and agribusinesses are working to reconcile
neo-liberal and ancestral philosophies. In response to the loss of land and
tino rangatiratanga, there have been two great resurgences of tikanga Māori
(Māori ways of doing things) in the past in New Zealand, which have helped
to shift the terms of the discussion.

The first of these took place at the turn of the twentieth century, in the
wake of the Land Wars, when it seemed that Māori might be heading for
extinction. This movement was led by the 'Young Māori Party' including
Apirana Ngata, a brilliant young lawyer from Ngati Porou who later became
Native Minister in the New Zealand Parliament; Te Rangihiroa (Peter Buck),
a medical doctor and reluctant politician who became the director of the
Bishop Museum in Hawai'i and a professor of anthropology at Yale; and

Maui Pomare, also a doctor and politician. Inspired by ancestral knowledge as well as modernist disciplines, these men worked to restore Māori people to health, revitalise ancestral tikanga including the Māori language, and to save the remnants of Māori land.

Among many other innovations, Apirana Ngata collected and published Māori chants and oral histories; revised and expanded the Māori dictionary first drafted by the missionary William Williams and his colleagues; fostered a resurgence of carving and building meeting houses; sought to restore the mana of his people by establishing a Māori Battalion that fought in two world wars; wrote about the Treaty of Waitangi and led the commemoration of its centennial in 1940; and fought to save the land by legislative changes that enabled fragmented rights to be consolidated, setting up co-operative businesses and adapting modern agricultural techniques for Māori purposes. Te Rangihiroa, an affable, charming man who often celebrated his dual heritage as a 'half-caste', served as director of Māori Health, entered Parliament and studied Māori material culture before becoming second-in-command of the Māori Battalion in World War I, winning the DSO. As mentioned earlier, with Ngata, Te Rangihiroa participated in the Dominion Museum expeditions, using cutting-edge technology to record vanishing tikanga (ways of living), before enjoying a brilliant international career in Pacific anthropology. Dr Maui Pomare became the director of Māori Health, and collected and published Māori oral traditions. Their philosophies were epitomised by Apirana Ngata in a whakataukī (saying) he wrote in a child's autograph book:

E tipu e rea, mo nga ra o tou ao
Ko to ringa ki nga rakau a te Pakeha, hei oranga mo to tinana
Ko to ngakau ki nga taonga a o tipuna Maori, hei tikitiki mo to mahuna
Ko to wairua ki te Atua, nana nei nga mea katoa.

Grow, child, in the days of your world
Your hand to the weapons of the Pakeha, as a livelihood for your body
Your heart to the treasures of your Maori ancestors, as a topknot for your
   head
Your spirit to God, who made all things.

During this period (roughly 1900–1930), Māori motifs were incorporated in contemporary public buildings and tikanga Māori (Māori culture) featured in international exhibitions, as the country presented itself to the wider world. European men (and a few Māori, including for instance Sir James Carroll and Te Rangihiroa) joined the 'Savage Club', wearing cloaks, brandishing patu (hand clubs) and taiaha (fighting staffs), led by their president the 'rangatira'. In their efforts to save Māori land and keep it productive, restore Māori to health and pass on tikanga Māori, Ngata and Te Rangihiroa had many influential European allies – lawyers, politicians, religious leaders, educationalists, ethnologists and economists. For a time, New Zealand was often referred to as 'Māoriland'. This national identification with indigenous customs, perhaps unique among settler societies, laid the foundation for contemporary ideas about 'bi-culturalism' and a willingness to address Treaty grievances, including the loss of land.

Old stadial ways of thinking are also resilient, however, ebbing and flowing in everyday life. During the 1930s, when assimilationist ideas and policies became resurgent in New Zealand, Ngata was pursued and disgraced for his oversight of Māori land development schemes and driven out of Cabinet in 1934, despite his stellar achievements. Te Rangihiroa was never appointed to a university post in New Zealand, despite a brilliant anthropological career outside the country. After the 1961 Hunn Report, which proposed many new assimilationist policies, a new generation of Māori leaders emerged, working alongside their elders in marches, occupations and other forms of protest to highlight grievances over breaches of the Treaty of Waitangi, and the loss of Māori language, tikanga and land.[67] Eruera Stirling, who was mentored by Ngata, was one of those elders, working closely with Nga Tamatoa, the young leaders at the front line of these protests.

In his book *Eruera: The Teachings of a Maori Elder*, based on interviews we did together in the late 1970s, Eruera spoke about his involvement in the Land March of 1975, led by Whina Cooper, sometimes referred to as 'the mother of the nation'; and the occupation of the Raglan golf course (1975) and of Bastion Point in Auckland (1977). At this time many Māori and other New Zealanders rallied to the cry of 'Not one more acre!', determined to stem the loss of Māori land. These events led to the establishment of the Waitangi Tribunal in 1975, and the amendment of its powers in 1985 to allow the adjudication of historic grievances (from 1840 to the present). Like the Young Māori Party, the Waitangi Tribunal seeks to work 'across worlds', aiming to bring together and balance Māori and modernist understandings of the past and present, reshaping possible futures in New Zealand.

Its meticulous, searching investigations, informed by evidence from elders as well as historians, anthropologists, linguists and lawyers, have led the way for settlements with the Crown that include the Whanganui River deed, discussed in the last chapter. The settlement process also sets many snares for participant iwi, however. As Margaret Mutu remarks:

> The process is not about settling claims at all. Nor is it about giving Maori many millions of dollars in compensation. Rather it is a unilaterally Crown-determined policy that aims to legally extinguish all historic Maori claims against the Crown as cheaply and as expeditiously as possible.[68]

Despite many obstacles, iwi including the Whanganui tribes and Tuhoe have made extraordinary efforts to operate the settlement process in a way that upholds ancestral philosophies and mana. In the agreement between the Crown and Tuhoe people in 2013, for instance, their Urewera rohe (or tribal territory) is described as a 'fortress', or ewe whenua, with an 'identity in and of itself' as their place of origin and return, the heart of the great fish of Maui, and the last district opened up for European settlement and governance in New Zealand. Backed by testimony from elders and the superb research of the historian Dame Judith Binney, Tuhoe tribal leaders have fought to restore their tino rangatiratanga over their ancestral lands. Binney's research is recorded in Tribunal reports and her book *Encircled Lands: Te Urewera 1820–1921*, which documents the engagements between Tuhoe and successive New Zealand governments, including broken promises of self-government, military invasions and later, invasions by police (particularly the arrest of Rua Kenana, a Tuhoe prophet, in 1916, and alleged terrorists in the Urewera raids in 2007).

Headed by a whakataukī (ancestral saying) '*ki te hāpai i tēnei manu o te rongomau*' – 'to carry on this bird of peace and quietness', the Tuhoe deed of settlement includes a preface that likens the agreement with the Crown to the process of entering a meeting house, a portal to the ancestral realm. Here, the front post of the house, the Pou Mataho, 'gazes past the paepae, across the marae, where there is no shelter from the fierce blaze of the sun or the bleakness of winter. It sees a century and a half of the pain-filled history of Tuhoe.' Moving forward, the Crown and Tuhoe meet together on the verandah of the meeting house and talk, 'protected from the elements but not yet within the comfort of the house'. As they enter the door (tatau pounamu – the greenstone door, or door of peace), they pass the Pou Tahu (front ridgepole post) inside the house that marks the compact with the Crown in 2011; the woven wall panels that represent various 'Relationship Statements' and other agreements; the Pou Tokomanawa, the central pole at the heart of the house, which represents the deed of settlement in 2013; and the Pou Tu a Rongo, the end post of the atua Rongo, of peace and goodwill. Together, these four posts hold up the ridgepole of the meeting house, supporting 'the shelter and comfort of those within, Tuhoe and the Crown'.

The deed itself, written in both Māori and English, is structured like the meeting house (an image of which is included in the text), with sections named after each of its key elements. The Pou Mataho section of the deed outlines the painful history of the relationship between Tuhoe and the Crown, with the Crown's acceptance of wrongdoing. The Pou Tahu summarises the history of Tuhoe's efforts to address their grievances, the findings of the Waitangi Tribunal, and Tuhoe's list of claims. The Pou Tokomanawa is at the heart of the settlement, addressing the mana motuhake (everlasting mana) and autonomy of Tuhoe, its relationship with the Crown, and the financial and cultural redress offered in the settlement; while the Pou Tu a Rongo records the Crown apology and Tuhoe's reply, with a statement of their aspirations.

The living heart of the agreement, Te Pou Tokomanawa, invokes the existential interlock between Tuhoe and Te Urewera, their ancestral lands:

Te Urewera is ancient and enduring, a fortress of nature, alive with history. Its scenery is abundant with mystery, adventure and remote beauty.

Te Urewera is a place of spiritual value, with its own mana and mauri.

Te Urewera has an identity in and of itself, inspiring people to commit to its care.

For Tuhoe, Te Urewera is the heart of the great fish of Māui. The name is derived from Murakareke, the son of the ancestor Tuhoe.

For Tuhoe, Te Urewera is their ewe whenua, their place of origin and return, their homeland.

Te Urewera expresses and gives meaning to Tuhoe culture, language, customs and identity. There, they hold mana by ahikāroa [fires alight on the land], they are tangata whenua and kaitiaki [guardians] of Te Urewera.

Te Kura Whare – Tuhoe's Living Building.

As a further expression of Tuhoe's philosophy of kaitiakitanga, their first collective act after signing the deed of settlement was to build Te Uru Taumata – a Whare Hou, or New House – at the heart of the Urewera. New Zealand's first 'living building', this large, contemporary complex is solar-powered, recycles water and is constructed largely from local materials harvested and processed by local people.

The process of designing and constructing Te Uru Taumata captures Tuhoe's commitment to make a new beginning and seek ora – lasting life and prosperity – for their land and people, recorded in a documentary film, *Ever the Land*. A contingent of Tuhoe people attended its premiere in Auckland in 2015, riveting the audience with their performance of a haka expressing their mana motuhake. Fittingly, the subtitle for this film is 'A People, A Place, Their Building.' The documentary also records the ceremony in 2014 when the Urewera was formally returned to the Tuhoe people, along with an apology from the New Zealand government, and an agreement to co-manage the Urewera into the future, taking care of waterways, plants, animals, people and the land. In the haka quoted in the deed, they chant:

Ehara taku mana i te mana hou
He mana tawhito tonu, taku mana

Ruru rawa mai, ka ruru mai
Ka mahora nga ture ki te maunga tapu

My authority [mana] is not of recent times
It is an ancient power, my sovereignty
When the compact was made
Our laws spread out across our whole region [over the sacred mountain].

Like other iwi across the country, from the time of the Declaration of Independence onwards, Tuhoe have sought to protect their ancestral territories as a whenua rangatira – a chiefly land, independent, prosperous and at peace.

As the last bastion of tino rangatiratanga to come under the rule of the nation-state in New Zealand, the Urewera also serves as a haven for te reo (the Māori language) and ways of thinking, contributing to the revival of te reo in kōhanga reo (Māori-language preschools), schools and universities, the Māori Language Commission/Te Taura Whiri i Te Reo Māori, Māori radio and television, and the resurgence of kapa haka, for instance. This has provided a wellspring of innovation in dealing with colonial and neo-colonial impositions of various kinds. As Tamati Ranapiri explained to the ethnologist Elsdon Best (who spent most of his time among Māori in the Urewera), the hau (life force) of the whenua (land), its waterways, forests and people (tāngata whenua) are inextricably intertwined. Tuhoe's determination to act as kaitiaki (guardians) for the Urewera, the heart of the 'great fish of Maui', like similar approaches by other iwi, are helping to inspire regenerative forms of land use that aim to bring about a state of ora (health, well-being, prosperity) for rivers, lakes, mountains and people alike, and not just in the Urewera, but across the land.

CHAPTER ELEVEN

Fountain of Fish

Moana / Sea

'[I]f something goes wrong, it's not only our beaches that get
ruined. It's everyone's.'

– TWEEDIE WAITITI, TE WHANAU-A-APANUI, *SUNDAY STAR-TIMES*

ON 23 APRIL 2011 A SMALL FLOTILLA OF PROTEST VESSELS HEADED
out to sea from the Eastern Bay of Plenty in New Zealand. Among
them was a fishing boat, the *San Pietro*, owned by the local iwi,
Te Whanau-a-Apanui, and skippered by Elvis Teddy, an iwi member.
Rikirangi Gage, a senior tribal leader, was also on board.

At that time, a large oil drilling ship, the *Orient Explorer*, contracted by
the Brazilian oil company Petrobras, was conducting a seismic survey of
the Raukumara basin, about 300 kilometres north of East Cape. In 2010,
Petrobras had been granted a permit by the New Zealand government to
carry out exploratory drilling in these waters, which traversed Te Whanau-
a-Apanui's ancestral fishing grounds. When they learned of this permit from
press reports, the iwi leaders were incensed.

As we have seen, under the Treaty of Waitangi, signed in 1840, Queen
Victoria had guaranteed their ancestors the 'full, exclusive, undisturbed possession of their Lands and Estates Forests Fisheries and other properties . . .
so long as it is their wish and desire to retain the same in their possession'.
Since 1975 the Waitangi Tribunal, established to inquire into breaches of
the Treaty, had held hearings around the country and investigated many
complaints by Māori kin groups, including those relating to fishing and the

ocean. The Tribunal had issued reports and made recommendations to governments of the day. Over this period, successive governments had offered apologies and settlements in cash and kind to many iwi around the country. When Te Whanau-a-Apanui leaders met with the prime minister to state their opposition to drilling for oil in their ancestral waters, he expressed sympathy, but refused to revoke the permit. Determined that their point of view should be heard, the tribe put out a call for assistance, and the environmental group Greenpeace responded, sending a flotilla of five protest vessels to the Bay of Plenty.[1]

As anger about the drilling increased, placards and signs sprang up on windows, fences and sheds along the road between Opotiki and Gisborne. Bonfires were lit in protest, and large-scale haka were performed on the beaches. On 10 April 2011, when Greenpeace protesters swam into the path of the *Orient Explorer*, they were watched by representatives of the New Zealand Air Force, Navy and Police. The police issued notices under the Maritime Transport Act 1994, ordering the protest boats and their crews to stay 200 metres from the ship, or to face a $10,000 fine or up to a year in jail.[2] In an interview with the *Sunday Star-Times*, Tweedie Waititi from Te Whanau-a-Apanui expressed surprise at the depth of feeling among her people: 'We are the most placid iwi on earth. And I tell you what, the government has awakened some sort of taniwha. It's quite a surprise to see my people react the way they are reacting. We're all virgins at doing this. We never fight.'[3]

Like other New Zealanders, tribal members had heard a great deal about the Deep Horizon blow-out in the Gulf of Mexico the previous year, and the damage done to the ocean, sea life, coasts and estuaries, and to the livelihoods of local people. They were fearful that a similar catastrophe might happen in their ancestral waters. Tweedie also expressed concern for the moki, a sacred fish that migrates every year from Hawaiki, the ancestral homeland, to Te Whanau-a-Apanui waters. 'That's the moki's home,' she said. 'Right where they want to drill. Every June, there is a star that shines in the sky and her name is Autahi, and that's our indication that the moki has come home.'[4] The story of the moki is told in paintings in the dining hall and carved meeting house at Kauaetangohia marae at Cape Runaway, executed by Te Whanau-a-Apanui artists Cliff Whiting and Para Matchitt.

I had also heard about this sacred fish many years earlier when I worked with Eruera Stirling (also from Te Whanau-a-Apanui) on our book about

San Pietro *confronting the oil prospecting ship* Orient
Explorer *on 23 April 2011, by Malcolm Pullman.*

his ancestors and his life. He told me about a time in his youth when a senior
elder, Manihera Waititi, invited him and his elder brother to catch the 'first
fish' to open the moki season. On that occasion, the two boys went to the
Whangaparaoa River before dawn and boarded Manihera's boat. With a
land breeze behind them, the elder took them to the moki fishing ground
about one hundred yards offshore from Ratanui, a beach where ancestral
voyaging canoes had landed. After catching several moki, they headed out to
a deep-water fishing ground, where they caught several more of the sacred
fish. Back on shore, the old man gave them the fish to take home to their
mother, Mihi Kotukutuku. As the tribe's senior leader, it was customary for
her to be presented with the first fish of the season.[5]

According to Eruera, the waters offshore from Raukokore, his home
village, are known as Te Kopua-a-Hinemahuru, the deep waters of
Hinemahuru, named after the ancestress of his people. Its fishing grounds
and shellfish beds are linked with the carved meeting house on shore, also
named after this high-born woman, whose mana extended over the land
and sea, and embodying the whakapapa (genealogy) of her descendants.
A rock named Whangaipaka stands in these waters, guarded by a kaitiaki,
or guardian, a large stingray. If a stranger went there without permission,
a great wave carrying the stingray would sweep over the rock, drowning the
intruder.[6] Eruera told me that in his time, shellfish beds and fishing grounds
were jealously guarded:

Each district had its own mussel beds, and they were reserved for the people of that place. If the people saw a stranger picking their mussels, look out! He'd be a dead man if he came ashore. Fishing was very tapu [imbued with ancestral presence], and each family had its own fishing grounds, no one else could fish there or there would be a big fight.

The old people were very particular about the sea, and nobody was allowed to eat or smoke out on the boats. If a man took food with him when he went fishing, he'd sit there all day with his hook and line empty and the fish would stay away.

Sometimes if the fishing was very bad the people would start asking questions, and if they found out the guilty man, he'd get into big trouble for breaking the sacred law of tapu. The people would just about knock him to pieces, and he wouldn't be allowed to go out to sea again for quite a while. If a thing like that happened at home, you were well marked by the people.[7]

Given the intensity of this bond between people, their land and their ancestral waters, and the way that whakapapa was entwined with both land and sea, it is not surprising that the leaders of Te Whanau-a-Apanui were outraged when, without any prior warning, the government issued a permit for an oil company to drill in their ancestral waters. As their protests were brushed aside, the tribal leaders became increasingly angry. As Tweedie Waititi remarked, it was as though a taniwha, a powerful ancestral being, had woken up and was thrashing around in the ocean.

When Rikirangi Gage, an acknowledged senior leader of the iwi, joined the protest flotilla, this gesture was ignored. Several days later, Te Whanau-a-Apanui's fishing boat *San Pietro* motored across the bow of the *Orient Explorer*, trailing tuna fishing lines and a string of buoys tied together with rope. When the captain of the survey ship told them to stay away, Gage replied, 'We won't be moving. We'll be doing some fishing.' Soon afterwards, police officers boarded the fishing boat and arrested the skipper, Elvis Teddy, charging him with an offence under the Maritime Transport Act and removing him from the vessel. Back on shore, Teddy defended his actions, saying that he was simply exercising his right under the Treaty of Waitangi to fish his ancestral waters. If his boat had come close to the *Orient Explorer*, it was the fault of the drilling ship's commander for not avoiding a fishing vessel.

Teddy was prosecuted, and during his trial in the district court, his lawyers argued that since the confrontation had happened outside New

Zealand's 12-mile territorial zone, the Maritime Transport Act did not apply. The judge agreed, and the charges were dismissed.[8] When the police appealed the judgment to the High Court, however, the judge ruled that as a New Zealand vessel, the *San Pietro* came under New Zealand jurisdiction, even on the 'high seas'. Although there was no specific provision in the Maritime Transport Act to this effect, the Act must apply beyond the 12-mile limit, or the New Zealand government would be unable to uphold its international obligations under the 1982 UN Convention on the Law of the Sea (UNCLOS).[9]

After this verdict, Teddy's lawyer issued a statement in reply, saying that by granting a drilling permit in their ancestral waters without consulting Te Whanau-a-Apanui, and by sending in the New Zealand Navy, Air Force and Police to stop Teddy and Gage from fishing in their ancestral waters, the New Zealand government had breached not only the Treaty of Waitangi but the UN Declaration on the Rights of Indigenous Peoples, which New Zealand has also signed. Soon afterwards, the New Zealand government took further steps to tighten its control over New Zealand vessels on the high seas, passing hotly debated legislation that prohibits protest at sea in the vicinity of oil exploration vessels.[10]

This clash between Te Whanau-a-Apanui on the one hand, and Petrobras and the Crown on the other, was yet another ontological collision, a clash between different 'worlds' or ways of being. At the same time, it is a complex story, with different resonances for different people. For many in New Zealand, the stand-off between the *San Pietro* and a large oil drilling ship recalled an episode in 1973 when the New Zealand government tried to stop French nuclear testing in the Pacific by sending two naval frigates, one with a Cabinet minister on board, to Moruroa Atoll, a testing site in the Society Islands. Several New Zealand yachts accompanied the frigates, and one of these was boarded off Moruroa and its skipper assaulted by French marines.[11] In 1984 when the New Zealand government declared the nation nuclear-free and refused to allow visits by US nuclear vessels, the country was ejected from the ANZUS alliance with the United States and Australia. A year later, French agents sank the Greenpeace vessel *Rainbow Warrior*, which was about to lead another protest flotilla to Moruroa, in Auckland harbour.[12] They were captured by the New Zealand Police and sent back to France without facing prosecution, where they were lauded by the French government, provoking much bitter comment.

In New Zealand, then, protest at sea is deeply entangled with national identity, and a concern for environmental issues. For many New Zealanders, by pitting its small boat against the oil drilling ship, Te Whanau-a-Apanui was following in that feisty tradition, fighting to protect the ocean. For many members of Te Whanau-a-Apanui, on the other hand, this was more a question of protecting their mana. The *San Pietro* and its crew were asserting the right of their iwi to safeguard ancestral fisheries against unwanted intrusion, based on the guarantee of 'full, exclusive and undisturbed possession' of their fishing grounds under Article Two of the Treaty of Waitangi. At the same time, for the government and many other New Zealanders, it was a matter of upholding the sovereignty of the Crown, and the government's right to manage the 200-mile Exclusive Economic Zone, to issue exploration permits to oil companies and to protect oil prospectors from unwarranted interference by protest vessels, including those owned by iwi.

Nevertheless, this was not an ethnic confrontation. Many of the protesters were not Māori, and as Tweedie Waititi remarked, '[I]f something goes wrong, it's not only our beaches that get ruined. It's everyone's. . . . I'm pretty sure that not only Maori have a connection to the sea.' Also, some iwi were flirting with the idea of supporting oil exploration: 'Like our lawyer said,' she added, 'our mana is not for sale and no amount of money could pay us off. Maybe some iwi you could dangle a carrot. But this one's not biting.'[13] In order to investigate these ontological collisions, and what they tell us about different relationships between people and the ocean in New Zealand, we can explore some of the deep, taken-for-granted presuppositions that underpin the positions adopted by different protagonists, along with previous alliances and confrontations.

Moana: the sea in te ao Māori

According to Māori ancestral accounts, the sea emerged at the very beginnings of the cosmos. As Teone Taare Tikao, a learned elder from Banks Peninsula in the South Island, told Herries Beattie in the early 1900s: 'The ocean came into existence before anything else. . . . It was the start of life in the universe. I believe this take [root] is correct, and that everything came from the water.'[14] In the beginning, he said, 'the sea lay like a vast, unbroken lake within the circle of the sand bank that ran right around it. There was no land and no sky, no sun nor moon, and no stars nor clouds. Darkness reigned.' It was only when Maku, or dampness, came together with Mahora-nuiatea, the wide expanse of the ocean, that earth and sky were created.

In the cosmological account given by Te Rangikaheke of Te Arawa, when Tawhiri, the wind god, attacked Tangaroa, the sea ancestor fled into the ocean while his offspring argued among themselves. Ikatere, the ancestor of fish, taunted his brother Tutewanawana, the ancestor of lizards, saying, 'You go inland, and be heaped up after fires in the fern!' and Tutewanawana retorted, 'You go to sea, and be hung up in baskets of cooked food!'[15] After this quarrel, Tangaroa's children went their separate ways. During this cosmic battle, only Tu, the ancestor of people, faced up to Tawhiri. For his temerity, he earned for his descendants the right to harvest the offspring of his brothers as food – birds, root crops, forest foods and trees, fish, crayfish and shellfish – although the ancestors concerned had to be propitiated with offerings.

The whakapapa link between people and the ocean features in many origin stories. These include the feats of the ancestor Maui, who set off with his older brothers from Hawaiki, the homeland, on a fishing expedition. After telling them to take their canoe out of sight of land, Maui dropped his line into the ocean, catching only small fish at first. When his brothers mocked him, he took a hook carved from his grandmother's sacred jawbone, baited it with blood from his nose and hauled up a great fish, Te Ika-a-Maui (Maui's fish), the North Island of New Zealand.[16] As Maui set off across the island to make an offering to Tangaroa, his brothers began to cut up his great fish, so they could eat it. As it writhed in agony, the new land convulsed, throwing up steep mountains and valleys. According to the tribes of the East Coast, Maui's canoe still lies at the top of Hikurangi, their ancestral peak, and his feats are not forgotten.[17] In 2000, pou (ancestral carvings) were erected on the summit of Hikurangi in honour of Maui and the star ances-tors who guided him across the ocean.

Like many East Coast people, Eruera Stirling traced his descent back to another great voyaging ancestor, Paikea, who had arrived in New Zealand on a whale.[18] After surviving an attempt by a jealous younger brother to kill him by sinking their canoe, Paikea recited a powerful karakia (incantation) and summoned a whale, which carried him to New Zealand (or he trans-formed himself into a whale, in another version). Arriving at Whangara on the East Coast, he named this locality and many of its features after places in the ancestral homeland.[19] Like Maui, Paikea's fame lives on. A carving of the ancestor riding his whale stands on the gable end of the meeting house

Paikea rides his whale on Whitireia meeting house, Whangara.

at Whangara, while an action song about him is so often sung that it is called the East Coast 'National Anthem'. His feats are also commemorated in *Whale Rider*, a novel by the contemporary Māori writer Witi Ihimaera who wove his story together with that of a young girl, also named Paikea, who grew up on the East Coast and, after many struggles, became a tribal leader. In its turn, *Whale Rider* became a movie that won international acclaim.

Other East Coast stories about the sea include that of Pou, whose son drowned in the Motu River. According to Timi Waata Rimini, a Bay of Plenty elder, who recounted this story in 1901, Pou searched for his son in Hawaiki, the ancestral homeland. When he arrived at the home of Tangaroa, a 'fountain of fish' seething with kahawai, and asked the sea god whether he had taken his son, Tangaroa denied it. In disbelief, Pou invited the sea god to attend his son's tangi (funeral). Upon his return to the Bay of Plenty, Pou told his people to make a great net. When the net was ready, the people looked out to sea and saw Tangaroa and his attendants, a huge shoal of kahawai, approaching, swimming inside Whakaari (White Island) to attend the tangi. As the shoal approached the mouth of the Motu River, Pou ordered his people to cast the great net. Thousands of Tangaroa's children were caught and fed to the crowds who had come to farewell Pou's son. As Rimini explained, when the kahawai arrive at the mouth of the Motu River every year, the story of Pou is re-enacted. In order to lift the tapu of Tangaroa, a chiefly youngster was taken to catch three kahawai, which were offered to Pou and the high chief of the region, a ritual re-enacted by Eruera and his brother in their youth.

By acknowledging the mana of Tangaroa, Maui, Paikea and Pou, these 'first fish' rituals guarded the fertility of the ocean. Rimini, for example, described catches of twenty or thirty thousand kahawai in the Bay of Plenty. When the kahawai shoals arrived at the mouth of the Motu River, he said, 'the fishing lines thrown out on one side of the river and the other are as close as the telephone lines in Wellington. The fish there are as thick as if packed in an oven. If a paua shell should be thrown out on the shoal, it would remain on the surface.'[20] For those familiar with today's depleted oceans, such tales seem incredible. Evidence presented to the Waitangi Tribunal hearings about kin-group relations with the ocean, however, has given a vivid impression of the prodigal quantities of fish that in earlier times were a staple item of diet, harvested by Māori in many parts of the country. The catches could be huge. In 1885, for instance, Major Gilbert Mair saw a fishing net 95 'chains' [approximately 1900 metres] long at Maketu in the Bay of Plenty. Hundreds worked to join sections of the net together, and two canoes carried it out to sea. After many shoals had passed, watched by an elderly tohunga from a high hill, he finally gave the signal to set the net. When the crowd on the beach, at least 1000 people, were unable to pull it in, the net had to be raised twice to let fish escape. On this occasion they caught 37,000 fish, three anchors and numerous sharks in one haul.[21]

Coastal iwi had an intimate knowledge of their tribal waters. In 1919, Colonel Thomas Porter, assisted by a local teacher at Te Kaha in the heart of Te Whanau-a-Apanui, published *The Maori as a Fisherman*, which recorded a wealth of information about ancestral fishing methods. Four years later, a party from the Dominion Museum invited by Sir Apirana Ngata, then the Native Minister, visited the East Coast to document various ancestral practices, many of which also related to fishing and the ocean. My great-grandfather James McDonald was also the film-maker and photographer for this expedition, working with Te Rangihiroa (Peter Buck), and McDonald's images were used to illustrate a paper about Māori

*Apirana Ngata and Peter Buck alongside a tukutuku panel at
Waiomatatini, by James Ingram McDonald, 1923.*

fishing techniques written and published by Te Rangihiroa after their journey. In this paper, Te Rangihiroa listed the names of fishing grounds and
channels in the reefs around the East Coast, and the fish that were caught in
those places. He described the methods used to catch each species, and the
times they were taken. Many of these fishing grounds also featured in tribal
stories of quarrels and battles between different kin groups when the restrictions on these grounds or channels were broken, collected and published by
Apirana Ngata.[22]

Among other sea lore, Te Rangihiroa described customs relating to the
kehe, or granite trout, a sacred fish that frequented rocky channels in the
reefs, grazing on kohuwai, a particular type of seaweed (*Tyndaridea anomala*).
A number of methods were used to catch this fish, including shaping named
channels in the reef with stones, waiting until the kohuwai grew back
again, and then using a hoop net to scoop up the kehe as they grazed on
the seaweed, or using a pole to drive them into the net. Te Rangihiroa also
described what happened when the chief's wife at Omaio became pregnant.
The rāhui, or sacred prohibition, on a famous kehe fishing ground called

Men fishing for kahawai on the East Coast, by James Ingram McDonald, 1923.

Te Wharau was lifted, and as people gathered on the beach, men with hoop nets were sent to stand on particular named rocks. When the tohunga called out 'Rukuhia!', people dived into the channels, swimming underwater and driving the kehe into the hoop nets, in an uproar of excitement. Afterwards, the fish were cooked and presented to the chieftainess as a delicacy.[23]

This link between the ongoing life and fertility of kin groups and that of the land and the seas off their coasts ran very deep. The sea itself was alive and breathing. At its heart lay Te Parata, a great taniwha (some say a gigantic whale), and when he breathed in, his mouth became a great whirlpool that swallowed canoes at sea.[24] When he breathed out, the tide began to flow, and children were born. According to an early manuscript collected by John White:

> Te Parata is the reason for the flow of the tides
> He draws breath into his belly
> when the tides flow, he is forcing breath
> out of his belly.

Te Parata is the most important *atua* of the ocean
He is also known as Tangaroa.
There is a reason for this name. It relates
to the length of the breath (*taanga manawa*)
he draws breath twice each day and night
This is the meaning of the name.[25]

In this way, the sea was linked with the rhythms of life and death. While the land was known as whenua (placenta), tidal waters were associated with amniotic fluid. Often, a chiefly child would be born as a certain star rose in the sky and the tide turned – for example, at Eruera's birth. According to Eruera, when he was born, his mother Mihi Kotukutuku had a long, difficult labour. Concerned for her safety, her attendants carried her to a place beside the sea where his older brother had been born. When the labour pains stopped, they consulted an old priestess named Hiria Te Rangihaeata who advised them to take her to a raupō (bulrush) house in the bush, and then to a karaka tree (*Corynocarpus laevigatus*) beside some ancestral gardens. There, she said, 'When the tides of Kirieke begin to flow and the star Poututerangi rises above Tihirau mountain, this child will be born.'[26] It happened as she had prophesied. When Eruera was about three years old, this old priestess and her husband Pera, the last tohunga from the Kirieke whare wānanga, took him away from his mother to live with them in the bush, teaching him ancestral stories, chants and genealogies, the lunar calendar, and the arts of gardening, eeling and fishing at sea.

The link between people and the tides was also associated with death. Wairua (spirits) left on the ebbing tide, and when a great chief died, he was farewelled with the chant, 'The eddy squall is gone, the storm is passed away, the Parata is gone, the big fish has left its dwelling place.'[27] If a traveller on the sea showed disrespect to its life force, his voyaging canoe might be sucked down into Te Parata, as was the case with the *Te Arawa* canoe when its captain Tamatekapua seduced the wife of the great priest Ngatoroirangi, who had power over the ocean. Fortunately Ngatoroirangi relented, and chanted a karakia that freed the canoe from this powerful vortex.[28] The name Te Parata was also given to the carved face at the base of a canoe prow, where it cut through the waves, and the carved face at the apex of a meeting house.[29] Te Parata is the powerful, interstitial vortex, associated with the ocean, where male and female, land and sea, east and west, dark and light mingle together.

Eruera Stirling often spoke about relations between people and the ocean, saying for instance that if a chief wanted to reserve a particular fishing ground, he would put a carved tōtara pole in the ground, and declare it off limits. 'After that if anybody took food from that place or pulled out the pole they were killed for their trouble, and the rāhui remained in force until the chief took away his pole and lifted his mana from the land.'[30]

The Ocean in 'the West'

As noted earlier, the gridding of the seas off New Zealand was initiated during the 1769–1770 *Endeavour* voyage around the coastline. As a leading hydrographer, Captain James Cook was a pioneer in the Enlightenment project that aimed to measure and mark out the world's vast expanses of ocean. When a coastline was drawn on the charts, this was at once a geographical description and a geopolitical statement. According to eighteenth-century conventions, European nation-states held *imperium*, or sovereignty, over territorial waters 3 miles out from their coasts, and the right to grant *dominium*, or property rights, within this zone, although this was rarely exercised. It was not until quite recently (in 1965 in New Zealand) that the Crown's sovereignty was extended out to 12 miles from the coast, and in 1982 by the United Nations Convention on the Law of the Sea out to 200 miles, defining an oceanic 'Exclusive Economic Zone'.

In eighteenth-century Europe, the 'high seas', that part of the ocean which fell outside territorial waters, were understood as a *mare liberum*, an expanse free for the ships of all nations to navigate. At that time the convention was quite recent, dating back to Grotius's *Mare Liberum* (1609), a work that argued for the freedom of the high seas, facilitating maritime exploration, trade and imperial expansion by European maritime powers.[31] Since none of its inhabitants were 'civilised', it was also assumed that the Pacific Ocean was a *mare nullius*, a vast, empty expanse whose inhabitants could exercise no sovereign rights over the ocean.[32] If a naval vessel from a European nation was the first to 'discover' an island in the Pacific, its representative (in this case, James Cook) could go ashore and raise a flag to claim it for his monarch – although according to some authorities in international law, he had to gain the consent of the local inhabitants before claiming sovereignty over the land.

At that time, European nation-states took it for granted that they had the right to determine the law of the sea, rather than the Pacific islanders who had invented blue-water sailing, and discovered, explored and inhabited this vast ocean for millennia before their arrival. In this way, they presupposed their right to exercise dominion over almost a third of the Earth's surface, an assumption that has continued into contemporary times. As the Tongan scholar 'Epeli Hau'ofa has pointed out, this transformation was profound. From a vantage point in Europe, on the opposite side of the globe, the Pacific Ocean seemed remote and empty, and its islands small and insignificant:

> [C]ontinental men – Europeans and Americans – drew imaginary lines across the sea, making the colonial boundaries that confined ocean people to tiny spaces for the first time.[33]

In their charts, Cook and his men abstracted and gridded this vast ocean, heedless of the sea paths, star paths, currents and sea markers familiar to island star navigators. These charts portrayed the Pacific as a vast empty space, waiting to be 'discovered' and explored, inscribed on the maps of the world and claimed by European powers. At the same time, like island navigators, Cook and his crew were also seafarers, with an intimate knowledge of the ocean (although their own home waters were very different from those in the Pacific). In part, their journals, sketches and collections restored the sea to life again, with meticulous depictions of local people in local seascapes, canoes and fishing gear, different species of fish, as well as recording tides and the temperature of the ocean.

At that time in Europe, too, kin-based communities in Ireland, Scotland and Norway managed inherited land/sea coastal domains in ways that were quite similar to those Māori kin groups who regarded reefs and fishing grounds as part of their ancestral domain, marked by seasonal movements across complex networks of mahinga kai, or places where particular kinds of food could be harvested at particular times of the year. During the eighteenth century in Britain, however, such kin-based coastal use rights and those who practised them were being displaced. Edmund Spenser, for instance, saw 'the refusal of the Irish to give up their barbarian customs and clannish pride' as evidence 'that they are a barbaric race who must be broken by famine and the sword'.[34] The use rights exercised by kin groups were being replaced by a regime that promoted the enclosure of land as private property, held by rights-bearing individuals, and of the sea out as far as cannon-shot (3 miles from the coast) as the property of the Crown, while the high seas and their fish were free for all to use, God's gift to humankind.

As Nonie Sharp has argued, this project of dismantling kin-based land/sea domains in Europe and replacing them with abstract property rights, held by individuals in the case of land and by nation-states in the case of territorial waters, had largely been accomplished by the end of the eighteenth century.[35] This regime was then transported to the Pacific, often by Europeans who had themselves suffered the loss of ancestral land/sea domains, displaced by the enclosure of the commons on land and the seizure of maritime use rights by the Crown.[36]

The whirlpool of time: ontological clashes at sea

These very different sets of assumptions about relations between people and the sea led to clashes from the outset. When the *Endeavour* arrived off the coasts of New Zealand, local people were at first unsure what this bizarre apparition might be. In Turanga (Poverty Bay in Gisborne), for instance, the first harbour they visited in New Zealand, the people thought the ship might be Waikawa, a sacred island off the end of the Mahia Peninsula, floating into their harbour. Nevertheless, they used their own time-honoured rituals for challenging the strangers, performing wero (ritual challenges), karakia (incantations) and haka (war dances).

There were many such clashes around the coastline of New Zealand. When the *Endeavour* arrived at Waikawa, for instance, off the end of the Mahia Peninsula, the site of a school of ancestral learning, priests chanted and warriors in canoes threw spears at the hull of the *Endeavour*, and Cook responded by ordering a cannon to be fired overhead. In reply a warrior turned around and exposed his naked backside to the ship, a gesture known as whakapohane. As they sailed across Hawke's Bay, flotillas of canoes came out, led by elderly chiefs wearing fine cloaks, chanting, making speeches, brandishing their weapons and preventing the Europeans from making a landing.[37] When the *Endeavour* headed north and arrived in the Bay of Plenty, a large canoe carrying 60 warriors came out from Tihirau peninsula, in Te Whanau-a-Apanui waters, and circled the ship, a priest reciting incantations as the crew performed a war dance. They cried out, 'Come to land and we will kill you', paddling at high speed to attack the *Endeavour* and stopping only when a volley of grapeshot was fired beside their canoe.

*Waka hourua (double canoe) under sail, chasing the Endeavour off
the Bay of Plenty, by Herman Diedrich Spöring, 1769.*

When a cannon loaded with round shot was fired overhead, they fled back
to the land.[38]

On the whole, Captain Cook respected these challenges, retorting with
warning shots rather than shooting the warriors. In his 'Hints', the Earl of
Morton had insisted that people in these new lands had the right to defend
their territories and, as we have seen, under European conventions territorial waters extended out to the 3-mile limit. Interestingly, it was Tupaia
who disputed the right of Māori to confront the *Endeavour*. Off the tip of
the Coromandel Peninsula, where another sacred site was located, when
warriors in two large carved canoes threw stones at the side of the vessel,
Tupaia warned them to stop this aggressive behaviour, or they would be
killed. According to Banks:

> They answerd him in their usual cant 'come ashore only and we will kill you
> all.' Well, said Tupia, but while we are at sea you have no manner of Business
> with us, the Sea is our property as much as yours.

In fact, it must have been Joseph Banks – Tupaia's translator – and not
Tupaia himself who introduced the idea of the sea as 'property' into these
early encounters. In Tahiti, as in New Zealand, the ocean was understood

as a great marae (sacred site), and islands as fish drawn up out of the ocean. Some sacred islands were thought to be capable of swimming from one place to another, and there was no idea that human beings could 'own' the ocean.[39]

Nevertheless, kin groups acted as guardians of their ancestral coastal waters. During recent legal contests between iwi and the Crown, although the Crown's lawyers have argued that in pre-European Māori times the ocean was a highway, open to all, their claim is not supported by the evidence of these first meetings between Māori and Europeans. And as one can see, Māori kin groups have long defended their rights over their ancestral waters. There is a powerful continuity between Rikirangi Gage's presence on board the *San Pietro* and their confrontation with the oil drilling ship, and those earlier clashes in which Te Whanau-a-Apanui asserted their mana over their tribal waters in the face of the *Endeavour*'s arrival, a mana they continue to uphold.

Those ancestral clashes have contemporary echoes in many parts of New Zealand. In 1985, for instance, the Hon. Matiu Rata, a Member of Parliament, wrote to the Waitangi Tribunal on behalf of the Muriwhenua people, alleging that the Ministry of Agriculture and Fisheries was about to breach the Treaty by introducing a fisheries management system that quantified fish stocks, enumerating different species of fish and turning them into 'quota' that could be bought and sold, in the process taking it for granted that Māori customary fishing rights had been extinguished.[40] A Waitangi Tribunal to hear the Muriwhenua Fishing Claim was established. During a long and exhaustive inquiry, a wealth of historical research and evidence from experts and knowledgeable elders was gathered about ancestral relations between iwi and the ocean. Wiremu Paraone, for example, described:

> the abundant fish-life in the Parengarenga Harbour, mullet jumping and splashing continuously, schools of kahawai appearing in the foam-filled waters, trevalli, parore, kingfish and all kinds of fish beneath the Te Hapua wharf...[41]

Fishing grounds and rocks were named and located, and the habits of particular species and customary fishing practices described. In their evidence, Muriwhenua people made many complaints about the devastation caused by large trawlers, expressing incredulity that the depletion and near-destruction of once-prodigal fisheries could be described as 'progress'; and fury that their own ways of fishing, which had preserved the rawa moana (bounty of the ocean), had been patronised, marginalised and often forbidden.[42]

Once again, however, this was not strictly an ethnic collision. The counsel for the claimants, Sian Elias (later chief justice of New Zealand) and David Baragwanath, and many of the witnesses to the Tribunal were not Māori. Their arguments and the evidence presented for and by Muriwhenua iwi proved to be compelling. After the hearings were over, the Tribunal found in favour of the Muriwhenua tribes, saying that their ancestral fisheries had extended beyond the perimeter of the continental shelf, and that during historic times their forebears were engaged in surplus as well as subsistence fishing, including whaling. In an historic overview, the Tribunal listed a long string of breaches by the Crown of the Article Two Treaty promise (in the English draft) that guaranteed to Māori kin groups the 'full, exclusive and undisturbed possession' of their fisheries, or their ancestral taonga (including fisheries by implication) in Te Tiriti.

Before 1840, for instance, some tribal leaders had charged harbour dues to visiting ships, but soon after the Treaty was signed, this was forbidden. In 1866, at the height of the Land Wars, the Oyster Fisheries Act forbade Māori to commercially harvest their oyster beds, although some kin groups had been sending thousands of kits of oysters to Auckland. Afterwards, their oyster beds were leased to non-Māori commercial interests. As Te Kawau, a leading Auckland rangatira protested, 'It was only the land I gave over to the pakeha, the sea I never gave, and therefore, the sea belongs to me.' Over the years, while some subsequent Acts of Parliament acknowledged Māori fishing rights, others ignored them, and in practice little was done to uphold them.[43] Although many tribes sought redress for the loss of their ancestral fisheries through the courts, none succeeded.[44] In 1963 when the Government removed licensing restrictions on fishing boats and encouraged investment in large commercial vessels, fisheries around the country were already depleted. By 1980, when it became clear that drastic action was needed to restore the fish stocks, Māori had been largely forced out of the fishing industry, and were finding it difficult to catch fish for their families.

While the Tribunal listed many historic breaches of the right of the Muriwhenua iwi to control their ancestral fisheries, however, they also considered that the Quota Management System (QMS) might not necessarily be in breach of the Treaty, since management arrangements based on the sovereignty of the Crown could change over time. The Tribunal urged the Crown to negotiate with the tribes, and find a mutually satisfactory arrangement. After a High Court ruling, this is more or less what happened. In a deal with Māori kin groups around the country, 10 per cent of the existing fishing quota was handed over to a Treaty of Waitangi Fisheries Commission to distribute, plus $10 million to create Aotearoa Fisheries; and in 1992 more quota and $150 million was given to the tribes to purchase half of Sealord, the country's biggest fishing company.[45] While these and other deals were used to settle Māori commercial fishing claims, however, they did not cover customary food gathering, which was recognised by establishing mātaitai and taiāpure, mechanisms for locally managing this kind of gathering by Māori kin groups, and by local Māori and non-Māori in partnership.

As the Muriwhenua Tribunal acknowledged, by quantifying and commoditising fish in ancestral waters, and by alienating the right to catch them to others, the QMS flew in the face of tribal relationships of kaitiakitanga, or guardianship, over ancestral stretches of the ocean. The so-called 'Sealord' deal also had the effect of corporatising Māori fishing, driving the management of fisheries towards a philosophy of 'maximising the return on assets' and often alienating local Māori communities from their control, an outcome that has caused disaffection in many kin groups. In 2005 in Northland, as Hone Sadler has noted, for example, Nga Puhi recreational fishers became concerned that stocks of kahawai, a favourite staple, were diminishing as a result of overfishing by commercial operators, including Aotearoa Fisheries and Sealord, which held quota owned by their own tribe. The Nga Puhi rūnanga (tribal council) joined the New Zealand Big Game Fishing Council in a legal challenge, asking that the commercial take of kahawai that had been set under the quota system be reduced and the recreational allocation increased, so that kahawai stocks could recover and ordinary Nga Puhi people could provide kahawai for their families and marae.[46]

A collision between ideas of kaitiakitanga and ideas of property in the ocean has also been at the heart of the recent clash between Māori and the Crown over the foreshore and seabed in New Zealand, another forerunner to the clash between Te Whanau-a-Apanui and the Crown. This saga began in the Marlborough Sounds, at the northern end of the South Island. Although the local tribes repeatedly applied to the local district council for licences to farm mussels in their ancestral rohe (territory), none were granted. Finally, in frustration, they applied to the Māori Land Court in

1997 to recognise their customary rights over the foreshore and seabed in the Sounds.[47]

In te ao Māori, the foreshore is understood as a fertile place. In this interstitial zone, where land meets sea and sky as the tides ebb and flow, new life is constantly emerging. At the time of the Treaty, kin groups moved from gardens and forests to wetlands, sandy beaches, rocky reefs and out to sea in seasonal migrations, harvesting at peak times of plenty. Particular groups held rights to particular resources at particular times of the year, creating complex, overlapping, shifting networks of rights that crossed the shoreline, binding people, land and sea together. According to English common law in 1840, on the other hand, land and sea were divided at the high-tide mark, and subject to different regimes of control. On land, the Crown held the right of *imperium*, or sovereignty, while *dominium*, or ownership, was generally held as private property; whereas, at sea, it was assumed that the Crown held both *imperium* and *dominium*, at least as far as 3 miles offshore, unless it had granted the right of ownership to other parties.

When land began to be surveyed, partitioned into blocks and sold in New Zealand, the government and European purchasers alike generally assumed that if they bought coastal land, they owned it to the high-tide mark, but that the foreshore or tidal zone and the seabed belonged to the Crown. From the beginning, however, Māori contested this assumption, which clashed with the Article Two Treaty promise about their control of ancestral fisheries. It was not until their rights to the foreshore and seabed were challenged in practice, however, that it became a matter for serious concern. In 1869, for instance, when the Crown tried to assert title to the Thames foreshore, where gold had been discovered, W. Taipiri petitioned the governor, saying:

> It . . . is a place from which we obtained flounders and cockles, and was a snipe preserve from the time of our ancestors even down to us. That land was considered valuable by our ancestors, it has been fought for, and men have been killed on account of those lands from which were obtained fish, cockles, and snipe. We still have the mana over those lands.[48]

Finally, the government negotiated with local Māori to purchase the Thames foreshore.

Over time, as Crown title to the foreshore and seabed was increasingly imposed by legislative fiat – the Harbours Act 1866, for example, which forbade the grant of any part of the foreshore without an Act of Parliament, Māori protests continued.[49] In 1885, for instance, Taiaho Ngatai said in a speech to the Minister of Native Affairs in Tauranga:

> Now, with regard to the land below high water mark immediately in front of where I live, I consider that that is part and parcel of my own land . . . part of my own garden. From time immemorial I have had this land, and had authority over all the food in the sea. Te Maere was a fishing-ground of mine. Onake, that is a place from which I have from time immemorial obtained pipis. Te Rona is another pipi-bed. My mana over these places has never been taken away . . . and no tribe is allowed to come here and fish without my consent being given. But now, in consequence of the word of the Europeans that all land below the high water mark belongs to the Queen, people have trampled upon our ancient Maori customs and are constantly coming here whenever they like to fish. I ask that our Maori custom shall not be set aside in this manner, and that our authority over these fishing-grounds may be upheld. . . . I am not making this complaint out of any selfish desire to keep all the fishing-grounds for myself; I am only striving to regain the authority which I inherited from my ancestors.[50]

From time to time, Māori appealed to the courts. In 1963, when the Court of Appeal ruled in a case over the Ninety Mile Beach that customary rights to the foreshore were extinguished when coastal lands were sold, the matter was assumed to be settled. The 1997 appeal by the Marlborough iwi to the Māori Land Court overturned that legal precedent. The judge in the Land Court held that the legislation cited by the attorney-general, including the Ninety Mile Beach case, had not in fact extinguished the customary rights of the Marlborough iwi, and that the Māori Land Court could consider their claim. The case was appealed, and then referred to the High Court, where the judge reversed that ruling, and then to the Court of Appeal, where the judges ruled unanimously that upon the signing of the Treaty, the Crown acquired only a radical right or 'imperium' over the sea with the acquisition of sovereignty (and now, as we have seen, the acquisition of sovereignty has also been challenged). Under the doctrine of continuity, in any case, according to the Court of Appeal, this was subject to any existing Māori customary property rights. Citing many local and international precedents, the judges ruled that unless these rights had been legally extinguished, they remained with Māori kin groups, and that this was also the case with the foreshore and seabed. Furthermore, the distinction in English common law between land above the high-water mark and land below it did not apply. As Judge Elias said:

> The common law as received in New Zealand was modified by recognised Maori customary property interests. If any such custom is shown to give interests in foreshore and seabed, there is no room for a contrary presumption derived from English common law. The common law of New Zealand is different.[51]

The judges referred the case back for the Māori Land Court to determine whether or not the Marlborough iwi had customary ownership of the foreshore and seabed in their ancestral territories. By this time, however, most New Zealanders took it for granted that, apart from riparian rights, the foreshore and seabed were owned by the Crown, and the decision caused a furore. Although some Māori leaders insisted that they only wished to exercise kaitiakitanga over the foreshore and seabed, and not treat them as private property, others were clearly interested in commercial possibilities, and a few made inflammatory statements.

Of all the sea-based ontological collisions discussed here, this is perhaps the most profound. Intimacy with the sea is, of course, not a Māori prerogative, although the cosmological underpinnings of the relationship may be different. Over the generations, many non-Māori New Zealanders have also formed close ties with particular beaches and stretches of coastline, echoing the ancestral Māori habit of going to coastal fishing camps in the summer by heading to seaside baches and camping grounds, and spending a great deal of time fishing, diving, surfing, surf life-saving and sailing in these places. Since the 1970s, moreover, the migration of Māori language, arts and writing into schools and the cultural mainstream have given wide currency to ideas such as kaitiakitanga and the stories of Papa and Tangaroa, Maui and the ancestral voyaging canoes, adding a new set of resonances to Kiwi relationships with the ocean.

For many non-Māori New Zealanders, then, the reaction to the Court of Appeal's decision in the foreshore and seabed case was visceral. Fearing that their recreational as well as commercial interests in these places might be lost to Māori, and that their relationship with particular beaches and harbours would be severed, many were outraged. There was also a wide streak of racist sentiment in the debate, fuelled by some politicians. Public anger was such that, in 2004, the government hastily passed legislation to ensure that the foreshore and seabed would be held in perpetuity by the Crown, with open access for all, subject to various regulatory restrictions.[52] In reaction, many Māori were also shocked by the tone of the debate. A judgment of the Court of Appeal had been overturned by legislative fiat, extinguishing any customary rights to ownership of the foreshore and seabed without apology or reparation, and vesting these in the Crown. When a hīkoi of thousands of protesters marched on Parliament, they were dismissed by the prime minister as 'wreckers and haters', a comment that hurt and horrified many of the elders who participated.

In the aftermath, however, as different iwi signed Treaty deeds of settlement with the Crown, anger on both sides gradually cooled.[53] When a new government formed a coalition with the Māori Party, which had been created in protest against the Foreshore and Seabed Act, new legislation gave Māori further customary (but not freehold) rights to these areas, while protecting public access and enjoyment. By the time that Te Whanau-a-Apanui's fishing boat confronted the *Orient Explorer*, then, they had many non-Māori supporters who shared their fears for the future of the ocean. In October 2011 when container ship the *Rena* ran aground on a reef in the western Bay of Plenty, it seemed that they had been prescient. A cargo including hazardous materials, fuel oil and diesel spilled into the sea, causing widespread environmental and economic damage.

In December 2013 there were more protests when the New Zealand government granted Statoil, Norway's state oil company, a licence to drill for oil in the Te Reinga basin, off Te Rerenga Wairua, the leaping-off place of wairua (spirits). Many Māori and other New Zealanders were infuriated by this action, given the tapu nature of this part of the sea, the fear that sonic testing would harm marine life including dolphins and whales, the threat of oil spills, and the role played by the fossil fuel industry in climate change. At a meeting in Northland attended by a Statoil executive, he was told that the company was not welcome in Northland, and that they had no support in the local community. As one of the elders exclaimed, 'this is the face of the monster with gold and silver teeth that was prophesised by our elders'.[54]

In 2014 a hīkoi against Statoil's drilling programme set off from Te Reinga (echoing the great Land March in 1975, during which thousands marched from Te Rerenga Wairua to Parliament to protest against the loss of Māori land), heading for Waitangi, arriving at the Treaty House on 6 February, the day that the Treaty had been signed in 1840. As the marchers posted on Facebook:

> Te Reinga is known historically and Nationally including Internationally as being a place of great importance and holds spiritual connection to Maori as Te Ara Wairua – A Spiritual Pathway which is Ancestral and Immemorial. . . . We object & oppose also on the grounds of concerns of detrimental affect and effect for and on all living species both below and above the sea.[55]

This was followed by a meeting in August 2014 attended by the Statoil vice-president, when a Māori veteran who had fought in World War II upended the tables at which the Statoil representatives were sitting; and by another hīkoi from Te Reinga to Auckland to an oil conference sponsored by Statoil. Recently, representatives of the Te Reinga protesters flew to Norway to ask the Saami Parliament, which has shares in Statoil, to tell the company to stop drilling in Māori ancestral waters, and to attend the Statoil AGM, to make known their opposition to Statoil's exploration of the Te Reinga basin. When this visit was reported on Māori TV, it was headlined 'Delegation takes on Norwegian *taniwha*'.

In a curious twist, however, in 2016 when the government announced in the United Nations their plan to create one of the world's largest marine sanctuaries around the Kermadec Islands, a haven for seabirds, whales, dolphins and fish covering 620,000 square kilometres of New Zealand's Exclusive Economic Zone, Te Ohu Kaimoana, the trust that acts as an advocate for Māori interests in fishing, filed a legal case against the plan in the High Court. Although the government had spoken with representatives of Ngati Kuri and Te Aupouri, the two far northern iwi with territorial interests in the Kermadecs, they had not consulted Te Ohu Kaimoana, who attracted heavyweight support from the leaders of other iwi in their decision to contest the government's move. Soon afterwards, the commercial fishing industry filed their own High Court challenge.

As in the case of the Nga Puhi contest over kahawai quota, concerns about commercial imperatives in Māori fishing (in this case advanced by Te Ohu Kaimoana and the leaders of other iwi, supported by the commercial fishing industry), and about a lack of consultation and precedents being set in relation to Māori fishing rights,[56] clashed head on with kaitiakitanga principles. Once again, modernist ideas of 'property' and profit have entangled in complex ways with mana and ancestral tikanga relating to the ocean.

Can different 'worlds' converge?

As one can see, in New Zealand, fundamentally different philosophies about human relations with the ocean have proved to be very resilient. At the same time, there have been significant transformations, both to Māori ideas and to modernist thinking. In the law, for example, at different times, the doctrine of continuity in relation to Māori rights has led to an insistence that when the Treaty of Waitangi was signed, English common law was transformed by the incorporation of Māori customary law, with its concepts and patterns of relations. One can see this in many New Zealand laws that cite tikanga (ancestral conventions), whether in general or in particular. As Judge Sian Elias put it succinctly: 'The common law of New Zealand is different.' At the same time, while particular tikanga may be cited in legislation, their content has often been transformed in the process. One can see this in the case of kaitiakitanga, for example, once exercised by non-human taniwha such as particular sharks and stingrays over particular ancestral stretches of the ocean. Today, a more anthropocentric version is common, with people regarding themselves as kaitiaki of these places.

On the other hand, the assumption that, with the signing of the Treaty, sovereignty was transferred to the British Crown has not been seriously disturbed, despite many challenges, since this provides a fundamental scaffolding for legal processes in New Zealand. In relation to the sea, this means that mechanisms such as mātaitai and taiāpure, where Māori kin groups either exercise or share limited rights over coastal subsistence fishing in conjunction with other community members, operate within strict limits, with ministers appointing tribal 'representatives' onto management groups and requiring that their arrangements do not clash with commercial fishing rights, for example. Simultaneously, however, the idea of the 'Crown' itself has also shifted, so that any pure opposition between Māori and the Crown is now difficult to sustain. For many years in New Zealand, Māori have been lawyers and judges, officials, members of Parliament and government ministers. In fact, it was a Māori Minister of the Crown, Matiu Rata, who helped to set up the Waitangi Tribunal and laid a major complaint on behalf of his Muriwhenua people in front of the Tribunal.

Again, the relation between iwi and the Crown is structural rather than strictly ethnic, and this is played out in fisheries management as well, with Māori as well as non-Māori managing fishing quota for iwi according to strictly commercial principles; while mātaitai and taiāpure, the management of customary fishing, is usually shared with non-Māori community members. At the same time, some non-Māori New Zealanders now speak of themselves as kaitiaki, or guardians, for rivers, beaches, endangered species or even vulnerable people. As Māori terms increasingly shift into Kiwi English, both European and Māori ways of thinking are being transformed. In New Zealand, it seems, the Treaty of Waitangi established a liminal zone in which experimentation 'across the pae' between Māori and non-Māori ancestral ways keeps creating new ideas and ways of doing things – in the law, in governance and in many areas of everyday life, from the arts to sport to public ritual.

This holds promise for the future, because in relation to the sea, experiments of this kind are urgently needed. While surfers, swimmers, divers and fishers still frequent our beaches and coasts, and sailors still cross the Pacific, their activities are increasingly at risk from water-borne pollution including gyres of plastic and other rubbish, the warming and acidification of the ocean, sedimentation, overharvesting of reefs, shellfish beds and fisheries, sea-level rise and the intense storms and current shifts driven by climate change, for example. Disciplinary modes of knowledge, characterised by partitions between the natural and social sciences, and the various disciplines (also born of the Order of Things), struggle to do justice to the cascading dynamics of complex oceanic systems in which people are also implicated, putting the future of many marine species and coastal human communities at risk.

The emerging science of complex networks, which is transforming the biological and social sciences, resonates closely with the relational systems of whakapapa, with their insistence on existential links between people and other forms of life. At present, collaborative efforts between Māori kin groups, marine scientists and local communities in many coastal areas around New Zealand are resulting in a growing (although far from universal) emphasis on protecting and enhancing the mauri ora (life force) of fishing grounds and harbours. After the sinking of the cargo ship *Rena* off the coast of Tauranga in 2011, for instance, when about 500 tonnes of heavy fuel oil, as well as floating containers and debris were released into the sea, killing birds and fish, infuriating iwi and many other local people, and harming the regional economy, a 'Long-term Environmental Recovery Plan' was developed with a goal to 'restore the mauri (life force) of the affected environment to its pre-Rena state'.[57] This emphasises the right of maritime ecosystems to exist in a state of ora.

In the Hauraki Gulf / Tikapa Moana, too, the Sea Change / Tai Timu Tai Pari (tides ebbing and flowing) project, a steering group of eight representatives of local iwi and eight representatives of local and central government, has been appointed to govern this prized waterway at the heart of Auckland City. The project aims to produce a spatial plan for managing the gulf, which is being degraded by overfishing, sedimentation and nutrient flows, to restore it to health. Although early indications are that gridded frameworks dominate the structure of the plan, Māori notions of kaitiakitanga and how to restore ora to seascapes are also influential.[58] Interestingly, Māori participants in such processes are speaking about the sea itself as an ancestor, Hinemoana, with her own rights to well-being. In New Zealand, at least, an idea of 'the rights of the sea', which helps to set ecological bottom lines to ensure its ongoing flourishing, and of people and oceanic life forms as kin, mutually dependent for their ongoing health and survival, might provide a counterpoint to extractive habits of mind that are damaging many maritime ecosystems, and putting human communities at risk. Such conceptions also have the virtue of being resonant with marine ecology, with its emphasis on symbiosis and complex living networks.

As for the wider Pacific, it is hard to see why the future of the world's greatest ocean should be dominated by ideas, conventions and strategies born out of continental Europe, especially when these are failing to safeguard its future. As 'Epeli Hau'ofa has insisted, for millennia before the first European ships ventured into its waters, this vast sea was explored and inhabited by Pacific islanders. Their ancestors were at home on the ocean, following the star paths and sea paths, discovering and settling new islands. Ancestral ideas about human relations with Te Moana-nui-a-Kiwa, in conjunction with contemporary science, may hold greater promise for its future than modernist extractive and management practices. It must be protected. With its whales, dolphins, birds and fish, and its tides, currents and vortices, the Pacific Ocean is our planet's beating heart.

CHAPTER TWELVE

Once Were Warriors
Tangata / People

U PON ITS RELEASE IN 1994, THE AWARD-WINNING FILM *ONCE WERE Warriors* (based on a novel by Alan Duff) shocked New Zealand and international audiences with its bleak, brutal portrayal of domestic relations in an urban Māori family. In the movie, the anti-hero 'Jake the Muss', although capable of tenderness, can't hold down a job or support his family. Still, he takes great pride in his reputation as a 'hard man', beating up those who challenge his authority, especially when he's drinking. Although Jake's wife Beth is a beautiful woman who tries to care for their children, she also drinks at times. One night when Jake invites his friends home for a riotous party, she gets drunk and defies him, refusing to cook for them. While the children listen upstairs, huddled together in a bedroom, Jake gives her a vicious beating. Contemptuous of his parents, their eldest son Nig decides to join a gang, while their younger son Boogie, who is in trouble with the police for a string of minor offences, has to face court proceedings without them. Their eldest daughter Grace, a gifted writer and a kind-hearted, gentle girl, supports Boogie in court. When he is sent away to an institution, a Māori social worker begins to mentor him, restoring his self-respect by teaching him the haka and other tikanga (ancestral customs).

On a trip to visit Boogie, who is now living in his mother's tribal area, the children catch sight of Beth's family marae. As she begins to reminisce about her childhood, Jake retorts that although she is descended from a rangatira family, he comes from 'a long line of slaves'. When they first fell in love, he tells their children, her whānau (extended family) decided that he was not good enough, and wouldn't allow him to marry her, so they ran away together to the city. Stung by the memory of past humiliations, Jake stops at a pub and gets drunk, and the visit to Boogie is abandoned. Afterwards, when he invites his mates back to the house for a boozy party, his 12-year-old daughter Grace is raped by one of Jake's best friends. When her father berates her for not treating this man with proper respect, Grace commits suicide, hanging herself from a tree in the back yard. Heartbroken, Beth decides to take her daughter back to her home marae to be buried. After the funeral, she finds Grace's journal and reads it, and discovers that her daughter had been raped. When Beth confronts his friend at the pub and gives Jake their daughter's journal to read, Jake beats this man to death. At the end of the movie, as police sirens begin to wail and Beth and her children drive away, heading back to her ancestral marae, Jake stands outside the pub raging. As a parting shot, Beth has told him that he is still a slave. Although her ancestors were warriors, they were not like him. They had mana (ancestral power) and wairua (spirit).

When *Once Were Warriors* was released, most viewers sympathised with Beth and her children. At the same time, many assumed that the violence shown in the film traces back in some way to ancestral Māori customs, and that *Once Were Warriors* accurately portrays life in many contemporary Māori families. In the aftermath of the movie, some scientists even went so far as to suggest that Māori might inherit a 'warrior gene', linked with a propensity to violence,[1] and that brutal treatment of Māori women and children dates back to ancestral times. This notion, however, is contradicted by a formidable array of historical evidence from the early contact period in New Zealand. As we will see, a stream of early European accounts of Māori life describe tender family relationships in which children enjoyed great freedom and domestic violence was rare. Likewise, early Māori sources describe male and female as complementary forces in the creation of the cosmos, in the landscape and in the human body. Violence against woman and children attacked the life force of their kin groups, and had to be requited. In order to investigate ancestral Māori ideas of the person and how these have changed, it is timely to return once again to the cosmological chants and narratives taught in the whare wānanga (houses of ancestral learning).

Ancestral ideas about men, women and children

As Te Rangikaheke explained in his account of the origins of the world, at the beginning, male sky and female earth were so closely entwined that they could not see each other. At once male and female, they were one ancestor:

> Friends, listen to me! *Kotahi anō te tūpuna Māori – ko Rangi raua ko Papa* (there is just one Maori ancestor, Rangi and Papa). According to the Maori people, Rangi and Papa were the take [roots, founding ancestors] of the past . . .
>
> There was no division between Rangi and Papa. They were clinging to each other. They could not perceive the infinite void. They could not perceive the infinite Night. Nor could they see each other.
>
> Now, time passed and Rangi and Papa began to stir. They still cleaved to one another in the darkness. They could not perceive the infinite void. They could not perceive the infinite Night. Nor could they see each other.
>
> Now, the time came that Rangi awoke, and that Papa awoke. They still cleaved to one another. They could not perceive the infinite void. They could not perceive the infinite Night. Nor could they see each other.[2]

During these long aeons of darkness, the different nights (pō) represent interminable hours of labour, as Papa gave birth to their children.[3] In this account, all of Rangi and Papa's offspring were male. In order to find their places and let light into the world, they force their parents apart, and fight with each other. At the same time, these contests are generative. Among the children of Rangi and Papa, Tane was the first to feel the need for a woman. He went around having sex with all kinds of creatures, but none of these unions yielded any offspring.

Finally, Tane seeks the help of his mother, Papatuanuku, who fashions the shape of a woman for him out of red earth at Kurawaka, an intensely tapu place where menstrual blood flows from her womb. Kura is the name for the red ochre used to mark people, places and objects in a state of tapu.[4] She tells Tane to breathe the hau, or wind of life, into the woman's nostrils, and he does so. As she stirs, he calls her Hineahuone – Hine of the heaped up earth – the seed bed of humanity (or sometimes Hinehauone – Hine of hau breathed into the earth). They sleep together and conceive a daughter called Hinetitama, the Dawn maiden. When Hinetitama grows up, Tane also sleeps with his daughter. One day, however, when she asks him, 'Well, my husband, who is my father?' Tane refuses to answer, telling her to ask the carved posts of their house instead. Realising that she has been deceived, and that her father is her lover, Hine flees aghast from the world of light into the underworld. When Tane begs her to return to him and their children, she cries out, 'You go back. I am sick with shame. I must stay here.' In Rarohenga, the underworld, she becomes Hinenuitepo, taking care of human beings after death – a mythic precedent for the tragic fate of Grace Heke in *Once Were Warriors*.

In this description of the world, women (in the forms of Papa and Hinenuitepo) are closely linked with te pō, the dark ancestral realm, and with the moon, stars and the tides; while men (Tane) are associated with the sky, the sun, and te ao mārama, the everyday world of light. Te pō is also linked with the womb (te whare tapu o te tangata – the sacred house of people); and many versions of the creation story tell of the evolution of the cosmos in the language of conception and childbirth. Women, then, are associated with both life and death. Likewise, sex is at once an act of creativity and betrayal. When the trickster hero Maui, determined to conquer death, wriggles into the vagina of Hinenuitepo as she lies sleeping, a watching fantail bursts out laughing. Waking up, she claps her legs together, crushing Maui between her thighs.[5] Hinenuitepo is the origin of death in the world, just as her mother Papatuanuku is the origin of life, caring for her children – the ū kai pō – the mother's night-feeding breast.

As in the case of Hinenuitepo, women's genitals cancelled the mana of men. After battle, warriors would crawl between the outstretched legs of a female tohunga to annul the tapu of death. On the door lintels of carved houses, the figure of a female ancestor was often carved, legs spread apart, so that those who entered the house became noa, free of tapu, or ancestral presence and power. We have already heard the story of Te Aokapurangi, a Te Arawa woman married to one of Hongi Hika's lieutenants. When her people were about to be attacked on Mokoia Island in Lake Rotorua, she asked Hongi to spare all those who passed between her legs. When he agreed, she ran ashore when their canoe grounded, climbed to the ridge-pole of her people's meeting house, and straddled the apex. All who passed through the door into this house were saved. Many of the creation stories also feature the mana of women. When the trickster ancestor Maui fishes up whenua (land) out of the depths of the ocean (Hinemoana or Sea Woman) – Te Ika-a-Maui (Maui's fish – the North Island of New Zealand), for instance

– he uses the sacred jawbone of his grandmother Murirangawhenua to perform this extraordinary feat.

Stories of the exploration and settlement of New Zealand also feature many high-born women. Hine-hakiri-rangi, for example, the sister of Pawa, commander of the *Horouta* canoe, carried the kūmara from Hawaiki ashore at Turanga, planting the prized tubers at Manawaru.[6] Kuiwai and Haungaroa, the sisters of Ngatoroirangi, the high priest navigator of the *Arawa* canoe, send volcanic fire from Hawaiki to revive their brother while he is freezing to death on top of Mt Tongariro.[7] Volcanic fire is a female power, kept in the body of Papatuanuku. Muriwai (or perhaps Wairaka) rescues the *Mataatua* canoe from being wrecked on the rocks off Whakatane, crying out as she picks up the paddle, 'Kia whakatāne au i ahau!' (Let me turn myself into a man!)[8] In these accounts, both male and female have their own mana (ancestral power), each within their own, complementary domains. There are as many female atua (powerful ancestors) as there are male. The world is ordered by whakapapa – vast, intricate patterns of relations based on complementary exchanges between male and female forces and beings, generating new forms of life. In this web of kinship, people trace their descent from all four grandparents, male and female, allowing them to activate different kin networks on different occasions; while others are bound into descent lines by adoption or alliance – actions often expressed in the language of weaving.

In her fine unpublished thesis 'Te Ira Wahine: The Female Principle', Waerete Norman describes a woven cosmos, with layers of skies and underworlds, comparing this with the fine mats (takapau wharanui) woven by women, laid one upon another – hence whakapapa, making layers:[9]

> Papa (earth) is the foundation source for the materials for the weaving of mats. For example, whiri means to plait, and a whiripapa is a flat plaited cord of three strands. The term for weave or weaving is raranga or whatu. The aho is the threadline, the genealogical thread that weaves shapes and flows in the design and patterning of the mat. The muka (flax fibre) are the delicate, fine fibres of aho (strands) that give colour, form, shape and meaning to the mat.
>
> The whakapapa itself stems at the very beginning from the tahuhu of the mat from which the ara (direction), the kaupapa (plan) of the weaving will flow and develop. This is evident in the initial weaving of the mat, which begins with maurua or hiki (interconnecting threads) and the integration of

the miro or aho (main threads) from one papa to another when sections of the mat are joined together.

In the warp and weft of each whariki takapau (fine mat) lie a cross section of landscapes, seascapes and skyscapes that reveal superimposed strata, foundation worlds.[10]

These intricate forms of order, in which genealogical lines and landscapes are intertwined, were also reflected in everyday life in ancestral times. Given their close relationship with Papatuanuku, the earth mother, it is not surprising that women did much of the garden work. The complementary relationship between men and women also governed the inheritance of root crops. As Samuel Marsden noted:

When the son of a chief attains the age of five or six years, his father gives him a basket of potatoes to plant. He either plants them himself or a slave cultivates them for him. The produce is his own sole property. From these potatoes he continues to plant ever after.

If the chief has a daughter, his wife supplies her in like manner with a basket of potatoes, and she continues to plant ever after from the same seed. The chief and his wife each grow their own potatoes and the produce is the private property of each.[11]

The balance between male and female was also expressed in the land itself, with the east coast of Northland being known as the tai tama wahine, the female coast, with its calm waters, for instance, while the west coast is the tai tama tāne (male coast), with its storm-tossed seas.[12] Like the land, according to Elsdon Best, the bodies of both men and women have male and female taha (sides), the right side being male, and the left side female.[13] The identity of a person is composed of different taha, allowing them to activate their different 'sides' (male or female, or different kin networks for example) at different times. This same pattern was reflected in chiefs' houses (and now in meeting houses), where the right side of the house by the window was known as tāne kaha (strong male), while the left side by the door was known as tamawahine (female child). Inside these houses, the tukutuku, or wall panels, woven by women alternate along the walls with the carved poupou, or ancestral figures, carved by men, while the painted kōwhaiwhai patterns on the rafters depict spiralling vines of ancestry and alliance, binding them together.[14]

This balance between men and women was reflected in even the most tapu of rituals. As we have noted, Hongi Hika told Samuel Marsden that during the ritual sacrifice of enemy leaders, parts of the body of a defeated male ariki (paramount chief) were ritually consumed by the victorious male ariki, while those of his senior wife were consumed by her female counterpart. Parts of the bodies of their children might also be consumed in these rituals. In this way, the victors acquired the mana of both male and female senior lineages on the losing side.[15] The same complementarity is echoed in Māori descent. While there is a preference to trace through senior male lines, a senior female descent line might trump a male line with less mana, although this varied across kin groups. A woman descended from senior lines on both sides might enjoy more mana than either her husband or father, and be regarded as intensely tapu. Such a woman was keenly sought after in marriage, for the mana she passed on to her children; and if she also married a high-born man, the mana of their children might exceed their parents'. Again, there are resonances with the kinship politics among the ruling families in early nineteenth-century Europe.

During his early visits to Northland, the missionary Samuel Marsden and his colleagues met a number of powerful female leaders, including Waitohirangi, the ariki Kaingaroa's mother, a tapu woman who had her own sacred seat at the heart of their pā at Lake Omapere, in front of a carved pātaka, or storehouse, raised 4 feet off the ground, that held her sacred food.[16] He also met Te Pahi's elderly wife; and Rahu, Ruatara's senior wife, an accomplished warrior, canoe paddler and weaver.[17] According to J.L. Nicholas, Rahu was 'considered no less a personage than a queen by all the people within [Ruatara's] territory'.[18] Indeed, when the first missionary wives landed at Hohi and were introduced to Rahu at Rangihoua pā, they curtsied to her as though they were meeting the British Queen.[19] Marsden also frequently commented upon the affectionate, tranquil relationships he observed in Māori families, between men and women, and parents and children. He remarked: 'I saw no quarrelling while I was there. They are kind to their women and children. I never observed either with a mark of violence upon them, nor did I ever see a woman struck.'[20] He added: 'The New Zealanders do not correct their children lest they should abate their courage or subdue their violent passions. Hence the children are in no subjection to their parents.'[21]

Children were the source of ongoing life for a kin group, and so it was important to ensure that their hau ora, or life force, was not diminished.

It was thought that the wairua of the child was implanted when the eyes of the foetus were formed, and that the unborn baby received their nourishment through the fontanelle – the most tapu part of the head. The sex of the unborn child was often revealed in dreams, with huia feathers indicating a female child, and kōtuku feathers a male child.[22] Near the end of her pregnancy, a chiefly woman would retire to a whare kōhanga (nest house), accompanied by her female relatives; and the birth of the child was surrounded by tapu restrictions, which increased with the mana of the parents. The goddess Hineteiwaiwa presided over both childbirth and weaving, and according to Elsdon Best the first tiki, or neck ornament, which represented a human foetus, was made and given to Hineteiwaiwa by her father.[23] For women who were not rangatira, childbirth was often unattended, and they kneeled on a mat and held onto a pole as they gave birth.

After contact with European settlers, Māori regarded the agonised contortions of the settler women when giving birth with a mixture of scorn and amusement. If the birth was difficult, this was a sign that the child would have a troublesome disposition; or that it was not the husband's baby, and could not emerge until its true whakapapa was recited. When the child was born and sneezed, a relative would exclaim 'Tihei, mauri ora!' – 'I sneeze, the source of life!' Although infanticide was sometimes practised – where there was a severe shortage of food; or if the mother already had many children, or wanted to avenge herself on her husband for infidelity, it happened at the moment of birth, before the first breath of life was taken, by pressing on the fontanelle or blocking the nose to prevent the hau ora from flowing into the child. Generally, babies were a welcome sign of the ongoing fertility of the kin group, and greeted with ceremony and feasting. Their bodies were massaged and their noses flattened; and the placenta and navel cord (iho) were taken away and buried in a sacred place, establishing their relationship with their ancestral land. Chiefly children were dedicated to their ancestors in a complex series of rituals.

These ancestors thus had an interest in their descendants' well-being; and if a child was harmed, whether deliberately or accidentally, they attacked the hau of the offender. The extended family might also take the child away from an offending parent. If a chiefly child was harmed, other members of the hapū would intervene, punishing the offender with a taua muru, or plundering party, singing angry songs to humiliate them and taking their property.

As a result of these sanctions, parents rarely punished their children. As Henry Williams remarked in 1825, a father could not compel his children to return things they had taken, 'nor do I believe that [he] can, by the customs of the land inflict any chastisement over them – so also with his wife'.[24]

Many European observers described the tender care with which men as well as women treated their offspring. J.L. Nicholas, for instance, remarked in 1814:

> The tenderest parental affection is remarkable among all classes, high and low, in this country. The chiefs carry their children upon their backs, taking them from their mothers at an early age, that they may not be an incumbrance to them in their laborious employments. It must be allowed that the men make excellent nurses, and have a peculiar art in the management of their infant offspring.[25]

As Joel Polack, a trader, wrote in the 1830s:

> The New Zealand father is devotedly fond of his children, they are his pride, his boast, and peculiar delight; he generally bears the burden of carrying them continually within his mat. . . .
>
> The children are seldom or never punished; which, consequently, causes them to commit so many annoying tricks, that continually renders them deserving of a sound, wholesome castigation.
>
> The father performs the duty of a nurse; and any foul action the embryo warrior may be guilty of, causes rather a smile than a tear from the devoted parent.[26]

> The obstinacy of the children exceeds belief; the son of a chief is never chastised by his parent. The boys are brought up entirely by the men; and it is not uncommon to see young children of tender years, sitting next to their parents in the war councils, apparently listening with the greatest attention to the war of words uttered by the chiefs. . . .
>
> They also ask questions in the most numerously attended assemblies of chiefs, who answer them with an air of respect, as if they were of a corresponding age to themselves. I do not remember a request of an infant being treated with neglect, or a demand from one of them being slighted.[27]

Augustus Earle, a visiting artist who travelled the North during the early 1840s, added:

> Both parents are almost idolatrously fond of their children; and the father frequently spends a considerable portion of his time in nursing his infant, who nestles in his blanket, and is lulled to rest by some native song. . . .
> The children are cheerful and lively little creatures, full of vivacity and intelligence. They pass their early years almost without restraint, amusing themselves with the various games of the country . . .[28]

From these and many other early European accounts,[29] it is clear that Māori children enjoyed considerable freedom, and that violence against both children and women was rare. Striking a child or a woman was regarded as a patu wairua, a blow to the spirit, that harmed not only the individual but their kin network, diminishing its life force. Because of this, such an offence had to be balanced (whakarite) and utu taken to restore the mana of the kin group, usually an attack or a muru (ritual plundering) raid on the offender. This applied even if the woman or child was hurt by accident, particularly if they were of senior descent.

Some high-ranking women had a series of love affairs, leaving one man after another. If a low-ranking woman committed adultery, attacking the mana of her husband, she and her lover might be killed or violently punished; but otherwise, assaults or insults to a wife were avenged by her kinsfolk – and the same applied to their children. If a husband mortally offended his wife, she might enter a state known as whakamomori (intense humiliation) and hang herself or kill one of their children, inviting utu against her husband by her family.[30] The severity of such responses meant that domestic harmony was highly valued, and women and children were rarely harmed by their husbands or parents. This did not apply, however, in times of war, or to taurekareka (war captives) within kin groups and households. The mana of their descent lines had been destroyed, and there are a number of accounts of war captives being abused, killed and sometimes eaten. Marsden was clearly not thinking about 'slaves' when he wrote about domestic relations in New Zealand.

Indeed, in many (perhaps most) kin groups, seniority of descent mattered more than gender. In whakapapa and oral histories, it can be difficult to know whether a person is male or female, because many ancestral names are not gender specific. This is also true of the Māori language, in which pronouns and possessives are gender neutral. For this reason, it may be very misleading to rely on reading Māori documents in translation, where a translator often uses 'him' or 'his' without noticing that the original Māori word might equally apply to a woman.

At huihuinga, or ceremonial gatherings, male and female complementarity was also expressed. The first voice raised during the ceremony was (and is) almost always that of an older woman, or kuia, who chanted a karanga, welcoming the visitors and summoning up ancestors to join their descendants. As the visiting kuia called in reply, occasionally an elder, or kaumātua, in their party might chant a waerea, clearing away hostile ancestral forces so that they can safely enter the marae. The speeches that followed were usually delivered by male orators, although in some tribal areas – for instance, the East Coast and Northland – chiefly women spoke on occasion.[31] In 1814, for example, during a heated dispute over an adulterous liaison in the Bay of Islands, Nicholas noted that the closing speeches were given by the three wives of Pomare, the offending rangatira.[32] These practices have carried on in these regions into contemporary times, although increasingly, women are expected to remain silent and sit behind their menfolk, who occupy the paepae (speakers' benches).

European ideas about men, women and children

In Māori families, then, the roles of men, women and children were complementary and interdependent with wider kin networks. When the first European settlers began to arrive in New Zealand, on the other hand, the ideal of an autonomous, self-contained family led by a strong father was taking shape in Europe – the idea that 'a man's home is his castle'. In part, this was based on religious doctrine. When William Williams and his colleagues began to translate the Bible into Māori, for instance, they began with Genesis. According to the Genesis account, God took a rib from Adam and 'made he a woman, and brought her unto the man'.[33] In the story of the Garden of Eden, when Eve was tempted by the serpent, she took apples from a forbidden tree and gave one to Adam. They ate, and saw that they were naked. For this sin God expelled them from Paradise, saying to Eve, 'I will greatly multiply thy sorrow and thy conception; in sorrow thou shalt bring forth children; and thy desire shall be to thy husband, and he shall rule over thee.'[34] When these texts were translated into Māori, God's own gender was not specified, and in speaking of 'man', the missionary translators used Adam's name.

From the outset, the Bible stories began to influence Māori thinking. In 1809, for instance, Ruatara, a young man who had sailed to England, told Samuel Marsden that the trickster hero Maui had made the first woman from a rib from his own body,[35] a detail almost certainly borrowed from the story of Genesis, which Marsden had just told him. Although Paul's Epistles were translated into Māori later than Genesis, these included instructions to the Ephesian women that included: 'Submit yourselves unto your own husbands, as unto the Lord. For the husband is the head of the wife, even as Christ is the head of the Church.' To Timothy, Paul wrote:

> Let the woman learn in silence with all subjection. But I suffer not a woman to teach, nor to usurp authority over the man, but to be in silence. For Adam was first formed, then Eve. And Adam was not deceived, but the woman being deceived was in the transgression.[36]

In New Zealand, the missionary families were expected to model Christian virtues, and to urge Māori to follow their example. Women should not preach or hold lay offices, but should submit themselves to their husbands. Adultery and fornication were forbidden. Children should honour their mothers and fathers, and as missionary children grew up, they should marry other Europeans. Part of the scandal of Thomas Kendall's marriage was that while Jane Kendall was the first to commit adultery, with their manservant Richard Stockwell, Thomas Kendall did even worse when he had an affair with a chiefly Māori woman.

In Britain at that time, the common law doctrine of *coverture* decreed that because Eve was made from Adam's rib, married women were literally part of their husbands; and that by seducing Adam, Eve had ensured the ongoing subjection of women. According to an early account of this doctrine:

> Man and wife are one person, but understand in what manner. A woman as soon as she is married is called *covert*, that is *veiled*, clouded and over-shadowed. . . . [T]o a married woman, her new self is her superior, her companion, her master. Eve, because she had helped to seduce her husband, had inflicted upon her special bane. . . . [Women] make no laws, they consent to none, they abrogate none. All of them are understood either married or

to be married and their desires are their husbands. The Common Lawe here shaketh hand with divinitye.[37]

Under this common law doctrine, as Sir William Blackstone explained in his *Commentaries on the Laws of England* (1765–1769), 'the husband and wife are one person in law; that is, the very being or legal existence of the woman is suspended during her marriage, or at least is incorporated or consolidated into that of her husband, under whose wing, protection and cover, she performs everything'.[38] Although the freedom of individual women varied widely according to social class, wealth and force of character, they were formally subordinate to men. Not surprisingly, it was also in this period that Mary Wollstonecraft wrote *A Vindication of the Rights of Women* (1792), arguing for greater freedom for women and the first steps towards female emancipation, although it was not until 1918 that women got the vote in Britain.

As the anthropologist Marilyn Strathern has argued, during the early modern period in the United Kingdom, men acquired an 'identity' as property-owning, rights-bearing individuals, linked with each other through relations that were external to themselves.[39] In this kind of 'possessive individualism',[40] as people were set apart from each other, and from the natural world, the identity of a married man as a separate entity came to include his wife and children. As Blackstone pointed out, under the common law, they had no independent legal existence. Under the law of equity, while women had greater rights including rights to their own property, these had to be awarded to them by men (usually their fathers), and were limited in practice to wealthy upper-class women and their families.[41] For this reason, most men controlled their wives' property and earnings. At least in theory, a woman could not dispose of these resources without her husband's consent. She could not sue or be sued, because if she was libelled, her husband was the injured party, and had to act on her behalf. Likewise, she could not sign contracts; and her husband was liable for her debts and any legal breaches. Their children were also the property of her husband, and so was her body – he could imprison his wife to secure his conjugal rights, for instance, and 'chastise' her short of death or serious injury. It was not until 1891 that a man was denied the right to imprison his wife, and not until 1991 that he was legally forbidden to rape her. If they divorced, he took the children, since they were his property.[42]

A group of children at Karioi School holding their drawings towards the camera.

In Britain at this time, too, many parents – although not all – held fast to a philosophy of 'spare the rod and spoil the child'. While they might love their offspring, it was widely supposed that children were inherently sinful, and in need of guidance. They had to be taught correct behaviour, and corporal punishment was used as a form of 'chastisement'. Working-class children were often sent to labour under very harsh conditions – up chimneys, down mines, on farms and in factories – while children under 10 could be imprisoned, transported or hanged for minor offences.[43] When compulsory education was introduced in Britain, this disciplinary power was extended to teachers.[44] Children sat in gridded rows in classrooms under the eye of their teacher, and were drilled by rote. If they stepped out of line, they were punished.[45] As one might expect, given these habits of mind, many early European visitors and settlers saw the indulgent treatment of children by Māori parents as foolishly lenient, making them unruly and undisciplined – despite the fact that they also found these children to be charming and polite.

At the same time, it is clear that rigid disciplinary approaches were not the only model for rearing children in Europe during this period, although they were dominant.[46] Romantic thinkers, including Jean-Jacques Rousseau, William Blake, William Wordsworth and others, saw children as uncorrupted and pure, innocent and close to nature.[47] In order to flourish, they needed protection and freedom. This idea of childhood was in fact quite close to ancestral Māori practices. As recent accounts have noted, however, Romantic ideas about childhood were most common among the aristocracy and upper middle classes in Europe. In his 'Histories of Childhood', for instance, John Clarke remarks, 'For the great mass of the population of Western European countries such as Britain and France, children's lives were characterized by poverty, hard labour and exploitation.'[48] Since most early European settlers came from working-class backgrounds, it was their ideas about childhood and the treatment of women that became dominant in New Zealand. In order to advance to civilisation, it was thought, Māori must adopt European ways of being. If they were recalcitrant, they should be punished and 'brought into line'.

Transformations in relations between men, women and children

Transformations in the roles of Māori men, women and children began very early after the arrival of Europeans. According to the old idea of the Great Chain of Being, Europeans were superior to Māori, and men were above both women and children. Given this kind of thinking, many Europeans regarded Māori as a lesser form of life, Māori women and children in particular. The early missionaries reported many incidents in which women were raped, abused and kidnapped by visiting sailors, their children harmed and their household goods stolen. Venereal diseases were introduced early to many Māori communities. Family life was transformed as some men began to barter female war captives, and even their wives and daughters for European goods, especially muskets.[49] One common consequence of contracting a venereal infection was infertility, a state known as whare ngaro (literally 'lost house'), in which a woman was no longer able to act as a sheltering 'house' for children, the source of ongoing life for her kin group.

After the introduction of potatoes, which cropped several times a year, and a growing barter of potatoes and flax with the crews of visiting ships, women's work on the land became increasingly arduous, and travelling taua began to capture women for this purpose. These female captives were sometimes killed as sacrifices, or humiliated and abused, and made to carry out heavy labour that left them weak, exhausted and infertile. If they were of high rank, they might be taken as junior wives. In addition, the introduction of muskets allowed those who acquired them early (like Hongi Hika and other northern rangatira) to attack other kin groups with relative impunity.

As taua roamed around the country, increasing numbers of women and children were killed or captured, radically disrupting domestic life in many kin groups across the country.[50]

When the missionaries arrived, they argued vehemently against the escalation of prostitution, slavery, cannibalism and fighting in New Zealand. At the same time, they were frequently puzzled about how to treat Māori women and children. This was the case with Thomas Kendall, the first schoolteacher in New Zealand. Because the Church Missionary Society sent inadequate supplies for his school, Kendall had to get his pupils to gather food, and while the boys felled trees and made fences, the girls wove cloaks as garments or as gifts for Kendall to send to the CMS in England. When they got bored with these activities, the young people went off to play with kites or tops, or to sing and dance, or left the school altogether.[51] Even in the classroom, it was almost impossible to control them. As Kendall lamented:

> My wild little pupils were all noise and play during the first four months.
> We could scarcely hear them read for their incessant shouting, singing and
> dancing. The first month they attempted to repeat their lessons in the school-
> house very well, but we soon had to follow them to a short distance in the
> bushes. I had no command over them, having at that time neither provisions
> nor rewards to give them.[52]

Kendall was also troubled by the relations between his male and female students. Māori children often went naked, and from about 12 years old it was common for young people to be sexually active. Until they were married or a girl had been set aside as a puhi (a high-born virgin, destined for an aristocratic marriage), this was not regarded with disfavour. In his school, he was unable to separate his male and female pupils, or to stop some of the girls from going to the ships. Here, one can detect a clash between ancestral Māori styles of instruction, in which boys and girls learned by working alongside adults and had great freedom, and early nineteenth-century schooling in Britain.

When Māori men and women joined missionary households, this was also challenging for both parties. Young rangatira women (such as Te Rakau's daughter Tungaroa) were expected to act as servants, which they found demeaning. Before marriage, Māori boys and girls were free to have affairs. This could threaten both marital fidelity in the missionary households, and family relationships. The missionaries believed that their children should marry other Europeans, and it was a cause of great trouble if they formed relationships with Māori partners. At the same time, some missionaries (Thomas Kendall, for example) had affairs with Māori women, scandalising the Church Missionary Society in London, and their peers.

The missionary wives worked hard to domesticate the 'girls' in their households, giving them European clothing to wear, encouraging them to adopt European standards of cleanliness and teaching them cooking, dress-making and housekeeping.[53] As one can see from Marianne Williams's letters and diaries, while her 'girls' enjoyed mastering European skills, they quickly became bored with staying indoors all the time and repeatedly performing the same tasks. Frequently, they left the household without warning, for reasons that their European hosts found inexplicable. Over time, however, some of these women began to conform to their 'Mata's' (Mother's) expectations. As Marianne Williams wrote five years after arriving in the Bay of Islands:

> My girls still take pets and run away for nothing. But they do not resist authority as much as they used to do. They do not attempt to bathe without leave . . . They do not now attempt to run outside of the fence when an English boat is on shore. They are tractable at school, and have yielded to us to determine when they shall sit and when stand, and whether they shall write large hand or small. They will consent to wear their gowns over their shifts without sulking about it, and though I have lost two of my best, I have two more who can . . . sew neatly, iron and fold all the week's linen, teach the others to wash when they like without any trouble.[54]

Likewise, as Jane Williams observed about the school that she and Marianne had established at Paihia for Māori girls:

> Twelve months ago the tumult and disorder of assembling for school was quite deafening and the contention about slates, pencils and seats very trying. But now order, submission and obedience are beginning to gain ground, and it is no trifling proof that when we enter the chapel, where we now keep school, we generally find each girl in her proper place, the slates and pen-cils are received quietly, and we are able to keep those unruly members, the tongues, in some subjection.[55]

Mananui Te Heuheu and Iwikau
Te Heuheu (seated) with the
palisades of their pā (Te Rapa)
at Taupo behind them, by
George French Angas, 1847.

When European men joined Māori families, they also brought with them expectations about marital behaviour and the ownership of property that could cause major difficulties. In order to attract European men with valuable skills into their communities, rangatira might match them with high-born women, with significant mana in their own right. Some European men tried to claim their wife's land, or expected them and their children to be docile and obedient, and not participate in public affairs. While some of these women conformed to their husbands' expectations, others carried on with their independent lives.

In the public sphere, the missionaries and early European officials also sought to impose their own standards of behaviour on Māori women and children. We know that the British Resident James Busby, for instance, took it upon himself to decide which rangatira would be permitted to speak at public gatherings where representatives of the British Crown were present, while excluding others. It is telling, then, that as far as we know, during the debates over the Treaty of Waitangi, no women or children participated in the discussions.

Nevertheless, at least 13 women signed Te Tiriti. As Henry Williams remarked, since this document forged an alliance with Queen Victoria, herself a woman, 'the ladies have expressed some disapprobation in not having a more prominent role in the Treaty with Her Majesty'.[56] While iwi descended from the *Arawa* canoe enforced restrictions upon women (including the right to speak in formal gatherings) that were more stringent than elsewhere in New Zealand, even here, many powerful women feature in tribal histories. It is striking that rangatira from these kin groups refused to sign Te Tiriti, and ally themselves with the queen. As Mananui Te Heuheu of Tuwharetoa declared, 'I will never consent to the mana of a woman resting upon these islands.'[57]

Te Tiriti was, however, signed in many other parts of the country where senior women played key leadership roles.[58] At Waitangi, for instance, three women signed the parchment – Takurua, Te Marama and Ana Hamu, the widow of the original patron of Williams's Paihia mission station. At Kaitaia, the female signatories included Marama and Ereonora, the high-born wife of Nopera Panakareao, the rangatira who famously declared that while the shadow of the land passed to Queen Victoria in Te Tiriti, the substance remained with the rangatira. As Hone Sadler remarks: 'In the world of Ngapuhi, men and women are of equal status.'[59] He and Waerete Norman have documented the lives of many wāhine rangatira (chiefly women) from Northland, including Hine-a-maru, Kahutianui, Whatuakaimarie, Waimirirangi and Muriwhenua. During the early contact period we can add Ruatara's senior wife Rahu, Hongi Hika's mother Tuhikura, his sister Waitapu, his senior wife Turikatuku and their daughter Rongo (another noted warrior who married Hone Heke and acted as his scribe and advisor),[60] along with many others. There is no doubt that at the time of the Treaty, there were many powerful female leaders in Northland.[61]

Further south, at Waikato Heads, Hana Riutoto signed a copy of the Treaty. The copy of Te Tiriti taken south by Henry Williams was signed by a number of female rangatira – at Kapiti, by Te Kehu and Rangi Topeora of Ngati Toa, the formidable sister of the great warrior Te Rangihaeata, a famous composer and lover who took the name 'Kuini Wikitoria' when she was baptised; at Port Nicholson, by Kahe Te Rau-o-te-rangi, famous for a heroic swim from Kapiti Island to the mainland; at Rangitoto (D'Urville Island), by Pari; and at Wanganui, by Te Rere-o-Maki. In this part of the country, wāhine rangatira often played important roles as diplomats – Te Pikenga, the wife of Te Rangihaeata, for example, often negotiated between Ngati Toa and her own Ngati Apa people; as did Waitohi, the sister of Te Rauparaha, the famous fighting chief.[62] At Cloudy Bay, however, when Major Thomas Bunbury refused to allow a Ngati Toa female rangatira to sign the Treaty, her husband also refused to sign the parchment.[63]

Surprisingly, the copy of Te Tiriti taken to the East Coast by William Williams was not signed by any female rangatira, although the Tai Rawhiti is famous for its powerful women leaders. These included Hinematioro at Uawa, who met Captain Cook and Tupaia, and in Marsden's time was described as a 'queen'. In the Tai Rawhiti, many kin groups and carved meeting houses are named after women, and in his Master's thesis for the University of Sydney, Apirana Mahuika documented the lives and careers of many great female leaders from this region, arguing that 'remove the female genealogies, and our genealogies will be made common [i.e. noa – common, profane]'.[64] To the south of the East Coast region, Turanga or Gisborne was known as Tūranga-tangata-rite, Turanga where all people are equal, a reference to the even-handed relations between men and women in that district. Nevertheless, no local women signed the Treaty there either. Later, however, female leaders like Riparata Kahutia and Keita Waere would play a prominent role in Land Court cases and politics in Turanga.

It appears, then, that the number of female rangatira who signed various copies of Te Tiriti depended largely on the views of the European men who controlled the signings. It is fascinating that Henry Williams, who by 1840 had spent 27 years in New Zealand, allowed more women to sign this document than any of the other European officials or missionaries involved in these transactions, including his brother William. Perhaps this was in part because of Henry's marriage to Marianne, herself a strong and eloquent woman, as well as the length and depth of his engagement with Māori people. It is clear that, by 1840, the freedoms of Māori women and children had already been curtailed. Indeed, the ceremonies of signing the Treaty around the country made a graphic statement that, in the eyes of the British authorities, women and children were subservient to men. While the text of Te Tiriti was gender neutral, the signing ceremonies were not.

The third article in the English draft of the Treaty of Waitangi, which gave Māori 'all the Rights and Privileges of British Subjects', had the effect of paving the way for the introduction of British common law to New Zealand; and as we have seen, the common law radically undermined the status of

Māori women and children. Under the third ture, or law, in Te Tiriti, on the other hand, in which the queen gave (tuku) to the Māori people (ngā tāngata Māori) customary practices exactly equal (ngā tikanga katoa rite tahi) to those of her people of England, Māori women might have expected their customary rights, and those of their children, to be protected. As far as we know, however, only Māori women protested their exclusion from the Treaty signings.

As British legal frameworks were progressively established in New Zealand, the opportunities for setting aside women, and marginalising female leaders, rapidly increased; and Māori men sometimes participated in this process. This has not been studied in depth and detail, but examples include some early land sales, where women's land rights were ignored or marginalised. There must also have been significant resistance to this subordination, however. When the Native Land Court was established in the 1860s, for instance, in the wake of the Land Wars, Māori women retained their land rights, although some European husbands tried to claim them; and leading women fought for their land, and often gave evidence in the court on land matters. In 1864, for instance, the Tainui female rangatira Timata, wearing a scarlet cloak, stood up at an auction to protest the sale of her ancestral lands at Ngaruawahia, supported by her European husband:

> Her voice and manner were striking and vehement, and the assembly listened attentively to the close of her speech, which few seemed to understand.
> Mr. W. Prior, her husband, then followed, and gave a translation of her protest in English [as follows]:
>
>   'I hereby protest against the sale of certain lands, known as Ngaruawahia. I claim the land for myself, my son, my daughters and other relatives. It is well known to thousands, that I have ever been a peaceable subject of the Queen; and I therefore claim protection as a British subject, my rights being guaranteed to me by the Treaty of Waitangi.
>
>   I protest against any of my lands being sold or disposed of in any way without my consent. And, if my protest is not attended to, and my rights respected, I shall appeal to the Queen, who is my great Chief.'[65]

In 1873, however, in the Native Land Act, husbands were made a legal party to all deeds executed by married Māori women, a provision that remained in place until 1881.[66] This caused great offence, and in 1876 Samuel Williams wrote to Sir Donald McLean to protest the injustice of this enactment:

We all of us know that according to Native usage and custom a Native woman can deal with her land without reference to her husband and Native women who have had their lands brought under these acts have in very many instances dealt with them without their husbands signing the deed they not considering that their husband had any voice in the matter and the husbands considering that they had no right to interfere.

These married women are now being told that according to English law they cannot deal with their own lands without their husbands being party to the deed. In regard moreover to previous transactions, vigorous efforts are now being made by certain individuals to induce them to repudiate contracts which they have entered into in that way and to make fresh arrangements with other persons.[67]

In the Native Lands Amendment Act 1882, this provision was changed, requiring reference to native custom in such matters, but now the Kotahitanga movement sought to bring all remaining Māori land under its control. Māori women, who had no formal representation in the Kotahitanga, feared their rights would be further eroded under this arrangement.[68] In May 1893 Meri Te Tai Mangakahia, a high-born woman from Hokianga and the wife of the Māori Parliament Premier, made an impassioned speech to the Māori Parliament:

I will explain the reason that I really want Maori women to have the vote and for women Members to stand in the Maori Parliament:

1. There are many women in New Zealand whose husbands have died and who own land
2. There are many women in New Zealand whose parents have died and who have no brothers, and who own land
3. There are many intelligent women in New Zealand who marry men who do not know how to run their land
4. There are many women whose parents have grown old, and who are intelligent women with land of their own
5. There are many male chiefs in this island who have appealed to the Queen over the problems affecting them, and we have never received any advantage from their appeals. For this reason I ask this House that women members be appointed. For perhaps the Queen will consent to the appeal of her Maori women advisers, since she is also a woman.[69]

The motion did not pass, although in September of that year women won the vote in New Zealand. When it was asked whether Māori women should be included, the House of Representatives answered with a roar of approval (although some Māori MPs opposed the measure). In this way, Māori women were among the group of New Zealand women who were first in the world to win the right to vote in general elections. They were finally able to vote in the Māori Parliament four years later, in 1897.[70]

All of these controversies were part of an ongoing transformation in the status of Māori women, and in relations between Māori people and the land. Once understood as inextricably tied together by complex, dynamic networks of whakapapa that gave them rights to use different resources at different times of the year, the Native Land Court quickly began to sort Māori into bounded groups of property-owning, rights-bearing individuals. In this way, they were separated from each other, as well as from their ancestral land.[71] It is a testament to the power of Māori women that, even under this system, they largely retained their rights to ancestral lands, at a time when married European women had no property rights of their own. In many regions, furthermore, Māori women led their kin groups. This disparity between Māori and European women must have added impetus to the emancipation of women in New Zealand, who became the first in the world to win the vote.[72]

In a number of tribal areas where senior women had long enjoyed the right to speak on the marae, they strongly resisted efforts to forbid them to do so. Eruera Stirling describes a dramatic confrontation in 1917 at a tangi in Rotorua between his mother Mihi Kotukutuku, the high-born leader of Te Whanau-a-Apanui in the Bay of Plenty, who often spoke for her people, and Mita Taupopoki, the aristocratic old chief of Te Arawa, where women were not permitted to speak on the marae:

> When they arrived at the marae a speaker from Te Arawa stood to welcome them, and then the elders of Te Whanau-a-Apanui didn't know what to do!
>
> My mother was the most senior one amongst them, and it was really for her to speak. Koopu of Maraenui and the other chiefs looked at each other, and the next thing my mother stood up on the marae in front of Tama-te-kapua meeting-house.
>
> As soon as she stood, the old chief of Te Arawa, Mita Taupopoki, called out, 'E tau! E tau, e tau, *e tau!* Sit down, sit down! Get your feet off my marae!

Meri Te Tai Mangakahia,
in the 1880s, by F.W. Mason
photographers, Napier.

It is not right for my marae, my tribal etiquette to be trampled by a woman!
E tau ki raro! Sit down!

It was not customary for women to speak on the marae in Te Arawa. Well,
my mother stood there and waited for Mita Taupopoki to finish, and when he
had stopped speaking she said,

'E Mita! You cannot talk to me! I am standing on *my* marae, in front
of *my* ancestor Tama-te-kapua – I am a descendant of his eldest son
Tuhoromatakaka, and I am a descendant of Apanui! It is not right for you
to speak to me – *you* sit down! You come from the junior line, from Tama-
te-kapua's younger son Kahumatamomoe – you, and all your people of
Te Arawa! And I think I heard you saying something about women – listen,
child, how do you think you were born into this world?'

My mother turned round and bent over, and she threw up her skirts and
said, 'Anei! Here is the place you came from, here between my thighs! Your

grey hairs come from a woman's belly, out into the world – so don't you speak to me!'

When my mother finished her whaikorero [oration] all the speeches were shut off. Wiremu Kingi the chief of Ngai Tai stood on the marae and said, 'Well, Te Arawa, this woman speaks according to her kawa, on her ancestral marae – who amongst us can answer her? Who?'

No one said a word.[73]

With this stunning gesture, Mihi Kotukutuku wiped out Mita Taupopoki's insult and silenced the marae. The practice of whakapohane, exposing the genitals and aiming them at an adversary, nullifying their mana, is an ancient one in Polynesia.[74] Female genitals served as a pathway between te ao and te pō, the ancestral realm of darkness and death, and this source of female tapu had the power to annihilate the mana of men.

Likewise, when the menfolk at Manutuke in Gisborne set up a paepae on the marae and told the women not to sit there, Heni Sunderland, a leading kuia was incensed:

> What they are saying to us is we are tapu men; we are so special that you women cannot come and sit here. I reacted badly, because I never ever saw it done to my Grannies, and I don't see why it should be done to me, and why it should be done to my children, because that was never our way.[75]

Despite their efforts to change the local tikanga, Heni continued to speak on behalf of her people – for instance, at the gathering when the Waitangi Tribunal was welcomed to her marae to open the proceedings for the Turanganui claims (although on that occasion, she spoke inside the meeting house).

Māori women also played leading roles during the first Māori renaissance at the turn of the twentieth century. Female leaders including Te Puea Herangi, the granddaughter of Tawhaio, the second Māori King, worked alongside Apirana Ngata to revitalise their people, economically, socially and culturally. In the wake of World War II, Te Puea became the first patroness of the Māori Women's Welfare League, formed to tackle many major issues affecting Māori families and communities. The second Māori renaissance from the 1970s onwards included a formidable array of female leaders – Dame Whina Cooper, Dame Te Ata-i-rangi-kaahu, Merimeri

Mihi Kotukutuku,
date unknown.

Penfold, Dame Mira Szazy, Dame Elizabeth Murchie, Dame June Mariu, Dame Tariana Turia, Hana Jackson, Titewhai Harawira, Donna Awatere and Ripeka Evans, and many others. This is captured by an iconic photograph taken at the beginning of the 1975 Land March at Te Hapua when Whina Cooper, hand in hand with her little grandchild, sets off down the long gravel road from Te Rerenga Wairua (the leaping place of spirits) in the far north of the North Island, heading for Parliament in Wellington to protest against the loss of Māori land.

In collaboration with their male peers, female Māori leaders created kōhanga reo, Māori language nests, in which preschool children speak Māori with elders and other speakers of te reo (the Māori language); kura kaupapa (Māori language schools); whare wānanga (Māori tertiary institutions); and Māori Studies departments in universities around the country. All of these institutions draw on the tikanga (protocols) of the old whare wānanga, or schools of learning, aiming to give Māori people the skills, knowledge and confidence to stand tall and succeed *as Māori* in the con-temporary world. In addition, women play major roles in the marae that are built and operated around the country, and kapa haka clubs (for practitioners of Māori performing arts), a major force in contemporary Māori life. There are also the waka ama (canoe paddling) clubs; Māori television and radio stations; Māori participation in government departments, regional govern-ment, museums, sports and the professions, film, writing and the arts; and many Māori businesses.

Nevertheless, and despite the resistance of so many Māori, it seems that early modern ideas about the relative roles of men, women and children and the 'savagery' of Māori remain potent in New Zealand. Often expressed by non-Māori in casual conversation and media such as talkback radio, these stereotypes have been internalised in gangs like Black Power and the Mongrel Mob, and in some Māori families. In the film *Once Were Warriors*, when Grace protests to her mother about her father's drunken violence, Beth Heke replies bitterly, 'It's just a woman's lot. That's all.' While Beth and her family may be fictitious, there has clearly been a radical shift in the lot of many Māori women and children over the past 200 years.

According to a recent report by Child, Youth and Family (CYF), for instance, 'a significant number of children and young people in New Zealand continue to experience distressing levels of abuse and neglect'; '[a]pproximately 57 per cent of children seen by CYF by the time they are five are Māori'; 'six out of every ten children in care are Māori'.[76] In an ironic counterpoint to neo-liberal talk about personal freedoms in New Zealand, the rates of incarceration of young Māori (especially young Māori men) are extremely high,[77] and many Māori children live in poverty in New Zealand. Compare this with the observation of Samuel Marsden: 'I saw no quarrel-ling while I was there. They are kind to their women and children. I never observed either with a mark of violence upon them, nor did I ever see a woman struck.'[78]

This loss of freedom and status is also evident in the changing roles of female Māori leaders – for instance, in many of the neo-tribal structures that have emerged from the Treaty settlement process. As Dame Mira Szazy once remarked: 'Māori women have allowed themselves to be marginal-ised and excluded from the Treaty resolution process for too long. Perhaps we have assumed our quiet persistent voices will be heard. They have not been.'[79] Tania Rangiheuea added:

Maori women's role in decision making processes, particularly within Maori institutions such as trust boards, councils, commissions and iwi authorities, is negligible. . . . There is no system of guarantee of a place for Maori women within our own institutions or within the new organisations which have evolved to manage our assets. Any talk of structural change sends the Government and our Maori men into a tailspin.[80]

Clearly, these transformations are linked with presuppositions about the roles of Māori women, the 'criminality' of Māori young men and women, the intellectual capabilities of Māori people, and the value of te reo Māori and ancestral Māori ways of thinking. These taken-for-granted assumptions, based on cosmic models such as the Great Chain of Being and stadial theories (which make a virtue of inequality), have proved remarkably resilient in New Zealand, continuing to blight the lives of many Māori people – men, women and children alike. As Hone Sadler has written in a parody of a whakapapa, based on Hone Mohi Tawhai's earlier satire:

Maori slept with the Maori Land Court and begat firstly Saddened Heart,
    and then Landlessness and Despair.
Saddened Heart slept with Urbanisation and begat Unemployment . . .
Unemployment slept with Alcohol and Drunkenness was born, followed by
    Abused Wife and Abused Children.
Unemployment slept with Drugs and begat Insanity followed by Trouble,
    and then the Court House.[81]

While this kind of vortex, like the throat of Te Parata, can take people down to te pō, it can also be reversed – a source of hope and resilience.

Voyaging Stars

. . . the paua eyes of gods and ancestors

whose real eyes, blinking in the light
of their lives millennia and centuries ago,

saw the vehicles themselves –
spacecraft, oxygen tanks, caravans led by elephants,

vehicles of concept, exploration, sails a vortex
ribbed by people shouting names down into the Great Sea.

– 'STAR WAKA 62', ROBERT SULLIVAN[1]

AS PATU HOHEPA HAS REMARKED, 'TIME IS A MOVING CONTINUUM if seen through Māori language, with ego being a particle whose own volition and direction is not bound to time. Time swirls like koru patterns, three dimensional spirals.'[2] These swirling currents carry the wairua of a person from the darkness of te pō into the body of a newborn child. As the baby enters te ao mārama, the world of light, it is greeted by its kinsfolk – 'Tihei, mauri ora!' (I sneeze, it is life!).

In ancestral times, during their passage through the world of light, a person was tied so closely to their ancestral land that it was identified with their own body. At the time of death, when they returned to the earth mother, te ū kai pō, the night-feeding breast, they were placed in caves, sepulchres or tapu trees. At the same time, the right eye of a rangatira might fly up into the heavens and become a star – kua whetūrangitia – twinkling as a sign to their descendants, sailing across the curved vault of the sky in their star waka (canoes), guiding travellers across the ocean. This sense of intimate connection with ancestors and the wider world is also fundamental to contemporary Māoritanga, linked as it is with the land, sea, marae and ancestral tikanga.

In this way, a person is always relationally connected. Self and identity are understood as a knot (here tangata) in the cloak of relationships, which is constantly being woven. As a person turns from one strand in their whakapapa to another, different taha, or sides, of themselves may be activated, each in its own way – my taha Māori (or Māori 'side'), or my taha pākehā (pakeha 'side'), for example, my taha Ngati Porou or my taha Nga Puhi. Here a person is the 'living face' of all their ancestors, who remain distinct and active within them.

In this networked world, a person is constantly negotiating their relations with others, striving to keep them in balance and good heart. For this reason, ideas of racial superiority and hatred are particularly virulent and destructive, endlessly generating negative and unequal exchanges. As we have seen, in ancestral times such transactions were known as hauhauaitu – harm to the hau, diminishing the life force. The result can be alienation, aggression, self-destruction and shame, a collapse of mana – as in the case of Jake Heke, for instance. Tracey McIntosh has graphically described this kind of negative spiral in contemporary institutions such as borstals, prisons and the courts, and in the education system, where Māori (and Pacific) students are often assumed to be less intellectually capable than their non-Māori counterparts, and steered towards the less demanding courses.[3]

In order to counter such destructive dynamics, contemporary institutions such as kōhanga reo ('language nests' where children are immersed in tikanga Māori), kura kaupapa (Māori medium schools), kapa haka clubs, Māori TV, the wearing of moko (tattoo) and the like, on the other hand, have been established to instil pride and confidence in young Māori, and to pass on tikanga Māori, or ancestral ways of being, enhancing the mana and hau ora of individuals and families. In these contemporary initiatives, many of those involved emphasise the need for Māori (and other New Zealanders) to draw upon all of their ancestral legacies in seizing the future. The act of whakahīhī – in which a person or group raises itself above others – invites an effort to restore more balanced relations, among different lines of ancestors within individuals as well as between different groups of people. The 'tall poppy' syndrome – a dislike of arrogance and pretension – is an old one in New Zealand, along with a liking for reciprocal relationships and shared decision-making.

The open-endedness (and vulnerability) of this kind of relational identity has also fostered experimentation – the very antithesis of fossilised 'tradition' – since first European arrival, posing very personal questions about whether and how individuals or groups might hold on to tikanga Māori, while exploring the wider world and forging relations with those who live differently. While te reo (the Māori language) is resurgent, relatively few still speak it fluently. Many Māori now live in other countries. They have Play Stations and cell phones; play rugby and netball; practise a wide range of professions, run successful businesses, star as opera singers on the world stage, or write poems and novels and make films enjoyed around the world.

Sometimes, ancestral conceptions are flexed to fit modernist presuppositions. As Marama Muru-Lanning has noted, during Treaty negotiations with the Crown, the Waikato River, formerly described as their tupuna awa (river ancestor) by Tainui leaders, was spoken about as an awa tupuna (ancestral river), thus transforming its nature and its relation with Tainui people.[4] Such shifts bring to light those simple, vivid, enduring and often hidden motifs that unfold onto-logically, underpinning different ways of being. The 'spiral of space-time' or the kin world of whakapapa in Māori philosophies; the 'Great Chain of Being' or the 'arrow of time'; the Nature/Culture split or the grid; possessive individualism or the atom in Western habits of mind – these ontological motifs or prototypes help to order a complex, constantly changing reality, making it intelligible and coherent.

When these underlying forms of order clash and mingle, strange things happen. As the Great Chain of Being comes into play, rivers and taniwha that were once the kaitiaki, or guardians, of people are relegated, so that people become the guardians of rivers. While it is often said that Māori walk backwards into the future with their eyes fixed on the past, this is based on a modernist linear idea of time, and reflects a seismic jolt in Māori semantics. As Patu Hohepa has pointed out, in ancestral conceptions, space-time (wā) 'swirls like koru patterns, three dimensional spirals', so that one faces the future (mua) and now the past (mua). Once the Western arrow of time is fired, however, time splits from space and becomes uni-dimensional, flying in a straight line from the past into the future. Wā (space-time) is laid down flat, and divided, measured and fragmented.

In other situations, modernist assumptions are adopted wholesale. Since the 1980s, for example, the neo-liberal conception of the cost-benefit calculating individual has become commonplace, eroding shared values and collective institutions from families to the state. Such an understanding of the self runs contrary to ancestral Māori ideas of a person as defined by their relationships with others, past and present, and values such as utu (reciprocity and balanced exchange); aroha (fellow feeling), manaakitanga (hospitality, care for others) and tino rangatiratanga (chiefly leadership) in which mana is exhibited in acts of generosity. This puts at risk institutions such as marae, founded as they are on the values of whanaungatanga (kinship) and manaakitanga; and iwi (tribes), hapū (sub-tribes) and whānau (extended families) as living networks in which kinfolk look out for each other.

This, one might think, is the predicament of te ao Māori – that in the ceaseless negotiation and questing of the descendants of founding ancestors, ancestral concepts – aroha, tapu, mana, utu, hau and the like – might be lost altogether, or transformed into entitative parodies of themselves, frozen into dogma. These risks are real, threatening ancestral Māori ways of being and ontological diversity in New Zealand. No doubt this is why Viveiros de Castro and his collaborators speak about the 'ontological self-determination of the world's peoples'[5] – acknowledging that it is not only 'Western' thinkers who ask ultimate questions and offer insights by exploring different kinds of realities.[6] In the Māori 'world', however, if space-time is a spiral, spinning in and out from the source, this is not a case of the 'eternal return', as Mircea Eliade would have it, in which the past is endlessly recapitulated.[7] A relational mode of being remains generative and dynamic, if marginalised in New Zealand; and effective relationships have been forged, mind-hearts changed, mana upheld and domination disrupted.

In Part One of this work, as we have seen, from the first arrival of Europeans and others in New Zealand, Māori thinkers vigorously tested and disputed Western forms of order and ideas about reality. These contestations, along with the impact they had on European visitors and settlers and their allies in Britain, led to the signing of the Declaration of Independence and the Treaty of Waitangi in New Zealand. In Part Two, such disputes over the nature of existence and the meaning of life, and the experiments 'across worlds' that they have provoked, were traced through particular spheres of existence, as Māori and incoming settlers from Europe and elsewhere tried to work out how to live together.

While stadial theories with their inexorable 'progress' from 'savagery' to 'civilisation' underpinned a post-Treaty refusal to include Māori in an emergent nation-state in New Zealand, these were vigorously contested by leaders including Hone Heke, Mananui Te Heuheu of Tuwharetoa, Potatau and Tawhiao (the first and second Māori Kings), along with the prophetic leader Te Kooti and many others. The Māori renaissance at the turn of the twentieth century led by Sir Apirana Ngata, Te Rangihiroa (Sir Peter Buck), Te Puea Herangi and their peers also radically shifted the wider society in New Zealand, introducing ideas of 'bi-culturalism' and the value of 'Māoritanga', and laying the groundwork for the Treaty settlements 50 years later. Challenges such as the 1975 Land March, the 1978 occupation of Bastion Point, the 2004 hīkoi in protest against the Foreshore and Seabed Bill, and the 2005 Tuhoe welcome to the Waitangi Tribunal, when naked warriors on horseback confronted Tribunal members, shots were fired and a New Zealand flag burned on the speaking ground, also led to lasting transformations.

These shifts were not achieved by Māori alone, however. As noted earlier, relational ideas and assumptions also exist in the Western tradition, and resonances between justice and tika, honour and mana, truth and pono, generosity and manaakitanga (all relational concepts) allowed alliances to be forged between Māori and pākehā, including lawyers, politicians, activists, artists and scholars, in the aftermath of the civil wars in New Zealand, at the turn of the twentieth century and in recent times. As on the marae, exchanges across the middle ground can be fertile and generative, as well as brutal and destructive. Today, a growing ease with terms like mana, tapu, utu, rangatiratanga and kaitiaki, as these words migrate into New Zealand English, reflects a willingness by a non-Māori majority in New Zealand to recognise the value of Māori conceptions, although this is always vulnerable to reversals.

Meanwhile in everyday life, Māori ancestral presence is marked by the performance of haka, or chants of challenge (and teaching the All Blacks, the national rugby team, to perform them properly); the kapa haka, or performing arts, festivals with their thousands of spectators; the act of wearing moko, or tattoo, as a statement of pride; waka ama paddling and voyaging by the stars; speaking Māori and cherishing ancestral taonga. These practices have become everyday aspects of life in contemporary New Zealand, increasingly shared with non-Māori New Zealanders. Pōwhiri (rituals of welcome) are almost routinely performed for distinguished guests; and the Treaty settlements are transferring significant capital, property and land to Māori kin groups.

As a result of the claim to the Waitangi Tribunal for a share of national broadcasting networks, Māori radio stations and Māori TV (often described as the best public television in New Zealand) have been established. Initiatives such as the kōhanga reo, or 'language nests', that link preschool children and their parents with native speakers of Māori, allowing them to learn the language and be immersed in tikanga Māori, are emulated by other indigenous groups around the world. Students in kura kaupapa (schools) and whare wānanga (tertiary institutions) explore ancestral knowledge alongside modernist disciplines, often generating new insights in the process. Here, assumptions of the superiority of 'Western' modes of knowledge are under siege.

Urban marae (ceremonial centres) in which the idiom of whakapapa (which has never been limited by 'blood', but is extendable by adoption, bond friendship and alliance) have sprung up in which those who run the marae work together as tāngata whenua, reaching out to Māori and others in the cities.[8] In 2016, for instance, during a crisis of homelessness in Auckland, Te Puea marae in Mangere opened its doors to families in need (including some non-Māori families) who were living in cars or on the streets, shaming the government by upholding the philosophy of manaakitanga powerfully articulated by Te Puea, the great female leader of Tainui after whom this marae and its meeting house are named.

The Māori Party, formed by Dame Tariana Turia and Sir Pita Sharples in an effort to advance Māori interests while promoting Māori language and values, holds the balance of power with other small parties in a coalition government, forcing a number of policy concessions, although it has not seriously contested neo-liberal philosophies in New Zealand, nor the rising gap between rich and poor among Māori as well as other New Zealanders. Programmes such as Whānau Ora (Wellbeing for Families), promoted by the Māori Party but supported by the government, seek to overcome the fragmentation of government agencies by introducing relational strategies into the state's own operations, wrapping interventions around whānau, or families, rather than vice versa, and revitalising kin networks. Ancestral values continue to shape life in New Zealand and elsewhere in a myriad of ways, some more visible than others.

As global citizens, Māori and Pacific people also engage in international debates and artistic, philosophical and political exchanges. Māori leaders are deeply involved with other indigenous peoples in programmes to advance indigenous rights, in the United Nations, for instance. Artistic creativity flourishes, whether in meetings of the 'SaVAge K'lub' featuring satirical parodies of *Pensée SauVAge* (Western fantasies about 'wild thought'), taking Polynesian ideas such as the Va (or wā in Māori–Polynesian space-time) and hurling them like spears into the heart of modernist myths about 'savages';[9] or artworks such as Lisa Reihana's *in Pursuit of Venus [infected]*, featuring in the 2017 Venice Biennale, which uses contemporary media to disrupt and question European images from James Cook's voyages around the world.[10]

In New Zealand, as elsewhere, life is moving in patterns that at once reinforce, and challenge, atomistic ideologies and their ruling ideas – that the world was created for human beings to dominate and control, a limitless resource to be exploited; that nation-states and cultures are bounded; that individuals exist solely to pursue their own goals and interests; and that social life can be understood as a market in which almost everything can be bought and sold.

Since the 1980s, the rapid increase in the wealth and power of corporates and global elites suggest a resurgence of the rule of the merchants, against which Adam Smith argued so vehemently in *The Wealth of Nations*.[11] Contemporary echoes of the Great Chain of Being, with its expectation that those at the bottom of the cosmic hierarchy (including land and sea, as well as people) must offer up tribute and deference to those at the top, and be grateful for what they receive in return, are proliferating – in corporate structures and bureaucracies, in top-down modes of surveillance and control, and in growing inequalities between 'the 1 per cent and the 99 per cent', for example. These patterns may be echoed in Māori corporations as well as other commercial entities in New Zealand, and in Treaty claims for the 'ownership' of 'assets' including rivers and the ocean – just as influential Māori leaders such as Sir Maui Solomon, Sir Tipene O'Regan, Dr Manuka Henare, Dr Ella Henry, Kingi Smiler and others are exploring ways of bringing together ancestral tikanga with contemporary capitalism.[12]

At the same time, the near-collapse and fragility of world financial systems is eroding confidence in the 'invisible hand of the market' and the virtuosity of cost-calculating, autonomous individuals. Global flows of refugees, students, workers, goods, ideas, information and capital move across nation-state boundaries, engendering trans-national and trans-cultural ways of living. Virtual networks of communication such as the World Wide Web, digital TV, Skype and sites like Facebook with their photographs and messages and many other relational media sprawl around the world, ignoring national borders and disrupting time-space distinctions.

In science, too, modernist disciplines with their silos (subjects, departments and faculties) struggle to illuminate the intricate dynamics of exchanges across networks of complex systems.[13] In an era dominated by the scale and intensity of anthropogenic impacts on other planetary systems, Cartesian divisions between mind and matter, people and nature, and the social sciences and the natural sciences are contradicted by the findings of contemporary science.[14] Debates about climate change, losses of bio-diversity, the acidification of the ocean, changing currents, air flows and gravitational fields are drawing attention to the interconnection of all forms of life – plants, animals, people and the planet they inhabit.[15]

Meanwhile, nation-states seem poorly organised to respond to these challenges. Fundamental presuppositions that underpin the 'autonomy' of the nation-state and its mechanisms are resilient, partly because these are taken for granted, embedded in unexamined habits of mind and practice, and in institutional frameworks at different scales – local, regional, national and global. It may be, however, that the worlds we inhabit are increasingly relational in character, and that a modernist style and the entitative modes of understanding and organisation it engenders are non-adaptive for many purposes.

As a number of theorists have pointed out, during encounters between people who live differently, taken-for-granted assumptions may come to light and be questioned. Different kinds of encounters become possible; and new kinds of questions, in a spiralling process of critical, searching exchanges. In New Zealand, a small country with a diverse population and access to very different philosophical traditions, new ways of thinking about global challenges can happen. In the Waitangi Tribunal and the settlement process, for instance, the attempt to restore some balance to relationships between Māori and other New Zealanders repeatedly brings to light contradictions between different habits of mind. As soon as fish are turned into quota, to be bought and sold on the market; or broadcasting frequencies are auctioned; or knowledge becomes intellectual property to be licensed and traded; or waterways are turned into units of water to be counted and sold for hydro-electric power, irrigation and water supplies for towns and cities, these transformations are contested by Māori in front of the Waitangi Tribunal. Other ways of negotiating these relationships are proposed, and sometimes enacted.[16]

In New Zealand, as elsewhere, shifts towards atomistic ways of being, anthropocentric models and extractionist habits of mind have been associated with fragmentation in social networks, growing inequalities between rich and poor, the incarceration of many young people (especially young Māori men), market failures in housing and finance, and the degradation of fresh water, land and maritime ecosystems – all signs of mate (dysfunction, ill health and disorder). The tears of Rangi themselves – lakes, aquifers and rivers – are becoming toxic, making people and animals sick.

These are not the only pathways that are open to us, however. It is possible that experimental links might be forged between cutting-edge science, technologies and relational thinking, and innovative modes of engagement among people and the wider world, in a quest for strategies that generate ora – lasting prosperity and well-being. Exchanges might occur between philosophies that recognise the importance of individual enterprise and striving, and those that recognise the need for communal flourishing. Here, ontological styles in which matter has never been dead or separated from people may prove helpful. When the physicist Jane Bennett urges us to 'picture an ontological field without unequivocal demarcations between human, animal, vegetable, or mineral' in which 'all forces and flows are or can become lively [and] affective',[17] I think of the nineteenth-century Māori philosopher Nepia Pohuhu, who said, 'All things unfold their nature [tupu], live [ora], have form [āhua], whether trees, stones, birds, reptiles, fish, quadrupeds or human beings.'[18]

It is possible to see the links between human communities, land and sea as patterned by complex, multi-dimensional, dynamic systems in which people are related to other life forms, and our fates are tied together. A river, for instance, might be understood as a living being, recognised as a legal person with its own rights – as in the case of the Whanganui River, where the local iwi say, '*Ko au te awa, ko te awa ko au. Kei te mate te awa, kei te mate ahau*' – 'I am the river, and the river is me. If the river is dying, so am I.' Relations between people and the Pacific Ocean might be informed by strategies evolved by islanders over millennia of oceanic living. We might experiment with more egalitarian, inclusive patterns of governance, and relations among land, sea, men, women and children based upon ideas of manaakitanga (mutual caring) and he whenua rangatira – a prosperous, abundant country, where people live in peace. As Henare [Salmond], Holbraad and Wastell suggest, '[we] might instead seize on these engagements as opportunities from which novel theoretical understandings can emerge'[19] – and perhaps, new ways of living.

As Eruera Stirling used to chant:

Whakarongo! Whakarongo! Whakarongo!	*Listen! Listen! Listen!*
Ki te tangi a te manu e karanga nei	*To the cry of the bird calling*
Tui, tui, tuituia!	*Bind, join, be one!*
Tuia i runga, tuia i raro,	*Bind above, bind below*
Tuia i roto, tuia i waho,	*Bind within, bind without*
Tuia i te here tangata	*Tie the knot of humankind*
Ka rongo te pō, ka rongo te pō	*The night hears, the night hears*
Tuia i te kāwai tangata i heke mai	*Bind the lines of people coming down*
I Hawaiki nui, i Hawaiki roa,	*From great Hawaiki, from long Hawaiki*
I Hawaiki pāmamao	*From Hawaiki far away*
I hono ki te wairua, ki te whai ao	*Bind to the spirit, to the day light*
Ki te Ao Mārama!	*To the World of Light!*

Eruera Stirling to Anne Salmond, 20 January 1981, on the publication of *Eruera: Teachings of a Maori Elder*, while I was on sabbatical leave at King's College, Cambridge with Jeremy and our children:

Now the day is over and night is Drawing nigh Shadows of the evening steals across the skies, the Long white clouds moving above with the glittering lights of Tamanuiitera [the sun] above the Great Sea of Te moananui a kiwa [the Pacific] and on the shores of Waitemata beneath the Great Hills of Tamaki maku Rau [Auckland].

There lies Beneath the Great City of Auckland and No 1 Amiria Street Herne Bay, the Lonely Home of your father and mother and family in the Atmosphere of a Home where we all met and Specially you Ani in our meeting together to enter in to the School of Learning of the Life and Histories of the Whare Wananga.

The Dawn of the Light came from the night when you first came to meet me Ani that Light of History glitters into the House, and I saw signs of faith with you that day still clings in my memory of you, and Amiria and I have you still our mokopuna [grandchild] and one of the Family, and Here we are all together.

You have Brought us into the world of History, the two Books, Amiria and Eruera is the Talk of the People of Auckland and all over New Zealand. Kia Pumau ai Te Kaha me te maramatanga ki runga ia koe me to Hoa Rangatira me te whanau mokopuna [May strength and enlightenment always be upon you and your husband and our great-grandchildren].

. . . Well my Dearest Ani I now will close my Letter on behalf of the whole family and extend to you our Greetings and our High Lights wishes for You. Ka mutu Ra i konei enei mihi atu kia korua me nga mokopuna i te [Let me close these greetings to you both and our great-grandchildren with the] Blessings of Allmighty God upon you and your Family.

Arohanui [Best love]
Na o Tipuna [From your Grandparents]
Eruera & Amiria Stirling

Portrait of Eruera Stirling by Marti Friedlander circa 1993.

Whakataukī from and to Eruera and Amiria Stirling:

E paru i te tinana, e mā i te wai,	If you're touched with mud, you can wash it off,
E paru i te aroha, ka mau tonu ē.	If you're touched with aroha, it lasts always.

NOTES

AJHR	*Appendices to the Journals of the House of Representatives*
APL	Auckland Public Library
ATL	Alexander Turnbull Library
AWMML	Auckland War Memorial Museum Library
BL	British Library
CMS	Church Missionary Society
CO	Colonial Office
GBPP	Great Britain Parliamentary Papers
HL	Hocken Library, Dunedin
ML	Mitchell Library, Sydney
SSRN	Social Science Research Network
UOAL	University of Auckland Library

Preface Voyaging Worlds

1   For accounts of Polynesian deep-sea voyaging, see Henry 1907, Frake 1985, Gell 1985, Gladwin 1995, Hutchins 1995, Finney 2000, Anne Salmond 2005, Di Piazza and Peathree 2007, Di Piazza 2010. In many oceanic systems of star navigation, the canoe is seen as standing still in the sea while the stars rise up overhead and islands move towards the vessel – rather like contemporary satellite navigation devices. Mimi George, who worked closely for many years with Kaveia, a leading Polynesian navigator from Taumako, writes vividly about how, at sea, he would *become* his ancestor Lata, the first canoe maker, responding to the interlocking patterns of swells, the different winds, *lapa* or streaks of underwater light, the flights of the birds and the starpaths or sequences of stars that rise up on the bearing of particular islands, guiding him to his destination (George 2012 and George n.d., pers. comm).
2   Viveiros de Castro, Holbraad and Pedersen 2014.
3   Irwin 2015.
4   On current estimates, early in the fourteenth century – see Wilmshurst, Hunt, Lipo and Anderson 2011, Johns, Irwin and Sung 2014, Jacomb, Holdaway, Allentoft, Bunce, Oskam, Walter and Brooks 2014, and Bell, Currie, Irwin and Bradbury 2015. Some of these first Polynesian arrivals (from the Cook Islands and the Marquesas) have been found in burials at Wairau Bar in Cloudy Bay, Marlborough. For an excellent recent survey of likely migration patterns across the Pacific, based on ancient DNA evidence, including contacts with South America, see Matisoo-Smith 2015.
5   Taylor 1968, Anne Salmond 2005.
6   Crosby 1986, Diamond 1997.
7   For a recent reflection on value as a creative force around which different groups of people organise their lives, feelings and desires, see Graeber 2013.
8   See, for instance, Descola on the 'nature–culture' divide (Descola 2013), and Capra and Mattei on 'mind–matter' and 'people–environment' divisions (Capra and Mattei 2015), along with many other critics of Cartesian dualism. In the 2015 Marilyn Strathern lecture, for instance, Viveiros de Castro explored a 'growing feeling that our own Modern ontology (singular) such as laid down by the scientific revolution of the 17th century not only was made largely obsolete by the scientific revolutions

418

of the early 20th century, but that it also turned out to have disastrous consequences when considered from its business end, i.e. as an imperialist, colonialist, ethnocidal and ecocidal "mode of production"' (Viveiros de Castro 2015).

9   In speaking of 'worlds' and 'realities,' I am not referring here to essentialised entities or objects ('the world'; 'reality'). Rather, I'm interested in how different people (including anthropologists) hold different assumptions about reality, and either try to work these through in shared projects of different kinds, or ignore or dismiss those held by others. Here, there are no external vantage points, no possibility of detached observation. As Amiria Salmond has written recently, 'ethnography comes *with a position on [ontological] difference and sameness built into it.* The challenge then is not to step outside this position – whether by trying to "see through the natives' eyes" and/ or by proposing a new meta-ontology of different worlds – but to work *through* it; to mobilise the methods at our disposal, recognising all the while that difference and sameness, as far as ethnography is concerned, are always relations of comparison rather than essential properties of [other] groups of people' (Amiria Salmond 2016; emphases in original).

10   See Strathern 2014b, for an illuminating discussion of two different kinds of relationality – internal (as in whakapapa), where the terms are mutually defining; and external, as in Euro-American cosmology, which relies on 'the prior distinctiveness of the "different" entities being related'. Here the entities are defined first, and then the relations as links between them. As Strathern muses while exploring historical transformations in European kinship and (and biology), 'the anthropologist might want to know why kin relations in some regimes [e.g. whakapapa] are the very exemplars of cosmology, while in this one [i.e. Euro-American kinship] they are repeatedly pushed to one side'.

11   Stirling as told to Anne Salmond 1980, 247. As Christopher Loperena points out in a recent reflection on engaged ethnographic research, 'doing things in the right way' is far from straightforward, given divergences and clashes of interests among community members. Nevertheless, he argues strongly for an anthropology that strives to make ethical choices: 'Moral communities are always in formation. From my perspective, we have more to gain from nurturing diverse epistemological registers that can foster original approaches and ultimately breathe new life into the discipline. . . . The ethical imperative to respond to social problems will continue to generate moral debate and encourage methodological transformations, leading to richer ethnographic engagements and a more honest anthropology' (Loperena 2016, 346).

PART ONE: EARLY ENCOUNTERS, 1769–1840

Chapter One Hau: Wind of the World

1   Or perhaps Tahitian dyes, as used by the *'arioi* artists in the Society Islands?

2   Joppien and Smith 1985, 60.

3   Banks to Dawson Turner 12 December 1812, quoted in Carter 1998, 133–4.

4   In describing his discovery, Carter writes, 'In her splendid study of the first meeting between Europeans and the Maori of New Zealand, *Two Worlds* . . . (1991), Professor Dame Anne Salmond made prominent use, as a symbolic icon, of the watercolour drawing in the British [Museum] Library Department of Manuscripts . . . usually described as "An English naval officer bartering with a Maori". . . . So it has remained until April 1997 when the writer of this note had occasion to re-examine the transcripts he had made twenty-five years ago of selected letters by Sir Joseph Banks . . . . The relevant paragraph in the letter is [quoted]. On 29 April 1997 the writer drew these details to the attention of Anne Salmond with the suggestion that a joint paper

on this discovery could be prepared . . .' (Carter 1998). This was generous of Harold
Carter, but the discovery was his.

5   For an account of the 'arioi and early Tahitian society, see Anne Salmond 2009.
6   Quoted in Anne Salmond 2009, 36, which sets Tupaia's life in the context of life in the
     Society Islands at that time, and discusses his chart. For a detailed account of Tupaia's
     life and career, see also Anne Salmond 2012b. For insightful discussions of Tupaia's
     chart of the Pacific, see Di Piazza and Peathree 2007 and Di Piazza 2010.
7   Sometimes called te hā – breath, taste.
8   Letter from Tamati Ranapiri to Peehi (Elsdon Best), 23 November 1907, p. 2,
     MS-Papers-1187-127, Alexander Turnbull Library, Wellington, trans. Anne
     Salmond. Original text in Māori: 'Taua mea te hau. Ehara i te mea ko te hau e pupuhi
     nei. Kaore, maku e ata whakamarama ki a koe. Na, he taonga tou ka homai e koe moku
     (kaore a taua whakaritenga utu mo te taonga) na ka hoatu hoki e ahau mo tetahi atu
     tangata, a ka roa pea te wa, a ka mahara taua tangata kei a ia ra taua taonga, kia homai
     he utu ki a au, a ka homai e ia, na ko taua taonga i homai nei ki a au. Ko te hau tena o te
     taonga i homai ra ki a au i mua. Ko taua taonga me hoatu e ahau ki a koe, E kore rawa
     e tika kia kaiponutia e ahau moku, ahakoa taonga pai rawa taonga kino ranei, me tae
     rawa taua i a au ki a koe, no te mea he hau no to taonga tenei taonga na, ki te mea ka
     kaiponutia e ahau tena taonga moku, ka mate ahau. Koina taua mea, te hau.'
9   Mauss, trans. Halls 1990.
10   Tregear 1891, 168.
11   Te Kohuora of Rongoroa 1854, collected by Richard Taylor, published in Taylor
     1855, 15–16.
12   Te Rangikaheke of Te Arawa, written for Governor George Grey, c. 1849, APL
     GNZMSS 43.
13   Hongi 1894.
14   For a meditation upon this theme, see Schrempp 1985.
15   For an exploration of these pairings and the patterns they form in shaping te ao
     Māori, based on an investigation of fundamental patterns in te reo (the Māori lan-
     guage) and some rituals, see Anne Salmond 1978.
16   As Strathern has argued for Hagen in the New Guinea Highlands: 'A person is held
     by the relation (and it is always a specific relation) of the moment: parties to a relation
     exist in that relationship to each other' (Strathern 2011, 94). Likewise in te ao Māori,
     identity is relational; the being of a named person is shaped by their various descent
     lines, the current state of their relationships with others, and the moment at which a
     specific relation is being negotiated.
17   For a detailed study of Māori ceremonial gatherings on marae, see Anne Salmond 1975.
18   Jones 1959, 232.
19   University of Auckland 1988.
20   Ibid., inner front cover. For further illumination about key named features of Waipapa
     marae, see Marsden ed. Royal 2003, 'Mātauranga Māori, Mātauranga Pākeha', 73–79.
21   Jensen 2011, 7, commentary on Viveiros de Castro 2007.
22   Sahlins 1985b, 195.
23   Barlow 1991, 26–27.
24   Also the ritual of kapukapu tūtata (snatching the hau) – see Takaanui 1894, 172–4.
25   See Best 1903, 83–84, who explains that the hau of an enemy could be a lock of hair,
     or the heart, offered up to the victors' atua (powerful ancestors) who live in the hau or
     wind.
26   Mead 2003, 27 describes the dynamic by which an act of wrongdoing is requited, and
     balance is achieved – kua ea.
27   Pohuhu in S. Percy Smith 1913, 13.
28   Equally, it was possible to attack the hau of such a place: see Best 1900, 197 for a kara-
     kia, or incantation, to destroy the hau of a particular territory.

29 Or as a tree; see Marsden ed. Royal 2003, 63.

30 Strathern 1995, 21.

31 For a recent instance of contemporary scientific reflection about the nature of life in biological systems (including human communities and ecosystems), see Dupré and O'Malley 2013.

32 Mattei and Kapra 2015.

33 Mohi Turei, *Te Pipiwharauroa*, January 1911, 4–5.

34 For a thoughtful reflection on 'states of existence' as fundamental forms of order in Māori realities, see Binney 1980, 9–10.

35 From this vantage point, it seems that current debates about 'detachment' versus 'engagement' in anthropology reflect modernist preoccupations (see, for instance, Candea, Cook, Trundle and Yarrow 2015), rather than universal dilemmas. In te ao Māori, it is not really possible to detach one's self from others. A relationship may be more or less distant or close at any moment, active or inactive, hostile or friendly, but people are always already enmeshed in relational networks, one way or another. Nor are these states binary, but graded on continua and constantly changing. It is the ways in which relationships are negotiated and balanced (or not) that really matter.

36 Hart 2007.

37 Cook ed. Beaglehole 1969, 653.

38 Anne Salmond and Amiria Salmond 2010.

39 A process referred to by Viveiros de Castro as 'equivocation' – which also applies to ethnographic encounters and anthropological interpretation, where it may be strategically deployed as 'controlled equivocation' (Viveiros de Castro 2004b).

40 In the contemporary social sciences, questions are often raised about how far human understandings of reality are based on universal patterns. Do human beings inhabit a singular 'world' (or 'universe'), for instance (i.e. we live in the same world, but have different 'views' of it), or many 'worlds' (i.e. a 'multiverse') – assumptions about realities that are radically different, even incommensurable? In his book *Cognitive Variations: Reflections on the University and Diversity of the Human Mind* (2009), for instance, Geoffrey Lloyd, an eminent scholar of ancient Chinese and Greek philosophies, sought to test these competing propositions – 'a one world thesis, where differences relate just to the views taken of that world, [or] the more radical idea that the worlds that different humans (let alone other sentient beings) inhabit themselves differ in the sense that they are incommensurable with one another' (Lloyd 2010, 207). In the end, Lloyd came down on the side of a 'one world' thesis, arguing that if the worlds inhabited by different groups of people were radically incompatible, mutual intelligibility and understanding across linguistic and cultural boundaries would be impossible.

When Amiria Salmond and I were invited to review this work (Anne Salmond and Amiria Salmond 2010), we were not so certain. From the evidence of a range of early encounters between Europeans and islanders in New Zealand, Hawai'i and the Society Islands, it seemed that impasses in understandings were commonplace, arising from very different assumptions about what is real and what matters; and incommensurable premises often proved to be resilient and enduring, generating misunderstandings and conflict, but also provoking new habits of mind and ways of living. If, as Roy Wagner has argued, 'the understanding of another culture involves the relationship between two varieties of the human phenomenon; it aims at the creation of an intellectual relation between them, an understanding that includes both of them' (Wagner 1981, 3), this is not the preserve of anthropologists alone. Such an experimental process does not annihilate or control philosophical differences; it is generative, creating understandings that are something new and different.

While 'bridgeheads of intelligibility' may be built, then, this is a process of trial and error that may take 'years, even generations, of exchanges, debate and often conflict between people holding competing assumptions' (Anne Salmond and Amiria

Salmond 2010). Indeed, it seems possible that Lloyd's dismissal of the 'multiple worlds' thesis was itself underpinned by a 'one world' conception of reality in which 'the world' is taken to be singular and bounded, and there can be just one ultimate reality against which all human understandings must be tested. As Lloyd himself observes, 'there is no theory-free way of accessing an answer to the question of what the world comprises' (Lloyd 2010, 210).

41   For example, Descola 2013.

42   For a lucid recent account of the ontological turn in anthropology, and critiques of its implications, see Jensen 2016. In discussing the work of this second group of anthropologists (including Strathern, Wagner, Holbraad and Viveiros de Castro), he remarks (10–12): '[T]he ontological turn is about the inherently uncertain process of trying to learn about the thoughts of different worlds *via* necessary detours through our own. . . . Rather than an ethnographic description of what people say, think and do, and how that is different from our ways of being in the world, ontology . . . is necessarily a synthetic product of their thoughts and actions parsed through our categories. . . . [T]he success criterion of this operation is precisely that something 'alter' remains, and that it is allowed to trouble our own thought.'

Chapter Two **Tupaia's Cave**

1   At the time I was chairperson of the board of the New Zealand Historic Places Trust (now Heritage New Zealand), and attended in that capacity.

2   Work on this chapter (and this book) began in 1980–81, while I was a Nuffield Fellow at King's College and the Department of Social Anthropology at the University of Cambridge. I had just completed an intensive period of work with Eruera Stirling on a book about his ancestors and life, which involved a deep immersion in aspects of wānanga, or ancestral knowledge. The juxtaposition of that experience with life as a scholar in Cambridge made me think hard about the relations between Māori and Western philosophies and forms of knowledge, and this in turn led to an inquiry into the first exchanges between Māori and Europeans. In drafting the book *Two Worlds: First Meetings between Maori and Europeans 1642–1772* (1991), the first fruit of those reflections, Eruera and other East Coast elders including Darcy Ria, Peggy Kaua and Bino and Frances Reedy helped me to understand the local context when the *Endeavour* commanded by James Cook arrived in Turanga, Anaura and Uawa in October 1769. A draft reconstruction of the events in Uawa (Tolaga Bay) was first presented for feedback and advice to a formal gathering at Hauiti marae in 1989, when I was accompanied by my mother Joyce, Lady Lorna Ngata, Peggy Kaua and Ingrid Searancke. The reconstruction of the events in Turanga (Gisborne) was presented (with Kiki Kerekere-Smiler) at a large formal gathering at Poho-o-Rawiri marae on the occasion of the *Endeavour* replica's visit to Gisborne in 1995. Later intensive work on Cook's visits to Tahiti and Tupaia's Tahitian background was carried out in Tahiti and published in *The Trial of the Cannibal Dog: Captain Cook in the South Seas* (2003) and *Aphrodite's Island: The European Discovery of Tahiti* (2009). Many thanks to Wayne Ngata of Te Aitanga-a-Hauiti, the Māori Language commissioner, for checking this chapter, and his insightful comments and edits. My thanks, too, to Brett Graham for helpful feedback, and permission to publish his brilliant image based on Pei Jones' sketch of the takarangi double spiral.

3   For the final archaeological report from the Cook's Cove excavation, see Walter, Jacomb and Brooks 2010.

4   For a recent account of Te Rawheoro, the school of learning at Uawa, and its founder Hingangaroa, with the story of Ruakapanga and his great birds, see *Te Nupepa Maori*, 7 December 2007, 27.

5   See Ruatapu 1993.
6   Polack 1838 II, 135. Wayne Ngata points out that the correct name is 'Te Ana o Tupaia' not 'Te Ana no Tupaia'.
7   Joel Polack described this 1835 visit to Uawa, and oral histories about Tupaia's visit in Polack 1838 II, 135–6.
8   See Weisner 2014 for a discussion of the way in which talk around the fire at night frees the imagination – in contrast with Plato's Cave, where prisoners chained in a cave were forced to watch the shadows of objects lit by a fire behind them flickering across a wall, mistaking these for reality (Plato, *The Republic* Book VII).
9   Cook ed. Beaglehole 1955, 514.
10 Ibid., cclxxix–cclxxxiv.
11 Ibid., cclxxxiii.
12 Banks ed. Beaglehole 1962 I, 396.
13 Ibid., I, 399.
14 This date is based on 'civil time' as kept at the time of the voyage, for instance in Banks's journal (which runs from midnight to midnight), rather than 'ship's time' (which runs from noon to noon, twelve hours ahead of civil time). Because they first landed on the east bank of the Turanganui River in the late afternoon, Banks recorded the date of their arrival in New Zealand as 8 October 1769 (civil time), while the ship's log gives the date as 9 October 1769 (ship's time). In this period, however, civil time (which runs from midnight to midnight) was used to date events on land.
    No extra day has been added for 'westing' (i.e. crossing the International Date Line heading west), because the Date Line did not exist at the time of Cook's voyage. Rather, as the *Endeavour* sailed westward around the world from Greenwich, Cook daily increased his hour-angles and time differences and longitudes to ensure that his charts remained accurate. Each day on board was thus slightly longer than the last, instead of making the correction all at once as travellers have done since 1884, when the International Date Line was established. Cook finally changed his dates at Batavia, rather than off the east coast of New Zealand, as is the current practice.
    For detailed accounts of the encounters in Poverty Bay, Hawke's Bay, Anaura and Tolaga Bay, see Anne Salmond 1991, 118–84; 2003, 113–28; 2012c, 69–77.
15 William Leonard Williams, from the Williams missionary family which lived nearby for many years, named the rock as Te Toka-Taiau (see Williams 1888, 393).
16 'Tupia understood them and made himself understood so well that he at length prevailed on one of them to strip of his covering and swim across – he landed upon a rock surrounded by the tide, and now invited us to come to him C. Cook finding him resolved to advance no farther, gave his musket to an attendant, and went towards him, but tho' the man saw C. Cook give away his weapon to put himself on a footing with him, he had not courage enough to wait his arrival, retreating into the water, however he at last ventured forward, they saluted by touching noses' (Monkhouse in Cook ed. Beaglehole 1955, 569).
17 Banks ed. Beaglehole 1962 I, 403.
18 'Several Canoes put off from shore and came towards us within less than a quarter of a mile but could not be persuaded to come nearer, tho Tupia exerted himself very much shouting out and promising that they should not be hurt. At last one was seen coming from Poverty bay or near it, she had only 4 people in her, one who I well remember to have seen at our first interview on the rock: these never stopd to look at any thing but came at once alongside of the ship and with very little persuasion came on board; their example was quickly followd by the rest 7 canoes in all and 50 men. They had many presents given to them notwithstanding which they very quickly sold almost every thing that they had with them, even their Cloaths from their backs and the paddles out of their boats; arms they had none except 2 men, one of whom sold his patoo patoo as he calld it' (Banks ed. Beaglehole 1962 I, 406); 'They were all kindly

treated and very soon enter'd into a traffick with our people for George Island Cloth &c giving in exchange their paddles (having little else to dispose of) and hardly left themselves a Sufficient number to paddle a shore, nay the People in one Canoe after disposing of the Paddles offer'd to sell the Canoe. After a stay of about two hours they went away' (Cook ed. Beaglehole 1955, 173–4).

19 For an investigation of this exchange and the current locations of many of these painted hoe (paddles) in European and other museums and collections, see Amiria Salmond 2015e, and PhD research by Steve Gibbs of Ngai Tamanuhiri.

20 For knowledgeable accounts of kinship relations in Uawa at the time of the *Endeavour*'s arrival, the relationship between Te Whakatatare-o-te-rangi and Hinematioro, and their encounters with Tupaia and the *Endeavour* crew, see Walker 2012 and Donald 2012.

21 Parkinson 1773, 97.

22 For recent discussions of botanical draughting and Parkinson's art, see Nickelsen 2006, Lack and Ibañèz 1997. Ewen Cameron, botanist at Auckland War Memorial Museum, and I have compiled a list of the plants collected at Poverty Bay (Taoneroa), based on evidence from Parkinson's sketches for the *Florilegium*, with their notes on where different species were collected, the herbaria of pressed plants and Solander's botanical manuscript in Latin, studied by Cameron. For a commentary on their zoological collecting, see Andrews 2012.

At present the Longbush Ecological Trust, which I chair, is planting a 1769 Garden at Longbush (upriver from the Cook landing site in Poverty Bay), designed by Philip Smith of o2 Landscapes and based on the plants collected during the *Endeavour*'s visit, combining contemporary botanical and Māori knowledge of these species in preparation for the two hundred and fiftieth commemoration of these first meetings between Māori and Europeans in 2019, and the convergence of these two botanical traditions (see www.longbushreserve.org). In this exercise we are being guided by Graeme Atkins of Ngati Porou, a fine field botanist and mātauranga expert who works for the Department of Conservation.

23 Banks ed. Beaglehole 1962 I, 419.

24 Ibid., I, 420.

25 Cook ed. Beaglehole 1955, 538–9.

26 Ruatapu 1993, 18 (Māori), 118 (English).

27 Banks ed. Beaglehole 1962 I, 420, 443.

28 For a detailed account of the 'arioi cult in the Society Islands, and Tahitian society at the time of early European contact, see Anne Salmond 2009.

29 Cook ed. Beaglehole 1955, 539.

30 Ibid., 186.

31 For Spöring's sketch of this canoe prow, with the dimensions of the canoe inscribed, see BL Add. MS 23920, f. 77b in Joppien and Smith 1985, 177. This canoe prow has not been located.

32 Parkinson 1773, 98.

33 Banks ed. Beaglehole 1962 I, 417.

34 Ibid., II, 32.

35 Frängsmyr, Heilbron and Rider 1990.

36 For a precursor to this 'objectification of the subject' which gave the subject mastery over an exterior, singular, mathematicised world, see Descola's 2013 discussion of the invention of linear perspective and its links with Descartes' *res extensa*, the split between Nature and human beings, and the invention of instruments such as the telescope, microscope and quadrant (Descola 2013, 59–63).

37 In this 'entitative' onto-logic, binaries are characterised by mutual exclusion and sharp boundaries (i.e. binary oppositions), whereas in a 'relational' cosmology such as te ao Māori, the pairs split out from an original whole (i.e. complementary dualisms)

are still fundamentally entangled in relations across a liminal zone – Rangi and Papa, sky father and earth mother; te ao and te pō; male and female; light and dark; tapu and noa, and so on. The structure of the cosmos itself reflects this pattern, with te ao and te pō mediated by te kore, the 'seedbed of the cosmos' which contains the potentiality for all forms of life, from which new life forms are continuously generated (see Anne Salmond 2012a, 123–6 for an extended discussion of the differences between 'entitative' and 'relational' ontological styles).

38 Foucault 1970.

39 For example, Henare [Salmond], Holbraad and Wastell eds 2007a, 10, 11.

40 Yeo 2001.

41 Blomley 2003. See also the physicist David Bohm's discussion of Cartesian logic, the grid, its link with a mechanistic view of the cosmos, and its viral spread, in *Wholeness and the Implicate Order*: '[The grid] is constituted of three perpendicular sets of uniformly spaced lines. Each set of lines is evidently an order. . . . A given curve is then determined by a *coordination* among the X, the Y and the Z orders. Coordinates are evidently not to be regarded as natural objects. Rather, they are merely convenient forms of description set up by us. As such, they have a great deal of arbitrariness or conventionality. . . . To use coordinates is in effect to order our attention in a way that is appropriate to the mechanical view of the universe. . . . [O]nce men were ready to conceive of the universe as a machine, they would naturally tend to take the order of coordinates as a universally relevant one, valid for all basic descriptions . . .' (Bohm 1980, xiv–xv, 113–114).

42 Lovejoy 1936, Hodgen 1971, Bennett 2010, 87–88.

43 It is interesting to note that in te ao Māori, while tiered structures and grids are not unknown, relational ideas of reciprocal exchange and complex networks are dominant. As mentioned earlier, ancestral Māori cosmological ideas included a structure of layered skies and underworlds, laid one upon the other (whakapapa – literally to make layers). Tukutuku panels in chiefs' houses (and now meeting houses) are gridded, with intersecting rows of raupō or wood bound together by strands of fibre coloured with dyes. Overwhelmingly, however, the ramifying networks of whakapapa order the world.

44 Reill 2005.

45 For an investigation of the complex traces of Enlightenment 'vitalism' in various post-Enlightenment life sciences, see Normandin and Wolfe eds 2013; and in philosophy, see Lash 2006.

46 Israel 2006.

47 Banks ed. Beaglehole 1962 II, 19–20.

48 Ibid., I, 312–13.

49 Cook ed. Beaglehole 1969, 175.

50 For analyses of surveying, the grid and imperial power, see Beamer and Duarte 2009, Bell 2005.

51 See papers in Mare Nullius session, 2015 European Society for Oceanists Conference, Brussels; Anne Salmond 2015.

52 For example: 'This manner of thinking has made us imagine an infinity of false relations between natural beings. . . . It is to impose on the reality of the Creator's works the abstractions of our mind' (Buffon 1749, 9a–b). See also Sloan 1976 for a discussion of the debate between Buffon and Linnaeus, and how Buffon ended up losing the argument – a classic case of a scientific paradigm shift in progress.

53 On Banks and Enlightenment science in the Pacific, see Gascoigne 2004; Hankins 1985; Jardine, Secord and Spary eds 1996; MacLeod and Rehbock eds 1988; Miller and Reill eds 1996. See Tim Ingold's recent meditation on the emergence of early modern science, with its split between 'the real' and 'the imaginary', and how 'Nature became amenable to the project . . . of classification. The lines were broken, but the

resulting objects could be ordered and arranged, on the basis of perceived likeness or difference, into the compartments of a taxonomy. One could speak, for the first time, of the building blocks of nature, rather than its weave . . .' (Ingold 2013, 743).

54 For accounts of botanical draughting, see Nickelsen 2006, Lack and Ibañèz 1997.

55 Directions for Seamen, bound for Far Voyages, 1666, *Philosophical Transactions* 1, 140–1.

56 Warren 1951, Wellman 2002. For an investigation of the complex variations among 'vitalist' thinkers in Enlightenment medicine and biology, see the papers in Wolfe ed. 2008.

    At that time in Europe, medical education typically covered natural history (including geology, zoology and botany, with field trips and study in botanical or physic gardens where the plants used for herbal medicines grew) as well as anatomy and surgery and the study of disease, alongside the classical texts of Hippocrates and Galen. Many physicians were trained in centres such as Edinburgh, Leyden and Montpellier, while relatively few British doctors graduated from Oxford or Cambridge, where dissenters were not admitted and classical studies dominated.

    In Edinburgh, Montpellier and Leyden, medical students were taught to observe and describe plants, landscapes and climates as well as people and their diseases, and to reflect upon the relationships among them. The Surgeon's Company in London, which employed the distinguished physician William Hunter among others and where William Monkhouse had studied, offered a more specialised training in anatomy and surgery, and examined naval surgeons, but candidates were often already well educated, with a keen interest in natural history.

57 Buffon 1749, 23b–24a.

58 Monkhouse in Cook ed. Beaglehole 1955, 564–87.

59 Pratt 1992.

60 Nicholas 1817 I, 72.

61 Parkinson 1773, 98.

62 Jones 1959, 232.

63 Tiramorehu 1849.

64 For example, in the famous waiata (song) that begins *E pā tō hau he wini raro, e homai aroha* – 'your hau comes to me as a northern wind, bringing aroha'.

65 Jones in collaboration with Graham 2012.

66 Kalamakūloa makes a similar point about Hawai'ian ki'i (ancestral figures): 'The Ki'i are portals connected to the Life force, where we can commune with our ancestors, our past and the future' (quoted in Tengan 2016, 63). The way in which this works is more like Karen Barad's surreal evocation of quantum entanglement than anything in classical space-time: 'mythic time / story time / inherited time / a time to be born / a time to die / out of time / short on time / experimental time / now / before / to come / . . . threaded through one another, knotted, spliced, fractured, each moment a hologram, but never whole' (Barad 2010).

67 This canoe prow has not yet been located. Another canoe prow, however, which may have also been sketched by Spöring in Tolaga Bay (see centre canoe, BM Add. MS 23920, f. 52b, notes in Joppien and Smith 1985, 175) appears very similar to a tauihu recently sold at Sotheby's and exhibited in 2014 in Frankfurt Museum.

    When he visited the exhibition, the Māori scholar Paul Tapsell realised that this canoe prow seemed oddly familiar (pers. comm. 2014). It reminded him of the prow on a canoe depicted in an old German engraving of a Māori war canoe at sea. It appears that this image was copied from an engraving published in Sydney Parkinson's journal of his voyage on board the *Endeavour* (see Joppien and Smith 1985, 201). This in turn was based on an imaginary pen and wash study of a canoe at sea (BM Add. MS 23920, f. 46), one of a series of such drawings completed by Parkinson on board the *Endeavour*. In all of these images, the canoe prow is dominated by the figure of an ancestral bird, wings furled, head originally fringed with feathers, as one can see from the sketch – surrounded by three large openwork double spirals. At this stage, however, it is not possible to authoritatively link these sketches from the voyage with this or other early surviving canoe prows from New Zealand.

68 For Parkinson's and Spöring's sketches of this canoe (BL Add. MS 23920, f. 52a–b) and a canoe prow seen in Tolaga Bay (BL Add. MS 23920, f. 77b; BM Prints and Drawings, folio 201, c. 5, no. 271), see Joppien and Smith 1985, 175–7.

69 For John Frederick Miller's 1771 sketch 'A Carved Plank from New Zealand' (BL Add. MS 23920, f. 75), see Joppien and Smith 1985, 216.

70 Tapsell 1997, 334.

71 Harms 2002, 435.

72 Anne Salmond 1991, 174.

73 Umbaur 1998.

74 See Scharrahs 2002.

75 Volker Harms (pers. comm. 2014). See a discussion of the emasculation of ancestral Kū figures in Hawai'i in Tengan 2016; in the case of this poupou, the head and arms of the ancestor were damaged.

76 Amiria Salmond [Henare] 2007. For references to the pioneering role of *Thinking Through Things*, see, for instance, Jensen 2016; Viveiros de Castro 2015; Vigh and Saudal 2014, 53–54, among others.

77 For detailed accounts of this series of these Te Aitanga-a-Hauiti projects, see Ngata, Ngata-Gibson and Amiria Salmond 2012; B. Lythberg, C. Hogsden and W. Ngata (2016). 'Relational systems and ancient futures: co-creating a digital contact network in theory and practice', in Engaging Heritage: Engaging Communities (Heritage Matters series), B. Onciul, S. Hawke and M. Stefano (eds). Boydell and Brewer. pp. 205–225.

78 Lythberg, Newell and Ngata 2015. In recent times, Paikea has also been brought to life in *The Whale Rider* (1987), a book by the Māori novelist Witi Ihimaera, and in a prize-winning feature film of the same name.

79 Amiria Salmond 2015e.

80 As one of the Te Ha trustees and one of their two representatives on the national co-ordinating committee, I am working with many others in planning the 2019 commemorations.

The following four chapters on Thomas Kendall and his relationship with Hongi Hika are dedicated to the historian Judith Binney, who wrote a ground-breaking account of Kendall's life (Binney 1968).

Chapter Three Ruatara's Dying

1 Praed 1824.

2 Also known as 'Oihi'.

3 For excellent accounts of the period between 1814 and 1840 in New Zealand, and the missionary enterprise, see Middleton 2014, which discusses the exchanges between missionaries and Māori in the Bay of Islands from a historical archaeological perspective; and O'Malley 2012 and Ballantyne 2015 from historical perspectives.

4 I was invited on this journey as patron of the contemporary sailing ship *R. Tucker Thompson*, and because I had written about the arrival of the first missionary party in an earlier book, *Between Worlds* (1997).

5 This paper, later published as Anne Salmond 1998, is updated and expanded in this chapter, based on much further reflection, reading and research.

6   Thomas Kendall to J. Pratt, 11 March 1815, HL MS 55/23, 1.

7   Kendall to Pratt, 11 March 1815, HL MS 55/23, 5; Kendall to Marsden, 6 July 1815, HL MS 55/12.

8   While Marsden was under the impression that Ruatara's father was Kaparu, recent research suggests he was the son of Te Aweawe, of Ngati Rahiri and Ngati Tautahi (Te Ara Encyclopedia of New Zealand www.teara.govt.nz/en/biographies/1r19/ruatara).

9   For a more detailed account of this era in New Zealand, including the attack on the *Boyd*, see Anne Salmond 1997.

10   For Kendall's accounts of the European depredations that led to the attack, see Kendall to Rev. B. Woodd, 28 December 1813, HL MS 54/23; and Kendall to J. Pratt, 25 March 1814, HL MS 54/35–36, 14–17.

11   For a recent, judicious weighing up of the evidence about responsibility for the attack on the *Boyd*, see Waitangi Tribunal 2014, 80–84.

12   Waitangi Tribunal 2014, 36.

13   Nicholas 1817 I, 51.

14   Genesis I:12, King James Bible.

15   For a discussion of 'dominion theology' and countervailing approaches in early nineteenth-century missionary accounts of Nature in New Zealand, see Beattie and Stenhouse 2007.

16   Observations and Journal of Rev. Samuel Marsden's First Visit to New Zealand, HL MS 176/1, 11.

17   Samuel Marsden in *Proceedings of the Church Missionary Society* 3, 1810, 123.

18   Marsden Papers, 25/10/1810, ML A1993, 3.

19   Rev. M. Atkinson to Marsden, 31 July 1802, Marsden Papers, Vol. 1, ML CYA 1992.

20   Waitangi Tribunal 2014, 26.

21   Dr John Mason Good to Marsden, 29 April 1810, Marsden Papers, Vol. 1, ML A1992, 485.

22   Nicholas 1817 I, 25.

23   Dr John Mason Good to Marsden, 29 April 1810, Marsden Papers, Vol. 1, ML A1992, 485.

24   Ibid.

25   Samuel Marsden quoted in *The Missionary Magazine for 1810*, 538–9.

26   15 November 1809, Some Account of New Zealand, obtained by the Rev. S. Marsden, from Duaterra, a young Chief of that Island; and communicated to a Friend in London, in *Proceedings of the Church Missionary Society for Africa and the East* III (1810–1812), 111–26.

27   Marsden to Pratt, 10 June 1813, HL MS 54/8.

28   Dr John Mason Good to Marsden, 16 August 1814, Marsden Papers, Vol. 1, ML CYA 1992.

29   Samuel Marsden, December 1814, Memoir of Duaterra, in McNab 1908 I, 344.

30   *Sydney Gazette and New South Wales Advertiser*, 11 December 1813, 1.

31   Quoted in Thomas Kendall, 1814, *A Journal of my proceedings during a Voyage from Port Jackson to New Zealand commencing March the 7th in the Year of our Lord 1814*, ML A1443; HL 54/66; also HL CMS 54m 312–13.

32   For Kendall's own account of his life until this point, see Kendall to B. Woodd, 23 January 1813, HL MS 54/1; and for his preparations for visiting New Zealand, including reading Savage's book 'An Account of the Island of New Zealand' (*Some Account of New Zealand, Particularly of the Bay of Islands and the Surrounding Country*, 1807) and his offer to learn Māori, see Kendall to Pratt, 20 October 1808, HL MS 498/11. For his account of his experiences since leaving England, including the loss of a baby, see Kendall to Woodd, 28 December 1813, HL MS 54/23, and Kendall to J. Pratt, 25 March 1814, HL MS 54/35–36.

33 For some background on John King and his wife Hannah, see Middleton 2008, 51–52.

34 Hall and King complained, for instance, that Marsden was making them work on his farm, along with his Māori visitors at Parramatta, instead of letting these men teach them the language (William Hall and John King to Pratt, 2 November 1811, University of Birmingham Special Collections, CMS C N/E 1-5, /4.

35 J. Pratt to Messrs. Hall and King, 16 December 1814, HL MS 54/78.

36 Reverend Samuel Marsden to Reverend Josiah Pratt, 15 November 1809, HL MS 498/233. For Pratt's reaction, see his confidential letter to Kendall, 18 March 1814, HL MS 54/31: 'Wm. Hall ought to have followed Mr. Marsden's directions, and to have gone thither [to New Zealand]. Do what you can, my good friend, to heal matters. They may think Mr. Marsden harsh with them: should even you think him so, you recollect . . . how needful that decisive character is to the discharge of his important duty. . . . I fear there is much obstinacy in William Hall, and perhaps not a little self-interest. . . . I fear the love which Hall and King once seemed to have for the heathen is gone!' Kendall shared his view of the matter with his friend Rev. Basil Woodd: 'Mr. Marsden has a great many enemies in this colony & too much business upon his hands' (Kendall to Woodd, 11 March 1814, HL MS 54/26, 4).

37 Kendall to Pratt, 6 September 1814, HL MS 54/66, 4.

38 Kendall to Pratt, 20 October 1808, HL MS 498/11.

39 Kendall to Woodd, 13 March 1814, HL MS 54/26.

40 Jane Kendall to Kendall, 19 March 1814, HL MS 54/43; Kendall to Pratt, 6 September 1814, HL MS 54/66, 9.

41 While Jones and Jenkins give this man's name as 'Tuai', Kendall generally called him 'To-i' or 'Toi', while Pratt called him 'Tooi'. In the letters he wrote in English, after he had worked with Professor Lee, Tui invariably signed his own name as 'Thomas Tooi' (Tui to Pratt, 17 September 1818, HL MS 56/96; Tui to Bickersteth, 14 December 1818, HL MS 56/112; Tui to Bickersteth, 8 January 1819, HL MS 56/127; Tui to Pratt, 12 July 1819, HL MS 56/179). Although in his first efforts to transcribe Māori, Kendall occasionally used 'i' to represent 'ai', he also used 'ay' for this sound. By 1818 both Kendall and Professor Lee in Cambridge were using a 'Continental' orthography for Māori vowels (close to Italian or Spanish), as did the missionary orthography for Tahitian. Thus, 'To-i' or 'Tooi' would equate to 'Tui' in Māori. Alison Jones now calls this man 'Tooi', using his own orthography (Jones pers. comm. 2016).

42 Muru had been ill-treated by the master of his ship, Captain Stuart, who did not give him enough food, and Kendall paid the five pounds that Muru owed to Stuart and persuaded the governor of Tasmania to give him permission to join the *Active* (Kendall to J. Pratt, 6 September 1814, HL MS 54/66, 6–7).

43 Kendall to Rev. B. Woodd, 11 March 1814, HL MS 54/26; Kendall to Pratt, 25 March 1814, HL MS 54/35–36, 6.

44 Ibid. See also the Māori vocabulary in Kendall to Pratt, 15 June 1814, HL MS 54/43.

45 Kendall to Woodd, 11 March 1814, HL MS 54/26, 3.

46 Kendall to Pratt, 25 March 1814, HL MS. 54/35–36: 'I have already collected several words chiefly from a Young Native whose name is To-i, and whom I have clothed, and fed for several weeks past, but he knows so little of English that I have not been able to make much progress, altho' he does all in his power to assist me.'

47 William Hall to Pratt, 15 June 1814, HL MS 54/44.

48 Kendall, 1814, Journal, MS 163, typescript, copy held in UOAL, 9.

49 For an excellent description of this pā, or fortified village, see Middleton 2014, 29–30.

50 Hall to the Secretary, 16 June 1814, ML MS 176a: 'From our knowledge of the language we are able to make him [Ruatara] understand us upon any common subject. We talked to them in their own language.'

51 William Hall to T. Smith, 4 October 1814, HL MS 54/69.

52 Kendall to J. Pratt, 6 September 1814, HL MS 54/66, 13–14.

53 Ibid.

54 Hall to Pratt, 15 June 1814, HL MS 54/44.

55 Kendall to Pratt, 15 June 1814, HL MS 54/43; also 6 September 1814, HL MS 54/66, 15, where this place is named as 'Motoo Terra' [Motutera?]. For a fine description of Māori gardening based at Rangihoua in this period, see Middleton 2014, 73–75.

56 Ibid., 15.

57 Kendall to J. Pratt, 6 September 1814, HL MS 54/66, 16.

58 Ibid.

59 Ibid., 17.

60 Ibid., 30. The *Active*'s crew were a polyglot lot, hailing from Ireland, Germany, America, Norway, Sweden, Hawai'i and Tahiti, with only two sailors from England.

61 Ibid., 18.

62 Ibid., 29.

63 Ibid., 24.

64 Ibid., 25.

65 Ibid., 28–29.

66 Ibid., 29–30.

67 Kendall, 1814, Journal, MS 163, typescript, copy held in UOAL, 25.

68 Pratt to Marsden, 18 August 1814, HL MS 54/66, 46.

69 Kendall to Pratt, 15 June 1814, HL MS 54/43, 13–20.

70 Kendall to Pratt, 3 October 1814, HL MS 54/51 and 54/67. The 'curious box' may be the 50-cm papahou treasure box AM 36720, 'owned by Rev Basil Woodd of the CMS before 1831', which Auckland Museum recently returned to Otago Museum (Neich 2014, 388). Many thanks to Rhys Richards for tracking down this taonga. See Kendall to Pratt, 19 October 1815, HL MS 55/22, 1 inquiring whether these artefacts had arrived safely; and reporting that he and his colleagues had sent further curiosities by the *Active* on 11 July 1815.

71 See Marsden to Pratt, 12 October 1814, HL MS 54/61 for a description of these objects, and a detailed account of how Hongi carved this self-portrait from the end of an old post with a modified iron hoop; along with a list of the rangatira, with a few details about each (e.g. 'Toohe – Brother to Coro Coro – a fine young man, of good parts, learns English very fast. His Father was Priest'). Also Dr John Mason Good to Samuel Marsden, 3 August 1815, Marsden Papers, Vol. 1, ML CYA 1992. This carving is now held in the collection of Auckland Museum. See Pratt to Kendall, 16 August 1815, HL MS 55/19, 1 for a letter of thanks, and asking for more 'curiosities' to be sent to the CMS.

72 Marsden to Pratt, 12 October 1814, HL MS 54/61, 2.

73 Rev. Samuel Marsden's Account of Proceedings to and from New Zealand, 20 June 1815, HL MS 55/4.

74 In a letter to Pratt on 12 October 1814, HL MS 54/61, Marsden listed the Māori who were living with him at Parramatta as 'Duaterra [Ruatara], is Chief, and possesses considerable influence; Shunghee [Hongi Hika] – Duaterra's uncle commands 17 Districts; Coro-coro [Korokoro], A war-like Chief on the opposite Shore in the Bay; Toohe [Tui] – Brother to Coro-coro, a fine young man, of good parts, learns English very fast, his Father was Priest; Parow – Related to old Tippahee, who was shot by Europeans; Repreero [Ripiro], Son of Shunghee – a fine boy; Warrakee – a common man; Mowhee – ditto, reads and writes the English Language; Pyhee – Servant to Duaterra; Tinnana – a fine young man, learning to make nails &c.; Whycatto – a common man.'

75 Marsden to Pratt, 30 September 1814, HL MS 54/55.

76 J.T. Campbell to S. Marsden, 17 November 1814, HL MS 54/71.

77 For Marsden's accounts of this voyage, see Marsden to Macquarie, 30 May 1815, HL
    MS 54/71; Samuel Marsden's Account of Proceedings, HL MS 55/4; Observations
    and Journal of Rev. Samuel Marsden's First Visit to New Zealand, HL MS 176/1.
78 Kendall to Pratt, 13 February 1815, HL MS 54/81.
79 Hall to Smith, 4 October 1814, HL MS 54/69.
80 Nicholas had come out from England as a settler on the *Earl Spencer* with Thomas
    Kendall, who regarded him as a friend (Kendall to Woodd, 13 February 1815, HL MS
    54/81).
81 Marsden to Pratt, 15 June 1815, HL MS 55/2; Marsden's Account of Proceedings,
    20 June 1815 HL MS 55/4.
82 Marsden to Pratt, 18 November 1814, HL MS 54/76.
83 Marsden's Account of Proceedings, 20 June 1815, HL MS 55/4.
84 Nicholas 1817 I, 23–24.
85 Marsden to Pratt, 26 October 1815, HL MS 55/34.
86 Ibid.
87 Marsden to Lachlan Macquarie, 30 May 1815, HL MS 54/71.
88 Nicholas 1817 I, 86–67.
89 Ibid., I, 184.
90 Ibid., I, 171–2.
91 Marsden's Account of Proceedings, 20 June 1815, HL MS 55/4, 24.
92 For example, Hongi Hika's sister Waitapu (Tapu water), who was killed defending her
    brother at the battle of Moremonui.
93 Marsden's Account of Proceedings, 20 June 1815, HL MS 55/4, 25.
94 Ibid., 26.
95 Ibid.
96 For a detailed and insightful analysis of this event, see Jones and Jenkins 2011,
    79–102.
97 See Middleton 2008, 39–64, and 2014 for accounts (based on archaeology, oral history
    and archival research) of the establishment of the Hohi mission.
98 See, for instance, Kendall to Pratt, 13 February 1815, in Kendall, 1814, Journal, MS
    163, typescript, copy held in UOAL; Kendall to Pratt, 6 November 1816, HL MS
    56/30.
99 Nicholas 1817 I, 274.
100 As Mason Durie has noted, 'Few tribes have . . . reduced [tikanga] to a simple set
    of rules. Instead the most appropriate tikanga for a group at a given time, and in
    response to a particular situation, is more likely to be determined by a process of
    consensus, reached over time and based both on tribal precedent and the exigencies of
    the moment.' Durie 1998, 3.
101 See Middleton 2014, 32–33 for an account of Te Puna at this time.
102 Many thanks to Angela Middleton for identifying this location.
103 Marsden's Account of Proceedings, 20 June 1815, HL MS 55/4, 30.
104 Ibid., 34.
105 Nicholas 1817 I, 346.
106 Ibid., 291.
107 Marsden's Account of Proceedings, 20 June 1815, HL MS 55/4.
108 Ibid.
109 Ibid.
110 John King to Rev. Daniel Wilson, 15 February 1815, quoted in Elder ed. 1934,
    57–58.
111 Kendall to Woodd, 13 February 1815, HL MS 54/81.
112 Nicholas 1817 I, 365–6.
113 Marsden's Account of Proceedings, 20 June 1815, HL MS 55/4, 80.
114 Ibid., 80–81.

115 Nicholas 1817 I, 395.
116 In Ludwig Binswanger, *Le Rêve et L'Existence* (Paris, Desclée de Brouwer, 1954), Introduction.
117 Observations and Journal of Rev. Samuel Marsden's First Visit to New Zealand, HL MS 176/1, 24.
118 Ibid., 25.
119 Nicholas 1817 II, 167.
120 Kendall to Pratt, 11 March 1815, HL MS 55/23, 4.
121 Ibid., 5.
122 Nicholas 1817 II, 178; see also Marsden's Account of Proceedings, 20 June 1815, HL MS 55/4.
123 Nicholas 1817 II, 179–80.
124 Ibid., 191.
125 Middleton 2014, 30.
126 Marsden to Macquarie, 30 May 1815, HL MS 54/71.
127 Nicholas 1817 II, 194.
128 Anne Salmond 1991c, Waitangi Tribunal D17.
129 Marsden's Account of Proceedings, 20 June 1815, HL MS 55/4.
130 Middleton 2014, 33.
131 Marsden to Pratt, 13 June 1815, HL MS 54/87:

> 'Revd Sir,
> I have sent you a Box containing Various articles principally wearing apparel Such as are manufactured and used by the natives of New Zealand. No. 1 named Neck'ho is worn by the Chiefs & the Ladies as a mantle, No. 2 [ditto], No. 3 is worn by the Common people universally, and in the nights and rainy weather the Chiefs also wear them. Some of them are exceeding large, and nearly cover them from head to Foot, and in the evening when they encamp they have the appearance of a number of Bee hives. If it should rain they draw them over their heads and when it is fine weather they put their heads out like a land Tortoise out of its shell. No. 5 ka'ka'how is worn by the Chiefs and their wives as a Great Coat in England. The thick Canvas [flax] mat is worn in the Field of Battle. [Four] of them will resist any Spear, and in action are Worn by the Chiefs, as a Coat of Mail. Before they put them on they wet them, in Order that they may resist the force of the spear more effectually. I recommend you to put the thick mat into water, and you will see an instantaneous effect produced. The Canvas [flax] will be rendered stiffer and more like a board, which appears to be the peculiar quality of the New Zealand Flax. . . . There is also in the case a stone To'kee or Adze, such as are used by the Chiefs in making their canoes, for the want [absence] of edge tools.[In the second list No. 6, 7 and 8 were cloaks Ra'pa, Pa'o'kow and Ka'ka'how on a lower list.] No. 9 named Ha'ha is mearly [sic] an ornament worn by the Chiefs, round their necks and is considered valuable by them. [Evidently the Hee'tik'kee, as are No. 11 and 12 named on the lower list.] No. 11 named Hee'tik'kee is worn as a belt by the Chiefs. [Actually a patu, named in the second list as a Pa'too'too (No. 10).] No. 14 War'ra' is a sleeping mat. No. 15 Shun'na is an upper Garment worn by the wives of the Chiefs. There is also a small wood funnel in the Box, which is used by the natives in putting their Oil into calabashes [, and a few fish hooks]. I shall also send a few spear [sic] in charge of Mr Wilkinson[,] Master of the Sydney Packet[,] and shall had [sic: add?] to your Collection of curiosities every opportunity that occurs.
> I have the honour to be[,] Revd. Sir[,]
> Your most Obedient Servant, Saml. Marsden.'

132 Kendall to Pratt, 11 March 1815, HL MS 55/23, 5; Kendall to Marsden, 6 July 1815, HL MS 55/12.

133 For a detailed analysis of the Te Puna site, see Middleton 2008, 119–51.
134 For an account of Ruatara's death, see Kendall to Pratt, 11 March 1815, HL MS 55/23; Kendall to Marsden, 6 July 1815, HL MS 55/12.
135 Kaingaroa was tapu for three days, Hongi for two days, Rakau for three days, Kanae ten days and Taapopo two months (Kendall to Pratt, 11 March 1815, HL MS 55/23, 6).
136 Ibid.; and Kendall to Marsden, 5 July 1815, HL MS 55/12.
137 Kendall to Pratt, 11 March 1815, HL MS 55/23, 10.
138 Marsden quoted in Nicholas 1817 II, 394.

Chapter Four Hongi Hika and Thomas Kendall

1 Erima Henare in Waitangi Tribunal 2014, 99.
2 Nicholas 1817 I, 27.
3 For a biography of Hongi Hika, see Cloher 2003. For excellent accounts of the intricate relations between different kin groups in the Bay during this period, see Sissons, Wihongi and Hohepa 1987 and Ballara 2003, 169–205.
4 Her uterus was cut out and her womb filled with burning sand, a terrible assault on her whare tangata (house of people), representing her family's mana and descent line (Kelly 1938, 178–9). See also S. Percy Smith 1910, 31–45; R.D. Crosby 1999, 46–49; and Ballara 2003, 182–6 for accounts of this battle.
5 For a fine and pioneering study of Kendall's life, see Binney 1968.
6 Kendall to Pratt, 11 March 1815, HL MS 55/23, 19.
7 King to Rev. Daniel Wilson, 6 July 1815, in Elder ed. 1934, 99; and ibid., in Elder ed. 1934, 111: 'They want to instruct us how to treat our children, to cook, and many other things, saying "It is very good in New Zealand", so that if we were in single families among them we could be of no use to them, for they are like bears when vexed. We should be in too much fear of them. Not only that, but it would be too strong a temptation for them; they would plunder us. No doubt they would kill us.'
8 King to Wilson, 6 July 1815, in Elder ed. 1934, 111; see also Kendall to Pratt, 11 March 1815, HL MS 55/23, 20–22; Kendall to Pratt, 18 December 1818, HL MS 56/117.
9 Kendall to Pratt, 11 March 1815, HL MS 55/23, 23–27.
10 King to Pratt, 9 July 1815, HL MS 55/27, 8.
11 Kendall to Pratt, 19 October 1815, HL MS 55/22, 4.
12 Kendall to Pratt, 19 January 1816, HL MS 55/45; Kendall to Pratt, 23 January 1816, HL MS 55/50; Kendall to Pratt, 6 November 1816, HL MS 56/30.
13 Proceedings of Magistrates' Court, 12 April 1815, ML MS 55/28; Marsden to Pratt, 15 June 1815, HL MS 55/3, 2–5.
14 Kendall to Pratt, 19 October 1815, HL MS 55/22, 4–5.
15 King to Pratt, 9 July 1815, HL MS 55/27, 8–9.
16 Kendall to Pratt, HL MS 55/23, 30–36; see also Kendall to Pratt, 20 January 1816, HL MS 55/46; Kendall to Pratt, 22 January 1816, HL MS 55/48.
17 Hall to Pratt, 17 June 1815, HL MS 54/80, 2. For a detailed account of Hall's building activities, see Middleton 2014, 44.
18 Hall to Pratt, 24 October 1815, HL MS 55/24; Hall to Pratt, 12 January 1816, HL MS 55/43; Kendall to Pratt, 22 January 1816, HL MS 55/48.
19 Kendall to Pratt, 11 March 1815, HL MS 55/23, 14; Kendall to Marsden, 6 July 1815, HL MS 55/12; Kendall to Marsden, 25 July 1817, in Elder ed. 1934, 139: 'They cannot endure the thought that they should lose the property which has descended to them from their forefathers and be driven into the bush, as they saw is the case of the natives of New South Wales.'
20 Hall to Pratt, 16 January 1816, HL MS 55/44; Kendall to Marsden, 6 July 1815, HL

MS 55/12, 22–23; Kendall to Captain Graham, 29 January 1816, HL MS 55/56.

21 Hall to Pratt, 16 January 1816, HL MS 55/44, 1; Kendall to Captain Graham, 29 January 1816, HL MS 55/56; Hall to Pratt, 22 August 1816, HL MS 56/22.

22 Many thanks to Angela Middleton for helping me to understand the relation between particular place names at that time and locations in the Bay of Islands.

23 Hall to Pratt, 22 August 1816, HL MS 56/22, 4.

24 Middleton 2014, 44.

25 Kendall, School List with General Remarks, April 1817, HL MS 56/56.

26 Kendall to Rev. Basil Woodd, 10 December 1818, *The Missionary Register 1820*, 308.

27 Kendall to Marsden, 27 October 1815, HL MS 55/37, 1–2; Kendall to Pratt, 20 January 1816, HL MS 55/46.

28 Kendall to Pratt, 6 November 1816, HL MS 56/30.

29 See Pratt to Kendall, 7 June 1817, HL MS 56/17.

30 Kendall to Pratt, 19 October 1815, HL MS 55/22, 6–7.

31 Kendall to Pratt, 19 January 1816, HL MS 55/45, 1–3 describes an attack on his house and himself by sailors from the *Phoenix*, Captain Parker. See also Kendall to Pratt, 6 November 1816, HL MS 56/30, 3.

32 King to Pratt, 25 January 1816, HL MS 55/53.

33 Ironically, Kendall had been very supportive of Stockwell, seeking a pardon for him on grounds of good behaviour and commenting that 'his services were very acceptable to Mrs. Kendall during my absence in the last voyage of the *Active*' (Kendall to Pratt, 15 May 1813, HL MS 54/5; Kendall to Woodd, 13 February 1815, HL MS 54/81; Kendall to Pratt, 3 July 1815, HL MS 55/13; Kendall to Pratt, 19 October 1815, HL MS 55/22, 10). It was not until 6 March 1818 that Kendall asked Marsden to have Stockwell removed from his house, adding that 'Mrs Kendall is averse to taking any more persons in to the house of any kind' (Kendall to Marsden, 6 March 1818, HL MS 56/73).

34 William Hall, 3 June 1816, ATL Micro-MS 0853, 9–11.

35 Ibid.

36 Kendall to Pratt, 15 May 1813, HL MS 54/5.

37 Kendall to Woodd, 16 October 1816, HL MS 56/24; Hall to Pratt, 22 August 1816, MS 56/22, 5.

38 See HL MS 56/23 for a listing of the pupils at Kendall's school, and Kendall to Rev. Basil Woodd, 16 October 1816, HL MS 56/24 and MS 56/25 for accounts of how the school was established, and requests for various items. See also lists from January 1817 in HL MS 59/39 and MS 59/60.

39 Kendall to Woodd, 16 October 1816, HL MS 56/24, 1–3. See also Kendall to Rev. Joshua Mann, 14 July 1817, HL MS 56/59: 'My wild little pupils were all noise and play during the first four months. We could scarcely hear them read for their incessant shouting, singing and dancing. The first month they attempted to repeat their lessons in the schoolhouse very well, but we soon had to follow them to a short distance into the bushes. I had no command over them, having at that time neither provisions nor rewards to give them.'

40 Middleton 2014, 46.

41 Foucault has written eloquently about the origins of this kind of physical discipline and constraint in Europe in Foucault 1995; see also May 2006.

42 King to Pratt, 23 July 1817, HL MS 56/61.

43 Kendall, School List with General Remarks, 4 April 1817, HL MS 56/56. See also William Hall to Pratt, 8 November 1818, HL MS 56/104: 'In respect to the language we can speak it sufficiently well to enable us to buy or sell anything to them or get our work done, in short we can speak pretty fluently upon any common subject. But as to writing it grammatically, or translating any part of the Scriptures, we are utterly unequal to this work. We wish very much to have a Minister or two amongst us.

Classically educated, and the more living languages they understand they will be the better qualified for their work'; and King to Pratt, 1 December 1818, HL MS 56/101: 'this is the great obstacle – not knowing the Language – and this will take a person of good abilities some years to learn'.

44 Kendall, General Remarks, January 1817, HL MS 56/39.

45 Sabean, Teuscher and Mathieu eds 2007, 16.

46 Kendall to Pratt, 6 November 1816, HL MS 56/30; see also Kendall to Rev. Joshua Mann, 14 July 1817, HL MS 56/59: 'My new situation has exposed me to various temptations and troubles, and the remains of a stubborn perverse nature from which I groan to be delivered . . .'

47 Kendall to Woodd, 1 February 1817, HL MS 56/40; Kendall, School List with General Remarks, 4 April 1817, HL MS 56/56; Kendall to Mann, 14 July 1817, HL MS 56/59.

48 Kendall to Pratt, 10 June 1817, HL MS 56/58.

49 Kendall to Mann, 14 July 1817, HL MS 56/59.

50 Kendall to Pratt, 10 June 1817, HL MS 56/58.

51 Kendall to Hall, 18 December 1819, HL MS 56/117.

52 For an account of this campaign, as told by Te Morenga and Hongi to Samuel Marsden, see Samuel Marsden's Journal of Proceedings at New Zealand from July 29 to October 19, 1819, HL MS 177/1, 46–48.

53 Cloher 2003, 63.

54 Kendall to Rev. Basil Woodd, 10 December 1818, HL MS 56/103.

55 Kendall to Pratt, 8 December 1818, HL MS 56/210.

56 Kendall to Pratt, 14 December 1818, HL MS 56/113; for the gift of a war trumpet, see Kendall to Pratt and Bickersteth, 15 May 1819, HL MS 56/155. Hall also sent Pratt a waka huia or carved feather box (Hall to Pratt, 8 November 1818, HL MS 56/104). On 4 June 1819 Pratt wrote back to Hall, saying that '[t]he curiosities which you sent by the "Catherine" are not yet passed through the Custom House. We are always thankful for such things, particularly such as explains any of the superstitions of the Natives' (HL MS 56/163). On 16 August 1819 Pratt wrote again, thanking Kendall for the curiosities, the specimens of Hongi's writing, and especially the self-portrait he had carved: 'Shunghee's head, sent us by Mr. Marsden, attracts great attention. Pray continue to send all that you can procure, for our Museum, and give us a description of their use' (HL MS 55/19).

57 Kendall to Pratt, 14 December 1818, HL MS 56/113, 5–6; Kendall to Pratt, 17 May 1819, HL MS 56/159; Kendall to Pratt, 20 May 1819, HL MS 56/162; and Pratt to Kendall, 20 July 1819, HL MS 56/184, when he told Kendall that the CMS had submitted his Catechism to Professor Lee at Cambridge, who had suggested some improvements. See Lachlan Paterson's interesting paper about missionary efforts to transcribe Māori (Paterson 2014).

58 Josiah Pratt to John King, March 1818, quoted in Middleton 2008, 63.

59 Rev. D. Wilson to John King, November 1816, Transcripts of Selected Items from the Four Volumes of Marsden Correspondence, 1814–1815, HL MS 0057a.

60 Kendall to Pratt, 29 July 1817, HL MS 56/64.

61 Pratt and Bickersteth to Kendall, 12 March 1818, HL MS 56/76.

62 Kendall to Pratt, 21 December 1818, HL MS 56/122, 1–2. Although Pratt wrote a letter on 4 June 1819 trying to console Kendall for these trials (Pratt to Kendall, 4 June 1819, HL MS 56/163, and Pratt to Kendall, 20 July 1819, HL MS 56/184), this would not have reached him for months.

63 In early 1818, for instance, Tete, the husband of Hongi's eldest daughter, and two of Kendall's pupils, Tawha, a son of Te Pahi, and Taungahuru, the son of the rangatira Okira, all embarked on the Active to visit Port Jackson (Kendall to Marsden, 3 March 1818, HL MS 56/72).

64 Marsden to Pratt, 24 February 1819, HL MS 56/136, 5–6.
65 Missionaries to Marsden, 5 November 1818, HL MS 57/10.
66 Kendall to Marsden, 25 July 1817, HL MS 56/63.
67 Agreement of settlers at Bay of Islands, 30 March 1819, HL MS 56/146.
68 Hall, Journal, 17 July 1819, in Elder ed. 1934, 221.
69 Ibid., 30 August 1819, 27.
70 Kendall to Marsden, 21 April 1819, HL MS 56/150.
71 For Marsden's accounts of these journeys, see Samuel Marsden's Journal of
    Proceedings at New Zealand from July 29 to October 19, 1819, HL MS 177/1; and
    Continuation of Samuel Marsden's Second Voyage to New Zealand in 1819, HL MS
    176/3.
72 Marsden's Journal of Proceedings at New Zealand from July 29 to October 19, 1819,
    13 August 1819, HL MS 177/1, 4.
73 Ibid., 9.
74 Ibid., 18 August 1819, 8.
75 See ibid., 19 October 1819, 101–2, when these complaints were repeated.
76 Marsden's Journal of Proceedings at New Zealand from July 29 to October 19, 1819,
    HL MS 177/1, 28 September 1819, 22.
77 Ibid., 4 September 1819, 30.
78 Ibid., 13 September 1819, 40–41.
79 Ibid., 15 September 1819, 48–49.
80 See also Marsden's later discussions with Murupaenga and Te Morenga in Waitemata,
    18 August 1820.
81 Marsden's Journal of Proceedings at New Zealand from July 29 to October 19, 1819,
    HL MS 177/1, 118–19. Or as Thomas McDonnell, who lived in the Hokianga in the
    1830s, was told: 'If [a man] won't kill his enemy when he catches him, what is the use
    of going to fight? A man goes to fish for whapuku. Well, he catches a fish. What does
    he do with it? Does he let it go again? That would be a foolish thing! No, for if he did,
    he would be laughed at, and people would say he was mad. So he eats it. What else did
    he catch it for? And so with fighting.' Petrie 2015, 43.
82 Marsden's Journal of Proceedings at New Zealand from July 29 to October 19, 1819,
    HL MS 177/1, 118.
83 Ibid., 29 September 1819, 64.
84 For example, John King, 15 August 1822, in Elder ed. 1934, 255: 'When an accident
    befalls them, they in general ascribe it to some fault of their own respecting their
    departed friends, whom they call atua – those who die on shore, of the gods of the
    land. Those who are drowned, their spirits are called Taneewha [taniwha] or atua, or
    gods of the sea, of the water, etc. The departed spirits are all the gods they know of as
    far as I can learn. When a great chief dieth he becometh a great god.'
85 For an exploration of vitalist ideas in contemporary as well as historic modernist
    science, see Normandin and Wolf eds 2013.
86 Marsden's Journal of Proceedings at New Zealand from July 29 to October 19, 1819,
    9 November 1819, HL MS 177/1, 124–5.
87 Ibid., 8 September 1819, 38.
88 Cruise 1824, 10 May 1820, 126–7.
89 Samuel Marsden's Journal from February 13 to November 25, 1820, 4 May 1820, HL
    MS 177/2, 8.
90 Cruise 1824, 21 July 1820, 179.
91 Marsden's Journal of Proceedings at New Zealand from July 29 to October 19, 1819,
    9 November 1819, HL MS 177/1, 125.
92 Ibid., 6 October 1819, 81.
93 Marsden's Journal from February 13 to November 25, 1820, 18 August 1820, HL MS
    177/2, 67.

94 Marsden's Journal of Proceedings at New Zealand from July 29 to October 19, 7 October 1819, HL MS 177/1, 84.
95 Ibid., 22 October 1819, 117.
96 Ibid., 9 September 1819, 107–8.
97 Ibid., 90.
98 Ibid., 2 October 1819, 74.
99 Ibid., 2 October, 4 October 1819.
100 Ibid., 22 October 1819, 111.
101 Ibid., 112.
102 See Marsden's conversation with Murupaenga, Te Morenga and other chiefs in Waitemata, Marsden's Journal from February 13 to November 25, 1820, 18 August 1820, HL MS 177/2, 77.
103 Marsden in Elder ed. 1932, 152.
104 Middleton 2014, 88.
105 Butler, 6 December 1819, in Barton ed. 1927, 54–55.
106 Ibid., 7 December 1819, 55.
107 Ibid., 27 December 1819, 62.
108 Ibid., 6 November 1819, 46.
109 Ibid., 18 November 1820, 106.
110 Ibid., 8 November 1819, 48.
111 Ibid., 18 November 1820, 106.
112 Ibid., 6 November 1819, 47–48.
113 Ibid., 15 May 1820, 80.
114 Woodd to Pratt, 10 November 1820, HL MS 498/99, 1.
115 Butler, 14 February 1820, in Barton ed. 1927, 70.
116 Marsden to Pratt, 7 February 1820, in Elder ed. 1932, 329–30.
117 Marsden to Secretary, *Dromedary*, 29 February 1820, in Elder ed. 1932, 155.
118 Kendall to Marsden, n.d., and Marsden to Butler, 12 January 1820, in Elder ed. 1934, 345, 347. See also Middleton 2014, 102.
119 Marsden to Kendall, 26 April 1820, HL MS 57/22; Marsden to Secretary, 24 April 1820, in Elder ed. 1932, 159; McRae in Chapman ed. 1928, 18.
120 Many thanks to Angela Middleton for pointing out that this was Thomas Hansen junior, not senior (see McNab 1908, 542).
121 Richards 2015.
122 Commissioner Bigge Inquiry, in McNab 1908, 501.
123 Butler, 24 February 1820, in Barton ed. 1927, 73.
124 Pratt and Bickersteth to Kendall, 12 March 1818, in Elder ed. 1934, 142.
125 Kendall had already sent his manuscript, 'The New Zealander's First Book', to the CMS, who forwarded this to Professor Lee to help him in his work on the Māori language.
126 Kendall to Jane Kendall, 27 May 1820, MS 71/8.
127 *Church Missionary Register* 1820, 326–7.
128 Ibid., 5 April 1820, 143.
129 Cruise 1824, 27 February 1820, 19–20.
130 McRae in Chapman ed. 1928, 15.

Chapter Five How D'ye Do, Mr. King Shunghee?

1 Parts of this chapter were delivered as a Winter Lecture at the University of Auckland and in the third Rutherford Lecture in Wellington 2014. For images of Carlton House at this time see http://the-lothians.blogspot.co.nz/2013/04/5-carlton-house-london.

2   *The Sydney Gazette and New South Wales Advertiser*, 16 June 1821.
3   Ibid.
4   Perkin 1989, 35–40.
5   Samuel Marsden's Journal of Proceedings at New Zealand from July 29 to October 19, 1819, 20 September 1819, HL MS 177/1, 54.
6   http://the-lothians.blogspot.co.nz/2013/04/5-carlton-house-london.
7   For accounts of this meeting between King George IV and Hongi and Waikato, see *Cambridge Chronicle and Journal*, 24 November 1820, 3; *The Sydney Gazette and New South Wales Advertiser*, 2 June 1821, 16 June 1821.
8   Te Rangikaheke trans. Curnow 2012, 13–28.
9   Anne Salmond 1997, 214.
10 See also Elder ed. 1932, 20 August 1820, 291, when Murupaenga and other chiefs at Kaipara gave Marsden a similar explanation: 'All the souls of the New Zealanders went when they died into a cave at the North Cape, and from thence descended into the sea to the next world.'
11 Anne Salmond 1997, 217.
12 Ibid., 230.
13 Marsden's Journal of Proceedings at New Zealand from July 29 to October 19, 1819, 27 August 1819, HL MS 177/1, 17–18.
14 *Sydney Gazette and New South Wales Advertiser*, 26 May 1805, 1.
15 Tapsell 1997. For a comparison with Samoan gift exchange, see Tcherkezoff 2012.
16 Anne Salmond 1997, 350.
17 Ibid., 351.
18 Ibid., 354.
19 Ibid., 360.
20 Boris Gorelik, pers. comm; and see Gorelik ed. 2015.
21 Cruise 1824, 20 February 1820, 13. This medal was described by Captain Vasily Golovnin, when he met Maa-Tara in Simon's Bay, Cape of Good Hope, on his way back to New Zealand in 1808.
22 For a discussion of the cognate Hawai'ian term 'aha, which brings together similar ideas to those in kaha in Māori, see Tengan 2016, 69.
23 For Kendall's account of a meeting between one of the whalers involved in this attack, Captain Parker of the *Phoenix*, and local Māori, who gave him a detailed account of what happened, see Kendall to Marsden, 6 July 1815, HL MS 55/12. See also Kendall to Pratt, 11 March 1815, HL MS 55/23, 9, reporting that according to the Whangaroa people, when they were killing the *Boyd*'s sailors, Te Pahi put his hand over his eyes and wept; Marsden's Account of Proceedings to and from New Zealand, June 1815, 20 June 1815, HL MS 55/4, who said that, according to Ruatara and Hongi, after the attack on the *Boyd*, Te Pahi rescued five sailors from the rigging of the ship, who were forcibly taken from him and killed when they went ashore; and that according to the Whangaroa people who had attacked the ship, 'Tippahee had no hand in this melancholy event. It was wholly their own act and deed'; and Kendall to Marsden, 6 July 1815, HL MS 55/12. For a detailed account of the attack on the *Boyd* and its aftermath, see Anne Salmond 1997, 368–97; see also Waitangi Tribunal 2014, 80–84.
24 *Sydney Gazette*, 1 August, 21 August 1819.
25 Cruise 1824, 37–38; McRae 1928, 12–17.
26 Kendall to Pratt, 3 July 1820, *New Zealander*, ML MS 0071/009.
27 Minutes of the Committee, 14 August 1820, quoted in Butler ed. Barton 1927, 89–90.
28 Kendall to the Secretary, 14 August 1820, Church Missionary House, Kendall Correspondence, HL.
29 Kendall to Pratt, 3 July 1820, *New Zealander*, ML MS 0071/009.
30 *Church Missionary Register*, 1820, 327–8.

31 Taylor 1855, 310.
32 Lee 1896.
33 Indeed, universities in New Zealand are known in Māori as whare wānanga.
34 Strachan 1870, 101–4.
35 Kendall and Lee 1820.
36 As Kendall wrote to Pratt, 8 September 1820, : 'I have 46 more pages ready which
    Professor Lee will examine today. Professor Lee wishes me to write a Vocabulary of the
    Language after I have done the Grammar and this will take me at least a month. It would
    not be right for me to give up my work now, especially as Professor Lee encourages me
    to go on, and takes so much pains in instructing me how to arrange my materials.'
37 Norwich to Pratt, 1 October 1820, HL MS 498/93; Kendall to Pratt, 4 October 1814,
    HL MS 498/94.
38 *The Sydney Gazette and New South Wales Advertiser*, 16 June 1821; Kendall to Pratt,
    16 October 1820, HL MS 498/96.
39 Information from Hugh Rihari, a Bay of Islands tribal expert (Angela Middleton,
    pers. comm).
40 *The Sydney Gazette and New South Wales Advertiser*, 2 June 1821.
41 Waitangi Tribunal 2014, 100.
42 Pratt to Marsden, 20 December 1820, in Elder ed. 1934, 268. See also Cloher 2003.
43 Te Rangikaheke trans. Curnow 2012, 18, 25.
44 Kendall to Pratt, 18 December 1820, HL MS 498/105; and Kendall to Pratt,
    22 December 1820, HL MS 498/106.
45 Pratt to Marsden, 20 December 1820, in Elder ed. 1934, 270.
46 Trans. Anne Salmond.
47 For Marsden's accounts of his remarkable journeys on this occasion, see Samuel
    Marsden's Journal from February 13 to November 25, 1820, HL MS 177/2; and
    Particulars of Samuel Marsden's Third Voyage to New Zealand, HL MS 176/4.
48 McRae ed. Chapman 1928, 23.
49 Marsden's Journal from February 13 to November 25, 1820, HL MS 177/2, 41–47.
50 Ibid., 55–58.
51 Ibid., 63.
52 S. Percy Smith 1910, 138–9.
53 Marsden's Journal from February 13 to November 25, 1820, HL MS 177/2, 79–80.
54 Ibid., 77.
55 Ibid., 80–83.
56 Ibid., 91.
57 Marsden ed. Elder 1932, 331.
58 Ibid., 335–6.
59 Waitangi Tribunal 2014, 52–53.
60 See Graham 1923, 94: 'It was in Australia that Te Hinaki and his son Penehe-reti
    met Hongi, who showed him his guns brought from England, and asked him, "*Mo
    hea ou pu?*" ("For what object are your guns?") Hongi replied, "*Mou aku pu.*" ("For
    you are my guns.") Then Te Hinaki knew that Hongi contemplated revenge for past
    wars, and for the Ngati-paoa raid against Ngapuhi when the great war canoe "Kahu-
    mauroa" was captured'; and S. Percy Smith 1899b, 201–2: '[Hongi-Hika] exhibited
    to his guests all his guns and powder brought from England, arranging the former in
    rows, and giving each its name, saying: – "*E mara ma!* O friends! O Te Horeta! and Te
    Hinaki! Behold! this gun is 'Te Wai-whariki,' this is 'Kaikai-a-tekaroro,' this is 'Wai-
    kohu,' this is 'Te Ringahuru-huru,' this is 'Mahurangi,'" thus naming all the battles in
    which Nga-Puhi had been defeated.'
61 S. Percy Smith 1899b, 201–2.
62 This account by Wharepoaka, one of Hongi's lieutenants, was given to Marsden on
    28 August 1823, HL MS 177/4, 32–34.

Chapter Six Decline and Fall

1   Macaulay 1840.
2   John Butler, 27 July, 18 August 1821, in Barton ed. 1927, 149.
3   Butler in Barton ed. 1927, 154.
4   Ibid., 22, 23 August 1821, 168.
5   Kendall to Marsden, 27 September 1821, in Elder ed. 1934, 173–4.
6   Butler, 23 August 1821, in Barton ed. 1927, 165–7.
7   Butler ibid., 443.
8   Butler, 7 April 1821, ibid., 120.
9   Kendall to Pratt, 12 November 1821, in Elder ed. 1934, 180.
10   For a detailed account of this campaign and how Hongi became involved in it, as told by Te Rakau's son Wharepoaka to Samuel Marsden, see Samuel Marsden's Personal Copy of the Journal of his Fourth Visit to New Zealand July 29 to November 30, 1823, HL MS 177/4, 32–39.
11   Wharepoaka to Samuel Marsden, 28 August 1823, in Marsden's Personal Copy of the Journal of his Fourth Visit to New Zealand July 29 to November 30, 1823, HL MS 177/4, 32–39, 356–358; Butler to Bickersteth, 216. See also S. Percy Smith 1900; Graham 1923.
12   S. Percy Smith 1910, 191–201; R.D. Crosby 1999, 104–5; Ballara 2003, 219–20.
13   White 1888, 158.
14   S. Percy Smith 1910, 200.
15   Francis Hall to CMS, 18 January 1822, ATL Micro-MS-Coll-04-052.
16   James Shepherd, Journal, 16 January 1822, ATL Micro-MS-Coll-04-058 [docs, vol. 2, 859]. For commentary on the impact of Māori ways of being on various missionaries, including the temptation to engage in sexual liaisons with Māori women, see Wanhalla 2008; Ballantyne 2015.
17   Francis Hall, Journal, 4 February 1822, CMS CN 049.
18   Marsden to Kendall, 17 January 1822, ML MS 0071/024, ARC 0031.
19   Kendall to Marsden, 26 February 1822, HL MS 57/74, 1–3.
20   S. Percy Smith 1910, 225–33.
21   White 1888, Vol. V, Ch. XII, 169.
22   R.D. Crosby 1999, 108–13; Ballara 2003, 220–22.
23   Francis Hall to Kendall, 3 April 1822, ML MS 0071/027.
24   William Hall to Pratt, 6 April 1822, HL MS 67/10.
25   Samuel Leigh to Secretaries of Wesleyan Missionary Society, 6 April 1822, CMS CN/M2, 324; Leigh to Marsden, 4 April 1822, HL MS 57/77.
26   Francis Hall to Marsden, 6 April 1822, HL MS 57/69.
27   Samuel Leigh to Marsden, 4 April 1822, HL MS 57/76.
28   Marsden to Kendall, 11 June 1822, received in Bay of Islands, 17 July 1822. See also Marsden to Pratt, 11 June 1822, HL MS 57/80, informing him of his actions in regard to Kendall.
29   Thomas Surfleet Kendall's Diary, 2 October 1822, ML MS 0071/0151.
30   Kendall to Jane Kendall, 30 July 1822, ML MS 0071/029.
31   See Marsden's account of Kendall's offences in his letter to Rev. Pratt of the Church Missionary Society, Marsden to Pratt, 7 September 1822, HL MS 57/83.
32   John Butler to Marsden, 8 January 1822, *Westmoreland*, Sydney Cove.
33   Francis Hall to Marsden, 6 April 1822, HL MS 57/69.
34   Kendall to Butler, 28 September 1822, in Barton ed. 1927, 211–12.
35   Butler, 29 September 1822, in Barton ed. 1927, 241.
36   Minutes of Special Meeting, 5 November 1822, CN/M2, 255–8.
37   Butler, 6–7 February 1823, in Barton ed. 1927, 257–8.
38   Kendall to John Eyre, 27 December 1822, HL MS 71/40.

39 See Te Morenga and Hongi to Samuel Marsden, in Marsden's Personal Copy of the Journal of his Fourth Visit to New Zealand July 29 to November 30, 1823, HL MS 177/4, 95–99, for an account of this battle.

40 According to Gilbert Mair, quoted by S. Percy Smith 1910, 254: 'Hongi Hika gave him his helmet, a Morian cap he had received from George IV on his visit to England in 1820, and which Te Awaawa's bullet had damaged. This helmet subsequently fell into the hands of an old Ngati-Parua chief named Tahuri-o-rangi, who showed it to me at Te Waerenga in 1867, but it was buried in the old man's house at his death in 1873.' See also Butler, 26 May 1823, in Barton ed. 1927, 274 for a reference to this incident.

41 For an account of this campaign as told by Te Morenga and Hongi to Samuel Marsden, see Marsden's Personal Copy of the Journal of his Fourth Visit to New Zealand July 29 to November 30, 1823, HL MS 177/4; Anon., 1962, How Aokapurangi Saved Her People, Te Ao Hou 41, 13–14.

42 Kendall to Pratt, 3 July 1820; Binney 1968, 132.

43 Kendall to Pratt, 11 April 1823, HL MS 71/50; see also Kendall to Pratt, 5 April 1823, ML MS 0071/048; Kendall to Pratt, 11 April 1823, ML MS 0071/050.

44 Kendall to Hassall, 9 April 1823, HL MS 71/49.

45 Marsden to Pratt, 19 April 1823, in Elder ed. 1934, 198–9.

46 Sydney Gazette, 1 April 1824; Binney 1968, fn. 133.

47 Kendall to Pratt, 3 June 1823, ML MS 0071/054.

48 Marsden to Pratt, 12 June 1823, in Elder ed. 1934, 200.

49 For the published letters and journals of Henry and Marianne Williams, see Carleton 1874; Rogers ed. 1961; Fitzgerald ed. 2004 and Fitzgerald ed. 2011.

50 For Marsden's accounts of this visit, see Marsden's Personal Copy of the Journal of his Fourth Visit to New Zealand July 29 to November 30, 1823, HL MS 177/4; Samuel Marsden's Journal from July 2 to November 1, 1823, HL MS 177/3; and Particulars of Samuel Marsden's Fifth [sixth] Voyage to New Zealand, 1830, and Observations on his Fourth Visit, written in 1836, HL MS 176/5.

51 Henry Williams to Pratt, 10 November 1823, HL MS 498/305; Henry Williams, 24 October 1823, in Fitzgerald ed. 2011, 27.

52 This was Kanae's only son, Harowe Morunga (Harold Morpeth) (information from Hugh Rihari; Angela Middleton, pers. comm).

53 Marianne Williams, 7 August 1823, in Fitzgerald ed. 2004, 54–56.

54 Marsden's Personal Copy of the Journal of his Fourth Visit to New Zealand July 29 to November 30, 1823, HL MS 177/4, 8.

55 Kendall to Marsden, 9 August 1823, HL MS 57/98.

56 The sequence of events as recorded by Marsden and Kendall differ – here I follow Kendall's version. Marsden suggests that he did not tell Kendall that he was dismissed from the mission until 12 August; but in fact he told Kendall on the 8th that he had to leave New Zealand, and Kendall wrote back a letter of protest about this on the 9th. Marsden's account is written to put his actions in the best possible light. For Marsden's letter of dismissal, see Marsden to Kendall, 9 August 1823, HL MS 57/97.

57 Marsden's Personal Copy of the Journal of his Fourth Visit to New Zealand July 29 to November 30, 1823, 12 August 1823, HL MS 177/4, 14.

58 Ibid., 15.

59 Kendall to Pratt, 13 August 1823, ML MS 0071/060.

60 Kendall to Marsden, 14 August 1823, a and b, ML MS 0071/062; Marsden to Pratt, 15 August 1823, ML 204.

61 Marsden's Personal Copy of the Journal of his Fourth Visit to New Zealand July 29 to November 30, 1823, 19 August 1823, HL MS 177/4, 20.

62 Ibid., 21.

63 Ibid., 23 August 1823, 23–24.
64 Ibid., 27 August 1823, 29–31.
65 Ibid., 21 August 1823, 22.
66 McRae ed. Chapman 1928, 14–15.
67 Marsden's Personal Copy of the Journal of his Fourth Visit to New Zealand July 29 to November 30, 1823, HL MS 177/4, 40.
68 John King, 3 May 1823, in Elder ed. 1934, 255.
69 Many thanks to Angela Middleton for clarifying this relationship.
70 Marsden's Personal Copy of the Journal of his Fourth Visit to New Zealand July 29 to November 30, 1823, HL MS 177/4, 48.
71 John Butler and Samuel Marsden to John King, James Kemp, and The Missionaries & Lay Settlers, 5 November 1823, ML MS 0057/101, 9.
72 Samuel Leigh to Pratt, 16 October 1823, HL MS 498/304, 4.
73 James Kemp, Journal, 9 October 1823, APL MS 60.
74 Marsden's Personal Copy of the Journal of his Fourth Visit to New Zealand July 29 to November 30, 1823, HL MS 177/4, 65.
75 See Marianne Williams' account of the shipwreck, 16 October 1823, in Fitzgerald ed. 2004, 65–66.
76 TVNZ News, 7 November 2002: tvnz.co.nz/content/145351/2556418/article.html.
77 Corbett 2002.
78 See a Landcare Research report on this controversy (Harmsworth 2005). As Barclay reports (Barclay 2005, 146), while he was filming the *Tangata Whenua* series in 1974, the master carver Piri Poutapu told the interviewer Michael King on camera that the last time he had seen a large congregation of taniwha was when King Mahuta died, in the Waikato River: 'There were all forms of taniwha came up the river, swimming against the current. One was a shark. One was a stingray. One was a snapper without a tail. Others were logs.' Other Tainui elders also talked on film about seeing taniwha, and one old woman told King that her brother had been taken by a taniwha as retribution for wrongdoing. The whakataukī for their ancestral river is '*Waikato taniwha rau, he piko he taniwha, he piko he taniwha*' – 'Waikato of a hundred taniwha'.
79 Barclay 2005, 146–8.
80 Resource Management Act 1991, Section 7: 'In achieving the purpose of this Act, all persons exercising functions and powers under it, in relation to managing the use, development, and protection of natural and physical resources, shall have particular regard to– (a) kaitiakitanga: (aa) the ethic of stewardship.'
    For a commentary, see Culbertson 2015; see also Strang 2010.
81 Marsden's Personal Copy of the Journal of his Fourth Visit to New Zealand July 29 to November 30, 1823, HL MS 177/4, 67–68; Marsden to Kendall, 9 October 1823, HL MS 57/98.
82 Marsden's Personal Copy of the Journal of his Fourth Visit to New Zealand July 29 to November 30, 1823, HL MS 177/4, 76–77.
83 Ibid., 94.
84 Many thanks to Angela Middleton for pointing out the location of this house.
85 Marsden's Personal Copy of the Journal of his Fourth Visit to New Zealand July 29 to November 30, 1823, HL MS 177/4, 84.
86 Ibid., 93.
87 James Kemp, Journal, 31 October 1823, APL MS 60.
88 Henry Williams, 13 November 1823, in Fitzgerald ed. 2011, 29.
89 Marianne Williams, 6 October 1823, in Fitzgerald ed. 2004, 68.
90 Marsden's Personal Copy of the Journal of his Fourth Visit to New Zealand July 29 to November 30, 1823, HL MS 177/4, 114.
91 Ibid., 125. Henry was thrilled with his son, calling him 'the handsomest boy I ever saw' (Henry Williams, 13 November 1823, in Fitzgerald ed. 2011, 29).

92 Henry Williams to Pratt, 10 November 1823, HL MS 498/305.

93 Butler, 5 November 1823, in Barton ed. 1927, 315.

94 Marsden's Personal Copy of the Journal of his Fourth Visit to New Zealand July 29 to November 30, 1823, HL MS 177/4, 120–1.

95 Butler, 3 November 1823, in Barton ed. 1927, 304–5.

96 Ibid., 320.

97 Marsden to Hongi, 11 November 1823, in Marsden ed. Elder 1932, 336.

98 Marsden to Pratt, 20 December 1823, HL MS 57/105, 2.

99 Marsden to Pratt, 22 December 1823, HL MS 57/106. During this visit, Marsden asked various of the missionaries to answer questions about Māori cannibalism in writing. When James Kemp, for example, was asked, 'What acts of the New Zealanders in eating human flesh having fallen under your observation?' he answered, 'I once observed some human flesh cooked and prepared to eat.' In reply to the question, 'On which occasion were those acts perpetrated?', he wrote, 'On their return from war they killed many of their slaves as a satisfaction for their friends that were killed in battle.' When asked, 'Is the Cannibalism of the New Zealanders confined to their prisoners of war?' he replied, 'I believe it is' (James Kemp, Correspondence, APL MS 59, Folder 1, Letter 2).

100 Marsden to Pratt, 20 December 1823, HL MS 498/251.

101 James Kemp, Journal, 27 November 1823, HL MS 70.

102 Ibid.

103 James Shepherd, Journal, 23 March 1824, ATL aMS-1798.

104 George Clarke, 30 May 1824, HL MS 60/90, 13–15.

105 Dumont D'Urville, quoted in Binney 1967, 129.

106 Kendall to Bickersteth, 27 July 1824, ML MS 0071/066, and Kendall to Pratt, 27 July 1824, ML MS 0071/064. For exceptional insights into Kendall's account of Māori cosmology, based on a close study of early Māori manuscripts, see Thornton 1987, and also Binney 1967, 1980.

107 Best 1976, 357.

108 George Clarke, 1 July 1824, HL MS 60/90, 23–24.

109 Marianne Williams, 3 July 1824, in Fitzgerald ed. 2004, 86; in Fitzgerald ed. 2011, 43–44.

110 James Kemp, Journal, 27 October, 1 November 1824, APL MS 60.

111 Ibid., 1–3 November 1824.

112 See also his contrite letter to Professor Lee, ML MS 0071/067.

113 Thomas Kendall, *Sydney Gazette*, 8 January 1831.

114 See Judith Binney's commentary on this letter in Binney 1986.

115 Marsden to Coates, 10 September 1832, HL MS 57/210.

116 R.D. Crosby 1999, 155–7.

117 James Kemp, 14 July 1825, HL MS 70.

118 Marsden, HL MS 176/5, 50 – written in 1830.

119 James Kemp, 8 September 1825, HL MS 70.

120 Richard Davis, 15 November 1825, HL MS 66/10; Conversations of the missionaries with the chiefs 'Shunghee, Rewa, Titori, Hihi, Uduroa, Pakida, Tenana', at Kerikeri, 15 November 1825, CN/M4, 48.

121 James Kemp, HL MS 70.

122 Marsden, HL MS 176/5, 48 – written in 1830.

123 Marianne Williams in Fitzgerald ed. 2004, 126–8; Jane Williams ibid., 130–1; William Williams ibid., 131–2.

124 R.D. Crosby 1999, 175.

125 Earle 1832, 65–66.

126 Ibid., 67–71.

127 Marsden, HL MS 176/5, 50 – written in 1830.

128 H. Williams, 11 April 1827, in Rogers ed. 1961, 52.
129 T. Kendall to J. Pratt, 25 March 1814, HL MS 54/35–36, 16: 'Coweetee is another friend of ours, he also has lived some time with Mr. Hall by desire of Mr. Marsden.'
130 E. Henare in Waitangi Tribunal 2014, 108.
131 James Stack in Fitzgerald ed. 2011, 99.
132 Earle 1832, 63.
133 George Clarke in Fitzgerald ed. 2011, 96. From research carried out by Angela Middleton, it appears that Hariata later acted as her husband Hone Heke's scribe, and may in fact have written the letters attributed to him (Middleton, pers. comm.).
134 See, for instance, Lloyd 2010, 207.
135 See Anne Salmond and Amiria Salmond 2010, 304.
136 For a fine study of the complexities of 'ontological crossings' between Vanuatu people and missionaries, which discusses 'that mixture of articulated juxtaposition and movement, exchange and hostility, which saturates those most vibrant and volatile of cosmological entanglements', and the 'reciprocal mutability of socio-political and sacred power in contexts of religious conversion', see J. Taylor 2010, and also Laugrand 2012 for an account of recent inquiries into some of the complexities of conversion processes.
137 Marsden's Journal of Proceedings at New Zealand from July 29 to October 19, 1819, HL MS 177/1, 96: 'When I was in the different districts and wished to note anything down, I had to steal away into the thicket . . . while I minuted down any circumstance or conversation that tended to throw any light upon their customs, manners or religion, but it was seldom that I could steal away unobserved, and that account was obliged often to write in the midst of a crowd.'
138 Kendall to Pratt, 1 December 1818, in Elder ed. 1934, 147.
139 Kendall to Pratt, 11 April 1823, ML MS 0071/051, Collected papers of and relating to Rev. Thomas Kendall (ARC-0031).
140 This idea of a layered universe is also reflected in a diagram drawn by the Tainui scholarly expert Pei Te Hurinui Jones, which shows the cosmos as a stepped structure, very like the ahu or 'altar' on marae in the Society Islands, this time with twelve levels.
141 White I 1887, endpaper.
142 Thornton 1989, 159.
143 Ibid., 150.
144 Kendall to Rev. Joshua Mann, 14 July 1817, HL MS 56/59. He added: 'When the clouds are beautifully chequered, the atua above, it is supposed, is planting sweet potatoes. When these are planted in the ground the planters dress themselves in their best raiment and say that as atuas on earth, they are imitating the atua in heaven. The head, being the seat of the atua, is sacred.'
145 See Viveiros de Castro for an exploration of a statement by a Piro woman that European and Piro bodies are 'different'. He concludes that the realities implied by Piro conceptions of the body may be unlike anything capable of being experienced by European bodies (Viveiros de Castro 2013, 497–9).

Chapter Seven The Spring of the World

1 E. Henare in Waitangi Tribunal 2010, 35.
2 K. Taurua in Waitangi Tribunal 2010, 15.
3 Salmond 1992.
4 For an insightful reflection on similar kinds of entanglements between Native Americans and government agencies, see Noble 2007.
5 Hohepa 2011, 138.
6 Ibid., 172.

7   E. Henare in Waitangi Tribunal 2014, 29.
8   Hohepa 2011, 147.
9   Edwards 2010, 54.
10 Hohepa 2011, 172.
11 Fitzgerald ed. 2004, 15.
12 Henry Williams ibid., 20.
13 Ibid., 57–58.
14 Marianne Williams, Journal, Auckland War Memorial Museum Library MS, 7 August 1823, 59–60.
15 Henry Williams to Pratt, 10 November 1823, HL MS 498/305.
16 Rountree 2000, 56.
17 Marianne Williams, 7 January 1824, in Fitzgerald ed. 2004, 70.
18 Ibid., 12 January 1824, 73.
19 Marianne Williams, Journal, Auckland War Memorial Museum Library MS, 10 August 1823.
20 Henry Williams in Fitzgerald ed. 2011, 45.
21 Marianne Williams, 12 January 1824, in Fitzgerald ed. 2004, 75.
22 Ibid., 76.
23 Ibid., 78.
24 Ibid., 1 October 1824, 89–92. See also James Kemp, Journal, 1 October 1824, APL MS 60, for an account of this quarrel.
25 Marianne Williams, 7 October 1824, in Fitzgerald ed. 2004, 94; 7 October 1824, in Fitzgerald ed. 2011, 49–50.
26 Carleton 1874, 48; Marianne Williams in Fitzgerald ed. 2011, 48 – although according to James Kemp, on 13 October when King retrieved a goat that a rangatira had plundered from him and brought it to Kerikeri, the rangatira seized a goat in reprisal, and when Shepherd tried to stop him, hit him twice with a stick and 'behaved very rude and impotent'; and on 22 October when George Clarke tried to protect a woman who had quarrelled with her husband, her husband tried to strike him. He commented, 'I see the natives are very ready to make any little excuse so that they might find an opportunity to plunder' (James Kemp, Journal, APL MS 60).
27 Marianne Williams, 16 April 1824, in Fitzgerald ed. 2004, 84.
28 Henry Williams, 26 July 1824, in Fitzgerald ed. 2011, 45.
29 Ibid., 19 September 1824, 46.
30 Ibid., 24 June 1825, 57.
31 Henry Williams in Carleton 1874, 53; Henry Williams to Edward Marsh, 12 July 1826, in Fitzgerald ed. 2011, 74–75.
32 Marianne Williams, 24 January 1826, in Fitzgerald ed. 2011, 97–98.
33 Henry Williams, 1 April 1826, ibid., 70.
34 Ibid.
35 Marianne Williams, 19 March 1828, in Fitzgerald ed. 2004, 143.
36 Henry Williams in Fitzgerald ed. 2011, 102–7.
37 George Clarke ibid., 113; Marianne Williams, 24 December 1829, in Fitzgerald ed. 2004, 165.
38 Marianne Williams, 16 February 1830, in Fitzgerald ed. 2011, 124–5.
39 Marsden, HL MS 176/5, 3 – written in 1830.
40 Ibid., 6.
41 Although Marsden says that about 20 were killed and wounded, he had not yet arrived in the Bay; see ibid., 6; see also accounts in Fitzgerald ed. 2004, 177–80, and Fitzgerald ed. 2011, 128–34.
42 Marianne Williams in Fitzgerald ed. 2004, 180.
43 For Marsden's account of this visit, see HL MS 176/5, 1–26 – written in 1830.

44   Henry Williams, 8 March 1830, in Fitzgerald ed. 2011, 131.
45   Henry Williams in Carleton 1874, 80.
46   Ibid., 84; Waitangi Tribunal 2014, 109–10.
47   S. Percy Smith 1910, 427–35.
48   Ibid.
49   Anne Salmond 1991, 221.
50   Marianne Williams, 3 October 1831, in Fitzgerald ed. 2004, 202; 3 October 1831, in Fitzgerald ed. 2011, 154–55.
51   Henry Williams, 1 October 1831, in Fitzgerald ed. 2004, 203.
52   My own (fairly free) translation from the text in Māori.
53   During his visit to the Bay of Islands in 1830, Samuel Marsden had rejoiced to see many such signs of conversion; see HL MS 176/5 – written in 1830.
54   'New Zealand', *Sydney Gazette and New South Wales Advertiser*, 8 December 1831, 2.
55   Henry Williams to Rev. E.G. Marsh, 4 September 1831, in Carleton 1874, 89.
56   Henry Williams, 27 August 1830, in Fitzgerald ed. 2011, 137.
57   Henry Williams, 29 January 1829, in Fitzgerald ed. 2004, 158.
58   Marianne Williams, 23 December 1835, ibid., 226.
59   Henry Williams in Rogers ed. 1961, 200; 31 October 1831, in Fitzgerald ed. 2011, 159–60.
60   Ibid., 160.
61   Henry Williams, 27 August 1830, ibid., 137.
62   Henry Williams, January 1832, ibid., 164.
63   Henry Williams, 6 January 1832, ibid., 166.
64   Fairburn, South Auckland Research Centre MNP MS 176, 5 January 1832, 10.
65   Ibid., 168.
66   Ibid., 171.
67   Fairburn, South Auckland Research Centre MNP MS 176, 27 January 1832, 14.
68   Henry Williams in Rogers ed. 1961, 226.
69   Henry Williams, 4 March 1832, in Fitzgerald ed. 2011, 172. See also Best 1976 I, 284–93 for accounts of such niu rituals.
70   Best 1976, 297.
71   Fairburn, South Auckland Research Centre MNP MS 176, 8 March 1832, 17.
72   Henry Williams, 10 March 1832, in Fitzgerald ed. 2011, 175.
73   Fairburn, South Auckland Research Centre MNP MS 176, 8 March 1832, 18.
74   Henry Williams, 13 March 1832, in Fitzgerald ed. 2011, 177.
75   Henry Williams in Rogers ed. 1961, 237.
76   Fairburn, South Auckland Research Centre MNP MS 176, 31 March 1832, 19.
77   Ibid., 20.
78   For a graphic account of this storm, see Fairburn, South Auckland Research Centre MNP MS 176, 6–7 April 1832, 22–23.
79   Ibid., 248, and Marsden, HL MS 176/5, 33 – written in 1830. See also Williams' later report, which blamed Waikato and Wharepoaka for spreading these rumours: Henry Williams in Rogers ed. 1961, 261.
80   For the origin of the Papahurihia [layer/earth turned upside down] movement, see Fairburn, South Auckland Research Centre MNP MS 176, 31 May 1832, 29.
81   Henry Williams in Rogers ed. 1961, 251.
82   Ibid., 254.
83   Henry Williams, 17 March 1833, in Fitzgerald ed. 2011, 200.
84   Henry Williams in Rogers ed. 1961, 306.
85   Ibid., 308.
86   Ibid., 309.
87   McNab 1908 I, 594.
88   New South Wales Act 4 Geo IV c.96.

89 Busby 1832, 62–63.
90 Ibid., 69.
91 Busby to his brother Alexander Busby, 10 August 1831, Box 7, Vol. 1, MS 46, AWMML. See this collection of typescripts of Busby's letters in AWMML.
92 Cited in Waitangi Tribunal 2014, 118.
93 Ibid.
94 Richard Bourke to James Busby, 13 April 1833, GBPP, 1840, Vol. 33 [238], 4.
95 Henry Williams in Rogers ed. 1961, 311–12.
96 Anne Salmond, free translation.
97 For a detailed, well researched, if early account of James Busby's trials and tribulations in New Zealand, see Ramsden 1942.
98 Henry Williams in Rogers ed. 1961, 313.
99 *Sydney Gazette and New South Wales Advertiser*, 2 July 1833.
100 Anne Salmond, free translation.
101 Cited in Waitangi Tribunal 2014, 73 (emphasis in original).
102 Busby to his brother Alexander, 22 June 1833, AWMML MS 46.
103 Henry Williams, 14 July 1833, in Fitzgerald ed. 2011, 209.
104 Fitzgerald ed. 2011, 329.
105 Henry Williams, 8 December 1830, ibid., 141.
106 Henry Williams, 14 February 1834, ibid., 230.
107 Henry Williams, 23 September 1833, in Fitzgerald ed. 2004, 212; and 1 December 1834, ibid., 217.
108 Hohepa in Te Kawariki 2012, 56.
109 Baron Karl von Huegel, Diary, trans. Reuel Lochore, ATL, 90-389-6/18, 432–38.
110 Marianne Williams, 30 April 1834, in Fitzgerald ed. 2004, 215; Henry Williams to Dandeson Coates, CMS, 1 May 1834, in Fitzgerald ed. 2011, 233.
111 W. Yate, Journal and diary, ATL MS-2544, June 1834, 116–117.
112 Quoted in P. Parkinson 2012, 60.
113 For an oral account from Kiritapu about Titore's suit of armour and other gifts, see Kelly 1938, 168–9. See also Parkinson 2012 for a detailed account of these gift exchanges.
114 Henry Williams in Rogers ed. 1961, 396.
115 Pomare to Busby, n.d., BR 1/1, 192, NA.
116 Orange 1987, 16–17.
117 For an interesting discussion of Papahurihia, see Waitangi Tribunal 2014, 30.
118 Henry Williams, 8 November 1833, in Fitzgerald ed. 2011, 216.
119 Henry Williams in Rogers ed. 1961, 425.
120 Henry Williams, 21 March 1835, in Fitzgerald ed. 2011, 254.
121 Busby detested McDonnell, describing him to his brother Alexander as 'that mad knave' (Busby to Alexander Busby, 9 May 1836, AWMML MS 46).
122 For a leading study of He Whakaputanga, the Declaration of Independence, see M. Henare 2003.
123 Busby to Bourke, 10 October 1835 (no. 68), qMS 0344, ATL, Wellington.
124 Busby 1835a.
125 Busby 1835b.
126 See Te Kawariki 2012, 96–101, for extensive argument about this point.
127 Marsden, cited in Waitangi Tribunal 2014, 14.
128 James Busby to his brother Alexander, 10 December 1835, AWMML MS 46.
129 Busby to Haddington, cited in Waitangi Tribunal 2014, 162.
130 Hohepa in Te Kawariki 2012, 31.
131 Waitangi Tribunal 2014, 173–8.

Chapter Eight **Our Words Will Sink Like a Stone**

1   Waitangi Tribunal 2014, 6. Parts of this chapter were drafted in Anne Salmond 2012a, and in Anne Salmond 2010a, my evidence on Te Tiriti to the Waitangi Tribunal.
2   Shawcross 1966, 350.
3   Waitangi Tribunal 2014, 6.
4   Ibid., 477.
5   A. Ferguson ed. Oz-Salzberger 1995; Kames 1807.
6   Blackstone 1765–1769, *Commentaries* II, 3.
7   Ibid., II, 2.
8   Moloney 2001.
9   Blackstone 1765–1769, *Commentaries* I, 39, 47.
10 See commentary in Waitangi Tribunal 2014, 42–43.
11 For detailed accounts of Busby's negotiations for land at Waitangi and elsewhere, and his speculative attempts to establish a township named 'Victoria' near the residency, with a bank and an 'Institution for the support and education of half-caste children' in the Bay of Islands, see his letters to Alexander Busby in AWMML MS 46.
12 For a fine survey of these exchanges, see Waitangi Tribunal 2014, Ch. 6.
13 Darwin 1959, 409.
14 Ibid.
15 Ibid., 410.
16 *Report of the Parliamentary Select Committee on Aboriginal Tribes (British Settlements)* 1837 (London, William Ball), 23–24.
17 Ibid., 136.
18 Wakefield and Ward 1837, 42.
19 Aboriginal Protection Society 1846.
20 Busby to Bourke, 18 January 1836 and 26 January 1836, ATL qMS 0345, 59–61.
21 Busby to Alexander Busby, 9 August 1836, AWMML MS 46.
22 Marsden, March 1837, in Fitzgerald ed. 2004, 235; see also Middleton 2014, 162–3.
23 Busby to the Colonial Secretary of New South Wales, 16 June 1837, in Beecham 1838, 33. See also Henry Williams in Fitzgerald ed. 2004, 235–6.
24 Busby to the Colonial Secretary of New South Wales, 16 June 1837, in Beecham 1838, 36.
25 Ibid., 42: '[I]t seems . . . consistent with the arrangements of Divine Providence that an infant people which, by its intercourse with a powerful state, is subject to all the injury and injustice which weakness and ignorance must suffer by being thrown into a competition of interests with knowledge and power, should as naturally fall under and be not less entitled to the protection of the powerful state than the weakness of infancy and childhood is entitled to the protection of those who were the instruments of bringing it into an existence which requires such protection.'
26 Henry Williams, 29 May 1837, in Fitzgerald ed. 2011, 278.
27 Hobson to Bourke, 8 August 1837, in Beecham 1838, 29.
28 See Busby's scathing comments on Hobson's 'factory' proposal and Bourke's support of it in a letter to his brother Alexander, 20 November 1838, AWMML MS 46, which ends: 'So much for Capt Hobson – What an edifying example it is of official confidence – that the Capt of a ship of war who had not been as many weeks in this country as I had been years, should be thought a more fit person to report the result of his observations on this country and to offer suggestions upon the subject, than a Functionary sent out in the King's name expressly for that duty.'
29 Bourke to Lord Glenelg, 9 September 1837, in Beecham 1838, 25.
30 Ibid., 5.
31 Hinds ibid., 12.
32 Henry Williams, 11 January 1838, in Fitzgerald ed. 2004, 244.

33 Henry Williams, 11 January 1838, in Fitzgerald ed. 2011, 283.
34 Henare [Salmond], Holbraad and Wastell eds 2007a, 10, 11.
35 Rewa to McDonnell, quoted in Waitangi Tribunal 2014, 215.
36 Shawcross 1966, 357–9.
37 Henry Williams in Rogers ed. 1961, 278.
38 Lord Normanby to Hobson, Instructions, 14, 15 August 1839, CO 209/4, 251–82.
39 Busby to Alexander Busby, 29 July 1839, AWMML MS 46.
40 William Williams, 13 November 1839, in Fitzgerald ed. 2011, 286.
41 Henry Williams, 7 November 1839, in Fitzgerald ed. 2011, 288.
42 Henry Williams in Rogers ed. 1961, 454. Henry Williams, 20 November 1839, in Fitzgerald ed. 2011, 292.
43 Henry Williams in Fitzgerald ed. 2011, 297.
44 Henry Williams, 18 January 1839, in Fitzgerald ed. 2011, 311.
45 William Broughton, Bishop of Australia, to Henry Williams, Sydney, 10 January 1840, in Fitzgerald ed. 2011, 314.
46 Sorrenson 1991, 16–17.
47 Henry Williams in Fitzgerald ed. 2011, 247.
48 Henry Williams ibid., 316–17.
49 Henry frequently lamented his inability to master the Māori language, compared with his brother William's sophisticated mastery and the fluency of his son Edward. See, for example, Henry Williams, 25 April 1827, in Fitzgerald ed. 2011, 90: 'I shall never be an orator among the natives. It is with much difficulty I speak to them in my own way, particularly to a number. Words which I know will fly away when I particularly want them. William will be a proficient. He appears to have no impediment. Edward speaks, and so will all the children.'
50 Statement of generic issues: www.naumaiplace.com/site/whakapara/file/page/statement-of-generic-issues-10-02-2012.pdf.
51 Rev. Richard Taylor, Journal, 1840, AWMML typescript, 188.
52 Colenso 1890, 13.
53 Rev. Richard Taylor, quoted in Buick 1914, 152.
54 Colenso 1890, 13.
55 Colenso, Waitangi, 5 February 1840, ATL MS-Papers-003103. See also Captain Robertson's report of Hobson's speech: 'His Excellency began by stating that England was, thank God, a free country. Englishmen could go to any part of the world they chose; many of them had come to settle here. Her Majesty always ready to protect, had also the power to restrain her subjects; and Her Majesty wished the Chiefs of New Zealand to protect as well as to restrain them, – he was sent by Her Majesty to request that object publicly; they themselves had often requested Her Majesty to extend her protection to them; what he did was open and above board; he did not go to one Chief in preference to another; he came to treat with all openly. He would give them time to consider the proposals he had come to offer; that what he was sent to do was expressly for their own good – and Her Majesty now offers them her protection by this Treaty; it was unnecessary to say more, but he would read it to them' (*Sydney Herald*, 21 February 1840).
56 Henry Williams in Fitzgerald ed. 2011, 317.
57 In this account, the tribal affiliations of the different speakers are those given by Colenso in his original manuscript account.
58 Sissons, Wi Hongi and Hohepa 1987, 37, 38, 49, 131.
59 Colenso, Waitangi, 5 February 1840, ATL MS-Papers-003103.
60 Sissons, Wi Hongi and Hohepa 1987, 33, 34, 48, 49, 131, 134, 137, 140, 141, 144, 145, 147, 149.
61 Lee 1983, 87.
62 Ibid., 151.

63 Binney 2004, 222.
64 Colenso 1890, 25.
65 Ibid., 18–19.
66 W. Hobson to Governor Gipps, *Herald*, Bay of Islands, 5 February 1840, GBPP
    311, 8–9, Encl. 3 in No. 4, Despatch #40/8; see also Rev. Henry Williams to Coates,
    13 February 1840, CMS Letters Received 1838–1840, CN/M12, 15–18, ATL Micro
    collection 4, Reel 33: 'Many of the Chiefs hung back for some time, having been
    told that they would be sent on to the roads to break stones, as the convicts of Port
    Jackson, and to labour as they do'; and Captain Robertson, *Sydney Herald*, 21 February
    1840: 'They had been told that if they signed the Treaty they would become slaves,
    hewers of wood and drawers of water, and be driven to break stones on the road.'
67 Colenso 1890, 19.
68 Ibid., 19.
69 Ibid., 20.
70 Ibid., 22.
71 Ibid.
72 Ibid., 22–23.
73 Ibid., 23.
74 Ibid.
75 According to Richard Cruise: 'In size and strength he seemed to surpass all his
    countrymen; though far from being corpulent, there was not an armchair in the
    country in which he could sit, and in Shunghie's tribe he was much looked up to for
    his bravery and skill in leading warriors to battle' (Cruise 1824, 65).
76 Colenso 1890, 24–25.
77 Ibid., 25.
78 Colenso, Waitangi, 5 February 1840, ATL. Note, however, that a number of other
    observers thought that Heke spoke against the governor. Rev. Ironside, for instance:
    '[Heke] was violent in his harangue against Captain Hobson, vociferating repeatedly
    in his native style, "*Haere e hoki*" (Go, return.). Tamati Waaka came to me and said
    his heart was *pouri* (grieved) with Heke's violence, and the way Captain Hobson was
    being treated. "Well," I said, "if you think so, say so!" whereupon Tamati sprang up
    and made his speech' (Ironside in Buick 1914, 116). This account is supported by
    comments written by William Baker on a (presumably printed) copy of Te Tiriti:
    'I remember distinctly being present during the whole of the meeting; that Hone
    Heke Pokai was very violent in his language, though he is not mentioned by Captain
    Hobson. . . . A war of words ensued between Tamati Waaka Nene, who came in at this
    crisis, and Heke, the result of which was that Waaka "removed the temporary feeling
    that had been created."' (Baker ibid., 116).
79 Ibid.; Colenso 1890, 26–27. Hobson's gloss on Nene's speech, which differs signifi-
    cantly from Colenso's account, is also worth quoting in full: 'At the first pause Neni
    came forward and spoke with a degree of natural eloquence that surprised all the
    Europeans, and evidently turned aside the temporary feeling that had been created.
    He first addressed himself to his countrymen, desiring them to reflect on their own
    condition, to recollect how much the character of the New Zealanders had been
    exalted by their intercourse with Europeans, and how impossible it was for them
    to govern themselves without frequent wars and bloodshed; and he concluded his
    harangue by strenuously advising them to receive us and to place confidence in our
    promises. He then turned to me and said, "You must be our father! You must not allow
    us to become slaves! You must preserve our customs, and never permit our lands to be
    wrested from us!"' (Hobson to Gipps, 5–6 February 1840, GBPP 311, 8–9, Encl. 3 in
    No. 4, Despatch #40/8). These divergences between Hobson's and Colenso's accounts
    of Nene's speech are another useful reminder of the futility of expecting Colenso's
    manuscript or published accounts to literally replicate what was said at Waitangi.

80   John Hobbs, Journal, 20 November 1827, AWMML MS 144.
81   Patuone, in Departmental of Internal Affairs 1991, 98; see also Patuone website, http://patuone.com.
82   Colenso 1890, 27.
83   Bishop Pompallier to Captain Lavau, July 1840, quoted in Low 1990, 192.
84   Orange 1987, 56.
85   Colenso 1890, 27–28.
86   Felton Mathew, Diary, Te Papa Tongarewa Museum of New Zealand, CA000373.
87   Colenso 1890, 29.
88   Henry Williams in Carleton 1874, 14.
89   Henry Williams in Fitzgerald ed. 2011, 318.
90   Colenso 1890, 32–33.
91   Sadler 2015.
92   As Williams recorded, Hone Heke was the first to sign the Treaty, and he urged the others to sign as well (Henry Williams in Fitzgerald ed. 2011, 317).
93   Edwards 2010, 6–7.
94   Henare in Waitangi Tribunal 2014, 447.
95   Ibid., 482.
96   Ibid., 526–7.
97   Ibid.
98   Fletcher 2015, thesis abstract.
99   Bennett and Quilliam 2014.
100 As an example of the challenges this poses to iwi, see Sadler and Mackinnon 2014 for an account of the difficulties in setting up post-settlement structures that reflect and respect tikanga Māori.

PART TWO: RIVERS, LAND, SEA AND PEOPLE

Chapter Nine Tears of Rangi: Awa / Rivers

1   Parts of this chapter were delivered as the Fourth Rutherford Lecture in the Whanganui Opera House (broadcast by Radio New Zealand) and in a Rivers Workshop at Koroniti marae on the Whanganui River in 2014, and drafted as a paper in *Hau: Journal of Ethnographic Theory* (Salmond 2014a).
2   See de la Cadena 2010; and a recent legal judgment in Ecuador (where the Constitution gives rights to Nature – Pacha Mama – as a living being), requiring a provincial government to remedy damage to the Vicabama River on these grounds (*Wheeler et al v Director de la Procuraduria General del Estado en Loja*, www.earthlawcenter.org/ literature/).
3   Tupua is something extraordinary, from the ancestral realm (for a discussion of tupua, see Tcherkezoff 2008, 141–4).
4   Literally white mānuka, the timber from which eel weirs across the river were built.
5   Literally, the autumn migration of eels.
6   In Māori: *te tino rangatiratanga o o ratou wenua o ratou kainga me o ratou taonga katoa* (see Anne Salmond 2010a and b for commentary); see also Waitangi Tribunal 2014, which reports on the history and import of the Declaration of Independence by Northern iwi in 1835, and the Treaty of Waitangi in 1840.
7   Contrary (at least in part) to Povinelli's 1999 argument that in late modern liberal imaginings, the 'state apparatuses … do not need to experience the fundamental alterity of indigenous discourses, practices or their potentially radical challenge to the nation' (Povinelli 1999, 581). Her more recent writings about 'indigenous critical theory' (or theory/practice), however, are more open to the possibility of such

irruptions: 'the ends of indigenous critical theory are to make this spacing [between law and justice?] practical in a world in such a way that they make the content of statements and practices practical and sane rather than impractical and mad – or if not mad, then mythological' (Povinelli 2012, 27–29).

8   Newshub, Key: No one owns the wind, www.newshub.co.nz/politics/key-no-one-owns-the-wind-2012091011, 10 September 2012.

9   See Muru-Lanning 2016, 130–8 on such strategic redefinitions of water in New Zealand.

10   Waitangi Tribunal 1999.

11   For an astute and illuminating account of people and politics relating to the Waikato River, see Muru-Lanning 2016.

12   Waitangi Tribunal 2012.

13   John Key quoted in *New Zealand Herald* 2012c.

14   Hide 2012.

15   King Tuheitia quoted in *New Zealand Herald* 2012b.

16   Judgment: NZ Māori Council and Others v Attorney-General, 27 February 2013, www.scoop.co.nz/stories/PO1302/S00285/judgment-nz-Māori-council-and-others-v-attorney-general.htm.

17   Frame 1999.

18   Tipa 2013, 44.

19   Viveiros de Castro 2007, 153 (emphasis in source).

20   Te Rangikaheke trans. Curnow, APL.

21   Matiu Mareikura quoted in Waitangi Tribunal 1999, 56; also John Tahuparae quoted in Waitangi Tribunal 1999, 76.

22   Norman n.d.

23   Turama Thomas Hawira in Waitangi Tribunal 2012, 57.

24   King Tawhiao quoted in Muru-Lanning 2010, 45; 2016, 59.

25   Mareikura, Matiu quoted in Waitangi Tribunal 1999, 57.

26   Viveiros de Castro, Holbraad and Pedersen 2014.

27   See Cameron, de Leeuw and Desbiens 2014 for an exploration of such possibilities.

28   For a thoughtful exploration of the complex relations between Seminole Indians and the Florida Everglades, and the 'naturalisation' of indigenous peoples and waterways alike, see Cattelino 2015, 246–8.

29   Glacken 1967; Descola 2013.

30   Byrnes 2001.

31   Blomley 2005; Bell 2005; Beamer and Duarte 2009.

32   For instance, Banner 1999; David Williams 1999; Boast 2013.

33   Martin 1860.

34   For commentary on this doctrine, see Waitangi Tribunal 1999, 23.

35   Blackstone 1765–1769 quoted in Taggart 2002, 110, 112.

36   For reflections on the term 'ecosystem services', see Kull, Anauld de Sartre and Castro-Larrañaga 2015; Dempsey and Robertson 2012.

37   For a commentary on guardianship under New Zealand law, see Family Court of New Zealand 2012, *Powers to Act on Behalf of Others*.

38   Frame 1999, 234 (emphasis in source).

39   Henare [Salmond] in Henare [Salmond], Holbraad and Wastell eds 2007b, 50.

40   Strathern 2014a.

41   Muru-Lanning 2016, 83–91.

42   Stone 1974.

43   For example, Frame 1999.

44   See Ruru 2009 for an excellent review of writing about Māori legal engagement with freshwater issues until that date.

45   Morris and Ruru 2010, 58.

46 Salmond 2012a.
47 Pedersen 2010.
48 'In keeping with its monotheistic origins, ours is an ontology of *one* ontology. . . .
    For if cultures render different appearances of reality, it follows that one of them
    is special and better than all the others, namely the one that best *reflects* reality.
    And since science – the search for representations that reflect reality as transparently
    and faithfully as possible – happens to be a modern Western project, that special
    culture is, well, ours' (Henare [Salmond], Holbraad and Wastell eds 2007a, 10–11;
    emphases in source).
49 See Bateson's discussion of the double bind in Bateson 1956, 251–4.
50 Maanu Wihapi quoted in Waitangi Tribunal 2012, 16.
51 Toni Waho, oral evidence, quoted by Crown counsel, closing submissions, Waitangi
    Tribunal 2012, 66.
52 Waitangi Tribunal 2012, 67 (emphasis in source).
53 Ibid., 66.
54 Bateson 1956.
55 Macalister 2006.
56 Henare [Salmond] in Henare [Salmond], Holbraad and Wastell eds 2007b, 49.
57 *Ruruku Whakatupua* 2014.
58 Tamihana 1865.
59 Fennell 2011.
60 Povinelli 2012.
61 Law 2011, 2 (emphasis in source).
62 Graeber 2014.
63 For discussions of strategies in other jurisdictions to address similar challenges in
    relation to rivers, see Ruru ed. 2010; Jackson and Barber 2013; Archer 2014; and for a
    suggestion that legal personhood might be extended to taonga in general, see Angelo
    1996.
64 Bennett 2010, ix–x.

Chapter Ten **Like a Bird on a Sandbank: Whenua / Land**

1   Te Kumara i tae ma ai ki enei Motu. Nga kupu tohetohe a nga iwi Māori mo te kumara
    i kawea mai ai ki enei motu, trans. John White, in White 1888, 3–26 (English), 3–19
    (Māori). Parts of this chapter were drafted in the second Rutherford Lecture, deliv-
    ered in Christchurch in 2014 and broadcast by Radio New Zealand.
2   Ropata Wahawaha in White 1888, 4. The chant of the *Horouta*'s journey is now being
    mapped by Hera Ngata-Gibson and others in virtual reality, assisted by Google in
    California.
3   Iraia Tutanga Waionui ibid., 4–5, trans. Anne Salmond.
4   Mohi Turei ibid., 5–6.
5   Te Rangikaheke trans. Curnow, GNZMMSS 85, APL: '*Anā ko te ngaki kai anō tētahi,
    ko te tangohanga anō tētahi, ko te karanga manuhiri anō tētahi, ko te kōrero manuhiri anō
    tētahi, ko te kōrero rūnanga anō tētahi; ko te atawhai anō tētahi. Nā reira ka karangatia ki
    ngā whenua, ko Mea te rangatira.*'
6   E. Stirling as told to Anne Salmond 1980, 89–91.
7   Anne Salmond 1991b, 196–207.
8   Agnes Sullivan n.d.
9   For excellent studies of seasonal migrations to harvest food at mahika kai (literally
    food working places) in the South Island, see Jim Williams 2010 and 2012.
10 Merimeri Penfold interview with Anne Salmond 1986 for the Muriwhenua Land
    Waitangi Tribunal, unpublished ms in the author's possession.

11 Wyatt 1991.
12 Anne Salmond 1991c.
13 Ibid., 5.
14 Mutu 1992; Metge 1992.
15 Waitangi Tribunal 1997.
16 Head 1992.
17 Holy Bible, Genesis 9.
18 Locke 1689, *First Treatise*, para. 29.
19 Ibid., para. 32.
20 Ibid., paras 24, 25.
21 Ibid., para. 44.
22 Ibid., *Second Treatise*, Chapter 2, para. 6.
23 Ibid., Chapter 5, paras 26, 31. See also discussion in Ian Shapiro, Resources, capacities and ownership: The workmanship ideal and distributive justice, in Brewer and Staves eds. 1995, 21–42.
24 Ibid., Chapter 5, para. 38: 'But if either the grass of his enclosure rotted on the ground, or the fruit of his planting perished without gathering and laying up, this part of the earth, notwithstanding his enclosure, was still to be looked on as waste, and might be the possession of any other.'
25 Ibid., Chapter 5, para. 48.
26 De Vattel 1758, Chapter 7, para. 81.
27 Rodgers et al. 2011.
28 Tamakihikurangi 1861, 18L.
29 Shawcross 1966, 352–3.
30 Riseborough and Hutton 1997, 8.
31 Ibid., 7.
32 David Williams 1989, 73.
33 Quoted in Orange 1987, 93.
34 Orange 2004, 48.
35 See the speech by Sir George Gipps, 9 July 1840, on second reading of the New Zealand Land Claims Bill, *GBPP* 1841 331, 63–64, in which he declared 'the uncivilized inhabitants of any country have but a qualified dominion over it, or a right to occupancy only, and that until they establish amongst themselves a settled form of government, and subjugate the ground to their own uses, by the cultivation of it, they cannot grant to individuals, not of their own tribe, any portion of it, for the simple reason, that they have no individual property in it'.
36 Governor Grey to Early Grey, 2 August 1847, *Daily Southern Cross*, 14 April 1849, 3.
37 Orange 2004, 48.
38 John William Pokai (Heke) quoted in Belich 1986.
39 Heke to Gilbert Mair, 16 October 1844, APL.
40 John William Pokai (Heke) to Governor FitzRoy, May 1845, in Caselberg ed. 1975, 63. See also Heke to FitzRoy, August 1844, ibid., 61.
41 Kawiti to Grey, 29 November 1845, ibid., 65.
42 Heke to Grey, 2 December 1845, ibid., 65–66.
43 For an excellent history of these conflicts, see Belich 1986.
44 The Rt Hon Earl Grey to Governor Grey, copy of a despatch, 23 December 1846, *AJHR*, A-3, 10.
45 Riseborough and Hutton 1997, 15–16.
46 Letters from Te Wherowhero and Earl Grey reproduced in Orange 2004, 55.
47 Hone Heke with commentary by Sadler in Sadler 2014, 102–11.
48 Hone Heke Pokai, Letter to Queen Victoria, 10 July 1849, *GBPP* 1280 (1850), 17.
49 Te Haeana, Rakorako, Ngamiro, Tikiku, Pakihautai and Arama Karaka in Whareroa to Sir Donald McLean, 6 November 1850, ATL MS-Papers-0032-0674F-03.

50 McHugh 2011, 27.
51 This account, given by Te Heuheu's lineal descendant to James Cowan, can be found in Smith 1920, 160–1.
52 Martin 1860, 64.
53 Gore Browne 1860, 13.
54 Ibid., 42.
55 Ibid., 9–10.
56 Renata Kawepo to Governor Gore Browne, Caselberg ed. 1975, 91–94 (emphasis in source).
57 Martin 1860, 90.
58 See R.D. Crosby 2015.
59 Belich 1986.
60 This history is retraced from a legal historical point of view in astute studies by Richard Boast and David Williams, among others, and many submissions to the Waitangi Tribunal.
61 Hone Mohi Tawhai quoted in Sadler 2014, 152–3, translated by Hone Sadler with some small edits by Anne Salmond.
62 *Bay of Plenty Times*, 23 May 1874, 2.
63 Cheater and Hopa 1997; Poata-Smith 2004; Muru-Lanning 2010.
64 McHugh 2011, 1 (emphasis added).
65 In his fine study of Aboriginal title, McHugh acknowledges this when he writes: '[I do] not seek to sideline those indigenous struggles, the magnitude and ongoing vicissitudes of which have a stature and nobility far greater than the intellectualism that is the subject of this book. The story here seeks to recount the means by which Anglo legalism (in all its arrogance, complacence, occasional but very uneven glory, and manifest imperfection) absorbed and refracted their concerns' (McHugh 2011, 16). For astute observations about why the focus on property and rights has not liberated most indigenous peoples from poverty and disaffection, see McHugh 2011, 13–14. For a fascinating study of colonial strategies towards land and indigenous resistance in Canada, see Harris 2002.
66 For a recent critique, see Naomi Klein's 2016 Edward Said Lecture: '[W]e are told we have altered the earth so much and on such a planetary scale that we are now living in the Anthropocene – the age of humans. These ways of explaining our current circumstances have a very specific, if unspoken meaning: that humans are a single type, that human nature can be essentialised to the traits that created this crisis. In this way, the systems that certain humans created, and other humans powerfully resisted, are completely let off the hook. Capitalism, colonialism, patriarchy – those sorts of system. Diagnoses like this erase the very existence of human systems that organised life differently: systems that insist that humans must think seven generations in the future; must be not only good citizens but also good ancestors; must take no more than they need and give back to the land in order to protect and augment the cycles of regeneration. These systems existed and still exist, but they are erased every time we say that the climate crisis is a crisis of "human nature" and that we are living in the "age of man"' (Klein 2016).
67 Jack K. Hunn, 'Report on the Department of Māori Affairs: with statistical supplement', Wellington, *Appendices to the Journals of the House of Representatives*, 1961, vol. 2, G-10. For observations on the steps towards renewed assimilationist policies from the 1960s onwards, and for Māori and activist responses, see McHugh 2011, 38–39, 58–64.
68 Mutu 2013.

Chapter Eleven The Fountain of Fish: Moana / Sea

1   Knight 2011. Parts of this chapter were delivered in draft as a keynote lecture at the
     New Zealand Studies Association Conference in Oslo in 2014; in the first Rutherford
     Lecture at the Tauranga Yacht Club in 2014, broadcast on Radio New Zealand; and in
     Anne Salmond 2015.
2   Ibid.
3   Tweedie Waititi quoted in *Sunday Star-Times*, 24 April 2011, www.stuff.co.nz/
     sunday-star-times/features/4916738/Enter-the-taniwha.
4   Ibid.
5   E. Stirling as told to Anne Salmond 1980, 106–11.
6   Ibid., 220.
7   Ibid., 106.
8   Webster and Monteiro 2013, 1.
9   Ibid., 2.
10   Devathasan 2013.
11   Thakur 1989.
12   Pugh 1987.
13   Knight 2011.
14   Tikao 1939, 27.
15   Te Rangikaheke trans. Curnow 1983, 254.
16   Ruatapu 1993, 122–4.
17   Jahnke 2009, 393.
18   E. Stirling as told to Anne Salmond 1980, 24–28.
19   Ruatapu 1993, 142–6.
20   Rimini 1901.
21   Major G. Mair quoted in Best 1929.
22   Ngata 1944.
23   Te Rangihiroa 1926. For an extensive discussion of contemporary applications of the
     rāhui, see Bambridge ed. 2016.
24   Colenso 1887, 418–22.
25   John White ms, ATL, transcribed and translated by Charles Royal, pers. comm.
26   E. Stirling as told to Anne Salmond 1980, 81–83.
27   Colenso 1887, 422.
28   Te Rangikaheke trans. Curnow 1983, 237.
29   Colenso 1887, 422.
30   E. Stirling as told to Anne Salmond 1980, 221.
31   Sharp 1996, 117–19; Sharp 1998, 57–58.
32   Mulrennan and Scott 2000.
33   Hau'ofa 1993, 153.
34   Quoted in Sharp 1996, 113.
35   Ibid., 116.
36   For a fascinating discussion of the historical intersection between enclosure on land
     and the 'freedom of the seas' (during which indigenous people lost their rights over
     the ocean), see Sharp 1998, 54–58.
37   Salmond 1991b, 144–55.
38   Ibid., 185–6.
39   Thomson c. 1840, 27–28.
40   Matiu Rata quoted in Waitangi Tribunal 1988, 19; see also Bess 2001, which describes
     how this regime was enacted in the Fisheries Amendment Act 1986.
41   Wiremu Paraone quoted in Waitangi Tribunal 1988, 31.
42   For an excellent account of successive stages in fisheries management in New Zealand
     from a lack of management (except by Māori) from first European arrival to the

mid-1880s; to a limited entry system between 1866–1962; to a regulated open entry system between 1963–1982; and the Quota Management System in 1983, see Bess 2001, 27.

43 Although Section 8 of the Fish Protection Act 1877 stated that 'Nothing in this Act contained shall be deemed to repeal, alter, or affect any of the provisions of the Treaty of Waitangi, or to take away, annul or abridge any of the rights of the aboriginal natives to any fishery secured to them thereunder', this was repealed by the Sea Fisheries Act 1894, which referred only to 'existing Maori fishing rights'; while the Fisheries Act 1908 included no reference at all to Māori fishing rights. This legal situation prevailed until the Fisheries Act 1983, which stated in Section 88(2) that 'nothing in this Act shall affect any Maori fishing rights' but when the Quota Management System was enacted in the Fisheries Amendment Act 1986, this once again included no reference to Māori fishing rights. See Bess 2001, 89.

44 Bess 2001, 27.

45 See the account in Bess 2001, 90.

46 Sadler 2008.

47 See Bess 2001, 90–93.

48 W. Taipiri in Waitangi Tribunal 2004, 37.

49 For an account of this legal history, see Bess 2001, 90.

50 Taiaho Ngatai in Waitangi Tribunal 2004, 35.

51 S. Elias in *Ngati Apa v Attorney General*, CA 173/01.

52 For a succinct history of the foreshore and seabed saga, see McHugh 2011, 202–11.

53 See Palmer 2006; Duxfield 2007, 6–10.

54 Kirk 2013.

55 www.facebook.com/gracelee.hnn/posts/632455636825057, 27 February 2014.

56 http://teohu.maori.nz/kermadec/FAQs_Kermadec.pdf.

57 Fa'aui and Morgan 2014.

58 See www.seachange.org.nz/.

Chapter Twelve Once Were Warriors: Tangata / People

1 Lea and Chambers 2007. Parts of this chapter were drafted in the 2015 J.C. Beaglehole Lecture for the New Zealand Historical Association, delivered in Christchurch; and in keynote addresses to the 2013 New Zealand Psychological Society Annual Conference in Auckland (Ahau: The Self in a Relational World) and the 2015 New Zealand Early Childhood Convention in Rotorua (Once were Warriors).

2 Te Rangikaheke trans. Curnow 1983, 3–4.

3 Norman n.d., Women and Childbirth.

4 Ibid., The Ways of Papa-tuanuku.

5 Te Rangikaheke trans. Biggs 1970, 70–71.

6 White III 1887, 69.

7 Stafford 1967, 22.

8 Tarakawa and Smith 1894, 60.

9 Norman n.d., Women in the Cosmos.

10 Norman's unpublished PhD thesis in Māori Studies at the University of Auckland, one of the most subtle and searching accounts of the role of women in te ao Māori to date, is currently being edited by Anne Salmond and Harry Burkhardt, Ngati Kuri for publication. See also Linda Tuhiwai Smith 1990; Brooks and Tennant 1992; Ralston 1993; Ballara 1993; Binney 2004; Mikaere 1994; Seuffert 2005; and Sadler 2014 (140–1) for insightful accounts of the shifting roles of Māori women.

11 Marsden ed. Elder 1932, 477. See also Kendall to Marsden, 25 July 1817, HL MS

56/63: 'The territorial possessions of the New Zealanders, as far as I can learn are hereditary, descending . . . from the father or mother to the eldest son or daughter.'

12   Norman n.d., Women in the Cosmos; Waitangi Tribunal 2014, 4.4.2.2.

13   Best 1982, 596.

14   Boyd 2010.

15   Marsden ed. Elder 1932, 173–4.

16   Ibid., 99; Nicholas 1817 I, 339. See also Heni Brown of Poverty Bay talking with Judith Binney about her great-grandmother Meri Puru, who spent time with the prophetic leader Te Kooti during the Land Wars: 'My great-grandmother was a kuia tapu [sacred female elder]. Te Kooti made her like that. When we have our kai (food), she doesn't have kai like us – she only has a little bit, just a cupful outside by herself. She was very sacred. She was a makutu [bewitching] old lady. She could destroy, you know – some kind of prayer that she uses and it reacts onto that person'; and reports of Waioeka Brown, a woman who was sent to one of the last whare wānanga in Poverty Bay to learn the genealogies and histories of her people (Binney 2004, 24–25).

17   Marsden 1815, HL MS 55/4, 19. See also Ralston 1993, 27–28.

18   Nicholas 1817 I, 177.

19   Ibid., 192.

20   Marsden 1815, HL MS 55/4, 69; Marsden ed. Elder 1932, 128. See also ibid., 408: 'You do not see the New Zealanders drinking and swearing and fighting and murdering one another, as is the case in civil society. I never saw a woman struck by a man in New Zealand, nor two men fighting together.'

21   Marsden ed. Elder 1932, 479.

22   Shortland 1856, 143.

23   Best 1976 I, 133.

24   Henry Williams in Fitzgerald ed. 2011, 59.

25   Nicholas 1817 II, 307.

26   Polack 1840 I, 374.

27   Ibid., 378–9.

28   Angas 1847, 91–92.

29   Given so much contemporary scepticism about the lack of domestic violence in Māori families and the freedom enjoyed by Māori children in early contact times, it is worth quoting a range of early eyewitness accounts on these topics by European visitors or settlers from that period: John Savage 1807, reprint 1966, 44–45: 'The children here appear to be treated with a great degree of parental affection. They are robust, lively, and possess, in general, pleasing countenances'; John Liddiard Nicholas 1817 I, 179–80: 'I have before given some instances of the tender affection subsisting between relations in this country, and no where else can it be found more ardent and sincere. The New Zealander loves his connections in the genuine warmth of his heart, and is never more happy than when he can enjoy their society'; II, 66–67: 'Far from being petulant or unruly, I observed on the contrary, all the children in New Zealand, both male and female, remarkably submissive and obedient towards their mothers and in the whole course of my observation among them, I never met with a single instance of undutiful behaviour. But, besides that my own eyes bore testimony to their docile and tractable dispositions, I found in answer to several inquiries I made on the subject, that they were never in the habit of treating their mothers with disrespect; nor, if inclined to do so, could I discover that they would be at all protected by their fathers against the punishment due to their irreverence'; II, 307–8: 'The tenderest parental affection (an impulse wisely ordained by nature) is remarkable among all classes, high and low, in this country. The chiefs carry their children upon their backs, taking them from their mothers at an early age, that they may not be an incumbrance to them in their laborious employments. It must be allowed, however, that the men make excellent nurses, and have a peculiar art in the management of their infant offspring.

I have never seen any father fonder of his child than the chief Wiveeah appeared to be of a fine boy, whom he brought with him on his back, in one of his visits to us; he evinced the gentlest attention to the little creature, while it clung with its arms round his neck, and seemed to rest perfectly happy in his indulgent care'; Richard Cruise 1824, 275–6: 'In the manner of rearing children, and in the remarkable tenderness and solicitous care bestowed upon them by the parents, no partiality on account of sex was in any instance observed. The infant is no sooner weaned than a considerable part of its care devolves upon the father: it is taught to twine its arms round his neck, and in this posture it remains the whole day, asleep or awake, suspended upon his shoulders, and covered with his mat; and in his longest journeys, or his most laborious occupations, it is his constant companion'; George Craik 1830, 386 (drawing on Cruise's description): 'In most of their labours the men take at least some share, although perhaps not quite an equal one. Of one important duty, however, the husband relieves the wife almost completely – namely, of the care of the children. As soon as the infant is weaned, it is taught to twine its arms round its father's neck; and so completely does it in a short time acquire the habit of trusting to this support, that, asleep or awake, it remains the whole day thus suspended, protected from the weather by the same mat which covers its parent; and in his longest journeys as well as his most laborious occupations, it is his constant companion'; Augustus Earle 1832, 257: 'They are kind and hospitable to strangers; and are excessively fond of their children. On a journey, it is more usual to see the father carrying his infant than the mother; and all the little offices of a nurse are performed by him with the tenderest care and good humour. In many instances (wherein they differ from most savage tribes) I have seen the wife treated as an equal and companion. In fact, when not engaged in war, the New Zealander is quite a domestic, cheerful, harmless character: but once rouse his anger, or turn him into ridicule, and his disposition is instantly changed'; Richard Taylor 1839–40: 'One of the finest traits I have noticed in the New Zealanders is that of parental love; the men appear chiefly to nurse their children, and are generally to be seen with one on their back covered up under their mats, the little things appear likewise sensible of their fathers' love for they seem principally to cling to them'; John Walton 1839, 63: 'The unbounded freedom in which the children are indulged, seems very favourable to their growth, which is much more rapid than that of European children, who are less strong and active at ten years of age than those in New Zealand are at six. The tuition of the children begins at an early period, for the development of their mental powers is as rapid as that of their physical. . . . One effect of the excessive fondness of parents for their children is, that they are very rarely punished for any impropriety of conduct whatever. This exemption from merited chastisement occasions no little annoyance to the parents from the mischievous tricks which it emboldens these spoiled children to perform'; Joel Polack 1840, I, 28: 'The child of a chieftain is regarded by his followers precisely as the Highlanders of the fastnesses of Scotland and Wales confided in their young chiefs. In New Zealand, presents are sent from various tribes to these young representatives of their people, either from friendship, pride of generosity, or as tribute to deprecate the ire of an enemy'; II, 153–4: 'Among the many redeeming traits in the character of the New Zealanders, may be instanced the endearing affection entertained by the parent for his children, the affection also which binds relationship together, with the gifts and presents that are continually interchanged among each other'; Jean-Simon Bernard 1844: 'The children here are completely free; the parents never do anything to them. They never beat them and do not allow anyone else to beat them'; Edward Shortland 1856, 156: 'Curbing the will of the child by harsh means was thought to tame his spirit, and to check the free development of his natural bravery. The chief aim, therefore, in the education of children being to make them bold, brave, and independent in thought and act, a parent is seldom seen to chastise his child, especially in families of rank.

Were he to do so, one of the uncles would probably interfere to protect his nephew, and seek satisfaction for the injury inflicted on the child by seizing some of the pigs or other property of the father'; William Colenso, 1868, 30: 'Their love and attachment to children was very great, and that not merely to their own immediate offspring. They very commonly adopted children; indeed no man having a large family was ever allowed to bring them all up himself – uncles, aunts and cousins claimed and took them, often whether the parents were willing or not. They certainly took every physical care of them; and as they rarely chastised (for many reasons) of course, petted and spoiled them. The father, or uncle, often carried or nursed his infant on his back for hours at a time, and might often be seen quietly at work with the little one there snugly ensconced.'

30 Yate 1835, 98; Marshall 1836, 13–14; Walton 1839, 65. Note also that infanticide occurred at times, when a woman had too many children, and too many female children in particular. The baby was killed immediately after birth by pressing on the fontanelle or pinching the nose – until it had taken its first breath, it was not yet in te ao mārama (Walton 1839, 39, 41).

31 But also in the colonial period. According to Ballara 1993, 130, for instance, Niniwa-i-te-rangi, a senior woman in the Wairarapa, often spoke on ceremonial occasions in the late nineteenth and early twentieth centuries; and Binney quotes a vivid account from Heni Sunderland in Poverty Bay describing how the menfolk on the marae at Manutuke tried to exclude women from speaking, but did not succeed (Binney 2004, 238–9).

32 Ibid., 111. See also Polack 1840: 'women also engage in oratorical displays'.

33 'Na ka hanga a Ihowa, te Atua, i te rara i tangohia mai ra e ia i roto i a Arama hei wahine, a kawea ana e ia ki a Arama' (Now God made a woman from the rib he had taken from inside Adam, and carried her to Adam).

34 King James Bible, Genesis 3:16.

35 Marsden 1809, 111–26.

36 1 Timothy 2:11–14.

37 *The Lawes Provision for Women* (London, 1632), 124–5.

38 Blackstone 1765–1769, *Commentaries* I, 442.

39 Strathern 2014c, 9.

40 Macpherson 1962.

41 Perkin 1989, 10–31, 50–75.

42 For a valuable account of the doctrine of coverture, and how it transformed the status of women in Hawai'ian society, see Gething 1977.

43 Pinchbeck and Hewitt 1973 II, 351–3.

44 Auerbach 2009.

45 Pinchbeck and Hewitt 1973.

46 Foucault 1995.

47 Clarke in Kassem, Murphy and Taylor eds 2010, 9–10.

48 Clarke ibid., 8.

49 See, for instance, Cruise 1824, 204, 219–20.

50 R.D. Crosby 1999.

51 Kendall to Woodd, 16 October 1816, HL MS 56/24, 4–5.

52 Kendall to Mann, 14 July 1817, HL MS 56/59, 4.

53 For a fascinating discussion of the relations between missionary wives and Māori 'girls', see Rountree 2000.

54 Marianne Williams, AWMML MS 189.

55 Jane Williams, AWMML MS 224.

56 Quoted in Orange 1987, 90.

57 Buick 1914, 179.

58 For detailed studies of the signatories on various versions of the Treaty of Waitangi,

see www.nzhistory.net.nz/politics/treaty/making-the-treaty/treaty-of-waitangi-signing-locations; and www.teara.govt.nz/en/interactive/36341/women-signatories-to-the-treaty-of-waitangi.

59 Sadler 2014, 140–1.
60 Maureen Lander and Angela Middleton have carried out fascinating (as yet unpublished) research into Hariata or Rongo Hongi, illuminating her role as a warrior, Hone Heke's scribe and advisor. Many thanks to them for sharing these insights with me.
61 Sadler 1999. See also Norman n.d., Women and Tribal Origins.
62 Hohepa and Williams 1996, 29–30. See also Law Commission 1999, 14–17.
63 Orange 1987, 90.
64 Mahuika 1973, 268.
65 *New Zealander*, 10 September 1864, 4. My thanks to Raewyn Dalziel for locating this source.
66 For an excellent discussion of these developments, see Ballara 1993, 134–5.
67 Samuel Williams to Sir Donald McLean, 4 July 1876, Williams Family Papers, Acc. 75-1, Box I: DOO252 15.4.75, Folder 2, ATL, quoted by Ballara 1993, 35.
68 Ballara 1993, 135–6.
69 Paremata Maori o Niu Tireni, Otaki 1893 [First Sitting], I tu ki te Waipatu, 18 Mei 1893. For background on Meri Te Tai Mangakahia, see McDonald 1991.
70 Rei 1993, 21.
71 Dallimore 1983; David Williams 1999; Boast 2013.
72 For an intriguing comparative account of how women gained the vote in New Zealand, Australia and Hawai'i, see Grimshaw 2000. Grimshaw argues that Māori men gained the vote because the settlers were afraid of what might happen if they were not given that right, but that their votes were limited to four Māori electorates. Thus when European women gained the vote in September 1893, there was enthusiastic support for Māori women to be given the vote as well, since their votes were sequestered in the same way. See also Rei 1993.
73 E. Stirling as told to Anne Salmond 1980, 44–45.
74 See, for instance, Salmond 2009, 51–54, which discusses the custom of genital exposure in Tahiti as a way of channelling ancestral power, either to disconcert an adversary or to bring about fertility in plants, animals and people.
75 Binney 2004, 28–29.
76 Ministry of Social Development 2015, 4, 7, 8. See also Wynd 2013 for the links between poverty and child abuse in New Zealand.
77 For a sobering account of domestic violence in some contemporary Māori families, based on women's oral accounts, see Glover 1993.
78 Marsden 1815, HL MS 55/4, 69; Marsden ed. Elder 1932, 128.
79 Szazy 1995.
80 Rangiheuea 1995, p. 107.
81 Sadler 2014, 154–5.

Afterword Voyaging Stars

1 Sullivan 1999.
2 Hohepa, pers. comm.
3 McIntosh 2005; Summative Report, Starpath Project, University of Auckland.
4 Muru-Lanning 2016, 147–77.
5 Viveiros de Castro, Holbraad and Pedersen 2014.
6 For a recent conversation between Peter Skafish and Eduardo Viveiros de Castro that explains my affinity with his approach to anthropology, see Skafish 2016. Here,

Viveiros de Castro describes Davi Dopenawa, a Yanomami shaman, as 'an anthropologist in his own right', who, like contemporary anthropologists and philosophers, reflects upon metaphysical questions. In the same way, Māori thinkers such as Tamati Ranapiri, Taare Teone Tikao, Eruera Stirling, Maori Marsden, Hone Sadler and many others reflect upon the nature of existence and being, and are teachers and philosophers in their own right. To regard them as the 'subjects' or 'objects' of anthropological inquiry is a hauhauaitu – a fundamental denial of reciprocity and philosophical exchange in the anthropological enterprise of learning about and from different ways of being.

7   See Sahlins 1983, 528.

8   Rosenblatt 2011.

9   Lythberg 2016.

10   Auckland Art Gallery 2015.

11   For example, Adam Smith 1776: 'Our merchants . . . complain much of the bad effects of high wages in raising the price, and thereby lessening the sale of their goods both at home and abroad. They say nothing concerning the bad effects of high profits. They are silent with regard to the pernicious effects of their own gains. They complain only of those of other people' (Book I, Chapter IX); 'That foreign trade enriched the country, experience demonstrated to the nobles and country gentlemen as well as to the merchants; but how, or in what manner, none of them well knew. The merchants knew perfectly in what manner it enriched themselves. It was their business to know it. But to know in what manner it enriched the country was no part of their business. This subject never came into their consideration but when they had occasion to apply to their country for some change in the laws relating to foreign trade' (Book IV, Chapter I); 'The proposal of any new law or regulation which comes from this order, ought always to be listened to with great precaution. It comes from an order of men, whose interest is never exactly the same with that of the public, who have generally an interest to deceive and even to oppress the public, and who accordingly have, upon many occasions, both deceived and oppressed it' (Book I, Chapter XI).

12   For example, O'Regan 2003; Solomon 2004; Manuka Henare 2011.

13   For comparative reflections upon European and Māori ways of talking about knowledge, see Salmond 1983a, 1985.

14   As Gilbert, Sapp and Tauber point out in their critique of the early modern idea of the autonomous biological individual (and its impact on evolutionary theory): 'Symbiosis is becoming a core principle of contemporary biology, and it is replacing an essentialist conception of "individuality" with a conception congruent with the larger systems approach now pushing the life sciences in diverse directions. These findings lead us into directions that transcend the self / nonself, subject / object dichotomies that have characterised Western thought' (Gilbert, Sapp and Tauber 2012, 326). See also their reflections on the conception of living beings (including people) as 'holobionts' – themselves communities of organisms, not bounded isolates; and Strathern's meditations on the invention of identity in early modern Europe, and the nature / culture split (e.g. Strathern 2014b).

15   See, for instance, Dupré and O'Malley 2013, who outline a biological framework for seeing life as 'the result of the intersection of lineage-forming, metabolically collaborate matter, organized within different interacting levels . . . [This] allows a smooth transition from the earliest living matter to standard examples of life and beyond them all the way to contemporary ecosystems' (335).

16   In some Māori businesses (see KPMG 2016), as well as iwi and hapū organisations and enterprises.

17   Bennett 2010, 116–17.

18   Pohuhu in S. Percy Smith 1913, 131.

19   Henare, Holbraad and Wastell eds 2007a, 1.

BIBLIOGRAPHY

Aboriginal Protection Society 1846. *On the British Colonization of New Zealand*. London, Smith, Elder & Co.

Andrews, John Robert Haydon 2012. The East Coast of the North Island – zoological collections of the *Endeavour* voyage. *Journal of the Royal Society of New Zealand* 42/2, 139–144.

Angas, George French 1847. *The New Zealanders Illustrated*. London, Thomas M'Lean.

Angelo, A.H. 1996. Personality and Legal Culture. *Wellington Law Review* 26, 395.

Anon. 1962. How Aokapurangi Saved Her People. *Te Ao Hou* 41, 13–14.

Archer, Jennifer L. 2014. Rivers, Rights and Reconciliation in British Columbia: Lessons learned from New Zealand's Whanganui River Agreement. Available at SSRN 2374454.

Auckland Art Gallery 2015. *Lisa Reihana: In Pursuit of Venus*. Catalogue, Auckland, Auckland Art Gallery.

Auerbach, Sascha 2009. 'Some Punishment should be Devised': Parents, Children, and the State in Victorian London. *The Historian*. Phi Alpha Beta, 757–779.

August, Wikitoria 2005. Māori Women: Bodies, spaces, sacredness and mana. *The New Zealand Geographer* 61, 117–123.

Ballantyne, Tony 2015. *Entanglements of Empire: Missionaries, Māori, and the Question of the Body*. Auckland, Auckland University Press.

Ballara, Angela 1993. Wahine Rangatira: Maori Women of Rank and their Role in the Women's Kotahitanga Movement of the 1890s. *New Zealand Journal of History* 27/2, 127–139.

—— 2003. *Taua: 'Musket Wars', 'Land Wars' or Tikanga? Warfare in Māori Society in the Early Nineteenth Century*. Auckland, Penguin Books.

Bambridge, Tamatoa ed. 2016. *Rahui: Legal Pluralism in Polynesian Traditional Management of Resources and Territories*. Acton, ACT, Australian National University Press.

Banks, Joseph in ed. J.C. Beaglehole 1962. *The Endeavour Journal of Joseph Banks 1768–1771*, Volumes I and II. Sydney, Angus & Robertson.

Banner, Stuart 1999. Two Properties, One Land: Law and Space in Nineteenth Century New Zealand. *Law & Social Inquiry* 24/4, 807–852.

Barad, Karen 2010. Quantum Entanglements and Hauntological Relations of Inheritance: Dis/continuities, SpaceTime Enfoldings, and Justice-to-Come. *Derrida Today*, 3/2, 240–268.

Barclay, Barry 2005. *Mana Tuturu: Maori Treasures and Intellectual Property Rights*. Honolulu, University of Hawai'i Press.

Barlow, C. 1991. *Tikanga Whakaaro: Key Concepts in Maori Culture*. Auckland, Oxford University Press.

Barton, R.J. ed. 1927. *Earliest New Zealand: The Journals and Correspondence of Rev. J. Butler*. Masterton, Palamontain & Petherick.

Bateson, Gregory and Don Jackson et al. 1956. Toward a Theory of Schizophrenia. *Behavioural Science* 1/54, 251–254.

Battaglia, B. 2011. Of Archipelagos and Arrows. *Common Knowledge* 17/1, 151–154.

Beamer, B. Kamanamaikalani and T. Kaeo Duarte 2009. I Palapala No Ia Aina – Documenting the Hawaiian Kingdom: A Colonial Venture? *Journal of Historical Geography* 35, 66–86.

Beattie, J. and J. Stenhouse 2007. Empire, environment and religion: God and the natural world in nineteenth-century New Zealand. *Environmental and History* 13/4, 413–446.

Beecham, John 1838. *Remarks upon the Latest Official Documents relating to New Zealand.* London, Hatchards.

Belich, J. 1986. *The New Zealand Wars and the Victorian Interpretation of Racial Conflict.* Auckland, Auckland University Press.

—— 1996. *Making Peoples: A History of the New Zealanders from Polynesian Settlement to the End of the Nineteenth Century.* Auckland, Allen Lane/Penguin.

—— 2004. *Paradise Reforged: A History of the New Zealanders from the 1880s to the Year 2000.* Auckland, Allen Lane/Penguin.

Bell, A., T. Currie, G. Irwin and C. Bradbury 2015. Driving Factors in the Colonisation of Oceania: Developing Island-level statistical models to test competing hypotheses. *American Antiquity* 80/2, 397–407.

Bell, Duncan S.A. 2005. Dissolving Distance: Technology, Space and Empire in British Political Thought 1770–1900. *Journal of Modern History* 77, 523–562.

Bennett, Adam and Rebecca Quilliam 2014. Crown still in charge: Minister Chris Finlayson on Waitangi Treaty ruling. *New Zealand Herald*, 14 November. www.nzherald.co.nz/nz/news/article.cfm?c_id=1&objectid=11358560

Bennett, Jane 2010. *Vibrant Matter: A Political Ecology of Things.* Durham, Duke University Press.

Bess, Randall 2001. New Zealand's Indigenous People and their Claims to Fisheries Resources. *Marine Policy* 25, 23–32.

Best, Elsdon 1900. Spiritual concepts of the Maori. *Journal of the Polynesian Society* 9/4, 173–199.

—— 1903. Notes on the art of war as conducted by the Maori of New Zealand, with Accounts of various customs, rites, superstitions, &c, pertaining to war, as practised and believed in by ancient Maori. *Journal of the Polynesian Society* 12/2, 65–84.

—— 1909. Forest Lore of the New Zealand Maori III. *Transactions and Proceedings of the New Zealand Institute* 42, 433–480.

—— 1929. *Fishing Methods and Devices of the Maori.* Wellington, Dominion Museum Bulletin.

—— 1976. *Maori Religion and Mythology* I. Wellington, Government Printer.

—— 1982. *Maori Religion and Mythology* II. Wellington, Government Printer.

Bidwill, J. 1841. *Rambles in New Zealand.* London, W.S. Orr & Co.

Biggs, Bruce 1970. Nga Tama a Rangi, GNZMSS 43, in *Working Papers* 15, Department of Anthropology, University of Auckland.

Biggs, Michael 1999. Putting the State on the Map: Cartography, Territory and European State Formation. *Comparative Studies in Society and History* 41/2, 374–405.

Bille, Mikkel 2015. Hazy Worlds: Atmospheric Ontologies in Denmark. *Anthropological Theory* 15/3, 257–274.

Binney, J. 1967. The Heritage of Isaiah: Thomas Kendall and Maori Religion. *New Zealand Journal of History* 1/2: 124–147.

—— 1968. *The Legacy of Guilt: A Life of Thomas Kendall.* Auckland, Oxford University Press.

—— 1980. The Lost Drawing of Nukutawahiti. *New Zealand Journal of History* 14, 3–24.

—— 1986. 'At Every Bend a Taniwha': Thomas Kendall and Maori Carving. *New Zealand Journal of History* 20, 132–146.

—— 2004. Tuki's Universe. *New Zealand Journal of History* 38/2, 215–232.

—— 2004. Some Observations on the Status of Maori Women. *New Zealand Journal of History* 38/2, 233–242.

—— 2009. *Encircled Lands: Te Urewera 1820–1921.* Wellington, Bridget Williams Books.

Blackstone, William 1765–1769. *Commentaries on the Laws of England.* Oxford, Clarendon Press. http://avalon.law.yale.edu/subject_menus/blackstone.asp

Blomley, Nicholas 2003. Law, Property and the Geography of Violence: The Frontier, the Survey, and the Grid. *Annals of the Association of American Geographers* 93/1, 121–141.

—— 2005. The Borrowed View: Privacy, Propriety and the Entanglements of Property. *Law and Society Inquiry* 30/4, 617–661.

Boast, Richard 2008. *Buying the Land, Selling the Land: Governments and Maori Land in the North Island 1865–1921*. Wellington, Victoria University Press.
—— 2013. *The Native Land Court 1862–1887: A Historical Study, Cases and Commentary.* Wellington, Thomson Reuters.
Bohm, David 1980. *Wholeness and the Implicate Order*. London, Routledge.
Bonacorsci, Andrea 2010. New Forms of Complementarity in Science. *Minerva* 48, 355–387.
Boyd, Peter 2010. Tukutuku: He whai toi, he toi tupu. In pursuit of an understanding of Maori art practices. PhD thesis, University of Auckland.
Brewer, John and Susan Staves, eds 1995. *Early Modern Conceptions of Property*. London and New York, Routledge.
Brookes, Barbara and Margaret Tennant 1992. Maori and Pakeha Women: Many Histories, Divergent Pasts? In eds Barbara Brookes, Charlotte Macdonald and Margaret Tennant, *Women in History* 2. Wellington, Bridget Williams Books, 25–48.
Buffon, Comte de 1749, ed. J. Piveteau, 1954. *Premier Discours de la manière d'etudier de la traiter l'histoire naturelle, Histoire naturelle I (Oeuvres Philosophique de Buffon)*. Paris, Presses Universitaire de France.
Buick, T. Lindsay 1914. *The Treaty of Waitangi*. Wellington, S. & W. Mackay.
Busby, James 1832. A Brief Memoir relative to the Islands of New Zealand [Submitted to the Right Hon. The Secretary of State for the Colonies]. In *Authentic Information Relative to New South Wales and New Zealand*. London, J. Cross.
—— 1835a. *The British Resident at New Zealand to H.B.M.'s Subjects who are Residing or Trading in New Zealand*. Paihia, CMS Press.
—— 1835b. Letter to the Rangatira. In *The British Resident: Letters 1835–1839*. Wellington, Alexander Turnbull Library.
Byrnes, Giselle 2001. *Boundary Markers: Land Surveying and the Colonisation of New Zealand*. Wellington, Bridget Williams Books.
Cameron, Emilie, Sarah de Leeuw and Caroline Desbiens 2014. Indigeneity and Ontology. Special issue of *Cultural Geographies* 21/1, 19–26.
Candea, M. 2008. Against the motion. In eds M. Carrithers, M. Candea, K. Sykes, M. Holbraad and S. Venkatesan, Ontology is just another word for Culture: Motion tabled at the 2008 Manchester Meeting of the Group for Debates in Anthropological Theory. *Critique of Anthropology* 30, 152–200.
Candea, Matei, Joanna Cook, Catherine Trundle and Thomas Yarrow 2015. *Detachment: Essays on the Limits of Relational Thinking*. Manchester, Manchester University Press.
Capra, Fritzjof and Ugo Mattei 2015. *The Ecology of Law: Toward a Legal System in Tune with Nature and Community*. Oakland CA, Berrett-Koehler Publishers.
Carleton, H. 1874. *The Life of Henry Williams: Archdeacon of Waimate*, Volumes I and II. Auckland, Upton and Co.
Carpenter, Samuel 2009. *Te Wiremu, Te Puhipi, He Wakaputanga me te Tiriti / Henry Williams, James Busby, a Declaration and the Treaty*. Wellington, Waitangi Tribunal. http://karuwha.org.nz/wp-content/uploads/2014/09/Henry-Williams-James-Busby-a-Declaration-and-theTreaty.pdf
Carter, H. in ed. Margaret Lincoln 1998. Note on the Drawings by an Unknown Artist on board HMS *Endeavour. Science and Exploration in the Pacific: European Voyages to the Southern Oceans in the 18th Century*. Suffolk, The Boydell Press in association with the Carleton, National Maritime Museum, 133–134.
Caselberg, J. ed. 1975. *Maori is my Name: Historical Maori Writings in Translation*. Dunedin, John McIndoe Ltd.
Cattelino, Jessica 2015. The cultural politics of water in the Everglades and beyond: Transcript of the Lewis Henry Morgan Lecture given on October 14, 2015. *Hau: Journal of Ethnographic Theory* 5/3, 235–250.

Cheater, A. and N. Hopa 1997. Representing Identity. In eds A. James, J. Hockley and A. Dawson, *After Writing Culture: Epistemology and Practice in Contemporary Anthropology*. London, Routledge, 208–223.

Clammer, J., S. Poirier and E. Schwimmer 2004. *Figured Worlds: Ontological Obstacles in Intercultural Relations*. Toronto, University of Toronto Press.

Clarke, John 2010. Histories of Childhood. In eds Derek Kassem, Lisa Murphy and Elizabeth Taylor, *Key Issues in Childhood and Youth Studies*. Oxford, Routledge, 3–12.

Cloher, Dorothy Urlich 2003. *Hongi Hika: Warrior Chief*. Auckland, Penguin Books.

Colenso, William 1868. On the Maori Races of New Zealand. *Transactions and Proceedings of the New Zealand Institute* 1, 30.

—— 1887. Ancient Tide Lore, and Tales of the Sea. *Transactions and Proceedings of the New Zealand Institute* 20, 418–422.

—— 1890. *The Authentic and Genuine History of the Signing of the Treaty of Waitangi, 5th and 6th of February 1840*. Wellington, Government Printer.

Cook, James in ed. J.C. Beaglehole 1955. *The Journals of Captain James Cook I: The Voyage of the Endeavour 1768–1771*. Cambridge, Cambridge University Press, for the Hakluyt Society.

—— in ed. J.C. Beaglehole 1969. *The Journals of Captain James Cook II: The Voyage of the Resolution and Adventure 1772–1775*. Cambridge, Cambridge University Press, for the Hakluyt Society.

Corbett, Jan 2002. Transit and the taniwha. *New Zealand Herald*, 9 November. www.nzherald.co.nz/nz/news/article.cfm?c_id=1&objectid=3003401

Craik, George 1830. *The New Zealanders*. London, Charles Knight.

Crosby, Alfred 1986. *Ecological Imperialism: The Biological Expansion of Europe 900–1900*. Cambridge, Cambridge University Press.

Crosby, R.D. 1999. *The Musket Wars: A History of Inter-Iwi Conflict 1806–45*. Auckland, Reed.

—— 2015. *Kūpapa: The Bitter Legacy of Māori Alliances with the Crown*. Auckland, Penguin.

Cruise, Richard 1824. *Journal of a Ten Months' Residence in New Zealand*. London, Longman, Hurst, Rees, Orme, Brown & Green.

Culbertson, Jake 2015. The Promise of Dragons: Urban Planning's intractable publics. *For Engagement*, the blog of the Anthropology and Environment Society, UC Davis California.

Curnow, Jenifer, 1983. Wiremu Maihi Te Rangikaheke. MA thesis, University of Auckland.

—— 2012. Transcriptions and Translations of nine Manuscripts by Wiremu Maihi Te Rangikaheke. GNZMMSS 85, APL, unpublished manuscript.

Dallimore, Gail 1983. The Land Court in Matakaoa. MA thesis, University of Auckland.

Darwin, Charles 1959. *The Voyage of the Beagle*. New York, Harper.

David, Andrew 1988. *The Charts and Coastal Views of Captain Cook's Voyages: Volume I: The Endeavour Voyage*. London, The Hakluyt Society in Association with the Australian Academy of the Humanities.

de la Cadena, Marisol 2010. Indigenous Cosmopolitics in the Andes. *Cultural Anthropology* 25/2, 334–370.

de Vattel, Emerich 1758. *Le Droit des Gens* (The Law of Nations). Switzerland.

Dempsey, Jessica and Morgan Robertson 2012. Ecosystem services: Tensions, impurities and points of engagement within neo-liberalism. *Progress in Human Geography* 36, 758–780.

Department of Internal Affairs 1991. *The People of Many Peaks: The Maori Biographies from the Dictionary of New Zealand Biography*. Auckland, Auckland University Press.

Descola, Phillippe 2013. *Beyond Nature and Culture*. Chicago, University of Chicago Press.

Derrida, Jacques, trans. David Clark 1995. *The Gift of Death*. Chicago, University of Chicago Press.

Devathasan, Anna 2013. The Crown Minerals Act 2013 and Marine Protest. *Auckland University Law Review* 19, 258–263.

Diamond, Jared 1997. *Guns, Germs, and Steel: The Fate of Human Societies*. New York, W.W. Norton & Co.

Diaw, Mariteuw 2008. From Sea to Forest: An Epistemology of *Otherness* and Institutional Resilience in Non-conventional Economic Systems. http://dlc.dlib.indiana.edu/dlc/ bitstream/handle/10535/312/diaw.pdf?sequence=1

Di Piazza, Anne 2010. A Reconstruction of a Tahitian Star Compass based on Tupaia's 'Chart for the Society Islands with Otaheite in the Centre. *Journal of the Polynesian Society* 19/4, 377–392.

Di Piazza, Anne and Erik Peathree 2007. A New Reading of Tupaia's Chart. *The Journal of the Polynesian Society* 116/3, 321–340.

Donald, Stephen 2012. Dual heritage, shared future: James Cook, Tupaea and the transit of Venus at Tolaga Bay. *Journal of the Royal Society of New Zealand* 42/2, 79–85.

Dupré, John and Maureen O'Malley 2013. Varieties of Life of Living Things: Life at the Intersection of Lineage and Metabolism. In eds Sebastian Normandin and Charles T. Wolfe, *Vitalism and the Scientific Image in Post-Enlightenment Life Science, 1800–2010*. Dordrecht, Springer, 311–343.

Durie, Mason 1998. *Te Mana Te Kāwanatanga: The Politics of Māori Self-Determination*. London, Oxford University Press.

—— 2001. *Mauri Ora: The Dynamics of Māori Health*. Auckland, Oxford University Press.

Duxfield, Flint 2007. The twin crises of climate change. *Going Under: Te korokoro o te Parata*, special issue of *Just Change: Critical Thinking on Global Challenges* 10, 6–10. www.gci.org.uk/Documents/Just_Change.pdf

Earle, Augustus 1832. *Narrative of a nine months' residence in New Zealand in 1827: together with a journal of a residence in Tristan D'Acunha, an island situated between South America and the Cape of Good Hope*. London, Longman, Rees, Orme, Brown & Longman.

Edwards, Rima 2010. Affidavit. WAI 1040, #A25, 16 April.

Elder, J.R. ed. 1932. *The Letters and Journals of Samuel Marsden 1765–1838, Senior Chaplain in the Colony of New South Wales and Superintendent of the Mission of the Church Missionary Society in New Zealand*. Dunedin, Coulls Somerville Wilkie.

—— 1934. *Marsden's Lieutenants*. Dunedin, Coulls Somerville Wilkie.

Englund, H. and J. Leach 2000. Ethnography and the Meta-Narratives of Modernity. *Current Anthropology* 41/2, 225–248.

Evens, T.M.S. n.d. Twins are Birds and a Whale is a Fish, a Mammal, a Submarine: Revisiting 'Primitive Mentality' as a Question of Ontology. Pers. comm.

Fa'aui, Tumanako Ngawhika and Te Kipa Kepa Brian Morgan 2014. Restoring the Mauri to the Pre-MV *Rena* State. *Mai Journal* 3/1, 3–17. www.journal.mai.ac.nz/sites/default/ files/MAI_Jrnl_V3_Iss1_Faaui_0.pdf

Fairburn, William. Letters to the Church Missionary Society London. South Auckland Research Centre MNP MS 176.

Fennell, Lee Anne 2011. Ostrom's Law: Property Rights in the Commons. *International Journal of the Commons* 5/1, 9–27.

Ferguson, Adam, ed. F. Oz-Salzberger 1995. *An Essay on the History of Civil Society*. Cambridge, Cambridge University Press.

Finlayson, Christopher 2012. www.beehive.govt.nz/release/whanganui-river-agreement-signed

Finney, B.R. 2000. Nautical Cartography and Traditional Navigation in Oceania. In eds D. Woodward and G.M. Lewis, *Cartography in the Traditional African, American, Arctic, Australian, and Pacific Societies, Vol. 3*. Chicago, University of Chicago Press.

Fitzgerald, Caroline 2004. *Letters from the Bay of Islands: The Story of Marianne Williams*. Auckland, Penguin Books.

—— 2011. *Te Wiremu – Henry Williams: Early Years in the North*. Wellington, Huia Press.

Fletcher, Ned 2015. A praiseworthy device for amusing and pacifying savages? What the
     framers meant by the English text of the Treaty of Waitangi. PhD thesis, University of
     Auckland.
Foucault, Michel 1970. *The Order of Things: An Archaeology of the Human Sciences*. London,
     Tavistock.
—— 1995. *Discipline and Punish: The Birth of the Modern Prison*. New York, Vintage Books.
Frake, Charles 1985. Cognitive Maps of Time and Tide among Mediaeval Seafarers.
     Man 20, 254–270.
Frame, Alex 1999. Property and the Treaty of Waitangi: A Tragedy of the Commodities?
     In ed. Janet McLean, *Property and the Constitution*. Oxford, Hart Publishing,
     224–234.
Frängsmyr, T., J.L. Heilbron and R. Rider 1990. *The Quantifying Spirit in the 18th Century*.
     Berkeley, University of California Press.
Gascoigne, John 1994. *Joseph Banks and the English Enlightenment: Useful Knowledge and
     Polite Culture*. Cambridge, Cambridge University Press.
Gell, Alfred 1985. How to Read a Map: Remarks on the Practical Logic of Navigation.
     Man 2, 271–286.
George, Marianne 2012. Polynesian Navigation and Te Lapa – 'The Flashing'. *Time and
     Mind: The Journal of Archaeology, Consciousness and Culture* 5/2, 135–173.
—— n.d. Te La o Lata and Gauging Performance of an Ancient Polynesian Sail.
     Pers comm.
Gething, Judith 1997. Christianity and Coverture: Impact on the Legal Status of Women
     in Hawaii, 1820–1920. *Hawaiian Journal of History* 1/1, 188–220.
Gilbert, Scott F., Jan Sapp and Alfred L. Tauber 2012. A Symbiotic View of Life: We Have
     Never Been Individuals. *The Quarterly Review of Biology* 87/4, 325–341.
Glacken, Clarence J. 1967. *Traces on the Rhodian Shore: Nature and Culture in Western
     Thought from Ancient Times to the end of the Eighteenth Century*. Berkeley and Los
     Angeles, University of California Press.
Gladwin, Thomas 1995. *East is a Big Bird: Navigation and Logic on Puluwat Atoll*.
     Cambridge, Harvard University Press.
Glover, Marewa 1993. *Te Puna Roimata: Maori Women's Experience of Male Partner Violence:
     7 Case Studies*. Hamilton, University of Waikato.
Gore Browne, Governor, in Proceedings of the Kohimarama Conference, 1860,
     Comprising Nos 13 to 18 of the *Maori Messenger*, 13.
Gorelik, Boris ed. 2015. *'An Entirely Different World': Russian Visitors to the Cape 1797–
     1870*. Van Riebeek Society.
Graeber, David 2013. It is value that brings universes into being. *Hau: Journal of
     Ethnographic Theory* 3/2, 219–243.
—— 2014. Anthropology and the rise of the professional-managerial class. *Hau: Journal of
     Ethnographic Theory* 4/3, 73–88.
Graham, George 1923. Fall of Mokoia and Mauinaina and the death of Kaea. *Journal of the
     Polynesian Society* 32/126, 94–95.
Green, Sarah ed. 2014. Anthropological knots: Conditions of possibilities and interven-
     tions. *Hau: Journal of Ethnographic Theory* 4/3, 1–113.
Grimshaw, Patricia 2000. Settler Anxieties, Indigenous Peoples, and Women's Suffrage
     in the Colonies of Australia, New Zealand, and Hawai'i, 1888–1902. *Pacific Historical
     Review* 69/4, 553–572.
Hankins, Thomas 1985. *Science and the Enlightenment*. Cambridge, Cambridge University
     Press.
Harms, Volker 2002. Ancestor Panel of the Maori dating from Cook's first South
     Seas Voyage 1768–1771, discovered in the Ethnographic Collection of Tuebïngen
     University. Baessler Archive XLVI.
Harmsworth, G.R. 2005. Roading Case Study: Transit New Zealand and Ngati Naho –

Meremere, Springhill Road, www.landcareresearch.co.nz/publications/researchpubs/
FinalMeremere_Roadingcasestudy.pdf

Harris, Cole 2002. *Making Native Space: Colonialism, Resistance, and Reserves in British Columbia*. Vancouver, University of British Columbia Press.

Harrison S. 2003. Culture Difference as Denied Resemblance: Reconsidering Nationalism and Identity. *Comparative Studies in Society and History* 45/2, 343–361.

Hart, K. 2007. Marcel Mauss: In Pursuit of the Whole. A Review Essay. *Comparative Studies in Society and History* 49.2, 473–485.

—— 2011. The Ethnography of Finance and the History of Money. Pers. comm.

Hau'ofa, 'Epeli 1994. Our Sea of Islands. *The Contemporary Pacific* 6/1, 147–161. https://scholarspace.manoa.hawaii.edu/bitstream/handle/10125/12960/v6n1-148-161-dialogue.pdf

Head, Lindsay 1992. An Analysis of Linguistic Issues raised in Margaret Mutu (1992) 'Tuku Whenua or Land Sale?' and Joan Metge (1992) 'Cross-cultural Communication and Land Transfer in Western Muriwhenua 1832–1840'. Muriwhenua Land Claim.

Henare, Manuka 2003. Changing Images of Nineteenth Century Māori Society – From Tribes to Nation. PhD thesis, Victoria University of Wellington.

Henare, Manuka, Chellie Spiller, Ljiljana Erakovic and Edwina Pio 2011. Relational Well-Being and Wealth: Māori Businesses and an Ethic of Care. *Journal of Business Ethics* 98/1, 153–169.

Henare, Manuka, H. Petrie and A.M.A. Puckey 2010. 'He Whenua Rangatira' Northern Tribal Landscape Overview (Hokianga, Whangaroa, Bay of Islands, Whāngārei, Mahurangi and Gulf Islands). Auckland, Crown Forestry Rental Trust (CRFT), UniServices Ltd.

Henry, Teuira 1907. Tahitian Astronomy (Recited in 1818 at Porapora, by Rua-nui [Great-pit], a Clever Old Woman): Birth of the Heavenly Bodies. *Journal of the Polynesian Society* 16, 101–104.

Hickford, Mark 2006. 'Decidedly the Most Interesting Savages on the Globe': An Approach to the Intellectual History of Maori Property Rights, 1837–1853. *History of Political Thought* 28/1, 122–167.

Hide, Rodney 2012. Tribunal enraptured by myths and folk legends. *New Zealand Herald*, 2 September. www.nzherald.co.nz/nz/news/article.cfm?c_id=1&objectid=10831075

Hikuroa, D., A. Slade and D. Gravley 2011. Implementing Māori indigenous knowledge (mātauranga) in a scientific paradigm: Restoring the mauri to Te Kete Poutama. *MAI Review* 3, 2–9.

Hodgen, Margaret 1971. *Early Anthropology in the Sixteenth and Seventeenth Centuries*. Philadelphia, University of Pennsylvania Press.

Hohepa, Patu 1999. My Missionary, My Musket and My Mana. In ed. Alex Calder, Jonathan Lamb and Bridget Orr, *Voyages and Beaches: Pacific Encounters, 1769–1840*. Honolulu, University of Hawai'i Press, 180–201.

—— 2011. *Hokianga: From Te Korekore to 1840*. Report commissioned by the Crown Forestry Rental Trust, Wai 1040, #E36.

Hohepa, Patu and David Williams 1996. *The Taking into Account of Te Ao Maori in Relation to Reform of the Law of Succession*. Wellington, Law Commission. www.lawcom.govt.nz/sites/default/files/projectAvailableFormats/NZLC%20MP6.pdf

Hone Heke to Gilbert Mair 16 October 1844. NZMS 724, APL, trans. Anne Salmond.

Hongi, Hare 1894. Notes on T. Tarakawa's paper 'The coming of Te Arawa and Tainui canoes'. *Journal of the Polynesian Society* 3/1, 37–40.

Hoskin, Keith 1995. The Viewing Self and the World We View: Beyond the Perspectival Illusion. *Organisation* 21/1, 141–162.

Howe, Kerry ed. 2006. *Waka Moana: The Discovery and Settlement of the Pacific*. Auckland, David Bateman Ltd.

Hutchins, E. 1995. *Cognition in the Wild*. Cambridge MA, MIT Press.

Ingold, Tim 2013. Dreaming of Dragons: On the Imagination of Real Life. *Journal of the Royal Anthropological Institute* 19, 734–754.

Irwin, Geoff 2008. Pacific Seascapes, Canoe Performance, and a Review of Lapita Voyaging with Regard to Theories of Migration. *Asian Perspectives* 47/1, 12–26.

—— with Richard Flay 2015. Pacific Colonisation and Canoe Performance: Experiments in the Science of Sailing. *Journal of the Polynesian Society* 124/4, 419–443.

Israel, Jonathan 2006. Enlightenment. Which Enlightenment? *Journal of the History of Ideas* 67/3, 523–545.

Jackson, Sue and Marcus Barber 2013. Recognition of indigenous water values in Australia's Northern Territory: current progress and ongoing challenges for social justice in water planning. *Planning Theory and Practice* 14/4, 435–454.

Jacomb, C., R.N. Holdaway, M.E. Allentoft, M. Bunce, C.L. Oskam, R. Walter and E. Brooks 2014. High-precision dating and ancient DNA profiling of moa (Aves: Dinornithiformes) eggshell documents a complex feature at Wairau Bar and refines the chronology of New Zealand settlement by Polynesians. *Journal of Archaeological Science* 50, 24–30.

Jahnke, Robert 2009. Review of *Paki Harrison: The Story of a Master Carver*. *Journal of the Polynesian Society* 118/4, 392–394.

Jardine, N., J.A. Secord and E.C. Spary eds 1996. *Cultures of Natural History*. Cambridge, Cambridge University Press.

Jensen, Casper Bruun 2011. Introduction, Comparative Relativism: Symposium on an Impossibility. *Common Knowledge* 17/1, 1–12.

—— 2016. New Ontologies? Reflections on Some Recent 'Turns' in STS, Anthropology and Philosophy. www.academia.edu/25710614/New_Ontologies_Reflections_on_ Some_Recent_Turns_in_STS_Anthropology_and_Philosophy

Johns, Dilys A., Geoffrey J. Irwin and Yun K. Sung 2014. An early sophisticated East Polynesian voyaging canoe discovered on New Zealand's coast. *PNAS Early Edition* 1–6. www.pnas.org/content/111/41/14728.full.pdf

Jones, Alison and Kuni Jenkins 2011. *Words between Us: He Kōrero: First Māori–Pākehā Encounters*. Wellington, Huia Press.

Jones, Pei Te Hurinui 1959. *King Potatau*. Wellington, The Polynesian Society.

—— in collaboration with Dr Brett Graham 2012. Takarangi loop: http://vimeo. com/40541652

Joppien, Rudiger and Bernard Smith 1985. *The Art of Captain Cook's Voyages, Volume I, The Voyage of the Endeavour 1768–1771*. Melbourne: Oxford University Press in association with the Australian Association of the Humanities.

Kames, Henry Home 1807. *Sketches of the History of Man*. Edinburgh, William Creech.

Kapferer, B. 2007. Anthropology and the Dialectic of Enlightenment: A Discourse on the Definition and Ideas of a Threatened Discipline. *The Australian Journal of Anthropology* 18/1, 72–94.

—— 2011. Strathern's New Comparative Anthropology: Thoughts from Hagen and Zambia. *Common Knowledge* 17/1, 104–110.

Kassem, Derek, Lisa Murphy and Elizabeth Taylor eds 2010. *Key Issues in Childhood and Youth Studies*. Oxford, Routledge.

Kawharu, Merata 2005. Te Tiriti and its Northern Context in the Nineteenth Century. Report commissioned by CFRT.

Kelly, Leslie 1938. Fragments of Ngapuhi History. *Journal of the Polynesian Society* 47/188, The Conquest of Ngare Raumati, 163–177; Moremu-nui, 173–181.

Kelso, J.A. Scott and David Engstrom 1960. *The Complementary Nature*. Cambridge MA, MIT Press.

Kendall, Thomas 1815. *A korao no New Zealand, or, the New Zealander's first book: being an attempt to compose some lessons for the instruction of the natives*. Sydney, G. Howe.

Kendall, Thomas and Samuel Lee 1820. *A Grammar and Vocabulary of the Language of New Zealand*. London, Church Missionary Society.

Kirsch S. 2011. Lost Worlds: Environmental Disaster, 'Culture Loss', and the Law. *Current Anthropology* 42/2, 167–198.

Kirk, Jenny 2013. Maori leaders meet with oil company executives. Māori TV, 11 December. http://puhipuhi.co.nz/maori-leaders-meet-with-oil-company-executives/

Klein, Naomi 2016. Let them Drown: The Violence of Othering in a Warming World. *London Review of Books* 38/11, 11–14.

Kohimarama Conference 1860. *Te Karere Maori: The Maori Messenger* 7, 13.

Knight, Kim 2011. Enter the taniwha. *Sunday Star-Times*, 24 April. www.stuff.co.nz/sunday-star-times/features/4916738/Enter-the-taniwha

KPMG New Zealand 2016. *Māui Rau: Adapting in a Changing World*. Auckland.

Kull, Christian, Xavier Arnauld de Sartre and Monica Castro-Larrañaga 2015. The political ecology of ecosystem services. *Geoforum* 61, 122–134.

Lack, H. Walter and Victoria Ibáñez 1997. Recording Colour in Late Eighteenth Century Botanical Drawings: Sydney Parkinson, Ferdinand Bauer and Thaddäus Haenke. *Curtis's Botanical Magazine* 14/2, 87–100.

Lash, Scott 2006. Life (Vitalism). *Theory, Culture & Society* 23, 323–329.

Latour, Bruno 2004. Whose Cosmos, Which Cosmopolitics?: Comments on the Peace Terms of Ulrich Beck. *Common Knowledge* 10/3, 450–462.

Laugrand, Frederic 2012. The Transition to Christianity and Modernity among Indigenous Peoples. *Reviews in Anthropology* 41/2, 1–22.

Law, John 2011. What's Wrong with a One-World World? heterogeneities.net www. heterogeneities.net/publications/Law2011WhatsWrongWithAOneWorldWorld.pdf

Law Commission 1999. *Justice: The Experiences of Māori Women. Te Tikanga o te Ture: Te Mātauranga o ngā Wāhine Māori e pa ana ki tēnei*. Wellington, Law Commission. www.lawcom.govt.nz/sites/default/files/projectAvailableFormats/NZLC%20R53.pdf

Lea, R. and G. Chambers 2007. Monoamine oxidase, addiction, and the 'warrior' gene hypothesis. *New Zealand Medical Journal*, 120/1250 PMID: 17339897.

Lee, Anna Mary 1896. *A Scholar of a Past Generation: A Brief Memoir of Samuel Lee D.D., Professor of Arabic, and Afterwards Regius Professor of Hebrew in the University of Cambridge, Canon of Bristol etc*. London, Seeley & Co.

Lee, Jack 1983. *'I have named it the Bay of Islands . . .'*. Auckland, Hodder & Stoughton.

Lee, Samuel and Thomas Kendall 1820. *A Grammar and Vocabulary of the Language of New Zealand*. London, London Missionary Society.

Lloyd, Geoffrey E.R. 2009. *Cognitive Variations: Reflections on the University and Diversity of the Human Mind*. Oxford, Oxford University Press.

—— 2010. History and Human Nature: Cross-cultural Universals and Cultural Relativities. *Interdisciplinary Science Reviews* 35/3–4, 201–214.

Locke, John (anon.) 1689. *Two Treatises of Government: In the Former, The False Principles, and Foundation of Sir Robert Filmer, and His Followers, Are Detected and Overthrown. The Latter Is an Essay Concerning The True Original, Extent, and End of Civil Government*. London.

Loperena, Christopher Antony 2016. A Divided Community: The Ethics and Politics of Activist Research. *Current Anthropology* 57/3, 332–346.

Lovejoy, Arthur 1936. *The Great Chain of Being: The History of an Idea*. Boston, Harvard University Press.

Low, Peter 1990. Pompallier and the Treaty: A New Discussion. *New Zealand Journal of History* 24/2, 190–199.

Lythberg, Billie 2016. 21st century South Sea Savagery: Rosanna Raymond's SaVAge K'lub at APT8. *Broadsheet* 45/1, 14–17.

Lythberg, Billie, Jenny Newell and Wayne Ngata 2015. House of Stories: The Whale

Rider at the American Museum of Natural History. *Museum and Society* 13/2, 195–220.

Macalister, John 2006. The Māori presence in the New Zealand lexicon, 1850–2000: Evidence from a corpus-based study. *English World-wide* 27/1, 1–24.

Macaulay, Thomas Babington 1840. Review of Van Ranke's *The Political and Ecclesiastical History of the Popes during the Sixteenth and Seventeenth Centuries*. *Edinburgh Review* 72, 228.

MacLeod, Roy and Philip. F. Rehbock eds 1988. *Nature in its Greatest Extent: Western Science in the Pacific*. Honolulu, University of Hawai'i Press.

Macpherson, C.B. 1962. *The Political Theory of Possessive Individualism: From Hobbes to Locke*. Oxford, Clarendon Press.

Madden, Rosemary 1992. Dynamic and Different: mana wahine. MPhil thesis, Massey University.

Mahuika, Apirana 1973. Nga Wahine Kai-hautu o Ngati Porou: Female Leaders of Ngati Porou. MA thesis, University of Sydney.

Mamdani, M. 2001. Beyond Settler and Native as Political Identities: Overcoming the Political Legacy of Colonialism. *Comparative Studies in Society and History* 43/4, 651–664.

Marsden, Maori, ed. Charles Royal 2003. *The Woven Universe: Selected Writings of Maori Marsden*. The Estate of Rev. Maori Marsden.

Marsden, Samuel 15 November 1809. Some Account of New Zealand, obtained by the Rev. S. Marsden, from Duaterra, a young Chief of that Island; and communicated to a Friend in London. *Proceedings of the Church Missionary Society for Africa and the East*, III (1810–1812), 111–126.

—— ed. J.R. Elder 1932. *The Letters and Journals of Samuel Marsden 1765–1838, Senior Chaplain in the Colony of New South Wales and Superintendent of the Mission of the Church Missionary Society in New Zealand*. Dunedin, Coulls Somerville Wilkie.

Marshall, W.B. 1836. *A Personal Narrative of Two Visits to New Zealand in His Majesty's Ship, Alligator, A.D. 1834*. London, James Nisbet & Co.

Martin, Sir William 1860. *The Taranaki Question*. Auckland, The Melanesian Mission.

Matisoo-Smith, Elizabeth 2015. Ancient DNA and the human settlement of the Pacific: A review. *Journal of Human Evolution* 79, 93–104.

Mauss, Marcel, trans. W.D. Halls 1990. *The Gift: The Form and Reason for Exchange in Archaic Societies*. London, Routledge.

May, Trevor 2006. *The Victorian School Room*. Riseborough, Shire Publications.

McDonald, C. 1991. Meri Mangakahia. In ed. Charlotte McDonald, Merimeri Penfold and Bridget Williams, *The Book of New Zealand Women: Ko Kui Ma Te Kaupapa*. Wellington, Bridget Williams Books, 413–415.

McHugh, Paul 2011. *Aboriginal Title: The Modern Jurisprudence of Tribal Land Rights*. Oxford, Oxford University Press.

McIntosh, Tracey 2005. Maori identities: Fixed, Fluid, Forced. In ed. James Hou-Fu Liu, Tim McCreanor, Tracey Mcintosh and Teresia Teaiwa, *New Zealand Identities: Departures and Destinations*. Wellington, Victoria University Press.

McNab, Robert ed. 1908. *Historical Records of New Zealand I and II*. Wellington, Government Printer.

McRae, Alexander, ed. Sir Frederick Evans Chapman 1928. *Journal Kept in New Zealand by Ensign Alexander McRae, of the 84th Regiment, together with relevant documents*. Wellington, Alexander Turnbull Library.

McRae, Jane 2017. *Māori Oral Tradition: He Kōrero nō te Ao Tawhito*. Auckland, Auckland University Press.

Mead, Hirini Moko 1997. *Landmarks, Bridges and Visions: Aspects of Maori Culture*. Wellington, Victoria University Press.

—— 2003. *Tikanga Māori: Living by Māori Values*. Wellington, Huia Press.

Metge, Joan 1992. *Cross-cultural Communication and Land Transfer in Western Muriwhenua*

1832–1840. Research report commissioned by the claimants, Wai 45, #F13.

Middleton, Angela 2008. *Te Puna – A New Zealand Mission Station: Historical Archaeology in New Zealand*. New York, Springer.

—— 2013. *Kerikeri Mission and Kororipo Pā: An Entwined History*. Dunedin, Otago University Press.

—— 2014. *Pewhairangi: Bay of Islands Missions and Māori 1814–1845*. Dunedin, Otago University Press.

Mikaere, Annie 1994. Maori Women: Caught in the Contradictions of a Colonised Reality. *Waikato Law Review* 2. www.waikato.ac.nz/law/research/waikato_law_review/pubs/volume_2_1994/7

Miller, D.P. and Peter Hanns Reill eds 1996. *Visions of Empire: Voyages, Botany, and Representations of Nature*. Cambridge, Cambridge University Press.

Mimica, J. 2010. Un/knowing and the practice of ethnography: A reflection on some Western cosmo-ontological notions and their anthropological application. *Anthropological Theory* 10/3, 203–228.

Ministry of Social Development (NZ) 2015. *Modernising Child, Youth and Family: Interim Report of the Expert Panel*. Wellington, Ministry of Social Development.

Mol, A. 2011. One, Two, Three: Cutting, Counting and Eating. *Common Knowledge* 17/1, 111–116.

Moloney, Pat 2001. Savagery and Civilization: Early Victorian Notions. *New Zealand Journal of History* 35/2, 153–176.

Morgan, Te Kipa Kepa Brian 2011. Waiora and Cultural Identity: Water Quality Assessment using the Mauri Model. *AlterNative: An International Journal of Indigenous Peoples* 3/1.

—— with T.N. Faʻaui 2014. Restoring the Mauri to the Pre M-V *Rena* State. *MAI Journal* 3/1, 3–17.

Morris, James D.K. and Jacinta Ruru 2010. Giving voice to rivers: Legal personality as a vehicle for recognising Indigenous peoples' relationships to water. *Australian Indigenous Law Review* 14/2, 49–62.

Mulrennan, Monica and Colin Scott 2000. *Mare Nullius:* Indigenous Rights in Saltwater Environments. *Development and Change* 31, 681–708.

Muru-Lanning, M. 2010. Tupuna Awa and Awa Tupuna: An Anthropological Study of Competing Discourse and Claims of Ownership to the Tainui River. PhD thesis, University of Auckland.

—— 2016. *Tupuna Awa: People and Politics of the Waikato River*. Auckland, Auckland University Press.

Mutu, Margaret 1999. *Tuku Whenua* and Land Sale in New Zealand in the Nineteenth Century. In ed. Alex Calder, Jonathan Lamb and Bridget Orr, *Voyages and Beaches: Pacific Encounters, 1769–1840*. Honolulu, University of Hawaiʻi Press.

—— 1992. *Tuku Whenua or Land Sale?* Research report commissioned by the Muriwhenua Research Committee, WAI 45, #F12.

—— 2008. Māori Issues. *The Contemporary Pacific* 20/1, 232–237.

—— 2013. Te Tiriti o Waitangi in a Future Constitution, Removing the Shackles of Colonisation. 2013 Robson Lecture, Napier, 22 April 2013, 8. www.converge.org.nz/pma/shackles-of-colonisation.pdf

Neich, Roger 2014. *Tradition and Change in Māori and Pacific Art: Essays by Roger Neich*. Auckland, Bridget Williams Books for Auckland War Memorial Museum.

New Zealand Herald 2012a. Agreement entitles Whanganui River to legal identity. 30 August. www.nzherald.co.nz/nz/news/article.cfm?c_id=1&objectid=10830586

New Zealand Herald 2012b. We own the water – Maori King. 14 September. www.nzherald.co.nz/nz/news/article.cfm?c_id=1&objectid=10833926

New Zealand Herald 2012c. Debate: Who owns the water? 26 September. www.nzherald.co.nz/nz/news/article.cfm?c_id=1&objectid=10836420

Ngata, Apirana 1944. Rauru-nui-a-Toi lectures, typescript.

Ngata, Wayne, Hera Ngata-Gibson and Amiria Salmond 2012. Te Ataakura: Digital Taonga and Cultural Innovation. *Journal of Material Culture* 17/3, 229–244.

Nicholas, John Liddiard 1817. *Narrative of a Voyage to New Zealand: Performed in the Years 1814 and 1815 in Company with the Rev. Samuel Marsden*, Volumes I and II. London, Hughes & Baynes.

Nickelsen, Kärin 2006. Draughtsmen, Botanists and Nature: Constructing Eighteenth-Century Botanical Illustrations. *Studies of History and Philosophy of Biological and Biomedical Sciences* 37, 1–25.

Noble, Brian 2007. Justice, Transaction, Translation: Blackfoot Tipi Transfers and WIP's Search for the Facts of Traditional Knowledge Exchange. *American Anthropologist* 109/2, 338–349.

Norman, Waerete n.d. Te Ira Wahine: The Female Principle. PhD thesis, University of Auckland.

Normandin, Sebastian and Charles T. Wolfe eds 2013. *Vitalism and the Scientific Image in Post-Enlightenment Life Science, 1800–2010*. Dordrecht, Springer.

Obeyesekere, Gananath 2005. *Cannibal Talk: The Man-eating Myth and Human Sacrifice in the South Seas*. Berkeley, University of California Press.

O'Malley, Vincent 2012. *The Meeting Place: Māori and Pākehā Encounters, 1642–1840*. Auckland, Auckland University Press.

Ong, Aihwa 2007. Neoliberalism as a Mobile Technology. *Transactions of the Institute of British Geography* 32, 3–8.

Orange, Claudia 1987. *The Treaty of Waitangi*. Wellington, Bridget Williams Books.

—— 2004. *An Illustrated History of the Treaty of Waitangi*. Wellington, Bridget Williams Books.

O'Regan, Tipene 2003. Transcripts of interviews and seminars conducted with Marcia Langton and Lisa Palmer. University of Melbourne.

Palmer, M. 2006. Resolving the Foreshore and Seabed Dispute. In eds Raymond Miller and Michael Mintrom, *Political Leadership in New Zealand*. Auckland, Auckland University Press, 197–214.

Parkinson, Phillip 2012. Tuku: Gifts for a King, and the Panoplies of Titore and Patuone. *Tuhinga* 2, 53–68.

Parkinson, Sydney 1773. *A journal of a voyage to the South Seas, in his Majesty's ship, the Endeavour. Faithfully transcribed from the papers of the late Sydney Parkinson, draughtsman to Joseph Banks, Esq*. London, Stanfield Parkinson.

Paterson, Lachlan 2014. Speech to text: Missionary endeavours 'to fix the Language of the New Zealanders'. Centre for Research on Colonial Culture, 10 November. https://blogs.otago.ac.nz/crocc/2014/11/10/speech-to-text-missionary-endeavours-to-fix-the-language-of-the-new-zealanders/

Pedersen, Morten Axel 2010. Non-identity Politics. *Common Knowledge* 17/1, 117–122.

Perkin, Joan 1989. *Women and Marriage in Nineteenth Century England*. London, Routledge.

Petrie, Hazel 2015. A Guide to Literature in Māori Relating to Te Ao Tawhito. Lodged in New Zealand research archives.

—— 2015. *Outcasts of the Gods? The Struggle over Slavery in Māori New Zealand*. Auckland, Auckland University Press.

Pinchbeck, Ivy and Margaret Hewitt 1973. *Children in English Society II: From the Eighteenth Century to the Children Act 1948*. London, Routledge & Kegan Paul.

Poata-Smith, E.S. 2004. The Changing Contours of Maori Identity and the Treaty Settlement Process. In eds J. Hayward and N. Wheen, *The Waitangi Tribunal*. Wellington, Bridget Williams Books.

Poirier S. 2005. *A World of Relationships: Itineraries, Dreams, and Events in the Australian Western Desert*. Toronto, University of Toronto Press.

Polack, J.S. 1838. *New Zealand, Being a Narrative of Travels and Adventures during a Residence in that Country between the Years 1831 and 1837*, Volumes I and II. London, Richard Bentley.
—— 1840. *Manners and Customs of the New Zealanders*, Volumes I and II. London, James Madden & Co.
Polynesian Voyaging Society, pvs.kcc.hawaii.edu
Povinelli, Elizabeth 1999. The State of Shame: Australian Multiculturalism and the Crisis of Indigenous Citizenship. *Critical Inquiry* 24/2, 575–610.
—— 2001. Radical Worlds: The Anthropology of Incommensurability and Inconceivability. *Annual Review of Anthropology* 30, 319–334.
—— 2012. The Governance of the Prior. *Interventions* 13/1, 13–30.
Praed, Winthrop Mackworth 1824. Australasia. Prize Poem, *Missionary Register*, April 1824, 198–199.
Pratt, Mary Louise 1992. *Imperial Eyes: Travel Writing and Transculturation*. New York, Routledge.
Pugh, Michael 1987. Legal Aspects of the Rainbow Warrior Affair. *International and Comparative Law Quarterly* 36, 3655–3659.
Pyyhtinen, O. and S. Tamminen 2011. We Have Never Been Only Human: Foucault and Latour on the Question of the Anthropos. *Anthropological Theory* 11/2, 135–152.
Quine, W.V. 1969. *Ontological Relativity & Other Essays*. The John Dewey Essays in Philosophy, ed. Department of Philosophy, Columbia University, New York and London, Columbia University Press.
Ralston, Caroline 1993. Maori Women and the Politics of Tradition: What Roles and Power Did, Do, and Should Maori Women Exercise? *The Contemporary Pacific* 5/1, 23–44.
Ramos, Alcida 2012. The Politics of Perspectivism. *Annual Review of Anthropology* 41, 481–494.
Ramsden, Eric 1942. *Busby of Waitangi: H.M.'s Resident at New Zealand 1833–1840*. Wellington, A.H. & A.W. Reed.
Rangiheuea, Tania 1995. The Role of Maori Women in Treaty Negotiations and Settlements. In ed. G. McLay, *Treaty Settlements: The Unfinished Business*. Wellington, New Zealand Institute of Advanced Legal Studies and Victoria University.
Rei, Tania 1993. *Māori Women and the Vote*. Wellington, Huia Publishers.
Reill, P.H. 2005. *Vitalizing Nature in the Enlightenment*. Berkeley, University of California Press.
Richards, Rhys 2015. *Tracking Travelling Taonga*. Sydney, Paremata Press.
Rimini, Tiimi Waata 1901. Te Puna Kahawai i Motu. *Journal of the Polynesian Society* 10/4, 183–190.
Riseborough, Hazel and John Hutton 1997. *The Crown's Engagement with Customary Tenure in the Nineteenth Century*. Rangihaua Whanui Series. Wellington, The Waitangi Tribunal.
Rodgers, Christopher P., Eleanor A. Straughton, Angus J.L. Winchester and Margherita Pieraccini 2011. *Contested Common Land: Environmental Governance Past and Present*. London, Earthscan.
Rogers, Lawrence ed. 1961. *The Early Journals of Henry Williams, 1826–1840*. Christchurch, Pegasus Press.
Rorty, Richard 1991. *Objectivity, Relativism, and Truth: Philosophical Papers, Volume 1*. Cambridge, Cambridge University Press.
Rosenblatt, Daniel 2011. Indigenizing the City and the Future of Maori Culture: The Construction of Community in Auckland as Representation, Experience, and Self-Making. *American Ethnologist* 38/3, 411–429.
Rountree, Kathryn 2000. Re-making the Maori Female Body: Marianne Williams's Mission in the Bay of Islands. *Journal of Pacific History* 35/1, 49–66.
Ruatapu, Mohi ed. Anaru Reedy 1993. *Ngā Kōrero a Mohi Ruatapu, tohunga rongonui o Ngāti Porou*. Christchurch, Canterbury University Press.

Ruru, Jacinta 2009. *The Legal Voice of Māori in Freshwater Governance: A Literature Review*. Lincoln, Landcare Research New Zealand.
— ed. 2010. Why it Matters: Indigenous Peoples, the Law and Water. Special issue of *The Journal of Water Law* 20, 5–6.
Ruruku Whakatupua – Te Mana o Te Awa Tupua 2014. http://nz01.terabyte.co.nz/ots/ DocumentLibrary/RurukuWhakatupua-TeManaoTeAwaTupua.pdf
Sabean, David Warren, Simon Teuscher and Jon Mathieu eds 2007. *Kinship in Europe: Approaches to Long-Term Development (1300–1900)*. Oxford, Berghan Books.
Sadler, Hone 1999. Ngā Wāhine Rangatira o Ngāpuhi. Master of Mātauranga thesis, Te Whare Wananga o Raukawa.
— 2007. Mātauranga Māori / Maori Epistemology. *International Journal of the Humanities* 4/10, 33–45.
— 2008. The Kahawai Legal Challenge: Ngāpuhi Iwi, Big Game Fishing & Recreational Fishing Unite. *The International Journal of Interdisciplinary Social Sciences* 2/6, 139–148.
— 2014. *Ko Tautoro te Pito o Tōku Ao: A Ngāpuhi Narrative*. Auckland, Auckland University Press.
— with Callum Manu Minto Mackinnon 2014. Pathways for Ngapuhi's Future: (PGSE) Post Settlement Government Entity. *International Journal of Arts & Sciences* 7/5, 749–779.
— 2015. Legitimacy of Sovereignty in Aotearoa New Zealand: Was it Ceded or Usurped – The Ngapuhi Tribunal Claim. *International Journal of Arts & Sciences* 8/3, 97–106.
Sahlins, Marshall 1983. Other Times, Other Customs: The Anthropology of History. *American Anthropologist* 85/3, 517–544.
— 1985a. *Islands of History*. Chicago, University of Chicago Press.
— 1985b. Hierarchy and Humanity in Polynesia. In eds A. Hooper and J. Huntsman, *Transformations of Polynesian Culture*. Auckland, The Polynesian Society.
— 1996. The Sadness of Sweetness. *Current Anthropology* 37/3, 395–415.
— 2012. Alterity and autochthony: Austronesian cosmographies of the marvelous. The 2008 Raymond Firth Lecture. *Hau: Journal of Ethnographic Theory* 2/1, 131–160.
Salmond, Amiria [publications from 2002 to 2007 published under the surname Henare].
— 2005a. Wai 262: A Maori 'Cultural Property' Claim. In ed. B. Latour, *Dingpolitik: Atmospheres of Democracy*. Karlsruhe, ZKM, 64–69.
— 2005b. Nga Aho Tipuna (Ancestral Threads): Maori Cloaks from New Zealand. In eds D. Miller and S. Kuechler, *Clothing as Material Culture*. Oxford, Berg, 121–138.
— co-edited with Martin Holbraad and Sari Wastell 2007a. *Thinking Through Things: Theorising Artefacts Ethnographically*. Oxford, Routledge.
— 2007b. *Taonga Māori*: Encompassing Rights and Property in New Zealand. In eds A. Henare, M. Holbraad and S. Wastell, *Thinking Through Things: Theorising Artefacts Ethnographically*. Oxford, Routledge, 46–67.
— 2007c. *Nga Rakau a te Pakeha*: Reconsidering Maori Anthropology. In eds Jeanette Edwards, Penny Harvey and Peter Wade, *Anthropology and Science: Epistemologies in Practice*. Oxford, Berg, 93–113.
— ed. with Rosanna Raymond 2008. *Pasifika Styles: Artists Inside the Museum*. Dunedin and Cambridge, Otago University Press and Cambridge University Museum of Archaeology and Anthropology.
— with Rosanna Raymond 2010. Show and Tell: Weaving a Basket of Knowledge. In eds Arnd Schneider and Christopher Wright, *Between Art and Anthropology: Contemporary Ethnographic Practice*. Oxford, Berg, 95–102.
— with Liana Chua 2011. Artefacts in Anthropology. In the *ASA Handbook of Social Anthropology*. London, Sage.
— 2013. Transforming translations (part 1): 'The owner of these bones'. *Hau: Journal of Ethnographic Theory* 3/3, 1–32.
— 2014. Transforming translations Part 2: Addressing ontological alterity. *Hau: Journal of Ethnographic Theory* 4/1, 155–187.

—— with M. Lander 2015. Ancestral threads: Seven Māori Cloaks. In *Artefacts of Encounter: Cook's Voyages, Colonial Collecting and Museum Histories*. Dunedin, Otago University Press.

—— 2016a. Posting on ASAONET, Association for Social Anthropology Bulletin Board (asaonet@listserv.uic.edu). 5 Jan. Ms. in files of author.

—— with J. Adams, B. Lythberg, M. Nuku and N. Thomas 2016b. In *Artefacts of Encounter: Cook's Voyages, Colonial Collecting and Museum Histories*. Dunedin, Otago University Press.

—— with N. Thomas 2016c. Weapons, Utensils and Manufactures of various kinds: Cambridge's collections. In *Artefacts of Encounter: Cook's Voyages, Colonial Collecting and Museum Histories*. Dunedin, Otago University, 29-42.

—— with B. Lythberg and M. Nuku, 2016d. Relating to, and through, Polynesian Collections. In *Artefacts of Encounter: Cook's Voyages and Colonial Collecting and Museum Histories*. Dunedin, Otago University Press, 43-55.

—— 2016e. 'Their paddles were curiously stained': Two Māori paddles from the East Coast. In *Artefacts of Encounter: Cook's Voyages, Colonial Collecting and Museum Histories*. Dunedin, Otago University Press, 118-121.

—— with G. Albert and C. Wilson 2016f. Maru, Kahukura and Hukere – Three named 'god-sticks' from New Zealand. In *Artefacts of Encounter: Cook's Voyages, Colonial Collecting and Museum Histories*. Dunedin, Otago University Press, 238-239.

—— with B. Lythberg and M. Nuku, 2016g. An Admirable Typology. In *The Material Cultures of Enlightenment Arts and Sciences*, eds. S. Schaffer and A. Craciun. Palgrave Studies in the Enlightenment, Romanticism and Culture of Print Series, eds. A. K. Mellor and C. Siskin. London, Palgrave MacMillan, 267-269.

—— 2016h. Contribution to Anthropology Discussion Group 5/1/2016.

Salmond, Anne 1975. *Hui: A Study of Maori Ceremonial Gatherings*. Wellington, A.H. & A.W. Reed.

—— 1976. Stirling, Amiria, as told to Anne Salmond. *Amiria: The Life Story of a Maori Woman*. Wellington, A.H. & A.W. Reed.

—— 1978. Te Ao Tawhito: A Semantic Approach to the Traditional Maori Cosmos. *Journal of the Polynesian Society* 87/1, 528.

—— 1980. Stirling, Eruera, as told to Anne Salmond. *Eruera: The Teachings of a Maori Elder*. Auckland, Oxford University Press.

—— 1983a. Theoretical Landscapes: on Cross-cultural Conceptions of Knowledge. In ed. David Parkin, *Semantic Anthropology*, ASA Monograph Series No. 22. London, Academic Press, 6587.

—— 1983b. The Study of Traditional Maori Society: The State of the Art. *Journal of the Polynesian Society* 92/3, 309331.

—— 1985. Maori Epistemologies. In ed. J. Overing, *Reason and Morality*. London, Tavistock Publications, 240-263.

—— 1989. Tribal Words, Tribal Worlds: The Translatability of *tapu* and *mana*. In eds Mac Marshall and John L. Caughey, *Culture, Kin, and Cognition in Oceania: Essays in honour of Ward Goodenough*. Washington, American Anthropological Association, 55-78.

—— 1991a. Tipuna: Ancestors: Aspects of Maori Cognatic Descent. In ed. A Pawley, *Man and a Half: Essays in Pacific Anthropology and Ethnobiology in Honour of Ralph Bulmer*. Auckland, The Polynesian Society, 343-356.

—— 1991b. *Two Worlds: First Meetings between Maori and Europeans 1642-1772*. Auckland, Viking.

—— 1991c. Likely Maori understanding of Tuku and Hoko. Wai 45, for the Waitangi Tribunal, Muriwhenua Land Claim, Doc #D17.

—— 1992. Maori Understandings of the Treaty of Waitangi. F19, for the Waitangi Tribunal, Muriwhenua Land Claim.

—— 1995. Self and Other in Contemporary Social Anthropology. In ed. Richard Fardon, *Counterworks: Managing the Diversity of Knowledge*. London, Routledge, 23–48.

—— 1997. *Between Worlds: Early Exchanges between Maori and Europeans 1773–1815*. Auckland, Viking.

—— 1998. Maori and Modernity: Ruatara's Dying. In ed. A.P. Cohen, *Signifying Identities: Anthropological Perspectives on Boundaries and Contested Values*. Edinburgh, University of Edinburgh, 37–58.

—— 2003. *The Trial of the Cannibal Dog: Captain Cook in the South Seas*. Auckland, Penguin.

—— 2005. Their Body is Different, Our Body is Different: European and Tahitian Navigators in the 18th Century. *History and Anthropology* 16/2, 167–186.

—— 2009. *Aphrodite's Island: The European Discovery of Tahiti*. Auckland, Penguin/Viking.

—— 2010a. Brief of Evidence of Distinguished Professor Dame Anne Salmond. WAI 1040, #A22, for the Waitangi Tribunal.

—— 2010b. Written Answers to Questions, for the Waitangi Tribunal.

—— 2011. *Bligh: William Bligh in the South Seas*. Berkeley, University of California Press; Auckland, Penguin.

—— 2012a. Ontological Quarrels: Indigeneity, Exclusion and Citizenship in a Relational World. *Anthropological Theory* 12/2, 115–141.

—— 2012b. Tupaia, the Navigator Priest. In eds Sean Mallon, Kolokesa Mahina-Tuai and Damon Salesa, *Tangata o le Moana: New Zealand and the People of the Pacific*. Wellington, Te Papa Press, 57–76.

—— 2012c. Back to the Future: First Encounters in the Tai Rawhiti. *Journal of the Royal Society of New Zealand* 42/2, 69–77.

—— 2014a. Tears of Rangi: Water, power and people in New Zealand. *Hau: Journal of Ethnographic Theory* 4/3, 285–309.

—— 2014b. Broadcast: The 2014 Rutherford Lectures. www.radionz.co.nz/national/programmes/rutherford-lectures/20141207

—— with M. Tadaki and T. Gregory 2014c. Enacting new freshwater geographies: *Te Awaroa* and the transformative imagination. *New Zealand Geographer* 70/1, 47–55.

—— 2015. The Fountain of Fish: Ontological Collisions at Sea. In eds Silke Helfrich and David Bollier, *Patterns of Commoning*. Amherst, Massachusetts, Off the Common Books.

Salmond, Anne and Amiria Salmond 2010. Artefacts of Encounter. *Interdisciplinary Science Review* 35/3–4, 302–317.

Savage, John 1807. *Some Account of New Zealand, Particularly of the Bay of Islands and the Surrounding Country*. London, J. Murray.

Scharrahs, Anke 2002. Beitrage zur Eraltung von Kunstwerken, Verbe der Restauratoren 10.

Schmidt, J.J. and Kyle R. Mitchell 2014. Property and the Right to Water: Towards a Non-liberal Commons. *Review of Radical Political Economics* 46/1, 54–69.

Schrempp G. 1985. Tū alone was brave: Notes on Maori cosmogony. In eds A. Hooper and J. Huntsman, *Transformations of Polynesian Culture*. Auckland, The Polynesian Society.

—— 1992. *Magical Arrows: The Maori, the Greeks, and the Folklore of the Universe*. Madison, Wisconsin, University of Wisconsin Press.

Scott, Joan Wallach 2001. Fantasy Echo: History and the Construction of Identity. *Critical Inquiry* 27/2, 284–304.

Scott, Michael W. 2007. *The Severed Snake: Matrilineages, Making Place, and a Melanesian Christianity in Southeast Solomon Island*. Durham, North Carolina, Carolina Academic Press.

Seuffert, Nan 2005. Nation as Partnership: Law, 'Race', and Gender in Aotearoa New Zealand's Treaty Settlements. *Law & Society Review* 39/3, 485–526.

Sharp, Nonie 1996. Reimagining Sea Space: From Grotius to Mabo. *Arena* 7, 111–129.

—— 1998. Terrestrial and Marine Space in Imagination and Social Life. *Arena* 10, 51–68.

Shawcross, Kathleen 1966. Maoris of the Bay of Islands 1769–1840: A Study in changing Maori attitudes towards Europeans. MA thesis, University of Auckland.

Shortland, Edward 1856. *Traditions and Superstitions of the New Zealanders, with illustrations of their manners and customs.* London, Longman, Brown, Green, Longmans & Roberts.

Shortland, Lieutenant 1845, Speeches of Hokianga Chiefs, encl. in Shortland to Stanley, 18 Jan. 1845, GBPP 108:10.414.

Sissons, Jeffrey, Patrick Hohepa and Wiremu Wi Hongi 1987. *The Pūriri Trees are Laughing: A Political History of Ngā Puhi in the Inland Bay of Islands.* Auckland, Polynesian Society.

Skafish, Peter 2016. The Metaphysics of Extra-Moderns: On the Decolonization of Thought. A Conversation with Eduardo Viveiros de Castro. *Common Knowledge* 22/3, 393–414.

Sloan, Phillip R. 1976. The Buffon-Linnaeus Controversy. *Isis* 67/3, 356–375.

Smith, Adam 1776. *An Inquiry into the Nature and Causes of the Wealth of Nations,* Volumes I and II. London, W. Strahan & T. Cadell.

Smith, Linda Tuhiwai 1990. Mana wahine, mana Maori: a case study. Auckland, Maori Education Research and Development Unit, University of Auckland.

—— 1999. *Decolonising Methodologies: Research and Indigenous Peoples.* London, Zed Books.

Smith, Ian, Angela Middleton, Jessie Garland and Naomi Woods 2012. *Archaeology of the Hohi Mission Station, Volume I: The 2012 Excavations.* Dunedin, University of Otago Studies in Archaeology N. 24.

Smith, Ian, Angela Middleton, Jessie Garland and Naomi Woods 2014. *Archaeology of the Hohi Mission Station, Volume II: The 2013 Excavations.* Dunedin, University of Otago Studies in Archaeology N. 26.

Smith, S. Percy 1899a. Wars of the Northern against the Southern tribes of New Zealand in the nineteenth century: Part I. *Journal of the Polynesian Society* 8/3, 141–164.

—— 1899b. Wars of the Northern against the Southern tribes of New Zealand in the nineteenth century: Part II. *Journal of the Polynesian Society* 8/4, 201–230.

—— 1900. Wars of the Northern against the Southern tribes of New Zealand in the nineteenth century: Part III. *Journal of the Polynesian Society* 9/1, 1–37.

—— 1900. Wars of the Northern against the Southern tribes of New Zealand in the nineteenth century: Part IV. *Journal of the Polynesian Society* 9/2, 85–120.

—— 1910. *Maori Wars of the Nineteenth Century.* Christchurch, Whitcomb & Tombs Ltd.

—— 1913. *The Lore of the Whare Wananga,* I & II. New Plymouth, The Polynesian Society.

—— 1920. Clairvoyance among the Maoris. *Journal of the Polynesian Society* 29/1, 49–161.

Solomon, M. 2004. Strengthening traditional knowledge systems and customary laws. In eds S. Twarog and P. Kapoor, *Protecting and Promoting Traditional Knowledge: Systems, National Experiences and International Dimensions.* United Nations, 155.

Sorrenson, M.P.K. 1991. Treaties in Colonial Policy: Precedents for Waitangi. In ed. William Renwick, *Sovereignty and Indigenous Rights: The Treaty of Waitangi in International Contexts.* Wellington, Victoria University Press.

—— 2014. *Ko te Whenua te Utu / Land is the Price: Essays on Maori History, Land and Politics.* Auckland, Auckland University Press.

Stafford, Don 1967. *Te Arawa: A History of the Arawa people.* Wellington, A.H. & A.W. Reed.

Stone, Christopher D. 1974. *Should Trees have Standing? Towards Legal Rights for Natural Objects.* Los Altos, California, W. Kaufmann.

Strachan, A. 1870. *Life of the Rev. Samuel Leigh, Missionary to the Settlers and Savages of Australia and New Zealand.* London, Wesleyan Mission House.

Strang, Veronica 2010. The Summoning of Dragons: Ancestral Serpents and Indigenous Water Rights in Australia and New Zealand. *Anthropology News* 51/2, 5–7.

Strathern, Marilyn 1980. No Nature, No Culture: The Hagen Case. In eds Carol MacCormack and Marilyn Strathern, *Nature, Culture and Gender.* Cambridge,

Cambridge University Press, 174–222.

—— 1990. Artefacts of History: Events and the Interpretation of Images. In ed. J. Siikala, *Culture and History in the Pacific*. Helsinki, Finnish Anthropological Society Transactions 27, 25–44.

—— 1995. *The Relation: Issues in Complexity and Scale*. Manchester, Prickly Pear Press.

—— 1997. Out of Context: The Persuasive Fictions of Anthropology. *Current Anthropology* 28/3, 251–281.

—— 2011. Binary License. *Common Knowledge* 17/1, 87–103.

—— 2014a. Anthropological reasoning: Some threads of thought. *Hau: Journal of Ethnographic Theory* 4/3, 23–37.

—— 2014b. Hiding its own Terms: Naturalism and the Invention of Identity. Paper presented at the International Union of Anthropological and Ethnological Sciences, Japan.

—— 2014c. Becoming enlightened about relations. ASA Firth Lecture 2014. Available at: www.theasa.org/publications/firth.shtml

Sullivan, Agnes n.d. The Maori Economy of Tamaki, 1820–1840. Draft PhD thesis, University of Auckland.

Sullivan, Robert 1999. *Star Waka*. Auckland, Auckland University Press.

Szazy, Dame Mira 1995. Comment. In *Treaty Settlements: The Unfinished Business*. Wellington, New Zealand Institute of Advanced Legal Studies and Victoria University.

Taggart, Michael 2002. *Private Property and Abuse of Rights in Victorian England: The Story of Edward Pickles and the Bradford Water Supply*. Oxford, Oxford University Press.

Tahana, Yvonne 2012. Simmering discontent threatens Maori unity. *New Zealand Herald*, 22 September. www.nzherald.co.nz/nz/news/article.cfm?c_id=1&objectid=10835738

Tamakihikurangi, Renata 1861. *Renata's Speech and Letter to the Superintendent of Hawke's Bay on the Taranaki War Question; in the original Maori, with an English translation*. Wellington.

Tamihana, Wiremu 1865. Letter to Donald McLean [but intended for the Governor], 23 May 1861, *Appendices to the Journals of the House of Representatives* 1865, E-11, 4, translated by Anne Salmond.

Tapsell, Paul 1997. The flight of Pareraututu: An investigation of Taonga from a tribal perspective. *Journal of the Polynesian Society* 106/4, 323–374.

Tarakawa, Takaanui 1894. Explanation of some matters referred to in the paper, 'The coming of the Arawa and Tainui canoes from Hawaiki to New Zealand', by Takaanui Tarakawa, translated by S. Percy Smith. *Journal of the Polynesian Society* 3/3, 171–175.

Tarakawa, Takaanui and S. Percy Smith 1894. Ko Te Rerenga Mai O Mata-Atua, Me Kurahaupo Me Era Atu Waka, I Hawaiki. / The Coming of Mata-Atua, Kurahaupo, and Other Canoes from Hawaiki to New Zealand. *Journal of the Polynesian Society* 3/2, 59–71.

Taylor, E.G.R. 1968. Navigation in the Days of Captain Cook. *The Journal of the Institute of Navigation* 21, 256–276.

Taylor, John 2005. Paths of Relationship, Spirals of Exchange: Imag(in)ing North Pentecost Kinship. *The Australian Journal of Anthropology* 16/1, 76–94.

—— 2010. The Troubled Histories of a Stranger God: Religious Crossing, Sacred Power, and Anglican Colonialism in Vanuatu. *Comparative Studies in Society and History* 52/2, 418–446.

Taylor, Richard 1839–40. Journal, MS 302, Auckland War Memorial Museum Library typescript.

—— 1855. *Te Ika a Maui, or, New Zealand and its Inhabitants*. London, Wertheim & McIntosh.

Tcherkezoff, Serge 2008. *First Contacts in Polynesia: The Samoan Case (1722–1848): Western Misunderstandings about Sexuality and Divinity*. Canberra, Australian National University Press.

—— 2012. More on Polynesian gift-giving: The Samoan sau and the fine mats (toonga), the Maori hau and the treasures (taonga). *Hau: Journal of Ethnographic Theory* 2/2, 313–324.

Te Aho, L. 2012. Ngā Whakatunga Waimāori: Freshwater Settlements. In eds N.R. Wheen and J. Hayward, *Treaty of Waitangi Settlements*. Wellington, Bridget Williams Books.

—— 2014. Review of Ruruku Whakatupua – Te Mana o Te Awa Tupua. *Māori Law Review*. Te Aurere, Te Aurere.org.nz

Te Kawariki & Network Waitangi Whangarei 2012. *Ngā Puhi Speaks: Independent Report on Ngā Puhi Nui Tonu claim, commissioned by Kuia and Kaumātua of Ngā Puhi*. Whangarei, Te Kawariki.

Te Rangihiroa (Peter Buck) 1926. The Maori Craft of Netting. *Transactions and Proceedings of the New Zealand Institute* 56, 597–646.

Te Rangikaheke c. 1849, trans. Jenifer Curnow. Te Whakapapa o te Ao [The genealogy of the world] and Nga Tama a Rangi [the children of Rangi]. APL.

Tengan, Tai P. Kāwika 2010. Genealogies: Articulating Indigenous Anthropology in/of Oceania. Special issue of *Pacific Studies* 33/2–3, 139–167.

—— 2016. The Mana of Kū: Indigenous Nationhood, Masculinity and Authority in Hawai'i. *New Mana: Transformations of a Classic Concept in Pacific Langauages and Cultures*. Canberra, ANU Press, 55–75.

Thakur, Ramesh 1989. Creation of the Nuclear-Free New Zealand Myth: Brinksmanship without a Brink. *Asian Survey* 29/10, 919–939.

Thomson, Rev. Richard c. 1840. Unpublished History of Tahiti, Alexander Turnbull Library Micro MS Collection 2, Reel 169, London Missionary Society 660, Salmond transcript.

Thornton, Agathe 1987. *Maori Oral Literature: As Seen by a Classicist*. Dunedin, University of Otago Press.

—— 1989. Some reflections on Traditional Maori Carving. *The Journal of the Polynesian Society* 98/2, 147–166

Tikao, Teone Taare, as told to Herries Beattie 1939. *Tikao Talks: Tales and Traditions as told by Teone Taare Tikao to Herries Beattie*. Dunedin, A.H. & A.W. Reed.

Tipa, G.T. 2013. Bringing the past into our future – using historic data to inform contemporary freshwater management. *Kotuitui: New Zealand Journal of Social Sciences Online* 8/1–2, 40–63, DOI: 10.1080/1177083X.2013.837080.

Tiramorehu, Matiaha 1849. Te Waiatanga mai o te Atua. Translation and commentary by Van Ballekom Manu and Harlow Ray. Christchurch, Canterbury Maori Studies 4.

Tregear, Edward 1891. *The Maori-Polynesian Comparative Dictionary*. Wellington, Lyon & Blair.

Umbaur, Konrad 1998. Maori Artwork from Captain Cook Voyage Discovered. Radio New Zealand News, 3 May 1998.

University of Auckland 1988. *Tane-nui-a-Rangi*. Auckland, University of Auckland.

Vigh, Henrik and David Saudal 2014. From Essence Back to Existence: Anthropology beyond the Ontological Turn. *Anthropological Theory* 14/1, 49–73.

Viveiros de Castro, Eduardo 1998. Cosmological Perspectivism in Amazonia and Elsewhere, four lectures delivered 17 February – 4 March at the Department of Social Anthropology, University of Cambridge.

—— 2003. *And*. Manchester, Manchester University Press.

—— 2004a. Exchanging Perspectives: The Transformation of Objects into Subjects in Amerindian Ontologies. *Common Knowledge* 10/3, 463–484.

—— 2004b. Perspectival Anthropology and the Method of Controlled Equivocation. *Tipiti* 2/1, 3–22.

—— 2007. The Crystal Forest: Notes on the Ontology of Amazonian Spirits. *Inner Asia* 9/2, 153–172.

—— 2011. Zeno and the Art of Anthropology: Of Lies, Beliefs, Paradoxes, and Other Truths. *Common Knowledge* 17/1, 128–145.

—— 2013. The Relative Native. *Hau: Journal of Ethnographic Theory* 3/3, 473–502.

—— with Martin Holbraad and Morten Axel Pedersen 2014. The Politics of Ontology: Anthropological Positions. In *Fieldsights – Theorizing the Contemporary*, *Cultural Anthropology Online*, 13 January 2014.

—— 2015. Who is afraid of the ontological wolf? Some comments on an ongoing anthropological debate. CUSAS Annual Marilyn Strathern Lecture, 30 May 2014. www.academia.edu/12865685/Who_is_afraid_of_the_ontological_wolf

—— with Martin Holbraad 2016. Ideas of Savage Reason, Glass Bead in Conversation with Martin Holbraad and Eduardo Viveiros de Castro. In Site O: Castalia, the Game of Ends and Means – Glass Bead. www.glass-bead.org/journal/ site-o-castalia-the-game-of-ends-and-means/?lang=enview

Waitangi Tribunal 1988. *Muriwhenua Fishing Claim Report*. Wellington, The Waitangi Tribunal (Wai 22).

—— 1992. *Mohaka River Report*. Wellington, The Waitangi Tribunal (Wai 119).

—— 1993. *Te Ika Whenua Report – Energy Assets Report*. Wellington, The Waitangi Tribunal (Wai 212).

—— 1997. *Muriwhenua Land Report*. Wellington, The Waitangi Tribunal (Wai 45).

—— 1999. *Whanganui River Report*. Wellington, The Waitangi Tribunal (Wai 167).

—— 2004. *Report on the Crown's Foreshore and Seabed Policy*. Wellington, The Waitangi Tribunal (Wai 1071).

—— 2010. Transcript, #4.1.1, Wai 1040, Hearing at Te Tii Marae, 12–14 May.

—— 2012. *The Stage I Report on the National Freshwater and Geothermal Resources Claim*. Wellington, The Waitangi Tribunal (Wai 2358).

—— 2014. *He Whakapūtanga me te Tiriti: The Declaration and the Treaty*. Wellington, The Waitangi Tribunal (Wai 1040).

Wagner, Roy 1981. *The Invention of Culture*. Chicago, University of Chicago Press.

Wakefield, Edward Jerningham and J. Ward 1837. *The British Colonization of New Zealand: Being an Account of the Principles, Objects and Plans of the New Zealand Association*. London, John W. Parker.

Walker, Victor 2012. Te Aitanga-a-Hauiti and the transit of Venus. *Journal of the Royal Society of New Zealand* 42/2, 105–112.

Walter, Richard, Chris Jacomb and Emma Brooks 2010. Final Report on Archaeological Excavations at Cooks Cove Z17/311, Tolaga Bay, East Coast, North Island. www.spar.co.nz/Reports/EastCoast/ FinalReportonArchaeologicalExcavationsatCooksCove,TolagaBay.pdf

Walton, John 1839. *Twelve Months' Residence in New Zealand, containing a correct description of the Customs, Manners, &c., of the Natives of that Island*. Glasgow, R.M. McPhun.

Wanhalla, Angela 2008. 'One White Man I Like Very Much': Intermarriage and the Cultural Encounter in Southern New Zealand, 1829–1850. *Journal of Women's History* 20/2, 34–56.

Warren, M.D. 1951. Medical Education during the Eighteenth Century. *Post-graduate Medical Journal* 27/308, 304–311.

Webster, Kerryn and Felicity Monteiro 2013. High Court clarifies jurisdiction over New Zealand ships on high seas, International Law Office. www.internationallawoffice.com/ newsletters/detail.aspx?g=96970d24-7159-4b4c-b41f-71d8c0f583bc

Weisner, Polly 2014. Embers of society: Firelight talk among the Ju/'hoansi Bushmen. *PNAS* 111/39, 14027–14035. www.pnas.org/content/111/39/14027.full.pdf

Wellman, Kathleen 2002. Physicians and Philosophes: Physiology and Sexual Morality in the French Enlightenment. *Eighteenth-Century Studies* 35/2, 267–277.

White, John 1887. *The Ancient History of the Maori, His Mythology and Traditions: Horouta, or Taki-tumu Migration*, Volumes I–III. Wellington, Government Printer.

—— 1888. *The Ancient History of the Maori, His Mythology and Traditions: Tai-Nui*, Vol. IV. Wellington, Government Printer.

Williams, David 1989. Te Tiriti o Waitangi: Unique Relationship between Crown and

Tangata Whenua? In ed. Hugh Kawharu, *Waitangi: Maori and Pakeha Perspectives of the Treaty of Waitangi*. Auckland.

—— 1999. *Te Kooti Tango Whenua: The Native Land Court 1864–1909*. Wellington, Huia Press.

Williams, Jim 2010. *Mahika Kai*: The Husbanding of Consumables by Māori in pre-contact Te Waipounamu. *Journal of the Polynesian Society* 119/2, 149–180.

—— 2012. Ngāi Tahu Kaitiakitanga. *MAI Journal* 2012, 1/2, 89–102.

Williams, W.L. 1888. On the visit of Captain Cook to Poverty Bay and Tolaga Bay. *Transactions and Proceedings of the New Zealand Institute* 21, 389–397.

—— 2012. Ngai Tahu Kai-tiakitanga. *Mai Journal* 1/2, 89–102.

Wilmshurst, Janet M., Terry L. Hunt, Carl C. Lipo and Atholl J. Anderson 2011. High-precision radiocarbon dating shows recent and rapid initial human colonization of East Polynesia. *PNAS* 108/5, 1815–1820.

Wolfe, Charles T. ed. 2008. Vitalism without Metaphysics? *Medical Vitalism in the Enlightenment*, special issue of *Science in Context* 21/4, 461–463.

Wyatt, Philippa 1991. The Old Land Claims and the Concept of 'Sale': A Case Study. MA thesis, University of Auckland.

Wynd, Donna 2013. *Child abuse: what role does poverty play?* Auckland, Child Poverty Action Group.

Yate, William 1833–1845. Journal and diary, MS-2544, Alexander Turnbull Library, Wellington.

—— 1835. *An Account of New Zealand, and of the Formation and Progress of the Church Missionary Society's Mission in the Northern Island*. London, R.B. Seeley & W. Burnside.

Yeo, Richard 2001. *Encyclopaedic Visions: Scientific Dictionaries and Enlightenment Culture*. Cambridge, Cambridge University Press.

LIST OF ILLUSTRATIONS

Colour plates

1   Marsden's mill and cottage, by J. Lycett, 1820. Mitchell Library, State Library of New South Wales, Sydney, PXD41F1

2   Plan of New Plymouth in New Zealand, by Frederick A. Carrington, 1842. Alexander Turnbull Library, Wellington, 832,295a

3   The missionary settlement Rangihoua, New Zealand, by unknown artist, c. 1832. National Library of Australia, Canberra, Rex Nan Kivell Collection, NK131

4   The Armoury in Carlton House, by Augustus Charles Pugin, 1814. Royal Collection Trust / © Her Majesty Queen Elizabeth II 2016, RCIN 917092

5   Augustus Earle meeting Hongi Hika at the Bay of Islands, by Augustus Earle, November 1827. Alexander Turnbull Library, Wellington, G-707

6   Tukopoto at Kaitoke, Te Wherowhero's pā, by George French Angas, 1844. National Library of Australia, Canberra, Rex Nan Kivell Collection, NK1111

7   Tui in European costume, by Jules LeJeune, 1824. Copied 1825 or 1826 by Antoine Chazal from an original by LeJeune for Duperrey's *Voyage autour du monde . . .* (Paris, 1822–25). Alexander Turnbull Library, Wellington, C-082-096

8   The Rev. Thomas Kendall and the Māori chiefs Hongi and Waikato, by James Barry, 1820. Alexander Turnbull Library, Wellington, G-618

9   Te Kara, the United Tribes ensign, Waitangi. Alexander Turnbull Library, Wellington, MS-1550-120

10   The mission station at Kerikeri, by Jules Lejeune, 1824. Copied 1826 by Antoine Chazal from a drawing by LeJeune for Duperrey's *Voyage autour du monde . . .* (Paris, 1822–25). Alexander Turnbull Library, Wellington, C-082-094

11   A hākari, or feast, in the Bay of Islands, by Cuthbert Clarke, 1849. National Library of Australia, Canberra, Rex Nan Kivell Collection, NK2004

12   'Owharawai. Pa of Hone Heke', copied from a drawing taken by Mr Symonds of the 99th Regt by Thomas Biddulph Hutton, 1845. Book of New Zealand sketches, Purewa, 1845–60. Alexander Turnbull Library, Wellington, E-137-q-006

13   Children on the banks of the Waipa, lithograph by Louisa Hawkins after George French Angas, 1847. Alexander Turnbull Library, Wellington, A-092-014

14   'He that chastiseth one, amendeth many', by H. Heath, 1831. Photo by Hulton Archive/Getty Images

15   No Drill No Spill – protests against oil drilling in Whanau-a-Apanui waters. *New Zealand Herald*

16   Foreshore and seabed hīkoi at Parliament, 5 May 2004. https://en.wikipedia.org/wiki/New_Zealand_foreshore_and_seabed_controversy#/media/File:Hikoi-foreshore.jpg

Page numbers in **bold** refer to illustrations.

rivers 302–03; claims for ownership
as 'assets' 412; Crown control of
navigable rivers and lakes 306, 308;
as legal persons 293–94, 298, 307,
309, 314, 315; modernist views of
rivers 304–07, 308–15, 408; people
as guardians 294, 295, 307, 408;
pollution 414; as taonga 315; tōku awa
(my river, I belong to this river) 309;
as tradeable units of water 413–14; *see
also* and names of individual rivers, e.g.
Whanganui River; freshwater debates
Awatere, Donna 403
awhe i te hau (gathering in the hau) 15
Awiri 146

Baker, Charles 273–74
Balneavis, Raumoa 303
Banks, Joseph **9,** 23, 24, 25, 27–28, 31, 32,
33, 42, 128, 134, 142; Enlightenment
science 37, 39, 41; Māori art 44–45,
48, 49, 50; Matara's visit 133; plants
collected 29–30, 53; President of the
Royal Society of London 8, 64, 133;
and Tupaia 6, 7, 8, 10, 16, 21, 43, 44,
366–67; in Uawa **6,** 7, 8, 10, 16, 29–30,
31–32, 53
Banks Peninsula 225
Baragwanath, David 368
Barlow, Cleve 203
Barry, James 141
Bastion Point occupation 346, 410
Bay of Islands 56, 63, 66–67, 69, 70–71,
83, 84, 85, 100, 108, 115, 121, 123,
141, 142, 143, 145, 159, 166, 204,
215, 216, 223, 239; capital shifted
to Auckland 333; Charles Darwin's
visit 250–51; European and Māori
population 247; land sold by
1840 331; lawless Europeans 255; *see
also* individual placenames
Bay of Plenty 255, 337, 351, 352, 358–59,
365, 366, 373, 400
Bean, William 108
Beattie, Herries 356
Best, Elsdon 10, 15, 184, 303, 304, 350,
383, 385
Bible stories, influence on Māori thinking 389; *see also* Genesis creation story
Bickersteth, Edward 141, 184
bi-culturalism 346, 410
Bigge, John, Commission of Inquiry 121,
148, 224

Binney, Dame Judith 347; *Encircled Lands:
Te Urewera 1820–1921* 347
Blackstone, William 249
Blackstone, William, *Commentaries on the
Laws of England* 249, 250, 306, 390
Blackwood, Price 230, 231
Bligh, William 135
Bounty mutineers 130
Bourke, Sir Richard 227, 228, 234, 237,
241, 242, 252, 253, 254
Boyd 56, 57, 73, 86, 135, 190, 193
Brampton 168–69, 171, 172, 173–75, 176,
189
Brind, William 213
British Army 332; 84th Regiment 120,
121, 123
British Parliamentary Select Committee
on Aboriginal Tribes 251–52
British presence in New Zealand 76,
80–82, 142–43, 147, 148; British
Resident 224–45, 250, 252, 253, 254,
261; European requests for protection 252, 253–55; letter from northern
rangatira to William IV 216–18,
227, 228–29, 230; Māori had little
say 255–56; northern rangatira
relationships with the British (generally) 148, 215, 216; rangatiras' fears of
land loss 77–78, 81–82, 88, 107, 177,
218, 236, 332; settlement 250, 253–55,
259–60, 261, 285, 305, 312, 328–31,
333, 335–36; Te Morenga's request for
British protection 148; Wakefield,
Edward, *The British Colonization of New
Zealand* 252; *see also* British Army;
kāwana (governors); missionaries; and
names of explorers, e.g. Cook, James
broadcasting, Māori 407, 411, 413
Brothers 98
Brown, Deidre 135
Browne, Thomas Gore 337–38, 339, 340
Bruce, George 135
Buck, Peter/Te Rangihiroa 303, 304, 344,
345, 346, 359, **360,** 360–61, 410
Buffalo 237
Buffon, Georges-Louis Leclerc, Comte
de 36, 40, 41
Bunbury, Thomas 397
Busby, Agnes 236
Busby, James **225;** *Brief Memoir Relative
to the Islands of New Zealand* 225,
226–27; British Resident 201, 224–28,
238, 239, 241, 243, 250, 254, 261; and

Dame Anne Salmond. Photograph by Jane Ussher.

DAME ANNE SALMOND is Distinguished Professor of Māori Studies at the University of Auckland and author of books including *Hui: A Study of Maori Ceremonial Gatherings* (1975, A.H. and A.W. Reed); *Amiria: The Life Story of a Maori Woman* (1976, A.H. and A.W. Reed); *Eruera: The Teachings of a Maori Elder* (1980, Oxford University Press); *Two Worlds: First Meetings between Maori and Europeans 1642–1772* (1991, Viking Press, University of Hawai'i Press); *Between Worlds: Early Exchanges between Maori and Europeans 1773–1815* (1997, Viking Press, University of Hawai'i Press); *The Trial of the Cannibal Dog: Captain Cook in the South Seas* (2003, Penguin UK, Penguin NZ, Yale University Press); *Aphrodite's Island: The European Discovery of Tahiti* (2007, University of California Press, Penguin NZ) and *Bligh: William Bligh in the South Seas* (2011, University of California Press, Penguin NZ). Among many honours and awards, she is an International Member of the American Philosophical Society, a Foreign Associate of the US National Academy of Sciences and a Corresponding Fellow of the British Academy; in 2013 she became New Zealander of the Year and winner of the Rutherford Medal from the Royal Society of New Zealand.